6HS

Computer Network Architectures and Protocols

Applications of Communications Theory
Series Editor: R. W. Lucky, *Bell Laboratories*

A Continuation Order Plan is available for this series. A continuation order will bring delivery of each new volume immediately upon publication. Volumes are billed only upon actual shipment. For futher information please contact the publisher.

Computer Network Architectures and Protocols

Edited by

Paul E. Green, Jr.

IBM Corporation
Yorktown Heights, New York

PLENUM PRESS • NEW YORK AND LONDON

Library of Congress Cataloging in Publication Data

Main entry under title:

Computer network architectures and protocols.

(Applications of communications theory)
  Bibliography: p.
  Includes index.
  1. Computer networks. I. Green, Paul Eliot, date   . II. Series.
TK5105.5.C638   001.64′404   82-5227
ISBN 0-306-40788-4   AACR2

First Printing—May 1982
Second Printing—May 1983

©1982 Plenum Press, New York
A Division of Plenum Publishing Corporation
233 Spring Street, New York, N.Y. 10013

Printed in the United States of America

To Doogie

Contributors

James D. Atkins
IBM Corporation, Research Triangle Park, North Carolina

H. V. Bertine
Bell Laboratories, Holmdel, New Jersey

Gregor V. Bochmann
University of Montreal, Montreal, Quebec, Canada

David R. Boggs
Xerox Corporation, Palo Alto Research Center, Palo Alto, California

Daniel Brand
IBM Zurich Research Laboratory, Rüschlikon, Switzerland

David E. Carlson
Bell Laboratories, Holmdel, New Jersey

James W. Conard
Control Data Corporation, Anaheim, California

D. D. Cowan
IBM Zurich Research Laboratory, Rüschlikon, Switzerland

André A. S. Danthine
University of Liège, Liège, Belgium

John D. Day
Cullinane Database Systems, Inc., Westwood, Massachusetts

Harold C. Folts
Omnicom, Inc., Vienna, Virginia

Mario Gerla
University of California, Los Angeles, California

James P. Gray
IBM Corporation, Research Triangle Park, North Carolina

Paul E. Green, Jr.
IBM Research Center, Yorktown Heights, New York

Brent T. Hailpern
IBM Research Center, Yorktown Heights, New York

Verlin L. Hoberecht
IBM Corporation, Kingston, New York

Leonard Kleinrock
University of California, Los Angeles, California

Robert M. Metcalfe
3Com Corporation, Menlo Park, California

Jonathan B. Postel
Information Sciences Institute, University of Southern California, Marina del Rey, California

David B. Rose
IBM Corporation, Research Triangle Park, North Carolina

Harry Rudin
IBM Zurich Research Laboratory, Rüschlikon, Switzerland

Antony Rybczynski
Bell Canada, Ottawa, Ontario, Canada

Gary D. Schultz
IBM Corporation, Research Triangle Park, North Carolina

Mischa Schwartz
Columbia University, New York, New York

John F. Shoch
Xerox Corporation, Palo Alto Research Center, Palo Alto, California

Thomas E. Stern
Columbia University, New York, New York

Carl A. Sunshine
Information Sciences Institute, University of Southern California, Marina del Rey, California

Edward A. Taft
Xerox Corporation, Palo Alto Research Center, Palo Alto, California

Fouad A. Tobagi
Stanford University, Stanford, California

Iwao Toda
Yokosuka ECL NTT, Yokosuka, Japan

Stuart Wecker
Technology Concepts, Inc., Sudbury, Massachusetts

Colin H. West
IBM Zurich Research Laboratory, Rüschlikon, Switzerland

Pitro Zafiropulo
IBM Zurich Research Laboratory, Rüschlikon, Switzerland

Hubert Zimmerman
IRIA/Laboria, Rocquencourt, France

Preface

This is a book about the bricks and mortar out of which are built those edifices that so well characterize late twentieth century industrial society—networks of computers and terminals. Such computer networks are playing an increasing role in our daily lives, somewhat indirectly up to now as the hidden servants of banks, retail credit bureaus, airline reservation offices, and so forth, but soon they will become more visible as they enter our offices and homes and directly become part of our work, entertainment, and daily living.

The study of how computer networks work is a combined study of communication theory and computer science, two disciplines appearing to have very little in common. The modern communication scientist wishing to work in this area finds himself in suddenly unfamiliar territory. It is no longer sufficient for him to think of transmission, modulation, noise immunity, error bounds, and other abstractions of a single communication link; he is dealing now with a topologically complex interconnection of such links. And what is more striking, solving the problems of getting the signal from one point to another is just the beginning of the communication process. The communication must be in the right form to be routed properly, to be handled without congestion, and to be understood at the right points in the network. The communication scientist suddenly finds himself charged with responsibility for such things as code and format conversions, addressing, flow control, and other abstractions of a new and challenging kind.

As for the computer scientist, he finds that his discipline has changed too. The fraction of computers that belong to a network involving terminals and computers is increasing all the time. And for a typical single computer, the fraction of its execution load, storage occupancy, and system management problems that are involved with being part of a network is also growing.

It is the objective of this book to provide a comprehensive text and reference volume that can be used in education, research and development in this combined field of computer networks. The aim is to be instructive and, within the limits imposed by space, encyclopedic.

The present status of the computer network art can be traced to three main sources: research networks built by universities, often operating under government support; private networks provided by the computer manufacturers; and public network offerings provided by common carriers. In this volume all three sources of expertise have been tapped. Cooperation between these communities has led to the establishment of a high level of world wide standardization on certain special aspects of network architectures and protocols, and these are described.

When I was asked by the Editor of this series to prepare a volume in this area, it was clear that two approaches were possible. The emphasis could either be on abstract and generic descriptions of network structure (the architecture) or on specific implementations and the functions they provide. The latter approach, in which one might describe how a given packet-switched common carrier network functions or how a piece of software offered by a computer manufacturer works, would provide a treatment of immediate help to the user of just that service or product. However, it seemed obvious that a more generally useful and less perishable volume would result if one took the first approach and dealt with structural concepts at the most basic and generally applicable level; this was the procedure adopted in preparing this volume.

There already exist several perfectly adequate treatises that cover parts of the area or cover all the areas fairly lightly or from the special point of view of the university, computer manufacturer, or common carrier. However, writing the really complete treatise that was wanted seemed not to be within the ability of any one author (at any rate not this author). A volume composed of invited contributions by experts was clearly called for. At the same time, a need emerged in the Institute of Electrical and Electronics Engineers (IEEE) to have a special journal issue on this very topic, so the two processes of book and journal issue were merged. The volume you are now reading is really a second iteration, the first being a Special Issue on Computer Networks Architecture and Protocols, the April 1980 issue of the IEEE Communications Transactions. This volume consists of revised versions of those papers, plus several new chapters, all organized into seven parts, each of which has a tutorial introduction. A comprehensive subject index and index of acronyms has been supplied.

The book is organized along the lines of the "layered" view which is always used today in dissecting network function and which will be introduced in Part I. According to this scheme, the structure within any network "node" or "machine" may be broken into layers with the raw transmission facilities of classical communications (for example, wires or satellite links) below the lowest layer and the using source and destination persons or programs above the highest one. Part II discusses the lowest layer, the Physical Layer, by which transmission connections are set up between nodes. Part III presents the Link Control Level, which operates to produce error-free sequential delivery of data messages or "packets" from a particular node to one of its neighboring nodes. In Part IV we see how packets make their way from the originating node to the destination node, a process which can be a complex one when there are intermediate nodes in between and when there are many simultaneous users of the network resources. When we get to Part V, the fact that the path of the messages has been a sequence of nodes and links is no longer visible because we are discussing high level functions by which the path provided by this sequence is exploited by just the two end users at the source and destination nodes, respectively.

Any treatment of computer network structure that aspires to completeness and timeliness cannot stop with just the internals of the layers. At least two other areas of great concern today were identified and are discussed here. Just in the last several years the difficult step of connecting together networks that were previously functioning separately has become most important as the number of networks proliferates and the breadth of interconnection freedom desired by end users becomes more ambitious. This problem is the subject of Part VI.

And finally, Part VII caps off our treatment of how the details of network function *should* work with a series of reports on the extent to which we are now able by formal methods to make sure in advance that they *will* work.

I have tried to get the best people available to write chapters on the different subtopics. This has inevitably meant a heavy drain on the schedules of very busy individuals, but the request has been met with a commendable responsiveness and generosity for which I am most grateful. I would also like to record my indebtedness to the referees of these chapters and especially to the three individuals who helped plan the volume: Alex A. McKenzie, Carl Sunshine, and Stuart Wecker. Dr. Sunshine made a particularly heavy contribution, since he managed the review and editing process for all the chapters in Part VII.

Mt. Kisco, New York   Paul E. Green, Jr.

Contents

PART IV: NETWORK LAYER

PART V: HIGHER-LAYER PROTOCOLS

PART VI: NETWORK INTERCONNECTION

PART I

Introduction

The introductory part of this volume consists of two chapters. In Chapter 1 the concept of layered computer network architectures is motivated and explained in a tutorial way. The way in which Parts II through V of the book relate to the various layers is also indicated.

A network *architecture* is a complete definition of all the layers necessary to build the network. The definition itself is expressed as a set of *protocols* that act within the same layer or between layers. A protocol, in turn, is a set of agreements for interaction of two or more parties and is expressed by three components, *syntax* (e.g., a set of headers, a set of commands/responses), *semantics* (the actions and reactions that take place, including the exchange of messages), and *timing*, the sequencing and concurrency aspects of the protocol.

While the book is intended to present the generic architectural view of networks, it was nonetheless felt important to include in Chapter 1 a bit of the history of some of the implementations, if only to show how the earlier ones suffered from an absence of the systematic layered approach. This discussion of implementations also gives some feel for the world of software and hardware products in which the architecture ceases to be a paper design and becomes an operational reality.

Chapter 2 serves to complete the introductory portion of this book by detailing the new proposed international reference model for layered network architecture, the Open System Interconnection, promulgated by the International Standards Organization, and known more succinctly as "ISO/OSI." This model is being widely adopted as a definitive framework for talking about layered network architectures.

OSI, as formally approved, takes the summary form presented in Chapter 2; details on syntax, semantics, and timing of protocol layers above level 3 (equivalent roughly to the X.25 packet standard) have not been agreed upon yet. Therefore, even though the reader will have to be content with OSI as a useful pedagogical model, it is to be expected that eventually the ISO model will be transformed into a full-fledged architecture in the sense defined above.

1

The Structure of Computer Networks

Paul E. Green, Jr.

I. Introduction

A computer network is a structure that makes available to a data processing user at one place some data processing function or service performed at another place. Such a computer network is exemplified superficially in Fig. 1. In this case one of the end users is a person sitting at a terminal. The other end user is a specific application program running on a computer. The network consists of a number of boxes or *nodes*, among them the terminal (A) and the computer (B), and includes also the intervening transmission lines connecting the nodes.

Ever since computer users began accessing central processor resources from remote terminals over 25 years ago, such computer networks have become more versatile, more powerful, and inevitably, more complex. Today's computer networks [1–6] range all the way from a single small processor that supports one or two terminals to complicated interconnections in which hundreds of processing units of various sizes are interconnected to one another and to tens of thousands of terminals, often with various forms of special multiplexors and controllers in between.

As this evolution has proceeded, so have attempts to replace ad hoc methods of network design with systematic ways of organizing, understanding, and teaching about computer network details. Today there is an orderly way of looking at networks in terms of *layered architectures*, which makes it possible to dissect the many interlocking functions of the network and then explain them one at a time. This book is organized in just this way, the various sections and chapters being devoted to the different layers. As we shall see, each layer in a layered architecture is a collection of defined interactions called *peer protocols*, and the boundaries between layers is another set of interactions called *interface protocols*.

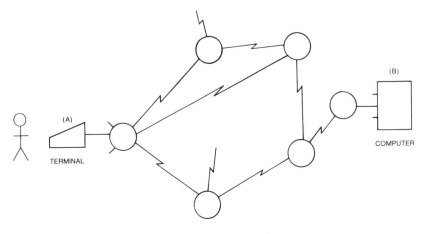

Fig. 1. A computer network.

It is appropriate to state at this point the difference between a protocol, an architecture, and an implementation. A *protocol* is a set of rules of procedure stating just how two or more parties are supposed to interact, for example, by sending messages to each other. A network *architecture* is a precise definition of the aggregated set of functions that the network and its components should perform. The architecture consists of a number of individual protocols. An *implementation* is a running version of which the architecture is the blueprint. Thus the architecture exists on paper and the implementation exists as actual hardware or software that runs. The emphasis in this book is on architectures and their component protocols, not on implementations.

This initial chapter has the objective of introducing the layering concept in a simple and plausible way and, by going into an intermediate level of detail, to set the stage for the various chapters to follow which will discuss individual layers in much greater depth. We shall do this by first briefly tracing the historical evolution of network implementations, and then by summarizing some of today's layered architectures.

In Section II, we analyze a list of the basic functions that the network provides in putting the parties that the network serves into communication with one another. This allows us to identify the layers and state what each of them is supposed to accomplish. Then, to prepare the ground for relating these structural abstractions to real life we review the history of network implementations. This is done in two pieces; Section III discusses commercially provided networks (and the influence of research networks on them) and Section IV treats the standards of the common carriers and related bodies. Finally, in Section V we review how three different implementation groups have filled in the details of certain of the layers of Section II in their own particular way to provide the services that were covered in Sections III and IV.

II. A Framework for Discussing Networks: The Total Access Path between End Users

A. Characterizing the Network

The basic function to be performed by any computer network is the provision of an *access path* by which an *end user* at one geographical location can access some other end user at another geographical location. Depending on the particular circumstances, the pair of end users might be a terminal user and a remote application program he or she is invoking (as with Fig. 1), two application programs interacting with one another remotely, one application program querying or updating a remote file, and so forth. It is important to understand that by *access path* we mean the sequence of functions that makes it possible for one end user not only to be physically connected to the other, but to actually *communicate* with the other in spite not only of errors of various types but also large differences in the choices of speed, format, patterns of intermittency, etc., that are natural to each end user individually. The distinction is important because it captures one of the key differences between classical communications (transmission and error control) and computer communications.

There are many ways of characterizing networks, for example, the following: (1) according to the particular application (banking, time sharing, etc.), (2) according to geography (in-plant, out-plant), and (3) according to ownership (public, private), and so forth. Another way of characterizing different network types is to examine the topological character of the web of transmission lines that connect together the nodes at which the different end users are located and/or which perform some connection and message forwarding function. (A *node* is a physical box such as a computer, controller, multiplexor, or terminal; an *end node* is one where an end user resides.) Topologically, we may distinguish various network types in the manner shown in Fig. 2.

None of these four approaches really reveals what the network is actually doing. A much better scheme is to examine the total repertoire of functions that the network must provide in making up an effective access path between two end users (Table I). By doing this in an ordered way, one is in a good position to characterize the important features of both common

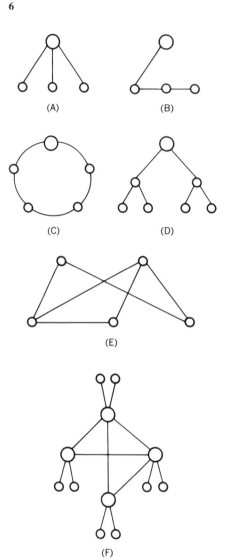

Fig. 2. Six network topologies. (A) Star,
(B) Multidrop, (C) Loop, (D) Tree, (E)
Mesh, (F) Mesh of trees.

carrier networks (of the leased, dial, fast circuit-switched, and packet-switched types that we shall define later in this chapter) and the network designs of computer manufacturers.

B. Access Path Requirements

First, someone must make sure that a set of physical transmission resources (lines) exists that run from the origin node to the destination

Table I. Access Path Requirements[a]

To give one end user access to another end user, someone must:

Make sure a transmission path exists	USING	Common carrier-provided lines
See that it talks in bits	USING	Modems
Provide electrical connection and control of modem	USING	Physical interfaces (II)
Provide economies during intermittent use	USING	Physical dialup; line sharing by multidropping or other multiaccess schemes (III)
Move individual messages without error	USING	Data link control; Error detection and retransmission (III)
Send messages to correct node and correct subsidiary address within node. Bypass failed or congested line or node.	USING	Addressing, routing (III, IV)
Accommodate buffer size. Avoid need to resend long messages	USING	Packetizing/depacketizing (IV)
Resolve mismatches between feasible rate of message flow across network and that desired by end user	USING	Buffering, flow control (IV)
Accommodate request – response patterns peculiar to the end user pair	USING	Set up, take down, and manage datagram, transaction, or session dialogue (V)
Make it possible for one end user to interpret and use the code, format, command convention, etc., used by the others	USING	Protocol conversions (V)

[a] Roman numerals indicate parts of the book in which each function is described in detail.

node, often by way of intermediate nodes. In out-plant situations (beyond one contiguous set of customer premises), this is done by common-carrier-provided links, either terrestrial or satellite.

Today it is still true that most common-carrier lines are analog lines that were originally designed to handle voice waveforms. Therefore, the next step is to see to it that the two ends of each line talk in bits by substituting for the bits certain waveforms whose energy lies in a frequency range accommodated by the lines. *Modems* (modulator–demodulator units) provide this function and some others. One modem at the sending end of the line converts bits to analog waveforms, and a second modem at the receiving end converts analog waveforms back to bits. Modems will not be discussed further in this volume. The interested reader should consult Ref. 7. The state of the modem must be controlled at all times by the remainder of the node to which it is attached. An electrical or *physical interface* must be provided to perform this function. Part II of this volume deals with this interface.

The next problem to be faced is to exploit the intermittent ("bursty") nature of most end user traffic in such a way as to economize on line costs. If each sending end user were always to generate a bit stream at a constant rate, networks made entirely of simple point-to-point leased lines of just the right capacity would be the appropriate solution. But since this is, in practice, hardly ever the case, one must either use an intermittently available *dial up* point-to-point line, or hang a number of end nodes along the same line and use *multidropping* or another of the wide variety of *multiple access* techniques that have been invented to interleave the bursty traffic. Especially attractive are the new *packet-switching* or *fast circuit-switching* (very fast dialup) services, which we shall return to presently. (Multidropping, multiple access, packet-switching and fast circuit-switching are all forms of time-division multiplexing.) In any of these functions there is a *calling* function at the end that initiates the connection and a *called* function at the other. The physical level calling and called function that make up the dialup function are not presented in this volume in Part II but are deferred until Part IV since they may be closely compared to other functions discussed there.

Next, a capability must be provided for making sure that the bit stream received is an accurate replica of the bit stream transmitted. This is done by adding redundancy bits for *error detection* every so often in the transmitted bit stream. If, upon checking the arriving redundancy bits against the string of immediately preceding arriving data bits (a "frame"), the receiver detects an error, the transmitter is asked by the receiver to resend the frame.

In most computer networks the multidropping function (if used) and the error detection/retransmission function are handled by *data link control* (DLC) elements, one at each point of connection of a node to a line. With multidropping of many nodes on the same leased line comes the need to add into the exchanges between DLC elements certain link address and control fields or characters to be used to avoid conflicting attempts to use the line and have the correct node absorb the message.

The three chapters of Part III discuss how classical data link controls, such as BISYNC and HDLC as well as some more recently introduced multiaccess protocols, accomplish the functions of line sharing and error-free node-to node message delivery.

The action taken in response to the *addressing* information is, of course, the *routing* operation, detailed in Chapter 12. We have just encountered a simple addressing/routing requirement on a single link connecting several stations. When the nodes at which the end users are located are separated not just by one line but by one or more intervening nodes and lines, messages must be forwarded from node to node, and addressing and routing then become quite elaborate, particularly if there is a multiplicity of possible routes between the two end nodes. In such a topologically complex network, upon failure of a node or link, alternate path rerouting provides a powerful tool for recovery.

Before leaving the subject of addressing and routing, it should be noted that a line connected to a node often carries traffic to or from more than one location within that node. To resolve the ambiguity, an intranode addressing and routing function is required in such cases.

The next function that must be provided is to accommodate the *buffering* of incoming messages from the line until they can be serviced, and the buffering of outgoing messages until they can be carried away by the transmission line. Limitations on available buffer size and the desire for fast response time, together with the aforementioned need to do error checking on a frame-by-frame basis (while seeing to it that the inevitable retransmissions do not take too long), lead to the need to segment (*packetize*) outgoing bit streams into frames of reasonable size and similarly to reassemble (*depacketize*) incoming bit streams.

Next, the rate of flow of outgoing packets has to be regulated so as neither to overflow the buffers at the receiving station nor to leave the receiving end user waiting for more traffic. This can be accomplished by feeding back along part or all of the access path from the receiving node to transmitting node special *pacing* or *flow control* signals. There are many options here, and these are discussed in Chapter 13. One may need to control rate of flow on an individual internode link to protect a buffer dedicated to that link at the same time that a completely different mechanism is controlling end-to-end flow to protect a buffer dedicated to an end user. The flow control signals sent from receiver to sender may simply turn off and on the emission of packets, they may tell the latter how many more packets can for the moment be safely sent, or there may be other strategies.

The next function needed is a way for the end user to use all the functions just listed to conduct a dialogue with the end user at the other end of the access path. The access path must be managed so that the dialogue between end users has the *request–response pattern* that the end users require. For example, the pair of users might be such that a single packet should flow in just one direction. This simplest case has been termed the *datagram* type of dialogue (actually a monologue). Or there might be a tightly structured *transaction* form of dialogue in which, for example, a single packet in one direction elicits a fixed number of reply packets in the other direction. A third possibility is a *session* between end users in which the flow of packets back and forth is part of a related series of transactions. By analogy with a telephone conversation, it would be as though an access path exists for each word, each sentence and its response, or for an entire telephone call, respectively. In managing the dialogue, there is the need not only to set up and take down the dialogue, but, while it is in progress, to associate related packets with one another, and to decide when an end user should listen and when it should talk.

The last function required is to make sure, for each end user at a node, that the access path accommodates its pecularities with respect to such things as format, character code, device control, and database access conventions. This is done by a *protocol conversion* to provide the right form of *presentation*. The four chapters of Part V discuss the dialogue management and protocol conversion processes.

Once all the elements just listed are provided, the access path can be considered complete. This is shown in Fig. 3 where the actions just discussed are listed in order. Character streams typed in by the terminal user undergo a protocol conversion, then have various control bits set and sequence numbers added for managing the dialogue, are arranged in packets

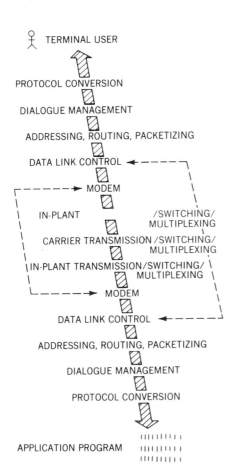

TERMINAL USER

PROTOCOL CONVERSION

DIALOGUE MANAGEMENT

ADDRESSING, ROUTING, PACKETIZING

DATA LINK CONTROL

MODEM

IN-PLANT   /SWITCHING/
                             MULTIPLEXING

CARRIER TRANSMISSION /SWITCHING/
                     MULTIPLEXING

IN-PLANT TRANSMISSION/SWITCHING/
                     MULTIPLEXING

MODEM

DATA LINK CONTROL

ADDRESSING, ROUTING, PACKETIZING

DIALOGUE MANAGEMENT

PROTOCOL CONVERSION

APPLICATION PROGRAM

Fig. 3. Access path elements with dashed lines showing two examples of peer interaction.

and are then provided with addresses, and so forth. Two interesting things are immediately obvious: the elements occur in pairs, and the two members of each pair talk essentially only to each other. For example, one modem talks to the other, ignoring both details of the transmission link and the meaning of bits it is forwarding. As another example, a DLC element ignores what its modem is doing about modulation and demodulation and also what the information field within a frame contains. A DLC element interacts only with the DLC element at the other end to convey the frame successfully from one sending node to the proper receiving node on the same line. This isolation of interaction into pairs is almost always true for all the functions we have been discussing.

C. Peer Interaction and Interfaces

This pairwise interaction, or *peer interaction*, is summarized in the *layer diagram* of Fig. 4, which is derived directly from Fig. 3. Another way of

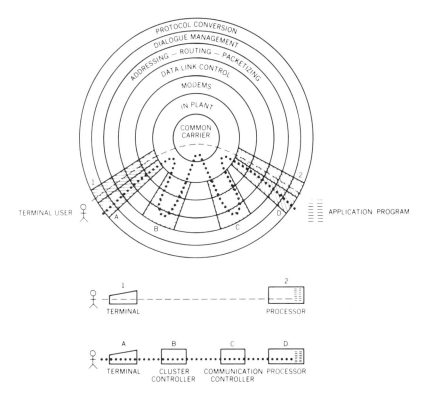

Fig. 4. Peer pairs of access path elements. (The modem may be absent in local in-plant connections.)

thinking of Fig. 4 is that it is the inverse of one end user's view of a network; instead of showing one end user at the center of his or her network, we show the transmission facilities at the center and the two end users at the periphery. The access path across the network is depicted at the bottom for illustrative cases of zero and two intermediate nodes. Note that when the access path goes through intermediate nodes, in each intermediate node it goes no higher in the layered structure than the routing operation.

The various members of a given layer communicate with each other by a *header* owned by that layer, as we shall see when we get to Figs. 9–11.

It is instructive to note that we can categorize these layers in terms of the role they play topologically. The modem, physical dialup, and DLC functions are two-party structures. They deal with successful conveyance of packets (frames) between adjacent nodes; the existence of nodes farther along the access path is invisible. The functions of dialogue management, protocol conversion and packetizing/depacketizing are also two-party structures, but here the two parties involved are at the end nodes; the existence of nodes in between is invisible. Addressing and routing are multinode functions; all nodes along the access path are involved as the message threads its way across the network from line to node to line to node, etc.

Layers up through (roughly) addressing-routing-packetizing provide a portion of the access path that hides from the end user much of the network detail. Functions outside this layer in Fig. 4 are often referred to as *higher-layer* functions. (These are discussed in detail in this book in Part V, while Parts II through IV discuss the lower layers and the physical interface.)

Several caveats are in order about this seemingly tidy picture. For example, some generic functions can occur in more than one layer. Consider, for example, *multiplexing*, the interleaving of several traffic streams as they flow through the same path. We have already met this function in data link control. It also occurs (invisibly to the nodes) buried within the common carrier's transmission system. Moreover, several end users can be multiplexed on one transmission path, and as one proceeds from a set of end users at a sending node inward in the concentric circles of Fig. 4, there is a choice of options as to the layer within which this merging might take place.

Another complication is that there is some interlayer communication of control information within the same node. This weakens the prior statements to the effect that the two peer-related members of a given layer at the two ends of the access path ignore the contents of the bit stream handed down by the next higher layer and are also not involved in the service provided to them by the next lower layer. For example, in an intermediate node, the routing function must supply to the DLC function an address it can use in forwarding a message to the proper choice of several stations on the same link. It is also appropriate to point out that some layers may be very simple or even null. For example, the routing function in a small end node such as a terminal is likely to be nonexistent. The physical (dialup) level will be completely absent for leased lines.

The term *interface* has been widely used to describe the interactions *between adjacent layers* of Fig. 4, and we shall adopt that convention here. Only two of these have been standardized. That lying between the modem and the DLC level is the *electrical* (or *physical*) *interface* as we have said, and this has been internationally standardized in the many flavors discussed in Chapter 3. The other interface that has enjoyed some standardization is that between the outer layer of Fig. 4 and the end user. In some product lines a reasonably stable *application program interface* has been defined on the CPU side; terminal user interfaces have fared more successfully, as discussed in Chapter 15. In the case of all other interfaces between the concentric layers of Fig. 4, essentially no uniformity exists; each implementation handles any one of these interfaces differently.

Not shown in Figs. 2 and 3 is *network control*, the set of functions that do the activation and deactivation of the various portions of the access path shown, provide some of the control parameters required in their operation, and manage recovery. Network control can to various degrees be centralized (in one node) or decentralized (no single node dominant). The many network control functions that are required in forming the access path can be classified into several phases. One such rough classification is the following.

(1) Establishing the electrical transmission path between nodes. This may involve dialup, which requires that appropriate telephone numbers be supplied to a participating node.

(2) Assigning data link addresses of stations, designating who is primary or secondary, and activating the DLC-level function.

(3) Establishing and updating routing tables that tell each node where to forward a message. If the message must proceed onward to another node, the table must say which outgoing link to use.

(4) Establishing and updating directories of all end users in the network, and providing name-to-address conversion.

(5) Establishing and later disestablishing the datagram, transaction, or session connection out to the end users. Parameters must be supplied at each end to set up the specific dialogue convention required by the end user. Queues of requests and responses within a session must be managed.

(6) Providing an interface to the human network manager. This includes coordinating upgrades, and problem determination functions, such as error reporting, testing, sending traces, making measurements.

In this section, we have introduced the notion of layers of function as they occur in peer-related pairs to form an access path through the network. We have also mentioned the control of these functions. Before discussing how these ideas are manifested in specific network protocols of the computer manufacturers and the public common carriers, let us return to a topological view of things and examine in a little more detail what computer networks look like from that standpoint.

III. Networks of Commercially Provided Access Paths

A. Early Systems

In order to discuss the rationale of access path implementations that have been of most interest, it is instructive to sketch the historical evolution of private networks since the 1960s. Let us look first at what has happened with large computers, then minicomputers, and then common carrier computer network services.

The earliest systems were single-processor batch systems that later evolved to support a few local terminals. True teleprocessing (remote access of a terminal end user to an application program in a processor) came with systems such as that shown in Fig. 5, of which a well-known example was the IBM System/360 running the Basic Telecommunications Access Method (BTAM). Essentially all the processing was concentrated in the central host processor, as befitted the technology available at that time. Of the various access path functions we have enumerated in Table I, only elementary DLC-level functions were performed outboard of the host, specifically in a *transmission control unit*, which was often hard-wired and not programmable. The other functions were never cleanly layered, as in Fig. 4, but were so spread out among the different software systems (as shown in Fig. 6) that a change in the configuration of a line or its attached terminal required reprogramming in all these software systems. Terminal cluster controllers performed the device control functions, but essentially none of the communication access path functions. What proved to be a particularly inconvenient restriction was the lack of *line sharing* or *terminal sharing*. By this is meant that, since a given line and all the terminals on it were part of the access path to only one and the same application program, if one user wanted to access two different applications (e.g., savings accounts and credit checking), he required two terminals and two lines (dotted circles in Fig. 5).

The next step in commercially provided networks came around 1974, with systems such as that of Fig. 7, of which a typical example was the System/370 with software and hardware releases referred to as Systems Network Architecture (SNA) generations 1 and 2 [5], [8]. The transmission

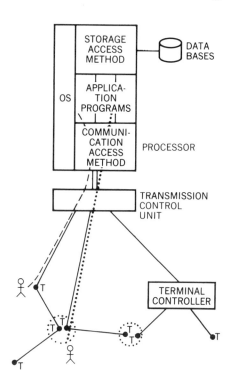

Fig. 5. Typical teleprocessing system of the 1960s such as System/360; dotted and dashed lines are access paths.

control unit gave way to a programmable *communication controller* that handled all data link control and a great deal more. In the communication controller code, the host communication access method code, and the cluster controller code, a significant attempt was made to delineate function into layers, as in Fig. 4. Thanks to the availability of microcomputers and the lowered cost of main and secondary storage, it began to be possible to execute limited application code, including that involving significant databases, in the cluster controllers, and (for some non-IBM realizations) in the communication controller. Most significantly, this design allowed terminals to share a line to separate applications located in the same host and to do the same thing with applications in the cluster controller. Moreover, it allowed access paths between host application programs and cluster controller application programs.

B. Computer Networking

It was soon clear that functions of commercially provided networks did not go far enough. The ARPAnet [9], developed under U.S. Defense Department sponsorship, had shown how a number of *resource-sharing*

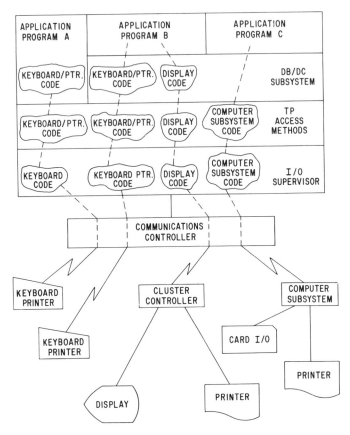

Fig. 6. Distribution of terminal-specific code in an early teleprocessing system.

functions could be provided, and it was soon found that such functions were needed by customers of the computer manufacturers. Specifically, many commercial network users had multiple processors individually serving *tree networks* such as the one in Fig. 7. These networks could not intercommunicate. A given terminal user frequently wanted an access path to an application *in a different host* from the one that normally served him, and it was either uneconomical or infeasible to run a second copy of that application in his own host just to provide this service. Moreover, it became desirable for one application to talk to a remote other application. These capabilities were needed for sharing processor resources among locations and for improving system availability through remote backup. These requirements led to the *computer networking* solution shown in Fig. 8(C), realized, for example, in IBM Systems Network Architecture with Advanced Communication Function (SNA/ACF), also known as SNA-3 [10] and the

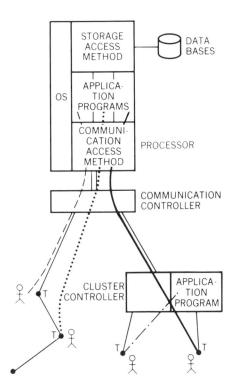

Fig. 7. Typical teleprocessing systems of the
1970s such as System/370 with SNA; dotted
and dashed lines are access paths.

later SNA 4.2 [11]. In this arrangement, any terminal can gain an access
path to any of the applications in any of the hosts. Application-to-application access paths are also supported. Figure 8(C) shows several of the tree
structures of Fig. 7 [schematized in Fig. 8(B), just as Fig. 8(A) abbreviates
Fig. 5] connected together into a mesh of trees [as in Fig. 2(F) by physical
paths between communication controllers. Thus, an SNA tree network can
be characterized as a *hierarchical* network with network control centralized
in the processor [actually in a module called the System Services Control
Point (SSCP) located in the communications access method]. SNA/ACF is
a *hybrid* peer-hierarchical structure, that is, hierarchical within each tree or
domain (with its own SSCP), but with peer interconnection between trees at
the level of the host-attached communication controllers. Not shown in the
diagram is the *multitail* capability of communication controllers, in which
one such controller can support more than one processor. (Also, one
processor can support several controllers.)

In the world of minicomputers, networks have evolved somewhat
differently. Originally, minicomputers were used individually for stand-
alone, real-time, or batch processing or for supporting a few simple terminals. When the need developed for connecting these together, it was found

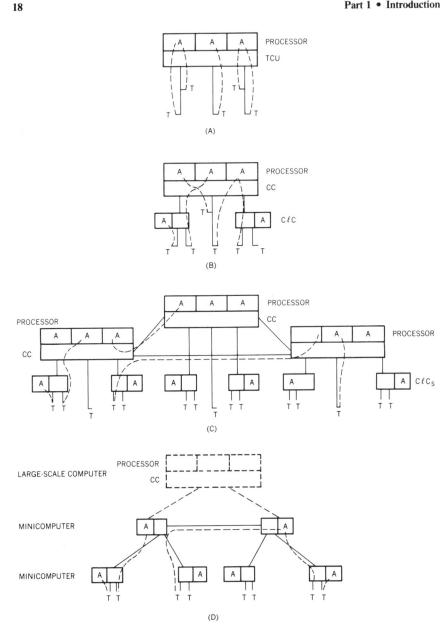

Fig. 8. Schematization of access paths. (A) abbreviates Fig. 5. (B) abbreviates Fig. 7. (C) Top-down network of trees. (D) Bottom-up approach of DECnet.

desirable to do this in a strictly *peer* style of interconnection rather than the peer-plus-hierarchical pattern just discussed. Peer connection had been used in the ARPAnet, and the flexibility of this mode of operation undoubtedly had a strong influence on minicomputer networking. In the peer mode of interconnection, no one computer does network control for the other; there is no master/slave distinction and there need be no identifiable central control point. Network control steps are managed in each node more or less symmetrically. In principle, this allows a wide range of topologies to be implemented, but requires special procedures for managing routing tables, flow control, directory functions, and recovery operations, especially when the network consists of a large number of nodes.

One of the better known of the peer computer network designs is the set of DECnet offerings of the Digital Equipment Corporation based on Digital Network Architecture (DNA) [21]. The DECnet design has been implemented not only for the minicomputers of the DEC product line (e.g., PDP-11), but also for the high end (e.g., DECSYSTEM-20). The ultimate objective is to connect the machines together in a mesh [as in Fig. 2(E)] or in a hierarchy [as in Fig. 8(D)], or other arrangements. In fact, a natural evolution for minicomputer users has been for independent users to start with stand-alone minicomputers of roughly equal power, later to connect them together, and still later to connect this set to a single large host. This *bottom-up* evolutionary pattern may be contrasted with the *top-down* pattern of network growth experienced by many users of large machines, as just described.

The ARPAnet [12], which had a great influence on all succeeding computer networks, whether commercially or carrier provided, embodied a mesh-connected backbone network of many small Interface Message Processors (IMP's), connected together by a packet switching (Section IV B) IMP-to-IMP protocol. Most computers were connected into the network by means of the Host-to-IMP protocol, very roughly equivalent to the later X.25 Interface, which we shall describe in the next section. (A third protocol, the ARPAnet Host-to-Host protocol is roughly equivalent to a *virtual circuit*.) Specially augmented IMPs, called Terminal Interface Processors (TIPs) provided the additional terminal handling software to allow terminal connection into the backbone network. Special higher-level software was provided in the hosts, for example, to support interactive terminals (TELNET) or to effect bulk file transfers (FTP).

IV. Networks of Access Paths Provided by Carriers

In commercially provided networks, such as the IBM and DEC offerings just described, the physical transmission-level function between nodes in the network is, of course, provided by the common carriers. The carriers have been investigating whether there is any technical reason why other functions of Fig. 4 at a higher level than the transmission level might not also be provided by them—for example, protocol conversion. Several references, e.g., [13], detail the recent status of common carrier offerings and data network interfaces.

A. Fast Circuit Switching

The common carriers are, in fact, taking steps not only to improve service at the transmission level, but to provide higher-level services. At the transmission level, an urgent need of the data processing community has been to have dialup service with much faster connect times and much shorter minimum billing increments than ordinary voice grade dialup service provides. There has also been the need to improve the space-division physical interface, such as V.24 (known in the United States as RS-232C), by providing a combined space- and time-division interface of wider generality. These needs have been met partially by the X.21 Recommendation of the international standards body, Comité Consultatif Internationale de Télégraphique et Telephonique (CCITT). The 21 (or fewer) wires of V.24, each performing one and only one function, are replaced in X.21 by up to eight wires, of which one is used in each direction to send bit patterns for specific control functions. By this means, the repertoire of control functions is flexible and expandable. But the real significance of X.21 is not as an electrical interface, but as a peer protocol below the DLC level, to be used for dialing and disconnecting at data processing bit stream speeds, thus serving as the basis of *fast circuit-switching* common carrier networks. In this volume, Chapter 7 describes X.21. In particular, it describes the properties of that portion of the total access path that "X.21 Circuit-Switched Service" can provide, and then compares these capabilities with those of X.25 packet-switching service.

B. Packet Switching

Packet switching [14] seems to have been inspired by the idea of sharing communication channel capacity across a number of users by implementing the same time-slicing philosophy that had earlier proved so successful in sharing the execution power of a single processor across many user processes. Every user node that connects to a packet-switched common carrier makes a contract with the carrier (i.e., follows standard protocols) to hand him bit streams already segmented (packetized) as we have described earlier, with each packet supplemented with a header saying, among other things, to which other user node he wishes the packet delivered. Widespread interest in packet switching on the part of the carriers has led them to standardize this contract in the form of the CCITT Recommendation X.25

[15], which is discussed further in the next section and in considerable detail in Chapters 8 and 9.

The contract includes an agreement on the physical level (not only from the interface point of view but the dialup point of view), the data link control, how the remote user is to be addressed, packet size, how the flow of packets toward and out of the carrier's network is to be regulated, and how certain recovery actions are to be effected. The contract also includes some network control functions such as protocols for establishing and disestablishing the access path. Thus, two user nodes (say A and B) each agree to exchange packets with the carrier network using the X.25 standard, and the carrier agrees to deliver to B properly addressed packets from A and vice versa. The combined actions of (1) the X.25 interface of A to the network, (2) the X.25 interface of B to the network, and (3) the network, provide a full duplex path, termed a *virtual circuit*, between the higher-level function at the two nodes.

Actually, if one adopts the definition of an *interface* we have been using (Section II C), then X.25 is not, strictly speaking, an interface (although often called one), but a set of layered *peer* interaction protocols, by which a machine talks to a packet network (as we shall see in Section V D).

There is currently some debate over whether a degenerate form of virtual circuit, called the *datagram* mode of operation and referred to earlier in this chapter, should be supported under X.25. There, the duration of the contract is essentially only one packet long. The datagram option of X.25 is described in Chapter 9.

Fast circuit switching and packet switching both offer the user the economies of paying for the transmission service only to the extent that it is used. Fast circuit switching has the particular advantage over packet switching that once the transmission path has been set up, it is totally transparent. That is, except for uncontrollable random errors, the bit stream out is the same as the bit stream in for a period of time whose duration is up to the user. Packet switching, although highly nontransparent (since the user is required to adhere to what the contract says about packet length, rate of flow, header structure, etc.) does allow the carrier to offer the user more of the access path function discussed earlier in this chapter than does fast circuit switching, and it allows him many freedoms in buffering, delayed delivery, etc.

V. Network Architectures and Protocols

A. Architecture Versus Implementation

The precise definition of the functions that a computer network and its components should perform is its *architecture*. Exactly by what software code or hardware these functions are actually performed is the *implementa-tion*, which is supposed to adhere to the architecture. Both the data processing and carrier communities have expressed their network ideas in layered peer architectures that in one way or another resemble Fig. 4. Communication architecture is different from processor architecture or storage subsystem architecture in that it usually involves a *pairwise* interac-tion of *two* parties (although there are a few exceptions, such as routing or distributed directory protocols [16], in which more than two parties are involved). For example, as we have said earlier in this paper, a DLC element in one node interacts with a DLC element in another; the flow control functions in two nodes interact specifically with each other, and so forth. The set of agreements for each of these pairwise interactions may be termed a protocol, and thus we find network architecture specified in terms of *protocols for communication between pairs of peer-level layers*. A network protocol consists of the following three elements: (1) *syntax*—the structure of commands and responses in either *field-formatted* (header bits) or *character-string* form; (2) *semantics*—the set of requests to be issued, actions to be performed, and responses returned by either party; and (3) *timing*—specification of ordering of events.

We shall now briefly discuss SNA, DNA, X.25, and the new Open System Interconnection from this point of view, saying something about semantics and syntax, but nothing about timing. All four of these structures make strict definitions of protocols between the two members of a pair of functions at the same level (although in different nodes), but usually leave details of interaction of adjacent layers in the same node (interfaces) to be decided by the implementer. They are all slightly different in the way they assign functions to the different layers, in spite of the fact that these assignments may at first glance appear to be equivalent. The SNA and DECnet architectures and the OSI Reference Model are different in kind from X.25. The former two manage the access path from end to end. On the other hand, as originally conceived, X.25 is not an end-to-end protocol, but a node-to-packet network protocol; it manages the access path from a user node to the immediately adjacent node internal to the packet network. End user to end user functions are built up by a concatenation of the two X.25 paths between each user and the network, plus the internal network paths, as noted in Section IV B. Recent work has strengthened the end-to-end message accountability provisions of common carrier networks that use X.25 into and out of the network, as discussed in Chapter 8.

B. SNA

Figure 9 shows the layers of two SNA nodes. No intermediate nodes are shown, but in practice one or more of these could exist along the access

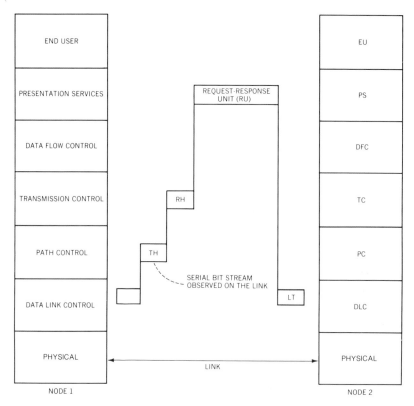

Fig. 9. SNA architectural layers. Compare with Fig. 4. The request–response unit (RU) is usually converted user information.

path. Furthermore, the layers at one end could be in more than one physical box. For example, at the host end, all functions could be in the host (as in the small System/370s, or functions roughly corresponding to Data Link Control and Path Control could be in the software of a separate communication controller and the rest in the host, the more usual situation. Or it might be possible to move almost all the access path functions out to a *front-end communications processor*, leaving the host processor freer to concentrate its resources on application processing. At the terminal end, all the functions shown might be in the same box in the case of an "intelligent terminal," or almost all except the upper layer might be in the cluster controller that supports a number of "dumb" terminals.

The functions of the SNA protocol layers are as follows [5], [11], [17].

1. *Data Link Control* (DLC) transfers packets intact across the noisy transmission facility. For every line attached, there is one instance of DLC

or *DLC Element* (DLCE). This protocol layer can be implemented either as SDLC or the 370 I/O channel.

2. *Path Control* (PC) routes incoming packets to the appropriate outgoing DLCE or to the correct point within its own node. It allows alternate path routing between nodes and the use of several sets of parallel DLC facilities ("transmission groups") between a node pair for better reliability and throughput. It also does packetizing of outgoing and depacketizing of incoming messages. There is one instance of PC per node. The pair of PCs at the two end nodes provide to the higher protocol layers a set of eight *virtual routes* upon which sessions may be built, with flow control within each virtual route. Chapter 11 describes all these functions.

3. *Transmission Control* (TC) manages pacing (flow control for an individual session), helps manage session establishment/disestablishment, and performs a number of other functions on behalf of one of the end users. There is one instance of TC, namely, a Transmission Control Element (TCE), per session per end user.

4. *Data Flow Control* (DFC) has the function of accommodating the idiosyncrasies of message direction and intermittency demanded by the end user. Such idiosyncrasies include, for example, whether a user wants to communicate duplex or half-duplex or whether the separate messages (RUs) are parts of larger units of work as seen by the end user. For example, different RUs flowing in one direction might represent different lines of text that make up a single display screen of text. A screen full of lines of text would be handled by SNA as a *chain*. A structured set of related screens, including messages flowing in both directions, would be handled by SNA as a *bracket*, i.e., a set of chains. There is one instance of DFC per end user session.

5. *Presentation Services* (PS) define the end user's port into the network in terms of code, format, and other attributes. The pair of PS realizations in the pair of nodes has the job of accommodating, for example, the totally different interfaces seen by a terminal end user (and his supporting device control hardware or code) and the application that is being accessed. The PS layer (and other layers as well) are designed for flexibility as to the fraction of the complexity that lives at each member of the peer pair. It is thus possible to have a small or even null PS function in a simple terminal while doing most of it in the processor. As has been mentioned, it is possible optionally to have not just one, but a number of concurrently operating "sub-end-users" for each end user (as we have employed the term *end user*), so that a form of multiplexing (using so-called *FM headers*) takes place at the PS level that is roughly analogous to that at the DLC level. Both Data Flow Control and Presentation Services are described in Chapter 16.

There are a number of other SNA functions that have to do with network control [18], but which are too detailed for a discussion here. These network control functions involve a separate family of access paths that emanate from the System Services Control Point, which might be in some other node not shown, and terminate in modules (also not shown) that control the various functions shown in Fig. 9.

The function of the various headers is shown in Fig. 9. The zig-zag strip shows the bit stream that would be observed on the line. On an outbound message, TC adds to the user data Request/Response Unit (RU) a Request/Response Header (RH) on behalf of itself and DFC, PC adds a Transmission Header (TH), and DLC adds a Link Header (LH) and Link Trailer (LT). Inbound, each layer strips off its appropriate header (and trailer) and forwards what is left. (If there is multiplexing within PS, there is still another header within the RU, namely, the Function Management (FM) header, not shown.) All of this illustrates the following important property of peer protocols: it is by means of the *header* that belongs to a given layer of the protocol that the interaction of the peer pair constituting that layer takes place.

C. DNA and DECnet

The architecture on which the DECnet implementations are based is DNA (Digital Network Architecture). Both DNA and the DECnet implementation are described in Chapter 10. In the DNA set of protocols, illustrated in Fig. 10, there are four basic layers, of which the bottom four are vendor-provided, and the top one is a user implementation, or (in the case of file access) vendor-supplied. The bottom three layers of DNA correspond roughly to the bottom three layers of SNA, as shown in Fig. 9, but with some interesting differences. The Data Link Level is exactly the DLC level of Figs. 4 and 9, the preferred realization being the DEC line control, Digital Data Communications Message Protocol (DDCMP). DDCMP is character-oriented (like BISYNC), but has many of the characteristics of bit-oriented DLCs. As in HDLC, for example, control and data characters are distinguished positionally.

The Transport Layer uses the Transport Packet Header (TPH) for its peer communication. Each packet, with its associated TPH, is handled as a datagram, i.e., each packet is handled by the *Transport Protocol* (TP) as a stand-alone unit, and TP guarantees only a "best effort" to deliver the packet. It will, however, guarantee that if the packet has not arrived by a certain time, then it will never arrive. Successive packets may follow different routes as the TP routing algorithm in each node responds to changing connectivity conditions in the network, so that packets may arrive out of order. Packet loss can occur due to temporary line outages, due to action of TP flow control (which allows for the relief of congestion by discarding packets), or because the packet had exceeded the age limit without being delivered and had to be subjected to euthanasia. The seeming disadvantages of uncertainty of delivery and ordering buys considerable simplicity in Transport Protocol, compared, for example, to SNA Path Control, where tight control is maintained over connectivity, sequentiality, and guaranteed arrival.

In DNA, sequentiality and guaranteed arrival are restored (if required by the user) in the Network Service Layer, using sequence numbers, acknowledgments, and *timeouts*, much as with Data Link Controls. That is, if a packet having a given sequence number arrives successfully, this is acknowledged to the sending *Network Services Protocol* (NSP), and transmission proceeds to the next packet; but if the sender has to wait longer than a certain delay before hearing from the receiver, it retransmits the missing packet. Other NSP functions include end-to-end flow control and packetizing/depacketizing.

The basic access path provided by the two NSPs at two end nodes (using a TP protocol pair per hop, in turn supported by a DDCMP protocol pair per hop) is called a *logical link*. The Application Layer of DNA provides a means for a number of concurrent user processes to communicate with partners across the network, each using a separate logical link. Usually this layer is user-implemented, but a number of file access and distributed file management options can be built using the vendor provided Data Access Protocol (DAP), as illustrated in Fig. 10.

The Network Control functions mentioned in Section II D are almost completely decentralized in DNA. For example, logical links are activated and deactivated by commands to the NSP from the Application level process. In SNA, a session between end users at separate nodes is set up and taken down by a third party, the System Services Control Point, which might be in one of the two nodes or might be in a third node.

D. X.25

The X.25 protocol is illustrated in Fig. 11. The X.21 protocol, mentioned earlier in this paper as an interface, is used as a peer protocol for providing the electrical connection between the user node and the nearest Data Circuit Terminating Equipment (DCE) node owned by the carrier. The X.25 specification allows for use of X.21 bis (in which the interface appears to each user as a V.24-interface) as an interim solution. In Fig. 11, stations 1 and 2 are the Data Terminal Equipments (DTEs), i.e., the user's end nodes. Packets P1 and P3 are intended for station (DTE) 2 and packet P2 is intended for some other station. The Link Control Level protocol, which manages error-free transfers of strings of packets to and from the packet network, is equivalent to the DLC layer of SNA and the Physical

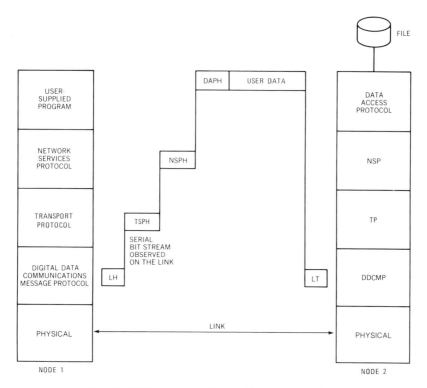

Fig. 10. DNA architectural layers. Compare with Fig. 4.

Link layer of DNA. The Link Control Level protocol uses the full-duplex Asynchronous Balanced mode of HDLC. Here each of the two DLC stations is neither solely a primary station nor a secondary station, but a "combined" station that is able to take responsibility unilaterally for transmission and recovery.

The Packet Level protocol produces the Virtual Circuits (VCs) referred to earlier. There may be one or many (as in Fig. 11) VCs multiplexed onto one access line. These may be *permanent* (assigned upon initial subscription to the service and always in place) or *switched* (invoked as needed). (A switched VC is also known as a *virtual call*.) These virtual circuits have end-to-end aspects during setup or takedown of the VC and end-to-network aspects otherwise. For example, flow control usually operates only to regulate traffic between the user node and the network. After a VC is initially set up, the addressing is between each node and the network, not between end users. These are clearly end-to-network functions. But in initially establishing the VC, the end-user node must know how to address the other end-user node. This is clearly an end-to-end function.

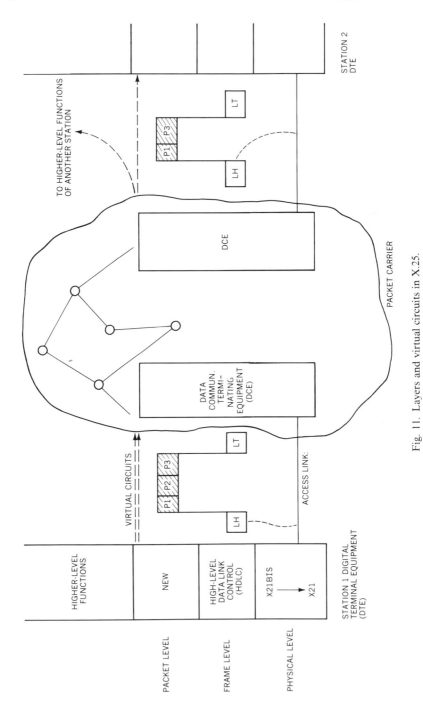

Fig. 11. Layers and virtual circuits in X.25.

As Fig. 11 shows, there are two X.25 protocols between each of the two customer-owned end nodes and the network. The packet carrier appears in this diagram in roughly the position where a single intermediate node would appear in Figs. 9 and 10. If an SNA or DECnet system operates across an X.25 packet carrier facility, there are some divided responsibilities. For example, the SNA and DECnet implementations have specific rules about packet size, addressing/routing, flow control, internal multiplexing of flows, and recovery from error and lost- or duplicated-message conditions. When X.25 services are used, these responsibilities may overlap with those that the carrier is willing to undertake. There is a growing literature (e.g., [19]) discussing how these overlaps may be resolved.

E. Open System Interconnection

Before ending this brief review of network protocols, architectures, and implementations, it should be mentioned that there is considerable interest and activity in the standards bodies that have defined HDLC, X.21, X.25, etc., in standardizing even higher-level functions than those represented by the Packet Level of X.25. The object is to allow any-to-any (i.e., *open*) interconnection capability for communication products. This is being attempted by adding four more layers above the X.25 Packet Level, making seven in all. The next chapter summarizes the available details. The lowest two layers correspond to the usual peer physical level and DLC, just as with SNA and DNA, Figs. 9 and 10. These are discussed in Parts I and II of this volume. The third *Network* level is equivalent to the Packet level of X.25. The fourth *Transport* layer exists only at the end nodes and provides the necessary high level of end-node to end-node integrity control to support sessions that require it. Part IV treats questions that appear in OSI Layers 3 and 4. The fifth *Session* layer corresponds roughly to TC and DFC of SNA; that is, it acts to bind the end users together in a session and then administers the rules of the dialogue. The sixth *Presentation* layer provides protocol conversion as in Figs. 4 and 9, and the end user's *Application* layer completes the structure. Part V corresponds to Layers 5 and 6. In OSI, network control, as defined earlier in Section II D, runs as an Application level function.

Since it is being built up carefully using a wide variety of inputs from many sources of earlier experience, the Reference Model should provide a fairly clear and comprehensive framework for discussion, analysis, and comparison.

VI. Concluding Remarks

Even though networks have been growing more complicated, they should be getting easier to dissect and understand as systematic formalization and layering become more pervasive in the implementations. One reason for persistence of complexity is that, until now, the architects have carried a heavier burden than is commonly realized of maintaining compatibility with individual software and hardware product offerings that antedated the evolution of systematic, clearly layered sets of network protocols. These earlier offerings are gradually disappearing or in later releases are adhering more and more to the strict terms of the architecture. The modularization means that new ideas ought to be more easily incorporated without producing system-wide disruptions. Continuing research will provide such new ideas.

References

[1]   A. S. Tanenbaum, *Computer Networks*, Englewood Cliff, N. J.: Prentice-Hall, 1981.
[2]   P. E. Green Jr., and R. W. Lucky, Eds., *Computer Communications*, New York: IEEE Press, 1975.
[3]   L. Kleinrock, *Queuing Systems, Vol. II*, New York: Wiley, 1976.
[4]   M. Schwartz, *Computer Communication Network Design and Analysis*, Englewood Cliffs, NJ: Prentice-Hall, 1977.
[5]   R. J. Cypser, *Communications Architecture for Distributed Systems*. Reading, MA: Addison-Wesley, 1978.
[6]   D. W. Davies, D. L. A. Barber, W. L. Price, and C. M. Solomonides, *Computer Networks and their Protocols*, New York: Wiley, 1979.
[7]   J. R. Davey, "Modems," *Proc. IEEE*, vol. 60, pp. 1284–1292, Nov. 1972. Reprinted in [2].
[8]   J. H. McFadyen, "Systems network architecture: An overview," *IBM Syst. J.*, vol. 15, no. 1, pp. 4–23. See also three companion papers in the same issue.
[9]   L. G. Roberts and B. D. Wessler, "Computer network development to achieve resource sharing," in *1970 AFIPS Conf. Proc (SJCC)*, vol. 36, pp. 543–549.
[10] *Introduction to Advanced Communication Function*, Order No. GC30-3033, IBM Data Processing Div., White Plains, NY, 10504.
[11] J. P. Gray and T. B. McNeil, "SNA multiple-system networking," *IBM Syst. J.*, vol. 18, no. 2, pp. 263–297, 1979.
[12] See, for example, the papers on ARPAnet reprinted in [2].
[13] J. Halsey, L. Hardy, and L. Powning, "Public data networks: Their evolution, interface, and status," *IBM Syst. J.*, vol. 18, no. 2, pp. 223–243, 1979.
[14] R. E. Kahn, Ed., *Special Issue on Packet Communication Networks*, *Proc. IEEE*, vol. 66, Nov. 1978.
[15] A. Rybczynski, B. Wessler, R. Despres, and J. Wedlake, "A new communication protocol for accessing data networks—The international packet mode interface," in *AFIPS Conf. Proc. (NCC)*, vol. 45, June 1971, pp. 477–482.

[16] J. Bremer and O. Drobnik, "Specification and validation of a protocol for decentralized directory management," IBM Research Ctr., Yorktown Hts., NY, Tech. Rep. RC-7800, Sept. 25, 1979.

[17] *SNA Format and Protocol Reference Manual*, Order No. SC30-3112.

[18] J. P. Gray, "Network services in systems network architecture," *IEEE Trans. Commun.*, vol. COM-25, pp. 104–116, Jan. 1977.

[19] F. P. Corr and D. H. Neal, "SNA and emerging international standards," *IBM Syst. J.*, vol. 18, no. 2, pp. 244–262, 1979.

2

A Standard Layer Model

Hubert Zimmermann

I. Introduction

In 1977, the International Organization for Standardization (ISO) recognized the special and urgent need for standards for heterogeneous informatic networks and decided to create a new subcommittee (SC16) for "Open Systems Interconnection."

The initial development of computer networks had been fostered by experimental networks such as ARPAnet [1] and CYCLADES [2], immediately followed by commercial networks [3], [4]. While experimental networks were conceived as heterogeneous from the very beginning, each manufacturer developed its own set of conventions for interconnecting its own equipment, referring to these as its "network architecture."

The universal need for interconnecting systems from different manufacturers rapidly became apparent [5], leading ISO to decide upon the creation of SC16 with the objective being to come up with standards required for "Open Systems Interconnection." The term "open" was chosen to emphasize the fact that by conforming to those international standards, a system will be capable of interacting with all other systems obeying the same standards throughout the world.

The first meeting of SC16 was held in March 1978, and initial discussions revealed [6] that a consensus could be reached rapidly on a layered architecture which would satisfy most requirements of Open Systems Interconnection with the potential of being expanded later to meet new requirements. SC16 decided to give the highest priority to the development of a standard Model of Architecture which would constitute the framework for the development of standard protocols. After less than 18 months of discussion, this task was completed, and the ISO Model of Architecture called the Reference Model of Open Systems Interconnection [7] was transmitted by SC16 to its parent Technical Committee on "Data Processing" (TC97) along with recommendations to start officially a number of projects for developing on this basis an initial set of standard protocols for Open Systems Interconnection. These recommendations were adopted by TC97 at the end of 1979 as the basis for the ensuing development of standard protocols for Open Systems Interconnection within ISO. The OSI Reference Model was also recognized by CCITT Rapporteur's Group on Public Data Network Services.

The present chapter describes the OSI Architecture Model as it was transmitted to TC97. Sections II–V introduce concepts of a layered architecture, along with the associated vocabulary defined by SC16. Specific use of those concepts in the OSI seven-layer architecture are then presented in Section VI. Finally, some indications on the likely development of OSI standard protocols are given in Section VII.

Note on an "Interconnection Architecture"

The basic objective of SC16 is to standardize the rules of interaction between interconnected systems. Thus, only the external behavior of Open Systems must conform to OSI Architecture, while the internal organization and functioning of each individual Open System are beyond the scope of OSI standards since these are not visible from other systems with which it is interconnected [8].

It should be noted that the same principle of restricted visibility is used in any manufacturer's network architecture in order to permit interconnection within the same network of systems with different structure.

II. General Principles of Layering

Layering is a structuring technique which permits the network of Open Systems to be viewed as logically composed of a succession of layers, each wrapping the lower layers and isolating them from the higher layers, as exemplified in Fig. 1. Each layer performs a specific set of functions which add to or enhance those performed by the lower layers. For instance, the transport layer (see Section VI) performs end-to-end transport control functions on top of packet switching functions performed by the lower layers.

An alternative but equivalent illustration of layering, used in particular by SC16, is given in Fig. 2 where successive layers are represented in a vertical sequence, with the physical media for Open Systems Interconnection at the bottom.

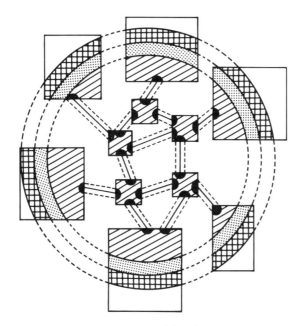

Fig. 1. Network layering.

Each individual system itself is viewed as being logically composed of a succession of subsystems, each corresponding to the intersection of the system with a layer. In other words, a layer is viewed as being logically composed of subsystems of the same rank of all interconnected systems. For instance, each system will logically comprise a physical circuit control subsystem; a data link control subsystem; a packet-switching subsystem; a

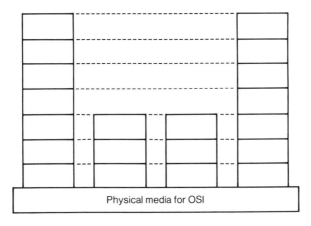

Fig. 2. An example of OSI representation of layering.

transport control subsystem; i.e., a transport station, etc. Conversely, all transport stations form collectively the Transport Layer.

Each subsystem is, in turn, viewed as being made up of one or several entities. In other words, each layer is made of entities, each of which belongs to one system. Entities in the same layer are termed *peer* entities. Entities in a layer represent the distributed processing capability of the layer in performance of its functions. On the other hand, entities of all layers within one single Open System represent the protocol processing capability of this system; i.e., its processing capability seen by the other Open Systems.

For simplicity of notation, any layer is referred to as the (N) *layer*, while its next lower and next higher layers are referred to as the $(N-1)$ layer and the $(N+1)$ layer, respectively. The same notation is used to designate all concepts relating to layers; e.g., entities in the (N) layer are termed (N) *entities*, as illustrated in Figs. 3 and 4.

The basic idea of layering is that each layer adds value to services provided by the set of lower layers in such a way that the highest layer is offered the set of services needed to run distributed applications. Layering thus divides the total problem into smaller pieces. Another major objective of layering is to ensure independence between layers. This is achieved by defining services provided by a layer to the next higher layer, independent of how these services are performed. This permits changes to be made in the way a layer or a set of layers operate, provided they still offer the same service to the next higher layer. (A more comprehensive list of criteria for layering is given in Section VI.) This technique is similar to the one used in structured programming where only the functions performed by a module (and not its internal functioning) are known by its users.

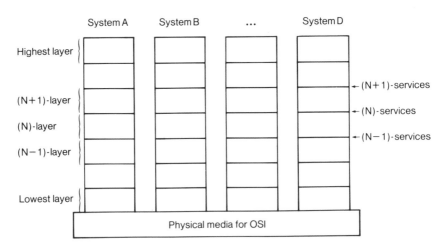

Fig. 3. Systems, layers, and services.

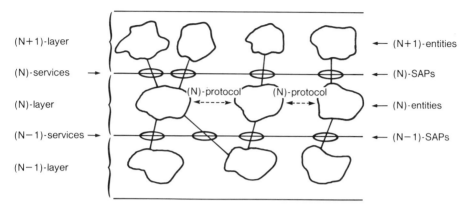

Fig. 4. Entities, service access points (SAPs), and protocols.

Except for the highest layer, which operates for its own purpose, (N) entities distributed in the (N) layer among the interconnected Open Systems work collectively to provide the (N) service to $(N + 1)$ entities as illustrated in Fig. 4. In other words, the (N) entities add value to the $(N - 1)$ service they get from the $(N - 1)$ layer and offer this value-added service, i.e., the (N) service, to the $(N + 1)$ entities. For instance, the Network Layer adds a relaying capability on top of point to point communication service provided by the Data link Layer. Similarly, the Transport Layer adds end-to-end control on top of the control cascade of the Network Layer.

Communication between the (N) entities makes exclusive use of the $(N - 1)$ services. In particular, direct communication between the $(N + 1)$ entities in the same system, e.g., for sharing local resources, is not visible from outside of the system and thus is not covered by the OSI Architecture. Entities in the lowest layer communicate through the Physical Media for OSI, which could be considered as forming the (0) layer of the OSI Architecture. Cooperation between the (N) entities is ruled by the (N) *protocols*, which precisely define how the (N) entities work together using the $(N - 1)$ services to perform the (N) functions which add value to the $(N - 1)$ service in order to offer the (N) service to the $(N + 1)$ entities. For instance, the transport protocol defines how transport stations cooperate to provide the transport service to session entities, making use of the network service.

The (N) services are offered to the $(N + 1)$ entities at the (N) *service access points*, or (N) SAPs for short, which represent the logical interfaces between the (N) entities and the $(N + 1)$ entities. An (N) SAP can be served by only one (N) entity and used by only one $(N + 1)$ entity, but one (N) entity can serve several (N) SAPs and one $(N + 1)$ entity can use

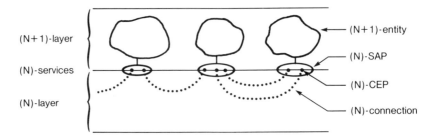

Fig. 5. Connections and connection end points (CEPs).

several (N) SAPs. (N) SAPs represent the means by which (N) entities and ($N + 1$) entities carry out their server/user relationship. In other words, SAPs are used to model relations between processing elements (entities) in each open system.

A common service offered by all layers consists of providing associations between peer SAPs (and thus between peer entities using these SAPs) which can be used in particular to transfer data. More precisely (see Fig. 5), the (N) layer offers (N) *connections* between (N) SAPs as part of the (N) services. The most usual type of connection is the *point-to-point* connection, but there are also *multi-end-point* connections which correspond to multiple associations between entities (e.g., broadcast communication). The end of an (N) connection at an (N) SAP is called an (N) *connection end point* or (N) CEP for short. Several connections may coexist between the same pair (or *n*-tuple) of SAPs. In the following, for the sake of simplicity, we will consider only point-to-point connections.

Connectionless communications (e.g., datagrams in the network service) which are important for transaction-oriented applications will be included later in the OSI Reference Model.

III. Identifiers

Objects within a layer or at the boundary between adjacent layers need to be uniquely identifiable, i.e., in order to establish a connection between two SAPs, one must be able to identify them uniquely. The OSI Architecture defines identifiers for entities, SAPs, and connections as well as relations between these identifiers, as briefly outlined below.

Each (N) entity is identified with a *global title** which is unique and identifies the same (N) entity from anywhere in the network of Open

---

*The term "title" has been preferred to the term "name," which is viewed as bearing a more general meaning. A title is equivalent to an entity name.

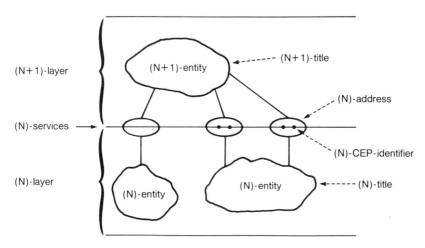

Fig. 6. Titles, addresses, and CEP identifiers.

Systems. Within more limited *domains*, an (N) entity can be identified with a *local title* which uniquely identifies the (N) entity only in the domain. For instance, within the domain corresponding to the (N) layer, (N) entities are identified with (N) *global titles* which are unique within the (N) layer.

Each (N) SAP is identified with an (N) *address* which uniquely identifies the (N) SAP at the boundary between the (N) layer and the $(N + 1)$ layer.

The concepts of titles and addresses are illustrated in Fig. 6.

Bindings between (N) entities and the $(N - 1)$ SAPs they use (i.e., SAPs through which they can access each other and communicate) are translated into the concept of (N) *directory* which indicates correspondence between global titles of (N) entities and $(N - 1)$ addresses through which they can be reached, as illustrated in Fig. 7. For instance, an information retrieval service on a network can be known by the global title of the corresponding application entity. A directory will permit one to deduce the corresponding address (presentation address), i.e., the address towards which the connection to the information retrieval service has to be established.

Correspondence between (N) addresses served by an (N) entity and the $(N - 1)$ addresses used for this purpose is performed by an (N) *mapping* function. In addition to the simplest case of one-to-one mapping, mapping may, in particular, be hierarchical, with the (N) address being made of an $(N - 1)$ address and an (N) suffix. Mapping may also be performed "by table." These three types of mapping are illustrated in Fig. 8. For instance, a one-to-one mapping is used by the Presentation Layer

(N)-title	(N−1)-address
A	352
B	237
B	015
C	015

Fig. 7. Example of an (N) directory.

which arranges for presentation of data but does not perform any specific addressing function on top of the session service, and thus simply maps, one-to-one, presentation addresses onto session addresses. Hierarchical mapping offers the advantage of simplicity and will normally be used by the Transport Layer to offer subaddressing capability within a host (usually identified with one network address). The price paid for simplicity of hierarchical mapping is that these subaddresses are tied forever with the address and thus cannot be moved. Mapping by table offers more flexibility since a change in configuration will be "easily" reflected in a change of

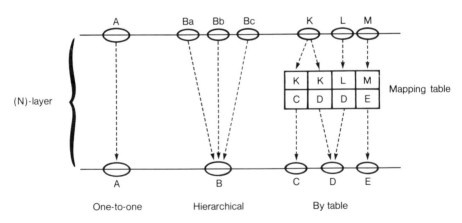

Fig. 8. Mapping between addresses.

mapping tables. Mapping by table might be used for instance in the Network Layer, where flexibility of reconfiguration is important.

Finally, each (N) CEP is uniquely identified within its (N) SAP by an (N) CEP *identifier* which is used by the (N) entity and the $(N + 1)$ entity on both sides of the (N) SAP to identify the (N) connection as illustrated in Fig. 6. This is necessary since several (N) connections may end at the same (N) SAP.

IV. Operation of Connections

A. Establishment and Release

When an $(N + 1)$ entity requests the establishment of an (N) connection from one of the (N) SAPs it uses to another (N) SAP, it must provide at the local (N) SAP the (N) address of the distant (N) SAP. When the (N) connection is established, both the $(N + 1)$ entity and the (N) entity will use the (N) CEP identifier to designate locally the (N) connection. For instance, a session entity A which wishes to get a connection with a session entity B needs to know the transport address $TA(B)$ (of the transport SAP) at which B can be reached. In order to have this connection established, session entity A requests the transport layer to establish a transport connection between the local SAP with address $TA(A)$ and the distant SAP with address $TA(B)$. When the connection has been established, each session entity A and B will simply refer to this connection at their respective end by the corresponding transport CEP.

(N) connections may be established and released dynamically on top of $(N - 1)$ connections. Establishment of an (N) connection implies the availability of an $(N - 1)$ connection between the two entities. If not available, the $(N - 1)$ connection must be established. This requires the availability of an $(N - 2)$ connection. The same consideration applies downwards until an available connection is encountered.

In some cases, the (N) connection may be established simultaneously with its supporting $(N - 1)$ connection provided the $(N - 1)$ connection establishment service permits (N) entities to exchange information necessary to establish the (N) connection. For instance, establishment of a transport connection requires the availability of a network connection (e.g., an X.25 virtual circuit). If it is not available, the network connection must be established prior to establishment of the transport connection or simultaneously, provided the establishment of the network connection permits one to transmit the transport control information necessary for establishing the transport connection (e.g., user data in call request and call indication packets in X.25).

B. Multiplexing and Splitting

Three particular types of construction of (N) connections on top of ($N - 1$) connections may be distinguished:

(1) One-to-one correspondence, where each (N) connection is built on one ($N - 1$) connection.

(2) Multiplexing (referred to as "upward multiplexing" in [7]), where several (N) connections are multiplexed on one single ($N - 1$) connection.

(3) Splitting (referred to as "downward multiplexing" in [7]), where one single (N) connection is built on top of several ($N - 1$) connections, the traffic on the (N) connection being divided between the various ($N - 1$) connections.

These three types of correspondence between connections in adjacent layers are illustrated in Fig. 9. In the Transport Layer, for instance, a one-to-one correspondence will be used when the Open System is a single terminal connected to an X.25 Public Data Network, thus implementing only one transport connection on a network connection (virtual circuit). In the case of a cluster of terminals, multiplexing of several transport connections on a single network connection may be used to reduce the cost of usage of the Public Data Network (this depends of course on its tariff structure). Finally, splitting one transport connection onto two (or more) network connections may permit one to have a higher throughput or a better reliability than that given by a single network connection.

C. Data Transfer

Information is transferred in various types of data units between peer entities and between entities attached to a specific service access point. The

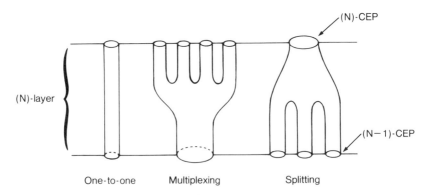

Fig. 9. Correspondence between connections.

	Control	Data	Combined
(N)-(N) Peer Entities	(N)-Protocol Control Information	(N)-User Data	(N)-Protocol Data Units
(N)-(N−1) Adjacent layers	(N−1)-Interface Control Information	(N−1)-Interface Data	(N−1)-Interface Data Unit

Fig. 10. Interrelationship between data units.

data units are defined below, with an example of what these data units would be for the Data Link Layer using HDLC as its Data Link protocol (see Section VII B). The interrelationship among these data units is shown in Fig. 10.

(N) *protocol control information* is information exchanged between two (N) entities, using an $(N-1)$ connection, to coordinate their joint operation; e.g., HDLC header and trailer.

(N) *user data* is the data transferred between two (N) entities on behalf of the $(N+1)$ entities for whom the (N) entities are providing services, e.g., data passed by network entities and transferred transparently in the information field of HDLC information frames by data link entities.

An (N) *protocol data unit* is a unit of data which contains (N) Protocol Control Information and possibly (N) User Data, e.g., HDLC frames.

(N) *interface control information* is information exchanged between an $(N-1)$ entity and an (N) entity to coordinate their joint operation, e.g., system-specific control information passed between network entities and data link entities running HDLC, such as buffer address and length, maximum waiting time, etc.

(N) *interface data* is information transferred from an $(N+1)$ entity to an (N) entity for transmission to a correspondent $(N+1)$ entity over an (N) connection, or conversely, information transferred from an (N) entity to an ($N + 1$) entity which has been received over an (N) connection from a correspondent ($N + 1$) entity, e.g., text to be transmitted transparently by data link entities.

(N) *interface data unit* is the unit of information transferred across the service access point between an ($N + 1$) entity and an (N) entity in a single interaction. The size of (N) interface data units is not necessarily the same at each end of the connection, e.g., one block (or a piece of block or a chain of blocks) of data to be transmitted by the data link entity serving a network entity.

($N - 1$) service data unit is the amount of ($N - 1$) interface data whose identity is preserved from one end of an ($N - 1$) connection to the other. Data may be held within a connection until a complete service data unit is put into the connection, e.g., a block of data transferred as such from one network entity to its correspondent network entity by their servicing data link entities (as the information field of an HDLC frame).

Expedited ($N - 1$) service data unit is a small ($N - 1$) service data unit whose transfer is expedited. The ($N - 1$) layer ensures that an expedited data unit will not be delivered after any subsequent service data unit or expedited data unit sent on that connection. An expedited ($N - 1$) service data unit may also be referred to as an ($N - 1$) expedited data unit. There

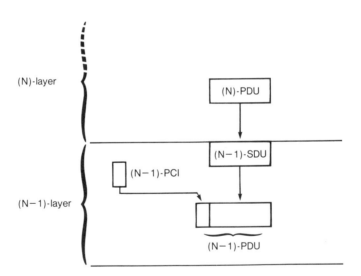

PCI = Protocol control information
PDU = Protocol data unit
SDU = Service data unit

Fig. 11. Logical relationship between data units in adjacent layers.

is no equivalent of data link expedited data units offered by HDLC, but proposals have been made for such an enhancement.

Note: An (N) protocol data unit may be mapped one-to-one onto an ($N - 1$) service data unit (see Fig. 11).

V. Management Aspects

Even though a number of resources are managed locally, i.e., without involving cooperation between distinct systems, some management functions require communication between systems.

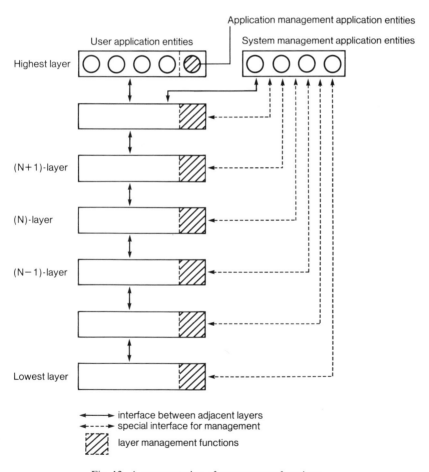

Fig. 12. A representation of management functions.

Examples of such management functions are:

configuration information,
cold start/termination,
monitoring,
diagnostics,
reconfiguration, etc.

The OSI Architecture considers management functions as applications of a specific type. Management entities located in the highest layer of the architecture may use the complete set of services offered to all applications in order to perform management functions. This organization of management functions within the OSI Architecture is illustrated in Fig. 12. For instance, updating routing tables (used by entities in the network layer to forward packets towards their destination) is a management function. Management entities in charge of this function must communicate to determine the proper contents of routing tables (e.g., destination unreachable through a given node). In order to communicate, these route management entities, located in the Application Layer (i.e., the highest layer) use the set of services provided by the lower layers (e.g., data formatted by the Presentation Layer, reliable transport of data ensured by the Transport layer, etc.). The updating of routing tables is itself a local function by which each route management entity in the Application Layer interacts with its local network entity (through the dotted arrow in Fig. 12).

VI. The Seven Layers of the OSI Architecture

A. Justification of the Seven Layers

ISO agreed on a number of principles to be considered for defining the specific set of layers in the OSI architecture, and applied these principles to come up with the seven layers of the OSI Architecture.

Principles to be considered are as follows:

1. Do not create so many layers as to make difficult the system engineering task of describing and integrating these layers.
2. Create a boundary at a point where the services description can be small and the number of interactions across the boundary is minimized.
3. Create separate layers to handle functions which are manifestly different in the process performed or the technology involved.
4. Collect similar functions into the same layer.

5. Select boundaries at a point which past experience has demonstrated to be successful.
6. Create a layer of easily localized functions so that the layer could be totally redesigned and its protocols changed in a major way to take advantage of new advances in architectural, hardware, or software technology without changing the services and interfaces with the adjacent layers.
7. Create a boundary where it may be useful at some point in time to have the corresponding interface standardized.
8. Create a layer when there is a need for a different level of abstraction in the handling of data, e.g., morphology, syntax, semantics.
9. Create for each layer interfaces with its upper and lower layer only.
10. Create further subgrouping and organization of functions to form sublayers within a layer in cases where distinct communication services need it.
11. Create, where needed, two or more sublayers with a common, and therefore minimum, functionality to allow interface operation with adjacent layers.
12. Allow bypassing of sublayers.

B. Specific Layers

The following is a brief explanation of how the layers were chosen:

(1) It is essential that the architecture permits usage of a realistic variety of physical media for interconnection with different control procedures (e.g., V.24, V.35, X.21, etc.). Application of principles 3, 5, and 8 leads to identification of a *Physical Layer* as the lowest layer in the architecture.

(2) Some physical communications media (e.g., telephone lines) require specific techniques to be used in order to transmit data between systems despite a relatively high error rate (i.e., an error rate not acceptable for the great majority of applications). These specific techniques are used in data link control procedures which have been studied and standardized for a number of years. It must also be recognized that new physical communications media (e.g., fiber optics) will require different data-link control procedures. Application of principles 3, 5, and 8 leads to identification of a *Data Link Layer* on top of the physical layer in the architecture.

(3) In the Open Systems Interconnection, some systems will act as final destinations of data. Some systems may act only as intermediate nodes (forwarding data to other systems). Application of principles 3, 5, and 7 leads to identification of a *Network Layer* on top of the Data Link Layer. Network-oriented protocols, such as routing, for example, will be grouped

in this layer. Thus, the Network Layer will provide a connection path (network connection) between a pair of transport entities (see Fig. 13).

(4) Control of data transportation from source end system to destination end system (which need not be performed in intermediate nodes) is the last function to be performed in order to provide the totality of transport service. Thus, the upper layer in the transport-service part of the architecture is the *Transport Layer*, sitting on top of the Network Layer. This Transport Layer relieves higher-layer entities from any concern with the transportation of data between them.

(5) In order to bind/unbind distributed activities into a logical relationship that controls the data exchange with respect to synchronization and structure, the need for a dedicated layer has been identified. So the application of principles 3 and 4 leads to the establishment of the *Session Layer*, which is on top of the Transport Layer.

(6) The remaining set of general interest functions are those related to representation and manipulation of structured data for the benefit of application programs. Application of principles 3 and 4 leads to identification of a *Presentation Layer* on top of the Session Layer.

(7) Finally, there are applications consisting of application processes which perform information processing. A portion of these application processes and the protocols by which they communicate comprise the *Application Layer* as the highest layer of the architecture.

The resulting architecture with seven layers, illustrated in Fig. 13, obeys principles 1 and 2. A more detailed definition of each of the seven layers identified above is given in the following sections, starting from the top with

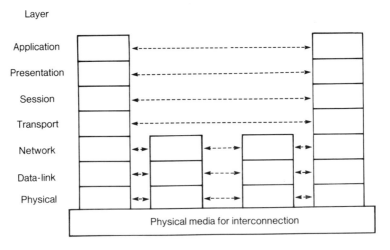

Fig. 13. The seven-layers OSI architecture.

the Application Layer described in Section VI C 1) down to the Physical Layer (described in Section VI C 7).

C. Overview of the Seven Layers of the OSI Architecture

(1) *The Application Layer.* This is the highest layer in the OSI architecture. Protocols of this layer directly serve the end user by providing the distributed information service appropriate to an application, to its management, and to system management. Management of Open Systems Interconnection comprises those functions required to initiate, maintain, terminate, and record data concerning the establishment of connections for data transfer among application processes. The other layers exist only to support this layer.

An application is composed of cooperating *application processes* which intercommunicate according to application layer protocols. Application processes are the ultimate sources and sinks for data exchanged.

A portion of an application process is manifested in the application layer as the execution of an application protocol (i.e., application entity). The rest of the application process is considered beyond the scope of the present layered model. Applications or application processes may be of any kind (manual, computerized, industrial, or physical).

(2) *The Presentation Layer.* The purpose of the Presentation Layer is to provide the set of services which may be selected by the Application Layer to enable it to interpret the meaning of the data exchanged. These services are for the management of the entry, exchange, display, and control of structured data.

The presentation service is location independent and is considered to be on top of the Session Layer which provides the service of linking a pair of presentation entities. It is through the use of services provided by the Presentation Layer that applications in an Open Systems Interconnection environment can communicate without unacceptable costs in interface variability, transformations, or application modification.

(3) *The Session Layer.* The purpose of the Session Layer is to assist in the support of the interactions between cooperating presentation entities. To do this, the Session Layer provides services which are classified into the following two categories:

a. Binding two presentation entities into a relationship and unbinding them. This is called session administration service.
b. Control of data exchange, delimiting, and synchronizing data operations between two presentation entities. This is called *session dialog service.*

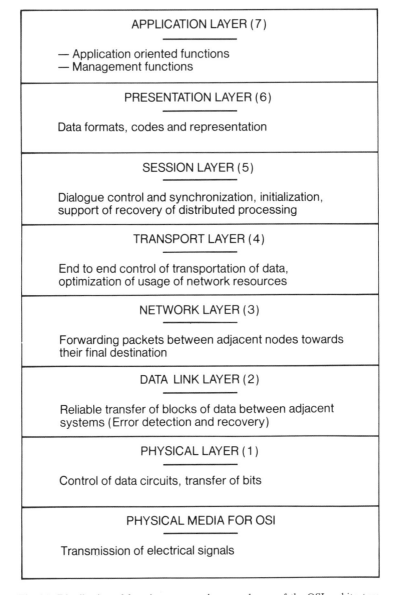

APPLICATION LAYER (7)

— Application oriented functions
— Management functions

PRESENTATION LAYER (6)

Data formats, codes and representation

SESSION LAYER (5)

Dialogue control and synchronization, initialization,
support of recovery of distributed processing

TRANSPORT LAYER (4)

End to end control of transportation of data,
optimization of usage of network resources

NETWORK LAYER (3)

Forwarding packets between adjacent nodes towards
their final destination

DATA LINK LAYER (2)

Reliable transfer of blocks of data between adjacent
systems (Error detection and recovery)

PHYSICAL LAYER (1)

Control of data circuits, transfer of bits

PHYSICAL MEDIA FOR OSI

Transmission of electrical signals

Fig. 14. Distribution of functions among the seven layers of the OSI architecture.

To implement the transfer of data between presentation entities, the
Session Layer employs the services provided by the Transport Layer.

(4) *The Transport Layer.* The Transport Layer exists to provide a
universal transport service in association with the underlying services provided by lower layers.

The Transport Layer provides transparent transfer of data between session entities. The Transport Layer relieves these session entities from any concern with the detailed way in which reliable and cost-effective transfer of data is achieved.

The Transport Layer is required to optimize the use of available communications services to provide the performance required for each connection between session entities at minimum cost.

(5) *The Network Layer*. The Network Layer provides functional and procedural means to exchange network service data units between two transport entities over a network connection. It provides transport entities with independence from routing and switching considerations.

(6) *The Data Link Layer*. The purpose of the Data Link Layer is to provide the functional and procedural means to establish, maintain, and release data links between network entities.

(7) *The Physical Layer*. The Physical Layer provides mechanical, electrical, functional, and procedural characteristics to establish, maintain, and release physical connections (e.g., data circuits) between data link entities.

Distribution of functions among the seven layers of the OSI architecture is illustrated in Fig. 14.

VII. OSI Protocol Developments

The model of OSI architecture defines the services provided by each layer to the next higher layer, and offers concepts to be used to specify how each layer performs its specific functions. Detailed functioning of each layer is defined by the protocols specific to the layer in the framework of the Architecture model. Most of the initial effort within ISO has been placed on the model of OSI. The next step consists of the definition of standard protocols for each layer.

This section contains a brief description of a likely initial set of protocols, corresponding to specific standardization projects recommended by SC16.

A. Protocols in the Physical Layer

Standards already exist within CCITT defining:

1. interfaces with physical media for OSI, and
2. protocols for establishing, controlling, and releasing switched data circuits.

Such standards are described in Chapters 3 and 7. The only work to be done will consist of clearly relating these standards to the OSI architecture model.

B. Protocols in the Data Link Layer

Standard protocols for the Data Link Layer have already been developed within ISO, which are described in Chapters 4 and 5. The most popular Data Link Layer protocol is likely to be HDLC [9], without ruling out the possibility of using also character-oriented standards. Just as for the Physical Layer, the remaining work will consist mainly of clearly relating these existing standards to the OSI Architecture model.

C. Protocols in the Network Layer

An important basis for protocols in the Network Layer is Level 3 of the X.25 interface [10] defined by CCITT and described in Chapter 8. It will have to be enhanced in particular to permit interconnection of private and public networks. Other types of protocols are likely to be standardized later in this layer, in particular, protocols corresponding to Datagram networks (Chapter 9).

D. Protocols in the Transport Layer

A universal transport protocol is expected to be standardized by ISO imminently [11] on the basis of a proposal made by the European Computer Manufacturers Association (ECMA).

E. Protocols for the Session Layer

A minimum session protocol sufficient to support initial requirements is under development within ISO on the basis of another proposal made by ECMA [12]. Standardization of this session protocol would closely follow standardization of the transport protocol mentioned in Section VII D.

F. Presentation Layer Protocol

So far, Virtual Terminal Protocols (VTPs) and part of virtual file are considered the most urgent protocols to be developed in the Presentation Layer. A number of VTPs are available (e.g., [13], [14]), many of them being very similar, and it should be easy to derive a Standard VTP from these proposals, also making use of the ISO standard for "Extended Control Characters for I/O Imaging Devices" [15]. These protocols are reviewed in Chapter 15. The situation is similar for File Transfer Protocols.

G. Management Protocols

Most of the work within ISO has been done so far on the architecture of management functions, and very little work has been done on management protocols themselves. Therefore, it is too early to give indications on the likely results of the ISO work in this area.

VIII. Conclusion

The development of OSI Standards is a very big challenge, the result of which will impact all future computer communication developments. If standards come too late or are inadequate, interconnection of heterogeneous systems will not be possible or will be very costly.

The work collectively achieved so far by SC16 members is very promising, and additional efforts should be expended to capitalize on these initial results and come up rapidly with the most urgently needed set of standards which will support initial usage of OSI (mainly terminals accessing services and file transfers). The next set of standards, including OSI management and access to distributed data, will have to follow very soon.

Common standards between ISO and CCITT are also essential to the success of standardization, since new services announced by PTTs and common carriers are very similar to data-processing services offered as computer manufacturer products, and duplication of incompatible standards could simply cause the standardization effort to fail. In this regard, acceptance of the OSI Reference Model by the CCITT Rapporteur's Group on Layered Architecture for Public Data Networks Services is most promising.

It is essential that all partners in this standardization process expend their best effort so that it will be successful and the benefits can be shared by all users, manufacturers of terminals and computers, and the PTTs/common carriers.

References

[1] L. G. Roberts and B. D. Wessler, "Computer network development to achieve resource sharing," in *Proc. SJCC*, 1970, pp. 543–549.
[2] L. Pouzin, "Presentation and major design aspects of the CYCLADES computer network," in *Proc. 3rd ACM-IEEE Commun. Symp.*, Tampa, FL, Nov. 1973, pp. 80–87.
[3] J. H. McFadyen, "Systems network architecture: An overview," *IBM Syst. J.*, vol. 15, no. 1, pp. 4–23, 1976.
[4] G. E. Conant and S. Wecker, "DNA, an architecture for heterogeneous computer networks," in *Proc. ICCC*, Toronto, Ont., Canada, Aug. 1976, pp. 618–625.

[5]   H. Zimmermann, "High level protocols standardization: Technical and political issues,"
      in *Proc. ICCC*, Toronto, Ont., Canada, Aug. 1976, pp. 373–376.
[6]   ISO/TC97/SC16, "Provisional model of open systems architecture," Doc. N34, Mar.
      1978.
[7]   ISO/TC97/SC16, "Reference model of open systems interconnection," Doc. N227, June
      1979. The OSI Reference Model had reached the stage of a Draft International Standard
      (DIS 7498) at the end of 1981.
[8]   H. Zimmermann and N. Naffah, "On open systems architecture," in *Proc. ICCC*, Kyoto,
      Japan, Sept. 1978, pp. 669–674.
[9]   ISO, "High level data link control—Elements of procedure IS 4335, 1977.
[10] CCITT, "X.25," Orange book, vol. VIII-2, 1977, pp. 70–108.
[11] ISO/TC97/SC16 Draft Transfer Protocol, Sept. 1980.
[12] ECMA, "Session protocol specification, Draft 4," Doc. ISO/97/16 N 375, Aug. 1980.
[13] IFIP-WGF 6.1, "Proposal for a standard virtual terminal protocol," Doc.
      ISO/TC97/SC16/N23, 56 pp., Feb. 1978.
[14] EURONET, "Data entry virtual terminal protocol for EURONET," VTP/D-Issue 4, doc.
      EEC/WGS/165.
[15] ISO, "Extended control characters for I/O imaging devices," DP 6429.

PART II

Physical Layer

In this section we begin to get into the details of what constitutes a fully developed set of protocols. Up to now the discussion has been at a global overview level, but now we shall see, for some real protocols, exactly what sort of actions and reactions occur using just what sorts of information-conveying mechanisms.

The physical layer is a good place to introduce protocol details, particularly to communication engineers who are more likely to be at home with physical signal manipulation notions than with the concepts from data processing which dominate the flavor of the higher protocol levels.

Practically every computer communications practitioner has encountered the EIA RS-232C interface (or its non-U.S. equivalent), but probably without realizing that it can be thought of in the same generic terms as data-link controls, session management, and other complex matters to be found in the layers above.

The syntax of the physical layer is stated in physical (or perhaps more accurately space-division) terms (which of several interconnecting wires have a high or low voltage) or in a mixture of physical and temporal terms (specific bit sequences on specific wires). The semantics is the set of actions and reactions that take place. These are called functional and procedural characteristics in Chapter 3, the semantics being expressed by the mechanical and electrical characteristics.

What the physical layer protocols are doing is basically two things:

1. A physical *interface* protocol is used by the data terminal equipment (DTE—a computer terminal or other data-processing box) to control the internal state, bit by bit, of the attached data circuit-terminating equipment (DCE, e.g., a modem in the case of voice grade lines) or vice versa, and

2. A physical *peer* protocol causes two DCEs at two ends of a physical connection between two DTEs to establish or disestablish the electrical connection ("dialup").

In this section of the book we emphasize the first of these two functions, deferring until Chapter 7 the peer protocol aspects of the physical level. This is done in order to allow in Chapter 7 a comparison of the services provided by the X.21 peer protocol and those of the network layer protocol X.25.

Chapter 3 reviews RS-232C (vintage 1969) very briefly and then details the more modern physical level protocols RS-449 and X.21.

3

Physical Interfaces and Protocols

H. V. Bertine

I. Introduction

The CCITT* Recommendation X.25 protocol for access to packet switched data networks is probably the first internationally recognized data communication protocol to use the concept of levels or layers. The 1976 version of Recommendation X.25 [1] defined the first level, which it designated level 1, as

> the physical, electrical, functional, and procedural characteristics to establish, maintain and disconnect the physical link between the DTE and the DCE.

CCITT, in its work on a layered model for public data network (PDN) applications, states [2]

> The physical layer represents the most basic level of the Model and describes transparent transmission of a bit stream over a circuit built in some physical communications medium.

> The physical layer provides mechanical, electrical, functional, and procedural characteristics to activate, maintain, and deactivate physical connections, referred to as data circuits for bit transmission between link functional units.

---

*International Telegraph and Telephone Consultative Committee. CCITT is a committee of the International Telecommunications Union (ITU), a specialized agency of the United Nations Organization. The CCITT work on data communications is focused in two study groups. CCITT Study Group XVII is responsible for data communications over telephone facilities. Its work is contained in V-series recommendations. CCITT Study Group VII is responsible for data communications over data networks. Its work is contained in X-series recommendations.

ISO,* in its work on open system interconnection, has developed a seven-layer architectural model [3]. This model defines the physical layer as

> The physical layer provides mechanical, electrical, functional and procedural characteristics to activate, maintain and deactivate physical connections for bit transmission between data link entities possibly through intermediate systems, each relaying bit transmission within the physical layer.

> A physical connection may allow duplex or half-duplex transmission of bit streams.

ISO also introduces the concept of a physical service data unit:

> A physical service data unit consists of one bit in serial transmission and of "n" bits in parallel transmission.

> The transmission of physical service data units (i.e., bits) can be performed by synchronous or asynchronous transmission.

These definitions are being reviewed. For example, an internal working document [4] within ISO proposes modifying the definition of the physical layer to read

> The physical layer provides the functional and procedural means to activate, maintain and deactivate physical connections for bit transmission between data link entities. Physical layer entities are interconnected by means of a physical media. Mechanical and electrical characteristics are defined at one or more points of interest (e.g., point of demarcation) along the physical media.

Several observations can be made from the above quotations. First, the two international sources of the quotations reflect the widespread interest in this subject. Second, at the present time, there is no precise consensus of what the physical level includes. However, it is clear that the physical level has four important characteristics which will be designated here as

- mechanical,
- electrical,
- functional, and
- procedural.

---

*International Organization for Standardization. ISO is a voluntary nontreaty group made up of the principal standardization body of each represented nation. The U. S. member body is the American National Standards Institute (ANSI). The ISO work on data communications is focused in two subcommittees of Technical Committee 97 (Information Processing Systems). ISO/TC97/SC6 is responsible for data communications. ISO/TC97/SC16 is responsible for open systems interconnection.

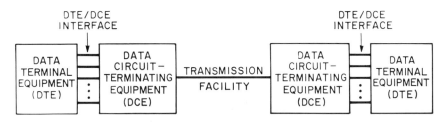

Fig. 1. DTE/DCE interface.

In Section II, each of these characteristics will be discussed in detail.

The physical level exists at a variety of places. A very important and widely standardized interface is the one between the DTE and the DCE as depicted in Fig. 1. The most familiar DTE/DCE interface in the U. S. is that described by EIA* RS-232-C [5]. There are other serial data DTE/DCE interfaces, such as EIA RS-449 [6], ccitt X.20 [7], and X.21 [7]. There are also what are known as parallel data DTE/DCE interfaces, such as ccitt V.19 [8] and V.20 [8]. Other types of data communication interfaces are important, such as EIA RS-366-A [9], which covers the DTE interface to automatic calling equipment (ACE). There is also a physical interface between the DCE (e.g., a modem) and the transmission facility (e.g., telephone line) as specified in ccitt V-series modem recommendations [8]. Another important interface is the signaling interface between networks such as that specified by ccitt Recommendation X.75 [7].

Space does not permit a description of the physical level characteristics of each of the interfaces of this chapter. However, two specific interfaces, EIA RS-449 and ccitt X.21, will be discussed in detail in Section III to provide a flavor for the considerations which go into the development of the physical level.

Parameters associated with the physical level also have been standard-ized. For example, EIA RS-269-B [10], ANSI† X3.1 [11] and X3.36 [12], and ccitt V.5 [8], V.6 [8] and X.1 [7] set forth the signaling rates (i.e.,

---

*Electronic Industries Association. EIA is a trade association that represents manufacturers in the U. S. electronics industry. The EIA work on data communications is carried out by Technical Committee TR30. EIA standards on data communications are published in the RS-series. In addition, EIA publishes supplementary material in Industrial Electronics Bulletins.

†American National Standards Institute. ANSI is a nonprofit, nongovernmental organization. It serves as the national clearing house and coordinating activity for voluntary standards in the U. S. The ANSI work on data communications is focused in two technical committees of Standards Committee X3 (Information Systems). Technical Committee X3S3 is responsible for data communications and Technical Committee X3T5 is responsible for open systems interconnection. American National Standards resulting from the work of these committees are contained in the X3.-series.

bits/s) for the physical level of the DTE/DCE interface. The alignment of data and timing signals for synchronous operation are specified in EIA RS-334-A [13]. Signal quality for asynchronous operation is specified in EIA RS-363 [14] and RS-404 [15] and ISO 7480 [16]. Space does not permit further discussion of these standards.

Work is continuing to further the standardization of the physical level. Section IV provides a look at this effort.

II. Characteristics of the Physical Level

As mentioned previously, the four principal characteristics making up the physical level are mechanical, electrical, functional, and procedural. Each is briefly described in this section.

A. Mechanical Characteristics

The mechanical aspects pertain to the point of demarcation. Typically, this is a pluggable connector, but other arrangements, such as screw terminals, are sometimes used. Included are the specifics of the connector, the assignment of interchange circuits (see Section II C) to pins, the connector latching arrangement, mounting arrangements, etc. The location of the interface connector (e.g., close to or on the DCE) is often specified as well as the provision of cabling (e.g., interface cabling is generally considered part of the DTE).

The following are the various mechanical interfaces that have been standardized by ISO:

- ISO 2110 [17]: 25-pin connector used for serial and parallel voice-band modems, public data network interfaces, telegraph (including Telex) interfaces, and automatic calling equipment. EIA RS-232-C and EIA RS-366-A are compatible with ISO 2110.
- ISO 2593 [18]: 34-pin connector used for the CCITT Recommendation V.35 [8] wide-band modem. Although there is no equivalent EIA standard, this interface is used within the U. S.
- ISO 4902 [19]: 37-pin and 9-pin connectors used for serial voice-band and wide-band modems. EIA RS-449 is compatible with ISO 4902.
- ISO 4903 [20]: 15-pin connector used for public data network interfaces specified by CCITT Recommendations X.20, X.21, and X.22 [7]. There is no equivalent standard in the U. S.

The various connectors and their relative sizes are illustrated in Fig. 2. All connectors, except for the 34-pin connector, belong to the same connector family.

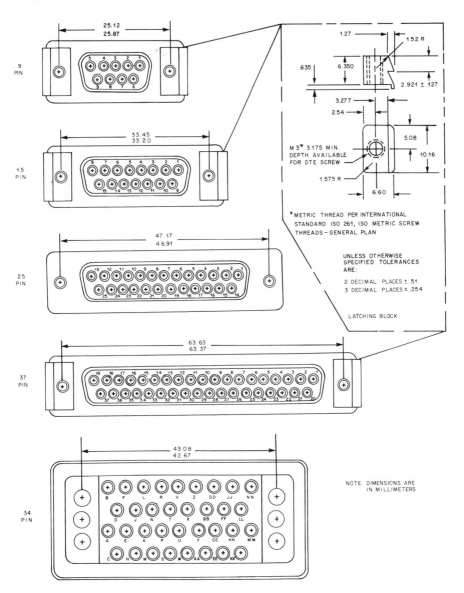

Fig. 2. Comparison of DCE connectors.

The newest standards (37/9-pin and 15-pin) contain additional specifications to solve many of the mechanical interface problems experienced with implementations of the earlier standards. A key provision is the specification of an inexpensive DCE latching block (see Fig. 2) which enables latching and unlatching to be done either with or without a tool. This innovation should eliminate the incompatibilities associated with the wide variety of latching devices in use today. Another improvement is the placing of limitations on the size of the DTE connector including cover, cable clamp, and latching arrangement. This permits compact mounting arrangements involving multiple DCE connectors while assuring adequate clearances.

The EIA RS-449 and CCITT X.21 interfaces discussed in Section III use these new connector specifications.

B. Electrical Characteristics

In the early standards (EIA RS-232-C, CCITT Recommendation V.28 [8]), the electrical characteristics were defined at the point of demarcation. More recent standards (EIA RS-422-A [21] and RS-423-A [22], CCITT Recommendations V.10 [8]/X.26 [7] and V.11 [8]/X.27 [7]) specify the electrical characteristics of the generators and receivers and give guidance with respect to the interconnecting cable. The latter situation, while simplifying the job of the integrated circuit manufacturer, has been criticized because there is no specification at the point of demarcation. The absence of this specification hampers sectionalization of trouble.

The following are the various electrical characteristics that have been standardized by CCITT:

- V.10/X.26: New unbalanced electrical characteristics. EIA RS-423-A, FED-STD 1030A [23], and MIL-STD 188-114 [24] are compatible with V.10/X.26.

- V.11/X.27: New balanced electrical characteristics. EIA RS-422-A, FED-STD 1020A [25], and MIL-STD 188-114 are compatible with V.11/X.27.

- V.28: Unbalanced electrical characteristics. EIA RS-232-C is compatible with V.28.

- V.31 [8]: Electrical characteristics for interchange circuits controlled by contact closure. Used in parallel modem (CCITT V.20 [8]). EIA RS-410 [26] is a similar standard.

- V.35 [8]: Balanced electrical characteristics used on the data and timing circuits of the CCITT V.35 modem. Although there is no equivalent EIA standard, this interface is used within the U. S.

The use of the latter two electrical characteristics is limited and, therefore, they will not be discussed further. Figure 3 provides a comparison of V.28, V.10, and V.11. The key item to note is that V.10 provides a transitional mechanism since it is interoperable with both V.28 and V.11.

The new unbalanced and balanced electrical characteristics were developed to provide improved performance in terms of supporting higher bit rates and longer cable distances compared with V.28 and RS-232-C. Integrated circuit manufacturers were active in the development of these new electrical characteristics to ensure their practical realization in state-of-the-art technology.

The electrical characteristics of V.28/RS-232-C specify a single-ended generator that produces a 5–15-V signal (negative for binary 1, positive for binary 0) with respect to signal ground (common return). A single common return lead is used for all interchange circuits. Generator rise time is relatively fast such that the time for the signal to pass through the ±3 V transition region does not exceed 1 ms and, for data and timing interchange circuits, also does not exceed 3% (for V.28; 4% for RS-232-C) of the nominal signal element duration. A single-ended receiver is specified having a dc resistance between 3 and 7 kΩ. These electrical characteristics are generally limited to data signaling rates below 20 kbit/s and cable distances shorter than 15 m.

The new unbalanced electrical characteristics specify a low-impedance (≤ 50 Ω) single-ended generator that produces a 4–6-V signal (negative for binary 1, positive for binary 0) with respect to the common return. A single common return lead for each direction of transmission can be used across the interface. Waveshaping of the generator output signal is used to control the level of near-end crosstalk to adjacent circuits in the interconnection. Data signaling rates up to 3 kbit/s can be used over cable distances up to 1000 m. For data signaling rates above 3 kbit/s, the cable distance decreases with increasing signaling rate to 10 m at 300 kbit/s.

The new balanced electrical characteristics specify a low-impedance (≤ 100 Ω) balanced generator that produces a 2–6-V differential signal (A terminal negative with respect to the B terminal for binary 1, opposite polarity for binary 0). Each interchange circuit requires a pair of wires for balanced operation. Data signaling rates up to 100 kbit/s can be used over cable distances up to 1000 m. For data signaling rates above 100 kbit/s, the cable distance decreases with increasing signaling rate to 10 m at 10 Mbit/s.

The new balanced and unbalanced electrical characteristics are identical for the receiver. They specify a differential receiver which has a high input impedance (≥ 4 kΩ) and a small transition region (±0.2 V).

The correlation between the binary 1 and 0 states given above for each of the electrical characteristics and the states of the interchange circuits is shown in Fig. 4.

CCITT V.28 (EIA RS – 232 – C)

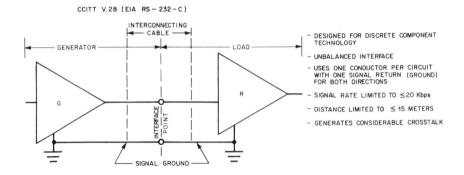

- DESIGNED FOR DISCRETE COMPONENT TECHNOLOGY

- UNBALANCED INTERFACE

- USES ONE CONDUCTOR PER CIRCUIT WITH ONE SIGNAL RETURN (GROUND) FOR BOTH DIRECTIONS

- SIGNAL RATE LIMITED TO ≤20 Kbps

- DISTANCE LIMITED TO ≤ 15 METERS

- GENERATES CONSIDERABLE CROSSTALK

CCITT V.10/X.26 (EIA RS–423–A)

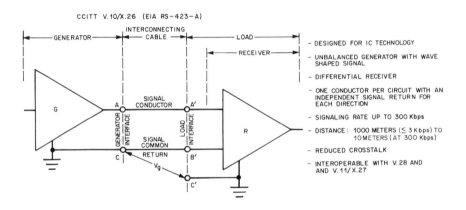

- DESIGNED FOR IC TECHNOLOGY

- UNBALANCED GENERATOR WITH WAVE SHAPED SIGNAL

- DIFFERENTIAL RECEIVER

- ONE CONDUCTOR PER CIRCUIT WITH AN INDEPENDENT SIGNAL RETURN FOR EACH DIRECTION

- SIGNALING RATE UP TO 300 Kbps

- DISTANCE: 1000 METERS (≤ 3 Kbps) TO 10 METERS (AT 300 Kbps)

- REDUCED CROSSTALK

- INTEROPERABLE WITH V.28 AND AND V.11/X.27

CCITT V.11/X.27 (EIA RS–422–A)

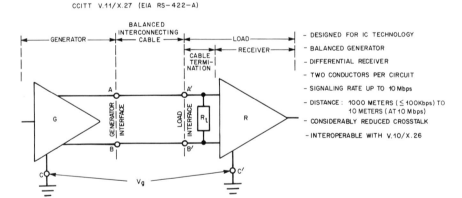

- DESIGNED FOR IC TECHNOLOGY

- BALANCED GENERATOR

- DIFFERENTIAL RECEIVER

- TWO CONDUCTORS PER CIRCUIT

- SIGNALING RATE UP TO 10 Mbps

- DISTANCE : 1000 METERS (≤100Kbps) TO 10 METERS (AT 10 Mbps)

- CONSIDERABLY REDUCED CROSSTALK

- INTEROPERABLE WITH V.10/X.26

Fig. 3. Comparison of electrical characteristics.

BINARY	1	O
DATA	MARK	SPACE
CONTROL	OFF	ON

Fig. 4. Signal state correlation table.

A key feature built into the new electrical characteristics is an evolution path from the existing V.28/RS-232-C electrical characteristics. The V.10/RS-423-A specifications were specifically designed to permit interoperation with both V.28/RS-232-C and V.11/RS-422-A. The EIA RS-449 and CCITT X.21 interfaces discussed in Section III make use of this capability.

C. Functional Characteristics

Interchange circuit functions are typically classified into the following broad categories: data, control, timing, and grounds. Further classification into primary and secondary channel functions are made for those DTE/DCE interfaces employing a secondary channel.

The following are the two CCITT recommendations which define the functions of interchange circuits:

- V.24 [8]: DTE/DCE and DTE/ACE interchange circuits. Originally developed for use with modems and automatic calling equipment associated with modems, they may also be used with digital networks. EIA RS-232-C and RS-449 are compatible with V.24 for DTE/DCE interchange circuits and EIA RS-366-A is compatible with V.24 for DTE/ACE interchange circuits.
- X.24 [7]: DTE/DCE interchange circuits. Developed for use with public data networks (CCITT Recommendations X.20, X.21, and X.22). There is no equivalent standard in the U. S.

The V.24 interchange circuits have been used for several decades. They employ the concept of one function per interchange circuit. Over the years, the list of interchange circuits has grown steadily. The 1980 version of Recommendation V.24 defines 43 interchange circuits for use in various DTE/DCE interfaces and 12 interchange circuits for the DTE/ACE interface.

In the 1968–1972 CCITT study period, work started on interface standards (X.20 and X.21) specifically designed for the emerging duplex data networks. The technology to be employed in these networks favored a "compact" interface where the ACE functions, DCE control functions, and data were multiplexed over a single "data" interchange circuit in each direction. The result of this work was Recommendation X.24, which defines a small set of interchange circuits. This set includes a data and a control circuit in each direction plus a single bit timing circuit from the DCE. An optional byte timing circuit from the DCE is also defined. The 1980 version of X.24 also defines a framing circuit from the DCE which is used in the new X.22 interface.

The EIA RS-449 interface described in Section III A uses V.24 interchange circuits and the CCITT X.21 interface described in Section III B uses X.24 interchange circuits.

D. Procedural Characteristics

The final aspect of the physical level is the set of procedures for using the interchange circuits. These procedures are the ones that need to be performed to enable the transmission of bits so that the higher-level functions (described in subsequent chapters) can take place. The exact division between which procedures are part of the physical level and which procedures are higher-level procedures is an area of considerable debate.

The following are the various CCITT recommendations which define procedures at the physical level:

- V.24: Procedures affecting the interrelationships between certain interchange circuits. EIA RS-232-C and RS-449 contain equivalent procedures.
- V.25 [8]: Procedures for use with automatic calling equipment. EIA RS-366-A contains equivalent procedures.
- V.54 [8]: Procedures regarding maintenance test loops. EIA RS-449 contains equivalent procedures.
- V-series modems [8]: Modem-specific procedures for the use of interchange circuits. Several Federal standards contain equivalent procedures.
- X.20: Procedures for asynchronous operation on a public data network. There is no equivalent standard in the U. S.
- X.20 bis [7]: Procedures for asynchronous operation on a public data network for DTEs designed to interface with V-series asynchronous modems. EIA RS-232-C contains equivalent procedures.
- X.21: Procedures for synchronous operation on a public data network. There is no equivalent standard in the U. S.
- X.21 bis [7]: Procedures for synchronous operation on a public data network for DTEs designed to interface with V-series synchronous modems. EIA RS-232-C and RS-449 contains equivalent procedures.

- X.22: Procedures for synchronous operation on a public data network whereby several circuits are time division multiplexed. There is no equivalent standard in the U. S.
- X.150 [7]: Procedures regarding maintenance test loops for public data networks.

Two examples of these procedures are given in Section III.

You may have wondered what happened to CCITT Recommendation X.25 [7], which was discussed on the first page of this chapter. X.25, which specifies the packet mode interface to packet switched public data networks, does contain a section on the physical level. This section, however, simply references the appropriate sections of X.21 and X.21 bis.

III. Examples of the Physical Level

In this section two examples are given of the physical level for DTE/DCE interfaces. The first is EIA RS-449, which was developed to replace EIA RS-232-C. The second CCITT Recommendation X.21, which was developed specifically as a synchronous interface to public data networks. In each example, the four characterists of the physical level—mechanical, electrical, functional, and procedural—are clearly evident.

Before taking up these new interfaces, it is appropriate to briefly review EIA RS-232-C, the dominant DTE/DCE interface in use today. The first version of this standard, RS-232, was adopted in May, 1960. It was revised three times—in October, 1963 as RS-232-A, in October, 1965 as RS-232-B, and in August, 1969 as RS-232-C.

RS-232-C defines 21 interchange circuits. Each circuit provides a single function as summarized in Fig. 5. Not all circuits are needed in every application. For example, the timing circuits are omitted for nonsynchronous applications, certain control circuits are omitted for nonswitched applications, and the five secondary channel circuits are omitted when secondary channel operation is not employed.

The interchange circuit procedures contained in RS-232-C are more fully described in a separate Application Notes document [27]. Included is a series of charts giving control circuit state diagrams for a number of applications. An example illustration of these procedures is given in Fig. 6. This figure, covering half duplex operation over the switched network, shows the major states and transitions for the six principal RS-232-C control circuits.

RS-232-C includes the specification of electrical characteristics for the interchange circuits. These unbalanced characteristics were described above

CIRCUIT		NAME	DIRECTION	DESCRIPTION
GROUND	AA	PROTECTIVE GROUND		ELECTRICALLY BONDS TOGETHER THE EQUIPMENT FRAMES
	AB	SIGNAL GROUND OR COMMON RETURN		ESTABLISHES THE COMMON GROUND REFERENCE POTENTIAL FOR ALL INTERCHANGE CIRCUITS
DATA	BA	TRANSMITTED DATA	TO DCE	CONVEYS DATA SIGNALS FOR TRANSMISSION TO THE COMMUNICATIONS CHANNEL
	BB	RECEIVED DATA	TO DTE	CONVEYS DATA SIGNALS RECEIVED FROM THE COMMUNICATIONS CHANNEL
CONTROL	CA	REQUEST TO SEND	TO DCE	REQUESTS ABILITY TO TRANSMIT DATA TO THE COMMUNICATIONS CHANNEL
	CB	CLEAR TO SEND	TO DTE	INDICATES WHETHER OR NOT THE DCE IS READY TO TRANSMIT DATA TO THE COMMUNICATIONS CHANNEL
	CC	DATA SET READY	TO DTE	INDICATES WHETHER OR NOT THE DCE IS IN THE DATA MODE
	CD	DATA TERMINAL READY	TO DCE	CONTROLS THE SWITCHING OF THE DCE TO AND FROM THE COMMUNICATIONS CHANNEL
	CE	RING INDICATOR	TO DTE	INDICATES WHETHER OR NOT A "RINGING SIGNAL" IS BEING RECEIVED BY THE DCE
	CF	RECEIVED LINE SIGNAL DETECTOR	TO DTE	INDICATES WHETHER OR NOT THE DCE IS RECEIVING A LINE SIGNAL FROM THE COMMUNICATIONS CHANNEL
	CG	SIGNAL QUALITY DETECTOR	TO DTE	INDICATES WHETHER OR NOT THERE IS A HIGH PROBABILITY OF ERROR IN THE RECEIVED DATA
	CH	DATA SIGNAL RATE SELECTOR (DTE SOURCE)	TO DCE	SELECTS BETWEEN TWO DATA SIGNALING RATES OR RANGES OF RATES
	CI	DATA SIGNAL RATE SELECTOR (DCE SOURCE)	TO DTE	INDICATES ONE OF TWO DATA SIGNALING RATES OR RANGES OF RATES
TIMING	DA	TRANSMITTER SIGNAL ELE-MENT TIMING (DTE SOURCE)	TO DCE	PROVIDES TIMING SIGNALS FOR TRANSMITTED DATA
	DB	TRANSMITTER SIGNAL ELE-MENT TIMING (DCE SOURCE)	TO DTE	PROVIDES TIMING SIGNALS FOR TRANSMITTED DATA
	DD	RECEIVER SIGNAL ELEMENT TIMING (DCE SOURCE)	TO DTE	PROVIDES TIMING SIGNALS FOR RECEIVED DATA
SECONDARY	SBA	SECONDARY TRANSMITTED DATA	TO DCE	EQUIVALENT TO CIRCUIT BA EXCEPT IT APPLIES TO THE SECONDARY CHANNEL
	SBB	SECONDARY RECEIVED DATA	TO DTE	EQUIVALENT TO CIRCUIT BB EXCEPT IT APPLIES TO THE SECONDARY CHANNEL
	SCA	SECONDARY REQUEST TO SEND	TO DCE	EQUIVALENT TO CIRCUIT CA EXCEPT IT APPLIES TO THE SECONDARY CHANNEL
	SCB	SECONDARY CLEAR TO SEND	TO DTE	EQUIVALENT TO CIRCUIT CB EXCEPT IT APPLIES TO THE SECONDARY CHANNEL
	SCF	SECONDARY RECEIVED LINE SIGNAL DETECTOR	TO DTE	EQUIVALENT TO CIRCUIT CF EXCEPT IT APPLIES TO THE SECONDARY CHANNEL

Fig. 5. EIA RS-232-C interchange circuits.

in Section II B. They apply at the point of demarcation between the DTE and DCE (i.e., at the 25-pin connector). Interface operation is generally limited to data signaling rates below 20 kbit/s and cable distances shorter than 15 m.

A. EIA RS-449

RS-232-C was recognized by EIA in 1973 to be a limiting factor in many user environments. The principal new capabilities and benefits desired were

- improved performance, longer interface cable distances, and a significantly higher maximum data rate (to be achieved with the new electrical characteristics);

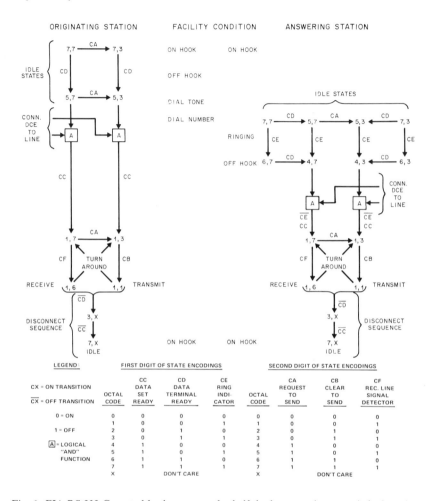

Fig. 6. EIA RS-232-C control lead sequences for half-duplex operation on switched service.

- additional interface functions, such as loopback testing; and
- resolution of the mechanical interface problems which had led to a proliferation of designs, many of which were incompatible with one another.

The first approach examined was to update RS-232-C. Creating an RS-232-D would require a degree of compatibility with RS-232-C which would have severely compromised the desired new capabilities and benefits.*

---

*The opposite was true for the automatic calling equipment interface, RS-366. It has been updated as RS-366-A.

Therefore, the decision was made to develop a new interface. Two major approaches for this new interface were studied at the outset and were reviewed many times thereafter. One was to follow the basic concepts of RS-232-C. The other was to seek alignment with the developing CCITT work on Recommendation X.21. (See Section III B.)

The principal advantage of the first approach is the ability to interoperate with RS-232-C. This would not be possible with the X.21 approach. The principal advantage of the X.21 approach is a lower cost interface achieved through a substantial reduction in the number of interchange circuits. However, as discussed in Section IV, there are significant technical and performance problems associated with the adoption of X.21 for the modem interface. Therefore, the first approach was taken with two principal objectives:

- the ability to interoperate the new equipment with the presently existing RS-232-C equipment (no modification to RS-232-C equipment permitted), and
- to obtain the new capabilities cited earlier when two new equipments are interfaced.

These objectives were satisfied (as described below) and RS-449 was published by EIA in November, 1977, after international agreement was reached in CCITT and ISO. To simplify the following discussion, the EIA terminology will be used. The listings given in Section II can be used for reference to the equivalent international standards.

1. Functional

One of the problems with RS-232-C was that many equipments included interface circuits in addition to those defined in RS-232-C. New Sync (now known as New Signal) is one example. More importantly, there was a strong need to incorporate additional capabilities in the interface for loopback testing and other functions. These problems were solved in RS-449 by the addition of new interchange circuits following the philosophy used in RS-232-C of one function per interchange circuit. Figure 7 provides a complete listing of the 30 RS-449 interchange circuits and gives the equivalent interchange circuits in RS-232-C and CCITT Recommendation V.24.*

A new set of interface circuit names and mnemonics is used in RS-449. The names were chosen to more accurately describe the function performed and to eliminate the term "data set," which is no longer appropriate. The

---

*CCITT is studying the addition to Recommendation V.24 of the one RS-449 interchange circuit (Terminal in Service) presently not included.

EIA RS-449		EIA RS-232-C		CCITT RECOMMENDATION V.24	
SG	SIGNAL GROUND	AB	SIGNAL GROUND OR COMMON RET.	102	SIGNAL GROUND OR COMMON RET.
SC	SEND COMMON			102a	DTE COMMON RETURN
RC	RECEIVE COMMON			102b	DCE COMMON RETURN
IS	TERMINAL IN SERVICE				
IC	INCOMING CALL	CE	RING INDICATOR	125	CALLING INDICATOR
TR	TERMINAL READY	CD	DATA TERMINAL READY	108/2	DATA TERMINAL READY
DM	DATA MODE	CC	DATA SET READY	107	DATA SET READY
SD	SEND DATA	BA	TRANSMITTED DATA	103	TRANSMITTED DATA
RD	RECEIVE DATA	BB	RECEIVED DATA	104	RECEIVED DATA
TT	TERMINAL TIMING	DA	TRANSMITTER SIGNAL ELEMENT TIMING (DTE SOURCE)	113	TRANSMITTER SIGNAL ELEMENT TIMING (DTE SOURCE)
ST	SEND TIMING	DB	TRANSMITTER SIGNAL ELEMENT TIMING (DCE SOURCE)	114	TRANSMITTER SIGNAL ELEMENT TIMING (DCE SOURCE)
RT	RECEIVE TIMING	DD	RECEIVER SIGNAL ELEMENT TIMING	115	RECEIVER SIGNAL ELEMENT TIMING (DCE SOURCE)
RS	REQUEST TO SEND	CA	REQUEST TO SEND	105	REQUEST TO SEND
CS	CLEAR TO SEND	CB	CLEAR TO SEND	106	READY FOR SENDING
RR	RECEIVER READY	CF	RECEIVED LINE SIGNAL DETECTOR	109	DATA CHANNEL RECEIVED LINE SIGNAL DETECTOR
SQ	SIGNAL QUALITY	CG	SIGNAL QUALITY DETECTOR	110	DATA SIGNAL QUALITY DETECTOR
NS	NEW SIGNAL				
SF	SELECT FREQUENCY			126	SELECT TRANSMIT FREQUENCY
SR	SIGNALING RATE SELECTOR	CH	DATA SIGNAL RATE SELECTOR (DTE SOURCE)	111	DATA SIGNALING RATE SELECTOR (DTE SOURCE)
SI	SIGNALING RATE INDICATOR	CI	DATA SIGNAL RATE SELECTOR (DCE SOURCE)	112	DATA SIGNALING RATE SELECTOR (DCE SOURCE)
SSD	SECONDARY SEND DATA	SBA	SECONDARY TRANSMITTED DATA	118	TRANSMITTED BACKWARD CHANNEL DATA
SRD	SECONDARY RECEIVE DATA	SBB	SECONDARY RECEIVED DATA	119	RECEIVED BACKWARD CHANNEL DATA
SRS	SECONDARY REQUEST TO SEND	SCA	SECONDARY REQUEST TO SEND	120	TRANSMIT BACKWARD CHANNEL LINE SIGNAL
SCS	SECONDARY CLEAR TO SEND	SCB	SECONDARY CLEAR TO SEND	121	BACKWARD CHANNEL READY
SRR	SECONDARY RECEIVER READY	SCF	SECONDARY RECEIVED LINE SIGNAL DETECTOR	122	BACKWARD CHANNEL RECEIVED LINE SIGNAL DETECTOR
LL	LOCAL LOOPBACK			141	LOCAL LOOPBACK
RL	REMOTE LOOPBACK			140	LOOPBACK/MAINTENANCE TEST
TM	TEST MODE			142	TEST INDICATOR
SS	SELECT STANDBY			116	SELECT STANDBY
SB	STANDBY INDICATOR			117	STANDBY INDICATOR

Fig. 7. Equivalency of interchange circuits.

mnemonics were chosen to be easily related to the circuit names and to be unique from those used in RS-232-C to avoid confusion. Briefly, the new circuits are

- Send Common (SC)—provides a signal common return path for all unbalanced interchange circuits employing one wire used in the direction toward the DCE.

- Receive Common (RC)—provides a signal common return path for all unbalanced interchange circuits employing one wire used in the direction toward the DTE.

- Terminal in Service (IS)—indicates to the DCE whether or not the DTE is operational. A major use is to make an associated port on a line hunting group busy if the DTE is out-of-service.

- New Signal (NS)—indicates to the DCE when the DCE receiver should be prepared to acquire a new line signal. A major use is to improve the overall response time of multipoint polling systems.

- Select Frequency (SF)—controls the DCE transmit and receive operation with respect to two frequency bands. Its purpose is to allow selection of the frequency mode of the DCE in multipoint circuits where all stations have equal status.
- Local Loopback (LL)—requests the DCE to initiate a loopback of signals in the local DCE toward the local DTE. Its purpose is to allow checking of the functioning of the DTE and the local DCE.
- Remote Loopback (RL)—requests the DCE to initiate a loopback of signals in the remote DCE toward the local DTE. Its purpose is to allow checking of the functioning of the DTE, local DCE, transmission channel, and the remote DCE.
- Test Mode (TM)—indicates to the DTE when a test condition has been established involving the local DCE. Its purpose is to distinguish test conditions from other nondata mode conditions of the DCE.
- Select Standby (SS)—requests the DCE to replace regular facilities with predetermined standby facilities. Its purpose is to facilitate the rapid restoration of service when a failure has occurred.
- Standby Indicator (SB)—indicates to the DTE whether regular facilities or standby facilities are in use. This may be in response to activation by circuit SS or by other means.

2. Procedural

The text of RS-449 contains the procedures for using the interchange circuits. The basic RS-232-C procedures were carried over into RS-449. The state diagrams (e.g., see Fig. 6) prepared in an application note to RS-232-C [27] can be applied to RS-449.

The procedures for the new test and standby interchange circuits are principally based on action–reaction pairs. For example, the local loopback circuit is turned ON by the DTE (the action) to request a local loopback. The DTE now waits. When the DCE has established the loopback, it turns the test mode circuit ON (the reaction), indicating that the loop has been established and any data sent by the DTE on the send data circuit should be returned to the DTE on the receive data circuit. The DTE can now begin sending test data. A similar action–reaction sequence is followed when deactivating the loopback.

3. Electrical

As stated earlier, interoperability with EIA RS-232-C was a principal objective in the design of EIA RS-449. This is achieved by permitting the use of the unbalanced RS-423-A electrical characteristics on interchange circuits when the data rate is less than 20 kbit/s, the upper limit for

RS-232-C. Unlike X.21 (see Section III B 1), this flexibility to use the unbalanced electrical characteristics is allowed for both the DTE and DCE. To provide good performance for data rates above 20 kbit/s (where interoperability with EIA RS-232-C does not apply), EIA RS-449 designates certain circuits which must be operated with the balanced RS-442-A electrical characteristics. This enables EIA RS-449 to be used for data rates up to 2 Mbit/s.

The key to obtaining this flexibility is the use of two wires for each of the following interchange circuits (designated by RS-449 as Category I circuits):

SD—Send Data
RD—Receive Data
TT—Terminal Timing
ST—Send Timing
RT—Receive Timing
RS—Request to Send
CS—Clear to Send
RR—Receiver Ready
TR—Terminal Ready
DM—Data Mode.

Either RS-422-A or RS-423-A generators can be used on these circuits for data rates below 20 kbit/s. For data rates above 20 kbit/s, these circuits are RS-422-A. All other interchange circuits (designated by RS-449 as Category II circuits) always use RS-423-A and thus have one wire per interchange circuit with a common signal return lead. Figure 8 summarizes this arrangement.

Two important benefits are achieved. For DTEs or DCEs designed for operation at speeds of 20 kbit/s or less, a manufacturer may choose to implement the unbalanced RS-423-A electrical characteristics on all interchange circuits. With this design, a single RS-449 implementation can operate with another RS-449 device or interoperate with an RS-232-C device (see Section III A 5). Alternatively, a manufacturer may choose to implement the balanced RS-422-A electrical characteristics on the Category I interchange circuits. With this design, a single RS-449 implementation can operate with another RS-449 device at all bit rates up to 2 Mbit/s with maximum performance. This is contrasted with the variety of different interfaces (RS-232-C, V.35, etc.) required in the past, each applying to a narrow range of data rates.

4. Mechanical

The RS-449 connectors come from the same connector family as the familiar 25-pin connector used with RS-232-C. This selection was made

CATEGORY I CIRCUITS–DATA SIGNALING RATE ≤ 20,000 BITS PER SECOND

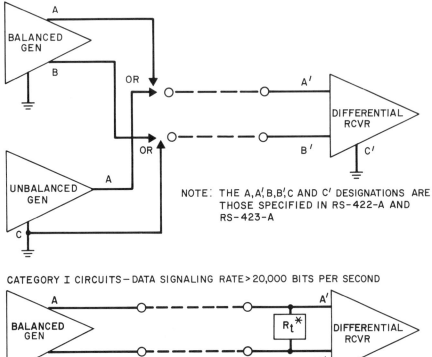

NOTE: THE A,A',B,B',C AND C' DESIGNATIONS ARE
THOSE SPECIFIED IN RS-422-A AND
RS-423-A

CATEGORY I CIRCUITS–DATA SIGNALING RATE > 20,000 BITS PER SECOND

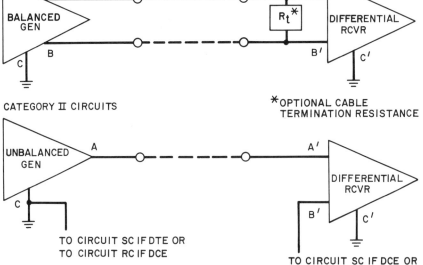

*OPTIONAL CABLE
TERMINATION RESISTANCE

Fig. 8. EIA RS-449 interface connections of generators and receivers.

because of the favorable experience associated with the use of the 25-pin connector. In order to satisfy the requirements of some foreign administrations, two connectors are used. A 37-pin connector is used for the basic interface. If secondary channel operation is used, these leads appear on a separate 9-pin connector. An important side benefit of the 9-pin and 37-pin connectors is that they are different from the present 25-pin and 34-pin connectors. This prevents the accidental interconnection of incompatible electrical characteristics which may result in physical damage to interface generators and terminators.

The mechanical enhancements described in Section II A involving standardization of the DCE latching block and maximum DTE connector envelope size are incorporated in RS-449. The pin assignment plan was carefully chosen to minimize crosstalk in multipair cable (i.e., one Category I circuit or two Category II circuits in the same direction are assigned to a pair) and to facilitate the design of an adapter when interworking with RS-232-C is desired.

Finally, provision was made for the use of shielded interface cable. Pin 1 of the interface connector is used to ensure continuity of the shields between tandem connections of shielded interface cable.

5. Interoperability

Interoperability with RS-232-C, when desired, may be accomplished by means of a simple passive adapter and a few additional design criteria for the RS-449 interchange circuits. The adapter specification and the detailed design criteria are contained in [19] and [28]. No modifications are needed for the RS-232-C equipment. Performance for interoperability is that associated with RS-232-C interfaces.

B. CCITT Recommendation X.21

CCITT Recommendation X.21 will be used in this section as a second illustration of the four characteristics of the physical level. To simplify the presentation, references, when made, will be to CCITT and ISO standards.

The 1980 version of CCITT Recommendation X.21 contains two distinct parts. One part specifies a "general purpose" DTE/DCE interface for synchronous operation on public data networks. This is the physical level part of Recommendation X.21. The second part of Recommendation X.21 specifies the call control procedures for circuit switched services. There is still debate in the standards arena about whether these are also part of the physical level. The emerging consensus is that the call control elements of X.21 involve link level (e.g., for character alignment and parity) and network level (e.g., for addressing and call progress signals) functions. This viewpoint is taken here and thus these functions are covered in Chapter 7.

1. Electrical

One of the objectives for Recommendation X.21 was to permit interface operation over distances considerably greater than that available with
Recommendation V.28. To achieve this objective at the synchronous data
rates given in X.1,* the new balanced electrical characteristics (Recommendation X.27) were specified for the DCE side of the interface. To allow
flexibility in DTE design at the four lower data rates, the DTE is permitted
to use either the new balanced or the new unbalanced (Recommendation
X.26) electrical characteristics. For the 48 kbit/s rate, only the balanced
electrical characteristics are permitted to ensure good performance.

2. Mechanical

The mechanical interface for X.21 is specified by ISO 4903. The
mechanical enhancements described earlier for RS-449 involving standardization of the DCE latching block, maximum DTE connector envelope size,
and the use of pin 1 for shield also apply to ISO 4903. Similarly, the 15-pin
interface connector comes from the same family of connectors as the
familiar 25-pin connector.

Another major enhancement is the result of careful assignment of
interchange circuits to connector pin numbers. The pin assignments provide
for the connection of interchange circuits to multipaired interconnecting
cable so that each interchange circuit operates over a pair. Of particular
importance is the use of two wires for each interchange circuit even when
interworking between a DTE using X.26 electrical characteristics and a
DCE using X.27 electrical characteristics. This eliminates the need for either
options inside the equipment or a special interface cord which connects
certain pins together. Also, this provides a performance level when interworking which approximates the performance level when X.27 is used by
both equipments.

3. Functional

Another objective in the design of Recommendation X.21 was to
considerably reduce the number of interchange circuits while at the same
time folding into the interface the automatic calling function. Thus, as
illustrated pictorially in Fig. 9, X.21 contains five basic interchange circuits.
A transmit (T) circuit and a receive (R) circuit are used to convey both user
data and network control information depending on the state of the control

---

*CCITT Recommendation X.1 specifies data rates of 600, 2400, 4800, 9600, and 48,000 bit/s for
Recommendation X.21.

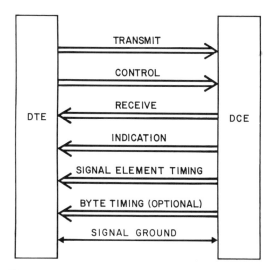

Fig. 9. CCITT Recommendation X.21 DTE/DCE interface.

(C) circuit and the indication (I) circuit. Bit timing is continuously provided by a signal element timing (S) circuit. A sixth interchange circuit which provides byte timing information is optional. A signal ground circuit is also provided. Detailed definitions of these interchange circuits are contained in CCITT Recommendation X.24.

4. Procedural

As mentioned earlier, some of the procedures in X.21 are considered above the physical level. However, the procedures associated with the quiescent phase of X.21 are generally agreed to be within the physical level. Two quiescent signals are defined for the DCE: *DCE not ready* and *DCE ready*.

DCE not ready indicates that no service is available. It is signaled whenever possible during network fault conditions and when network test loops are activated. *DCE not ready* is signaled with continuous binary 0 on circuit R and the OFF condition on circuit I.

DCE ready indicates that the DCE (network) is ready to enter operational phases. *DCE ready* is signaled with continuous binary 1 on circuit R and the OFF condition on circuit I.

A major feature incorporated into X.21 is the definition of three quiescent signals for the DTE. Two DTE not ready signals are defined to distinguish between a nonoperational DTE and a condition in which the DTE is operational but is temporarily out of service.

DTE uncontrolled not ready indicates that the DTE is unable to enter operational phases because of an abnormal condition. *DTE uncontrolled not ready* is signaled with continuous binary 0 on circuit T and the OFF condition on Circuit C.

DTE controlled not ready indicates that, although the DTE is operational, the DTE is temporarily unable to enter operational phases. *DTE controlled not ready* is signaled with a continuous bit stream of alternate binary 0 and binary 1 bits (i.e., $0101\ldots$) on circuit T and the OFF condition on circuit C.

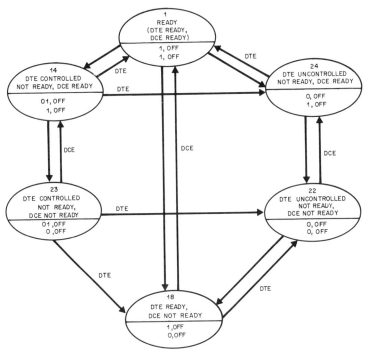

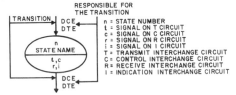

Fig. 10. CCITT Recommendation X.21 quiescent states.

DTE ready indicates that the DTE is ready to enter operational phases. *DTE ready* is signaled with continuous binary 1 on circuit *T* and the OFF condition on circuit *C*.

To ensure proper detection of these signals, X.21 requires that the DTE and DCE be prepared to send these signals for a period of at least 24 bit intervals. Detection of these signals for 16 contiguous bit intervals is required.

The various combinations of the two DCE quiescent signals and the three DTE quiescent signals provide for the six quiescent states of the X.21 interface as shown in Fig. 10. The implementations of X.21 by some networks do not allow all the possible transitions between these states. Therefore, Fig. 10 only shows those transitions that are valid for all networks.

X.21 also contains provisions to ensure proper interpretation of the interface under fault conditions (e.g., power off, disconnection of the interface cable, failure of an interchange circuit, and loss of incoming line signal to the DCE). Finally, X.21 (and X.150) defines the interface state for each of the various maintenance test loops.

IV. The Future

The preceding sections have reviewed the basic characteristics of the physical level and have described two recently standardized DTE/DCE interfaces. However, one should not assume that the physical level work is complete. In fact, three major activities are presently underway:

- direct DTE-to-DTE operation,
- tandem DCE-to-DCE operation, and
- " universal" DTE/DCE interface and the " mini" interface.

The first activity is being pursued with both EIA RS-449 and with CCITT Recommendations X.20 and X.21. Present thinking for synchronous interfaces is to use a data, timing, and control circuit in each direction with a simple crossover adapter between the two DTEs. Asynchronous interfaces would omit the timing circuits and, for X.20, also omit the control circuits. This arrangement is straightforward for EIA RS-449 and CCITT X.20 but requires the addition of a new timing interchange circuit for the X.21 DTE. A draft standard based on this thinking is presently being voted on by the ISO [29].

The second activity is being spurred by the multiplexing capability provided by the 9600 bit/s modem specified in CCITT Recommendation V.29 [8]. Tandem DCE-to-DCE operation would allow any number of the derived channels from the V.29 modem to be extended to a distant location by means of a pair of modems. The principal issue is which interchange circuits need to be interconnected through a simple crossover adapter and the proper slaving of the timing circuits in the DCEs. These issues are presently being addressed in CCITT Study Group XVII.

The third activity is the most ambitious of the three. The objective is to define a single "universal" DTE/DCE interface suitable for use both on public data networks and on telephone networks. This interface would include the automatic calling capability and utilize only a small number of interchange circuits.

The major driving force for the "mini" interface for modems is to reduce the cost of the interface by reducing the number of interchange circuits. This translates to the elimination of the separate ACE interface, fewer wires in the interface cable, a smaller connector, and fewer generators/receivers. The X.21 interface has been proposed as a candidate for the "mini" interface but there are several significant problems. One major problem is the significant reduction in throughput for half-duplex operation and for multipoint polling systems [30]. This occurs since X.21 does not provide immediate recognition of a specific control signal. That is, X.21 requires the recognition of a bit pattern in contrast to the instant recognition of a signal level on a individual control lead.

A second problem with using X.21 is the loss of functionality because there is no means to pass control information during data transfer. Two examples concerning signaling to the DTE while the receive direction is in the data transfer phase illustrate this problem. In this situation, X.21 circuit I is ON (indicating data transfer phase) and circuit R carries user data. Thus, there is no way to convey to the DTE information about the receive direction, such as Signal Quality (RS-232-C circuit CG, RS-449 circuit SQ, and V.24 circuit 110). In addition, there is no way to convey to the DTE information about the transmit direction, such as Clear to Send (RS-232-C circuit CA, RS-449 circuit CS, and V.24 circuit 105). The impact of this latter problem is illustrated by a centralized multipoint system operating with the use of continuous carrier from the master station. After the remote DTE detects its poll, it responds by turning circuit C ON (a function equivalent to Request to Send in present day modems). However, as discussed above, there is no means to convey to the DTE when the DCE is prepared to accept data (i.e., the Clear to Send function). Since this time interval varies with modem type, this loss of capability is significant.

Other flexibilities of the EIA RS-232-C and RS-449 interfaces, such as separate send and receive timing circuits, would be lost if X.21 were used without change. Also, quite a few RS-232-C, RS-449, and V.24 interchange circuit functions that apply outside of the data transfer phase are not presently accommodated by X.21. Examples include data signaling rate selection, selection and indication of standby facilities, select frequency, and loopback testing. Either these functions will be lost or X.21 must be modified to accommodate them. In addition, a way must be provided for handling a secondary channel. A separate connector for the secondary channel will probably be needed.

An alternative proposal for the "mini" interface, called the encoded control approach, was introduced by the U. S. in June, 1981 [31]. This proposal reduces the number of interchange circuits to two in each direction plus signal ground. Only customer data appears on the two data circuits and all control information is exchanged on the two control circuits via time division multiplexing techniques. Time-critical control functions are serviced more often to avoid throughput penalties. All present control functions, including the autocalling functions, are accommodated along with spare capacity for expanded functions. Timing information is imbedded in the data and control circuits in each direction via differential Manchester encoding. Balanced electrical characteristics (V.11) and a 9-pin interface connector are used in a manner which facilitates DTE–DCE, DTE–DTE, and DCE–DCE operation.

While this alternative approach has many attractive attributes, it also has drawbacks. Differential Manchester encoding doubles the signaling rate across the interface and the control circuits need to operate at eight times the rate of the data circuits to avoid a throughput penalty. This reduces the interface cable distance at the higher data rates and reduces the maximum interface data rate. Also, it is a completely new interface—it is not compatible with any existing equipment.

The debate is continuing both nationally (EIA, ANSI) and internationally (ISO, CCITT). Some favor the immediate adoption of a modified version of X.21 for the "mini" interface so as to achieve the "universal" interface objective. Modifications to X.21 are proposed to reduce or eliminate some of the drawbacks cited above but a fully "universal" interface is not achieved since an X.21 "mini" interface used for asynchronous operation does not align with the public data network asynchronous interface (X.20). Others feel that the encoded control approach offers a quantum step forward and is flexible to accommodate future needs as they become identified. Still others prefer to retain the status quo pending development of the interface requirements for the Integrated Services Digital Network by CCITT. They are concerned about standardizing a "mini" interface which may have a short life.

At this point, the only certainty is that the debate will continue. However, it is hoped that the strong desire that has been expressed for the "universal" interface will lead to the necessary agreements in the 1980s.

References

[1]   CCITT Recommendation X.25, in CCITT Orange Book, vol. VIII. 2 (Public data networks), 1977.

[2]   CCITT COM VII No. R6, Appendix 1 to Annex 4, "Proposed draft recommendation—
      Reference model for public data network applications," May 1981.
[3]   ISO Second Draft Proposal 7498, "Data processing—Open systems interconnection—
      Basic reference model," Dec. 1980.
[4]   ISO/TC97/SC6 N2132, "Physical layer and physical media for OSI," Oct. 1980.
[5]   EIA Standard RS-232-C, "Interface between data terminal equipment and data com-
      munication equipment employing serial binary data interchange," Aug. 1969.
[6]   EIA Standard RS-449, "General purpose 37-position and 9-position interface for data
      terminal equipment and data circuit-terminating equipment employing serial binary data
      interchange," November, 1977, and Addendum 1 to RS-449, Feb. 1980.
[7]   CCITT X-Series Recommendations, in CCITT Yellow Book, vols. VIII.2 and VIII.3 (Data
      communication networks), 1981.
[8]   CCITT V-Series Recommendations, in CCITT Yellow Book, vol. VIII.1 (Data communica-
      tion over the telephone network), 1981.
[9]   EIA Standard RS-366-A, "Interface between data terminal equipment and automatic
      calling equipment for data communication," March 1979.
[10] EIA Standard RS-269-B, "Synchronous signaling rates for data transmission," January
      1976.
[11] ANSI X3.1, "Synchronous signaling rates for data transmission," 1976.
[12] ANSI X3.36, "Synchronous high-speed data signaling rates between data terminal
      equipment and data communication equipment," 1975.
[13] EIA Standard RS-334-A, "Signal quality at interface between data processing terminal
      equipment and synchronous data circuit-terminating equipment for serial data transmis-
      sion," Aug. 1981.
[14] EIA Standard RS-363, "Standard for specifying signal quality for transmitting and
      receiving data processing terminal equipments using serial data transmission at the
      interface with non-synchronous data communication equipment, May 1969.
[15] EIA Standard RS-404, "Standard for start–stop signal quality between data terminal
      equipment and non-synchronous data communication equipment," March 1973.
[16] ISO Draft International Standard 7480, "Information processing start–stop transmission
      signal quality at DTE/DCE interfaces," Nov. 1981.
[17] ISO International Standard 2110, "Data communication—25-pin DTE/DCE interface
      connector and pin assignments" (Revision of ISO 2110-1972), 1980.
[18] ISO International Standard 2593, "Connector pin allocations for use with high-speed
      terminal equipment," 1973 (being revised as "Data communication—34-pin DTE/DCE
      interface connector and pin assignments, DIS 2593, Nov. 1981).
[19] ISO International Standard 4902, "Data communication—37-pin and 9-pin DTE/DCE
      interface connectors and pin assignments," 1980.
[20] ISO International Standard 4903, "Data communication—15-pin DTE/DCE interface
      connector and pin assignments," 1980.
[21] EIA Standard RS-422-A, "Electrical characteristics of balanced voltage digital interface
      circuits," Dec. 1978.
[22] EIA Standard RS-423-A, "Electrical characteristics of unbalanced voltage digital inter-
      face circuits," Dec. 1978.
[23] FED-STD 1030A, "Electrical characteristics of unbalanced voltage digital interface
      circuits," Jan. 1980.
[24] MIL-STD 188-114, "Electrical characteristics of digital interface circuits," March 1976.
[25] FED-STD 1020A, "Electrical characteristics of balanced voltage digital interface circuits,"
      Jan. 1980.
[26] EIA Standard RS-410, "Standard for the electrical characteristics of Class A closure
      interchange circuits," April 1974.

[27] EIA Industrial Electronics Bulletin No. 9, "Application notes for EIA Standard RS-232-C," May 1971.

[28] EIA Industrial Electronics Bulletin No. 12, "Application notes on interconnection between interface circuits using RS-449 and RS-232-C," Nov. 1977.

[29] ISO Draft International Standard 7477, "Data processing requirements for DTE to DTE physical connection using 15- and 37-pin connectors," Dec. 1981.

[30] CCITT COM XVII No. 214, U. S. contribution, "Methods of control information interchange for the mini-interface," Oct. 1979.

[31] U. S. working paper to ISO/TC97/SC6/WG3 "Approaches to the DTE/DCE physical interface," June 1981.

PART III

Link Control Layer

Data link control (DLC) protocols manage the successful conveyance of messages from one node to the next. The underlying physical layer that was described in Part II provides only the transport of a stream of bits from transmitter to receiver (or receivers) on a link (usually noisy) interconnecting two or more nodes. It is up to the DLC protocol partners of transmitter and receiver to jointly exploit this bitstream capability for error-free message conveyance.

To do this the protocol must accomplish several things. First, *synchronization* at the byte level must usually be provided by the DLC, bit synchronization having been handled at the physical level by the DCE (typically a modem). Second, the information bits or bytes must be *delimited* on transmission in some way so that the receiving DLC protocol partner can separate off those constituting the message intended for the higher protocol levels from those intended for itself.

The delimitation function can become complicated when it depends on unique bit patterns that belong to the protocol exchange between DLC partners, for then means must be provided (called *transparency* function) to take care of the fortuitous appearance of just these bit patterns in the message actually intended for the higher layers.

Third, since there may be more than one receiver listening to the same bitstream on a shared transmission medium, and since the choice of which station is transmitting must change from time to time, a transmission-reception *control* function must be provided. This typically includes polling to solicit messages, addressing to vector messages to the right station, and, in some cases, simply allowing stations to contend independently for the shared medium using some prearranged scheme for resolving any "collision" between contenders.

Fourth, the occasional bit errors must be corrected. Because forward error correction usually expends too many bits in providing the needed redundancy, it is customary to use only enough redundant bits for error detection at the receiver; the detection of an error then triggers in some way repeated retransmissions of the same message until it is received properly.

These four DLC functions are the routine ones that occur during "steady state" operation of the protocol. In addition there are "transient" ones that involve activating or deactivating the DLC software, hardware, or microcode. Also, providing downline IPL (initial program load) function and exchange of certain parameter settings used at the DLC level are also commonly regarded as part of the required function of modern DLCs.

The art of Data Link Controls has advanced considerably from the simple but inefficient and inflexible asynchronous (start–stop) DLCs in which precious line capacity was wasted in adding to each character fixed bit patterns for synchronization. Synchronous character-oriented DLCs (such as BISYNC) alleviate many of the problems with start–stop, and are described in Chapter 4.

These character-oriented protocols have proved to retain several disadvantages, notably that the same alphabet set (for example, ASCII or EBCDC) and the same positions in a frame are used for line control characters, text characters, and device control characters. Thus, a character of text could be spuriously converted by noise into a character that signals the end of a frame, for example, Another disadvantage of having line control characters drawn from the same alphabet as device control and text characters is that every time a new choice of alphabet is made for the peculiar needs of some particular end user, a new and different variant of the line control results. These difficulties as well as bit efficiency problems and other problems were alleviated in the new "bit-oriented" DLCs of Chapter 5, such as the High Level Data Link Control (HDLC) and its relatives. In these protocols, line control information always occurs at its own same place in a frame. Thus, the time origin of the entire frame must be knocked out of line in order for link control and data to become confused, a much less likely circumstance than to have a character in error. The line control commands and responses are specified as bit patterns that have nothing to do with any alphabet set.

The byte-oriented DLCs of Chapter 4 are still the most widely used class in today's computer networks. As the new network architectures take over, the bit-oriented DLCs, described in Chapter 5, are gradually supplementing them. Also gaining widespread use, particularly for shared satellite or local area communications, are the contention-oriented "multiaccess" protocols detailed in Chapter 6. In these two situations there is a single sharable transmission resource that provides an any-to-any topological connectivity between stations. Also, the bandwidth of the medium is very much larger than the average data rate between station pairs. This combination of circumstances leads to a set of contention based DLC-level protocols with a much more probabilistic flavor than the more classical ones of Chapters 4 and 5.

4

Character-Oriented Link Control

James W. Conard

I. Overview

A data link control protocol is a set of very specific rules governing the interchange of data over an interconnecting communication link between business machines.

The business machines may be computers, terminals, message or packet switches, concentrators, or any of a broad range of data terminal equipment in any mix. The interconnecting communication links may be assembled in any of several arrangements and may be comprised of private or common carrier multipoint, point to point, switched (dial), or nonswitched (dedicated) facilities using cable, land line, microwave, or satellite channels. The data being interchanged can be represented in many forms and can serve batched, conversational, processor to processor, inquiry/response, or other typical applications.

The link control protocol rules typically define initialization of an already established physical link, control of normal data interchange, termination of the link at the end of the transaction, and, perhaps most important from the point of view of the user, techniques to control recovery from abnormal conditions such as invalid or no response, loss of synchronization, and faults resulting from anomalies in the communication link.

Link control protocols have traditionally been character-oriented. They utilize, either singularly or in sequence, defined character structures from a given code set to convey the information necessary to frame the data and supervise its interchange. Protocols which use defined character structures for supervisory control are also known as byte-oriented protocols.

Many variations of the basic character-oriented protocol are possible and form the subject of this chapter. A major subset, perhaps a separate class, uses combinations of characters and byte-length fields to supervise the link. These are known as byte-count or count-framed protocols. A totally different class of link control protocols uses positionally located control fields rather than code set combinations for supervisory control. These are known as bit-oriented link control protocols and are dealt with in Chapter 5.

Strictly speaking, the term link control excludes other levels within the commonly recognized standard layer model of communication control discussed in Chapter 2. Ideally, the link control level should be independent of the other levels, should be distinct as to functions performed and services offered, and should have clearly delineated interfaces with the physical level protocol below it and the network level protocol above it. Character-oriented protocols, having evolved with rapidly changing communication requirements, have certain characteristics such as intermixed message, device, and link control, which tend to blur the interface between logically independent layers. These characteristics led to the development of the many variation of character-oriented protocols and ultimately to the now emerging bit-oriented protocols.

It must be remembered that character-oriented protocols as control mechanisms are concerned solely with the transfer of data over an established communications link. They are not concerned with the physical processes necessary to establish a link at Level 1. Nor are they network protocols. They do not control the flow of information between end points of a multinodal network. They can, however, be applied between nodes or between a node and an end point user.

Character-oriented protocols are suitable for two-way alternate and, less often, for two-way simultaneous operation using a variety of data link configurations, including full and half-duplex, multipoint, switched, and dedicated. The two facility configurations most commonly encountered in association with character-oriented link control are illustrated in Fig. 1. A point-to-point facility is one which interconnects two and only two stations. Point-to-point facilities may be either nonswitched, sometimes referred to as private line or dedicated, or they may be switched. The difference between switched and nonswitched is one of facility acquisition. In the switched case the facility must be acquired by the lower physical level protocol prior to the transfer of data and released at the end of the transfer. Nonswitched facilities are dedicated and usable on demand.

A multipoint facility very common for these applications, consists of a single master and two or more remote stations. Transmissions from the master are received by all remotes. Transmissions from the remotes are received only by the master. This multipoint arrangement normally requires four-wire channels.

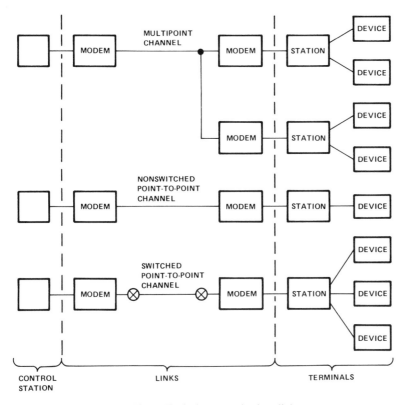

Fig. 1. Typical communications links.

Many special and hybrid combinations of interconnect arrangements are possible and often encountered. The system designer must be aware of the type and characteristics of the interconnecting link since these characteristics often directly influence the choice of protocol and its operational procedures.

II. Protocol Perspective

Data link control protocols are as old as data communications. Over the years these protocols have been evolving typically to fulfill the requirements of a particular application. Early systems, using Baudot code, had no inherent link control capability. They relied totally on sequences of data

characters to implement supervisory functions. The advent of other character sets led to protocols using controls derived from these sets. Each
manufacturer developed protocols reflecting the needs of its product line
and usually optimized for a specific implementation. Many users groups
also developed protocols to meet their unique requirements. All of these
various protocols were character-oriented in approach and generally incompatible with each other.

Standards organizations in the United States and abroad recognized
the problem and struggled to resolve the incompatibilities. The American
National Standards Institute (ANSI) and the International Standards
Organization (ISO) were especially active in this effort. For lack of standardization, the protocols developed by the larger dominant manufacturers
tended to fill the vacuum by becoming, in effect, de facto standards. This
has certainly been the case with IBM's BSC (Binary Synchronous Communication) developed in the late 1960s.

The standards organizations finally reached agreement with the publication in 1971 of ANSI's X3.28 on the use of ASCII control characters for
link control and of ISO's IS1745. These activities, among standards bodies,
manufacturers, and users groups, continue to produce revised, updated, and
even new character-oriented protocols to keep pace with evolving technology and requirements. At the present time the most widely used and
familiar link protocols are those briefly described in the following paragraphs:

ANSI X3.28 [1]: This protocol standard carries the rather lengthy title
of "Procedures for Use of the Communication Control Characters of
American National Standard Code for Information Interchange in Specified
Data Communication Links." It was first promulgated in 1971 and updated
in 1976. This standard specifies a group of control protocols, called categories, each designed to meet the requirements of a specific combination of
link configuration and message transfer application. These procedures are
based on the use of ten communication control characters provided in the
ASCII code set.

ISO IS1745 [2]: This internationally accepted protocol is titled "Basic
Mode Control Procedures for Data Communication Systems." It, too, is
based on the use of ten communications control characters to supervise a
data link. Link control is organized into phases of connection, link establishment, information transfer, termination, and disconnect. The standard
defines formats of messages and supervisory sequences for each of these
phases. It is designed for two-way alternate operation. The current version
of this standard was released in 1975.

ECMA-16 [3]: The European Computer Manufacturers Association
(ECMA) also standardized a character-oriented protocol: "Basic Mode
Control Procedures for Data Communication Systems Using the ECMA

7-bit Code." This standard closely resembles IS1745 in definition of formats, supervisory sequences, and phases.

IBM BSC [4]: The Binary Synchronous Communication (BSC) protocol is the most widely implemented of the protocols developed by the various manufacturers. It is character-oriented and designed for two-way alternate operation over point-to-point or multipoint links. It can be implemented using control characters from any of three code sets: EBCDIC, ASCII, or Six-bit Transcode. BSC utilized nine of the "standard" communication control characters and supplements these with six additional two-character sequences to provide additional link control functions.

IATA SLC [5]: Less well known but very widespread in use is the Synchronous Link Control standardized by the International Air Transport Association. This protocol supervises two-way simultaneous data transfer over full duplex links. It utilizes a combination of communication control characters and character length fields to form control blocks for link supervision. The control blocks permit identification of message blocks, sequence numbers, priorities, and other parameters.

DEC DDCMP [6]: Digital Equipment Corporation's "Digital Data Communications Message Protocol" (DDCMP) is, perhaps, the best known of the byte-count oriented protocols. It combines communication control characters and control fields to frame information blocks with supervisory controls. Complete transparency to the information is achieved through the use of a byte-count mechanism rather than the more common escape sequences. DDCMP constitutes the data link control level of Digital Equipment Corporation's DNA architecture described in Chapter 10.

The protocols listed above represent only a very small sample of the character-oriented protocols in use today. Many variations have been developed and implemented. Often a protocol will be developed and optimized for a very specific parameter such as response time, efficiency over a specific facility, or throughput. While satisfying a particular requirement, such specialization usually limits widespread application.

III. Protocol Characteristics

Character-oriented protocols, despite the wide variety of application and implementation parameters, generally share a common set of characteristics. They are much alike in basic structure, functions performed, phases of operation, code set utilization, and control character definition. The various protocols differ in how these fundamental characteristics are applied to a particular situation. Before examining the details of protocol operation it is apropos to review these basic characteristics.

A. Functions

The fundamental task of any link control protocol involves the interchange of information between senders and receivers over a given interconnecting link. The integrity of the information being transferred is a paramount consideration. Garbled or lost information is of no value to the user and can often be disastrous. If the data interchange always took place between two stations over an error-free point-to-point facility only a rudimentary data link control procedure would be necessary. The data communications environment is, however, far from ideal and exhibits characteristics which must be accommodated by the protocol.

In addition to the requirements imposed by the link itself, the protocol must contend with requirements which derive from the application, the nature of the information, i.e., conversational, batch, inquiry/response, the need for transparent operation, recovery techniques, flow control, and others. To accomplish this task a basic set of link protocol functions have evolved. These are described next.

Frame Control delimits the beginning and end of transmission blocks by the use of delimiting characters and a character count in byte-count-oriented protocols. This is necessary since extremely long blocks of information are unlikely to survive transmission through the electrically noisy medium without error. The block mechanism provides a method of implementing and controlling a block length chosen as most likely to survive and thus keep retransmission to a minimum. The mechanism also provides the ability to identify when information should, but may not, be present, and finally, provides a convenient method of signaling when the checking mechanism is to be active. Frame control characters are also commonly used to acquire, maintain, and if necessary, reestablish synchronization between sender and receiver. This is absolutely essential if the receiver is to decode the information correctly. Note that bit synchronization, which is no less critical, is a physical level function.

Error Control provides for the detection of errors, the acknowledgement of correctly received blocks and messages, and the requests for retransmission of incorrectly received messages. The most commonly used error detection techniques are vertical and longitudinal parity checks, and cyclic redundancy checks. These are described later in this chapter. Another method of error control is sequence control. Sequence control mechanizes a method of numbering blocks and messages to facilitate proper retransmission and to eliminate or at least identify lost or duplicate messages.

Initialization Control governs the establishment of an active data link over a communication facility that has been idle. It usually involves an exchange of sequences identifying a particular sender or receiver among the many present on a multipoint facility or among the almost infinite number connectable through a switched facility. Polling and calling are typical of initialization control.

Flow Control sequences regulate the flow of information across the data link. They permit a receiver to exercise some control of the amount and rate of information flowing into his system so as to avoid overwhelming his capacity to accept and process the incoming data. At link level, flow control is limited to the ability to accept or not accept information transfers.

A further discussion of flow control at the data link level and other flow control mechanisms at higher levels is given in Chapter 13.

Link Management sequences are used to supervise the links, by controlling transmission direction, establishing and terminating logical connections, and identifying which station is going to send and which is going to receive. Link management responsibility usually resides in a master or control station.

Transparency is a characteristic of some, but not all, character-oriented protocols. It allows the link control to be totally independent of the pattern or code structure of the information being transmitted. A transparent link control is able to transfer machine language data streams without the information interfering with link control functions. Character-oriented link protocols require escape or count mechanisms to implement transparent operation.

Abnormal Recovery controls supervise action to be taken to recover from abnormal occurrences such as illegal sequence, cessation of block flow, loss of responses, and other protocol defined exception conditions. Time-outs are a common method of detecting such conditions.

How the functions are implemented is the basis for the more detailed review of protocol operation in a later section.

B. Code Sets and Control Characters

Character-oriented protocols make use of defined characters from a given code set to execute communications supervisory functions. The most common code set in use is the American National Standard Code for Information Interchange (ASCII) which is defined in ANSI X3.4-1976 and reproduced here as Fig. 2. This code set is basically identical to the CCITT Alphabet 5 and the ISO Standard 646.

Of interest to the communicator are the ten characters of these code sets which are designated as communication control characters. The primary functions of these characters will be defined next, but first it will be useful to clarify the terms "message" and "block." A message is an ordered sequence of characters arranged to convey information from originator to user. A message may be contained in one or more blocks. A block is a group

b7 b6 b5 → B b4 b3 b2 b1 \ COLUMN / ROW	0 0 0 0	0 0 1 1	0 1 0 2	0 1 1 3	1 0 0 4	1 0 1 5	1 1 0 6	1 1 1 7
0 0 0 0 0	NUL	DLE	SP	0	@	P	`	p
0 0 0 1 1	SOH	DC1	!	1	A	Q	a	q
0 0 1 0 2	STX	DC2	''	2	B	R	b	r
0 0 1 1 3	ETX	DC3	#	3	C	S	c	s
0 1 0 0 4	EOT	DC4	$	4	D	T	d	t
0 1 0 1 5	ENQ	NAK	%	5	E	U	e	u
0 1 1 0 6	ACK	SYN	&	6	F	V	f	v
0 1 1 1 7	BEL	ETB	'	7	G	W	g	w
1 0 0 0 8	BS	CAN	(	8	H	X	h	x
1 0 0 1 9	HT	EM	)	9	I	Y	i	y
1 0 1 0 10	LF	SUB	*	:	J	Z	j	z
1 0 1 1 11	VT	ESC	+	;	K	[	k	(
1 1 0 0 12	FF	FS	,	<	L	\	l	¦
1 1 0 1 13	CR	GS	–	=	M	]	m	)
1 1 1 0 14	SO	RS	.	>	N	^	n	~
1 1 1 1 15	SI	US	/	?	O	___	o	DEL

Fig. 2. ASCII Code Set: Communications control characters are outlined.

of characters arranged for technical or logical reasons to be transmitted as a unit. A block may contain an entire message or part of a message.

SOH (Start of Heading). A control character which identifies the beginning of a sequence of characters which constitutes the heading of message. The sequence usually contains addressing and routing information.

STX (Start of Text). A character delimiting that part of a message which constitutes the text. An STX is often used to terminate the header which began with SOH.

ETX (End of Text). A control character used to delimit the end of a series of characters constituting the text of a message.

EOT (End of Transmission). This control character signifies the end of a transmission which may have contained one or more messages. It usually implies relinquishment of the data link.

ENQ (Enquiry). A communications control character used to solicit a response from another station. It may be used as a status request or as a request for identification, or both.

ACK (Acknowledgment). A control character which represents an affirmative response to a sender. It acknowledges error-free reception of a block or segment of a message.

DLE (Data Link Escape). A control character which changes the meaning of a limited set of contiguous following characters. It is used to provide supplementary control the most common of which is transparent operation.

NAK (Negative Acknowledgment). This character represents a negative response from the receiver to the sender. It indicates that a block of information has been received with errors and must be retransmitted.

SYN (Synchronous Idle). A communications control character used to establish and to maintain character synchronization between the sender and the receiver. It is also often used as a transmission idle in the absence of any data.

| | | | Most Significant Bits (Bit 8 Transmitted Last) | | | | | | | | | | | | | | | |
| | | | bit Positions 8,7,6,5) | | | | | | | | | | | | | | | |
Bit Positions 4321	CR	0000 0	0001 1	0010 2	0011 3	0100 4	0101 5	0110 6	0111 7	1000 8	1001 9	1010 10	1011 11	1100 12	1101 13	1110 14	1111 15
0000	0	NUL	DLE	DS		SP	&	−						{	}	\	0
0001	1	SOH	DC1	SOS						a	j	~		A	J		1
0010	2	STX	DC2	FS	SYN					b	k	s		B	K	S	2
0011	3	ETX	DC3							c	l	t		C	L	T	3
0100	4	PF	RES	BYP	PN					d	m	u		D	M	U	4
0101	5	HT	NL	LF	RS					e	n	v		E	N	V	5
0110	6	LC	BS	ETB	UC					f	o	w		F	O	W	6
0111	7	DEL	IL	ESC	EOT					g	p	x		G	P	X	7
1000	8		CAN							h	q	y		H	Q	Y	8
1001	9	RLF	EM					\		i	r	z		I	R	Z	9
1010	10	SMM	CC	SM	¢	!	¦	:									
1011	11	VT				.	$	,	#								
1100	12	FF	IFS		DC4	<	*	%	@								
1101	13	CR	IGS	ENQ	NAK	(	)	_	'								
1110	14	SO	IRS	ACK		+	;	>	=								
1111	15	SI	IUS	BEL	SUB			¬	?	"							

Fig. 3. EBCDIC code set.

ETB (End of Transmission Block). This character signifies the end of block of data for communication control purposes.

These ten control characters are, in some protocols, combined with other characters to form a sequence for additional control purposes. For example DLE is combined with STX to indicate the beginning of a transparent data sequence which would end with the sequence DLE ETX.

Another code set commonly encountered is the Extended Binary Coded Decimal Interchange Code (EBCDIC). This code set also contains the communication control characters defined above. See Fig. 3.

C. Transmission Error Control

The three most common error detection methods used by character-oriented protocols are the Vertical Redundancy Check (VRC), the Longitudinal Redundancy Check (LRC), and the Cyclic Redundancy Check (CRC). VRC and LRC are often combined.

VRC is simply a parity scheme in which a bit is appended to the bits which comprise the character. The value of the appended bit is calculated to provide either an "odd" number of 1 bits in the character or an "even" number of 1 bits in the character. The transmitter calculates and appends the parity bit. The receiver also calculates the correct parity bit and compares it with the bit appended to the incoming character. Failure to compare indicates that a transmission error has occurred. VRC schemes can only detect an odd number of bit errors in a character.

LRC is identical in implementation to VRC except that it is computed on a sequence of successive characters. The result is transmitted as an extra check character called an LRC character. LRC schemes are vulnerable to double-bit errors in the row of characters.

Even when VRC and LRC techniques are combined there are many possibilities for errors to occur in such a way as to be undetected by the error detection technique. This shortcoming led to the development of the much more powerful detection technique known as Cyclic Redundance Check (CRC).

A complete treatment of the theory of cyclic codes is beyond the scope of this article. Very simply stated, however, a cyclic redundancy code is one which makes use of the mathematical properties of the block of data being transmitted. Any sequence of bits represents the coefficients of a polynomial. If the polynomial representing the message is divided by another polynomial which represents the cyclic generator polynomial the result will be a remainder which can be appended to the message as check bits and transmitted as part of the block. An identical process performed by the receiver on the incoming block should result in the same remainder. If it does not, a transmission error has occurred. Generator polynomials are very carefully chosen to be immune to the particular error properties of the transmission medium. The most commonly used CRCs in character-oriented protocols are the CRC-16 and the CCITT V.41 polynomial. CRC-16 is represented by the algebraic expression $X^{16} + X^{15} + X^2 + 1$. It will detect all errors occurring in bursts up to 16 bits in length and over 99% of bursts longer than 16 bits. The V.41 polynomial is represented as $X^{16} + X^{12} + X^5 + 1$ and has performance capability similar to that of CRC-16. Both have 16 check bits which are appended to the block as two 8-bit characters.

D. Phases of Link Control

Character-oriented protocols are generally structured as a series of well-ordered logical processes as illustrated in Fig. 4. ANSI calls these

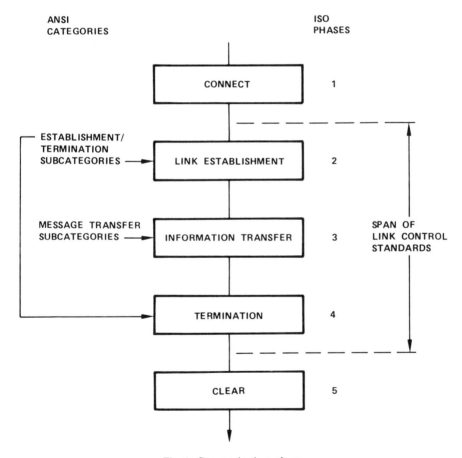

Fig. 4. Communications phases.

processes subcategories while ISO calls them phases. In X3.28, in fact, ANSI creates protocols by combining an information transfer category with an establishment/termination category. Note that of the five phases illustrated, two, the connect and clear phases, are associated with the level 1 protocol. Let's look at each of these phases:

Connect. The connect phase consists of those processes associated with establishing a connection over a switched facility such as provided by a common carrier. The process normally includes off-hook signaling, switching, and an exchange of identification. These functions, as stated, are normally provided by level 1 protocol and are not required on dedicated facilities.

Link Establishment. Link Establishment is the first phase in the span of link control protocols. This phase includes processes required to initialize data transfer over an already established physical link. Polling (inviting to send) and selecting (calling) are typical processes.

Information Transfer. This phase includes processes associated with the objective of link control; the transfer of data. It begins following link establishment and terminates with the end of the message or data transfer. It includes the actual transfer between connected station comprising the message and also includes the acknowledgment process.

Termination. The termination process consists of those functions associated with relinquishing control of the link following transmission of the message or messages. Control is normally returned to the master or control station in a multipoint link who can then return to link establishment phase to initialize transfer to another station. The termination phase can also initiate physical disconnect on a switched connection.

Clear. The clear phase functions to release the facility by signaling on-hook. These functions, like the connect phase, are normally part of level 1 protocol.

IV. Protocol Operation

Having reviewed the characteristics which form the common framework for the various character-oriented protocols we can now examine in more detail the "how" of these protocols.

A specific category of ANSI X3.28 has been chosen as being typical of the most common character-oriented protocols. This protocol will be described in terms of the establishment, information transfer, and termination phases described earlier.

The objective of this protocol is to supervise the transfer of messages over a two-way alternate dedicated multipoint link. One station is designated as the control or master station. The blocks of data being transferred may constitute an entire message of a part of a message. VRC/LRC is used as an error detection technique.

A. Establishing the Data Link

Since a dedicated communications facility has been assigned to the link, the control station may initiate the link without the need to acquire a facility as would be necessary on a nondedicated switched network. The control station may establish the link at any time by either polling or calling. The control procedure is illustrated in Fig. 5. Polling and calling are distinguished by the use of unique addresses in the prefix preceding ENQ. The control station [Fig. 5(1)] wishing to solicit input messages from one of the tributary stations sends a polling sequence [Fig. 5(2)] consisting of the control character ENQ and the address of the selected station.

The addressed tributary responds in one of two ways. If it has no message to send it responds with the terminating control character EOT [Fig. 5(5), (14)], thus returning control to the control station, which may then poll or call another station.

If the addressed tributary has a message to send it enters the information transfer phase [Fig. 5(4)] described later.

A third possibility is that the control station receives either no reply or an invalid reply to its poll [Fig. 5(6)]. In this event, usually detected by a timeout, the control station terminates with an EOT [Fig. 5(14)] before resuming polling or calling.

The control station having messages to deliver to one of the tributaries selects or calls that tributary by sending a calling sequence [Fig. 5(7)] consisting of the control character ENQ preceded by SYN characters and the tributary's call address.

The addressed tributary, recognizing its call address, has one of two choices. If it is ready to receive messages it sends the acknowledgement sequence ACK 0 [Fig. 5(8)], which is represented by the sequence DLE 0. The control station, upon detecting this reply, enters the information transfer phase.

The two-character acknowledgment sequence is a technique used to provide an additional check on transmission integrity by the use of alternating acknowledgments. The first and all odd-numbered blocks of a received sequence are acknowledged with the sequence ACK 1 transmitted as DLE 1. The second and all even-numbered blocks of the sequence are acknowledged by the sequence ACK 0. The receipt of two successive even or odd acknowledgment, e.g., ACK 0, ACK 0, indicates the loss of a transmission block. To return to our called tributary, if it is not ready to receive traffic it responds with the control character NAK [Fig. 5(9)]. The control station has now the option of calling the same tributary again [Fig. 5(11), (7)] or terminating the exchange with an EOT [Fig. 5(12), (14)].

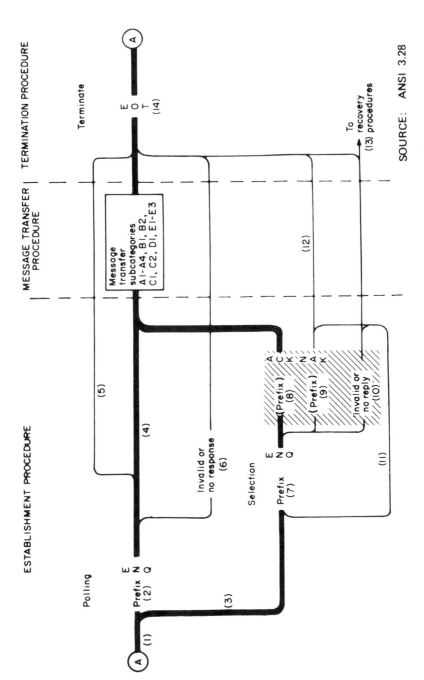

Fig. 5. Subcategory 2.4: Two-way alternate, nonswitched multipoint with centralized operation. Cross-hatched area is slave response.

Again the possibility exists that the control station will receive an invalid reply of no reply [Fig. 5(10)] to its calling sequence. In this event the control station may either terminate with an EOT [Fig. 5(14)], recall the same tributary [Fig. 5(11), (7)], or exit to a recovery procedure [Fig. 5(13)]. Usually a number of retries are made before initiating recovery.

B. Information Transfer

Information transfer begins under control of the master station following successful establishment of the data link. The master station can be the control station which has messages to send and which has successfully selected a tributary station. The master station could also be one of the tributary stations which has been successfully polled and assigned master status when it responded with an indication that it had traffic to send.

The information transfer phase is illustrated in Fig. 6. The station begins transmission of the first message block with either SOH [Fig. 6(2)] if the message has a heading, or STX if it does not [Fig. 6(3), (4)]. Following blocks which continue the heading are initiated with SOH. Following, i.e., intermediate blocks, which begin or continue the text of a message are started with STX.

Transmission of the block continues with data characters until the system-defined block length is reached. At this point the station appends the end-of-block sequence ETB BCC [Fig. 6(5)] or the end-of-message sequence ETX BCC [Fig. 6(6)] if the block is the last block of the message. The *BCC* is the block check character, in this case a single LRC character. At the receiver this incoming stream of characters is examined and appropriate action taken. The SOH character is recognized as both the start of block and the start of message character. As the start of block character it initiates the parity-checking mechanism. The STX character was recognized as the start of block character and initiated parity accumulation. ETB and ETX initiate parity check comparison and line turnaround for a reply.

If the first block is received correctly and the station is ready to receive another block it transmits the positive acknowledgment sequence ACK 1 [Figure 6(8)]. ACK 0 would be used as the positive reply to the second block using the alternate acknowledgment method discussed earlier. The master station receiving the acknowledgment may transmit the next block [Fig. 6(7)] or, if the acknowledged block was the last of the message, initiate termination [Fig. 6(9)].

Were the block received incorrectly and not accepted, the receiving station would respond with NAK [Fig. 6(10)], indicating to the master station that retransmission is required. Usually a particular block will be retransmitted [Fig. 6(11), (7)] several times before a recovery procedure [Fig. 6(12)] is invoked. Note that the NAK does not alter the sequence of the

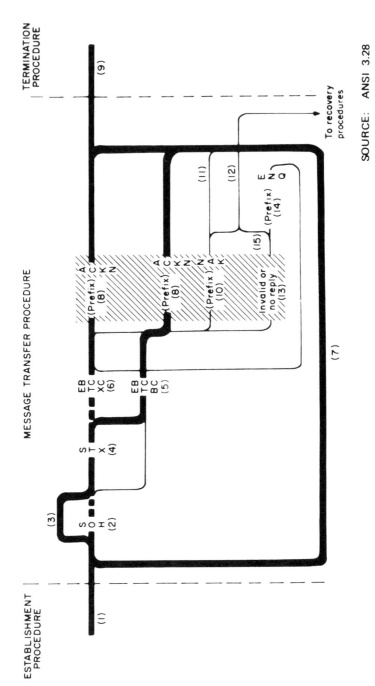

Fig. 6. Subcategory B2: Message-associated blocking, with longitudinal checking and alternating acknowledgments.

alternating acknowledgments. The receiver acknowledges the retransmitted block with the same ACK 1 or ACK 0 it would have used for a successful first transmission. Were the master to receive the wrong ACK, e.g., ACK 1 when ACK 0 was expected, it would retransmit that block as though a NAK had been received.

If the master station fails to receive a reply or received an invalid reply [Fig. 6(13)] to a transmitted block it will usually send an ENQ [Fig. 6(14)] after an appropriate timeout. The receiving station will then repeat its last reply. Several unsuccessful attempts at sending an ENQ to solicit a reply will result in initiation of a recovery procedure [Fig. 6(15)].

C. Termination of the Data Link

The data link is terminated by the transmission of the control character EOT. Termination may be initiated by the master following reception of a positive acknowledgment to the last block of a message. Termination is also initiated by a control station which has received an invalid or no reply to a poll or a call, or a NAK to a call. Termination can be initiated by a polled station which has no traffic to send.

D. Abnormal Conditions and Fault Recovery

Any of several causes such as line noise, line breaks, operator errors, or equipment malfunction may cause operation to violate the established protocol procedures. This usually results in an abnormal or fault condition. Recovery procedures are intended to aid in reestablishing normal operation. Recovery procedures can often only detect the condition and sometimes require normal intervention to correct the problem. More sophisticated systems may permit a degree of automatic recovery.

Timers play a very significant role in the detection of and recovery from fault conditions. In the protocol just described the prudent system designer would have implemented at least two timers. These timers and their role in fault recovery are as follows:

1. Response Timer. This timer protects a sending station against an invalid or missing response. It would be started with the transmission of any control character requiring a response such as ETX, ETB, or ENQ. It would be stopped when the valid reply was received. If it expires appropriate action such as retransmission N times is initiated. If link recovery does not occur, higher-level intervention by an operator or recovery program is required. Typical values for a response timer are in the range of 2–3 s. Timer values are, of course, highly dependent on the properties and parameters of the specific system.

2. Receive Timer. A receive timer will protect against failure to receive or recognize an end-of-block character ETB or ETX. Such a timer is started on detection of a start of block character SOH or STX, restarted with continuing data input, and stopped upon recognition of an end-of-block character. Expiration of this timer, usually in the range of 500 ms, initiates a search for character synchronization, discarded of the faulted block, and notification to higher level.

Other possible timer uses are to detect no activity on a line and to detect a missed DLE EOT where this sequence is used to initiate a switched circuit disconnect. Failure to clear a switched circuit connection can be very expensive!

E. Variations

Many variations in procedure and many options to the standard procedure are available. Most are designed for particular applications and situations but those described here have come into fairly widespread use. Most are subject to bilateral agreement, which is to say that both stations involved in the interchange must be aware of their presence.

1. Block Abort. A block abort occurs when the sending station in the process of sending a block decides for whatever reason to end transmission and terminate prior to the normal end of block. An abort is accomplished by transmitting the control character ENQ and then halting. The receiving station detects the ENQ (instead of ETB or ETX), discards the partial block, sends a NAK, and waits for the sender to resume.

2. Send Abort. Should a sending station decide to terminate a transmission after receiving an acknowledgment for a block but before sending the next block it may do so by sending EOT. This will cause the receiving terminal to discard the incomplete incoming message and wait for the control station to reestablish the link.

3. Receive Abort. A receiving station can abort a sequence of incoming blocks by sending EOT in lieu of its normal acknowledgment response. It may do this, for example, if it has become unable to receive owing to a fault or lack of storage. The sending station would normally try to recall the station and resend the message.

4. Temporary Delay. This variation allows a receiver to temporarily delay blocks coming from a sender. It is signaled by sending DLE; in place of the usual acknowledgment. This sequence, known as WACK, indicates to the sender that the block has been received correctly but that a temporary delay is required. The sender will send an ENQ to which the receiver will respond with another DLE;. This will continue until the receiver responds to an ENQ with the appropriate ACK or until the sender loses patience and the initiates recovery procedures.

5. Reverse Interrupt. Another variation in procedure allows a receiving station to ask a sending station to terminate the transmission so that the receiving station may gain access to the line. This would be useful for high-priority traffic as an example. The receiver asks for a reverse interrupt by transmitting the sequence DLE < in lieu of its normal acknowledgment sequence. The sender treats the DLE < as a positive acknowledgment and releases the line by transmitting EOT at the earliest opportunity.

6. *Synchronization Sequence.* If the receiver is to accurately locate and decode data characters from an incoming bit stream it must acquire and maintain character synchronization with the transmitter. In synchronous systems this is accomplished by the transmission of a synchronizing character called SYN at the beginning of a data stream, or following any period when no characters have been transmitted. Since there is a high probability that the first character of a stream of data will be distorted or errored, most protocols require that a minimum of two SYN characters precede the control or data characters. Many implementations require three or even four SYN characters. This allows the receiver to search for two successive SYN characters before declaring that synchronization has been acquired.

For the sake of simplicity, the SYN characters have been omitted from control sequences described in this chapter. It must be remembered that sequences such as ENQ, SOH, STX, EOT, and ACK are actually transmitted with two or more preceding SYNs, as for example SYN SYN ENQ or SYN SYN EOT.

7. *Pad Characters.* Pad characters are used by some protocols to assure that the first and last characters of a transmission are fully and properly transmitted by the associated data set. At the start of a data stream the pad assures that the receiver is prepared to receive and searching for synchronization. At the end of the data stream, the pad guarantees that the last significant character has been transmitted by the data set before it turns off for line turnaround. Most protocols define the leading pad as a SYN character and the trailing pad as an all-1's character.

8. *Prefixes.* In many protocols the control sequences consist of a prefix followed by the communication control character. The use of a prefix must be by bilateral agreement. When used they usually consist of up to 15 characters, which must be other than communication control characters. Prefixes are often used to convey status information or station identity especially when operating on switched network facilities where it is important to verify proper connection. The control character EOT is never preceded by a prefix. DLE EOT, however, is often used in switched network operation to initiate a disconnect of the switched circuit.

F. Transparency

One of the major and most often encountered variations to the basic data link control protocol is transparent operation. As defined earlier, transparent operation provides the link control with the ability to treat all transmitted and received characters, including normally restricted control characters, as data.

In character-oriented protocols transparent operation is implemented by the use of the Data Link Escape (DLE) character to form what are known as code extension sequences. Transparent operation is illustrated in Fig. 7 and operates as described next.

In the transparent mode each control character is preceded by a DLE character to form two-character sequences, examples of which are:

DLE STX Initiates the transparent mode for the following data block.

DLE ETB Terminates a block of transparent data.

DLE ETX Terminates the last block of transparent data.

DLE SYN Character synchronization sequence inserted into transparent transmitted blocks at approximately 1-s intervals; not accumulated in the BCC.

DLE ENQ Aborts the transmission of a block of transparent data; used by the transmitting terminal.·

DLE DLE Permits the transmission of a DLE as data within a transparent block.

The DLE character effectively instructs the receiver to recognize the next character as a control character and to ignore control characters (which may appear in transparent text) not preceded by DLE. Since the character DLE itself may appear in transparent text, the receiver would decode the following character as a control character. This is prevented by having the transmitter insert an extra DLE following one which appears in text, creating the two-character sequence DLE DLE. The receiver recognizing this sequence deletes one DLE, restoring the original data stream, and treats the other as valid data.

G. Byte Count Protocols

The use of escape sequences, based on DLE, introduces considerable complexity to the character-oriented protocols. Great care is required in either hardware or software implementation to avoid misinterpretation of control sequences.

Protocols, such as DDCMP, described in Chapter 10, have been devised which solve the transparency problem without the use of escape characters. These protocols are known as byte-count-oriented protocols since they achieve transparency by keeping track of character count and transmitting this information with each block.

The character count is normally transmitted as a positionally located field usually immediately following the SYN characters. The field length is

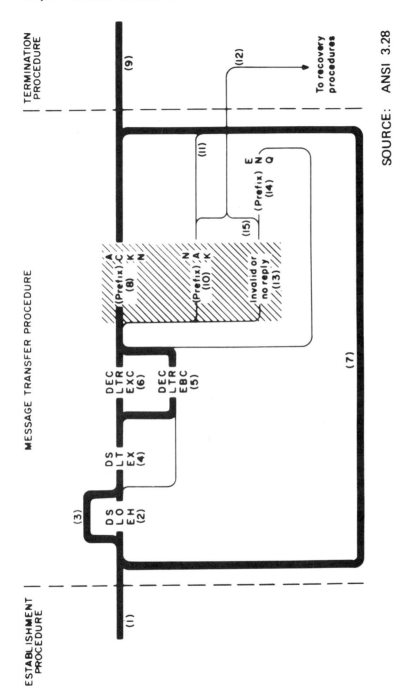

Fig. 7. Subcategory D1: Message-independent blocking, with cyclic checking, alternating acknowledgments, and transparent heading and text.

in character increments and indicates the number of characters comprising the block. The receiver then counts characters instead of searching for a control character to determine the location of the check characters and the end of the block.

H. Acknowledgment

Variations in the technique used to acknowledge blocks are quite common. The majority of these fall into one of the following categories:

No Acknowledgment. Protocols are in operation which use no acknowledgment method at all. Usually these would be found in situations where only one-way facilities may be used and where the data itself is highly redundant so that the receiver could discard an obviously errored block.

Single Acknowledgment. In this method the transmitter sends a block of information and waits for a reply. The reply is a single character providing a positive (ACK) or negative (NAK) reply. If positive the transmitter sends the next block. If negative the transmitter retransmits the last block.

Alternating Acknowledgments. This technique is the same as the single acknowledgement method with the exception that positive acknowledgments alternate odd and even blocks with a two-character sequences such as ACK 1 and ACK 0. This provides an additional protection against lost blocks.

Block Numbering. A much more sophisticated acknowledgment technique involves the numbering and sequencing of each transmitted block. Using this method, sometimes referred to as "pipelining," the transmitter may send blocks continuously, each block having been assigned and identified with a block number. The receiver, using a reverse channel, sends acknowledgments containing the block numbers correctly received. A NAK from the receiver causes the transmitter to retransmit all blocks sent after the last correctly received block. Many variations of this technique have been implemented. They all require a backward channel, usually a full duplex channel. This technique is of course much more efficient than block-by-block acknowledgment.

V. Implementation Considerations

Despite the existence of standards, the link control implementor must be aware of the many characteristics of the communications environment that are either subject to bilateral agreement or influence the behavior of the control protocol. Among these are the following:

- The physical facility and its interface requirements.
- The precise characteristics of the stations on the link in terms of the protocol options and variations implemented.

- The actual code set utilized.
- The formats of the messages being interchanged.
- Additional or optional link controls being implemented.
- The recovery procedures being used by all stations.
- The requirement for synchronization.
- The maximum block length accommodated and provisions for short blocks.

One way to assure that all parameters, characteristics, and functional behavior are well understood is to create a protocol specification for the specific application. This specification can be based on the "standard" protocol but is expanded to include all options, timers, bilateral agreements, and unique characteristics if any. The document can then be reviewed and revised until all parties sharing the communication link agree on its content.

VI. Limitations

Even though character-oriented protocols represent the vast majority of link control protocols in use today, it has long been recognized that they suffer from many deficiencies. Among these are the following:

1. The necessity to distinguish between data and control characters within a code set places a burden on hardware and software implementation.
2. The assignment of characters for link control subtracts from the combinations otherwise available for information transfer.
3. The character orientation meant that they were not naturally transparent to the structure or encoding of the text.
4. Transparency could only be achieved by invoking complicated escape techniques and at the expense of incompatibility with nontransparent protocols.
5. The mixture of message control, device control, and link control forced a significant amount of processing at a low functional level, and blurred the interface between these logically independent functions.
6. Error checking is usually done only on the text, thus exposing supervisory sequences to undetected errors which complicate error recovery.
7. The inherent two-way alternate nature of these protocols does not economically utilize full-duplex facilities.
8. The rigid structure of character-oriented protocols lacks flexibility and expandability.

Many deviations and variations have been devised in attempts to improve the character-oriented protocols. To a great extent these have been unsuccessful. The explosion in information technology combined with the rapid evolution in hardware have begun to overwhelm the ability of character-oriented protocols to keep pace.

This inability to overcome the inherent deficiencies of the character-oriented protocols was the impetus for the development of a whole new family of link control protocols now known as bit-oriented protocols.

Despite their deficiencies and despite the rapid emergence of the bit-oriented protocols, the character-oriented protocols can be expected to be with us well into the future, primarily because of widescale implementation. They have served our industry well.

References

[1] ANSI X3.28-1976: "American National Standard procedure for the use of the communication control characters of American National Standard code for information interchange in specified data communication links." American National Standards Institute, Inc., New York.

[2] IS 1745-1975, "Basic mode control procedures for data communication systems," International Standards Organization, Geneva, Switzerland.

[3] ECMA-16, "Basic mode control procedures for data communication using the ECMA 7 bit code," European Computer Manufacturing Association.

[4] IBM BSC, "General information—Binary synchronous communications," Publication GA27-3004-1, IBM System Reference Library.

[5] IATA SLC, "Synchronous Link control procedures," ATA/IATA Interline Communications Manual, International Air Transport Association, Montreal, Canada.

[6] DEC DDCMP, "Digital Data Communication message protocol," Digital Equipment Corporation.

[7] ANSI X3.4-1977, "American National Standard code for information interchange," American National Standards Institute, New York.

5

Bit-Oriented Data Link Control

David E. Carlson

I. Introduction

A new breed of data link control is emerging today. Known under a variety of names and mnemonics—ADCCP, HDLC, LAPB, BDLC, SDLC, UDLC, etc.—it is based on a bit-oriented, rather than character-oriented, organization and format. It offers a high level of flexibility, enhanceability, adaptability, reliability, and efficiency of operation for today's as well as for tomorrow's synchronous data communications needs.

A. Historical Background

Bit-oriented data link control procedures had their beginnings approximately a decade ago. It was then that it became evident that the various existing character-oriented data link control procedures (Chapter 4) that had served so well in so many applications (and still do in some) were not well suited for many of the newer interactive applications being pursued. Technology had provided more reliable transmission facilities, more intelligent and cost-effective computers and terminals, and new frontiers for their use in almost every segment of the business, industry, government, and academic environments. Extending or modifying the existing protocols to satisfy these needs was found to be generally inadequate. The character-oriented procedures were, from a control standpoint, basically two-way alternate ("half-duplex") in nature and batch-oriented in operation. They were inherently tied to the transmission code being used, and generally utilized unprotected control codes and sequences to perform link control management functions. Generally, only a single data link function was performed with each transmission unit sent [e.g., transfer data, acknowledge data, solicit (poll) data, etc.] and so large numbers of logical link turnarounds were often required. This, in turn, would lead to an unsatisfactory ratio of data transfer exchange to control exchange capability in many cases. Often, a character-oriented procedure would vary so much in format and function from one type of application or use to another, that for all intent and purposes they were no longer the same data link control procedure.

All in all, it was time for a new approach to data link control, an approach that would correct and improve the identified shortcomings present in the existing protocols, provide the features and services that this new environment demanded, and offer the ability for extension and enhancement in order to provide for the future. The bit-oriented data link control described in this paper seems to provide a satisfactory solution to these problems for many synchronous data communications needs.

B. General Requirements and Capabilities

The principal requirement for this new data link control was that it support the emerging interactive operations. To this end, the following capabilities were identified as being essential:

1. code-independent operation (transparency),
2. adaptability to various applications, configurations, and uses in a consistent manner,
3. both two-way alternate and two-way simultaneous ("full duplex") data transfer,
4. high efficiency (throughput), and
5. high reliability.

Code independence means that the user should be able to choose the code set or bit patterns to be used for data transfer without concern for the data link control procedure being used. There should be no need to dedicate certain codes or bit patterns from the user's set for data link control purposes (as had been the case with character-oriented protocols). The user's choice should be predicated solely on satisfying user-identified objectives.

Adaptability to various applications, configurations, and uses means that the composition of the procedures should be such that they are readily applicable to two-wire or four-wire equivalent physical circuits, in point-to-point or multipoint configurations, on switched or nonswitched circuits.

Adaptability and code independence also mean that there should be a sense of station independence as well, in that stations of different degrees of sophistication can coexist on the same link, so long as the controlling station is aware of the capabilities and limitations of each individual station and the station operations themselves do not interfere with one another. This should allow the combining of stations on a link on the basis of geographic location and traffic requirements, without concern for the type of stations involved.

The inclusion of *two-way simultaneous data transfer* capability means that more efficient operation should be possible, resulting in increased throughput and probably lower cost where two-way traffic flow requirements exist. It also means that fewer overall transmission paths should be needed in the resultant system configuration. Two-way simultaneous capability can be vitally important when operating in a long propagation delay situation, such as over satellite connections or very high speed links.

High efficiency means that the ratio of data transfer exchange to control exchange per unit of time should be high. The organization of the data link controls should allow multiple functions to be conveyed in each transmission, for example, transfer of data, acknowledgments for data received in earlier transmissions, plus in the case of a controlling station, a solicitation (poll) for a return transmission. High efficiency should also be realized by the use of a data link control organization that holds down the number of logical turnarounds required in the operation of the data link.

High reliability means that all transmissions, data and control, should be protected from transmission errors by a powerful error detection and correction mechanism. Recovery from transmission errors should be an automatic aspect of the procedures (for example, the execution of up to some design number N retransmission attempts before alarming). High reliability also means that data transfer sequence integrity should be maintained with respect to the order of the data that is passed to the higher level at the receiving station. Also, no data should be lost or duplicated without appropriate notification to the higher level.

C. Organization of Chapter

The balance of this chapter is presented in terms of the American National Standards Institute (ANSI) bit-oriented data link control procedure standard—ADCCP, the Advanced Data Communication Control Procedures (X3.66-1979) [1]. ADCCP is compatible with the High-Level Data Link Control (HDLC) standard that was developed by the International Organization for Standardization (ISO).

ADCCP is used as the baseline because it covers a wide scope of possible bit-oriented data link control procedure applications and has had the benefit of a broad base of input and comment from a large cross section of providers, users, and general interest organizations and individuals. This chapter describes the various link configurations, modes of operation, and station types that are covered by ADCCP. The composition of this bit-oriented procedure is described, including the frame structure, the repertoire of commands and responses, and the classes of procedure defined to date. To illustrate some of the principles of bit-oriented procedure operation, a few typical examples of operation are examined. The status of similar bit-oriented data link control procedure activity by other standards bodies (e.g., ISO, CCITT, etc.) is reviewed. The subject of compatibility with proprietary bit-oriented protocols (BDLC, SDLC, etc.) is touched on briefly. Finally, there is a crystal-ball view of possible future development and standardization in the subject area.

Throughout all sections of this chapter certain liberties have been taken in the level and completeness of description of the general operation so as not to cloud the overall picture with details of operation. The goal is to provide an overview of bit-oriented data link control operation in general, not an in-depth presentation of the ADCCP standard in particular. For details of specific ADCCP operation under various operating conditions, [1] should be consulted.

II. Configurations, Modes and Station Types

During the development of the bit-oriented data link control procedure approach, every attempt was made to identify the needs and requirements of a general data link control procedure that would have widespread applicability in today's and tomorrow's marketplace. Taken into consideration were point-to-point and multipoint configurations, using two-way alternate and two-way simultaneous operation over switched and non-switched transmission lines. Both terrestrial and satellite connections were recognized as being part of the problem. Also included was communication between logical equals and communication between logical unequals.

To satisfy the above needs, three different data transfer modes of operation evolved and three different types of stations were identified. The three modes are:

1. the normal response mode (NRM) for use in point-to-point or multipoint configurations,
2. the asynchronous response mode (ARM) for use in point-to-point or multipoint configurations, and
3. the asynchronous balanced mode (ABM) for use in point-to-point configurations.

The three types of stations are:

1. the primary station (one per NRM or ARM operation),
2. the secondary station (one or more per NRM or ARM operation), and
3. the combined station (two per ABM operation).

The normal and asynchronous response modes (NRM and ARM) provide an unbalanced type of data transfer capability between logically unequal stations (a single primary station and one or more secondary stations) operating in a centralized control environment. In both NRM and ARM, the role of the primary station is to control the overall data link operation. The primary station is responsible for initializing the link [activating the secondary station(s)], controlling the flow of data to and from the secondary station(s), recovering from system errors not recoverable by retransmission of the same data, and logically disconnecting the secondary station(s) when required. The secondary stations are subservient to the primary station at the data link level. Their role is generally passive and they have little or no capability for recovery from system errors. As a rule (and in many cases as an objective), the extent of their logical complexity is such that they can be significantly simpler and less costly than their primary station counterpart.

A primary station issues commands and receives expected responses. A secondary station receives commands and issues responses in accordance with the nature of the command received and the mode of operation used. In NRM, a secondary station initiates transmission *only* as a result of receiving explicit permission to do so from the primary station. Once permission is received, a secondary station response transmission must be initiated, with the end of the transmission being explicitly identified. The transmission may or may not include the transfer of data from the secondary station to the primary station, depending on the availability of data to transmit and the form of the explicit permission to send. In ARM, a secondary station is not required to receive explicit permission from the primary station in order to initiate transmissions (responses) of its own. ARM operation, therefore, is more freewheeling and less disciplined than NRM operation.

The normal response mode (NRM) is ideally suited for polled multipoint operation where ordered interaction between a central location and a number of outlying stations is required, or any situation where it is desirable for one station to be able to control the transmittability of other related station(s). Similarly, the asynchronous response mode (ARM) seems ideally suited for situations where a single primary station and a single activated secondary station wish to transmit freely to one another without the overhead of a polling control discipline.

Because of the asynchronous nature of secondary station transmissions when ARM is utilized in a multipoint environment, only one secondary station can be activated (on-line) at a time. Other secondary stations on the multipoint link must be kept in a quiescent disconnected mode (off-line) so as not to interfere with any transmission in progress.

The asynchronous balanced mode (ABM) provides a balanced type of data transfer capability between two logically equal stations (two combined stations) in a balanced control environment. Each combined station is capable of initializing the link, activating the other combined station, and logically disconnecting the link (deactivating the other combined station) when required, and is responsible for controlling its own data flow and recovering from its own system errors. A combined station can both issue commands and responses, and receive commands and responses. The asynchronous nature of the balanced mode of operation means that there is no operational overhead required to control transmission (start and stop data transfer) from the other combined station.

For a point-to-point configuration, the asynchronous modes (ARM and ABM) are usually more efficient than the normal response mode (NRM) because there is no polling overhead required. The choice of which asynchronous mode to specify is dependent on the relative level of data link control capability that is provided in each station: ABM operation for logical equals, ARM operation for logical unequals.

In a great many instances of NRM or ARM application, the primary station will be a host computer. The secondary stations will be operator-controlled terminals, simple data collection or data display devices, or the like, depending on the needs of the data system. In many ABM applications, each combined station will be a host computer, an intelligent network node (e.g., a packet-switching node), or at least a highly intelligent terminal that has the capability to control the data link itself.

In addition to the data transfer modes cited above, there are also non-data-transfer modes that have been defined to complete the complement of bit-oriented data link control procedures. They include two disconnected modes and an optional initialization mode.

In the optional initialization mode, a primary/combined station may initialize or regenerate the link control of a secondary/combined station. Details regarding the nature of such initialization activities have been deemed to be system dependent and, therefore, are not structured or specified in a standard manner at this time.

Both disconnected modes have the stations logically disconnected from the link. The normal disconnected mode (NDM) applies to primary and secondary stations only. In the normal disconnected mode, the secondary station may not initiate any form of transmission until explicitly requested to respond by the primary station. When so requested, the response can only be one of a limited set of responses that either accepts the command, refuses the command, or requests some alternative action on the part of the primary station. The asynchronous disconnected mode (ADM) applies to combined stations as well as to primary and secondary stations. In the asynchronous disconnected mode, the secondary/combined station may generate a particular response on an asynchronous basis as a request for a mode setting command in order to establish a data transfer mode.

The choice and evolution of the data transfer modes provided by these bit-oriented data link control procedures was not driven totally by technical considerations. Other factors played a role as well. For instance, political considerations provided some of the motivation for inclusion of the asynchronous balanced mode (ABM). The NRM and ARM modes had been defined first, and were pretty well fixed in place, and generally accepted internationally, when it was observed that they did not quite satisfy all of the "requirements." True, they supported point-to-point and multipoint configurations, two-way alternate and two-way simultaneous operation over switched and nonswitched facilities. They also provided transparent, efficient, and reliable data transfer. However, each was built on a primary station/secondary station relationship that had the negative aspect associated with it that in two-station configurations one of the stations was operationally "secondary" to the other. The overall control of data flow and responsibility for system recovery resided in only one of the stations—the designated primary station. For many applications, this was considered to be unacceptable. For example, when interconnecting governments, corporations, independent systems, etc., the thought of being the "secondary" to another, dependent upon another for one's operation and livelihood, was generally unacceptable. Hence the asynchronous balanced mode (ABM) was defined to support fully balanced, independent data transfer between logical equals. As noted later, ABM has become a vital part of the bit-oriented data link control procedure solution.

III. Composition of the Bit-Oriented Procedures

This section provides a brief sketch of the major elements that make up the composition of bit-oriented data link control procedures. Included are the frame structure and transmission formats; the commands, responses, and parameters; and the resultant classes of procedures.

A. Frame Structure

The basic transmission unit is called a frame. All transmissions (data, control, or both) are in frames, and each frame conforms to one of the two following formats:

1. if there is an information field to transport,

$$F, A, C, Info, FCS, F$$

2. if there are only data link control sequences to transport,

$$F, A, C, FCS, F$$

where

$$F = \text{flag sequence}$$

$$A = \text{address field}$$

$$C = \text{control field}$$

$$\text{Info} = \text{information field}$$

$$\text{FCS} = \text{frame check sequence}$$

The *flag sequence* (F) is a unique eight-bit pattern (a 0 bit followed by six 1 bits ending with a 0 bit) used to synchronize the receiver with the incoming frame. It delimits the start and close of each transmitted frame and is also used by the sender to fill time between frames during a transmission of multiple frames.

To achieve transparency, the unique flag sequence is prohibited from occurring anywhere in the address, control, information, and FCS fields by having the transmitter and receiver perform the following action after sending and receiving, respectively, the opening flag sequence:

- Transmitter: insert a 0 bit following five contiguous 1 bits anywhere before sending the closing flag sequence ("bit stuffing").
- Receiver: delete the 0 bit following five contiguous 1 bits following a 0 bit anywhere before receiving the closing flag sequence ("destuffing").

The closing flag for one frame may also serve as the opening flag for the next frame.

The *address field* (A) identifies the station (secondary or combined) on that link that is to receive (or is sending) the frame. Command frames are always sent with the receiving station's address. Response frames are always sent with the sending station's address. Hence, the address field identifies a secondary station in the normal and asynchronous response modes and the response-generating portion of a combined station in the asynchronous balanced mode.

Two mutually exclusive address field options are defined—single octet and multiple octet addressing. Single octet addressing provides for up to 256 different addresses. Multiple octet addressing provides for greater than 256 addresses and also allows for character-oriented encoding of the address field where such may be desirable. In the case of multiple octet addressing, the address field is recursively extendable with the first bit of each octet used to indicate which is the final octet of the address field. The final octet will have its first bit set to "1," and each preceding octet will have its first bit set to "0."

CONTROL FIELD BITS

CONTROL FIELD FOR	1	2	3	4	5	6	7	8
INFORMATION TRANSFER COMMAND / RESPONSE (I FRAME)	0	N(S)			P/F	N(R)		
SUPERVISORY COMMANDS / RESPONSES (S FRAME)	1	0	S	S	P/F	N(R)		
UNNUMBERED COMMANDS / RESPONSES (U FRAME)	1	1	M	M	P/F	M	M	M

Fig. 1. Control field formats.

The all-ones address is specified as a global (broadcast) address that all stations will be responsive to. The all-zeros address is specified as a null address that no station will be responsive to. Group addressing is possible on a system-by-system basis.

The *control field* (C) identifies the function and purpose of the frame. Three different control field formats are defined: information transfer, supervisory, and unnumbered. Figure 1 depicts the general organization of the control field formats.

Bit 1 set to "0" identifies the I frame format. Bit 1 set to "1" with bit 2 set to "0" or "1" identifies the S frame format or the U frame format, respectively. Only the I frame format has a send sequence number $N(S)$ to uniquely identify the frame and to allow it to be kept in sequential order during the data transfer operation. Both the I and S frame formats have a receive sequence number $N(R)$, so both formats are usable to acknowledge I frames received. The two S bits in the S frame format provide for the specification of four supervisory functions. The five M bits in the U frame format provide for the specification of up to 32 commands and 32 responses to cover the remaining control functions required. The P/F bit in each format provides for a checkpointing mechanism that allows a response frame to be logically associated with the appropriate initiating command frame. (The bit is considered to be the P bit if the frame is a command and the F bit if it is a response.) Checkpointing is accomplished by setting the F bit equal to "1" in the response frame that is to be treated as the logical counterpart of the command frame sent with the P bit set to "1."

In the normal response mode, the P bit set to "1" serves to poll the secondary station(s) to which it is addressed. Similarly, in NRM, the F bit set to "1" serves to identify the final frame in a series of frames sent by the secondary in response to a received P bit set to "1". In the asynchronous response mode and asynchronous balanced mode, the receipt of a frame with the P bit set to "1" will cause the secondary station (ARM) or combined station (ABM) to set the F bit equal to "1" in the next appropriate frame transmitted.

The *information field* (Info) contains the data that are to be transferred across the link. The data may be of any length and may consist of any code or grouping of bits. The bit stuffing protocol ensures "transparency," i.e., it allows the information field to include any patterns, even patterns that look to the end users like flags (01111110), without producing a spurious action at the receiving end.

All frames include a 16-bit *frame check sequence* (FCS) field prior to the closing flag sequence to assist in the detection of transmission errors. The FCS (described in the preceding chapter) is performed on the contents of the address, control, and information fields of the frame, using the well-known CCITT V.41 generator polynomial: $x^{16} + x^{12} + x^5 + 1$. Prior to initiating the FCS check at the transmitter (and the receiver), the FCS register (or equivalent) is preset to all ones. In the absence of transmission errors, a unique, nonzero 16-bit pattern is then detected at the receiver. Frames failing to pass the FCS check are discarded and ignored.

An optional 32-bit FCS is now available for those applications requiring a higher degree of detection of transmission errors. The 32-bit generator polynomial is:

$$x^{32} + x^{26} + x^{23} + x^{22} + x^{16} + x^{12} + x^{11} +$$

$$x^{10} + x^8 + x^7 + x^5 + x^4 + x^2 + x + 1.$$

Should the transmitter of a frame determine during the course of the transmission that the frame should be discarded and ignored by the receiver, it may accomplish this in either of two ways. One method involves premature termination of the frame in the normal manner with a flag sequence, but purposely causing an incorrect FCS field to be included in the frame. The other method involves aborting the frame in progress by transmitting a continuous ones state (with no inserted zeros) that persists for at least seven bit intervals in length. Aborted frames are ignored by the receiver.

If the ones state on the link persists for 15 bit times or more, an idle link state is defined. The idle link state indicates that the sending station has relinquished the right to continue transmission. It is often used in conjunction with two-way alternate operation on half-duplex transmission facilities. The reappearance of a flag sequence defines reentry into the active link state, wherein an operational mode may be established and information transferred between stations.

B. Elements of Procedure

Each frame contains a command or a response that is either an information transfer frame, a supervisory frame, or a miscellaneous unnum-

Table I—Specified adccp I, S, and U Format Control Field Bit Encodings[a]

Frame format	Command	Control field bits								Response
		1	2	3	4	5	6	7	8	
I	I	0	$N(S)$			P/F	$N(R)$			I
S	RR	1	0	0	0	P/F	$N(R)$			RR
	REJ	1	0	0	1	P/F	$N(R)$			REJ
	RNR	1	0	1	0	P/F	$N(R)$			RNR
	SREJ	1	0	1	1	P/F	$N(R)$			SREJ
U	UI	1	1	0	0	P/F	0	0	0	UI
	SNRM	1	1	0	0	P	0	0	1	
	DISC	1	1	0	0	P/F	0	1	0	RD
	UP	1	1	0	0	P	1	0	0	
		1	1	0	0	F	1	1	0	UA
	Nonreserved	1	1	0	1	P/F	0	0	0	Nonreserved
	Nonreserved	1	1	0	1	P/F	0	0	1	Nonreserved
	Nonreserved	1	1	0	1	P/F	0	1	0	Nonreserved
	Nonreserved	1	1	0	1	P/F	0	1	1	Nonreserved
	SIM	1	1	1	0	P/F	0	0	0	RIM
		1	1	1	1	F	0	0	1	FRMR
	SARM	1	1	1	1	P/F	0	0	0	DM
	RSET	1	1	1	1	P	0	0	1	
	SARME	1	1	1	1	P	0	1	0	
	SNRME	1	1	1	1	P	0	1	1	
	SABM	1	1	1	1	P	1	0	0	
	XID	1	1	1	1	P/F	1	0	1	XID
	SABME	1	1	1	1	P	1	1	0	

[a] Note: All unassigned unnumbered control field bit encodings are reserved for possible future standardization.

bered control frame. Although the list of commands and responses seems long, in most cases only a few are needed and used to any extent in the provision of normal operation. The majority of them are of the unnumbered format variety and are either associated with various link establishment/disconnect procedures or the provision of optional features and capabilities to satisfy special needs. A brief description of the various commands and responses that are defined in the ADCCP standard are listed below. (The specific control field bit encodings are given in Table I)

Information (I) Command/Response (I Format): I frames are used to transfer sequentially numbered information fields across a data link, and to acknowledge I frames already received from the other station.

Receive Ready (RR) Command/Response (S Format): RR frames are used to indicate readiness to receive I frames and to acknowledge I frames already received from the other station.

Receive Not Ready (RNR) Command/Response (S Format): RNR frames are used to indicate a temporary busy condition and to acknowledge I frames already received from the other station.

Reject (REJ) Command/Response (S Format): REJ frames are used to request retransmission of all I frames starting from a designated point in the numbering cycle and to acknowledge I frames already received from the other station.

Selective Reject (SREJ) Command/Response (S Format): SREJ frames are used to request retransmission of a single designated I frame previously transmitted and to acknowledge I frames already received from the other station.

Unextended Numbering Set Mode (SXXM) Commands (U Format): Unextended numbering set mode commands are used to establish the particular Modulo 8 sequence numbering mode of operation to be used. Upon accepting and acknowledging a set mode command, the receiving station's send and receive state variables are set to zero. Three unextended numbering set mode commands are defined:

SNRM—Set Normal Response Mode
SARM—Set Asynchronous Response Mode
SABM—Set Asynchronous Balanced Mode

Extended Numbering Set Mode (SXXME) Commands (U Format): Extended numbering set mode commands are used to establish the particular Modulo 128 sequence numbering mode of operation to be used. Upon accepting and acknowledging a set mode command, the receiving station's send and receive state variables are set to zero. Three extended numbering set mode commands are defined:

SNRME—Set Normal Response Mode Extended
SARME—Set Asynchronous Response Mode Extended
SABME—Set Asynchronous Balanced Mode Extended

Set Initialization Mode (SIM) Command (U Format): The SIM command is used to establish the initialization mode of operation, during which the link control may be initialized or regenerated, or operational parameters exchanged.

Disconnect (DISC) Command (U Format): The DISC command is used to logically terminate a previously established operational mode, and to cause the stations involved to assume the system predetermined disconnected mode.

Reset (RSET) Command (U Format): The RSET command is used to reset the send state variable at the transmitting station and the receive state variable at the receiving station to zero. The values of the state variables associated with the other direction of transmission remain unaffected.

Unnumbered Poll (UP) Command (U Format): The UP command is used to solicit response frames from one or more stations by establishing a special logical operational condition that exists at each addressed station for one respond opportunity. (Loop operation [2] is typical of the type of application that could utilize the UP command.) The UP command does not acknowledge any I frames (or UI frames) received from the other station.

Unnumbered Information (UI) Command/Response (U Format): UI frames are used to transfer information fields across a data link without impacting the send or receive state variables at any station. There is no specific link level acknowledgment provided for UI frames.

Exchange Identification (XID) Command/Response (U Format): XID frames are used to request and/or report a station's identity and, optionally, to convey the parameters, operational capabilities, and characteristics of the transmitting station.

Request Initialization Mode (RIM) Response (U Format): The RIM response is used to request that the initialization mode be established.

Request Disconnect (RD) Response (U Format): The RD response is used to request that the link be put in a disconnected mode.

Unnumbered Acknowledgment (UA) Response (U Format): The UA response is used to acknowledge receipt and execution of a mode setting, initializing, resetting, or disconnecting command.

Disconnected Mode (DM) Response (U Format): The DM response is used to indicate a request for a set mode command, or, if used in reply to a set mode command, as an indication that the set mode cannot be acted on at this time.

Frame Reject (FRMR) Response (U Format): The FRMR response is used to indicate that a frame received (command or response) was in error in a manner not recoverable by retransmission of the identical frame, such as

1. receipt of a control field that is invalid or not implemented, or
2. receipt of an information bearing frame with an information field that exceeds the maximum established length, or
3. receipt of an $N(R)$ which either points to an I frame which has been transmitted and acknowledged or to an I frame which has not been transmitted and is not the next sequential I frame awaiting transmission.

In addition, the ADCCP standard sets aside four unnumbered command/response code points as *Nonreserved Commands* and *Nonreserved Responses*. This provides implementors of the standard with a set of unnumbered code points that can be used to define special system-dependent data link functions, that may be necessary for a particular application but that do not have general applicability and hence were not standardized, with the assurance that said code points will *not* at some future time be assigned to a standard function or feature by ANSI.

C. Classes of Procedure

The three modes of operation, NRM, ARM, and ABM, provide the framework for the definition of three corresponding classes of procedure—the Unbalanced Normal Class (UNC), the Unbalanced Asynchronous Class (UAC), and the Balanced Asynchronous Class (BAC), respectively. Classes of procedure are defined in order to provide organization and direction for the application of the bit-oriented data link control procedures. Certain commands and responses are identified as belonging to the basic repertoire of these classes. Other commands and/or responses are viewed as being optional, either adding capability to the basic set or restricting utility of a general function for specific applications. Figure 2 depicts the three classes of procedures, the basic command and response repertoire, plus the optional functions, that are presently defined in the ADCCP standard.

In addition to certain of the commands and responses being optional functions, there is also an optional function concerning addressing (option 7) and two optional functions that deal with restrictions on the use of the I frame as a command only or a response only (options 8 and 9).

The following notation is used to identify a class of procedures and the optional functions that are supported:

- UNC,3,4—depicts the unbalanced, normal response mode class of procedures with the selective reject (SREJ) feature plus the ability to send nonsequenced unnumbered information (UI) frames.
- BAC,2,8—depicts the balanced, asynchronous balanced mode class of procedures with the reject (REJ) feature plus a restriction on the use of *I* frames as commands only.

Class UNC,3,4 might be typical of a multipoint configuration where the two-way alternate data transfer requirements are such that each secondary station transmission consists of multiple I frames, where the transmission error statistics indicate that the occurrence of transmission errors is low and that when errors do occur they generally only affect one frame out of a multiple frame transmission, and where there is occasionally a need to send some useful but not indispensable information to all secondary stations. Class BAC,2,8 might be typical of a point-to-point configuration involving two computers where balanced, equal control by both parties is important, where the two-way simultaneous data transfer requirements are such that the ability to request retransmission on the fly is desirable, and where the transfer of I frames is used as a continual data link level check that an inadvertent loopback has not occurred somewhere in the system. (BAC,2,8 is the class of procedure with optional functions that is used as the basis for the CCITT Recommendation X.25 Level 2 LAPB procedures described in Chapter 8.)

IV. Examples of Typical Operations

Figures 3–6 illustrate some typical on-line operations, with and without transmission errors, for the two classes of procedure identified above.

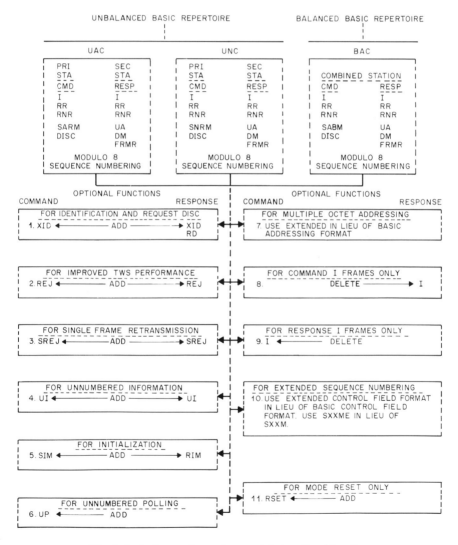

Fig. 2. Basic classes of procedures and their optional functions.

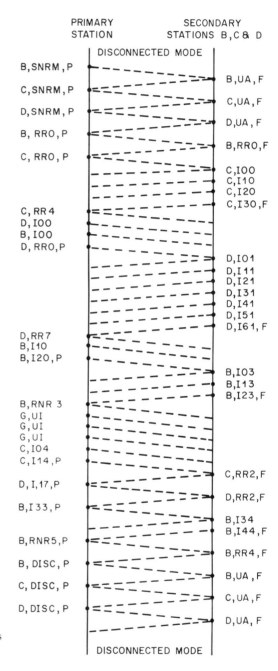

Fig. 3. Class UNC,3,4—examples of error-free operation.

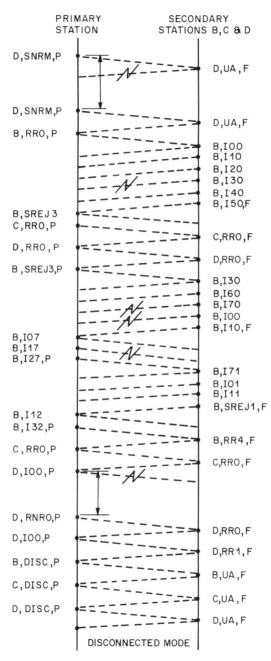

Fig. 4. Class UNC,3,4—examples of recovery procedures.

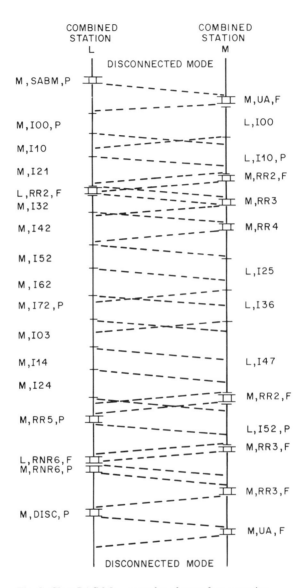

Fig. 5. Class BAC,2,8—examples of error-free operation.

Figures 3 and 4 depict an unbalanced, two-way alternate, multipoint operation (UNC,3,4) involving three secondary stations (B, C, and D). Figures 5 and 6 illustrate a balanced, two-way simultaneous, point-to-point operation (BAC,2,8) involving two combined stations (L and M). The examples cover normal, error-free operation as well as various error re-

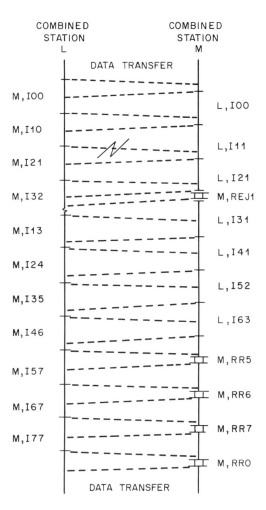

Fig. 6. Class BAC,2,8—example of
REJ recovery procedures.

covery situations. Many of the principles of the bit-oriented data link
control concept are illustrated by these examples. The vertical scale has been
dramatically reduced so as to allow illustration of various frame exchanges
during operations such as link setup, data transfer, recovery from transmission errors, and disconnect. The shorthand used in the figures should be
interpreted in the following way:

Consider frame X, Ysr, Z.

X represents the address associated with the frame. Primary station
transmissions will use the address of the secondary station for whom the
frame is intended. Secondary station transmissions will include the address

of the secondary station that is transmitting. Combined station transmissions will use the remote station address when a command frame is sent and will use the local station address when a response frame is sent.

Y represents the abbreviation for the command or response (for example, I, RNR, SNRM, UP, etc.). The "sr" following Y represents the send and receive sequence number values $N(S)$ and $N(R)$, respectively, that are an integral part of I and S format frames. If only a single number is present, it represents the receive sequence number $N(R)$.

Z, when present, indicates that the P or F bit is set to "1" in that fame. When not shown, it means that the value of the P or F bit is set equal to "0."

A. Unbalanced, Two-way Alternate Multipoint (UNC,3,4)

1. Example of Error-Free Operation

As indicated in Fig. 3, the primary station activates the secondary stations by addressing a SNRM command to each of them individually with the P bit set to "1." Each secondary station acknowledges the set mode command by returning the UA response with the F bit set to "1." (The P bit set to "1" grants the addressed secondary station the right to transmit an appropriate response, and the F bit set to "1" identifies the final frame in the corresponding response transmission.) As each secondary station (B, C, and D) is activated, its data link to the primary station is activated and that primary–secondary relationship is in the normal response mode (NRM).

As depicted, after setting up the entire link, the primary station polls B for information (traffic). B responds that it has no traffic to send by returning the RR response frame. The primary station then polls C, and receives four I frames from C. (A basic characteristics of these bit-oriented procedures is that a station may send more than one I frame before an acknowledgment is required. In fact, up to the modulus minus one I frames may be sent before an acknowledgment frame is required.) Each I frame has a different in-sequence send sequence number (first digit), plus a receive sequence number (second digit) that identifies the next I frame expected from the other (primary) station. Upon receipt of C,I30,F from C, the primary station acknowledges the receipt of four frames by issuing frame C, RR4. The 4 indicates that I frames numbered 0–3 were received correctly. Because the P bit is *not* set to "1," this frame does not grant C permission to send. It only acknowledges I frames received.

Before continuing the polling cycle with D, the primary station finds that it has received information for D from some other link and so delivers it to D. Prior to completion of the I frame transmission to D, information is received for B. Consequently, the delivery to B is performed before resuming the polling cycle with D (P bit set to "1"). The primary station will check the responses to subsequent polls for acknowledgments from B and D for the I frames delivered to B and D. (If the information for B and D had both been present when the C,RR4 frame was sent, the primary station could have sent B,I00 first and then combined the poll of D with the delivery to D by sending a D,I00,P frame.) D responds to the poll with the maximum number of response I frames (the modulus minus one = seven). When the primary station receives the seventh frame with the F bit set to "1," it acknowledges the transmission by sending D,RR7.

The primary station delivers two I frames to B, setting the P bit to "1" in the second I frame to affect the polling function. B responds with three I frames, identifying the final I frame with an F bit set to "1." The primary station returns B,RNR3, acknowledging the I frames received, but also indicating that the primary station is "not ready" to receive additional I frames from B.

At this point, the typical operation depicted indicates that the primary station has three frames worth of information that should be sent to all of the secondary stations on the link, but that the information is not so important to the operation of each secondary station that it warrants individual delivery, with individual acknowledgments. The nature of the information is such that should it be lost in transit, it will not cause a serious problem at any of the secondary stations. Examples of such information might include (1) some sort of updated hourly production report (missing one out of a series of such updated reports may not pose a problem), or (2) periodic time checks or weather reports. The use of the unnumbered information (UI) frame (option 4) plus the global address G (all ones) allows the information to be sent to all three secondary stations at the same time without impacting the send or receive state variables at any of the stations. Following the UI frames, the primary station sends two I frames to C. A series of exchanges with D and B follow. After receipt of B,I44,F from B, the primary station decides that it wishes to go into the disconnected mode. The primary station will check that all secondary station transmissions have been properly acknowledged. The check indicates that the B,I34 and B,I44,F frames have not been acknowledged, so the primary station issues a B,RNR5,P frame. The 5 acknowledges I frames up through 4. The P bit set to "1" will result in a response frame from B acknowledging receipt of the RNR frame. The RNR frame serves to inhibit any additional I frame transmissions from B. Upon receipt of B,RR4,F from B, the primary station initiates a DISC-UA exchange with each of the secondary stations, resulting in the link being returned to the normal disconnected mode.

2. Examples of Error Recovery Procedures

Figure 4 illustrates some typical error recovery actions that are possible with the unbalanced normal class of operation. Assume that secondary stations B and C have already been set up. The primary station sends D,SNRM,P to activate D. As noted, D responds with a UA response, but the response is subject to a transmission hit causing it to fail the FCS check at the primary station and, consequently, to be discarded. To determine when sufficient time has elapsed while waiting for an expected response, the primary station would probably activate a time-out function when it sends the D,SNRM,P frame. When this time-out function runs out, the primary station may initiate an appropriate recovery action. In the case shown, the recovery action is to issue the D,SNRM,P frame again and activate the time-out function again. Although D is already in the data transfer mode as a result of the first D,SNRM,P frame that it acknowledged, D is reactivated and returns another D,UA,F frame to the primary station. The arrival of this second acknowledgment at the primary station without error before the time-out function runs out, stops the time-out function, and completes the setup procedure. Normal polling and delivery functions then follow.

As depicted, the primary station polls B, and B responds with six I frames, the last of which contains an F bit set to "1." To guard against a "no response," the primary station would activate the response time-out function when it sent the B,RR0, P frame. The time-out function could then have been stopped with the reception of each I frame and then restarted in the case of the first five I frames when it was determined that the F bit was not set to "1" in that I frame. As indicated, I frame B,I30 sent by B was received in error and was discarded. The two following I frames were received free of error, and so only B,I30 is needed by the primary station to complete the data transfer of the six I frames. The first three I frames received can be passed along to the higher level. The last two I frames received are held, awaiting correct reception of the fourth I frame, B,I30. The primary station sends a selective reject frame (B,SREJ3) to acknowledge reception of I frames up through I frame numbered 2. B can then free up the buffers holding I frames 0–2. The SREJ also tells B that I frame numbered 3 will have to be retransmitted when permission to transmit is again granted.

As illustrated, the primary station has decided to complete the polling cycle before giving B permission to retransmit its I frame numbered 3. (Alternately, the primary station could have initiated retransmission immediately if it had wished to do so.) When the polling of C and D results in "no traffic" responses from each station, the primary station requests retransmission of the missing I frame numbered 3 from B by sending the B,SREJ3,P frame.

B responds by retransmitting B,I30, but does not retransmit I frames numbered 4 and 5 that were transmitted originally. Since its last transmission, B has obtained some additional I frames for transfer to the primary station. The SREJ command provided B with the opportunity to transmit new I frames up to the point where it would have the modulus minus one unacknowledged I frames outstanding. Consequently, B follows the I30 frame with I frames numbered 6, 7, 0, and 1. The I frame numbered 1 has the F bit set to "1" to identify it as the final frame in the transmission. As indicated, frames numbered 7 and 0 are subjected to transmission errors.

When the primary station receives these I frames, it treats them in the following manner. Upon correct receipt of B,I30, the primary station passes it plus I frames B,I40 and B,I50 from the original transmission up to higher level. When B,I60 is received, it is passed to higher level also. Frames B,I70 and B,I00 are identified as missing when B,I10, F is received out of sequence. In this instance, there are two frames requiring retransmission. The primary station will evaluate this situation to determine the type of recovery action to initiate.

If the SREJ function is used, it will have to be used twice. First, it would be used to have B,I70 retransmitted. Then, after B,I70 is received correctly, it would be used to acknowledge B,I70 and to have B,I00 retransmitted. After the successful transmission of B,I00, I frame B,I10 would *not* have to be retransmitted since it was received correctly in the original transmission.

On the other hand, if the SREJ function is not used, the primary station can utilize the checkpointing mechanism that is available with I, RR, and RNR frame transmissions with the P/F bit set to "1" to indicate which I frames have been acknowledged and where in the numbering sequence retransmission of I frames should begin. With this approach, only a single control exchange is required, but any already successfully transmitted I frames (such as B,I10,F) will be retransmitted. When this approach is chosen, the retransmitted I frame (B,I11) should be passed up to higher level, not the originally received I frame (B,I10,F). There is no link level assurance that the contents of an I frame are not altered (updated or made more current) at the time of its retransmission. The link control ensures sequence integrity at the data link level, but depending upon implementation, may not have complete control concerning the contents of I frames ready for transmission or retransmission.

In the case being considered here, the primary station detects that I frames 7 and 0 are missing, chooses not to use the SREJ recovery action, and has I frames of its own to deliver to B. The primary station sends three I frames to B, acknowledging receipt of I frames numbered 3–6 from B. (The middle frame is subject to a transmission error, resulting in an out-of-sequence condition at B as well.) The primary station gives B permission to transmit by setting the P bit equal to "1" in the third I frame sent to B. This causes a checkpoint to take place at B. The P bit is complementary to the earlier F bit sent by B. Since the $N(R)$ associated with this P bit does not acknowledge all of the I frames sent by B since B last sent an F bit set to "1," it is interpreted by B as an indication of where in B's send sequence numbering the retransmission of I frames should begin. The subsequent transmission from B includes all of the I frames from the number identified (7) and acknowledges only the first of the three I frames sent by the primary station. B concludes its transmission with an SREJ frame that requests the retransmission of primary station I frame numbered 1. The primary station retransmits frame B,I12 and adds frame B,I32,P. All of B's frames are acknowledged and a response from B has been requested. B acknowledges the primary station I frames and indicates "no traffic" to send.

The primary station polls C. C responds "no traffic." The primary station sends an I frame to D and requests in the same frame that D respond (P bit set to "1"). The time-out function at the primary station runs out waiting for the response. In a situation like this, the primary station does not know if it was its transmission or D's response that was lost (hit by a transmission error). The primary station could assume that D did not receive the I frame and simply retransmit it, or as is indicated here, the primary station could send a supervisory command with the P bit set to "1" to find out the number of the I frame that D next expects to receive. By sending the RNR command, the primary station restricts D's response to a supervisory frame. Hence, with the exchange of two short frames, the primary station is able to determine if retransmission is required or not. In this case, the primary station has to retransmit the I frame. However, in many instances, the primary station will determine that retransmission is not required (that is, the acknowledging response frame was lost), and occasionally, will discover that D is in a condition in which it would not be able to accept an I frame anyway (for instance, in a disconnected mode because of a power failure or equipment failure at the secondary station). As a general rule, it is considered to be a wise decision to first inquire as to the status of a secondary station before retransmitting unacknowledged I frames. This is even truer if the transmission consisted of multiple I frames.

After receiving the acknowledgment for frame D,I00,P, the primary station in this example initiates the disconnect procedure with each secondary station. Unlike the situation in Fig. 3 where the primary station needed to initiate an exchange of supervisory frames first in order to complete the acknowledgment cycle with a secondary station, in Fig. 4 the primary station knows that all of the secondary stations are in step with the primary station and so proceeds directly with the disconnect procedure.

B. Balanced, Two-Way Simultaneous Point-to-Point (BAC,2,8)

1. Examples of Error-Free Operation

In order to illustrate the interplay of two independent transmission flows in a balanced, two-way simultaneous operation, a slightly different representation of frames is used in Figs. 5 and 6. I frames are shown as having random lengths (solid vertical bars between horizontal boundary lines) and S and U format frames are shown as very short, fat vertical bars. In this way the interactions can be more reasonably noted. The angling lines between the columns serve to indicate where a frame begins or ends at the receiver relative to the receiver's transmissions as well as to its beginning and end at the sender. Many of the operational characteristic cited for the unbalanced case described above also apply here, but are activated in a continuous manner instead of only at the point of P/F exchanges.

As indicated in Fig. 5, combined station L activates the data link by sending an SABM command to combined station M. (In the general case, either station may initiate this action.) M responds with a UA response, acknowledging receipt of the mode setting command. Because of the asynchronous nature of these procedures, a P bit set to "1" is not necessary in order for the receiving station to respond. In this example, however, the F bit is set to "1" in the UA response because the P bit was set to "1" in the SABM command. As soon as M returns the UA response, it is in the information transfer state and may initiate transmission of frames to L. In this instance, M has two I frames ready to send and sets the P bit to "1" in the second frame in order to get an immediate response acknowledgment concerning their arrival at L. On the other hand, L enters the information transfer state when it receives the UA response to its SABM command.

Because of the two-way simultaneous nature of the operation, I frames may be flowing in both directions at the same time as shown. Because option 8 restricts I frames to being command frames only, I frames from L to M will always have the address M and I frames from M to L will always have the address L. Hence, the reception of an I frame with the remote station's address is an indication of a fault in the system, probably an inadvertent loopback somewhere between the two stations.

As each station prepares I frames for transmission, it increases the send sequence number $N(S)$ by one on each successive I frame as long as it does not have more than the modulus minus one unacknowledged I frames outstanding, and it sets the receive sequence number $N(R)$ to the value of the I frame next expected, thereby indicating acknowledgment of I frames number $N(R) - 1$ and below. Hence, a continual I frame flow from each station automatically acknowledges I frames received from the other station (freeing buffers at that station for other use) along with exercising its own information transfer. In the absence of errors and as long as both stations have I frames to send, the process is self-perpetuating.

As long as a station does not have an unanswered P bit outstanding, a station may decide to set the P bit equal to "1" in any one of the I frames transmitted. In the example, M has done so on its last of two I frames and L has done so on its first I frame. (Such action might be taken for a variety of reasons, including, in L's case, to check that an operational data link is present, and in M's case, to get an acknowledgment response that is logically associated with the frame that initiated it, or to provide a P/F exchange protected frame for the transfer of a REJ response in the case of errors, etc.)

After the frame with the P bit set to "1" is sent, the station may continue to send I frames to the other station. Since the receiving station cannot send an I frame with an F bit set to "1" (it would be a response I frame), the receiving station must interrupt its sequence of command I frames to insert a supervisory response frame (for example, L,RR2,F) that will convey both the F bit set to "1" and the $N(R)$ indicating the sequence number of the I frame next expected. I frames $N(R) - 1$ and below are acknowledged. The $N(R)$ should acknowledge at least all I frames transmitted up through the I frame sent with the P bit set to "1." In some instances, the $N(R)$ may acknowledge I frames beyond the $N(S)$ at the time that the P bit was set to "1," but less than or equal to the $N(S)$ at the time that the $N(R)$ is received. (The M,I72,P and M,RR2,F exchange shown later in this example illustrates this.)

When one of the stations runs out of I frames to send, then it will generate appropriate supervisory frames, (such as M,RR3 and M,RR4 in the example) in order to acknowledge I frames received. When I frames again become available, I frame transmission will resume with the next highest $N(S)$ and then current value of $N(R)$. The $N(S)$ sequence will be ever increasing (except during recovery—Fig. 6), incremented by one with each new I frame. The $N(R)$ value contained in each frame will be the current value of the receive state variable and may be incremented by more than one from frame to frame as a result of the transmission of different length I frames by the two stations involved (illustrated by the transmission of L,I10,P and L,I47).

In the example, L has concluded its transmission of I frames with M,I24 and is interested in disconnecting the link. After having sent M,I24,L receives M,RR2,F that is the reply to the earlier P bit (M,I72,P). Except for M,I24, all of L's transmitted I frames have been acknowledged. Hence, L transmits M,RR5,P to get an acknowledgment report on its last outstanding I frame. In the process, L acknowledges receipt of the I frame numbered 4 from M by setting $N(R)$ equal to 5 in M,RR5,P. While L is cleaning up its records in this fashion, M transmits an I frame L,I52,P with the P bit set to

"1." When M receives the P bit set to "1" from L, it generates the M,RR3,F response as a reply. L receives the P bit set to "1" from M, generates an RNR response (L,RNR6,F) in an effort to preclude further I frame transmission by M. In addition, as soon as L receives the F bit frame M,RR3,F in response to its P bit frame (M,RR5,P), L sends M,RNR6,P to stop any further I frame transmission by M. As soon as the F response frame M,RR3,F is received from M, L initiates the disconnect procedure by sending M,DISC,P. When M transmits the M,UA,F frame and L receives it, the link is in the disconnected mode.

2. *Examples of Error Recovery Procedures*

Many of the error recovery principles that were explained for the primary station in the unbalanced case are applicable to both combined stations in the balanced type of operation as well. Included are time-out functions associated with P bit transmissions, automatic retransmission of S or U format frames, and inquiry of status with a supervisory command before retransmitting I format frames. Consequently, they are not be reiterated here.

Because of the two-way simultaneous nature of the operation and the asynchronous mode of operation, the only way to determine when a response received is a response to a command sent is to set the P bit equal to "1" in the command frame for which a response is required. Otherwise, because of propagation delays and offset of possibly different length I frames, it is possible for frame n to be acknowledged in an I or RR frame after I frame numbered $n + x$ has been transmitted. It is also possible for several I frames in a row to have the same $N(R)$ value because of a long frame having been sent in the other direction. If the last I frame in a series is sent without the P bit set to "1," then the lack of a receipt of a response frame from the other station should not of itself be considered grounds for automatic retransmission. An enquiry of the other station's status first (using P/F bit exchange) is the recommended operation. In general, the use of P bits in both directions helps ensure an orderly operation of the two-way simultaneous exchange of data.

The REJ command/response function provides a mechanism for the receiving station to indicate to the sending station that the transmission in progress should be halted and retransmission should begin from the I frame number indicated by the $N(R)$ value in the REJ frame. It provides a mechanism for reporting an error condition prior to the point where a P/F exchange would provide for reporting the same condition from the receiving station. (As mentioned earlier, the repeat of the same $N(R)$ value in non-P/F frames cannot be construed in any way as a request for retransmission of I frames from that specified point.)

Figure 6 shows how the REJ function can be used to initiate retransmission earlier than waiting for the P/F cycle to be activated or for the number of outstanding unacknowledged I frames to equal the modulus minus one. Having the ability to send multiple frames between acknowledgments is a valuable asset of the bit-oriented procedures. Using the REJ function where two-way simultaneous capability exists helps remove what might otherwise be considered to be a negative aspect of the multiple frame transmission capability.

The examples of bit-oriented operation that are given here provide a brief insight into the capabilities of such procedures. Needless to say, many points have not been covered. The ADCCP standard is offered as a more complete description of the general features and capabilities of this new breed of data link control.

V. Related Standards Activities

The American National Standards Institute approved ADCCP in January, 1979. A proposal for enhancements and extensions to ADCCP is presently scheduled for consideration for adoption in mid 1982.

There are related efforts in the area of bit-oriented data link control standards development that also will likely influence the destiny of bit-oriented procedures. These are the International Organization for Standardization (ISO) HDLC, the International Telegraph and Telephone Consultative Committee (CCITT) Recommendation X.25 Level 2 (LAPB) and Recommendation X.75 Level 2, the Federal Government FIPS 71/Fed Std 1003, and the Institute of Electrical and Electronics Engineers (IEEE) Project 802.

The ISO bit-oriented activity is known as HDLC, High-Level Data Link Control. The related ISO documents [3]–[8] cover essentially the same material that is covered by the ANSI ADCCP standard. Not included are (1) switched network conventions, and (2) four reserved U frame format commands and responses that ADCCP sets aside for system designer use. The four reserved U frame format code points are reserved for implementor use to provide data link functions that are not included in the standard but that may be required in certain applications, with assurance that the selected code points will not be assigned to a standard function at some later time.

Consolidation efforts are presently underway within ISO to combine [4], [5], and [6], concerned with elements of procedures into one replacement standard [9]. Similarly, the two classes of procedure documents [7] and [8] are being consolidated into one standard under one cover [10]. When completed, it is anticipated that there will be an even greater correlation between the ISO and ANSI descriptions of these bit-oriented data link control procedures. Like ADCCP, HDLC is general in scope and broad in possible applications.

The CCITT bit-oriented activity that is consistent with the standards activities takes the form of Recommendation X.25 Level 2 LAPB and Recommendation X.75, Level 2. (The Recommendation X.25 Level 2 LAP procedures are not cited here because the LAP procedures are predicted on a different (nonstandard) definition and use of the SARM command than that recognized by the ADCCP or ISO standards.)

Recommendation X.25 defines a DTE/DCE interface to public data networks. Recommendation X.75 defines the interface between two network signaling terminals (gateways). In both cases, the bit-oriented procedures employed were adapted from the ISO balanced class of procedures (BAC) with optional functions 2 (REJ) and 8 (I Frames as Commands Only). To date, none of the other classes or optional functions have been utilized by CCITT in any of its Recommendations. Future studies of CCITT needs may result in reconsideration of other classes and/or optional functions.

The potentially large scale of applications of the BAC,2,8 class of procedure makes it a front runner when it comes to those classes of procedure that will likely find themselves "engraved in silicon" and hence will become major factors in the design of data link control procedure IC chips for link level operation between "logical equals."

The Federal Government also plays a significant role in the development of bit-oriented data link control procedures. FIPS 71/Fed Std 1003 is essentially the ADCCP standard, with a few minor exceptions. For example, the four reserved U frame format commands and responses are not supported.

FIPS 71/Fed Std 1003 is intended to serve as the basis for all future bit-oriented data link control equipment procurement throughout the government. For that reason, the large number of optional functions that are defined presents a potential nightmare when it comes to the interconnection of stations, or when it is necessary to move a station from one use and application to another. At present, in order for a piece of equipment to satisfy the condition in FIPS 71/Fed Std 1003 that will ensure a certain level of interoperability, it must, as a primary or combined station, be capable of (1) accepting a FRMR response from the other station that indicates that a command/response received was not implemented, (2) resetting the data link, and (3) following a revised data link procedure that does not involve the use of the nonimplemented command or response. A future alternative is being considered wherein the federal standard would specify only a limited set of classes with specified optional functions. If this latter course of action is followed, there would likely be a significant amount of pressure to rethink the subject of bit-oriented data link control procedure standards from the standpoint of standardizing only a minimal

set of fairly specifically spelled out classes of procedures instead of standardizing a general framework and the elements of a much larger group of
possible combinations of classes and optional functions. Whether such
action would be in the best interest of the data communication community
at this time is not clear.

Beginning early in 1980 an intense effort to define bit-oriented data
link control procedures for local area network applications was initiated by
the Institute of Electrical and Electronics Engineers (IEEE) Project 802. In
general, these local area network applications covered communications
between multiple stations operating in a "peer" relationship in a noncentralized, multiaccess environment on a common medium, running at speeds in
the tens-of-megabits range. The "peer" relationship has identified a number
of necessary and desirable extensions and enhancements to the present
bit-oriented data link control definition. Examples include (1) provision for
both "destination" and "source" addressing in each frame, and (2) control
of station access to the medium. To maximize the likelihood of satisfying
the needs of the local area network applications in an evolving bit-oriented
data link control definition, close liaison has, and is, being maintained with
ANSI, ISO, CCITT and others. There is every hope that this coordinated
effort will result in a fuller and more widely applicable bit-oriented data
link control standard.

High Level Compatability with Proprietary Protocols

The principles and concepts of this bit-oriented approach to data link
control seems to be well received by the data communications community as
a whole. Based on available literature, the principal proprietary bit-oriented
data link protocols that are around today are compatible with the ADCCP
standard, or some subset of it.

An important distinction must be understood here. A *standard* like
ADCCP is by definition broad in scope and minimally restrictive in what can
or cannot be done with its elements. A *protocol*, on the other hand, is
generally aimed at satisfying a particular need or application. A proprietary
protocol, by its very name, is something that is designed by an individual or
organization with a particular purpose in mind. The proprietary protocols
developed by various equipment manufacturers, for instance, are designed
with a significant influence from the marketplace as each of them sees the
marketplace. Of course, all manufacturers do not eye the general marketplace in an identical fashion. Hence, although a standard like ADCCP or
HDLC attempts to embrace the widest possible view of the marketplace, the
proprietary protocols that evolve based on views of that marketplace from
differing vantage points will likely include different subsets of the standard,

and possibly require additional elements that the standard did not include in its breadth of coverage.

Such is believed to be the case with proprietary protocols such as BDLC, SDLC, UDLC, and others. Burroughs has long been on record as intending that the Burroughs Data Link Control (BDLC) will be compatible with the ADCCP and HDLC standards. One might thus assume that as Burroughs needs and applications emerge, BDLC will satisfy those needs in a manner that utilizes the features and capabilities provided for in ADCCP and HDLC where possible. IBM's Synchronous Data Link Control (SDLC) claims to conform with the Unbalanced Normal Class of Procedures, a subset of ADCCP and HDLC. The basic repertoire of commands and responses in this class is the same as in the Unbalanced Normal Class of Procedures defined in ADCCP and HDLC. The product lines for which SDLC [11] is presently defined support some of the optional functions, but not all of them. In many countries, IBM has announced their intention to offer compatibility with the CCITT X.25 LAPB access procedure to public data networks. As other IBM marketplaces are identified, support for other standard bit-oriented features and functions may be announced. In the case of Univac, like Burroughs, there has been a long time statement of intended compatibility of Univac's Universal Data Link Control (UDLC) with the ADCCP and HDLC Standards. In addition, UDLC claims conformity with the IBM SDLC as well.

In line with the literature available, it would seem that most bit-oriented protocol providers claim compatibility with the whole or a part of the ADCCP and HDLC standards. However, claiming compatibility with an intentionally designed broad-scoped standard should not be misinterpreted as meaning that any two things rightly claiming such compatibility will necessarily be compatible with each other. The standards provide a guideline and a framework in which to develop and design specific protocols to answer an identified need and application in the marketplace. It is generally hoped that as bit-oriented data link controls become much better understood and their range of application comes into clearer focus, the number of necessary variations and perturbations will naturally reduce to the point where the essence of the then existing standard is cost-effectively expressible in a minimum of fixed variations. The economic impact of having an entire data link control protocol on an IC chip may well be the catalyst that will force the decision as to what limited list of features and capabilities will be available, with what classes of procedures.

VI. The Future

Work is still going on in the area of bit-oriented data link control standardization. Additional commands and responses are under consideration. Some of the existing functions (e.g., XID, Initialization Mode) are being examined in greater detail to identify if there are additional aspects of their utility that warrant definition and standardization.

A multilink operating capability has been approved by CCITT and is in its final stages of approval within ISO [12]. Multilink operation provides a mechanism that interfaces the higher level (Level 3) with a multiplicity of individually operating single link data link control procedure packages in such a manner that the group of single links appears to be the higher level as a single data link of greater bandwidth and increase reliability and integrity. The multilink procedures provide for the automatic distribution of information fields to the single link data link controls for transmission to the remote station where the information fields will be returned to their original sequence before delivery to the higher level. The nature of the multilink procedure is predicated on the high level of data transfer integrity of the single link procedures and relies on the capabilities of the higher levels to recover from any error situations that could result from infrequent equipment malfunctions or system errors that might occur above the single link data link level.

There has also been an increasing interest in possible extension to, or other applications of, these bit-oriented procedures. To date, the procedures are designed for application in synchronous systems operating in either a centralized control environment or a two-equal-party environment. There is some interest in applying the procedural concepts to asynchronous (start–stop) environments. There is also great interest (as is evidenced by the IEEE efforts to define a "peer" protocol for local area network applications) to determine what needs to be done to these bit-oriented procedures to make them applicable to noncentralized control environments as well. Use of bit-oriented procedures in areas of application like facsimile, TELETEX, text processing, electronic mail, etc., may also result in additions, extensions, or modifications to the bit-oriented procedures in the future.

The secure nature of the data link frame—its transparency (bit stuffing), its high level of error protection (16-bit or 32-bit CRC), plus its directability (address field assignment)—make it attractive for other applications besides transferring end user data. From a Level 1 maintenance and operations point of view, the bit-oriented frame appears to be an ideal vehicle for use in activating and deactivating Level 1 (physical line level) loopbacks or initiating other Level 1 related functions. Similarly, data link frames seem to be natural vehicles for Level 3 (and higher) use in exchanging user/network information relative to the establishment of a user-to-user (end-to-end) data transfer exchange. Consideration of uses such as these appear to be subjects of near-future activities. What impact they may have on the present organization of bit-oriented data link level procedures is not clear.

VII. Conclusions

After nearly a decade of inventing, evaluating, deliberating, and comprising, a bit-oriented data link control approach has emerged that satisfies the general requirements cited earlier for interactive operation. Although known by many names at the moment (ADCCP, LAPB, SDLC, etc.), this new breed of data link control contains the necessary features, capabilities, characteristics, and growth potential, and has the level of acceptance nationally and internationally to make it *the* Data Link Control approach for use in providing a high-integrity, transparent data transfer mechanism at the data link level that will satisfy today's as well as tomorrow's synchronous data communication needs.

References

[1] ANSI Standard X3.66-1979, "Advanced Data Communication Control Procedures," (Copies obtainable from American National Standards Institute, 1430 Broadway, New York, NY 10018).

[2] R.J. Cypser, *Communications Architecture for Distributed Systems.* Reading, MA: Addison-Wesley, 1978, p. 385.

[3] ISO-3309, "HDLC, Frame structure," (References [3]–[10] and [12] are available from Computer and Business Equipment Manufacturers Assoc., 1828 L St. N.W., Washington, DC 20036).

[4] ISO-4335, "HDLC, Elements of procedures."

[5] ISO-4335/AD1, "HDLC, Addendum 1 to ISO-4335."

[6] ISO-4335/AD2, "HDLC, Addendum 2 to ISO-4335."

[7] ISO-6159, "HDLC, Unbalanced classes of procedure."

[8] ISO-6256, "HDLC, Balanced class of procedure."

[9] ISO/TC97/SC6 N2100, "Consolidation of HDLC elements of procedures." (ISO/DIS 4335 Revised).

[10] ISO/TC97/SC6 N2099, "Consolidation of HDLC classes of procedures." (ISO/DIS 7809).

[11] "IBM Synchronous Data Link Control," General Info., IBM form GA27-3093.

[12] ISO/TC97/SC6 N2121, "Multilink control procedures." (ISO/DIS 7478).

6

Multiaccess Link Control

Fouad A. Tobagi

I. Introduction

The need for multiaccess protocols arises whenever a resource is shared (and thus accessed) by a number of independent users. One main reason contributing to such a situation is the need to *share scarce and expensive resources*. An excellent example is typified by time-sharing systems. Time-sharing was developed in the 1960s to make the powerful processing capability of a large computer system available to a large population of users, each of whom has relatively small or infrequent demands so that a dedicated system cannot be economically justified. Two advantages are gained: the smoothing effect of large populations on the demand, an effect resulting from the law of large numbers, and a lower cost per unit of service resulting from the (almost always existing) economy of scale.

A second major reason contributing to the multiaccess of a common resource by many independent entities is the need for communication among the entities; we refer to this as the *connectivity requirement*. An excellent example today is the telephone system, the main purpose of which is to provide a high degree of connectivity among its subscribers. The multiaccess protocol used in the telephone system is conceptually simple; it merely consists of placing a request for connection to one or several parties, a request which gets honored by the system if all the required resources are available.

Packet Communication

Let us now consider data communication systems. Communications engineers have long recognized the need to multiplex expensive transmission facilities and switching equipment. The earliest techniques for doing this were synchronous time-division multiplexing and frequency-division multiplexing. These methods assign a fixed subset of the time-bandwidth space to each of several subscribers and are very successful for stream-type traffic such as voice. With computer traffic, however, usually characterized as *bursty*, fixed assignment techniques are not nearly so successful, and to solve this problem, *packet communication systems* have been developed over the past decade [1]–[7]. Packet communication is based on the idea that part or all of the available resources are allocated to one user at a time but for just a short period of time. Here each component of the system is itself a resource which is multiaccessed and shared by the many contending users. To achieve sharing at the component level, customers are required to divide their messages into small units called packets which carry information regarding the source and the intended recipient.

One type of packet communication network, known as the *point-to-point store-and-forward* network, is one where packet switches are interconnected by point-to-point data circuits according to some topological structure. Packets are transmitted independently and pass asynchronously from one switch to another until they reach their destination. The multiplexing of packets on a channel is done by queueing them at each switch until the outgoing channel is free. Typical examples are the ARPAnet [7], the Cigale subnetwork [8], TELENET [9], and DATAPAC [10].

Another type of packet transmission network is the (single-hop) *multiaccess/broadcast* network typified by the ALOHA network [11], SATNET [12], and ETHERNET [5]. Here a *single* transmission medium is shared by all subscribers; the medium is allocated to each subscriber for the time required to transmit a single packet. The inherent single-hop broadcast nature of these systems achieves full connectivity at small additional cost. Each subscriber is connected to the common channel through a smart interface which listens to all transmissions and absorbs packets addressed to it.

Yet a third type of packet network can be identified. It is the (multihop) *store-and-forward multiaccess/broadcast* type which combines the features exhibited (and problems encountered) in the two types just mentioned. The best and perhaps only example of this type is the packet radio network (PRNET) sponsored by the Advanced Research Projects Agency [13], [14]. The concept of the PRNET is an extension of that of the ALOHA network in that it includes many added features such as direct communication by a ground radio network between mobile users over wide geographical areas, coexistence with possibly different systems in the same frequency band, antijam protection, etc. The key requirement of direct communication over wide geographical areas renders store-and-forward switches, called repeaters, integral components of the system. Furthermore, for easy communication among mobile users and for rapid deployment in military applications, all devices employ omnidirectional antennas and share a high-speed radio channel; hence the multiaccess/broadcast nature of the system.

The main issue of concern in this chapter is how to control access to a common channel to efficiently allocate the available communication bandwidth to the many contending users. The solutions to this problem form the set of protocols known as *multiaccess protocols*. These protocols and their performance differ according to the environment in question and the system requirements to be satisfied. We devote the next few paragraphs to summarizing the basic relevant characteristics underlying these environments.

Consider first *satellite channels*. A satellite transponder in a geostationary orbit above the earth provides long-haul communication capabilities. It can receive signals from any earth station in its coverage pattern and can transmit signals to all such earth stations (unless the satellite uses spot beams). Full connectivity and multidestination addressing can both be readily accommodated. The many characteristics regarding data rates, error rates, satellite coverage, channelization, and design of earth stations have been fully discussed in a paper by Jacobs *et al.* [12]. Perhaps the most important characteristic relevant to this discussion is the inherent long propagation delay of approximately 0.25 s for a single hop. This delay, which is usually long compared to the transmission time of a packet, has a major impact on the bandwidth allocation techniques and on the error and flow control protocols.

In *ground radio* environments, the propagation delay is relatively short compared to the transmission time of a packet, and as we shall see in the sequel, this can be of great advantage in controlling access to a common channel. It is important, however, to distinguish single-hop environments where direct full connectivity is assumed to prevail, and more complex user environments where, due to geographical distance and/or obstacles opaque to UHF signals, limited direct connectivity is achieved. Clearly, the latter situation is significantly more complex as it gives rise to a multihop system where global control of system operation and resource allocation (whether centralized or distributed) is much harder to accomplish. Another dimension of complexity results from the fact that, unlike satellite environments where earth stations are stationary, ground radio systems must also support mobile users. With mobile users, not only does demand on the system exhibit relatively fast dynamic changes, but the radio propagation characteristics are subject to important variations in received signal strength so that system connectivity is at all times difficult to predict; with these considerations it is important to devise access schemes and system control mechanisms that allow the system to adapt itself to these changes. Furthermore, multipath effects in urban environments can be so disastrous that special signaling schemes, such as spread spectrum, may be in order. Finally, another point of growing concern today is RF spectrum utilization. This is becoming an increasingly predominant factor in determining the structure of radio systems, both in satellite and ground environments. A packet radio system which allows the dynamic allocation of the spectrum to a large population of bursty mobile users needs flexible high-performance multiaccess schemes which can take advantage of the law of large numbers, and which permit coexistence of the system with other (possibly different) systems in the same frequency band.

Finally, we consider *local area communication* systems. These span short distances (ranging from a few meters up to a few kilometers) and usually involve high data rates. The transmission medium can be privately owned and inexpensive, such as twisted pair or coaxial cable. Local area environments are characterized by a large and often variable number of devices requiring interconnection, and these are often inexpensive. These situations call for communication networks with simple topologies and simple and inexpensive connection interfaces that can provide great flexibility in accommodating the variability in the environment and that achieve the desired level of reliability. With these constraints, we again face the situation in which a high bandwidth channel is to be shared by independent users. Short propagation delays and high data rates are the main characteristics that are exploited in devising multiaccess schemes appropriate to local area environments.

Multiaccess schemes are evaluated according to various criteria. The performance characteristics that are desirable are, first of all, high bandwidth utilization and low message delays. But a number of other attributes are just as important. The ability for an access protocol to simultaneously support traffic of different types, different priorities, with variable message lengths, and differing delay constraints is essential as higher bandwidth utilization is achieved by the multiplexing of all traffic types. Also, to guarantee proper operation of schemes with distributed control, robustness, defined here as the insensitivity to errors resulting in misinformation, is also most desirable.

Having so far discussed briefly the basic characteristics and system requirements underlying the various communication environments, we now proceed with a discussion of the multiaccess protocols appropriate to these environments. These protocols differ by the static or dynamic nature of the bandwidth allocation algorithm, the centralized or distributed nature of the decision-making process, and the degree of adaptivity of the algorithm to changing needs. Accordingly, these protocols can be grouped into five classes. The first class, labeled *fixed assignment techniques*, consists of those techniques which allocate the channel bandwidth to the users in a static fashion, independently of their activity. The second class is that of *random access techniques*. In this class the entire bandwidth is provided to the users as a single channel to be accessed randomly; since collisions may result which degrade the performance of the channel, improved performance can be achieved by either synchronizing users so that their transmissions coincide with the boundaries of time slots, by sensing carrier prior to transmission, or both. The third and fourth classes correspond to *demand assignment* techniques. Demand assignment techniques require that explicit control information regarding the users' need for the communication resource be exchanged. A distinction is made between those techniques in which the decision making is centralized (constituting the third class in question), and those techniques in which all users individually execute a distributed algorithm based on control information exchanged among them. The latter constitute the fourth class. The fifth class, labeled *adaptive strategies and mixed modes*, including those techniques which consist of a mixture of several distinct modes, and those strategies in which the choice of an access scheme is itself adaptive to the varying need, in the hope that near-optimum performance will be achieved at all times.

We describe the various protocols known today, either implemented or proposed, and discuss their performance and applicability to the different environments introduced in this Section. For this we consider the (conceptually) simplest situation consisting of M users wishing to communicate over a channel. This situation arises typically in satellite communication, in a single-hop ground radio environment, or in a shared bus local network.

II. Fixed Assignment Techniques

Fixed assignment techniques consist of allocating the channel to the users, independently of their activity, by partitioning the time-bandwidth space into slots which are assigned in a static predetermined fashion. These techniques take two common forms: *orthogonal*, such as frequency division multiple access (FDMA) or synchronous time division multiple access (TDMA), and *"quasiorthogonal"* such as code division multiple access (CDMA).

A. *FDMA and TDMA:* FDMA consists of assigning to each user a fraction of the bandwidth and confining its access to the allocated subband. Orthogonality is achieved in the frequency domain. FDMA is relatively simple to implement and requires no real time coordination among the users.

TDMA consists of assigning fixed predetermined channel time slots to each user; the user has access to the entire channel bandwith, but only during its allocated slots. Here, signaling waveforms are orthogonal in time.

A number of disadvantages exist for both FDMA and TDMA. FDMA wastes a fraction of the bandwidth to achieve adequate frequency separation. FDMA is also characterized by a lack of flexibility in performing changes in the allocation of the bandwidth and certainly the lack of broadcast operation. The major disadvantages in TDMA are the need to provide A/D converters for analog traffic such as voice, and rapid burst synchronization and sufficient burst separation to avoid time overlap. However, it has been shown that guard bands of less than 200 ns are achievable (as in INTELSAT's MAT-1 TDMA system, for example) and many operational systems are moving towards the use of TDMA [16]. Timing at an earth station is provided by a global time reference established either explicitly by a reference station, or implicitly by measurement of the propagation delay from the earth station to the transponder. In order to allow the TDMA modems to acquire frequency, phase, bit timing and bit framing synchronization for each received burst, a preamble is included in front of each burst requiring typically from 100 to 200 bit times. Thus clearly, TDMA is more complex to implement than FDMA, but an important advantage is the connectivity which results from the fact that all receivers listen to the same channel while senders transmit on the same common channel at different times. Accordingly, many network realizations, both in ground and satellite environments, are easier to accomplish.

From the performance standpoint it has also been established that TDMA is superior to FDMA in many cases of practical interest. I. Rubin has shown that the random variable representing packet delay is always larger in FDMA than in TDMA for comparable systems [17]. Lam derived the average message delay for a TDMA system with multipacket messages and a nonpreemptive priority queue discipline [18]. There, too, it was shown that TDMA is superior to FDMA.

For both FDMA and TDMA, the fixed preallocation of the frequency or time resource does not have to be equal for all users, but can be tailored to fit their needs (assumed constant). Kosovych studied two TDMA implementations [19]. In the first, called *contiguous assignment*, the users are cyclically ordered in the time sequence in which they have access to the channel. Each user is periodically assigned its *own* fixed time duration. In the second implementation, called *distributed allocation*, all access periods are of equal time duration, but the frequency of accesses can be different from one user to the other. It was shown that for situations in which the transmission overhead (defined as guard time and synchronization preamble time) is large, the contiguous fixed assignment implementation is better suited and provides substantially better performance than distributed fixed assignments, while when the transmission overhead is small, distributed fixed assignments provide slightly better performance.

Finally we note that, even though the allocation can be tailored to the relative need of each user, fixed allocation can be wasteful if the users' demand is highly bursty, as we shall explicitly see in the sequel. Given these limitations, one may increase the channel utilization beyond FDMA and

TDMA by using asynchronous time division multiple access (ATDMA), also known as statistical multiplexing [70]. Basically the technique consists of switching the allocation of the channel from one user to another only when the former is idle and the latter is ready to transmit data. Thus the channel is *dynamically* allocated to the various users according to their need. The performance of ATDMA in packet communication systems corresponds to that of a work-conserving single server queueing system, and is the best we can achieve under unpredictable demand. Unfortunately, it is not always possible to accomplish the necessary coordination among the users. This mode of multiplexing is possible only when several collocated users (such as the same earth station) are sharing a single point-to-point channel.

B. *CDMA*: Unlike FDMA and TDMA, code division multiple access allows overlap in transmission both in the frequency and time coordinates. It achieves orthogonality by the use of different signaling codes in conjunction with matched filters (or equivalently, correlation detection) at the intended receivers. Multiple orthogonal codes are obtained at the expense of increased bandwidth requirements (in order to spread the waveforms); this also results in a lack of flexibility in interconnecting all users (unless, of course, matched filters corresponding to all codes are provided at all receivers). However, CDMA has the advantage of allowing the coexistence of several systems in the same band, as long as different codes are used for different systems. Moreover, it is also possible to separate, by "capture," time overlapping signaling waveforms with the same code, thus achieving connectivity and efficient spectrum utilization. This interesting possibility falls into the class of random access techniques and is addressed in the following subsection.

III. Random Access Techniques

In computer communication, much data traffic is characterized as bursty (e.g., interactive terminal traffic). Burstiness is a result of the high degree of randomness seen in the generation time and size of messages and of the relatively low-delay constraint required by the user. If one were to observe the user's behavior over a period of time, one would see that the user requires the communications resources rather infrequently; but when he does, he requires a rapid response. That is, there is an inherently large peak-to-average ratio in the required data transmission rate. If fixed sub-channel allocation schemes are used, then one must assign enough capacity to each subscriber to meet his peak transmission rates, with the consequence that the resulting channel utilization is low. A more advantageous approach is to provide a single sharable high-speed channel to the large number of users. The strong law of large numbers then guarantees that, with a very high probability, the demand at any instant will be approximately equal to the sum of the average demands of that population. As stated in the introduction, packet communication is a natural means to achieve sharing of the common channel. When dealing with shared channels in a packet-switched mode, one must be prepared to resolve conflicts which arise when more than one demand is placed upon the channel. For example, in packet-switched radio channels, whenever a portion of one user's transmission overlaps with another user's transmission, the two collide and "destroy" each other (unless a code division multiple-access scheme is used). The existence of some positive acknowledgment scheme permits the transmitter to determine if his transmission is successful or not. The problem is how to control the access to the common channel in a fashion which produces, under the physical constraints of simplicity and hardware implementation, an acceptable level of performance. The difficulty in controlling a channel which must carry its own control information has given rise to the so-called random-access protocols, among others. We describe these here by considering again single-hop environments.

A. ALOHA [20]–[22]. Historically, the *pure* ALOHA protocol was first used in the ALOHA system, a single-hop terminal access network developed in 1970 at the University of Hawaii, employing packet-switching on a radio channel [11], [20]. The simplest of its kind, pure ALOHA permits users to transmit any time they desire. If within some appropriate time-out period following its transmission, a user receives an acknowledgment from the destination (the central computer), then it knows that no conflict occurred. Otherwise it assumes that a collision occurred and it must retransmit. To avoid continuously repeated conflicts, the retransmission delay is randomized across the transmitting devices, thus spreading the retry packets over time. A slotted version, referred to as *slotted* ALOHA, is obtained by dividing time into slots of duration equal to the transmission time of a single packet (assuming constant-length packets) [21], [22]. Each user is required to synchronize the start of transmission of its packets to coincide with the slot boundary. When two packets conflict, they will overlap completely rather than partially, providing an increase in channel efficiency over pure ALOHA. Owing to conflicts and idle channel time, the maximum channel efficiency available using ALOHA is less than 100 percent, 18 percent for pure ALOHA and 36 percent for slotted ALOHA. Both schemes are theoretically applicable to satellite, ground radio, and local bus environments. The slotted version has the advantage of efficiency, but it has the disadvantage that synchronization may be hard to achieve, especially in multihop ground radio.

Although the maximum achievable channel utilization is low, the ALOHA schemes are superior to fixed assignment schemes when there is a large population of bursty users. This point is illustrated in comparing for

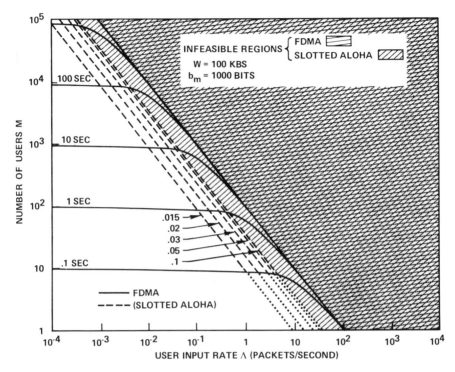

Fig. 1. FDMA and slotted ALOHA: performance with 100-kbit/s bandwidth and 1000-bit packets. Contours are for constant delay [23].

example the performance of FDMA with that of slotted ALOHA when M users, each of which generates packets at a rate of Λ packets per second, share a radio channel of W Hz [23]. Figures 1 and 2 display the constant delay contours in the (M, Λ) and (W, Λ) planes, respectively. These figures clearly show the important improvement gained in terms of bandwidth required, population size supported and delay achieved when the users are bursty.

B. Carrier Sense Multiple Access (CSMA) [24], [25]. In ground radio environments the channel can be characterized as wideband with a propagation delay between any source–destination pair that is small compared to the packet transmission time. In such an environment one may attempt to avoid collisions by listening to the carrier due to another user's transmission before transmitting, and inhibiting transmission if the channel is sensed busy. This feature gives rise to a random access scheme known as carrier sense multiple access (CSMA) [24], [25]. While in the ALOHA scheme only one action could be taken by the terminals, namely, to transmit, here many strategies are possible so that many CSMA protocols exist differing accord-

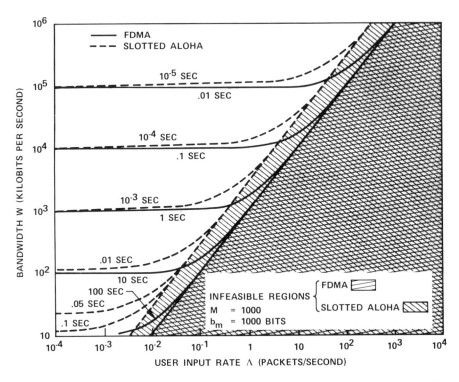

Fig. 2. FDMA and slotted ALOHA bandwidth requirements for 1000 terminals and 1000-bit packets. Contours are for constant delay [23].

ing to the action that a terminal takes to transmit a packet after sensing the channel. In all cases, however, when a terminal learns that its transmission had incurred a collision, it reschedules the transmission of the packet according to the randomly distributed delay. At this new point in time, the transmitter senses the channel again and repeats the algorithm dictated by the protocol. There are two main CSMA protocols known as *nonpersistent* and *p-persistent* CSMA depending on whether the transmission by a station which finds the channel busy is to occur later or immediately following the current one with probability p. Many variants and modifications of these two schemes have also been proposed. Thus, in nonpersistent CSMA, a ready terminal (i.e., a terminal with a packet ready for transmission) senses the channel and operates as follows:

1. If the channel is sensed idle, it transmits the packet.
2. If the channel is sensed busy, then the terminal schedules the retransmission of the packet to some later time according to the retransmission delay distribution. At this new point in time, it senses the channel and repeats the algorithm described.

The 1-persistent CSMA protocol, a special case of p-persistent CSMA, was devised in order to (presumably) achieve acceptable throughput by never letting the channel go idle if some ready terminal is available. More precisely, a ready terminal senses the channel and operates as follows:

1. If the channel is sensed idle, it transmits the packet with probability one.
2. If the channel is sensed busy, it waits until the channel goes idle and then immediately transmits the packet with probability one (i.e., persisting on transmitting with $p = 1$).

A slotted version of these CSMA protocols can also be considered in which the time axis is slotted and the slot size is τ seconds where τ is the maximum propagation delay among all pairs. Note that this definition of a slot is different from that used in the description of slotted ALOHA. Here a packet transmission time is equivalent to several slots. We make this distinction by referring to a slot of size τ seconds as a "minislot." All terminals are synchronized and are forced to start transmission only at the beginning of a minislot.

In the case of a 1-persistent CSMA, we note that whenever two or more terminals become ready during a packet transmission period, they wait for the channel to become idle (at the end of that transmission) and then they all transmit with probability one. A conflict will also occur with probability one. The idea of randomizing the starting time of transmission of packets accumulating at the end of a transmission period seems reasonable for interference reduction and throughput improvement. Thus we have the p-persistent scheme which involves including an additional parameter p, the probability that a ready packet persists, $(1 - p$ being the probability of delaying transmission by τ seconds, the propagation delay). The parameter p is chosen to reduce the level of interference while keeping the idle periods between any two consecutive nonoverlapped transmission as small as possible.

More precisely, the p-persistent CSMA protocol consists of the following: the time axis is minislotted and the system is synchronized such that all terminals begin their transmission at the beginning of a minislot. If a ready terminal senses the channel idle, then with probability p, the terminal transmits the packet; and with probability $1 - p$, the terminal delays the transmission of the packet by τ seconds (i.e., one minislot). If at this new point in time, the channel is still detected idle, the same process is repeated. Otherwise some packet must have started transmission, and the terminal in question schedules the retransmission of the packet according to the retransmission delay distribution (i.e., acts as if it had conflicted and learned about the conflict). If the ready terminal senses the channel busy, it waits until it becomes idle (at the end of the current transmission) and then operates as above.

Packet broadcasting technology has also been shown to be very effective in satisfying many local area in-building communication requirements. A prominent example is ETHERNET, a local communication network which uses CSMA on a tapped coaxial cable to which all the communicating devices are connected [5]. The device connection interface is a passive cable tap so that failure of an interface does not prevent communication among the remaining devices. The use of a single coaxial cable achieves broadcast communication. The only difference between this and the single-hop radio is that, in addition to sensing carrier, it is possible for the transceivers, when they detect interference among several transmissions (including their own), to abort the transmission of colliding packets. This is achieved by having each transmitting device compare the bit stream it is transmitting to the bit stream it sees on the channel. This variation of CSMA is referred to as carrier sense multiple access with collision detection (CSMA-CD) [26].

While until recently most of the concepts described in this section had been realized in experimental systems (namely, the ALOHA System, the PRNET, and Xerox's experimental ETHERNET), it is important to note that today contention systems of the ETHERNET type are available on the market, and new ones have been announced to be soon available. Examples are the Hyperchannel and the Hyperbus of Network Systems Corporation [73], and Z-Net of Zilog, and ETHERNET itself. Highly publicized, the latter has been recently announced as a product to be soon made available jointly by Xerox Corporation, Digital Equipment Corporation, and INTEL. Complete specifications of the data link and physical link protocols have been issued, and constitute, among other schemes, a proposal for a standard to the IEEE committee on standardization of local networks. A key feature that distinguishes this product from other already available systems is the LSI implementation of many of the data link and physical link protocols. LSI implementation of network protocols clearly marks a trend in the evolution of computer networking, a trend which is indicative of the existence of a wide market and the need to provide reasonably priced components.

C. Performance of Random Access. Many theoretical studies have been carried out to determine the performance of these random access schemes [20]–[22], [24]–[29]. We summarize here the most important results. Let S denote the aggregate rate of packet generation from the entire population of users, G the rate of packet transmissions (new and repeated, hence $G \geq S$), and D the packet delay (defined as the time elapsed between the time that the packet is originated and the time it is successfully received at the destination), all normalized to the (fixed) packet transmission time T. Analytic and simulation models provide us, for each random access scheme, with a relationship between S and G (displayed in Fig. 3), and the throughput delay tradeoff (displayed in Fig. 4) for a normalized propagation delay $a = \tau/T = 0.01$. We note that the behavior of these schemes is

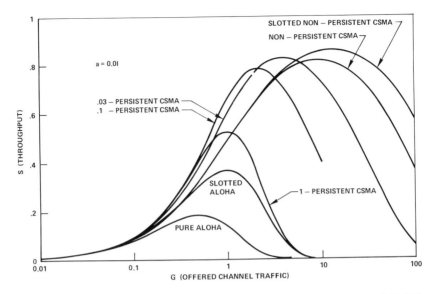

Fig. 3. Throughput for the various random access modes (propagation delay $a = 0.01$) [24].

typical of contention systems, namely, that the throughput increases as the offered channel traffic increases from zero, but reaches a maximum value for some optimum value of G, and then constantly decreases as G increases beyond that optimal value. Maximizing S with respect to the channel traffic rate G for each of the access modes leads to the channel capacity for that mode. From Fig. 4 we clearly note that D increases as the throughput increases, and reaches infinite values as the throughput approaches the

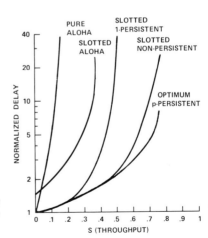

Fig. 4. CSMA and ALOHA: throughput-delay tradeoffs from simulation (propagation delay $a = 0.01$) [24].

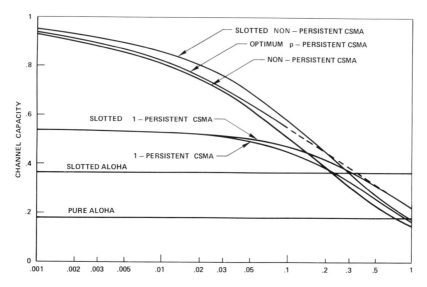

Fig. 5. CSMA and ALOHA: effect of propagation delay a on channel capacity [24].

channel capacity. These results show the evident superiority of CSMA over the ALOHA scheme. The CSMA channel capacity in some cases may be as high as 90 percent of the available bandwidth. It is clear, however, that, as expected, the channel capacity and the throughput-delay tradeoff for the CSMA schemes degrade as the normalized propagation delay $(a = \tau/T)$ increases. Figure 5 illustrates the sensitivity of the channel capacity to a.

CSMA-CD offers even more improvement. A system parameter affecting this improvement is the time required to detect collisions and abort ongoing colliding transmissions. The smaller this parameter is, the better the improvement is [26].

The results displayed in the above figures have two important assumed conditions, namely (1) acknowledgments are instantaneous, always received correctly and for free (i.e., do not occupy any channel time), and (2) all devices are within range and in line-of-site of each other so that sensing of all transmissions on the channel is perfect. While Condition (1) is relevant to both ALOHA and CSMA, Condition (2) is mostly relevant to CSMA. We discuss these issues in the following.

D. Acknowledgment Procedures and Their Effect. Basically, errors in multiaccess channels are due to two major causes: (1) random noise on the channel and (2) multiuse interference in the form of overlapping packets. A very reliable method ensuring the integrity of the transmitted data is the use of an error-detecting (e.g., cyclic) block code in conjunction with a positive acknowledgment of each correctly received message. Each packet contains a field for the cyclic checksum. Each receiver responds to a complete packet addressed to it with a correct checksum by transmitting an acknowledgment packet back to the originating terminal. This acknowledgment contains (among other things) the unique identification of the originating terminal along with a checksum to ensure the integrity of the acknowledgment packet itself.

It is all too evident that acknowledgments will use part of the total available bandwidth (our limited resource). The amount of overhead introduced, as well as the degradation in delay incurred, varies with the mode of operation. When the available bandwidth is provided as a single channel to be shared by both information and acknowledgment packets, then the channel performance will further suffer from interference between information packets and acknowledgment packets unless some kind of priority scheme is provided. Concerning the degradation in channel capacity due to the overhead created by the error control traffic, it has been shown [30] that, in a common-channel configuration with nonpriority acknowledgment traffic, the channel capacity of slotted ALOHA drops to 14 percent of the channel bandwidth. However, if by some means acknowledgment traffic can be given priority so as to guarantee its transmission free of conflict, then the channel capacity for slotted ALOHA can be maintained at around 26 percent (assuming here that an acknowledgment packet uses an entire slot). The effect of acknowledgment traffic on CSMA channels need not be as dramatic since it is very simple to implement schemes which give priority to acknowledgments packets. One mode of operation is as follows [30, 74].

1. If a terminal, with a packet ready for transmission, senses the channel idle, then the terminal transmits its packet τ seconds (the propagation delay) later if and only if the channel is still sensed idle.

2. If such a terminal senses the channel busy, then it follows the protocol in question (nonpersistent, 1-persistent,...) repeating step (1) whenever the channel is sensed idle.

3. All acknowledgment packets are transmitted immediately, without incurring the τ seconds delay.

The capacity of the nonpersistent CSMA protocol with priority acknowledgment and $a = 0.01$ drops gradually from 0.85 to about 0.45 as the acknowledgment packet size increases from 0 to a full packet size.

E. The Hidden Terminal Problem in CSMA and the Busy-Tone Multiple Access (BTMA) [28]. We now relax the assumption that all users are in line of sight and within range of each other. Typically, two terminals can be within range of the intended receiver, but out of range of each other or separated by some physical obstacle opaque to radio signals. The existence of hidden terminals in a radio environment significantly degrades the performance of CSMA. To illustrate this effect, consider a population of users, each of which is communicating with a central station. This station is

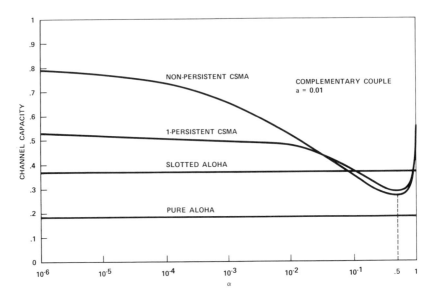

Fig. 6. An example of the hidden terminal situation: complementary couple configuration. Channel capacity versus α, the relative sizes of the two decoupled populations [28].

in line-of-sight communication with the entire population, but this population is divided into two groups (or relative sizes α and $1 - \alpha$) such that the radio connectivity exists only between users in the same group. Figure 6 displays the CSMA channel capacity versus α, showing that the channel capacity drops drastically as α increases from 0 and reaches a minimum of $\alpha = 0.5$ [28].

Fortunately, in environments where all users communicate with a single central station such as in the ALOHA system, the hidden-terminal problem can be eliminated by frequency-dividing the available bandwidth into two separate channels: a busy-tone channel and a message channel, thus giving rise to so-called *busy-tone multiple access* (BTMA). The operation of BTMA rests on the fact that, by definition, there exists a central station which is within range and in line of sight of all users. As long as the central station senses carrier on the message channel it transmits a (sine wave) busy-tone signal on the busy-tone channel. It is by sensing carrier on the busy-tone channel that the users' terminals determine the state of the message channel. The action that a terminal takes pertaining to the transmission of the packet is again prescribed by the particular protocol being used.

In CSMA, the difficulty of detecting the presence of a signal on the message channel when this message occupies the entire bandwidth is minor and is therefore neglected. This is not realistic when we are concerned with the (statistical) detection of the (sine wave) busy-tone signal on a narrow-band channel. In BTMA, the system's design involves a more complex set of system variables, namely the window detection time, the false alarm probability F, and the fraction of bandwidth devoted to the busy-tone signal. For a detailed analysis of this scheme, the reader is referred to [28]. The throughput-delay tradeoff for BTMA is slightly degraded in comparison to CSMA with no hidden terminals, but still exhibits relatively good performance.

F. Dynamic Behavior and Dynamic Control of Random Access Schemes. The performance results reported upon above were based on renewal theory and probabilistic arguments, assuming that steady-state conditions exist. If one examines in more detail the (S, G) relationships displayed above, one can see that the steady state may not exist because of an inherent *instability* of these random access techniques. This instability is simply explained by the fact that statistical fluctuations in the offered traffic increase the level of mutual interference among transmissions which in turn increases total G, which increases the frequency of collisions, and so forth. Such positive feedback causes the throughput to decrease to very low values. Extensive simulation runs performed on a slotted ALOHA channel with an *infinite population* of users have indeed shown that the assumption of channel equilibrium is not strictly speaking valid; in fact after some finite period of quasistationary conditions, the channel will drift into saturation with probability one [31]. Thus a more accurate measure of channel performance must reflect the tradeoffs among stability, throughput, and delay. To that effect, Markov models have been formulated to analyze slotted ALOHA and CSMA when M interactive users are contending for the channel [31]–[34]. These models permit one not only to derive analytic expressions for the average throughput-delay performance, but also to understand the dynamic behavior of these systems. In particular, it was observed that even in a finite population environment, if the retransmission delay is not sufficiently large, then the stationary performance attained is significantly degraded (low throughput, very high delay), so that, for all practical purposes, the channel is said to have failed; it is then called an unstable channel. With an infinite population, stationary conditions just do not exist; the channel is always unstable, thus confirming the results obtained from simulation, as just discussed. For unstable channels, Kleinrock and Lam [32] defined a stability measure which consists of the average time the system takes, starting from an empty channel, to reach a state determined to be critical. In fact, this critical state partitions the state space into two regions: a safe region, and an unsafe region in which the tendency is towards degraded performance. The stability measure is the average first exit time (FET) into the unsafe region. As long as the system operates in the safe region, the channel performance is acceptable; but then, of course, it is only usable over a finite period of time with an average equal to FET. For more details concerning the determination of FET and the numerical results, the reader is referred to [32], [33].

In the above discussion, it was furthermore assumed that the system parameters were all fixed, time invariant, and state independent. These systems are referred to as *static*. It is often advantageous to design systems that dynamically adapt to time-varying input and to system state changes, thus providing improved performance. Dynamic adaptability is achieved via dynamic control consisting of time and state-dependent parameters. The basic problem then is to find the control functions which provide the best system performance. Markov decision theory has successfully been applied by Lam and Kleinrock to the design and analysis of control procedures suitable to slotted ALOHA in particular and random access techniques in general [35]. Two main types of control are proposed: an *input* control procedure (ICP) consisting of either accepting or rejecting all new packets generated in the current slot, and a *retransmission* control procedure (RCP) consisting of selecting a retransmission delay; in both cases the action taken is a function of the current system state, defined as the number of active users with outstanding packets. In order to implement such control schemes, each channel user must individually estimate the channel state by observing the channel outcome over some period of time. The control is of a distributed nature, as there is no central station monitoring and broadcasting state information or control actions. In the context of slotted ALOHA, Lam and Kleinrock give some heuristic control-estimation algorithms which prove to be very satisfactory [35]. With appropriate modification and extensions, these algorithms can be applied to CSMA channels as well. These algorithms are best suited to fully connected single-hop-type environments. The dynamic control problem in multihop environments is more complex and little progress has yet been made in this area.

G. Capture. In the preceding discussions it was assumed that whenever two packet transmissions overlap in time, these packets destroy each other. This assumption is pessimistic as it neglects *capture* effects in radio channels. Capture can be defined as the ability for a receiver to successfully receive a packet (with nonzero probability) although it is partially or totally overlapped by another packet transmission. Capture is mainly due to a discrepancy in receive power between two signals allowing the receiver to correctly receive the stronger; both distance and transmit power contribute to this discrepancy. Clearly capture improves the overall network performance, and, by the means of adaptive transmit power control, it allows one to achieve either fairness to all users, or intentional discrimination. Some of these effects have been addressed in [27], [36].

H. Spread Spectrum Multiple Access (SSMA): Spread spectrum multiple access (SSMA) is the most common form of CDMA whereby each user is assigned a particular code sequence which is modulated on the carrier with the digital data modulated on top of that. Two common forms exist: the frequency-hopped SSMA and the phase-coded SSMA. In the former, as its name indicates, the frequency is periodically changing according to some known pattern; in the latter the carrier is phase modulated by the digital data sequence and the code sequence. SSMA has many applications: it is useful in satellite communications, mobile ground-radio, and computer communication networks [37]. In a recent article Kahn *et al.* addressed many of the issues concerning the use of SSMA in packet radio systems. Security, coexistence with other systems, and ability to counteract the effects of multipath are key factors contributing to the choice of SSMA in the PRNET; however, one main point of interest in this presentation is the benefit of capture in asynchronous SSMA. Even when several users employ the same code, the effect of interference is minimized by the "capture effect," defined here as the ability of the receiver to "lock on" one packet while all other overlapping packets appear as noise. The receiver locks on a packet by correctly receiving the preamble appended in the front of the transmitted packet. As long as the preamble of different packets do not overlap in time, and the signal strength of the late packets is not too high, capture of the earliest packet can be guaranteed with a high probability. In essence SSMA allows a packet to be captured at the receiver, while CSMA allows a user to capture the channel. CSMA can still be used in conjunction with SSMA. This mode will have the benefit of keeping away all users within hearing distance of the transmitter and thus help keep the capture effect and antijamming capability of the system at the desired level. For a complete discussion of all these issues, the reader is referred to [14].

IV. Centrally Controlled Demand Assignment

We have so far discussed the two extremes in the bandwidth allocation spectrum as far as control over the user's access right is concerned: the tight fixed assignment, which has the most rigid control, is nonadaptive to dynamically varying demand, and can be wasteful of capacity if small-delay constraints are to be met; and random access, which involves no control, is simple to implement, is adaptive to varying demand, but which, in some situations, can be wasteful of capacity due to collisions. In this and the following subsections, we examine demand assignment techniques which require that explicit information regarding the need for the communication resource be exchanged. We distinguish those demand assignments which are controlled by a central scheduler from those which employ a distributed algorithm executed by all users. We address centrally controlled assignments in the present subsection.

A. Circuit-Oriented Systems. In these systems, the bandwidth is divided into FDMA or TDMA subchannels which are assigned on demand. The satellite SPADE system, for example, has a pool of FDMA subchannels which get allocated on request [38]. It uses one subchannel operated in a TDMA fashion with one slot per frame permanently assigned to each user to handle the requests and releases of FDMA circuits. Intelsat's MAT-1 system uses the TDMA approach [39]. TDMA subchannels are periodically reallocated to meet the varying needs of earth stations.

The Advanced Mobile Phone Service (AMPS), recently introduced by Bell Laboratories, is yet another example of a centrally controlled FDMA system [40]. The uniqueness of this system, however, lies in an efficient management of the spectrum based on space division multiple access (SDMA). That is, each subchannel in the pool of FDMA channels is allocated to different users in separate geographical areas, thus considerably increasing the spectrum utilization. To accomplish space division, the AMPS system has a cellular structure and uses a centralized handoff procedure (executed by a central office) which reroutes the telephone connections to other available subchannels as the mobile users move from one cell to another.

Given the significant setup times required in allocating subchannels, the above systems are attractive only when applications have stream-type traffic. When traffic is bursty, we again turn to packet-oriented systems, such as in the following.

B. Polling Systems. In packet oriented systems, polling is one of two modes used to centrally control access to the communication bandwidth, again provided as a single high-speed channel. A central controller sends polling messages to the terminals, one by one, asking the polled terminal to transmit. For this the station may have a polling list giving the order in which the terminals are polled. If the polled terminal has something to transmit, it goes ahead; if not, a negative reply (or absence of reply) is received by the controller, which then polls the next terminal in sequence. Polling requires this constant exchange of control messages between the controller and the terminals, and is efficient only if (1) the round-trip propagation delay is small, (2) the overhead due to polling messages is low, and (3) the user population is not a large bursty one. Polling has been analyzed by Konheim and Meister [41], and their analysis has been applied to the environment of M users sharing a radio channel in [23]. Denoting by L the ratio of the data message length to the polling message length, and by a the ratio of propagation delay to message transmission time, Fig. 7 displays numerical results corresponding to some typical values of L and a. These curves show that indeed as the population size increases, thus containing more and more bursty users, the performance of polling degrades significantly. Channel utilization can reach 100 percent of the channel

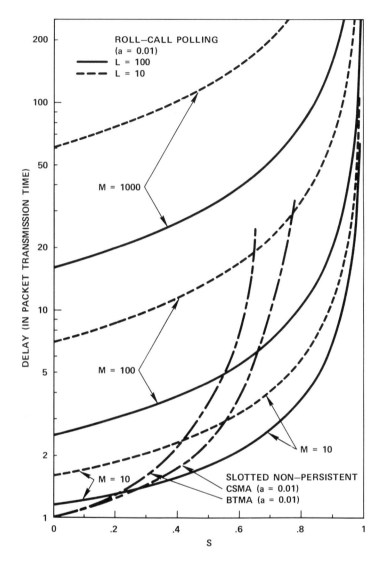

Fig. 7. Packet delay in roll-call polling. L = ratio of data message length to polling message length, a = normalized propagation delay, M = number of stations [23].

if the terminals are allowed to empty their buffers when they are polled. But as a result, the variance of packet delay can become intolerably large.

C. Adaptive Polling or Probing [*42*]. The primary limitation of polling in lightly loaded systems is the high overhead incurred in determining which of the terminals have messages. In order to decrease this overhead, a modified polling technique, based on a tree searching algorithm, and referred to as *probing*, has been proposed. This technique assumes that the central controller can *broadcast* signals to all terminals. First the controller interrogates all terminals, asking if any of them has a message to transmit, and repeats this question until some terminals respond by putting a signal on the line. When a positive response is received, the central station breaks down the population into subsets (according to some tree structure) and repeats the question to each of the subsets. This can be performed simply, for example by using binary addresses for the terminals and by transmitting as probing signal the common prefix of the addresses of a group of terminals. The process is continued until the terminals having messages are identified. When a single terminal is interrogated, it transmits its message.

Assume that the number of terminals is a power of 2, say $M = 2^n$. Let a cycle be recursively defined as the time required for the polling and transmission of all messages that were generated in the preceding cycle. If a single terminal has a message to transmit, probing requires $2n + 1$ inquiries per cycle as opposed to 2^n for conventional polling; but if all terminals have messages, probing requires $2^{n+1} - 1$ inquiries as opposed to 2^n for conventional polling. To avoid incurring such a penalty when the system is heavily loaded, the probing technique can be made adaptive whereby the controller starts a cycle by probing smaller groups as the probability of terminals having messages increases. In particular, the group size may be considered a function of the duration of the immediately preceding polling cycle. Simulation of the adaptive probing technique has shown that this scheme is always superior to polling in that its mean cycle time is always smaller than that of polling. Figure 8 displays the mean cycle time (obtained from simulation) as a function of the message arrival rate for both polling and probing [42]. Reference [42] did not provide any results concerning the message delay, but it is intuitively clear that the smaller the mean cycle time is, the lower is the average delay.

D. Split-Channel Reservation Multiple Access (SRMA) [23]. An attractive alternative to polling is the use of explicit reservation techniques. In dynamic reservation systems, it is the terminal which makes a request for service on some channel whenever it has a message to transmit. The central scheduler manages a queue of requests and informs the terminal of its allocated time.

Since the channel is the only means of communication among terminals, the main problem here is, once again, how to communicate the request to the central scheduler. The contention on the channel of these request packets is of exactly the same nature as the contention of the data packets themselves. Fixed assignment and random access techniques suggest themselves, but it is clear from previous results that random access modes for multiplexing the requests on the channel would be more efficient. Furthermore, in order to prevent collisions between the requests and the actual

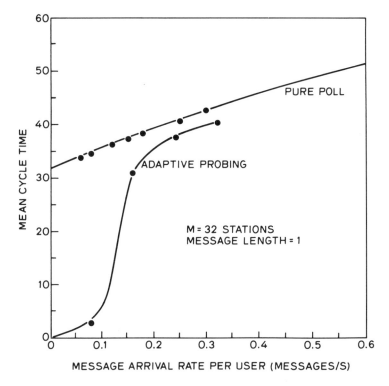

Fig. 8. Polling and adaptive probing: mean cycle time versus message arrival rate (simulation results—32 stations) [42].

message packets, the available bandwidth is either time divided or frequency divided between the two types of data. In the split-channel reservation multiple access (SRMA) scheme, frequency division of a ground radio channel is considered [23]. The available bandwidth is divided into two channels; one used to transmit control information, the second used for the data messages themselves. With this configuration, there are many operational modes. In the request/answer-to-request/message scheme (RAM), the bandwidth allocated for control is further divided into two channels: the request channel and the answer-to-request channel. The request channel is operated in a random access mode (ALOHA or CSMA). Upon correct reception of the request packet, the scheduling station computes the time at which the backlog on the message channel will empty and transmits an answer packet back to the terminal, on the answer-to-request channel, containing the address of the terminal and the time at which it can start transmission. Another version of SRMA, called the RM scheme, consists of having only two channels: the request channel and the message channel.

When correctly received by the scheduling station, the request packet joins the request queue. Requests may be serviced on a "first-come first-served" basis (or any other scheduling algorithm). When the message channel is available, an answer packet (containing the ID of a queued terminal scheduled for transmission) is transmitted by the station on the message channel. After hearing its own ID repeated by the station, the terminal starts transmitting its message on the message channel. If a terminal does not hear its own ID repeated by the scheduling station within a certain appropriate time after the request is sent, the original transmission of the request packet is assumed to be unsuccessful. The request packet is then retransmitted.

We now examine the performance of SRMA. Let η denote the ratio of request packet length to data packet length, this representing a measure of the overhead due to control information. In Fig. 9 we plot the (RAM) SRMA system capacity versus η for the following access modes: pure ALOHA SRMA, slotted ALOHA SRMA, and slotted nonpersistent carrier sense SRMA. In addition, we show the system capacity for both ALOHA and CSMA. We note that the system capacity in SRMA reaches 1 for very small η. Typical values for η fall in the range $(0.01, 0.1)$. Figure 9 shows that a high improvement is gained when the request channel is operated in slotted nonpersistent CSMA as compared to ALOHA. The delay for ALOHA SRMA and slotted nonpersistent carrier sense SRMA (normalized to b_m/W, where

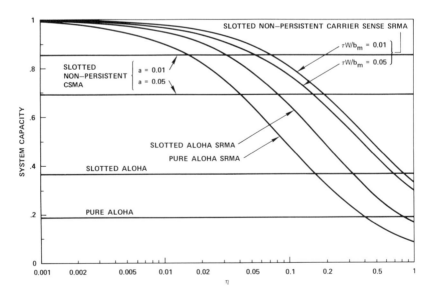

Fig. 9. SRMA: channel capacity versus η, ratio of request packet length to data packet length (normalized propagation delay of 0.01 and 0.05) [23].

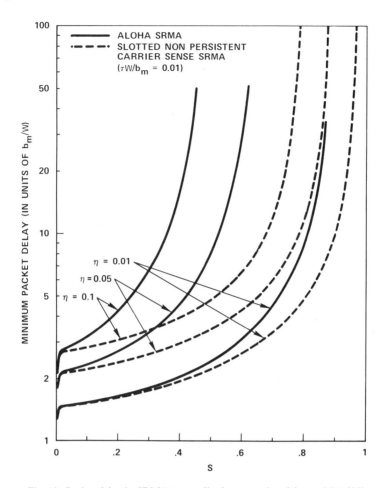

Fig. 10. Packet delay in SRMA (normalized propagation delay = 0.01) [23].

W denotes again the total channel bandwidth, and b_m is the number of bits per packet) is shown in Fig. 10 as a function of S for various values of η. We again note an important improvement in using CSMA for the request channel. Finally, in Fig. 11 we compare carrier sense SRMA with the random access modes ALOHA, CSMA, BTMA, and $M/D/1$, the perfect scheduling with fixed size packets and Poisson sources. We note that unless η is large (0.1 and above), there is a value of S below which CSMA or BTMA performs better than SRMA and above which the opposite is true.

E. Global Scheduling Multiple Access (GSMA) [*43*]. GSMA is a conflict-free reservation multiaccess scheme suitable for a high-speed data bus, which is based on the time-division concept for reservation. Here too a

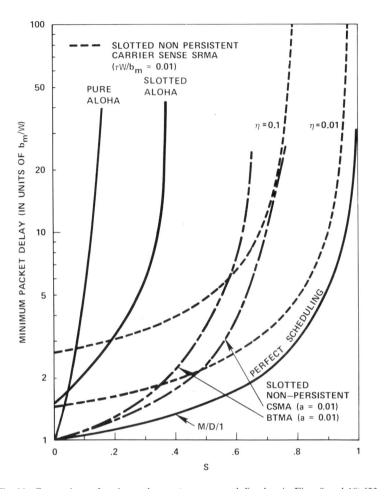

Fig. 11. Comparison of various schemes (parameters defined as in Figs. 9 and 10) [23].

scheduler oversees all scheduling tasks. The users, all connected to the same line, listen for scheduling assignments and transmit in accordance with the slot allocation initiated by the scheduler. The channel time is divided into frames (of variable lengths). A frame is partitioned into two subframes: a subframe of status slots statically assigned to the users (in a fixed TDMA mode) to request data slot allocation, and a subframe of data slots, each sufficient to transmit a data packet of P bits. The fixed assignment of the status slots removes the need to transmit users' IDs and thus reduces the size of these slots. In each frame, a user can be allocated a number of data slots which does not exceed the number of packets generated at the user during the preceding frame or a maximum number specified, whichever is

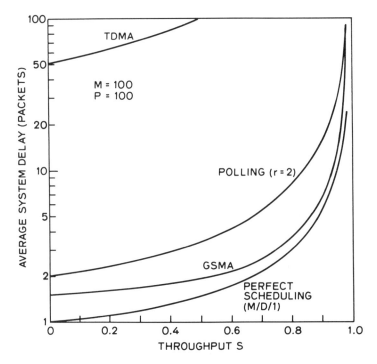

Fig. 12. GSMA: throughput delay performance (M = number of stations, P = number of bits per data packet) [43].

smaller. As a consequence each active user is guaranteed at least one slot per frame. Figure 12 displays the performance of GSMA (with $P = 100$ and number of stations $M = 100$) in comparison to polling (for some typical parameter values regarding the polling overhead r) and $M/D/1$ (the perfect scheduling). This illustrates some improvement gained in GSMA over polling [43].

V. Demand Assignment with Distributed Control

There are two reasons why distributed control is desirable. The first is *reliability*: with distributed control the system is not dependent on the proper operation of a central scheduler. The second is improved *performance*, especially when dealing with systems with long propagation delays, such as those using satellite channels. Indeed, if an earth station were to play the role of a scheduler, the minimum packet delay in a packet reservation scheme would be three times the round-trip propagation delay.

(Of course, this can be decreased if on-board processing is available.) With distributed control, this minimum delay can be brought down to twice the round-trip delay or less without affecting the bandwidth utilization. Clearly, in slotted ALOHA, the best random access scheme available for satellite channels, the minimum packet delay is exactly one round-trip delay; but this is guaranteed only for a channel utilization approaching zero! In fact, the inherent long propagation delay in satellite channels is really the nasty characteristic that makes this environment "more distributed" than the single-hop ground radio or local area environments. In the latter, we have seen that efficient random access schemes, such as CSMA, are available; and the shorter the propagation delay, the better the CSMA performance. With zero propagation delay, collisions in CSMA can be completely avoided and CSMA's performance then corresponds to that of an $M/D/1$ queue,* the best we can achieve under random demand. In fact, when the propagation delay is zero we no longer have a distributed environment, and the cost of creating a common queue disappears.

The basic element underlying all distributed algorithms is the need to exchange control information among the users, either explicitly or implicitly. Using this information, all users then execute independently the same algorithm resulting in some coordination in their actions. Clearly, it is essential that all users receive the same information regarding the demand placed on the channel and its usage in order to achieve a global optimum, and thus distributed algorithms are most attractive in fully connected systems. This attribute is not always present in ground radio environments, but certainly exists in satellite environments due to their inherent broadcast nature.† The long-delay/broadcast combination of attributes is one of the reasons why many distributed control algorithms have been proposed in the context of satellite environments. We examine in this section distributed control algorithms suitable for each of our three environments (satellite, ground radio, and local area), starting with satellite channels.

A. Reservation-aloha [45]. Reservation-ALOHA for a satellite channel is based on a slotted time axis, where the slots are organized into frames of equal size. The duration of a frame must be greater than the satellite propagation delay. A user who has successfully accessed a slot in a frame is guaranteed access to the same slot in the succeeding frame and this continues until the user stops using it. "Unused" slots, however, are free to be accessed by all users in a slotted ALOHA contention mode. An unused slot in the *current* frame is a slot which, in the *preceding* frame, either was idle or contained a collision. (Note again the effect of long delays on the control

---

*This correspondence applies to CSMA and fixed size packets and Poisson sources.
†This is valid unless the satellite uses spot beams, in which case we may lose on the connectivity requirement but gain the benefits of space division multiple access (SDMA).

procedure.) Users need to simply maintain a history of the usage of each slot for just one frame duration. Since no request is explicitly issued by the user, this schemes has been referred to as an *implicit reservation* scheme. Clearly Reservation-ALOHA is effective only if the users generate stream-type traffic or long multipacket messages. Its performance will degrade significantly with single-packet messages, as every time a packet is successful the corresponding slot in the following frame is likely to remain empty.

B.   A First-in First out (FIFO) Reservation Scheme [46]. In this scheme, reservations are made explicitly. Time division is used to provide a reservation subchannel. The channel time is slotted as before, but every so often a slot is divided into V small slots which are used for the transmission of reservation packets (as well as possibly acknowledgments and small data packets); these packets contend on the V small slots in a slotted ALOHA mode. All other slots are data slots and are used on a reservation basis, free of conflict. The frequency of occurrence of reservation slots can be made adaptive to the load on the channel and the need to make new reservations. This adaptivity can be achieved as a result of the time division of bandwidth between reservations and data packets.

To execute the reservation mechanism properly, each station must maintain information on the number of outstanding reservations (the "queue in the sky") and the slots at which its own reservations begin. These are determined by the FIFO discipline based on the successful reservations received. Each successful reservation can accommodate up to a design maximum of, say, eight packets, thus preventing stations from acquiring exclusivity of the channel for long periods of time. To maintain synchronization of control information at the proper time, and to acquire the correct count of packets in the queue if out-of-sync conditions do occur, each station sends, in its data packet, information regarding the status of its queue. This information is also used by new stations which need to join the queue. The robustness of this system is achieved by a proper encoding of the reservation packets to increase the probability of their correct reception at *all* stations. Furthermore, to limit the effect of errors, a station reacquires synchronization if it detects a collision in one of its reserved slots or an error in a reservation packet.

Figure 13 compares the throughput-delay tradeoff of the FIFO reservation scheme (operated with either a TDMA or a slotted ALOHA reservation subchannel) to that of TDMA and slotted ALOHA [66]. FIFO-Reservation offers delay improvements over TDMA. When compared to ALOHA, we note that higher system capacity is achieved but at the expense of a higher delay at low channel throughputs (due to a higher overhead).

C.   A Round-Robin (RR) Reservation Scheme [47]. The basis of this scheme is fixed TDMA assignment, but with the major difference that "unused" slots are assigned to the active stations on a round-robin basis.

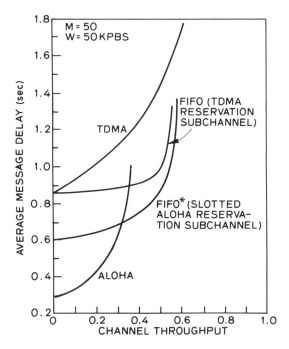

Fig. 13. Slotted ALOHA, TDMA, and FIFO reservation: delay throughput tradeoff for 50 users and single-packet messages in a satellite environment [66].

This is accomplished by organizing packet slots into equal size frames of duration greater than the propagation delay and such that the number of slots in a frame is larger than the number of stations. One slot in each frame is permanently assigned to each station. To allow other stations to know the current state (used or unused) of its own slot, each station is required to transmit information regarding its own queue of packets piggybacked in the data packet header (transmitted in the previous frame). A zero count indicates that the slot in question is free. All stations maintain a table of all stations' queue lengths, allowing them to allocate among themselves free unassigned slots in the current frame. Round-robin is the discipline proposed by Binder [47], but other scheduling disciplines can be used as well. A station recovers its slot by deliberately causing a conflict in that slot which other users detect. For a station which was previously idle, initial acquisition of queue information is required and is achieved by having one of the stations transmit its table at various times. However, it is interesting to note that in this scheme, while acquiring queue synchronization, a station can always reclaim and use its own assigned slot.

The above three schemes have been proposed for satellite channels. All of them assumed fixed size slots and thus can be implemented in systems which have been built for synchronous TDMA. The effect of large propagation delay is important. Framing is used in two of the schemes to deal with it, with the frame duration being equal to or longer than the propagation delay. Due to their dynamic nature, these protocols perform better than synchronous TDMA. However, when compared to random access (namely, ALOHA here), they offer higher capacity, but also higher delay at low throughput. If used in systems with small propagation delay, such as ground radio, then they will perform significantly better, and are expected to have a performance comparable to SRMA. In fact, due to the inherent small propagation delay in ground radio environments, other access modes with distributed control are also possible if all devices are in line-of-site and within range of each other. We describe these in the following.

D. Minislotted Alternating Priorities (MSAP) [48]. MSAP is a conflict-free multiple access scheme suitable for a *small* number of data users. In essence, MSAP is a "carrier-sense" version of polling with distributed control. The time axis is slotted with the minislot size again equal to the maximum propagation delay. All users are synchronized and may start transmission only at the beginning of a minislot. Users are considered to be ordered from 1 to M. When a packet transmission ends, the alternating priorities (AP) rule assigns the channel to the same user who transmitted the last packet (say user i) if he is still busy; otherwise the channel is assigned to the next user in sequence [i.e., user $(i, \bmod M + 1)$]. The latter (and all other users) detects the end of transmission of user i by sensing the absence of carrier over one minislot. At this new point in time, either user $(i \bmod M + 1)$ starts transmission of a packet (which will be detected by all other users) or he is idle, in which case a minislot is lost and control of the channel is handed to the next user in sequence. The overhead at each poll in this scheme is simply one minislot.

Scheduling rules other than AP are also possible, namely, round-robin (RR) or random order (RO). MSAP, however, exhibits the least overhead incurred in switching control between users. On the other hand, MSRR may be more suitable to environments with unbalanced traffic since then smaller users will be guaranteed more frequent access than with MSAP. These scheduling rules have also appeared in the literature as BRAM, the broadcast recognizing access method. For details, see [72].

E. The Assigned-Slot Listen-before-Transmission Protocol [49]. MSAP, being a "carrier sense" version of polling, behaves like polling. In particular, as the system load decreases, the overhead incurred in locating a nonidle user increases, and so does the delay. The assigned-slot listen-before-transmission protocol has been proposed to improve on MSAP by allowing several users to share common minislots. In such a case, there exists a tradeoff between the time wasted in collisions, and the time wasted in control overhead. Time is divided into frames, each containing an equal number of minislots (say, L). To each minislot of a frame is assigned a given subset of M/L users. A user with a packet ready for transmission in a frame can sense the channel only in his assigned minislot. If the channel is sensed idle, transmission takes place; if not, the packet is rescheduled for transmission in a future frame. A packet transmission spans T slots. The parameter M/L is adjusted according to the load placed on the channel. For high throughput, $M/L = 1$ is found to be optimum. In fact, with $M/L = 1$, the scheme becomes a conflict-free one which approaches MSAP and gives nearly identical results [49]. For very low throughput, $M/L = M$ (i.e., $L = 1$) is found to be optimum; this corresponds to pure CSMA. In between the two extreme cases intermediate values of M/L are optimum. Figure 14 displays the throughput-delay performance of this scheme for

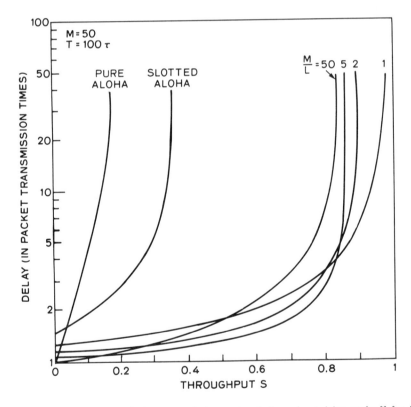

Fig. 14. Assigned-slot listen-before-transmission protocol: throughput delay tradeoff for 50 users and $T = 100$ (propagation time $a = 0.01$) [49].

various values of M/L when $M = 50$ and $T = 100$. It also shows how this scheme (and thus, MSAP) compare to CSMA.

F. Distributed Tree Retransmission Algorithms in Packet Broadcast Channels [71]. In many of the multiaccess protocols examined above, conflict resolution is achieved by retransmitting randomly in the future. Such a rescheduling discipline in slotted ALOHA achieves a 36 percent bandwidth utilization, but exhibits some sort of instability unless the rescheduling is controlled, as discussed in Section III. Tree algorithms are based on the observation that a contention among several active sources is completely resolved if and only if all the sources are somehow subdivided into groups such that each group contains at most one active source. (Such observation is similar to that made in the probing technique discussed in Section IV.) In its simplest form, the tree algorithm consists of the following. Each source corresponds to a leaf on a *binary* tree. The channel time axis is slotted and the slots are grouped into pairs. Each slot in a pair corresponds to one of the two subtrees of the node being visited. Starting with the root node of the tree, we let all terminals in each of the two subtrees of the root transmit in their corresponding slot. If any of the two slots contains a collision, then the algorithm proceeds to the root of the subtree corresponding to the collision and repeats itself. This continues until all the leaves are separated into sets such that each of them contains at most one packet. This is known to all users, as the outcome of the channel is either a successful transmission or an idle slot. Collisions caused by the left subtree (first slot of a pair) are resolved prior to resolving collisions in the right subtree. This scheme provides a maximum throughput of 0.347 packets/slot, and all moments of the delay are finite if the aggregate packet arrival rate is less than $1/3$ packets/slot [71].

Clearly, a binary tree is not always optimum. If, each time we return to the root node, we allow the tree to be reconfigured according to the current traffic conditions, it can be shown that the optimum tree is binary everywhere except for the root node whose optimum degree depends on traffic conditions [71]. The dynamic scheme achieves a throughput of 0.430 packets/slot, and all the moments of the delay are finite for $\lambda < 0.430$ packets/slot. Tree algorithms are implementable in both ground radio and satellite channels as long as the broadcast capability is available.

G. Distributed Control Algorithms in Local Area Networks: In addition to the random access schemes described previously in Section III, the above two algorithms are also applicable to local area (broadcast) *bus* networks as these exhibit the required characteristics of small propagation delay and full connectivity. But in local area communication, a slightly different topology has also been widely considered, namely, the *ring* (or loop). In the ring topology, messages are not broadcast but rather passed from node to node along unidirectional links until they reach their destination or, if required by the protocol, until they return to the originating node. Each subscriber is attached to the cable by means of an active tap which allows the information to be examined before it proceeds on the cable. To avoid excessive transit delays, messages are not stored in their entirety, but rather forwarded onto the cable as soon as possible. The delay incurred at each intermediate node can thus be limited to a small number of bit times. Messages are removed from the cable by the receiver (or the originator if the receiver is inactive).

A simple access scheme suitable for a ring consists of passing the access right sequentially from node to node around the ring. (Note that in a ring, the physical location of the nodes defines a natural ordering among them.) One implementation of this scheme is exemplified by the Distributed Computing System's network where an eight-bit control *token* is passed sequentially around the ring. Any node with a ready message may, upon receiving the control token, remove the token from the ring, send the message, and then pass on the control token [50]. Another implementation consists of providing a fixed number of message slots which are continuously transmitted around the ring. A message slot may be empty or full; a node with a ready message waits to see an empty slot pass by, marks it as full, and uses it to send its message [51–53]. A still different strategy is known as the *register insertion* technique [3], [54], [55]. Here a message to be transmitted is first loaded into a shift register. If the ring is idle, the shift register is just transmitted. If not, the register is inserted into the network loop at the next point separating two adjacent messages: the message to be sent is shifted out onto the ring while the incoming message is shifted into the register. The shift register can be removed from the network loop when the transmitted message has returned to it. The insertion of a register has the effect of increasing the transport delay of messages on the ring.

VI. Adaptive Strategies and Mixed Modes

We have so far examined quite a large number of multiaccess schemes and compared their performance. One thing is clear: each of these schemes has its advantages and limitations. No one scheme performs better than all others over the entire range of system throughput (except, of course, the hypothetical perfect scheduling, which is clearly unachievable in a distributed environment). If a scheme performs nearly as well as perfect scheduling at low input rates, then it is plagued by a limited achievable channel capacity. Conversely, if a scheme is efficient when the system utilization is high, the overhead accompanying the access control mechanism becomes large at low utilization. Although some characteristics of a system (propagation delay, channel speed, etc.) are unlikely to vary during operation, it is certain that the load placed upon the system will be time varying. In the case of a single subscriber type (say with periodic traffic, stream-type traffic, or bursty traffic) the volume of the traffic may be varying; if several subscriber types are simultaneously present, the volume of traffic introduced by each, and therefore the proportional mix of traffic types, may also be time varying.

We have discussed at several points in this paper the dynamic control of a specific access scheme which improved its performance to a certain extent; but such an adaptive control did not change the nature of the access scheme nor the nature of its limitation. Dynamically controlled random access schemes provide improved packet delay over uncontrolled versions, but still exhibit channel capacity less than 1. The adaptive polling technique decreased the overhead at low throughput but only to a certain extent. Actually, what one really needs is a strategy for choosing an access mode which is itself adaptive to the varying need so that optimality is maintained at all times. Clearly, in order to accomplish adaptivity, a certain amount of information is needed by the distributed decision makers. The type and amount of information required by an adaptive strategy, as well as the implementation of the information acquisition mechanism are among the most crucial factors in determining the performance and robustness of the strategy. A great deal of effort has been spent in recent years on such adaptive strategies. We devote this subsection to schemes which fall into this category.

A. The Urn Scheme [56]. We start with this more recent scheme because of its simplicity, elegance, and the smoothness by which it adapts to varying loads. It has been proposed for fully connected ground radio environments. The time axis is divided into packet slots, and all users are synchronized. Assuming that all users know the exact number n of busy users, the scheme consists of giving full access right (i.e., the right to transmit with probability 1) to some subset of k users. A successful transmission will result if there is exactly one busy user among these k. The probability of such an event is maximized when $k = \lfloor M/n \rfloor$, where $\lfloor M/n \rfloor$ denotes the integer part of M/n. This is in contrast to the controlled slotted ALOHA scheme, where all users are given the same partial access right: the right to transmit with probability $p = 1/n$. If the system is lightly loaded, then a large subset of users is given access right, but only a few, and hopefully only one user, will make use of it. As the load increases, k decreases and the access right is gradually restricted. If $n = 1$, for example, then $k = M$ and a successful transmission takes place. For the extreme case of $n = M$, $k = 1$ and the scheme converges to TDMA. If the sampling of the k users is random, the Urn scheme converges to random TDMA; if the sampling is without repetitions from slot to slot until all users have been sampled once, the Urn scheme converges to round-robin TDMA.

Two important questions remain: how to estimate n, and how to reach a consensus on who the k users are. One possible means for estimating n with good accuracy is to include a single reservation minislot at the beginning of each data slot. An idle user who turns busy sends a standard reservation message of few bits. All users are able to detect the following three events: no new busy users, one new busy user, and more than one new busy user (termed an erasure). As it is impossible with this minimal overhead to estimate the exact number of new busy users when the latter is greater than one, errors in estimation result; however, analysis and simulation have shown that this error is negligible, and that the scheme is insensitive to small perturbations in n. This last statement is even more important with respect to the robustness of the scheme since it means that all users need not have exactly the same estimate for n. As for coordinating the selection of the k users, an effective mechanism is the use of synchronized pseudorandom generators at all users which allow them to draw the same k pseudorandom numbers. Another mechanism, referred to as a round-robin slot-sharing window mechanism, consists of having a window of size k move over the population space. When a collision occurs, the window stops and decreases in size. When there is no collision, the tail of the window is advanced to the head of the previous window, and the size is again set to k as determined by n.

The improvement obtained by this scheme over slotted ALOHA and TDMA can be seen in Fig. 15, where the throughput-delay performance of all these schemes is displayed for a population size $M = 10$ [56].

B. Another Adaptive Strategy for the Dynamic Management of Packet Radio Slots [57]. Another way to achieve adaptivity is as follows. The time axis is again slotted with the slot size equal to a packet transmission time. Slots are grouped into k equivalence classes or subchannels. Slots are furthermore grouped into frames of m slots, $m \geq k$, each containing at least one slot for every equivalence class. Let M be again the number of users. Each user is at any one time assigned to one of the k equivalence classes. All stations in a given class use a random access mode to access slots assigned to their class. If CSMA is used as the contention scheme, then time slots are minislots of size τ, assigned to the k equivalence classes just as before. By dynamically varying the size of the frame and the assignment of slots within the frame to classes of users, one can vary the access mode to best fit the situation. At low load, for example, choosing $k = m = 1$ with all users in the same class leads to a pure random access mode of low delay. Choosing $k = m = M$ with each user constituting a separate class leads to TDMA. Increasing the parameter k has the effect of decreasing the rate of collisions among users of the same class. The frame size m can be used to allow a smooth changeover between the schemes. By partitioning the frame into two subframes, both contention and pure TDMA can coexist simultaneously.

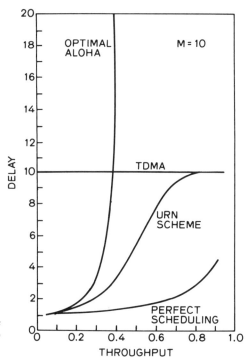

Fig. 15. Throughput-delay performance for the Urn scheme (example for 10 users) [56].

The information used in adapting to the situation is the collision rate and the rate of empty slots (or minislots) for the randomly accessed slots, and the rate of empty slots for the TDMA assigned slots. For example, when one minislot of a TDMA slot goes empty, the remainder of the TDMA slot may be canceled and reassigned to some other groups (then to be used via CSMA).

Schemes other than CSMA and TDMA can be combined by this adaptive strategy. One may, for example, mix CSMA with MSRR. In [57], Ricart and Agrawala studied, via simulation, some typical adaptation algorithms of this type. Some of their simulation results for a CSMA/TDMA combination are shown in Fig. 16. These results exhibit clearly the improvement gained over the entire throughput range by using the adaptive strategy.

C. The Reservation upon Collision Schemes (RUC) [58]. The basic concept in these schemes is to switch back and forth between contention mode and reservation mode. The channel time is divided into slots of fixed length, which in turn are divided into two parts: a data subslot SSO for transmission of information packets and a subslot SS1 for the transmission of (signaling) information regarding the transmitting user(s). The data subchannel can be in one of two states: the contention state or the reserved

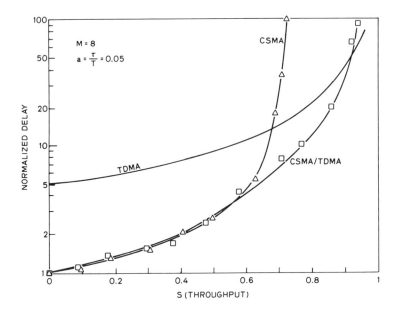

Fig. 16. Simulation results for an adaptive CSMA/TDMA strategy (eight stations, normalized propagation delay of $a = 0.05$) [57].

state. It is normally in the contention state and users can access the slots in a slotted ALOHA mode as long as no collisions occur. When a collision is detected, then the data subchannel switches to the reserved state and remains in that state until the queue of reservations is cleared, at which time it switches back to the contention state. That is, if a collision is detected, reservations are automatically implied for the colliding users. To accomplish this, the signaling information identifying the users must be received by all users free of interference, and thus a conflict-free use of the SS1 subslots must be devised. CDMA and TDMA have been proposed in [58]. When the number of users is large, a particularly suitable approach is to consider grouping the slots into a frame of, say, L slots. Each of the L SS1 subslots is assigned to a group of size M/L users instead of M users, thus decreasing the degree of multiplexing signaling information over the SS1 subslots. TDMA or CDMA still needs to be used. In this approach, users need not transmit their identification as this is implied from the position of the SS1 subslot. However, each user has to send the number of packets transmitted in the frame, and this information requires at most $\log_2(L + 1)$ bits. This scheme is referred to as the split reservation upon collision (SRUC).

   Figure 17 shows the performance of SRUC in a satellite environment as compared to slotted ALOHA and pure reservation for two values of the overhead Ψ required per frame for the signaling information. Clearly, this

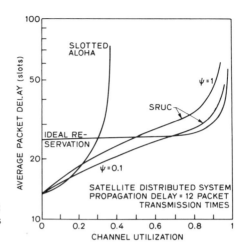

Fig. 17. Split reservation upon collision: throughput-delay performance for various values of the overhead Ψ [58].

performance degrades as Ψ increases. More detailed results can be found in [58].

Since slotted ALOHA and reservations are both suitable for satellite channels, RUC schemes are also particularly suitable for these as well as ground radio channels.

D. Priority-Oriented Demand Assignment (PODA) [12]. In the context of a satellite channel, PODA has been proposed as the ultimate scheme which attempts to incorporate all the properties and advantages seen in many of the previous schemes. It has provision for both implicit and explicit reservations, thus accomodating both stream and packet-type traffic. It may also integrate the use of both centralized and distributed control techniques thus achieving a high level of robustness.

To accomplish this flexibility, channel time is divided into two basic subframes, an information subframe and a control subframe. The information subframe contains scheduled packets and packet streams, with the packets also containing, piggybacked, control information such as reservations and acknowledgments. The control subframe is used exclusively to send reservations that cannot be sent in the information subframe in a timely manner. In order to achieve integration of centralized and distributed assignments, the information subframe is further divided into two sections, one for each type.

Access to the control subframe (which is divided into slots accommodating fixed size control packets) can take any form that is suitable to the environment. It can be by *fixed assignment* (TDMA) if the number of stations is small (giving rise to the so-called FPODA), or by *contention* as in ALOHA if the stations have a low-duty cycle (giving rise to CPODA), or a combination of both. The boundary between the control subframe and the information subframe is not fixed, but varies with the demand placed on the channel. As in the FIFO and RR reservation schemes, distributed control is achieved by having all stations involved in this type of control keep track of their queue length information. Priority scheduling can thus be achieved. For stream traffic, a reservation is made only once, and is retained by each station in a stream queue. Centralized assignment may be used when delay is not the crucial element. This scheme has been proposed in the context of a satellite channel but may be applied to other environments as well.

E. More on Mixed Modes. Other studies have appeared in the literature that also deal with integrating several different access modes into the same system.

The *Mixed* ALOHA *Carrier Sense* (MACS) scheme consists of allowing a large user to steal, by carrier sensing, slots which are unused by a large population of small users accessing the channel in a slotted ALOHA mode [59]. Analysis has shown that the total channel utilization is significantly increased with MACS, and that the throughput-delay performance of both the large user and the background ALOHA users is better with MACS than with a split-channel configuration in which the larger user and the ALOHA users are each permanently assigned a portion of the channel [59].

Group Random Access (GRA) procedures consist of using only certain channel time periods to allow some network terminals to transmit their information-bearing packets on a random access basis. The channel can then be utilized at other times to grant access to other terminals or other message types, by applying, as appropriate, group random access, reservation procedure, or fixed assignment. The idea is simply a fixed time-division assignment among groups utilizing different access schemes. For more details on and analysis of GRA, the reader is referred to [60], [61].

Finally, we consider satellite systems with on-board processing capability. These have recently received increased attention and are being considered as a means to increase the capacity of packet satellite channels [62]–[65]. One example is typified by the integration of slotted ALOHA on several uplink channels, with TDMA on one or several downlink channels. The on-board processing capability is used to filter out all collisions and thus improve the utilization of the downlink channels. The overall spectrum efficiency is also improved especially if the ratio of uplink channels to downlink channels is properly chosen. Analysis of these disciplines is given in [62], [63]. Additional improvement over these disciplines is possible by providing buffering capability on board the satellite to smooth the input and more completely fill the downlink channels.

VII. Conclusion

Tremendous advances have been made in recent years in devising multiaccess schemes suitable to a variety of data communication environments. In this paper, we have briefly reviewed a large number of these protocols which we have grouped into five categories according to (1) the degree of control exercised over the users' access (2) the (centralized or distributed) nature of the decision-making process; and (3) the degree of adaptivity of the algorithm to the changing need. We have seen that these link level protocols have a great impact on the utilization of the communication resource in particular and the overall system performance in general. We have also briefly discussed their suitability to various traffic characteristics.

Although an attempt has been made to render the presentation complete, it is by no means exhaustive of all existing schemes, and the field is still so wide open that new schemes are constantly being introduced. Throughout the paper, an emphasis was placed on that class of packet communications that service very many bursty users, since this has been a major concern for many years. It is important, however, to note that there is a growing interest in the support of applications which lend themselves to stream-type traffic (such as packetized voice, facsimile, video data for remote conferencing, etc.) and which may also require real-time communications service on the part of the network. Moreover, with an even greater interest in integrating the many different applications onto the same network structure, it is becoming important to devise multiaccess protocols which can provide all the capabilities and features required for this integration. The adaptive strategies discussed in this paper provide an attempt at solving this problem but it is still far from being completely resolved.

Another point of great importance is the impact that these link level protocols have on the design of higher-level protocols. Indeed, owing to the basically different nature and behavior of some of these multiaccess schemes, one is faced with the necessity to find new ways to deal with many of the higher level functions. To briefly illustrate this point, we consider for example store-and-forward multiaccess/broadcast systems. The routing problem in these systems is significantly different from the well-known routing algorithms devised for point-to-point store-and-forward networks; here the transmitted packet should carry, at each transmission, the next node's address, and each *receiving* node has to decide as to whether to relay or ignore the packet. A discussion of routing schemes appropriate to these systems can be found in [14]. Clearly, in single-hop broadcast systems, and in local area ring architectures, the routing problem is absent.

Acknowledgment procedures may also have to be handled differently in broadcast networks. In the PRNET, for example, hop-by-hop acknowledgments can be passive, in the sense that, due to the broadcast nature of transmission, the relaying of a packet over a hop constitutes the acknowledgments for the transmission over the previous hop. Acknowledgments may also be active in the sense that an acknowledgment packet is actually created and transmitted. If acknowledgment packets are given priority, the active acknowledgment procedure has the benefit of minimizing buffering requirements at the repeaters since the acknowledgments are sent at the earliest opportunity, and possibly minimizing channel overhead since the additional transmissions beyond success resulting from delayed acknowledgments can then be kept to a minimum [67]. (In fact, it was found that if acknowledgments were instantaneous, then a few buffers in each packet radio unit appear to be sufficient to handle the storage requirements, indicating that the system becomes more channel bound than storage bound [68], [69].) In satellite environments, PODA achieves the same objective by piggybacking acknowledgments, whenever possible, on pending reservation requests which are heard by all users including the sender.

To conclude, we can say that despite the many advances already accomplished, this area still presents many challenging open problems, and that to best make use of the progress already achieved in link level protocols, one also needs to turn one's attention to the many unresolved issues concerning higher-level protocols.

References

[1] D. W. Davies, K. A. Bartlett, R. A. Scantlebury, and P. T. Wilkinson, "A digital communication network for computers giving rapid response at remote terminals," presented at ACM Symp. Operating System Principles, Gatlinburg, TN, Oct 1–4, 1967.

[2] W. D. Farmer and E. E. Newhall, "An experimental distributed switching system to handle bursty computer traffic," in *Proc. ACM Conf.*, Pine Mountain, GA, Oct. 1969.

[3] M. T. Liu and C. C. Reames, "Communication protocol and network operating system design for the distributed loop computer network (DLCN)," in *Proc. 4th Annu. Symp. Computer Architecture*, Mar. 1977, pp. 193–200.

[4] M. T. Liu, "Distributed loop computer networks," in *Advances in Computer Networks*, M. Rubinoff and M. C. Yovitts, Eds. New York: Academic, 1978.

[5] R. M. Metcalfe and D. R. Boggs, "ETHERNET: Distributed packet switching for local computer networks," *Commun. Ass. Comput. Mach.*, vol. 19, pp. 395–403, 1976.

[6] L. Pouzin, "Presentation and major design aspects of the CYCLADES computer network," presented at Datacom 73, ACM/IEEE, 3rd Data Commun. Symp., St. Petersburg, FL, Nov. 1973, pp. 80–87.

[7] L. G. Roberts and B. D. Wessler, "Computer network developments to achieve resource sharing," in *1970 Spring Joint Comput. Conf., Proc. AFIPS Conf.*, vol. 36, 1970, pp. 543–549.

[8] L. Pouzin, "CIGALE, The packet switching machine of the CYCLADES computer network," presented at IFIP Congress, Stockholm, Sweden, Aug. 1974, pp. 155–159.

[9] H. Opderbeck and R. B. Hovey, "Telenet—Network features and interface protocols," in *Proc. NTG-Conf. Data Networks*, Baden-Baden, West Germany, Feb. 1976.

[10] W. W. Clipshaw and F. Glave, "Datapac network review," in *Int. Comput. Commun. Conf. Proc.*, Aug. 1976, pp. 131–136.

[11] N. Abramson, "The Aloha system," in *Computer Communication Networks*, N. Abramson and F. Kuo, Eds. Englewood Cliffs, NJ: Prentice-Hall, 1973.

[12] I. M. Jacobs, R. Binder, and E. V. Hoversten, "General purpose packet satellite networks," *Proc. IEEE,* vol. 66, Nov. 1978.

[13] R. E. Kahn, "The organization of computer resources into a packet radio network," in *Nat. Comput. Conf., AFIPS Conf. Proc.,* vol. 44. Montvale, NJ: AFIPS Press, 1975, pp. 177–186; also in *IEEE Trans. Commun.,* vol. COM-25, Jan. 1977.

[14] R. E. Kahn, S. A. Gronemeyer, J. Burchfiel, and R. C. Kunzelman, "Advances in Packet radio technology," *Proc. IEEE,* vol. 66, Nov. 1978.

[15] D. Clark *et al.*, "An introduction to local area networks," *Proc. IEEE,* vol. 66, Nov. 1978.

[16] W. G. Schmidt, "Satellite time-division multiple access systems: Past, present and future," *Telecommun.,* vol. 7, pp. 21–24, Aug. 1974.

[17] I. Rubin, "Message delays in FDMA and TDMA communication channels," *IEEE Trans. Commun.,* vol. COM-27, May 1979.

[18] S. Lam, "Delay analysis of time-division multiple access (TDMA) channel," *IEEE Trans. Commun.,* vol. COM-25, Dec. 1977.

[19] O. Kosovych, "Fixed assignment access technique," *IEEE Trans. Commun.,* vol. COM-26, Sept. 1978.

[20] N. Abramson, "The ALOHA system—Another alternative for computer communications," in *1970 Fall Joint Comput. Conf. AFIPS Conf. Proc.,* vol. 37. Montvale, NJ: AFIPS Press, 1970, pp. 281–285.

[21] L. G. Roberts, "ALOHA packet system with and without slots and capture," *Comput. Commun. Rev.,* vol, 5, pp. 28–42, Apr. 1975.

[22] L. Kleinrock and S. Lam, "Packet-switching in a slotted satellite channel," *Nat. Computer Conf., AFIPS Conf. Proc.,* vol. 42. Montvale, NJ: AFIPS Press, 1973, pp. 703–710.

[23] F. A. Tobagi and L. Kleinrock, "Packet switching in radio channels: Part III—Polling and (dynamic) split channel reservation multiple access," *IEEE Trans. Commun.* vol. COM-24, pp. 832–845, Aug. 1976.

[24] L. Kleinrock and F. A. Tobagi, "Packet switching in radio channels: Part I–Carrier sense multiple access modes and their throughput-delay characteristics," *IEEE Trans. Commun.,* vol. COM-23, pp. 1400–1416, Dec. 1975.

[25] F. Tobagi, "Random access techniques for data transmission over packet switched radio networks," PH.D. dissertation, Comput. Sci. Dep., School of Eng. and Appl. Sci., Univ. California, Los Angeles, Rep. UCLA-ENG 7499, Dec. 1974.

[26] F. Tobagi and V. B. Hunt, "Performance analysis of carrier sense multiple access with collision detection," in *Proc. Local Area Commun. Network Symp.,* Boston, MA, May 1979; also *Computer Networks,* Vol. 4, No. 5, Oct./Nov. 1980.

[27] N. Abramson, "The throughput of packet broadcasting channels," *IEEE Trans. Commun.,* vol. COM-25, pp. 117–128, Jan. 1977.

[28] F. Tobagi and L. Kleinrock, "Packet switching in radio channels: Part II—The hidden terminal problem in carrier sense multiple access and the busy tone solution," *IEEE Trans. Commun.,* vol. COM-23, pp. 1417–1433, Dec. 1975.

[29] F. A. Tobagi, M. Gerla, R. W. Peebles, and E. G. Manning, "Modeling and measurement techniques in packet communication networks," *Proc. IEEE,* vol. 66, pp. 1423–1447, Nov. 1978.

[30] F. Tobagi and L. Kleinrock, "The effect of acknowledgment traffic on the capacity of packet-switched radio channels," *IEEE Trans. Commun.,* vol, COM-26, pp. 815–826, June 1978.

[31] S. S. Lam, "Packet switching in a multiaccess broadcast channel with application to satellite communication in a computer network," Ph.D. dissertation, Dep. Comput. Sci., Univ. California, Los Angeles, Mar. 1974; also in Univ. California, Los Angeles, Tech. Rep. UCLA-ENG-7429, Apr. 1974.

[32] L. Kleinrock and S. S. Lam, "Packet switching in a multiaccess broadcast channel; Performance evaluation," *IEEE Trans. Commun.,* vol. COM-23, pp. 410–423, Apr. 1975.

[33] F. Tobagi and L. Kleinrock, "Packet switching in radio channels: Part IV—Stability considerations and dynamic control in carrier sense multiple access," *IEEE Trans. Commun.*, vol. COM-25, pp. 1103–1120, Oct. 1977.

[34] G. Fayolle, E. Gelembe, and J. Labetoule, "Stability and optimal control of the packet-switching broadcast channels," *J. Ass. Comput. Mach.*, vol. 24, pp. 375–386, July 1977.

[35] S. S. Lam and L. Kleinrock, "Packet switching in a multiaccess broadcast channel: Dynamic control procedures," *IEEE Trans. Commun.*, vol. COM-23, pp. 891–904, Sept. 1975.

[36] J. Metzner, "On improving utilization in ALOHA networks," *IEEE Trans. Commun.*, vol. COM-24, Apr. 1976.

[37] Special Issue on Spread Spectrum Communications, *IEEE Trans. Commun.*, vol. COM-25, Aug. 1977.

[38] B. Edelson and A. Werth, "SPADE system progress and application," *COMSAT Tech. Rev.*, vol. 2, pp. 221–242, Spring 1972.

[39] W. Schmidt *et al.*, "Mat-1: INTELSAT's Experimental 700-channel TDMA/DA system," in *Proc. INTELSAT/IEEE Int. Conf. Digital Satellite Commun.*, Nov. 1969.

[40] N. Erlich, "The advanced mobile phone service," *IEEE Commun. Mag.*, vol. 17, Mar. 1979.

[41] A. G. Konheim and B. Meister, "Service in a loop system," *J. Ass. Comput. Mach.*, vol. 19, pp. 92–108, Jan. 1972.

[42] J. F. Hayes, "An adaptive technique for local distribution," *IEEE Trans. Commun.*, vol. COM-26, Aug. 1978.

[43] J. W. Mark, "Global scheduling approach to conflict-free multiaccess via a data bus," *IEEE Trans. Commun.*, vol. COM-26, Sept, 1978.

[44] L. Kleinrock, "Performance of distributed multiaccess computer communication systems," in *Proc. IFIP Congress*, 1977.

[45] W. R. Crowther, R. Rettberg, D. Walden, S. Ornstein, and F. Heart, "A system for broadcast communication: Reservation-ALOHA," in *Proc. 6th Hawaii Int. Syst. Sci. Conf.*, Jan. 1973.

[46] L. Roberts, "Dynamic allocation of satellite capacity through packet reservation," in *Proc. AFIPS Conf.*, vol. 42, June, 1973.

[47] R. Binder, "A dynamic packet switching system for satellite broadcast channels," in *Proc. ICC'75*, San Francisco, CA, June 1975.

[48] L. Kleinrock and M. Scholl, "Packet switching in radio channels: New conflict-free multiple access schemes for a small number of data users," in *ICC Conf. Proc.*, Chicago, IL, June 1977, pp. 22.1-105–22.1-111.

[49] L. W. Hansen and M. Schwartz, "An assigned-slot listen-before-transmission protocol for a multiaccess data channel," *IEEE Trans. Commun.*, vol. COM-27, pp. 846–857, June 1979.

[50] D. C. Loomis, "Ring communication protocols," Univ. California, Dep. Inform. and Comput. Sci., Irvine, CA Tech. Rep. 26, Jan. 1973.

[51] J. R. Pierce, "Network for block switching of data," *Bell Syst. Tech. J.*, vol. 51, pp. 1133–1143, July/Aug. 1972.

[52] A. Hopper, "Data ring at computer laboratory, University of Cambridge," *Computer Science and Technology: Local Area Networking*. Washington DC: Nat. Bur. Stand., NBS Special Publ. 500-31, Aug. 22–23, 1977, pp. 11–16.

[53] P. Zafiropoulo and E. H. Rothauser, "Signalling and frame structures in highly decentralized loop systems," *Proc. Int. Conf. on Comput. Commun.* (Washington, DC), IMB Res. Lab., Zurich, Switzerland, pp. 309–315.

[54] E. R. Hafner *et al.*, "A digital loop communication system," *IEEE Trans. Commun.*, p. 877, June 1974.

[55] M. V. Wilkes, "Communication using a digital ring, "in *Proc.* PACNET *Conf.*, Sendai, Japan, Aug. 1975, pp. 217–255.

[56] L. Kleinrock and Y. Yemini, "An optimal adaptive scheme for multiple access broadcast communication," *ICC Conf. Proc.*, Chicago, IL, June 1977.

[57] G. Ricart and A. Agrawala, "Dynamic management of packet radio slots," presented at *Third Berkeley Workshop on Distributed Data Management and Comput. Networks*, Aug. 1978.

[58] F. Borgonovo and L. Fratta, "SRUC: A technique for packet transmission on multiple access channels," in *Proc. Int. Conf. Comput. Commun.*, Kyoto, Japan, 1978.

[59] M. Scholl and L. Kleinrock, "On a mixed mode multiple access scheme for packet-switched radio channels," *IEEE Trans Commun.*, vol. COM-27, pp. 906–911, June 1979.

[60] I. Rubin, "A group random-access procedure for multi-access communication channels," in *NTC'77 Conf. Rec. Nat. Telecommun. Conf.*, Los Angeles, CA, Dec. 1977, pp. 12:5-1–12:5-7.

[61] —"Integrated random-access reservation schemes for multi-access communication channels," School Eng. Appl. Sci., Univ. California, Los Angeles, Tech. Rep. UCLA-ENG-7752, July 1977.

[62] J. K. DeRosa, and L. H. Ozarow, "Packet switching in a processing satellite," *Proc. IEEE*, vol. 66, pp. 100–102, Jan. 1978.

[63] R. E. Eaves, "ALOHA/TDM systems with multiple downlink capacities," *IEEE Trans. Commun.*, vol. COM-27, pp. 537–541, Mar. 1979.

[64] S. F. W. Ng and J. W. Mark, "A multiaccess model for packet switching with a satellite having some processing capability," *IEEE Trans. Commun.*, vol. COM-25, pp. 128–135, Jan. 1977.

[65] —, "Multiaccess model for packet switching with a satellite having processing capability: Delay analysis," *IEEE Trans. Commun.*, vol. COM-26, pp. 283–290, Feb. 1978.

[66] S. S. Lam, "Satellite multi-access schemes for data traffic," in *Proc. Int. Conf. Commun.*, Chicago, IL, 1977, pp. 37.1-19–37.1-24.

[67] F. Tobagi *et al.*, "On measurement facilities in packet radio systems," in *Nat. Comput. Conf. Proc.*, New York, NY, June 1976.

[68] F. Tobagi, "Analysis of a two-hop centralized packet radio network: Part I—Slotted ALOHA," *IEEE Trans. Commun.*, vol. COM-28, pp. 196–207, Feb. 1980.

[69] ——"Analysis of a two-hop centralized packet radio network: Part II—Carrier sense multiple access," *IEEE Trans. Commun.*, vol. COM-28, pp. 208–216, Feb. 1980.

[70] W. W. Chu, "A study of asynchronous time division multiplexing for time-sharing computer systems," in *1969 Spring Joint Comput. Conf. AFIPS Conf. Proc.*, vol. 35, 1969, pp. 669–678.

[71] J. I. Capetanakis, "Tree algorithms for packet broadcasting channels," *IEEE Trans. Inform. Theory*, vol. IT-25, pp. 505–515, Sept. 1979.

[72] I. Chlamtac *et al.*, "BRAM: The broadcast recognizing access method," *IEEE Trans. Commun.*, vol. COM-27, pp. 1183–1190, Aug. 1979.

[73] J. E. Thornton, "Overview of Hyperchannel," *18th IEEE Comp. Soc. Int. Conf. (Comp Con 79 Spring)*, San Francisco, February 1979, pp. 262–265.

[74] M. Tokoro and K. Tamaru, "Acknowledging Ethernet," *Proc. CompCon 77*, pp. 320–325, Sept. 1977.

PART IV

Network Layer

In this part we deal with some protocol questions that one would call real "network" questions, in the following sense: The Physical Layer division of Part II dealt mostly with a particular interface within one node, and the Data Link Control discussion of Part III dealt with two protocol partners, and so does the Part V discussion of end-to-end higher level protocols. In other words, in Parts II, III, and V, the multinode character of the network is invisible. But here we shall be dealing with matters involving the interaction of all nodes, both end nodes and intermediate nodes, to produce a reliable connection path between parties resident in the end nodes. Such a connection serves as a base on which the protocols described in Part V can build complete paths allowing dissimilar end users to not only be connected but to communicate.

The nature of the services provided by the protocols described in the different chapters of this section varies considerably, being arranged in Chapters 7 through 11 in order of their complexity and thereby functionality. Chapter 7 takes the simplest point of view about this, describing the one-hop fast circuit switched connection provided by the peer physical level X.21 protocol and comparing it to those provided by an X.25-based packet network, this being the subject of the next chapter, Chapter 8. The fast circuit switched services provide, on an intermittent basis, a synchronous bit pipe supporting the higher protocol layers of Section V. The line error recovery features of DLC are missing, since their protocol level is omitted in the end-to-end services described in Chapter 7, and must be provided by the higher layers.

In the case of the X.25 packet-switched facilities, whose most recent state of evolution is described in Chapter 8, the services provided to the next higher layer are called a *virtual circuit*, a connection that conveys properly addressed packets in a full duplex connection between two parties, in proper sequential order. This is done by adding a third layer, the X.25 packet layer, on top of the physical and DLC levels, the latter providing the usual mechanisms for recovery from line errors. While logically the virtual circuit looks like a single pipe transporting packets, physically it consists of three pieces, first one set of three-level X.25 peer protocols working between one end node and the public data network, then the internal mechanisms of that network, and third the three X.25 peer protocols between the network and the other end node.

In actual use, it is most convenient to set up either the X.21-based fast circuit switched service or the X.25-based packet switched virtual circuit and then send a number of messages through it before taking it down again. The overhead connected with path establishment and disestablishment, particularly with virtual circuits, is clearly unattractive if a single isolated message must be sent, say a 1000-bit packet representing a credit card number being entered to a credit checking program. Special variants of X.25 have been developed to handle this "short message" problem, the *datagram* and *fast select* facilities, and these are described in Chapter 9.

The Digital Network Architecture of Chapter 10 provides as its form of service a *logical link*. A logical link provides almost the same functionality as a virtual circuit but has the added feature that instead of controlling the rate of flow on a packet-by-packet basis, the user can exercise the option of having the flow control respond to "messages," i.e., groups of packets.

In the case of System Network Architecture (Chapter 11), the services provided to the higher protocol layer take the form of a *class of service* interface. A session desiring a connection providing particular properties (say low delay even if at the expense of bit rate), is mapped onto a combination of *virtual route* and *priority level* within that route. This class of service appearance is supported by several underlying functions that are different from those provided by the four other approaches described in Chapters 7 through 10 (fast circuit switch connection, virtual circuits, short message virtual circuit variants, and logical links.) For one thing, the physical route between intermediate nodes (a so-called *explicit route* onto which a virtual route is mapped) is fixed, not dynamically varying from message to message, as with DNA logical links; and there are a number of other differences.

An important issue in a network of any significant topological complexity is just this issue of routing. Fully dynamic routing may send successive packets by different routes as the load and the topology change with time. Dynamic routing has its advocates who argue their case on the basis of fast response to changes in topology, and the objective of keeping all lines as full of packets as possible for economic reasons. Fixed routing advocates argue that reliability is actually lost by doing this since, for one thing, accountability of message paths is lost, and this is required for managing failure recovery. Chapter 12 discusses these tradeoffs and the many specific algorithms proposed and in use for actually carrying out the node by node routing of messages in response to address information.

The last chapter in this section discusses the other big technical issue which, in addition to routing, enters most prominently into the design of the services provided to the higher protocol layers, namely, flow control. This is a large and confusing subject for the reason that, unlike routing, flow control crops up in different protocol layers, and, in fact, in any practical network there are to be found several different flow control mechanisms working more or less independently but concurrently. Since much of the flow control function is of a multinode character, we choose to include it in this section of the book.

Reduced to its simplest terms, flow control is simply a mechanism for adjusting the rate of flow of packets in some part of the network in an attempt to keep down the congestion of the end users and the resources within the network (for example lines or buffers) while at the same time keeping up their utilization so that they are not idle.

Much of the complication of flow control can be traced to multiplexing. If every line between adjacent nodes and every route between end nodes carried only one end-to-end message stream (i.e., if there were only one such stream active in the network at any one time) flow control could in principle be exerted at any point along the route. However, in practice every DLC protocol pair is carrying multiplexed traffic between several source and destination node pairs, and every X.25 virtual route, DNA logical link or SNA virtual route is carrying traffic for a multiplicity of higher-level protocol pairs. From this fact, one can appreciate that there is no one protocol layer at which flow control could be exerted completely; it must be exerted at several simultaneously and independently. For example, it would not do to have all the control only at the DLC level because some higher-level resource might be congested while the DLC buffers were not, and because if they did become congested, only one of the multiplexed streams might be at fault, and it is impossible to tell which one from DLC level information. Chapter 11 provides a flow control mechanism toxonomy based on an association of different mechanisms with different protocol layers and also discusses the performance of different schemes.

7

Circuit-Switched Network Layer

Harold C. Folts

I. Introduction

CCITT Recommendation X.21 has been developed as "The General Purpose Interface between Data Terminal Equipment (DTE) and Data Circuit-terminating Equipment (DCE) for Synchronous Operation on Public Data Networks" [1]. The only "general purpose" part, however, is the designation of the physical elements which include the electrical (X.26/X.27), functional (X.24), and mechanical (ISO 4903) characteristics described in Chapter 3 (Bertine). Additionally, the basic family of quiescent signals and states for the interface is specified. These provide the fundamental components of X.21 which will apply to all modes of operation in new data communications applications for circuit-switched, packet-switched, and general purpose integrated services [2].

The remainder of X.21 includes procedures for leased circuit service (both point-to-point and multipoint) and for circuit-switched services. In relation to the OSI Reference Model of the ISO architecture, discussed in Chapter 2, the leased circuit procedures are a specific application at the Physical Layer, while the circuit-switched procedures involve the Data Link Layer and the Network Layer. The focus of this paper will be on the Network Layer call establishment procedures of Recommendation X.21.

II. Background

Extensive activity by telecommunications administrations around the world is taking place implementing public data networks which will provide tailored data communication services to the user community. In recognition of this new evolution, the International Telegraph and Telephone Consultative Committee (CCITT) established a study program in 1968 by forming a Joint Working Party for New Data Networks (JWP/NRD) to set the basis for international standardization. In 1972, the resulting first X-series of Recommendations, including the original version of X.21, was approved by the Fifth CCITT Plenary Assembly. These Recommendations dealt primarily with circuit-switching technology.

To further refine and expand this work, CCITT then established Study Group VII, Public Data Networks. The main thrust of the work continued toward circuit switching with only a minor question directed toward the emerging packet-switching technology. In 1976, however, a major diversion in direction started to take place with the sudden appearance of the X.25 Virtual Call packet-switched service, described in Chapter 8.

As a result, the emphasis on the circuit switching in public data networks has been subsequently overshadowed by the fascination for packet-switching technology. This does not mean, however, that circuit switching has passed into oblivion, but circuit switching is, in fact, being actively pursued by the Nordic Countries (Sweden, Norway, Denmark, and Finland), Japan, the Federal Republic of Germany, Italy, Hungary, and Canada (Infoswitch). Experience and proven technology may very likely lead in the future to an expansion of circuit-switched services in public data networks.

III. Architecture

The architecture of Recommendation X.21 has been a subject of considerable misunderstanding and controversy in the ISO and CCITT work developing the OSI Reference Model, which was introduced in Chapter 2. While X.21 provides the essential physical elements of an interface, it also provides the circuit-switched network control procedures. Some have argued that these procedures are also within the Physical Layer because they result in the establishment of a physical circuit which is the used for data transfer.

By analyzing the X.21 call establishment procedures in comparison with the call establishment procedures of X.25, it will become clear that the basic functionality of each is identical. It is technically possible to use the X.21 call establishment for a packet-switched virtual circuit as well as to use the X.25 call establishment for a circuit-switched physical circuit. Both are Network Layer control procedures.

The necessity for consistent distribution of functionality among layers for all switched network services was set forth by the United States to ISO. This consistency is essential if the goal of a universal interface for integrated services is to be realized [2]. ISO has now endorsed this determination and includes the provisions at the Network Layer in the OSI Reference Model for establishment of connections through a switched network regardless of the implemented technology: circuit-switched for physical circuits or packet-switched for virtual circuits.

IV. CCITT **Recommendation X.21**

When work on Recommendation X.21 began in 1969, during the early days of JWP/NRD, it was recognized that use of any CCITT V-series interfaces (equivalent of RS-232-C and RS-366) would not be satisfactory for the new generation of digital public data networks. Therefore, an initial objective was established to develop a new interface that is compatible with advancing technology and tailored for circuit-switched networks providing full transparency (bit sequence and protocol independence) for the transfer of user data.

For call control purposes, use of International Alphabet Number 5 (IA5) was adopted to maintain consistency with the character-oriented data link layer basic mode control procedures of ISO 1745 and ANSI X3.28, discussed in Chapter 4. At the time, work on the new bit-oriented procedures described in Chapter 10 (ISO HDLC and ANSI ADCCP) was in its infancy.

The first version of X.21 approved by the CCITT Fifth Plenary Assembly in 1972, was little more than an outline of procedures. It was not complete enough at that time for practical implementation. During 1973–1976, however, substantive work was completed to produce a usable Recommendation [3]. This version was approved by the CCITT Sixth Plenary Assembly in 1976 and appears in the Orange Book [4].

Subsequently, work continued to further refine and expand the Recommendation, as well as to include adjustments resulting from implementation experience. The new version of X.21 was completed at the CCITT Study Group VII meeting in February 1980. In addition to significant technical and editorial enhancements, the new revision of X.21 has been completely reorganized to track with the work in developing the standard architecture for Open System Interconnection (OSI). The presentation in this paper will relate to the latest revision which was approved by the CCITT VIIth Plenary Assembly, November 1980 [1].

A. General Purpose Physical Layer

1. Basic Elements

The physical elements for X.21 as discussed in chapter 3 include application of the X.26 and X.27 electrical characteristics, together with

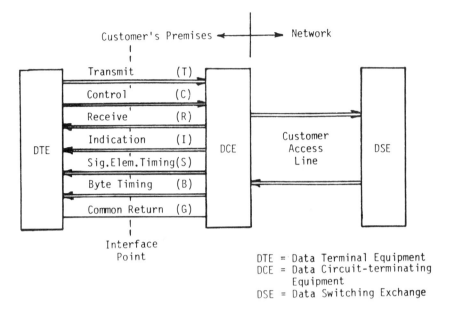

Fig. 1. X.21 interface.

functional circuits defined by X.24. The mechanical element of the interface
is the 15-pin connector specified by ISO 4903 which is from the same family
of connectors as the commonly known 25-pin connector used for RS-232-C
and the CCITT V-series interfaces. The physical configuration of the
DTE/DCE interface for X.21 consists of six circuits as shown in Fig. 1.

Circuits T and R convey data and control information, while circuits C
and I provide control functions similar to "OFF/ON hook" indications.
This simple out-of-band control provides an effective mechanism for maintaining full transparency during data transfer. Circuit S provides signal
element (bit) timing from the network, and optionally in some networks,
circuit B provides an octet byte alignment with the network.

2. Quiescent Phase Signals

The signals during the quiescent phase indicate the ability of the DTE
and the DCE to enter the operational phases such as the call control phase.
The two basic signals used indicate READY and NOT READY.

B. Circuit-Switching Procedures

For circuit-switched operation, X.21 defines four phases—quiescent,
call control, data transfer, and clearing. Within the phases there are a

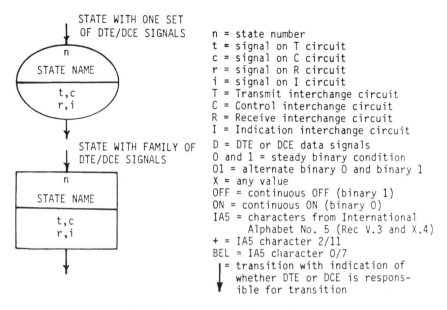

Fig. 2. Conventions for X.21 state diagrams.

number of states which are defined by the signals appearing on circuits *T*, *C*, *R*, and *I*. Each state is essentially a "snapshot" in time of the interface signals presented by the DTE and the DCE as described in Fig. 2. The interface procedures are then illustrated by state diagrams to present a coherent picture of the operations.

1. Data Link Layer Elements

X.21 does not support the full richness of the Data Link Layer functions of the OSI Reference Model but provides only the minimum necessary elements for basic operation. These include character synchronization and error detection.

As X.21 is intended for synchronous operation, the first Data Link Layer function provides for correct alignment of the IA5 character sequences used during the call control phase. The actual method of achieving character alignment was an issue of intense debate for several years [3], but was finally resolved in 1976. One proposal was to provide for character alignment as typically used for synchronous character-oriented operation. This provided for use of two or more contiguous SYN characters preceding each sequence of call control characters. The alignment for each direction of transmission would be independent. The other proposal was to use a separate byte alignment interchange circuit (circuit *B*, Fig. 1) from the DCE to the DTE. Circuit B provides the indication of the last bit of an 8-bit byte which represents an IA5 character with parity. The byte alignment information is used both to align characters received on circuit R and to align characters transmitted on circuit T. Each direction of transmission is then dependent on the byte alignment information provided by the network (DCE).

The compromise which resulted in agreement essentially recognized that either method of operation could be provided, but it requires two or more contiguous SYN characters to be present before each call control sequence in all cases, even when byte timing is provided by circuit B. Where byte alignment with the network is required, the DTE must still align transmitted call control characters to the synchronization of either circuit B, when used, or received SYN characters from circuit R.

This compromise now makes it practical to design a new DTE which can work with all X.21 network implementations where the provision is included in the DTE for alignment of transmitted characters to the synchronization of the received characters. The use of the byte timing circuit B, when offered by a network, then becomes a purely optional matter, and operation with a nonbyte aligned network is therefore possible.

Another provision of the compromise agreement allows ready adaptation of existing designs of synchronous character-oriented DTEs to X.21. This requires, for an intermediate period, that all networks accommodate convential SYN character alignment independent of direction of transmission. The intermediate period is to be determined by customer demand and other relevant factors as interpreted by the network provider.

The other Data Link Layer element of X.21 provides an elementary means of error checking using odd parity according to CCITT Recommendation X.4 [1]. Before the decision was made to employ parity, a thorough study was made as to how powerful an error control was needed. The conclusion showed that with the low error rates expected in public data networks, the use of parity is quite adequate and cost effective.

2. Network Layer Procedures

The character-oriented procedures used during the call control phase establish a connection to one or more distant subscribers through a circuit-switched public data network. To clearly define the procedures, a state diagram, Fig. 3, is used to show the relationship among the various call control phase states which are defined by the text. Only the recognized transitions among the states under normal operating conditions are shown by Fig. 3. As further clarification of the procedures, illustrative time sequence diagrams are also provided in the X.21 documentation. One of these examples is shown in Fig. 4.

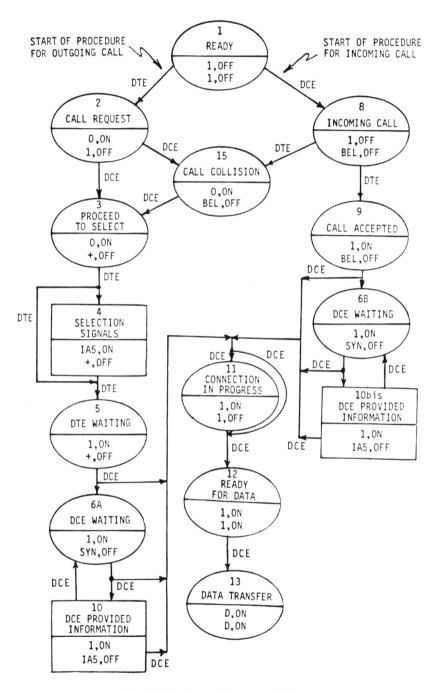

Fig. 3. State diagram for call establishment.

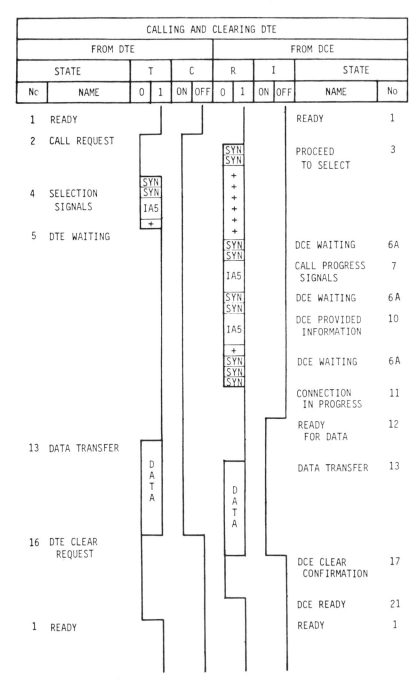

Fig. 4. Example of sequence of events: successful call and clear.

Call establishment can begin only from the READY state (state 1). Both the DTE and DCE must be READY before either INCOMING CALL (state 8) or CALL REQUEST (state 2) can be signaled across the interface. It was proposed that the DTE and DCE be allowed to enter the call establishment phase directly either from or toward a NOT READY state to allow more flexibility in operation. Some proposed network designs, however, precluded these additional state transitions.

The process for the calling DTE starts with the signaling of CALL REQUEST with $t = 0$ and $c = $ ON. The simple steady-state signal rather than a character sequence was used to alert the DCE of the request. As a result, only a minimum of intelligence for detection of the signal is needed. Next, in response to CALL REQUEST, the DCE signals PROCEED TO SELECT (state 3), $r = +$, $i = $ OFF.

It is possible for an INCOMING CALL and CALL REQUEST to be inadvertently signaled at the same time. Therefore the CALL COLLISION (state 15) has been included. There was considerable debate as to how a CALL COLLISION should be resolved. In following the principle of simplicity, only one means of resolution was desired. It was finally agreed that CALL REQUEST should always win because a DTE preparing for an outgoing call may not be able to readily reallocate its internal resources to handle an incoming call. Accordingly, the only exit transition from state 15 is toward PROCEED TO SELECT where the network continues to process the outgoing call and abandons the incoming call.

The DTE can then proceed with the SELECTION SIGNAL SEQUENCE for the specific call. During the SELECTION SIGNAL SEQUENCE, the DCE continues to signal $r = +$, $i = $ OFF, while the DTE sends a family of signals containing facility and address information. The formats for these signals are specified in detail in X.21 using the Backus Normal Form. For a simplistic description, Table I presents an example illustration of the format.

The FACILITY REQUEST enables selection of special service features for each call. It consists of a FACILITY REQUEST CODE followed by one or more FACILITY REQUEST PARAMETERS all separated by the "/" character. Multiple FACILITY REQUESTS are separated by "," characters. The last FACILITY REQUEST is ended with a "−" character. The list of recognized international facilities is given in CCITT Recommendation X.2, while the actual coding is specified in Annex 7 of X.21. A further discussion on optional user facilities is presented in a later section of this chapter.

The full address signals are in accordance with the format of the International Numbering Plan for public data networks of CCITT Recommendation X.121 [1]. ABBREVIATED ADDRESS signals can be used to represent, with a reduced number of characters, designated FULL ADDRESS signals as established by agreement with the specific network. A single ABBREVIA-

Table I. Simplified Example of Selection Signals

− = End of facility request
+ = End of selection signal
. = Beginning of abbreviated address
/ = Parameter separator
, = Facility request and address separator
Selection signal sequence = facility requests − addresses +
Facility requests = facility request code/facility parameter
  / ... / ...,... −
Addresses = full address signal,...,... or
  .abbreviated address signal,...,
   ... +
Facility registration or cancellation = facility request code/
    parameter/parameter/
    parameter − +

TED ADDRESS code may represent either a single address or a group of multiple addresses. Each ABBREVIATED ADDRESS signal is preceded by the "." character. Multiple FULL or ABBREVIATED ADDRESSs, which can be intermixed, are separated by "," characters. The last ADDRESS signal is followed by the "+" character as the "end of selection."

If there is no FACILITY REQUEST in the SELECTION SIGNAL SEQUENCE, the sequence will start immediately with the ADDRESS signals without any "−" character. If there is no ADDRESS signal, but there is a FACILITY REQUEST, the sequence is ended by the "−" followed by the "+" character.

As shown in Fig. 3, the SELECTION SIGNAL SEQUENCE may be bypassed. This provides for a direct calling feature similar to an "OFF-HOOK" or "hot line" service which may be used as either a fixed mode of operation or on a dynamic per-call basis. After receiving the PROCEED TO SELECT signal, the DTE signals DTE WAITING (state 5); then the DCE proceeds to establish a connection to a predesignated address or group of addresses. If the choice of direct call or addressed call is allowed dynamically on a per-call basis, the DTE can enter either state 5 or state 4 depending on the service desired.

Once the DCE has the request and necessary information to establish a connection through the network, the DCE signals $r = $ SYN, $i = $ OFF (state 6a) as it processes the call. If establishment of the call is successful, there will normally not be any CALL PROGRESS SIGNALS (state 7), and in the absence of any special facilities, there will not normally be any DCE PROVIDED INFORMATION (state 10).

Depending on how fast the connection is made, the DCE may bypass state 6a and proceed directly to CONNECTION IN PROGRESS (state 11) or READY FOR DATA (state 12). The difference will be whether the connection is made to a subscriber within the same switching center, the same network, or through an international connection to another network where the processing time would be greater. The procedure allows a great deal of flexibility in this respect.

The term CALL PROGRESS SIGNALS in state 7 is perhaps a misnomer because they primarily indicate the reasons for "nonprogress" or unsuccessful completion of the call. The CALL PROGRESS SIGNALS are defined by CCITT Recommendation X.96. The 1980 revision of X.96 has now established a great deal of commonality with the CALL PROGRESS SIGNAL definitions used for packet-switching operation. The coding for the two applications, however, are quite different. Figure 5 gives a list of the CALL PROGRESS SIGNALS applicable to X.21, together with the respective coding. Initially, a two-digit

CODE GROUP	CODE	SIGNIFICANCE	CATEGORY
0	00	RESERVED	WITHOUT CLEARING
	01	TERMINAL CALLED	
	02	REDIRECTED CALL	
	03	CONNECT WHEN FREE	
2	20	NO CONNECTION	WITH CLEARING DUE TO
	21	NUMBER BUSY	SHORT TERM CONDITIONS
	22	SELECTION SIGNALS PROCEDURE ERROR	
	23	SELECTION SIGNAL TRANSMISSION ERROR	
4&5	41	ACCESS BARRED	WITH CLEARING DUE TO LONG TERM CONDITIONS
	42	CHANGED NUMBER	
	43	NOT OBTAINABLE	
	44	OUT OF ORDER	
	45	CONTROLLED NOT READY	
	46	UNCONTROLLED NOT READY	
	47	DCE POWER OFF	
	48	INVALID FACILITY REQUEST	
	49	NETWORK FAULT IN LOCAL LOOP	
	51	CALL INFORMATION SERVICE	
	52	INCOMPATIBLE USER CLASS OF SERVICE	
6	61	NETWORK CONGESTION	WITH CLEARING DUE TO NETWORK SHORT TERM CONDITIONS
7	71	LONG TERM NETWORK CONGESTION	WITH CLEARING DUE TO NETWORK LONG TERM CONDITIONS
	72	RPOA OUT OF ORDER	
8	81	REGISTRATION/CANCELLATION CONFIRMED	WITH CLEARING DUE TO DTE-NETWORK PROCEDURE
	82	REDIRECTION ACTIVATED	
	83	REDIRECTION DEACTIVATED	

Fig. 5. Coding of call progress signals.

code is applied where the first digit indicates a general category of signal. This enables a relatively simple terminal to translate only the basic category of the CALL PROGRESS SIGNAL. The second digit indicates the more specific reason which can be translated by more intelligent terminals. In the future, it will be possible to expand the number of digits if further enrichment is needed.

The CALL PROGRESS SIGNAL SEQUENCE must be preceded by at least two "SYN" characters as described earlier for the character synchronization. These "SYN" characters will be sent during state 6a. If there is more than one block of signals, the period between them will be filled by additional "SYN" characters during state 6a.

In the 1976 issue [4] of X.21, state 10 was named CALLED LINE IDENTIFICATION. Further study, however, showed that more flexibility will be needed for future enhancements providing a family of signals that may be provided to the DTE from the network. Therefore, the name was changed to DCE PROVIDED INFORMATION. The only signal presently designated for state 10 is the original CALLED LINE IDENTIFICATION. In effect, CALL PROGRESS SIGNALS are really a subset of the more general DCE PROVIDED INFORMATION. This logically suggests a possible merger of states 7 and 10 for a simplification of the state diagram, which was done at the very last minute during the meeting of Study Group VII in February 1980 and therefore is part of the 1980 revised Recommendation.

While the above actions have been occurring at the calling DTE/DCE interface, the state diagram also shows the procedures unique at the called DTE/DCE interface in states 8, 9, and 10bis. The INCOMING CALL signal (state 8) with $r =$ BEL, $i =$ OFF is presented to a READY DTE where $t = 1$, $c =$ OFF. The DTE answers the call by signaling the steady-state conditions of $t = 1$, $c =$ ON for CALL ACCEPTED (state 9).

At this point, the network may wish to provide the called DTE additional information relating to the call (state 10bis). Similar to state 10 as earlier described, state 10bis was originally named CALLING LINE IDENTIFI-CATION in the previous version of X.21 [4], but further work has now changed the name to DCE PROVIDED INFORMATION. The new state 10bis includes the original CALLING LINE IDENTIFICATION and the new addition of CHARGING INFORMATION which will be described later. Consideration in the future will be given to further enhancing state 10bis to include additional capabilities such as subaddressing and a means for acceptance of reverse charging calls.

Another feature under future consideration will be a means for positive and negative acknowledgment of the DCE PROVIDED INFORMATION. As presently defined, negative acknowledgment due to error or rejection is only possible with a complete clearing of the call. It is felt that this may be too drastic where a simple retransmission could solve the problem.

Upon acceptance of the call, DCE WAITING (state 6b) is signaled. Then after at least two SYN characters being signaled in state 6b, DCE PROVIDED INFORMATION (state 10bis) may be signaled. As with state 6a, state 6b may be bypassed when connection time is very fast and no DCE PROVIDED INFORMATION will be sent.

The transition to states 11 and 12 is the process known as "connect-through" in the original version of X.21 in 1972. This was a issue of great confusion and debate which resulted in a carefully constructed agreement. The concerns were related to the danger of losing bits of user data and the possible presence of spurious bits during the "connect-through" process.

As the "connect-through" procedure is very complex to describe, the following extracted text from X.21 is presented to assist understanding:

All bits sent by a DTE after receiving READY FOR DATA and before sending DTE CLEAR REQUEST will be delivered to the corresponding DTE after that corresponding DTE has received READY FOR DATA and before it has received DCE CLEAR INDICATION (provided that the corresponding DTE does not take the initiative of CLEARING).

All bits received by a DTE after receiving READY FOR DATA and before receiving DCE CLEAR INDICATION or receiving DCE CLEAR CONFIRMATION were sent by the corresponding DTE. Some of those may have originated as DTE WAITING before that corresponding DTE has received READY FOR DATA; those bits are binary 1.

In effect, the result of the process of the transition on circuit R from "SYN" in state 6, or from "+" of state 5, to "1" of states 11 and 12 is the completion of the end-to-end connection. The "SYN" (or "+") is generated internally within the network, while the "1" originates from the distant DTE on circuit T and is carried through the network and presented to the local DTE on circuit R. Because the transition on circuit I may not be concurrent with the transition on circuit R, owing to network signaling differences, state 11 has been included but, as shown, may be bypassed. The significant state is READY FOR DATA (state 12) where a guaranteed transparent end-to-end path is established and ready for transfer of user data in state 13.

3. Clearing

In the proposed OSI Reference Model, a disconnection function is defined for each layer to terminate operational phases. In the case of X.25, there is a disconnection function at each of the first three layers, each of which serves a specific purpose. X.21, being a greatly simplified procedure for circuit-switched applications, does not provide for any disconnection function at either the Data Link or the Network Layers. Instead, the basic Physical Layer NOT READY functions of $t = 0$, $c =$ OFF, and $r = 0$, $i =$ OFF serve to terminate the operational phases of a call.

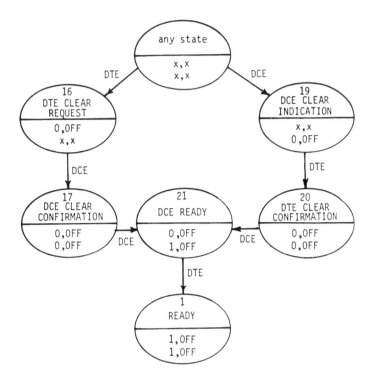

Fig. 6. Clearing phase.

Figure 6 shows the state diagram for clearing a circuit-switched connection and return to the READY state. Clearing can be initiated at any time by either the DTE or the DCE from any state in Fig. 3 except READY. A DTE initiates clearing by sending DTE CLEAR REQUEST (state 16) and the DCE responds with DCE CLEAR CONFIRMATION (state 17) followed at least 24 bit times later by DCE READY (state 21). The DCE initiates clearing by sending DCE CLEAR INDICATION (state 19), and the DTE responds with DTE CLEAR CONFIRMATION (state 20). The DCE then responds with DCE READY (state 21). In a normal clearing sequence, regardless of whether the DTE or the DCE initiates clearing, the DCE must first indicate DCE READY (state 21) $r = 1$, $i = $ OFF before the DTE can signal READY $t = 1$, $c = $ OFF to enter state 1. This was necessary due to the operation of the network signaling system in CCITT Recommendation X.60. Once READY (state 1) is reached, a new call can then be processed.

4. DTE Time-Limits and DCE Time-Outs

In order to detect error or fault situations and provide a recovery mechanism, a family of DTE time-limits and DCE time-outs has been specified. Each timer is started by a transition into a particular state. For normal operation within the specified time, the timer stops when the designated next state is entered. If the timer expires before the recognized normal transition, then a recovery action can be initiated. As a result, lock-up or endless loop operations are avoided so when the problem clears, normal operation can resume.

It should be noted that these time-outs and time-limits are not an indication of typical response times, but are used to determine when most probably a failure in operation has occurred in either the DTE or DCE. Much faster response times under normal operation are expected for efficient network operation.

5. Optional User Facilities

There are a number of optional user facilities (special service features) defined for circuit-switched service by CCITT Recommendation X.2. These may be selected on a per-call basis by a facility request in the SELECTION SIGNAL SEQUENCE. A list of these facilities is given in Table II.

The Closed User Group provides for communication only among a designated group of subscribers. A subscriber may belong to more than one such group, and therefore, a calling DTE must then designate to which group the subscriber being called belongs. A particular closed user group can be designated by the DTE as preferential to enable the network to process a call to the requested called subscriber in the preferential group without having to receive a facility request. Calls within nonpreferential groups would then need a facility request to specify the applicable closed user group desired.

Multiple Address Calling is allowed for circuit-switched service. This enables establishment of conference or broadcast types of communication. Additionally a centralized multipoint connection can be arranged on an addressed call basis.

Table II. Optional User Facilities

Closed user group
Multiple address calling
Charge advice
Calling line identification
Called line identification
DTE inactive
Redirection of call
Abbreviated addressing
Direct call
Facility registration/cancellation

Charge Advice is a new facility established to provide a calling DTE with the charging information related to an immediately preceding call. Upon clearing of a call for which the charge advice has been requested by a facility request, the network will, within 200 ms, return the charging information to the DTE by means of an INCOMING CALL (state 8). When the call is accepted by the DTE (state 9), the DCE will provide the charging information in state 10bis. At the present time, there is no generalized error recovery defined if the DTE fails to receive the information correctly. One means under consideration is to repeat the information two or more times or until the DTE clears.

Called Line Identification can be requested by a DTE on a per-call basis so the network will verify the called number during state 10. Additionally, Calling Line Identification can be provided on a continuing basis to called DTEs as part of state 10 bis. This feature is intended to facilitate screening of incoming calls by a DTE to avoid unauthorized access.

A new facility to appear in X.21 is the DTE Inactive facility. It would be invoked when a subscriber is to be out of operation for a period of time. The DTE would notify the network of certain information indicating the reason and when normal operation will resume. The network would forward this information to a calling DTE through the DCE PROVIDED INFORMATION state 10. The detailed formats and procedures for this facility will be further developed between 1981 and 1984.

Another facility that has been defined is Redirection of Call. This enables a subscriber to have incoming calls rerouted to an alternate number when desired, such as during nonbusiness hours. Other facilities that are also included in X.2 for circuit-switching service are Abbreviated Addressing and Direct Call. These have been discussed in detail earlier.

Facilities can be initiated on a per-call basis using a facility request or continuously on a subscription basis. Additionally, there is a procedure defined where a DTE can dynamically change or modify a particular facility. This is the Facility Registration/Cancellation procedure. It can be applied to reallocate or change full X.121 addresses for assigned abbreviated address codes. It can also be used to add and delete subscribers from closed user groups.

6. Test Loops

The new CCITT Recommendation X.150 has been developed to define a family of test loops to assist in the location of faults in an interconnection. These are shown in Fig. 7.

The DTE test loop 1 is implemented in the DTE and is under the full control of the DTE.

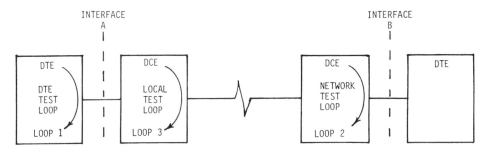

Fig. 7. Test loops.

The local test loop 3 types are located in the DCE and provides a loop toward the DTE. This enables the DTE to verify the operation of the DTE/DCE interface. Loop 3 can only be activated by a switch on the DCE, although a means for automatic activation across the interface is being studied.

Finally, network test loop 2 types are implemented in the DCE and provide a loop toward the network. This can also be activated manually by a switch on the DCE. A provisional procedure was proposed for use in some networks but was rejected before the new version of X.21 got approved. Automatic activation of loops through the network is very controversial with many of the nations and will probably not be universally agreed on.

V. Future Evolution

As circuit-switched networks commence operation, practical experience will be gained as to the efficacy of this technology for data communications applications. As a result, the question can then be answered within the next few years as to whether an efficient, fast circuit-switched operation will prove to be more effective than the popularized packet-switched service of X.25 for a number of applications.

One significant issue that must be dealt with in future work is the convergence toward common protocols to satisfy all modes of operation. It is not a practical matter on a continuing basis to have two very different protocols satisfying identical functions, i.e., X.21 call establishment and X.25 call establishment. As the general purpose physical elements of X.21 become the established universal Physical Layer interface for all data communications applications in the future, universal Data Link and Network Layer protocols should also be established accordingly. HDLC (AD-CCP) appears appropriate for the Data Link Layer, but considerable study remains to be done for establishment of a universal Network Layer standard [2].

References

[1] CCITT Yellow Books, CCITT Seventh Plenary Assembly, Vols. VII.2 and VII.3, November 1980, Geneva, Switzerland.
[2] H. C. Folts, "Evolution toward a universal interface for data communications," in Proceedings on International Conference of Computer Communications, Kyoto, Japan, Sep. 1978, pp. 675–680.
[3] H. C. Folts, "X.21—The international interface for new synchronous data networks," in Conference Record of the International Conference on Communications, IEEE, Vol. 1, San Francisco, June 1975, pp. 15–19.
[4] H. C. Folts and H. R. Karp, Eds., McGraw-Hill's Compilation of Data Communications Standards. New York: McGraw-Hill, 1978.

8

Packet-Switched Network Layer

Antony Rybczynski

I. Introduction and General Description

A. Introduction

The 1970s heralded the beginning of the development of public networks either in the form of experimental networks (e.g., France: RCP, U.K: EPSS) or commercial networks (e.g., Canada: Datapac, U.S.A: Telenet). The basis of all of these networks was the belief that packet switching was an appropriate technology for public data networks (PDNs). However, in their embryonic stages, the designs of each of these networks incorporated substantially different terminal access procedures for both host computers and slow speed character terminals. It was recognized that the commercial viability of these networks hinged largely on the development and adoption of standard access protocols. These standards would facilitate the connection of varying types of data terminal equipments (DTEs) to the various public networks being developed as well as facilitate international internetworking.

The International Telegraph and Telephone Consultative Committee (CCITT), a permanent organ of the International Telecommunications Union, is responsible for establishing Recommendations applicable to various aspects of international communications, including public data networks. A number of Recommendations related to PDN services have been approved within the last six years, most notably X.25 for packet-mode DTEs accessing packet-switching PDNs. Without these standards, users would almost definitely not be benefiting from the establishment of public data networks on a worldwide basis.

The year 1980 found us with PDNs offering X.25 packet-mode services being available in the U.S.A., Canada, the U.K., France, and Japan and on the verge of being established in a large number of other countries [1]. Furthermore, international services have already been established among a number of these countries. In order to meet the market need of gaining access to X.25 services, a number of mainframe and terminal manufacturers have announced products supporting X.25.

CCITT Recommendation X.25 was first approved in March 1976. The next formal revision took place in 1977 with the addition of data link control procedures that are compatible with the High-level Data Link Control (HDLC) procedures standardized by the International Organization of Standardization (ISO). The last formal revision of X.25 took place in the Fall of 1980. This paper conveys the important enhancements to X.25 which have been agreed upon and are currently contained in the text of the revised Recommendation.

B. General Description of X.25 Interface

CCITT Recommendation X.25 is titled: "Interface between Data Terminal Equipment (DTE) and Data Circuit-terminating Equipment (DCE) for Terminals Operating in the Packet Mode on Public Data Networks." However, applying the concepts of the standard layer model introduced in Chapter 1, X.25 is not strictly speaking an interface. In fact, X.25 is a set of three peer protocols as follows (see Fig. 1):

1. a peer protocol between Physical Level entities in the DTE and the DCE;
2. a peer protocol between Link Control Level entities in the DTE and the network node; and
3. a peer protocol between Packet-Switched Network Level entities in the DTE and the network node.

Each of these levels functions independently of the other levels, with the exception that failures at a level may affect the operation of higher levels.

The Physical Level specifies the use of a duplex, point-to-point synchronous circuit, thus providing a physical transmission path between the DTE and the Network. It also specifies the use of Recommendation V.24 (i.e., the EIA RS-232-C standard) between the DTE and a data set or modem. Therefore, no changes to the communications hardware of the DTE are required. The Physical Level also specifies the use of Recommendation X.21 though this capability is not yet widely available. Physical level protocols have been discussed in Chapter 3.

The Link Control Level specifies the use of data link control procedures which are compatible with HDLC and with the Advanced Data Communications Control Procedure (ADCCP) standardized by the U.S.

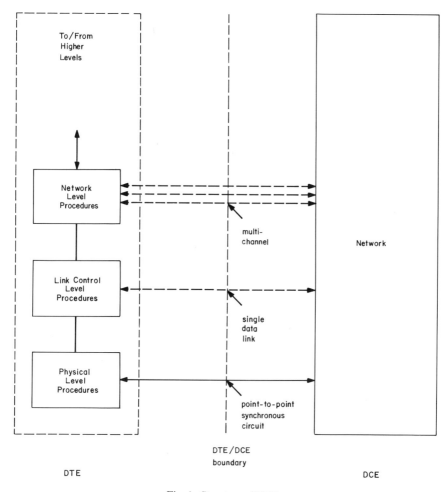

Fig. 1. Structure of X.25.

American National Standards Institute (ANSI) (see Chapter 5). The Link Control Level uses the principles of an ISO Class of Procedures for a point-to-point balanced system; in X.25, these procedures are referred to as the Balanced Link Access Procedures (LAPB). The use of this data link control procedure ensures that packets provided by the Packet-Switched Network Level and contained in HDLC information frames (see Fig. 2) are accurately exchanged between the DTE and the Network. The functions performed by the Link Control Level include

1. the transfer of data in an efficient and timely fashion;
2. the synchronization of the link to ensure that the receiver is in step with the transmitter;

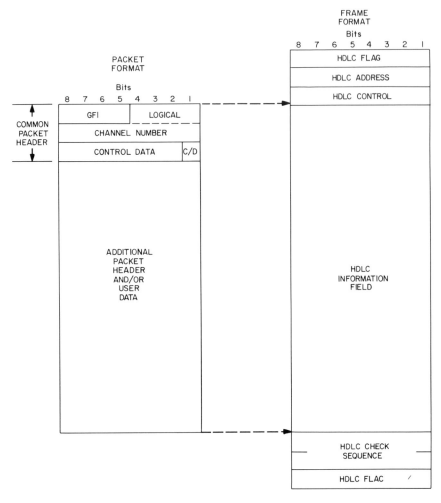

Fig. 2. General X.25 packet and frame formats. GFI, General Format Identifier; C/D-0 for user DATA packet, 1 for control packet.

3. the detection of transmission errors and recovery from such errors; and

4. the identification and reporting of procedural errors to higher layers for recovery.

The major significance of the Link Control Level is that it provides the Packet-Switched Network Level with an error-free, variable delay link between the DTE and the Network. The Packet-Switched Network Level is the highest level in X.25 and specifies the manner in which control information and user data are structured into Network Protocol Data Units called packets. The control information, including addressing information, is contained in the packet header field and allows the network to identify the DTE for which the packet is destined. It also allows a single physical circuit to support communications to numerous other DTEs concurrently.

The characteristics of the Packet-Switched Network Level Peer Protocol are further described in Section III.

C. Packet-Switched Network Level Services Available to X.25 DTEs

A distinction must be made between the X.25 access protocol and the Network Level services provided on a PDN operating in the packet mode and accessed by the DTE via X.25. Recommendation X.25 defines a set of three peer protocols to be used between the packet-mode DTE and the common-carrier equipment, generally referred to as the DCE. The X.25 Recommendation provides access to the following Network services that may be provided on public data networks:

1. switched virtual circuits (SVCs), also called virtual calls;
2. permanent virtual circuits (PVCs); and
3. datagrams.

A *virtual circuit* (VC) is a bidirectional transparent, flow-controlled path between a pair of logical or physical ports. A *switched virtual circuit* is a temporary association between two DTEs and is initiated by a DTE signaling a call request to the network. A *permanent virtual circuit* is a permanent association existing between two DTEs which does not require call setup or call clearing action by the DTE.

A *datagram* (DG) is a self-contained user data unit containing sufficient information to be routed to the destination DTE (independently of all other data units) without the need for a call to be established. At this time, the datagram service is not provided on any PDNs. This service is described in the next chapter.

The characteristics of virtual circuits are now presented.

II. X.25 End-to-End Virtual Circuit Service Characteristics

A. Introduction

The Network Level virtual circuit service characteristics are currently specified in a nonsystematic way in various sections of Recommendation X.25. This section attempts to consolidate the specification of VC characteristics. The perspective for this discussion is a view of the DTE-to-DTE services provided by VCs rather than a view of the signaling performed between the DTE and the network.

B. Establishment and Clearing of a Virtual Circuit

A switched virtual circuit is established when the call request issued by the calling DTE is accepted by the called DTE (see Fig. 3). A permanent virtual circuit is always established and therefore no establishment procedures are required. The call request identifies the called and calling addresses and facilities requested for the call, and may include user data. The user data sent during the call establishment phase is available for use by the higher layers (e.g., system passwords).

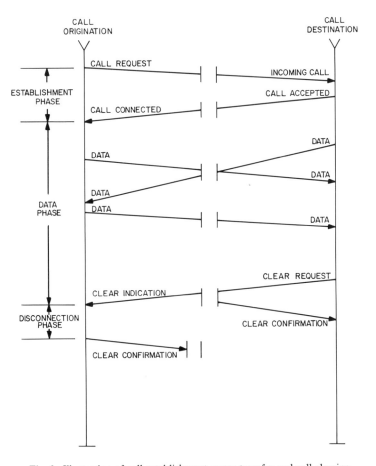

Fig. 3. Illustration of call establishment, DATA transfer and call clearing.

During the call establishment phase, the calling DTE may request certain optional user facilities (e.g., reverse charging) to be associated with the VC. In some cases (e.g., throughput class) the called DTE may wish to alter the facility values requested by the caller. Thus, the VC service provides mechanisms for facility negotiations during call setup. Optional user facilities are discussed in Section IV.

If the call is refused by the called DTE, the DTE can signal the reason for call clearing to the calling DTE in a diagnostic code. If the call attempt fails for some other reason, a call progress signal is transmitted across the network indicating one of the causes specified in X.25 and given in Table I. As will be seen in the next section, the diagnostic code is also used by the network to provide extra information to the DTE when it has made a local procedure error. This latter use is a characteristic of the X.25 Network Level protocol rather than of the virtual circuit itself.

Once the call has entered the data transfer phase, either DTE can clear the call using the diagnostic code to signal to the remote DTE the reason for the clearing. If the call is cleared by the network, it will signal this fact and indicate a call progress signal (Table I). When a call is cleared, data may be discarded by the network since the clear is not sequenced in respect to user data. All data generated by the DTE before initiation of a clear procedure will either be delivered to the remote DTE before completion of the clearing procedure at the remote DTE, or be discarded by the network. When a DTE initiates a clear, all data which were generated by the remote DTE before it has received the corresponding indication will be either delivered to the initiating DTE before the clear procedure is completed locally, or discarded by the network.

C. Data Transfer

In the data transfer phase, user data which are conveyed in DATA and INTERRUPT packets are passed transparently through the network. DTEs wishing universal operation on all networks should transmit all packets with data fields containing only an integral number of octets.

Virtual circuit flow control is a mechanism provided to ensure that the transmitting DTE does not generate data at a rate that is faster (on average) than that which the receiving DTE can accept. This is achieved by the receiving DTE controlling the rate at which it accepts DATA packets, noting that there is an upper limit on the number of DATA packets which may be in the network on a virtual circuit. Thus, flow control has end-to-end significance in that back-pressure exerted by a receiving DTE is reflected back to the sending DTE.

A considerable debate has taken place in the past on whether the DTE or the network should determine the maximum number of DATA packets

Table I. Clearing Call Progress Signals

Call progress signal	Explanation
DTE Originated	Called DTE has refused the call or remote DTE has cleared it.
Number busy	The called DTE is engaged in other calls and cannot accept the incoming call.
Out of order	The remote number is out of order. (X.25 Physical and/or Link Control Levels not in operation.)
Remote procedure error	An X.25 procedure error has occurred at the remote DTE/network boundary.
Reverse charging acceptance not subscribed[a]	Network has blocked the call because the called DTE does not accept reverse charged calls.
Incompatible destination	The remote DTE does not support a user or facility requested.
Fast select acceptance not subscribed[a]	The network has blocked the call because the called DTE does not support fast select calls.
Invalid facility request	Facility request invalid (e.g., a request for a facility which has not been subscribed to or is not available in the local network).
Access barred	The calling DTE is not permitted the connection to the called DTE (e.g., incompatible closed user group).
Local procedure error	A procedure error is detected at the local DTE/network boundary (e.g., incorrect format, expiration of a time-out).
Network congestion	Temporary network congestion or a temporary fault condition has occurred within the network.
Not obtainable	Called number not assigned.
RPOA Out of Order[a]	The RPOA nominated by the calling DTE is unable to forward the call.

[a]Received only if the corresponding facility is requested by the caller.

which may be in the network on a virtual circuit. On the one hand, there is a need for the network to assign resources to the VC based on information available to it (e.g., call routing) and on performance, specifically throughput, characteristics associated with the service. In this case, the network determines the maximum number of DATA packets that can be on a VC and the DTE need not be concerned with this aspect. On the other hand, there is

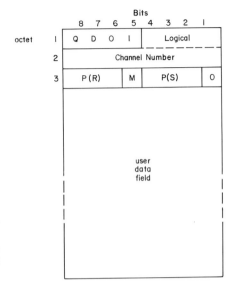

Fig. 4. DATA packet format. Q = data qualifier bit; D = delivery confirmation bit; M = more data bit; $P(S)$ = packet send sequence number; $P(R)$ = packet receive sequence number.

a need to allow DTEs to select the maximum number of DATA packets that can be on a VC and thus be able to ascertain whether certain DATA packets have been delivered to the remote DTE. This information can be used in conjunction with a higher level DTE-to-DTE error control protocol. With the addition of the Delivery Confirmation procedure in X.25, both objectives can be met simultaneously.

It has been agreed that DTE-to-DTE acknowledgment of delivery be available as a standard characteristic of X.25 virtual circuits. Specifically, if a DTE wishes to receive end-to-end acknowledgment for data it is transmitting, it uses an indicator called the Delivery Confirmation or D bit contained in the header of DATA packets (see Fig. 4). The D bit is always associated with the last octet in the DATA packet in which it is set by the DTE; this relationship is preserved by the network on an end-to-end basis even when the maximum packet lengths by the DTEs at each end of a VC are not the same. The acknowledgment is signaled via the packet receive sequence number $P(R)$, discussed in Section III.

If a DTE does not wish to receive end-to-end acknowledgment for data it is transmitting, it sets the D bit to zero. In this case, the network determines the maximum number of DATA packets which it is willing to accept bearing in mind the throughput requirements of the communicating DTEs.

The enhancement of X.25 by the addition of the Delivery Confirmation procedure increases the robustness of virtual circuits by providing a DTE-to-DTE acknowledgment scheme. The communicating DTEs can maintain strict control on the amount of unconfirmed data, thus facilitating error recovery in the event of failure.

Since the network may perform packet-length conversion, X.25 defines a "complete packet sequence" which is a sequence of DATA packets which may be combined by the network. The only DATA packets which can be combined with subsequent DATA packets are those that are full, have the D bit set to zero, and have an indication set by the sending DTE that More Data is to follow (see Fig. 4); the D bit has priority over the More Data Indication in packet combination so that a DATA packet with the D bit set to one is never combined with a subsequent packet. The More Data Indication may only be set by the DTE in full DATA packets or in partially full DATA packets which also have the D bit set to one. A sequence of DATA packets each carrying a More Data Indication except for the last one will be delivered as an equivalent sequence of DATA packets.

Two independent mechanisms are provided to transfer user control information between a pair of DTEs outside the normal flow of data on a VC. The first mechanism transfers user control data within the normal flow control and sequencing procedures on a virtual circuit. This is called the Data Qualifier procedure, uses the Q bit, and applies to "complete packet sequences."

The second mechanism bypasses the normal DATA packet transmission sequence and provides an out of band (nonsequenced) signaling channel on VCs. The INTERRUPT packet, which is used in this case, may contain one octet of user data and is always delivered at or before the point in the stream of DATA packets at which it was generated, even when DATA packets are being flow controlled.

The maximum attainable throughput of a virtual circuit may vary due to the statistical sharing of transmission and switch resources and is constrained by

1. the access line speed, local flow control parameters, and traffic on other calls at the local DTE/network boundary;
2. the access line speed, local flow control parameters, and traffic on other calls at the remote DTE/network boundary; and
3. the maximum throughput achievable through the network independent of access line characteristics. This limit may differ for national and varying types of international calls.

The above throughput will generally be reached if: (a) the DTE access data links of both ends of the VC are traffic engineered properly, (b) the receiving DTE is not flow controlling the DCE, and (c) the transmitting DTE is sending DATA packets which have the maximum data field length. In addition, excessive use of the D bit will constrain VC throughput since, in this case, the rate of packet transfer will be determined by the rate of packet delivery confirmation by the receiving DTE.

D. Error Recovery

The reset procedure is used to reinitialize the virtual circuit and in so doing removes in each direction all user data which may be in the network. When the reset is initiated by the DTE, it may convey to the remote DTE the reason for the resetting via a diagnostic code. If it is a network-generated reset, the reason is conveyed to both DTEs. Table II lists call progress signals associated with resetting in X.25.

All data generated by a DTE before initiation of a reset with either be delivered to the remote DTE before the corresponding indicator, or discarded by the network; all data generated after local completion of a reset procedure will be delivered after completion of the corresponding reset procedure at the remote end. When a DTE initiates a reset procedure, all data which were generated by the remote DTE before its receipt of the corresponding indication are either delivered to the initiating DTE before the procedure is completed locally, or discarded by the network. Multiple and simultaneous resets are handled at the local interface as defined by the procedures for single resets.

The maximum number of packets which may be discarded when the clearing or resetting procedure has been invoked is a function of network

Table II. Resetting Call Progress Signals

Call progress signal	Explanation
DTE Originated	Remote DTE reset the VC
Out of order (PVC only)	The remote DTE is out of order (e.g., X.25 Physical and/or Link Control Levels not in operation).
Remote procedure error	The call is cleared because of a procedure error at the remote DTE/network boundary.
Local procedure error	A procedure error is detected at the local DTE/network boundary (e.g., incorrect format, expiration of a time-out).
Network congestion	Temporary network congestion or temporary fault condition has occurred within the network.
Remote DTE operational (PVC only)	Remote DTE is ready to resume normal operation after a temporary failure or out of order condition.
Network operational (PVC only)	Network is ready to resume normal operation after a temporary failure or congestion.
Incompatible destination	The remote DTE does not support a function used.

end-to-end delay and network resources assigned in conjunction with the provided throughput. The maximum number of packets with the D bit set is a parameter of an X.25 interface (i.e., the local DTE transmit window size discussed in Section III D).

III.   X.25 Packet-Switched Network Peer Protocol Characteristics

A. Introduction

Recommendation X.25 specifies the peer protocol to be used by DTEs in establishing, maintaining, and clearing virtual circuits. This section now discusses this packet-switched network level protocol.

Packet Formats for the various types of packets are introduced during the discussion, while Table III summarizes the usage of various packet fields.

B. Multiplexing at the X.25 Interface

In order to allow a DTE to establish concurrent virtual circuits with a number of DTEs over a single physical access circuit, the X.25 Packet-Switched Network Level employs packet-interleaved Statistical Multiplexing. This multiplexing technique is used to exploit the fact that a typical virtual circuit to a remote DTE may actually be carrying data for only a

Table III. Usage of X.25 Packet Fields[a]

Packet type	Common[b]	Cause	Diagnostic	Addresses and address length	Facilities and facility length	Data
CALL REQUEST	REQ	—	—	REQ	REQ	OPT (16)
CALL CONNECTED	REQ	—	—	OPT	OPT	—
DATA	REQ	—	—	—	—	OPT (128)
INTERRUPT	REQ	—	—	—	—	REQ (1)
RR/RNR	REQ	—	—	—	—	—
RESET/CLEAR RESTART REQUEST	REQ	REQ	OPT	—	—	—
INTERRUPT/ RESET/CLEAR/ RESTART CONFIRMATION	REQ	—	—	—	—	—

[a] REQ: required; REQ (X): required, of maximum length X octets; OPT: Optional (only if all subsequent optional fields are not present); OPT (X): optional, of maximum length X octets; —: not applicable.
[b] Three octet Common Packet Header Field.

small percentage of the time. Each packet contains a logical channel number which identifies the packet with a switched or permanent virtual circuit, for both directions of transmission.

A *logical channel* is a conceptual access path between a DTE and the network. A logical channel, when not in use, can be dynamically assigned for a new call either originated by the local DTE or by a remote DTE. A logical channel, assigned to a call, is busy until the call is cleared. Logical channels can be viewed as analogous to dial ports in a conventional timesharing network.

The range of logical channel numbers that can be used for virtual circuits is established at subscription time by agreement between the DTE and the network.* If the DTE can only support a single VC, then logical channel number one will be used. If both PVCs and SVCs are used, then individual PVCs are statically assigned logical channel numbers in a range starting from number one, while logical channels for calls are assigned a range above this. Logical channel numbers for SVCs are dynamically assigned during call establishment and identify all packets (i.e., control and data) associated with the VC. The logical channel numbers are only significant for a particular DTE.

Every packet consists of a three octet common packet header field as shown in Fig. 2.

C. Establishing and Clearing a Virtual Circuit

A signaling method is provided to allow a DTE to establish switched virtual circuits to other DTEs, using logical channel numbers at each end to locally designate these switched virtual circuits.

A DTE initiates a call by sending a CALL REQUEST packet, Fig. 5, to the Network. The CALL REQUEST packet includes the logical channel number chosen by the DTE to be used to identify all packets associated with the call. It also includes the network address of the called DTE. A facility field (to be discussed in Section IV) is present only when the DTE wishes to request an optional user facility requiring some indication at call setup. Reverse charging is an example of such a facility. User data may follow the facility field and may contain up to a maximum of 16 octets.

The calling DTE will receive a CALL CONNECTED packet as a response indicating that the called DTE has accepted the call (Fig. 6).

If the call is refused by the called DTE or if the attempt fails, the calling DTE will receive a CLEAR INDICATION (Fig. 7) indicating the ap-

---

*Datagrams (see Chapter 9) are defined in X.25 as being carried on a datagram logical channel assigned at subscription time; this allows concurrent support for datagrams and VCs.

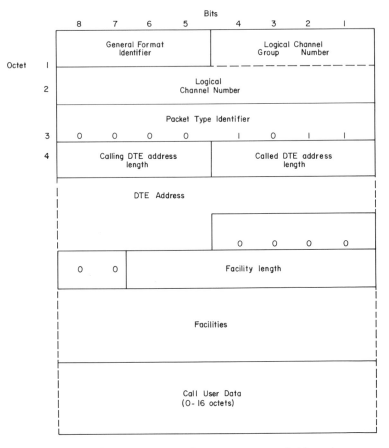

Fig. 5. CALL REQUEST and INCOMING CALL packet format.

propriate call progress signal, and a one octet diagnostic field, generated by the DTE and by the network in the former and latter cases, respectively.

Call clearing once the call enters the data phase, may be initiated by either DTE (or by the network in case of failure).

In any event, the logical channel number can be used again for another call when the clearing procedure is completed, normally by the transfer of a CLEAR CONFIRMATION packet. The CLEAR CONFIRMATION packet is three octets long and identifies the logical channel for which the clear procedures is completed.

Figure 8 illustrates the signaling and states associated with call setup and clearing on a particular logical channel.

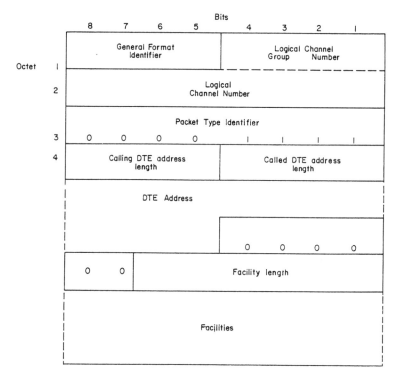

Fig. 6. CALL ACCEPTED and CALL CONNECTED packet format.

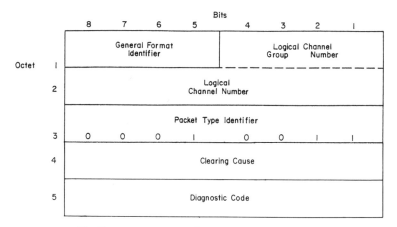

Fig. 7. CLEAR REQUEST and CLEAR INDICATION packet format.

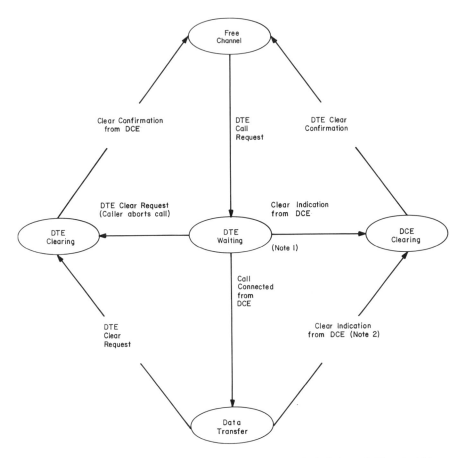

Fig. 8. Illustration of call establishment and clearing over a logical channel. Note 1: Either called DTE refused call or call attempt has failed. Note 2: Either called DTE cleared down call or call cleared due to network failure (reason signaled as call progress signal).

D. Data Transfer

DATA packets, illustrated in Fig. 4, can only be transferred across a logical channel, after the virtual circuit has been established and if flow control constraints are not violated.

$P(S)$ is the packet send sequence number of the packet. Only DATA packets are numbered, the numbering normally being performed modulo 8. The maximum number of sequentially numbered DATA packets that the DTE (or DCE) may be authorized to transmit, without further authorization from the network (or DTE), may never exceed seven. The actual maximum value, called the window size W, is set for the logical channel either at subscription time or at call setup time (using the facility described in Section IV B 2). The default value for W is 2.

Each DATA packet also carries a packet receive sequence number, $P(R)$, which authorizes the transmission of W DATA packets on this logical channel starting with a send sequence number equal to the value of $P(R)$. If the DTE or the network wishes to authorize the transmission of one or more DATA packets, but there is no data flow on a given logical channel in the reverse direction on which to piggyback this information, it can transmit a RECEIVE READY (RR) packet. If, on the other hand, the DTE or the network wishes to confirm the acceptance of a DATA packet with the D bit set to one, but does not wish to authorize the transmission of any more data, it can transmit a RECEIVE NOT READY (RNR) packet. RR and RNR packets are three octets long and identify the logical channel number and a $P(R)$ value. Flow control based on the conveyance of $P(R)$ numbers across a logical channel ensures that a sending DTE does not transmit data at an average rate which is greater than that at which the receiving DTE can accept that data.

The data field of a DATA packet may be any length up to some maximum value. The latter may be established independently at each end of a virtual circuit. Every network will support a maximum value of 128 octets.

When the Delivery Confirmation or D bit is set to zero, the $P(R)$ number is used to locally convey flow control information. When the D bit in Fig. 4 is set to one, the corresponding $P(R)$ is used to convey delivery confirmation information and therefore has DTE-to-DTE significance.

For example, if the D bit is set to one in a DATA packet numbered p [i.e., $P(s) = p$] which it is transmitting, then a $P(R)$, which is received in a DATA, RR, or RNR packet and is greater than or equal to $p + 1$, confirms acceptance by the remote DTE of the DATA packet. The receiving DTE indicates acceptance of a DATA packet with the D bit set to one by transmitting the corresponding $P(R)$ value to the Network.

In order to allow two communicating DTEs to each operate at their locally selected packet sizes, the user may indicate, in a full DATA packet or any DATA packet with the D bit set to one, that there is a logical continuation of his data in the next DATA packet on a particular logical channel. This is done with the More Data "M" bit contained in the DATA packet header as indicated in Fig. 4. Only a full DATA packet may have a More Data indication since a partially full packet is treated as if it had the M bit off.

Table IV defines the network treatment of DATA packets with various settings of the M and D bits.

The procedures used in conjunction with the Data Qualifier procedure are identical to those that apply to DATA packets. The format used in this procedure is identical to that of the DATA transfer packet except that the "Q" bit is set in the DATA packet header (see Fig. 4).

Table IV. Treatment of DATA Packets with *M* and *D* Bits

Data packet sent by source DTE			Combining with subsequent packet(s) is performed by the network when possible	Data packet[a] received by destination DTE	
M	*D*	Full		*M*	*D*
0 or 1	0	No	No	0	0
0	1	No	No	0	1
1	1	No	No	1	1
0	0	Yes	No	0	0
0	1	Yes	No	0	1
1	0	Yes	Yes[b]	1	0
1	1	Yes	No	1	1

[a]Refers to the delivered data packet whose last bit of user data corresponds to the last bit of user data, if any, that was present in the data packet sent by the source DTE.

[b]*Note*: If the data packet sent by the source DTE is combined with other packets, the *M* and *D* bit settings in the data packet received by the destination DTE will be according to that given in the two right-hand columns for the last data packet sent by the source DTE that was part of the combination.

INTERRUPT packets (Fig. 9), on the other hand, may be transmitted by the DTE even when DATA packets are being flow controlled. They contain neither send nor receive sequence numbers. Only one unconfirmed INTERRUPT may be outstanding at a given time.

E. Error Recovery

1. Reset Procedure

The reset procedure is used to reinitialize the flow control procedure on a given logical channel to the state it was in when the virtual circuit was established (i.e., all sequence numbers equal to zero and no data in transit). To reach this state, all DATA and INTERRUPT packets which may be in transit at the time of resetting are discarded. RESET REQUEST and RESET CONFIRMATION packets are used in the reset procedure.

2. Restart Procedure

The restart procedure provides a mechanism to recover from major failures. The issuance of a RESTART REQUEST packet is equivalent to sending a CLEAR REQUEST on all logical channels for switched virtual circuits and a

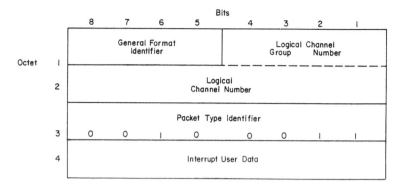

Fig. 9. INTERRUPT packet format.

RESET REQUEST on all logical channels for permanent virtual circuits. Thus, the restarting procedure will bring the DTE and the Network to the state they were in when service was initiated.

3. Error Handling

Recommendation X.25 (1976) laid the groundwork for further study on how packet level errors were to be handled at the X.25 interface. The following principles were established:

1. procedural errors during call establishment and clearing are reported to the DTE by clearing the call;
2. procedural errors during the data transfer phase are reported to the DTE by resetting the VC;
3. a diagnostic field is included in the reset packet to provide additional information to the DTE;
4. timers are essential in resolving some deadlock conditions;
5. some DTE procedural errors are a result of the DTE and DCE not being aligned as to the subscription options provided at the interface; and
6. rudimentary error tables define the action of the DCE on receiving various packet types in various states of the interface.

Several important error conditions were still not covered. Consequently, a major effort was expended to expand the error tables in X.25, to reach agreement on timeout strategies, and to increase the amount of information provided to DTEs via diagnostic codes and via a newly defined DIAGNOSTIC packet mechanism. These will now be briefly discussed.

Error tables were enhanced in two ways. Firstly, the number of error conditions handled was increased significantly. Secondly, the information content was increased by indicating not only the action taken by the DCE on detecting an error condition but also the state which the DCE enters.

A number of special error cases (e.g., packet received on unassigned logical channel) have been identified in X.25 for which it is inappropriate to inform a DTE of a procedural error by resetting or clearing the logical channel. In this case it has been agreed that a DIAGNOSTIC packet be used. The DIAGNOSTIC packet is nonprocedural in nature and solely for DTE logging. The DIAGNOSTIC packet identifies the logical channel number on which an error condition has been detected, and includes a diagnostic code.

Two areas associated with timeouts have been addressed. The first area relates to the length of time the DTE has to respond to an incoming call. On one hand, the network wishes to minimize its resources. On the other hand, short timeout values are not reasonable due to the interaction between calls on a single interface, and between the Network and Link Control Levels, and due to user processing within higher layers. A minimum value of three minutes has been agreed.

The second area relates to the action of the DCE when no confirmation has been received to an indication packet (i.e., during resetting, clearing, and restarting). In order to avoid long looping conditions, it has been agreed that the DCE will not retransmit indication packets. Instead, the DCE will take the following actions:

1. On expiry of a 60-s timer after issuing a RESET INDICATION, the DCE will clear the call, indicating the reason for clearing via the diagnostic code and call progress signal. On a PVC, a DIAGNOSTIC packet is sent.

2. On expiry of a 60-s timer after issuing a CLEAR INDICATION, the DCE will issue a DIAGNOSTIC packet and should eventually enter the ready state. In this state, the DCE does not ignore any packets sent by the DTE.

3. On expiry of a 60-s timer after a RESTART INDICATION has been issued, the DCE will issue a DIAGNOSTIC packet. The DCE considers this condition serious and will stay in this state indefinitely.

Diagnostic codes have been defined for reset, clear, and restart packets. The contents of the diagnostic code field provide nonprocedural information which do not alter the meaning of the call progress signal also provided. A DTE is not required to undertake any action on the content of the diagnostic code field. However, the DTE is advised to log the diagnostic to facilitate the correction of the problem.

Network-generated diagnostic codes are hierarchical. That is, for any specific diagnostic code there is always a code which is of a more general nature. The specific codes provide information allowing the DTE implementor to quickly diagnose problems. The more general codes are used when relatively uncommon or unanticipated problems occur. To accelerate trouble resolution, the X.25 error tables have been further enhanced by indicating the diagnostic code generated under each error condition.

F. Interrelationship between Levels

Changes of operational states of the Physical and Link Control Levels do not implicitly change the state of each logical channel at the Network Level; such changes when they occur are explicitly indicated by the use of Network Level restart, clear, or reset procedures as appropriate.

A failure at the Physical and/or Link Control Levels is defined as a condition in which the DCE cannot transmit and receive any frames because of abnormal conditions caused by, for instance, a line fault between the DTE and the DCE. When a failure is detected, the DCE will transmit to the remote end a RESET INDICATION indicating Out of Order for a permanent virtual circuit and a CLEAR INDICATION indicating Out of Order for an existing VC. During the failure, the DCE will clear any incoming calls.

When the failure is recovered, the DCE will send a RESTART INDICATION packet indicating Network Operational to the local DTE; this will result in a RESET INDICATION indicating Remote DTE Operational being transmitted to the remote end of each permanent virtual circuit.

IV. Optional User Facilities

A. Introduction

CCITT Recommendation X.2 defines the availability of various optional user facilities as being universally available or only available in some countries. Recommendation X.25 defines the procedures associated with all optional user facilities, irrespective of their availability.

This section describes only those optional user facilities which are proposed to be universally available.

B. Optional User Facilities

1. Closed User Group Facility

Closed User Group (CUG) is an optional user facility agreed to for a period of time between the Administration and a group of users. This facility permits the users in a CUG to communicate with each other, but precludes communication with all other users. A DTE may belong to more than one closed user group.

The calling DTE specifies the closed user group selected for a call using the optional user facility parameters in the CALL REQUEST packet. The closed user group selected for a call is indicated to a called DTE using the optional user facility parameters in the INCOMING CALL packet.

2. Flow Control Parameter Selection

Flow Control Parameter Selection is an optional user facility agreed to for a period of time which can be used by a DTE for its logical channels. The flow control parameters considered are the packet and window sizes for each logical channel for each direction of data transmission.

When the DTE has subscribed to the facility, it may, in a CALL REQUEST packet, separately request packet sizes and window sizes for each direction of data transmission. The maximum packet sizes that may be supported on public data networks are 16, 32, 64, 128, 256, 512, and 1024 octets. If a particular packet or window size is not explicitly requested, the DCE assumes default requests of 128 octets and 2, respectively.

When the DCE transmits a CALL CONNECTED packet, it indicates in the facility field the flow control parameters to be used by the calling DTE. The only valid facility indications in the CALL CONNECTED packet as a function of the facility requests in the CALL REQUEST packet are specified by the following general negotiation rules:

1. window sizes can be changed in the direction of $W = 2$; and
2. packet sizes can be changed in the direction of 128 octets.

When the called DTE subscribes to the facility, the DCE transmits flow control parameter facility indications to be used by the called DTE in selecting the flow control parameters for the call. The called DTE can change the indicated values using the above negotiation rules.

The flow control parameters for logical channels used for PVCs are established at subscription time.

The network may have to constrain the available parameter ranges in order to allow the call to be established. In this case, the network is involved in the negotiations discussed above. This would occur, for example, if a requested packet size, though available domestically, was not available on a particular international call.

3. Throughput Class Negotiation

Throughput Class Negotiation is an optional user facility agreed for a period of time which can be used by a DTE for virtual circuits. This facility permits negotiation on a per call basis of the throughput classes. The throughput classes are considered independently for each direction of data transmission.

A *throughput class* for one direction of transmission is an inherent characteristic of a virtual circuit, related to the amount of network resources allocated to it. This characteristic is meaningful when the D bit is set to zero in DATA packets. It is a measure of the throughput that is not normally exceeded on the VC. However, owing to the statistical sharing of transmission and switching resources, it is not guaranteed that the throughput class can be reached 100% of the time.

Default values are agreed between the DTE and the network. The default values correspond to the maximum throughput classes which may be associated with any virtual circuit.

4. One-Way Outgoing Logical Channel

One-way Outgoing Logical Channel is an optional user facility agreed for a period of time. This user facility restricts the use of a range of logical channels to outgoing calls. One-way logical channels retain their full duplex nature with respect to data transfer.

5. Incoming or Outgoing Calls Barred

Incoming or Outgoing Calls Barred are two optional user facilities agreed for a period of time. These facilities apply to all logical channels used for switched virtual circuits.

Incoming Calls Barred prevents incoming calls from being presented to the DTE. The DTE may originate outgoing calls. Outgoing Calls Barred prevents the DCE from accepting outgoing calls from the DTE. The DTE may receive incoming calls.

V. Concluding Remarks

A. A Common X.25 DTE

Network implementations of X.25 have come under considerable criticism in technical papers, such as one from IBM [2], which question whether a sufficient degree of commonality exists in the various X.25 implementations. The revised CCITT Recommendation X.25, which has been approved by Study Group VII in February 1980, resolves a number of key areas which led to network differences.

From a DTE implementation point of view, a common X.25 interface can be defined [3], [4], which consists of the following universally available features:

- an ISO-compatible frame level procedure (i.e., LAPB);
- use of Logical Channel Number one as the starting point for logical channel assignment;
- modulo 8 packet level numbering;
- dynamic $P(R)$ significance by use of the Delivery Confirmation bit;
- a standard procedure for selecting packet and window sizes, with defaults of 128 octets and 2, respectively;
- two mechanisms for user control data transfer (i.e., qualified DATA and INTERRUPT packets); and
- a standard way of specifying required call throughput.

What remains is for various network implementors to announce their implementation plans of the above features.

B. Relationship of X.25 to the Open System Interconnection

Chapter 2 has discussed a Standard Layer Model, specifically the Model for Open System Interconnection currently being defined by ISO. At the same time, the CCITT is developing a "Layered Model of Public Data Network Service Applications" for the purpose of facilitating DTE inter-working or gaining access to network services (e.g., directory assistance, electronic mail). A high degree of compatibility between CCITT's and ISO's Models is desirable; in fact, both ISO and CCITT agree on a seven-layer architecture. A major difference has been in the interpretation of the services provided by the Network and Transport layers and their relationship to X.25 virtual circuits.

The current view of the CCITT Rapporteur's Group studying OSI is that the services provided by the Transport and Network layers are identical except perhaps in the quality of service provided, and can be provided by X.25 virtual circuits; these can be provided by packet switching networks, or by using X.25 between DTEs in leased line and circuit switching networks. Quality of service becomes an issue since the Network layer may vary in its success in reaching the performance level required by the Transport layer (e.g., error rates, reliability, cost, throughput). When a Transport connection of higher reliability than that provided by the Network layer is required, this may be provided by the use of additional procedures within the Transport layer. Since these procedures do not add service features, but only increase an aspect of the quality of service, these procedures may be contained in a sublayer within the Transport layer.

The current ISO view appears to be that the services provided by the Network layer are somewhat primitive, resulting in distinctly different services being provided by the Network and Transport layers. The services of the Network layer can be provided by X.25 virtual circuits. However, in this model, many of the VC characteristics discussed in Section II are not used; instead, these functions are provided by the Transport layer.

The above discussion reflects two views of the relationship of X.25 to the Standard Layer Model. Alignment between the two models is in the process of being achieved.

C. Future Developments

Future activity and further work are required in the following areas:

(1) The characteristics of virtual circuits are defined in X.25, though much would be gained by having a separate CCITT Recommendation addressing them.

(2) The X.25 specification has become functionally complete after nearly six years of network operational experience. Further work will concentrate on new optional user facilities, and the addition of multiple line procedures defined for the Link Control Level.

(3) Presently, some networks require the data fields of DATA packets to contain an integral number of octets. The transmission by the DTE of data fields not containing an integral number of octets to the network may cause a loss of data integrity. Further considerations regarding the trends of future requirements and implementations toward either bit orientation (any number of bits) or octet orientation (an integral number of octets) for data fields in X.25 packets are under study in CCITT.

(4) The evolving Standard Layer Model provides a basic structure on which future work in ISO and CCITT can be built. The view that X.25 virtual circuits can provide the basic Transport layer services required by the Session layer must be studied further.

(5) There is a real need to select meaningful performance criteria, bearing in mind that the meaningfulness of criteria is viewed differently by network users and by the network providers. Once these criteria have been defined, realistic performance objectives should be set based on user requirements as well as on operating experience. The costs associated with meeting these objectives must also be considered.

References

[1] P. T. F. Kelly, "Public packet switched data networks, international plans and standards," *Proc. IEEE*, vol. 66, No. 11, Nov. 1978, pp. 1539–1549.

[2] M. L. Hess, *et al.*, "A comparison of four X.25 public data networks," *Proc. Int. Conf. Commun.* Boston, June 1979.

[3] A. M. Rybczynski and J. D. Palframan, "A common X.25 interface to public data networks," *Comput. Networks J.*, vol. 4, No. 3, pp. 97–110, July 1980.

[4] Z. Drukarch, *et al.*, "X.25: The universal packet network interface," *Proc. Int. Conf. Comput. Commun.* Atlanta, October 1980.

9

Packet-Switched Network Layer for Short Messages

Harold C. Folts

I. Introduction

The original version of X.25 [1] which was approved in 1976 provided two basic Virtual Circuit services described in the preceding chapter. The Permanent Virtual Circuit service provides a fixed end-to-end connection analogous to a point-to-point leased circuit, while the Virtual Call service provides for the establishment of switched connections to destination subscribers. In Permanent Virtual Circuit service, data packets can only be transferred between the two end-subscribers. In Virtual Call service, call establishment and clearing procedures are necessary to provide and release a switched connection. Permanent Virtual Circuit service is efficient when there are large volumes of data to be exchanged between two points. Virtual Call service, on the other hand, is efficient for exchange of data packet sequences periodically with a number of other subscribers.

While Virtual Call and Permanent Virtual Circuit services satisfy a large number of data communication applications, there are other applications requiring a different set of characteristics to provide a more optimum service. Where short units of data need to be exchanged frequently with a large number of other subscribers, the overhead of a Virtual Circuit call establishment becomes significant compared to the amount of data being transferred. Such applications which use short enquiry/response messages include point-of-sale, electronic funds transfer, credit checking, meter reading, reservation systems, directory searches, and inventory control. Additionally, process control systems need an effective means to handle sporadic movement of short units of data in such applications as position and sensor data, alarms, and telemetry. To satisfy these transaction and short one-way message applications, two additional capabilities have been added to the 1980 version of X.25 which was approved by the CCITT Seventh Plenary Assembly [2]. One enhancement is an extension to the Virtual Call service and is called the Fast Select facility. This allows conveyance of up to 128 octets of data within the call establishment and clearing packets. The other enhancement is the provision of Datagram service for the transport of independent "message" type of packets without the necessity of preestablishment of a connection. The new features of X.25 are complementary to the Virtual Call and Permanent Virtual Call services and significantly enrich the capability of X.25 to satisfy the broadest range of applications using packet-switching technology.

II. Fast Select Facility

As the United States was attempting to convince the CCITT to proceed with the inclusion of Datagram service in X.25, Japan proposed a variation of Virtual Call service to serve transaction-oriented applications. Known as the Fast Select facility, this variation provides for the exchange of up to 128 octets of data during the call establishment and clearing procedures for Virtual Call service. Fast Select effectively extends the capability of Virtual Call service to satisfy more transaction-oriented applications where at least one inquiry and one response is needed for communication. On the other hand, Fast Select does not as efficiently satisfy applications where there may be delays in the response or where there is a requirement for originating a large number of packets, each for different destinations. Support for Fast Select, however, finally grew to the point where it was agreed to provide it in X.25 along with Datagram service.

When the Fast Select facility is activated for a Virtual Call, the Call Request packet contains a facility request, indicating the Fast Select with one of two possible parameters. The parameters indicate whether there is a restriction on the response allowed to the Incoming Call at the destination.

The Fast Select call without restriction to response, shown in Fig. 1, processes the Call Request packet and delivers the maximum 128 octet call user data field to the destination in the Incoming Call packet. The destination then responds with either a Call Accepted packet or a Clear Request packet containing up to the maximum of 128 octets of user data. If a Call Accepted packet is sent, the maximum 128 octets of data are delivered to the call originator in the Call Connected packet. Subsequent packets during the remainder of the call are processed as defined for normal Virtual Call service.

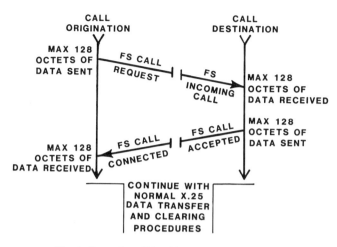

Fig. 1. Fast select (FS) with call accepted response.

When a Clear Request with a maximum of 128 octets of data is issued by the destination, the data are delivered to the call originator in a Clear Indication packet. Thus, a two-way transaction is completed, terminating the call. With the second parameter value in the facility request, the response to the incoming Fast Select call can be restricted to a Clear Request as shown in Fig. 2. This allows the network to process the Fast

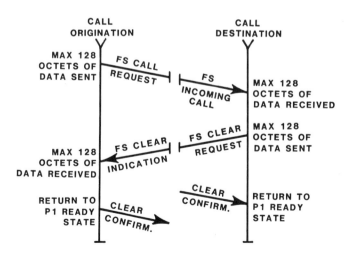

Fig. 2. Fast select (FS) with immediate clear response.

Select call more efficiently, leaving the originator knowing exactly the type of response to expect. This variation could be related to the same service as provided by a Datagram in each direction with about the same efficiency and overhead. There are two additional packets, however, in Fast Select with Clear Request response. These are the short three-octet Clear Confirmation packets shown in Fig. 2 to reinitialize the logical channels at each end of the connection.

In effect, Fast Select accelerates the Virtual Call process in establishing a communication. Additionally, inquiry–response applications can be more efficiently satisfied within the Virtual Call mode of operation common to the majority of X.25 network implementations.

III. Datagram Service

The Datagram mode of operation for packet-switching networks has long been the subject of extensive debate, particularly in the academic and research world. Pouzin [3] became a strong proponent of Datagrams when CCITT established the direction toward Virtual Call service with X.25 in 1976. Many member countries, in open CCITT debate, however, expressed doubt as to the true commercial viability of such a service.

Support for Datagram service in the United States began to expand in 1977 with the development of a proposal by the American National Standards Institute (ANSI) Task Group X3S37 on Public Data Networks. This proposal was subsequently presented to the International Organization for Standardization (ISO) and the CCITT for consideration. As a result, sufficient interest emerged to support furthering the development effort to included Datagram service in X.25 [4].

The United States proposal defined Datagram service, in general, as in the following paragraphs:

1) A Datagram is self-contained, carrying sufficient information to be routed from source DTE to destination DTE without reliance on earlier exchanges between source or destination DTE and the transporting network.

2) A Datagram is delivered in such a way that the receiver can determine the boundaries (i.e., beginning and end) of the Datagram as it was entered by the source DTE. The simplest way to achieve this is to deliver the Datagram intact as one unit to its destination, but other methods are not ruled out.

3) A Datagram is delivered with high probability to the desired destination, but it may possibly be lost.

4) The sequence in which Datagrams are entered into a network by a source DTE is not necessarily preserved upon delivery at a destination DTE.

5) If a Datagram cannot be delivered to the destination or is detectably lost, the network will attempt to advise the source DTE through provision of a "nondelivery notice" which indicates, to the best of the network's knowledge, why the Datagram could not be delivered. To distinguish among Datagrams for the purpose of providing error indications, the network will employ a Datagram identification supplied by the source DTE in each Datagram. The uniqueness of this identifier, if desired, is the responsibility of the source DTE and is not necessarily guaranteed.

The United States did not continue the arguments of Datagram versus Virtual Call [3], but instead conveyed the realization that Datagram service is a complement to Virtual Call service. In combination, therefore, a greatly extended range of user applications can be effectively satisfied through a single X.25 protocol supporting both services.

With this philosophy in mind, the ANSI Task Group developed the extensions to X.25 incorporating Datagrams. In maintaining the essential commonality with Virtual Call service, the same architecture was followed using multiple logical channels at the packet level. As shown in Fig. 3, the Physical Layer and the Data Link Layer are common to both Datagram and Virtual Call services. At the packet level, Datagrams are sent over designated logical channels where Virtual Calls and Datagrams cannot be intermixed within any logical channel. (Note that the term "packet level" is used here as defined by X.25 and does not fully correlate to the Network Layer of the OSI Reference Model, Chapter 2.)

The format used for a Datagram packet (Fig. 4) has been carefully designated to enable two different implementations. The first, considered the most practical, is as a self-contained independent service distributed

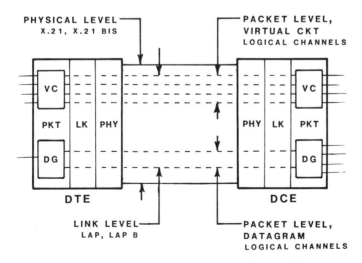

Fig. 3. Model of X.25 DTE/DCE interface supporting virtual circuit and Datagram operation.

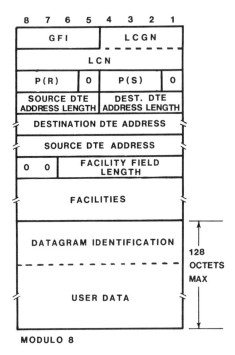

MODULO 8   Fig. 4. Datagram packet format.

among the network nodes. The second builds a Datagram out of a data packet on a Permanent Virtual Circuit to a centralized Datagram function within a network.

Figure 4 shows that the first two octets are common with all packets in an X.25 interface (see Fig. 2 of Chapter 8). The third octet is common with a data packet providing the sequence numbers $P(S)/P(R)$ for logical channel flow control. The $P(R)$ acknowledgment is always returned from the immediately adjacent network node, since the notion of an end-to-end connection does not apply within the definition of Datagrams.

The address and the facility field of the Datagram packet are identical to those of a Virtual Call, Call Request packet. These provide the information for the network to route the Datagram to its destination and indicate any particular service feature needed. The remainder of the Datagram packet is for the User Data field, which has a standard maximum length of 128 octets. There are not other optional maximum sizes. This is specifically to avoid the extreme complexity of handling fragmented and combined Datagrams.

The first two octets of the user data field are reserved for a Datagram identification which can be used to uniquely identify the packet associated

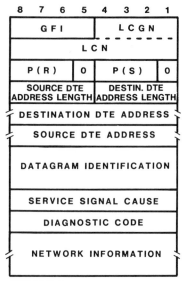

Fig. 5. Datagram service signal packet format.   **MODULO 8**

with the destination address. As discussed later, these two octets will be returned to the source within Datagram Service Signal packets from the network. Use of the Datagram identification is not mandatory, but is for the convenience of the user. When the Datagram identification is used, only 126 octets remain available in the user data field.

The other packet related to Datagram service is the Datagram Service Signal packet shown in Fig. 5. A Datagram Service Signal-Specific is generated by the network relative to a specific Datagram issued by a DTE. A Datagram Service Signal-General is generated by the network relative to the overall Datagram operation of the DTE or network.

There are three classes for the Datagram Service Signal-Specific packet. The first is "Datagram Rejected," indicating that a Datagram has been discarded by the network for some error or inconsistency in the issued Datagram. Such causes include local procedure error, invalid facility request, access barred, not obtainable, etc. Another class is "Nondelivery Indication" when a Datagram has been discarded by the network. This is an optional feature which is provided either by subscription for all Datagrams sent or by Facility Request on a per-Datagram basis. The last class of Datagram Service Signal-Specific packets provides "delivery confirmation," which is also optional either by subscription or by facility request.

The Datagram Service Signal-General is sent when there is some problem associated with the Datagram service. It can be used to indicate network congestion and to request a DTE to stop sending Datagrams either in general or to certain parts of the network. This enables the network to exercise a degree of control over being flooded with Datagrams under overload conditions.

The first three octets of a Datagram Service Signal packet (Fig. 5) are the same as for the Datagram packet. The address field is also the same format except that the source address is either the network, in the case of general signals, or the original destination from the related Datagram packet. The Datagram identification contains the first two octets of the user data field of the related Datagram packet to uniquely identify the associated Datagram. The user data field contains the reason for the service signal, and the diagnostic code provides a further explanation. The network information field has a maximum length of 16 octets and provides detail to help identify the problem; e.g., for a diagnostic of "invalid address," the address field of the related Datagram would be provided in the network information field.

A number of additional packets are also applicable for Datagram service. These are all common to the other X.25 services and include Flow Control, Reset, Restart, and Diagnostic packets discussed in Chapter 8. Since Datagrams utilize logical channels in a similar way to the other services, the logical channel related functions are identical.

For incoming Datagrams, the network maintains a queue for each Datagram logical channel. When the queue becomes full, additional arriving Datagrams or Datagram Service Signals are discarded. The maximum length of the queue is a subject for agreement with the specific network. Datagram Service Signals have priority over incoming Datagrams and are, therefore, inserted at the beginning of the queue. This may lead to discarding the last Datagram of the queue if the maximum queue length has been exceeded.

It is normally considered that only one logical channel is necessary for Datagram service because each Datagram is considered a totally independent entity, and the notion of end-to-end connection does not exist. If there is a need, however, for additional levels of precedence associated with Datagrams, multiple channels can then be effectively used, one for each level. Flow control procedures can thus be varied according to the associated precedence. Additionally, it may be desirable to receive Datagram Service Signals expeditiously on a separate logical channel to facilitate closer control on the overall Datagram operation.

The Datagram extension to X.25 does not provide the simplistic interface envisioned for some theoretical and some experimental networks where only a basic Datagram transport is provided with the operational functionality contained in the upper layers of the architecture. X.25 Datagrams represent a pragmatic solution to the problem of providing commercially viable public data network services. A single host computer interface can now communicate most efficiently with the broadest range of user applications in a common compatible way. Further work has been initiated to consider a simplified Datagram-only interface for less intelligent terminals in the field to either communicate with an X.25 host or communicate among themselves via an X.25 network. So far such an effort has received little interest.

IV. Fast Select/Datagram Interoperability

For further flexibility in implementing these two optional capabilities, it is feasible for Fast Select in one network to interoperate with Datagrams in another network via a gateway interface. The gateway would issue a Datagram to the next network in response to an incoming Fast Select call and vice versa; see Fig. 6. Either end would not realize that such a conversion had taken place. For each Datagram arriving at the gateway, a Fast Select call request with restricted response (clear request) would be issued to the next network. All the procedures for such interoperability have not yet been defined in CCITT Recommendation X.75, but work will continue in this area during the 1981–1984 CCITT Study Period.

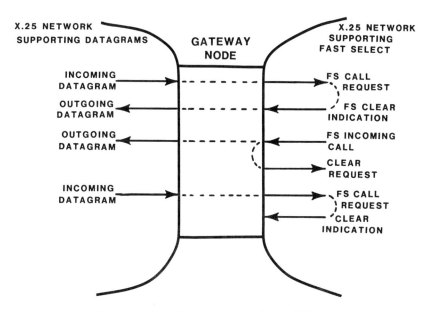

Fig. 6. Interoperation between fast select and Datagrams.

V. Conclusion

Fast Select and Datagram operations provide significant enhancement to the X.25 interface procedures. Since both capabilities are optional, not all networks will have either or both available. Only Virtual Call and Permanent Virtual Circuit services are mandatory in public packet-switched data networks. In the end, only time and the marketplace will tell the amount of acceptance the various services will receive in the real world by the users.

References

[1] H. C. Folts and H. R. Karp, Eds., McGraw-Hill's Compilation of Data Communications Standards. New York: McGraw-Hill, 1978.
[2] CCITT Yellow Books, CCITT Seventh Plenary Assembly, Volume VII.2, November 1980, Geneva, Switzerland.
[3] L. Pouzin, "Virtual circuits vs. datagrams—Technical and political problems," in Proceedings of the National Computer Conference, June 7–10, 1976, pp. 483–494.
[4] P. T. Sevcik, "Why the Datagram is needed—And how it will operate," Data Communications, McGraw-Hill, Mar. 1978.

10

DNA—The Digital Network Architecture

Stuart Wecker

I. Introduction

The extremely attractive price, capabilities, and performance of mini- and microcomputers have been major factors in automating a wide variety of applications that were previously done manually, by expensive electronic logic, or not at all. In some applications these computers operate stand-alone, interacting only with locally connected terminals and I/O devices. In other applications they communicate with other computer systems in the performance of their tasks, in order to share data, access remote functions and programs, and utilize resources located at remote computer sites. Networks supporting these distributed applications must provide a flexible communication mechanism that can accommodate a broad set of applications requirements, flow characteristics, and communication components. Creating such networks requires an architectural framework or structure designed to meet these requirements. The architecture serves as the specification for the implementations on the individual communicating computer systems.

Network architectures create a common user application communication interface independent of the internal structure and topology of the network, and standard internal interfaces and peer protocols to interconnect the components of these communicating systems (See Chapters 1 and 2). Digital Equipment Corporation's Digital Network Architecture (DNA), the standard structure for DECnet network products, supports the flexible interconnection of Digital's families of computers while providing an easy-to-use interface. DNA is the definition of the interfaces, structure, and protocols that compromise the design of the network intercomputer communication mechanism. This chapter presents an overview of this architecture.

II. Design Goals

DNA was designed to create a communication mechanism supporting a wide range of user applications, host computer systems, and interconnect technologies. Specifically, DNA has the following goals:

1. Create a Common User Interface. The application interface to the network should support a broad spectrum of application communication requirements and should be common across the varied implementations. Within such a network environment, applications may be moved among the systems in the network, with the common interface hiding the internal characteristics and topology of the network.

2. Support a Wide Range of Communication Facilities. The network should be adaptable to changes in communication technology and operate with a variety of communication channels (e.g., satellite channels, fiber optic links, local network links, value-added carrier services).

3. Be Cost Effective. A network built using DNA should approach the efficiency and performance of a network designed specifically for a given application.

4. Support a Wide Range of Topologies. The architecture should support communication between users, independent of the physical structure of the underlying data transport network.

5. Be Highly Available. The overall operation of the network should not be adversely affected by the failure of a topologically noncritical node and/or channel. Critical functions such as message routing, communication establishment, and network maintenance should use distributed algorithms.

6. Be Extensible. The architecture should allow for the incorporation of future technology in hardware and/or software.

7. Be Easily Implemented. The architecture should be independent of the internal characteristics of the hosts and their operating systems and be easily and efficiently implemented on a wide variety of heterogeneous hardware and software.

In addition to the above were the design goals applicable to any good development effort, especially modularity and maintainability.

III. Design Principles

These goals and previous (prior to 1974) research results, notably the ARPA network [1], the National Physical Laboratory Network [2], and other research activities [3], led to a set of design principles which guided the architecture design. These are as follows:

1. Be Highly Distributed. The communication functions should not be centralized or have centralized components that would be potential single points of failure.

2. Structure via a Layered Communication Hierarchy. This will create a highly flexible structure with ease of layer replacement and peer layer protocol communication.

3. Provide Uniformity among All Nodes. The network topology should not restrict node access. Nodes should be characterized only by the functions they perform, and not by their location in the network. The goals of uniformity and distribution imply an equality and symmetry among the network nodes.

4. Make Tradeoffs in Favor of Flexibility. Functions should be implemented at the highest practical efficient level within the structure where they can use the services of the network itself. Such functions as network control and maintenance should execute at the level of application programs.

5. Be Dynamic. Protocols should be flexible to change; new modules and functions should be easily added within the structure; and the network should be self-configuring.

These principles were applied both to the basic architectural structure and to the individual layers and the protocols of the architecture.

IV. Logical Link Communications

The properties and characteristics of network applications (e.g., file access and transfer, terminal access, distributed computing) were studied [4]. This study led to the basic capability of DNA: a common, general purpose, process-to-process communication mechanism, upon which network applications can be built. This communication mechanism creates a sequential, full-duplex, error-free, message-oriented communication path, a DECnet *logical link*, connecting processes in the network. This path is independent of the underlying network topology and characteristics of the individual communication channels. Processes in DNA represent either user application programs, providing for direct program to program communication, or other network resources (e.g., disk files, I/O devices, terminals) providing for program to network resource communication (see Fig. 1).

A. Logical Link Characteristics

One process requests, via the network interface that a logical link be created between itself and a remote process. The network requests communication with the remote process and, assuming no conflicts and an

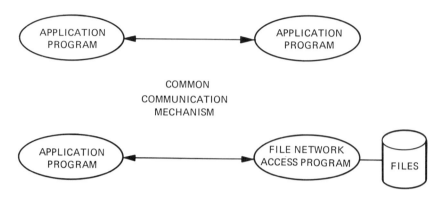

Fig. 1. Common communication mechanism between application programs and network resources.

acceptance by the remote process, the logical link is created. The two processes are then free to send and receive messages sequentially over the link.

Flow control functions allow the data receiver to control the rate of transfer over the link to match buffer availability. Data may be sent in either short segments (part of a message) or longer message blocks. The network divides these longer message blocks into smaller segments for transmission, reassembling them at the destination.

In addition to the normal logical link sequential data path, there is an interrupt data path over which short, high-priority messages may be sent and used to notify the remote process of special conditions and events occurring within the application. This interrupt data bypasses the normal data flow control mechanism and, in some implementations, actually initiates a program interrupt or trap to the receiving process. When communication is complete either process may disconnect and terminate the logical link.

B. Object Addressing

An important component of logical link operation is the addressing of the communicating processes (resource objects) within the network. Objects are referenced via a two-component address. The first part is the address of the system within which the object resides, the *node address*; the second part is the address of the object within that system, the *object address*. DECnet does not provide for global addressing of objects without knowing their node (system) address. This function can be easily added by creating a global network directory and resource manager which would be accessed to map global name references to specific "node, object" address pairs.

The object-addressing mechanism of DNA combines, within a common scheme, the advantages of global network address mechanisms and local node address mechanisms. The socket addressing mechanism used in the ARPA network is an example of a global scheme. In these networks users see a uniform network address space but require a directory information operator to provide the network address by mapping a local name or service request onto a network address prior to access. A local addressing scheme requires remote users to know the local format of names within each computer system they wish to access, but eliminates the need for a directory operator. In DNA object references are divided into two categories. User application programs are addressed via their local names. Common generic services (e.g., file access, maintenance functions) are addressed via global, generic service names.

The address of a user application program is the name of that program as defined in the system where the program resides. Thus, users must know the name of the remote application program for reference in creating a logical link. For common resources or service functions such as disk files, terminals, and file transfer functions, the remote name of the function or resource managing program need not be known. Instead there is a global generic name (service type number) for such objects. The user specifies the name of the service or resource requested to the specified system, and that system translates the generic name into a local address.

C. Local Link Interface

The interface between processes and the network communication service consists of five generic commands for operation of the logical link:

Connect. Create a logical link to the specified object. Objects may be either network resources (accessed via generic names), or user application programs (accessed via their local system names).

Transmit. Send a message over a logical link. If the message is longer than the maximum transmission block size, the network will segment it for transmission over the communication channels. Flow control options may cause the message to remain queued at the sending system until requested by the receiver. These options allow the user to trade off throughput, delay, and buffer utilization. They can be set to optimize the specific requirements of an application. They are set independently for each direction of a logical link.

Receive. Request a message from a logical link. This will queue a receiver buffer to the link and, depending on flow control settings, may cause a request message to be sent to accommodate the receive.

Transmit Interrupt. Send a short, interrupt message over a logical link. This message will be sent independently of the normal data flow control settings in effect.

Disconnect. Destroy a logical link. Normally, transmissions in progress will be completed and the logical link will be terminated. In the case of a program abort, the link is terminated immediately without completing transmissions in progress.

There may also be additional commands as part of the local system network interface used to receive incoming *Connect Request* and *Interrupt* messages. In addition, if a buffer sharing or pooling technique among a group of logical links is being used, then there will also be local commands to add buffers to and release buffers from the pool.

Commands on all systems are semantically equivalent; they cause the same actions to occur within the network. The syntax and operating system interfaces for these commands are implementation specific. In some systems they appear as user-callable subroutines from high-level languages; in others they are accessed via system service calls or traps. In some systems, they are transparent, hidden from the user, the user accessing higher-level functions such as file access services via the file system and the file system accessing the network via the network interface commands. Synchronization and completion notification are also implementation specific, some systems use a polling technique while others interrupt the program upon completion of a command. The reader should refer to specific implementation documentation on DECnet products for such details.

V. Node Addressing and Topological Considerations

DNA was designed to support a wide range of topologies. Specifically, the architecture supports networks as small as two LSI-11 microcomputers directly connected by an asynchronous data channel, and as large as global networks with a separate communication backbone network consisting of high-speed switching nodes and communication channels. Data message addressing on a logical link is via a two-part address: the node (system) address and the logical link address within that node. The node address is used by the transport (routing) communication mechanism of DNA. Logical link addressing is an end-to-end mechanism and is only known to the nodes within which the link terminates. The basic transport function of DNA is a node-addressed datagram communication mechanism as in the Cyclades research network [5].

All nodes in a DECnet network are addressed uniformly. The network has no inherent notion of a physical backbone communication network. Nodes take on specific characteristics based on the applications or functions they perform. Thus, for example, a node may support host functions (application programs), concentrator functions (terminal access), or switching functions (routing). These notions are logical ones; a single physical node can support multiple functions and, for example, be a host, switch, and concentrator simultaneously. A network can initially consist of a group of directly connected communicating end nodes and in time grow to a network with front-end nodes and switching nodes added between these communicating end nodes without affecting the users or network software in these nodes. The transport communication protocol and addressing is the same, for example, between hosts directly connected or between a host and a front-end communication system. This addressing scheme gives DNA the topological flexibility required to implement networks with dynamically changing configurations. Figure 2 shows some topological examples.

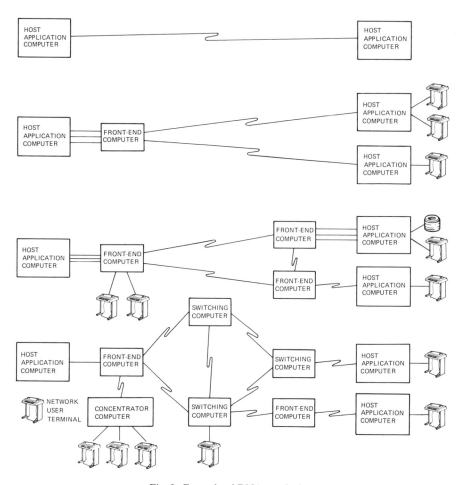

Fig. 2. Example of DNA topologies.

The control of a DNA network is totally distributed. That is, there is no inherent central control function in the network. To achieve high flexibility and topological independence, control and maintainance functions execute at the level of user applications within the DNA structure. At this level, topological considerations are transparent.

A requirement of every node is its ability to be addressed for the purpose of performing control and maintenance functions, such as dumping error counters and setting parameters. The uniform addressing of nodes in DNA and the execution of maintenance functions as user application level programs supports this access to control and maintenance information from all nodes. Thus, small networks that do not need such maintenance and control facilities may omit them, while larger networks may have control and maintenance nodes (network control center) for overall control of the network, located independent of the topology. Control and maintenance functions may even be partitioned among the nodes in the network.

VI. Structure

A layered hierarchical modular approach was applied to the design of DNA. That is, the functions necessary to create the user logical link communication facilities have been divided into a *layered hierarchy of functions*. Higher-level functions are built on lower-level ones. Each level or layer in the structure performs a well-defined set of communication functions and presents those functions to the layer above it via a well-defined interface. Each layer uses the functions of the layer or layers beneath it in the performance of its communication functions.

This structure is similar to that employed in many current operating systems. The structure defines layers of abstraction within the architecture. That is, higher layers in the structure use only the functions provided by interfaces to lower layers. The higher layers are unaware of the algorithms and protocols used by the lower layers. Lower layers use only the information passed in parameter blocks from the higher layers. This creates an independence of the layers, so that a layer module may be replaced by an equivalent new module as long as the new module retains the same functions and interfaces as the old one, even though it may execute a new algorithm and protocol. A *protocol* is a construct local to a layer, examined and used by that layer in communication with its peer counterparts in other nodes to create a distributed function within that layer. A given layer may not use information in other layer protocol headers. That information must be passed separate from the message in a parameter block across the interface. This concept, *protocol purity*, allows the easy replacement and independence of layer modules.

The Digital Network Architecture is divided into six functional layers: physical link layer, data link layer, transport layer, network services layer, session control layer, and application layer. The functions performed by each of these layers are distributed among the nodes and reflected in protocols that are used to communicate between and synchronize the peer layers in the nodes. The DNA layers and their names were designed prior to the efforts of the ISO committee described in Chapter 2. The DNA structure corresponds very closely to the ISO architectural model but unfortunately differs and conflicts in the names of some of the layers. The DNA transport layer corresponds to the ISO network layer and the DNA network services layer corresponds to the ISO transport layer. The DNA layers perform the following functions:

1. Physical Link Layer. This layer manages the physical transmission of information over a data channel. It is concerned with the physical characteristics of the media, signaling techniques, clocking on the channel, and the interfaces to the computer system and communication carrier services. It creates a channel-independent interface for the transmission and reception of data blocks. Protocols applicable here are communication interface standards such as RS-232C and RS-449 as described in Chapter 3.

2. Data Link Layer. This layer creates a sequential error-free communication path between adjacent nodes (connected by a single direct channel) over which data blocks may be transferred. In addition, this layer manages the transmission and reception on multipoint, multiaccess, and half-duplex channels. It creates a single-channel error-free sequential interface. The standard protocol for this layer is the Digital Data Communications Message Protocol (DDCMP). Other protocols to be supported in the future include X.25 value-added carrier services and the Ethernet multiaccess channel.

3. Transport Layer. This layer transports messages from source to destination nodes. It provides a routing function so that a path between two end nodes can be constructed from the individual node to node paths provided by the data link layer and associated communication channels (see Fig. 3). The path is not guaranteed to be sequential or error-free. The routing function switches messages from incoming channels to outgoing channels via a node route table. The creation and updating of this table is independent of the actual switching and is performed by the routing function algorithm. An overview of routing algorithms is presented in Chapter 12. The particular algorithm used in DECnet is dynamic and adaptive, changing paths when channels fail and using a lowest cost (a measure of performance) criteria in selecting those paths. The algorithm is

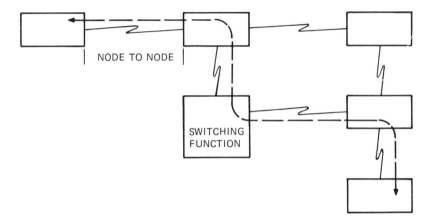

Fig. 3. End-to-end path from node-to-node paths.

distributed and uses the transport protocol to exchange routing information among the switching nodes of the network.

4. Network Services Layer. This layer creates and manages the user communication logical link paths. It uses the transport layer to move message blocks from source node to destination node. Within a node, it manages the logical link message queues and performs such functions as flow control, error control, message segmentation, and buffer management. The protocol for this layer is the Network Services Protocol (NSP).

5. Session Control Layer. This layer performs the system-dependent functions of logical link communications. These include node name to address translation, local process addressing, generic object name addressing, and, in some systems, process activation and authorization/security functions. The interface to this layer is the communication service by which programs communicate independent of their physical location in the network.

6. Application Layer. This is the layer at which user application programs, resource managing programs, and function-oriented programs execute. Data exchanges at this level use logical links for sequential communication. Many logical links operate simultaneously, each supporting an independent conversation. Generic function and resource managing programs, part of the DECnet product offerings, executing within this layer include the remote system loader, file access and file transfer programs, and maintenance and control functions. The Data Access Protocol (DAP) for network file access is an example of an application layer protocol.

The functions provided by layers 1–5 are part of the standard DECnet offerings. Layer 6, the application layer, is the only layer where both user- and DECnet-provided software coexist. Different products include different

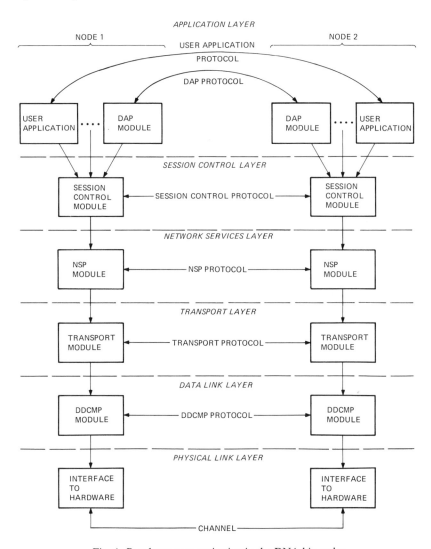

Fig. 4. Peer layer communication in the DNA hierarchy.

function programs at this layer. Table I gives a list of offerings from the current releases of DECnet.

Layer functions are realized by peer protocols, implemented within layer modules, used to synchronize and transfer data between corresponding layers within the DNA structure hierarchy. This peer layer communication is shown in Fig. 4. Further details on the structure of DNA can be found in the protocol specification documents [8], [12], [13], [14], [16], [17].

Table I. DECnet System Functions[a]

	DECnet-11 M Version 3	DECnet-11 S Version 3	DECnet-11 M -PLUS Version 1	DECnet-IAS Version 2	DECnet/E Version 1	DECnet-RT Version 1	DECnet-VAX Version 2	DECnet-20 Version 2
Task-to-Task	Yes	Yes	Yes	Yes	Yes	Yes	Yes	Yes
Network Command[b] Terminal	Yes	Yes[b]	Yes	No	Yes	No	Yes	No
File Transfer	Yes	No	Yes	Yes	Yes	Yes	Yes	Yes
Command/[c] Batch File Submission	Yes/Yes	No/No	Yes/Yes	Yes/Yes	No/Yes	No/Yes	Yes/Yes	Yes/No
Command/ Batch File Execution	Yes	No	Yes	Yes	Yes	No	Yes	Yes
Remote File Access	Yes	Yes[d]	Yes	Yes	No	Yes	Yes	No
Down-Line System Loading	Yes	No	Yes	Yes	No	No	Yes	No
Down-Line Task Loading	Yes	No	Yes	Yes	No	No	Yes	No
Routing Support	Yes	Yes	Yes	No	No	No	Yes	No

DECnet Functions

- *Task-to-Task Communications*—Programs or tasks can create logical links and exchange data with programs or tasks on other systems.
- *Network Command Terminal*—Local users can log onto systems in the network as though their terminal were directly connected to the remote system.
- *Intersystem File Transfer*—Data files may be moved between systems, at either program or operator request. The common file type supported across systems is sequential ASCII.
- *Command/Batch File Submission*—Local users can submit batch or command files to remote systems for execution.
- *Command/Batch File Execution*—Local users can cause a batch or command file that resides at a remote node to be executed.
- *Remote File Access*—Users or programs can remotely access sequential files on a record-by-record basis.
- *Down-Line System Loading*—Initial memory images for DECnet-11 S systems can be stored on the local system, and loaded on request into an adjacent 11/S system. Remote systems require the presence of a network bootstrap loader, implemented in read-only memory.
- *Down-Line Task Loading*—Programs to be executed on DECnet-11 S systems can be stored on the local system, and loaded on request, under the joint control of the operating systems at both ends of the logical link. This and the preceding feature simplify the operation of network systems that do not have mass storage devices.
- *Routing Support*—Node can route messages from incoming to outgoing channels, functioning as a network switching node.

[a]Table I provides the information for determining if the preceding functions are available on a particular DECnet system. Note that the above descriptions define the minimum capabilities provided by a given function. Additional capabilities, above those described as the minimum for a function, may be available between two of the same or different DECnet systems.

[b]Terminals on these systems may log onto other DECnet systems of the same type. DECnet-11S does not support connections from remote command terminals, only to 11M/11M-PLUS.

[c]Commands may be received by this node/commands may be sent by this node.

[d]Offers local users network access to remote file systems. Does not allow users on remote systems to access local files.

VII. Data Flow Within the Architecture

The communication functions managed by DNA have been divided into a hierarchy of layered modules. User data messages pass down through the hierarchy, each layer adding a communications capability and a protocol header to the message. This protocol header carries control information to the corresponding (peer) layer in the destination node for that layer. The message is then transmitted over the data channels and back up through the layer hierarchy to the destination user, the protocol headers being removed and processed along the way. Adhering to the rule of protocol purity, each layer only examines its own protocol layer header. A general description of this layered network architecture structure can be found in [6] and Chapter 1.

Figure 5 shows this data flow through the architecture. The letters near the arrows refer to the description below. In this description the name

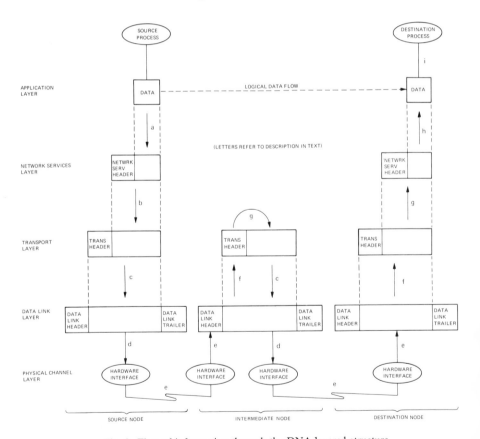

Fig. 5. Flow of information through the DNA layered structure.

"source" refers to the process sending a data message and "destination" to the process receiving it. Both processes may be sending and receiving data simultaneously as logical links are full duplex communication paths. For this example, however, a simple one-way flow will be described. Assume that the source process has already created a logical link to the destination process and the destination process has issued a receive request and is now waiting for data.

(a) The source process issues a transmit data command passing the local address of the message buffer and a local logical link reference number to the network services layer via its interface. (The session layer has been omitted here for simplicity. It is used during logical link creation and is essentially transparent during data transfers.)

(b) The network services layer adds a protocol header including the logical link identifier and a message sequence number. Since the destination process has already issued a receive command, permission to transmit is already pending at the source. This releases the message and the network services layer passes it to the transport layer specifying the destination node address.

(c) The transport layer adds a header consisting of the destination and source node addresses and selects an outgoing channel for this message based on its routing table information. It then passes the message to the data link layer specifying the outgoing channel address and, if a multistation channel, the logical station address of the receiving node on the channel.

(d) The data link layer adds its protocol header consisting of framing and synchronization information, a transmission block sequence number, and a cyclic redundancy check (CRC) trailer. It then passes this block to the physical link layer for transmission on the channel.

(e) The physical link layer transmits the message block over the data channel. It is received at the next node and passed up to the data link layer at that node.

(f) The data link layer checks the block, via the cyclic check, for bit errors in transmission and, via the message number, for proper sequence. If there were errors, a correction procedure, retransmission in DDCMP, will be used by the data link protocol to recover and receive the correct block. When correct, the data link header and trailer are removed from the message block, which is then passed up to the transport layer.

(g) The transport layer checks the destination address in the header, testing whether this is the destination node. If not, it selects the next outgoing channel from its routing table and proceeds as in Step (c), passing the message to the data link layer. The transport layer has switched the message from an incoming channel to an outgoing one. This will continue until the message finally arrives at the destination node. At the destination node, the transport header is removed and the message is passed to the network services layer in that node.

(h) The network services layer examines its header, the logical link identifier and sequence number. If the message is the next expected, it selects the next buffer queued for that logical link for reception of the data message, puts the message into the buffer, and passes the message to the destination process by completing the outstanding receive command. If the received message was in error (usually wrong sequence number), then a recovery procedure (retransmission) is invoked at the network services layer.

(i) The destination process interprets the data according to the specific higher-level protocol being used.

To summarize, the logical link presented at the end user application interface uses an underlying node-by-node transport mechanism for transmission of messages from the source to destination node. The internal network transports datagrams, independent message blocks addressed to a destination node, on a best efforts basis, much like the postal system. The network services layer performs error control, end-to-end sequencing, and flow control functions, correcting any message loss and sequence errors by the transport layer.

The remainder of the paper describes each of the major communication layers and specific protocols of the DNA architecture: the data link layer and DDCMP, the transport layer and routing algorithm, and the network services layer and NSP. This will be followed by some example facilities and applications of DECnet. It should again be noted that this paper describes the architecture of DECnet. Individual DECnet products implement varying subsets of this architecture.

VIII. The Data Link Layer and DDCMP

The data link layer of the architecture is responsible for maintaining the integrity and sequentiality of data sent over a single communication channel. In addition, on multipoint, multiaccess, and half-duplex channels this layer is responsible for the orderly management of the channel (which station can transmit next and which station is addressed to receive). Any algorithm and corresponding protocol providing such functions would be acceptable for use within the basic architectural framework of DNA, for example, those described in Chapters 4 and 5. Specifically, the Digital Data Communications Message Protocol (DDCMP) has been designed to perform these functions and is the standard data link protocol of DECnet.

A. Data Link Layer Goals

In addition to meeting the basic requirements of creating an error-free message-oriented sequential data channel, the DDCMP design was driven by the following set of goals:

(1) Operate over a wide variety of communications channels (e.g., synchronous and asynchronous) in both bit serial and bit parallel modes. The protocol should be independent of the physical characteristics of the data channel, and should operate on existing (1974, pre-"bit-stuffing") hardware.

(2) Operate on point-to-point and multipoint channels in both full- and half-duplex modes using a common set of messages and operating procedures.

(3) Offer high performance on all channels. That is, it should make maximum use of channel bandwidth even on channels with long delay characteristics (e.g. satellites), and should be efficient in transmitting binary (transparent) data.

(4) Provide a positive initialization indication so that if one of the communicating DDCMP modules on a channel reinitializes, that information is positively known to the other corresponding communicating module on the channel.

(5) Provide error recording features so that degradation of a channel can be detected and repaired prior to channel failure.

(6) Provide a basic mode so that bootstrapping and testing functions may be performed over the channel with a minimum amount of hardware and/or software required in the system to be bootstrapped.

(7) Create a protocol that is easily implemented on small mini- and microcomputers and even within an LSI chip.

B. Data Link Functions

The functions of DDCMP are divided into three components: (1) message framing, (2) channel management, and (3) sequential error-free data exchange [7].

Framing. Message framing uses a byte count technique. That is, messages are either fixed in length (control messages), or contain a length field within a fixed length protocol header which denotes the length of the succeeding variable length data field (data messages). This is in contrast to protocols that use a pattern detection scheme for framing. DDCMP does not search for special ending bit patterns and there are no escape mechanisms needed to achieve data transparency.

Byte synchronization is outside the basic protocol message framing mechanism and is specific to each channel type. For synchronous channels a conventional sync character approach is used, making DDCMP compatible with pre-"bit-stuffing" synchronous hardware interfaces. For asynchronous channels, byte synchronization is inherent in the 8-bit transmission format, so no additional information is needed. The same is true for 8-bit oriented parallel channels. The message framing is thus independent of the channel characteristics and can operate equally well on serial synchronous, asynchronous, and parallel data channels.

In addition to channel independence, byte count framing has a number of other advantages over the bit-stuffing or zero bit-insertion technique of HDLC as described in Chapter 5. One is better error detection properties of the CRC block check due to a constant block length with all data bit errors. In certain cases bits in error in HDLC frames cause inserted framing bits (zeros) not to be deleted or data bits to be deleted as framing bits. This has the appearance of a long burst error to the CRC and may go undetected based on the properties of the CRC. Another advantage of byte count framing is its message length independence from the data content. HDLC frame length is content dependent and changes (number of inserted zero bits) with different data values. This property allows transmission of DDCMP fixed length message blocks, a requirement in many satellite multiaccess slotted reservation schemes as described in Chapter 6.

Channel Management. In keeping with the design principle of node uniformity and symmetry, and the goal of supporting varied topologies, DDCMP assumes no master/slave or primary/secondary relationships between the communicating stations. Data transfer is a symmetric operation. In fact, using a physical loopback connector on a full duplex point-to-point channel, DDCMP will initialize and transmit to itself without knowing it is in such a configuration. This feature, symmetrical operation, is used in a loop-back test mode to check proper operation of the data channel, modem, and interfaces.

The channel management component of the protocol is used on half-duplex point-to-point channels and on multipoint channels where multiple transmitters and receivers are connected to a single channel. On half-duplex channels, permission to transmit (channel ownership) is passed alternately between the two attached stations. On multipoint channels, DDCMP uses a polling technique with the main end station designated the polling control station and the others tributary stations. On such channels, data blocks only flow between the control station and the tributaries. There is no direct tributary-to-tributary data flow (this can be accomplished via routing through the control station at higher levels of the architecture). The polling algorithm (which station is chosen next to transmit) is independent of the data exchange and framing portions of DDCMP and can be selected to provide a mechanism for either priority operation among the tributaries or a more equal, round-robin scheme. Channel management and data exchange are distinct components of the protocol. The channel management component of DDCMP determines when a given station on a channel may transmit, but what is transmitted is the same for all channel configurations. Thus, the protocol is still data symmetric even when one station is controlling the channel flow.

Data Exchange. To achieve data integrity and sequentiality over the channel, DDCMP uses a positive acknowledgment retransmission technique. The protocol assigns each message a sequential number, inserted in the protocol header, and computes a CRC block check added to the end of the message. The message is transmitted on the channel and an error recovery timeout timer is started. The receiver checks each message block check for bit errors and the sequence number for proper sequence. If there are no errors, the receiving DDCMP returns a positive acknowledgment containing the number of the message successfully received. If the transmitter does not receive such an acknowledgment within its timeout period, it initiates error recovery. If the original message was received in error, this will result in retransmission of the message. Additional features, for performance improvement, include pipelining of messages, piggybacking of acknowledgment information within data messages being sent in the reverse direction, a negative acknowledgment message used to decrease the time waiting to initiate error recovery, and a synchronization message used to recover from acknowledgment messages received in error. These are similar techniques to the ones used in HDLC.

C. Message Formats

DDCMP message formats are of three types: data, control, and maintenance. User data (information from the next higher layer in the architectural hierarchy) is sent within the data message format. Acknowledgment and initialization messages use the control message format. A special mode of the protocol, called maintenance mode, provides a simple framing envelope, via the maintenance message format, used for such functions as downline loading and loop testing. The three message types are identified by three special bytes which begin each of the three types. The data message format is shown in Fig. 6.

A DDCMP data message consists of a header, header block check, user data field, and data field block check. The header includes the count field used for framing, the transmit sequence number of the message, a piggybacked acknowledgment number, and a polling flag and station address used for channel management. The header is followed by a CRC-16 block check used to verify the integrity of the header fields. This separate header block check allows verification of the count field prior to using it to receive the succeeding data field and allows the remaining header fields to be used prior to receiving the remainder of the message. So, for example, the receive number field (the piggybacked acknowledgment) can be used to release transmit buffers and the station address (for multipoint channels) can be checked against the station's address as soon as the header block check is verified. Since the header is usually much shorter than the data field the

SOH	COUNT	FLAGS	RESP	NUM	ADDR	BLKCHK1	DATA	BLKCK2

Number of bits: 8   14   2   8   8   8   16   8*count   16

SOH   =   the numbered data message identifier
COUNT   =   the byte count field
FLAGS   =   the link flags (polling flag)
RESP   =   the response acknowledgment number
NUM   =   the transmit number
ADDR   =   the station address field
BLKCK1   =   the block check on the numbered message header
DATA   =   the numbered message data field
BLKCK2   =   the block check on the data field

Fig. 6. DDCMP data message format.

probability of bit errors in the header is significantly lower and, thus, usually without error. Fields such as the receive number and channel management (polling) flags are independent of the included user data and provide valuable information even with a corrupted user data field following. The data field block check is computed only over the data field. In software implementations, it can be added to the message prior to passing it to DDCMP, saving processing time during actual transmission.

DDCMP has five control messages as shown in Fig. 7. They are as follows:

ACK—Positive Acknowledgment. Used to acknowledge correct receipt of a sequential data message without bit errors.

NAK—Negative Acknowledgment. Used to notify the data transmitter of a received error and cause retransmission. A reason field in the NAK message gives the reason for the NAK and is used for error recording functions. Reasons are: received message with CRC error, buffer temporarily unavailable, receive overrun, message too long for buffer, header format error, and REP response.

REP—Reply to Message Number. Used to resynchronize after a timeout. After a timeout period (the timer, started after sending a message, has expired and no positive acknowledgment information has been received), the transmitter sends a REP with the number of the last sequential transmitted message. The receiver replies with an ACK or a NAK, depending on whether or not the message with that number was properly received. The NAK triggers any retransmission.

STRT—Start Initialization. Used to initialize the channel and reset message numbering.

Acknowledge Message (ACK) Format

ENQ	ACKTYPE	ACKSUB	FLAGS	RESP	FILL	ADDR	BLKCK3
8	8	6	2	8	8	8	16

Negative Acknowledge Message (NAK) Format

ENQ	NAKTYPE	REASON	FLAGS	RESP	FILL	ADDR	BLKCK3

Reply to Message Number (REP) Format

ENQ	REPTYPE	REPSUB	FLAGS	FILL	NUM	ADDR	BLKCK3

Start Message (STRT) Format

ENQ	STRTTYPE	STRTSUB	FLAGS	FILL	FILL	ADDR	BLKCK3

Start Acknowledge Message (STACK) Format

ENQ	STCKTYPE	STCKSUB	FLAGS	FILL	FILL	ADDR	BLKCK3

ENQ = the control message identifier
ACKTYPE = the ACK message type with a value of 1
NAKTYPE = the NAK message type with a value of 2
REPTYPE = the REP message type with a value of 3
STRTTYPE = the STRT message type with a value of 6
STCKTYPE = the STACK message type with a value of 7
ACKSUB = the ACK subtype with a value of 0
REASON = the NAK error reason
REPSUB = the REP subtype with a value of 0
STRTSUB = the STRT subtype with a value of 0
STCKSUB = the STACK subtype with a value of 0
FLAGS = the link flags
RESP = the response number used to acknowledge correctly
         received messages
FILL = a fill byte with a value of 0
ADDR = the station address field
BLKCK3 = the control message block check

Fig. 7. DDCMP control message formats.

STACK—Start Acknowledgment. Used to acknowledge a received start message. This message, the START, and the ACK form the initialization sequence.

DDCMP operates in one of three modes: startup, running, and maintenance. Stations are in startup mode during the initialization phase of the protocol. To ensure that there is a positive indication of startup on both ends of the channel a three-way symmetric startup handshake is used. This involves the alternate exchange of START, STACK, and ACK messages. With this sequence neither station can go through an initialization sequence without the other doing the same. Figure 8 shows this startup handshake sequence. After completing startup, the stations are in running mode. This is the mode in which data messages, ACKs and NAKs are exchanged. The REP message is used in this mode in the event of a transmitter timeout. Figure 9 shows a typical message flow for DDCMP.

Maintenance mode is a simplified mode of the protocol using the framing technique and channel management functions outlined earlier but without the acknowledgment and sequential numbering features. That is, either a message is delivered without bit errors or it is not delivered. A simple higher level protocol, MOP (Maintenance Operation Protocol), operates within this mode of DDCMP and performs such functions as downline loading and testing. Further details on the operation of DDCMP can be found in the protocol specification [8].

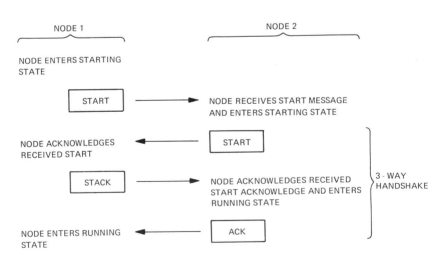

Fig. 8. Symmetric DDCMP startup sequence.

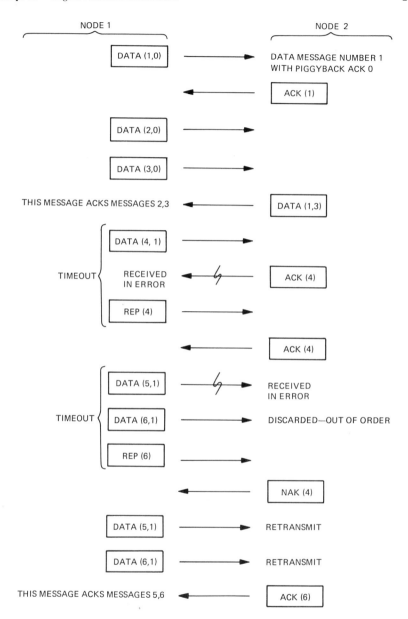

Fig. 9. Typical DDCMP message flow.

IX. The Transport Layer and Routing Algorithm

The transport layer of DNA creates network pathways via a routing function among the nodes of the network. That is, using the data link layer for transmission of message blocks over individual channels, the transport layer routes messages among the network channels, connecting them into a path between a source and destination node. This path is not maintained on a per user pathway basis, as in circuit-switched systems, but on a node addressed basis by having the transport layer at each intermediate node examine the transport header of the routed message and determine the outgoing channel that forms the best path to the destination node based on its routing table. Each message given to the transport layer is treated individually. The routing algorithm and table determine whether all messages to a given destination follow the same route or whether that route changes based on the occurrence of specified events, such as operator command, channel failures, queue delays, etc. The routing technique used by DNA is the distributed hop-by-hop piecewise technique described in Chapter 12.

The transport layer makes a best effort to deliver all messages presented to it. It does not guarantee delivery, sequentiality, or destruction of messages in a bounded amount of time. This service requires higher levels of the architecture to use a message numbering, acknowledgment, and retransmission mechanism to recover from lost messages, and to be concerned with old duplicates caused by their own retransmissions. The transport level itself does not duplicate messages. It operates much the same as the postal system. In addition, the transport layer manages the global flow of packets in the network through a simple congestion control mechanism. The DNA transport layer is similar in function to the network layer of the ISO model described in Chapter 2.

A. Transport Goals

The goals of the transport layer were driven by the overall goals of DNA. In addition to its basic functions of (1) accepting and delivering packets to reachable destinations, (2) avoiding congestion in the network, and (3) helping limit the lifetime of packets in the network, the transport layer goals were as follows:

1. Be Distributed. The routing algorithm and switching function should be distributed within the nodes of the network so that there is no central routing supervisor and single point of failure.

2. Be Efficient. The routing algorithm and switching function should not consume large amounts of channel bandwidth in protocol operation and should not consume much processing time in the route determination and switching function.

3. Be Simple. The algorithm should be simple so that it can be easily implemented, maintained, and tuned for optimal performance.

4. Be Stable. The algorithm should be stable so that after a change in the network (node or channel failure, for example), routing path changes do not oscillate but settle down to a stable set of paths.

5. Be Adaptable. It should adapt to topological changes in a reasonable amount of time and should recover from transient errors such as lost routing messages.

6. Support Heterogeneity. It should operate over a mixture of network node types, communication channels, and topologies.

B. Transport Functions

The transport layer functions are divided into three components:

1. Routing. The process of forwarding messages toward reachable destinations. It consists of the router which does the real time switching and the routing algorithm which updates the switching table of best paths.

2. Congestion Control. The control of total traffic flow in the network so that resources are not overloaded and performance reaches a steady state under heavy load rather than degrading with increased offered load.

3. Message Lifetime Control. The probabilistic bounding of the time a message will exist in the network before being discarded. This function helps higher-level protocols solve the message number problem of old messages being mistaken for current ones.

C. Transport Algorithms

Routing. The distributed routing algorithm is based on the premise that the best total path from a source node to a destination node, calculated in a distributed fashion, is the sum or the concatenation of the many individual node-to-node best paths. Each node individually maintains a list of its best next hop (outgoing channel) to each destination. Messages to be routed are transmitted via that best next hop. The next node does the same, thus building a total best path from the source node to the destination node. The determination of best path is based on a cost function. Each outgoing channel from a node is assigned a cost to route a message through that node over that outgoing channel. The better the route, the lower the cost. Cost is usually based on line quality characteristics such as delay, throughput, or error rate, but may also include characteristics of the switching node such as buffer resource availability and processing capacity. These cost values are assigned by an offline algorithm and can be changed by an operator or program. If the costs of all channels are set to the same value, the path chosen will be the one with the minimum number of hops (intermediate nodes).

For each channel (j) terminating at a node, the node maintains both a path length, HOPS, and a performance or quality measure, COST, to each destination node (i) in the network from that node. This is stored in the form of two matrices:

> HOPS(i, j)—path length to node (i) via channel (j)
> COST(i, j)—path cost to node (i) via channel (j)

From these can be calculated (1) the existence of a path to a given destination (i) if there are reachable values is some entry of HOPS row (i), and (2) the best path to that destination, the channel corresponding to the minimum value in COST row (i) with a reachable value for that entry in the HOPS matrix. These values of number of hops, cost, and channel (j) are saved. The channel is used to route messages toward the specified destination node. The hops and cost values are sent to adjacent (neighbor) nodes to inform them of a node's best routing values to a given destination.

Whenever an event that potentially changes paths occurs (e.g., a channel or node going down or coming up, or the reception of new path information from adjacent nodes via routing messages), a node determines if its paths have changed, or if there are new values for number of hops or cost. If a change has occurred, the node sends its new best route information to all of its neighbors via a routing message. This routing information is exchanged between adjacent nodes whenever the best cost/hops value changes and at periodic time intervals. The routing information message contains the minimum cost and corresponding number of hops from the node sending the routing message to all destinations. Upon receiving these messages from its adjacent nodes, a node will update its HOPS and COST matrices by adding to the received information its own channel cost and incrementing the hop count. It will then select its best path based on the minimum of the cost information in its revised matrices. Thus, a path is built using a distributed piecewise algorithm. Each node gathers input from its neighbor nodes via routing messages, adds its own cost values, sends this information to its neighbors, and computes its best routing paths. Figure 10 shows a typical routing data base.

The path length information, HOPS, is used to detect routing loops computed by the routing algorithm. A loop path may be computed by the routing algorithm when, in reality, the destination node is really unreachable. What happens, due to transmission timing delays, is that routing messages sent to update the HOPS and COST matrices in a node from other

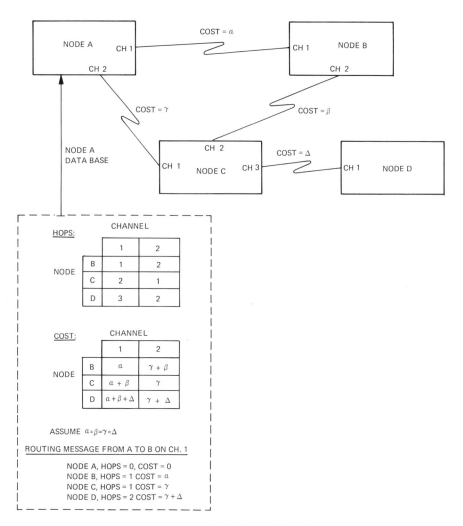

Fig. 10. Transport routing database and routing message.

nodes are not always received in proper time sequence. These updates generate new routing messages which circulate around the network sometimes in a closed loop. The nodes in the loop think they have a path to a given destination when in reality there is no path. Each time such a routing message traverses a node during the update, the hops count value will be incremented by one. Eventually, the hops count will exceed the longest possible nonredundant path in the network. When this occurs, the algorithm determines that the specified destination is really unreachable and stops circulating routing messages, marking the node unreachable in the HOPS matrix.

Congestion Control. The congestion control algorithm is used to control global flows among the nodes in the network and to prevent the depletion of resources within the network so that, under heavy offered load, the network reaches a steady state of performance rather than a decreasing one. Many techniques for controlling congestion have been researched. These include permit schemes [9], limiting the total number of messages in transit in the network, and feedback mechanisms [10], notifying the source nodes causing congestion to limit their input rates to the network. DECnet has chosen a simpler scheme: limiting the buffer utilization within the network. When the length of an output channel queue exceeds a specified threshold value [11], input messages (messages originating at this node) are delayed and transit messages (messages being routed) are discarded. Measurements using this technique have verified its effectiveness and simplicity in preventing buffer depletion and congestion.

Message Lifetime Control. The message lifetime control algorithm counts the number of nodes a data message has visited using a visit count field in the transport header of messages. Each intermediate node increments this field for each routed message. If the value of this field exceeds the maximum node visit limit, usually as the result of the message having followed a temporary loop formed in the routing path, the message will be discarded. Eventually, the routing algorithm will also detect this loop via the hop count, as described above, so future messages will not follow the loop. This puts some probabilistic limit on the maximum life of a message. The higher layers take additional measures as well to solve the old message detection problem.

D. Message Transport Header

The transport layer prefixes messages passed to it for transmission with a transport routing header. This routing header, shown in Fig. 11, contains the following information:

Routing Flags. Control flags used by intermediate routing nodes, including a "return to sender request" for returning messages addressed to unreachable destinations, and an indication of the routing header format type for future extensions.

Destination Node. The destination node address of this message.

Source Node. The source node address of this message.

Visit Count. The number of nodes "visited" by this message, as described above.

RTFLG	DSTNODE	SRCNODE	VISIT CNT
8	16	16	8

RTFLG   = the routing control flags

DSTNODE   = the destination node address

SRCNODE   = the source node address

VISIT CNT = the number of nodes this packet has visited

Fig. 11. Packet route header format.

Routing Message Format

CTLFLG	SRCNODE	RTGINFO	CHECKSUM
16	16	16n	16

Hello and Test Message Format

CTLFLG	SRCNODE	TEST DATA
16	16	8-1024

Initialization Message Format

CTLFLG	SRCNODE	INITFO
16	16	8n

CTLFLG   = Transport control flag, with the following types (bits 1-3):

    0 = Initialization message

    2 = Hello and Test message

    3 = Routing message

SRCNODE   = identification of source node's Transport

RTGINFO   = path length and path cost to all destinations

CHECKSUM   = one's complement add check on routing information

TEST DATA = sequence of up to 128 bytes of data to test the line

INITFO   = node type, maximum Data Link layer receive block size, Transport version.

Fig. 12. Transport protocol message formats.

E. Transport Layer Protocol Messages

The transport protocol sends and receives a number of control messages, in addition to the routed data messages, in performing its routing functions. These are shown in Fig. 12:

Routing Message. Sent to an adjacent node, it contains the minimum cost and number of hops to all destination nodes from the node sending this message.

Test Message. Used for channel and node integrity testing.

Initialization Message. Used to set parameters between adjacent nodes, such as node name and address, maximum data channel block size, and version identification; and cause the transport module to initialize its data base with respect to the channel on which this message arrived.

More details on the operation of the transport layer can be found in the specification [12].

X. The Network Services and Session Control Layers

The network services layer of the architecture creates and manages the logical link communication paths connecting processes in the network. Once a logical link is established, both processes may send and receive messages (groups of bytes) over the logical link simultaneously. The network services layer maintains message sequentiality without loss or duplication independently for each logical link. Any change, by the transport mechanism in routing of messages for a logical link, due to channel and/or node failures, is transparent to the users of the link. If it is not possible to maintain the logical link path due to, for example, unreachability of a node in the network, the link will be disconnected. The session control layer, residing above the network services layer, provides the system-dependent communication functions. These functions bridge the gap between the generic network services, the system-independent logical link mechanism, and the system-specific functions required by processes executing within the operating system environment. Thus, session control is the point of integration of DNA with the operating system. The session control functions include identifying the requested end user process, activating or creating processes, and validating incoming logical link connection requests. The relationship of session control to the operating system, users, and the network is shown in Fig. 13. To simplify the following discussion, the network services and session control layers are considered as a single service in the creation and management of logical links.

The network services layer performs its functions via the network services protocol (NSP). It uses the communications service provided by the

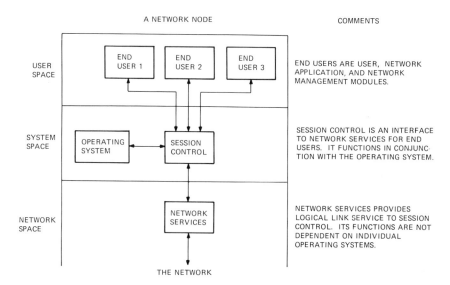

Fig. 13. Session control within DNA.

transport layer, that is, delivering messages on a best effort basis. NSP must create a reliable communication mechanism so that it can offer its users no-loss, sequential logical links. The techniques used by NSP are much the same as those used by DDCMP in creating an error-free channel from a communication medium that may corrupt information. That is, it numbers messages sequentially, checks for proper sequence at the receiving node, returns a positive acknowledgment to notify the sender of proper receipt, and uses a timeout to recover from lost messages via retransmission. The only function not needed by NSP is the block error check (CRC) used by DDCMP. NSP assumes the switching nodes do not corrupt individual message bits.

The design of the network services layer protocol is more complex, however, than the data link protocol due to the nonsequentiality and the unbounded lifetime of messages. On a physical channel message blocks are sequential with a well-defined lifetime. The protocol need only wait that maximum lifetime to ensure that there are no outstanding messages in the channel. At the network services layer this is not true because of the lack of sequentiality and service guarantees provided by the transport layer. The network services protocol must recognize out-of-sequence messages and discard old messages that arrive at a later point in time, rather than mistaking them for current messages. These problems are solved probabilistically via a large message number and small valid acceptance window. Other additional techniques used by NSP for performance include dynamic flow control options and holding out of sequence messages.

A. Network Services Goals

NSP was designed to support the basic architectural principles of DNA. The goals specific to NSP were as follows:

1. User-Oriented Performance. Users and/or NSP can trade off buffer requirements against throughput and delay on a logical link. That is, using the flow control mechanism, users may either provide one buffer at a time for receipt of messages or they may provide many buffers in advance. Larger numbers of buffers allow message pipelining and usually result in higher throughput on the link. By using these flow control options, the user can tailor the performance and characteristics of the logical link to the requirements of the application. In some implementations, the user has direct access to these options. In others, the NSP module does intermediate buffering for the user and takes into account the user-provided buffers in setting appropriate flow control parameters.

2. Fairness. All logical links should provide equal service. That is, a user with low data rate requirements should receive the same minimum level of performance (delay, minimum throughput) as a user with high data rate requirements. No single user should be able to monopolize the network service.

3. Extensibility. The network services protocol should be designed to accommodate future additions and extensions. These may come in the form of hardware and/or software. If possible, new versions of NSP should operate with old versions as well.

4. Efficiency. As with all the protocols, NSP should be relatively simple, easy to implement, use minimal amounts of CPU time, and be efficient on the channel in terms of number of messages exchanged and size of protocol headers.

5. Ease of Use. The interface to the network services layer should be simple. An unsophisticated user should be able to easily use the services of the network.

B. User Service Functions

The functions of NSP can be divided into two categories: those that are externally visible to the user (user interface commands resulting in protocol actions); and those which are usually transparent (internal functions used by the protocol).

The external functions are as follows:

1. Connection Management. NSP manages logical links on a dynamic basis. Links are created and destroyed on command from the communicating processes much the same way people control the telephone system via dialing and hanging up.

2. Data Transfer. Once a logical link is created, users may send and receive data over the link.

3. Interrupt Transfer. NSP provides a low-throughput low-delay sub-link part of a logical link used to send short high-priority alarm signal messages (interrupts).

C. Network Service Functions

The internal functions of NSP are those needed to create and manage the logical links using the transport mechanism. These are as follows:

1. Error Control and Sequentiality. NSP creates a sequential, no loss, no duplication communication mechanism using an underlying transport mechanism which is inherently unreliable.

2. Flow Control. NSP controls the flow of information from the sender to the receiver on a logical link so that data messages are not sent until actually requested by the receiver. (In some implementations, NSP modules may buffer some messages ahead for the users.) This gives the receiver control of its available buffers.

3. Segmentation/Reassembly. NSP divides large messages into smaller segments for transmission through the network. Reassembly takes place at the destination node. In some implementations, the reassembly is directly into user buffers. In others, the user receives the individual segments along with an indication of the last segment of a message. This reassembly into user buffers combined with the flow control mechanism results in a deadlock-free technique for application layer buffer management.

D. NSP Operation

The operation of NSP can be divided into three basic states shown in Fig. 13.

1. Connection

The establishment of a logical link. The user (program) requests a connection to a destination application program or generic service. It does this by specifying the node address and either a process name or generic service type in a connect command to the session layer which builds an appropriate connect request to the network service layer. The connection information is sent in a *connect initiate* message containing the address of the requested destination object, as provided by the user, the address of the source object, a local, dynamically assigned logical link number (identifier), and some optional data provided by the user. This information is sent to the destination NSP module via the transport service.

At the destination node this information is presented to the requested object. The destination object may examine the name of the requestor and the included optional data in deciding whether or not to accept the link. The optional data may contain, for example, information specific to the service requested of the destination object or an authorization account and password. If the requested object accepts the link, it notifies session control and a *connect confirm* message is returned by NSP. This message includes a locally assigned logical link number used to reference the link in this destination direction.

Each link has two logical link reference numbers, one for each direction of transmission. This reference address is similar to the one used in the X.25 interface described in Chapter 8, but consists of two addresses rather than one, so there are no conflicts or collisions during multiple simultaneous link creations, making the addressing symmetric. This symmetry allows direct physical connections between equal host systems creating logical links without requiring intervening switching nodes or interfaces. In fact, if two objects issue link creation commands to each other at the same time, with the local NSPs choosing the same local numbers, two links will be created without conflict.

In response to the *connect confirm* message, a third message, *data acknowledge*, acknowledging the confirm, is returned, completing the logical link. This forms a three-way handshake, similar to that of DDCMP, and is used to assure synchronization at logical link establishment. During the link establishment procedure, processes are directly addressed by name rather than by a global port address mechanism. This technique eliminates the need for a directory service or initial connection protocol used to find the address of an available port for a particular process or service.

2. Data Transfer

Once the link is established, both processes may send and receive normal data and interrupt data on the logical link. The transfer of data on the link uses the error control, flow control, and segmentation/reassembly functions of NSP.

(*a*) *Error Control.* The error control mechanism uses a positive acknowledgment retransmit scheme. Data messages sent on a link are numbered sequentially (modulo 4096). A retransmit timer is started upon transmission. When properly received, messages are acknowledged by number. If an acknowledgment is not received by the message sender when the timer expires, the message is retransmitted. In addition, such features as piggybacking and multiacknowledge are used for performance improvement. These techniques are similar to the ones used at the data link layer.

(*b*) *Segmentation/Reassembly.* For transmission through the network, NSP divides long messages into multiple smaller segments. These segments are reassembled at the destination node. Each message segment is numbered and sent as an NSP *data* message. In each segment, there are flags denoting whether this segment is the first, middle, or last segment of a message. The segment size is set in the connection procedure. For interrupt data there are *interrupt request*, *interrupt*, and *acknowledgment* messages used to request, transmit, and acknowledge interrupt information on the link.

(*c*) *Flow Control.* Flow control is used to manage buffer resources at the receiving end of a logical link. As part of the connection procedure a flow control option may be chosen to control the rate at which data blocks are transmitted for each direction on a logical link. The flow control options are (1) none, (2) segment, or (3) message. If no flow control is chosen then data will be sent immediately in response to a transmit command by the remote user. If segment flow control is chosen the receiver specifies the number of segments requested, usually via receive commands. When transmits are issued, those segments that correspond to receive requests will be sent over the logical link. Transmits issued prior to these requests will wait at the transmitting node pending corresponding requests. This segment request count is conveyed in a *data request* message. If message flow control is chosen, then the flow is based on complete messages rather than on segments of messages. In this case, the specified number of messages will be sent over the logical link. These will physically be sent as individual segments and reassembled at the destination node into the specified number of messages, transparent to the user. In addition to the flow control option settings, there is an on/off flow control switch which may be used to start and stop flows irrespective of the option chosen.

The choice of flow control setting and the correspondence of user receive commands and actual segment or message requests being sent by NSP is an implementation-dependent option. In some implementations the flow control mechanism is transparent to the user and is used internally by NSP to control flows based on a combination of its own buffer availability and user receive commands (user buffers). In other implementations the flow control mechanism is used directly by the user. That is, each receive command, specifying a buffer, results in a specific flow control request. In this case, these requests can be used to effectively manage and trade off buffer resources and logical link performance at the destination user. The choice of using message or segment flow control is based on the characteristics of the application protocol being sent over the logical link. Segment flow control gives the user the option of controlling the reception of information in small pieces, a useful mechanism for receiving messages of unknown variable length using a small number of segment buffers. Message flow control leaves the segmentation and reassembly to NSP, transparent to the user, useful for uniform or known length messages.

3. Disconnection

Either process may request disconnection of the logical link. This results in a *disconnect initiate* message being sent and a *disconnect confirm* message being returned to terminate operation of the specified logical link.

Figure 14 shows an example of an NSP protocol exchange and Table II shows the NSP message types. Figure 15 shows the connect message information built by the session layer which is passed to NSP and sent in the *connect initiate* message. Additional information on the operation of NSP can be found in the NSP protocol specification [13].

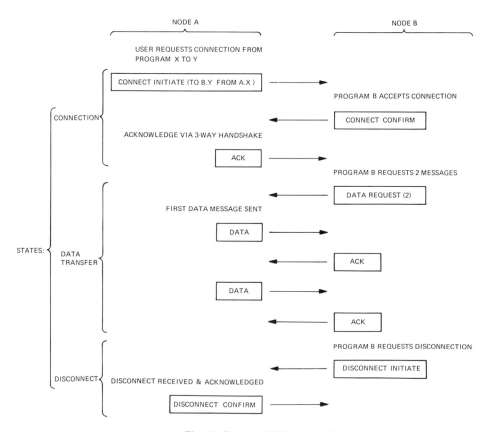

Fig. 14. Example NSP message flow.

Table II. NSP Messages

Type	Message	Description
Data	Data Segment	Carries a portion of a Session Control message. (This has been passed to Session Control from higher DNA layers and Session Control has added its own control information, if any.)
Data (also called *Other Data*)	Interrupt	Carries urgent data, originating from higher DNA layers.
	Data Request	Carries data flow control information (also called Link Service message).
	Interrupt Request	Carries interrupt flow control information (also called Link Service message).
Acknowledgment	Data Acknowledgment	Acknowledges receipt of either a Connect Confirm message or one or more Data Segment messages.
	Other Data Acknowledgment	Acknowledges receipt of one or more Interrupt, Data Request, or Interrupt Request messages.
	Connect Acknowledgment	Acknowledges receipt of a Connect Initiate message.
Control	Connect Initiate	Carries a logical link connect request from a Session Control module.
	Connect Confirm	Carries a logical link connect acceptance from a Session Control module.
	Disconnect Initiate	Carries a logical link connect rejection or disconnect request from a Session Control module.
	No Resources	Sent when a Connect Initiate message is received and there are no resources to establish a new logical link (also called Disconnect Confirm message).
	Disconnect Complete	Acknowledges the receipt of a Disconnect Initiate message (also called Disconnect Confirm message).
	No Link	Sent when a message is received for a nonexisting logical link (also called Disconnect Confirm message).
	No Operation	Does Nothing

DSTNAME	SRCNAME	MENUVER	RQSTRID	PASSWRD	ACCOUNT	USRDTA

BYTES: 19   19   1   39   39   39   16

DSTNAME = the destination end user name
SRCNAME = the source end user name
MENUVER = the field format and version format
RQSTRID = the source user identification for access verification
PASSWRD = the access verification password
ACCOUNT = the link or service account data
USRDATA = the end user connect data

Fig. 15. Connect message format.

XI. Higher Levels

Distributed applications execute at higher levels in the hierarchical structure using function-oriented protocols to transmit information over logical links. Functions executing at this level include file transfer, transaction processing, and distributed application communication. One of the standard DNA protocols executing at the application layer is the Data Access Protocol (DAP) creating a network file access mechanism. File access was chosen as a more basic or primitive mechanism than file transfer. File transfer is built on file access via a utility program that uses the access mechanism to sequentially access a file and transfer it. The example below outlines a use of this mechanism. This paper does not include any specific information on DAP; details can be found in the literature and specification [14], [15].

XII. Example Facilities

In a brief description such as this, it is impossible to present all the details and options of a design and set of products as large as DECnet. The inclusion here of a few brief examples of its facilities will help in understanding its operation.

(*a*) *File Access and Transfer*. File access in DECnet is accomplished by a communication between two programs: (1) the File Access Listener (FAL), and (2) the Network File Access Routines (NFARs) using the DAP protocol sent over an NSP logical link (see Fig. 16). The NFARs provide the interface that convert user file access commands (e.g., Open, Get, Put, Close) into the DAP protocol messages used to convey this information to the FAL on the remote system where the file actually resides. FAL then

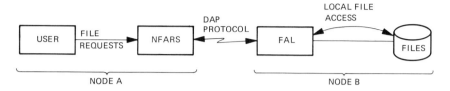

Fig. 16. File access via FAL and NFARs.

issues these commands to the local file system. The NFARs execute as part of the user program. A user could implement the DAP protocol (NFARs) directly in user code but with minimal saving in overhead and the added burden of tracking future protocol changes.

The user requests a file to be accessed by issuing an Open access request. The NFARs create a logical link to FAL by issuing an NSP connect request (via the session control layer), specifying the FAL generic object type. The FAL program checks permission to access the file using the user account number and password specified in the connect optional data field. If permission is granted the link is accepted and the connection completed. Using the DAP protocol, the FAL program and the NFARs exchange DAP messages (*file block request* and *file block data* messages) to access blocks of the file. The underlying network services layer, transport layer, and data link layer are used to transport these messages from source to destination sequentially and without errors.

In the transfer of a file, the DAP protocol is used in a mode where *file block request* DAP messages are omitted; instead, the flow control mechanism of NSP is used directly to control the flow of file blocks and the utilization of buffers. This creates an efficient file transfer function via a file access mechanism. More details on this can be found in [15]. Table III presents a list of the DAP messages and their functions. They are exchanged over DECnet logical links in the access of a file. Figure 17 shows a typical DAP exchange for a requested file retrieval.

In some implementations of DAP, the NFARs are accessed directly via subroutine calls from high-level languages (e.g., CALL NFOPEN). In other systems, e.g., VAX/VMS, these routines have been built into the file system and are accessed indirectly and transparently via normal I/O statements (e.g., Read, Write).

(*b*) *Network Management and Downline Loading.* The network management functions of DECnet control and monitor network operation. They perform the functions of loading and dumping of remote system memory; examining and changing network parameters, error counters, and event logs; testing physical channels and logical link paths; and setting and

Table III. DAP Messages

Message	Description
Configuration	Exchanges system capability and configuration information between DAP-speaking processes. Sent immediately after a link is established, this message contains information about the operating system, the file system, protocol version, and buffering ability.
Attributes	Provides information on how data are structured in the file being accessed. The message contains information on file organization, data type, format, record attributes, record length, size, and device characteristics.
Access	Specifies the file name and type of access requested.
Control	Sends control information to a file system and establishes data streams.
Continue-Transfer	Allows recovery from errors. Used for retry, skip, and abort after an error is reported.
Acknowledge	Acknowledges access commands and control connect messages used to establish data streams.
Access Complete	Denotes termination of access.
Data	Transfers the file over the link.
Status	Returns the status and information on error conditions.
Key Definition Attributes Extension	Specifies key definitions for indexed files.
Allocation Attributes Extension	Specifies the character of the allocation when creating or explicitly extending a file.
Summary Attributes Extension	Returns summary information about a file.
Date Time Attributes Extension	Specifies time-related information about a file.
Protection Attributes Extension	Specifies the file protection code.
Name	Sends name information when renaming a file or obtaining a directory listing.

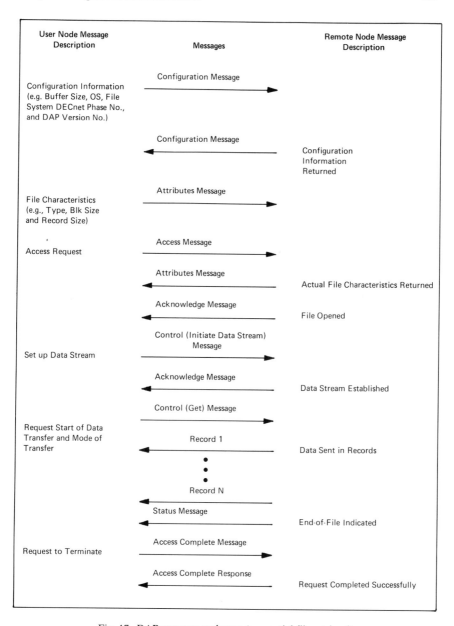

Fig. 17. DAP message exchange (sequential file retrieval).

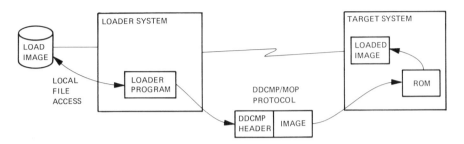

Fig. 18. Down-line loading via DDCMP.

displaying the status of nodes and channels in the network. Network management modules are distributed within the nodes of the network. They execute at the application level of the architecture, communicating via the Network Information and Control Exchange (NICE) protocol over logical links [17], [18]. The NICE messages and their functions are shown in Table IV.

Memory-only nodes in a DECnet network are downline loaded via the Maintenance Operation Protocol (MOP) [16]. This is a simple protocol which sends a load address and memory image to a system executing a small bootstrap program (usually a 100–200-word ROM). Table V is a list of the MOP messages and their functions. MOP messages are sent within DDCMP maintenance framing envelopes from one node (the loader system) to an adjacent node (the target system). If the loader node contains the file image on a local disk, the loader program accesses it directly. The loader program has a direct interface to DDCMP used to send and receive messages via DDCMP maintenance mode (see Fig. 18).

If the file is not local, the loader uses the NFARs and DAP to access the file from a remote file image system. This is a normal file access as explained above. The ability to access a remote file rather than having to first transfer the entire file image allows the loader node to itself be a system without any local mass storage, allowing for a cascaded load of nodes in the network.

The down-line load can be initiated from (1) the system to be loaded, by causing the system to execute the bootstrap and send a MOP *request program* message, initiating loading by the loader system; (2) a local command to the loader program on the loader system which will initiate loading; or (3) a command entered at another node running the NICE protocol. This is the protocol used for control and maintenance of DECnet networks, part of the management and control function component of DNA. It operates at the application layer much the same as any user

Table IV. NICE Messages

Message	Description
Request Down-line Load	Requests a specified executor node to down-line load a target node.
Request Up-line Dump	Requests a specified executor node to dump the memory of a target node.
Trigger Bootstrap	Requests a specified executor node to trigger the bootstrap loader of a target node.
Test	Requests a specified executor node to perform a node or line loopback test.
Change Parameter	Requests a specified executor node to set or clear one or more Network Management parameters.
Read Information	Requests a specified executor node to read a specified group of parameters, counters, or events.
Zero Counters	Requests a specified executor node to either read and zero or zero a specified group of line or node counters.
System Specific	Requests a system-specific Network Management function.
Response	Provides request status and requested information in response to a NICE request.

program. The NICE program in the remote system communicates to the NICE program running in the loader system to pass the request for loading to the loader program and eventually to be returned a completion notification. Thus, a user sitting at a terminal at a network control center node can control the loading of a remote node via a loader node with a file image located on a fourth, file image node system. Figure 19 shows an example of such a load; the numbers in the figure are the sequence of message and command flows. This complex structure is built from the basic logical link communication mechanism and function access programs of the DECnet architecture.

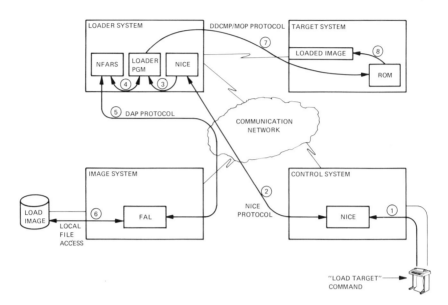

Fig. 19. Down-line loading via NICE with a remote file image.

XIII. Example User Application

This is an example of an actual implemented emergency telephone network in a large midwestern city using DECnet. It is included to show a typical application of the DNA structure and use of logical link communication paths. The objective was to establish a standardized number 911 which subscribers can reach from any telephone to contact an appropriate dispatcher at police or fire department headquarters.

A conventional approach connects all 911 calls to dispatchers at police headquarters, organizing them into zones corresponding to telephone exchange boundaries. The responding officer ascertains the location of the phone and type of emergency from the caller. There were deficiencies with this approach. The telephone network structure did not coincide with police or fire department boundaries. Certain classes of callers were unable to tell the dispatcher where help was needed (because of language, age, etc.) Some callers would not provide the necessary identification, making it difficult for the dispatcher to distinguish between crank calls or false alarms and anonymous Good Samaritans. The goals for the system were as follows:

1. Selective routing of calls to dispatchers;
2. Automatic location identification of the source of calls without verbal communication;
3. Dispatch to responsible agencies: fire or police;
4. Extremely high availability;

Table V. MOP Messages

Message	Description
Memory Load with Transfer Address (Deposit Memory and Transfer)	Causes the contents of the image data to be loaded into memory at the load address, and the system to be started at the transfer address.
Memory Load without Transfer Address (Deposit Memory)	Causes the contents of the image data to be loaded into memory at the load address.
Request Memory Dump (Examine Memory)	Requests a dump of a portion of memory to be returned in a memory dump data message.
Enter MOP Mode	Causes a system not in the MOP mode to enter MOP mode if the password matches. Usually transfers control of the satellite to a MOP program. Used for unattended satellite systems.
Request Program	Requests a program to be sent in some unspecified number of memory load messages.
Request Memory Load	Requests the next load in a loading sequence and provides error status on the previous load.
MOP Mode Running	Indicates to a host that the system is in the MOP mode and supports the features indicated in the message.
Memory Dump Data	Returns the requested memory image in response to a Request Memory Dump message.
Parameter Load with Transfer Address	Loads system parameters and transfers control to the loaded program.
Loopback Test	Tests a link by echoing the message sent by the host.
Looped Data	Returns the test message data in response to a Loopback Test message. Returned by the passive side if the message is looped from a computer.

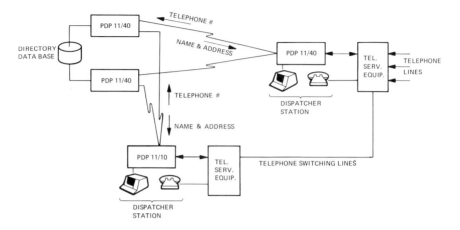

Fig. 20. 911 communication network example.

5. Capacity to process at least 40,000 calls per day, with up to 5,600 calls during any one busy hour, and provide response within 1 s;

6. Restriction of access to the telephone company master directory (to safeguard privacy).

The design chosen for the application was a network of semiautonomous systems. PDP-11 minicomputers are located at telephone company, police, and fire department locations. The network is connected in a star topology (Fig. 20) The data base for the location directory is at the telephone company. Switching processors are located at police and fire dispatch centers. All communication is via DECnet using 4800 bps synchronous communication channels. The telephone company installation acts as a directory manager. Many of the systems are dual processors for high availability.

When a 911 call is recognized at a local exchange, it is switched through the telephone network to the switching equipment at police headquarters along with the identification of the originating number. That system sends a request to the central data base for the corresponding address and zone. The information is extracted from the master directory and returned to the police system. The zone is used to determine routing to the proper dispatcher. When the dispatcher answers the call, the telephone number and address are displayed at the dispatcher station. If the call is for the police, the dispatcher handles it locally. If the caller indicates a fire, the dispatcher presses a button which transfers the call, including the number, to the appropriate fire department processor. The call is routed to the designated dispatcher there in a manner analogous to the initial transfer. Voice communication is unnecessary to establish location. The address display can be held by the system after the phone is hung up at the point of origin.

The operational availability of the network system has exceeded 99.95 percent. The system has met its performance and throughput goals and has maintained a response time of within 0.25 s. The system was installed without any major changes in the line structure of the existing 911 network. The network structure offers the benefit that each data base is under the control of the appropriate agency, thereby maintaining the security requirements of the telephone company, and accommodating establishment and shifting of boundaries by the police and fire departments.

XIV. Observations

Measurements of DECnet systems and comments from its many users have verified the effectiveness of the architecture. Implementations now exist on the 16-bit PDP-11, 32-bit VAX, and 36-bit DECsystem-10 and -20. Interfacing the DNA structure into a wide variety of operating systems has not proven particularly difficult. The architecture has undergone a number of minor revisions and modifications from its original 1974 design to the present. Throughout these changes the structure has remained flexible and extensible. The architecture and protocols have met their goals and expectations. Future requirements and additions to increase the capabilities of DECnet and keep pace with advancing technology will continue to verify its architectural strengths.

References

[1] L. Kleinrock, "Principles and lessons in packet communications," *Proc. IEEE*, Nov. 1978.
[2] D. Davies and D. Barber, *Communication Networks for Computers*. Somerset, NJ: Wiley, 1973.
[3] R. Metcalfe, "Packet communication," Massachusetts Institute of Technology, MIT Project MAC, MAC TR-114, Cambridge, MA, Dec. 1973.
[4] J. Licklider and A. Vezza, "Applications of Information Networks," *Proc. IEEE*, Nov. 1978.
[5] L. Pouzin, "Presentation and major design aspects of the Cyclades computer network," in *Proc. Third Data Commun. Symp.*, Tampa, FL, 1973.
[6] S. Wecker, "Computer network architectures," *Computer*, vol. 12, pp. 58–72, Sept. 1979.
[7] S. Wecker, "Components of a data communication protocol," presented at Intelcom '77, Atlanta, GA, Oct. 1977.
[8] "DNA: Digital data communications message protocol functional specification," Digital Equipment Corp., Maynard, MA, AA-D599B-TC, 1980.

[9] D. Davies, D. Barber, *et al.*, *Computer Networks and Their Protocols*. Somerset, NJ: Wiley, 1979.

[10] J. Majithia *et al.*, "Experiments in congestion control techniques," in *Proc. Int. Symp. Flow Control in Computer Networks*, Versailles, France, Feb. 1979.

[11] M. Irland, "Analysis and simulation of congestion in packet switches networks," Univ. Waterloo, Waterloo, Canada, CCNGT-61, 1977.

[12] "DNA: Transport functional specification," Digital Equipment Corp., Maynard, MA, AA-J059A-TK, 1980.

[13] "DNA: Network services functional specification," Digital Equipment Corp., Maynard, MA, AA-D600B-TC, 1980.

[14] "DNA: Data access protocol functional specification," Digital Equipment Corp., Maynard, MA, AA-D601B-TC, 1980.

[15] J. Passafiume and S. Wecker, "Distributed file access in DECnet," in *Proc. Second Berkeley Workshop on Distributed Data Management and Computer Networks*, Berkeley, CA, May 1977.

[16] "DNA: Maintenance operation protocol functional specification," Digital Equipment Corp. Maynard, MA, AA-D602B-TC, 1980.

[17] "DNA: Network management functional specification," Digital Equipment Corp., Maynard, MA, AA-J060A-TK, 1980.

[18] B. Stewart and S. Wecker, "Network Management in DECnet," *Proc. COMPCON 80*, Wash. DC, Sept. 1980.

11

Path Control—The Network Layer of System Network Architecture

James D. Atkins

I. Introduction

A person sits at a terminal and keys a logon sequence. A response is seen that indicates communication with a computational facility, but it is not obvious whether the computational facility is located within the terminal itself, in a controller to which the terminal may be attached, or in some processor remote to the terminal. Nor is the person aware of how the communication actually occurs. It may also be that the application, with which the terminal user is in communication, is unaware of the physical characteristics of the terminal in use, as well as of the transmission medium that provides the connection between the terminal and the application. This transparency is achieved by defining a framework or a set of rules within which product designs must conform. Systems network architecture (SNA) is an example of such a set of rules [1], defined to provide end user to end user communication.

To accomplish transparency, the management of function as seen by the end user is separated from the management of the transport network. This chapter will focus on the structure of the transport network of SNA, specifically the path control layer, that provides this communications facility. The layers of SNA above path control are described in Chapter 16.

After an overview of the role and positioning of the path control layer in SNA, the elements of path control will be discussed in more detail as well as a form of the network connectivity provided by *transmission groups* (parallel links). The remainder of the chapter will concentrate on the routing aspects of the path control network by mapping the end user's interface, *class of service*, onto the underlying architectural concepts, *virtual routes* and *explicit routes*. The rationale for using multiple static routes rather than adaptive routing techniques will also be discussed. Virtual routes are the logical end-to-end paths through the transport network; the actual physical paths are called explicit routes. Path activation, path selection, and path flow control will be described in these terms.

II. SNA Structure

The intent of this chapter is to examine the architectural characteristics of SNA. The discussion will center around the formats and protocols that make up the formal definition of the path control layer of SNA. It is not the intent of this chapter to discuss or describe product specifications. Typically, products implement only a subset of the formal architecture as described here. As an example, different program products may implement different layers or subsets of functions within layers. Product specifications should be referenced to determine the level or scope of SNA support in a given implementation.

SNA is structured as a layered architecture. The benefits of layering are generally accepted with respect to modularity of function and flexibility for enhancement. Detailed discussions of layering may be found in [3]–[8]. Figure 1 shows the five layers of SNA and the corresponding heading. The highest layer, abbreviated here as Presentation Services, defines the end user interface for each session. This layer is discussed in detail in Chapter 16.

Data flow control [1], [3] and transmission control [1], [3], [10] are also provided as per-session, end-to-end services. Data flow control (see Chapters 16 and 25) maintains the order of the messages flowing between two end users, including such functions as chaining of requests, management of session sequence numbers, response protocols, and concurrency of end user send/receive traffic flows. The transmission control elements manage the actual rate of flow of data within sessions by a session pacing mechanism. This mechanism is referred to in SNA as local flow control and regulates the entry of traffic into the transport network. The transmission control layer also participates in session establishment and termination. Other functions performed by this layer include the creation of request/response headers (RH in Fig. 1).

The subarea path control layer and data link control layer form the transport network of SNA. There is one instance of path control per node and one instance of data link control per local attached device, rather than one per session or per end user. Path control is responsible for routing and the segmenting and blocking of messages. Global flow control is also part of this layer of SNA, providing regulation of the flow of traffic through the

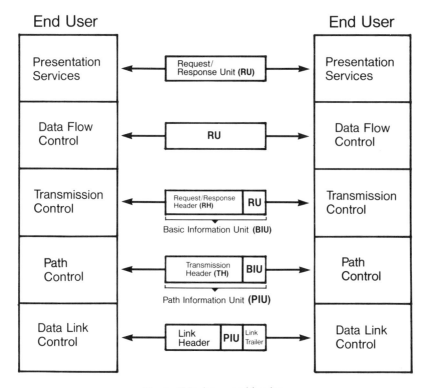

Fig. 1. SNA layers and headers.

transport network. The protocols for the accomplishment of these functions use the transmission header generated by path control. The data link control layer [1], [9] is defined to provide integrity and efficiency in the transmission of data across potentially noisy communications facilities. Data link control adds a link header and link trailer to messages to facilitate error recovery for each physical communications link in the network. The link header and trailer are appended and removed for each link the message traverses.

III. Network Environment

Before delving into the architectural specifics of path control it is appropriate to discuss the environment in which path control exists [10], [11]. SNA is a network architecture, where the network is composed of nodes interconnected by communications facilities (see Fig. 2). The nodes may be of widely varying functional capability, ranging from terminals with minimal native processing capability to complex multiprocessors. The com-

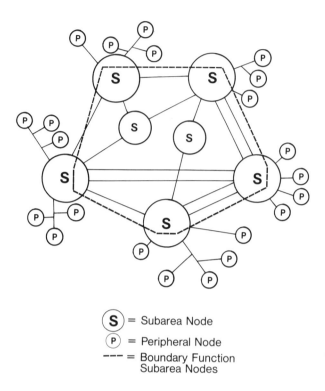

$\left(\text{S}\right)$ = Subarea Node
$\left(\text{P}\right)$ = Peripheral Node
--- = Boundary Function
        Subarea Nodes

Fig. 2. Network configuration.

munications facilities also come in a number of varieties ranging from high-speed I/O channels to low-speed, point-to-point telephone lines and including such media as satellite links and wide-band optical fibers.

The nodes that comprise a network may be partitioned in many ways. One such partitioning classifies nodes according to the address generation and recognition capability associated with the node. SNA categorizes nodes this way and defines multiple levels of addressing within the network, two of which are at the path control level. The higher of these two levels, called the network addresses, consists of two fields. These are called subarea address and element address. The second form of addressing uses only abbreviated versions of network addresses for the associated nodes. Nodes that are capable of recognizing full network addresses are called subarea nodes and are indeed assigned unique subarea values in their network addresses. In formal SNA terminology [1], these are physical unit type 4 (PU_T4) and physical unit type 5 (PU_T5) nodes and are usually realized as communications controllers or hosts, respectively. The network of sub-area nodes forms the transport network of SNA. Terminals and cluster controllers, called peripheral nodes, are attached to a subarea node and share the subarea address of that node. The subarea nodes represent the boundary of the SNA transport network shown by the dotted line in Fig. 2 as seen by these peripheral nodes (physical unit type 1 and physical unit type 2, abbreviated PU_T1 and PU_T2 nodes). Peripheral nodes support only abbreviated addressing.

Although the support of multiple levels of addressing may appear to be an unnecessary complexity, the result is in reality a simpler, more stable interface for the attachment of peripheral (PU_T1 and PU_T2) nodes. These peripheral nodes may be assigned a permanent local address for their implementations. This local address will be translated to a network address by boundary function path control in the adjacent subarea node. Changes in network addresses, e.g., as a result of changes in network configuration or the physical movement of peripheral nodes to a different subarea node, are transparent to the peripheral nodes. The new network address for the peripheral node is absorbed by its boundary function support.

The management of functionally different addressing capabilities of nodes is one of the responsibilities of the path control layer of SNA. Other path control tasks include the establishment of the paths for message transmission (see Sections X and XI) and the control and management of these paths (see Section XII).

IV. Path Control Functions

A. Peripheral Node Path Control

Elements of path control are found in each node in an SNA network. This includes both subarea nodes (PU_T4 and PU_T5) and peripheral nodes (PU_T1 and PU_T2). Path control in a peripheral node consists of packaging a message for transmission to the associated subarea node and routing messages received from the subarea node to the appropriate end user in the peripheral node. The packaging function consists of generating and appending a transmission header to the basic information unit (BIU) created by the transmission control element of the peripheral node to form a path information unit (PIU) as shown in Fig. 1. There are two formats of transmission headers generated by peripheral nodes. The first is a minimum header consisting of 2 bytes of information, providing some control data and a 1 byte address field (see Fig. 3). This transmission header, referred to as a format identifier type 3 (FID3) header, is generated by low function terminals or cluster controllers (PU_T1 nodes), and the 1 byte address field (local session identifier) identifies a specific session for that device.

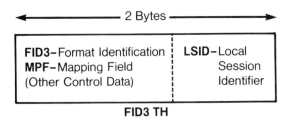

FID3 TH

LSID Bit:	0	1	2	3	4	5	6	7
Session Type	LU/SSCP (1/0)	LU/PU (1/0)	◄———— Local Address ————►					
SSCP–PU	0	0	0	0	0	0	0	0
SSCP–LU	0	1	X	X	X	X	X	X
LU–LU	1	1	X	X	X	X	X	X
Reserved	1	0	X	X	X	X	X	X

LSID Field Values in FID3 TH

Fig. 3. Transmission header format 3.

The local session identifier (LSID) is formatted to allow the support of 64 unique end users, or logical units (LU's), in these nodes (see Fig. 3). Note that the first two bits in the LSID indicate whether the message is for a control session (SSCP-LU or SSCP-PU) or an application session (LU-LU) for an end user. The all-zeros value for LSID specifies that the message is for the control session with the physical unit of the device (SSCP-PU).

The transmission header shown in Fig. 4 is used by higher function terminals and cluster controllers (PU_T2 nodes). This transmission header, referred to as format identifier type 2 (FID2), contains abbreviated forms of both origin and destination address fields as well as a session sequence number field. Session sequence numbers enhance session level integrity for these peripheral nodes by providing correlation for requests and responses. Peripheral nodes using FID3 transmission headers must rely on the data link control sequence numbers for integrity along the path between the peripheral node and its boundary subarea node.

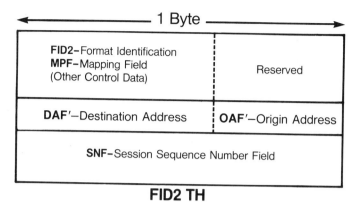

FID2 TH

Fig. 4. Transmission header format 2.

B. Boundary Node Path Control

Certain path control functions of subarea nodes may be classified as either boundary function or intermediate function. The dotted line in Fig. 2 passes through the subarea nodes providing boundary function. Intermediate network node function is provided by all the subarea nodes in this diagram. Boundary function is an example of economical distribution of function from peripheral nodes to subarea nodes. Intermediate function is concerned primarily with the continued transmission of a transport network message unit to its destination. As noted above, boundary function performs address translation to minimize the impact of network reconfiguration by shielding the peripheral nodes from the management of network addresses. Boundary function path control also provides path selection (see Section IX) and global flow control (see Section XII) for sessions that terminate in attached peripheral nodes. Boundary function transmission control elements provide session services for attached peripheral nodes such as local flow control (session pacing) and session sequence number management, as well as session activation/deactivation support. All of these components of boundary function result in fewer computational and storage requirements for peripheral nodes and a simpler interface for these nodes to the transport network.

Boundary function path control further supports the attachment of peripheral nodes in the sense that messages received from peripheral nodes are repackaged for distribution through the transport network. Once the messages have been repackaged, boundary function provides the initial routing determination for the transport network message units (see Fig. 2).

The repackaging of a message by boundary function path control is accomplished by replacing the FID2 or FID3 transmission header with a

2B	**FID4**–Format Identification Transmission Group Sweep Indicator Network Priority Indicator (Other Control Data)	Reserved
2B	(Other Control Data) **ERN**–Explicit Route Number	**VRN**–Virtual Route Number **TPF**–Transmission Priority Field
2B	**VR-CWI**–Virtual Route Change Window Indicator (Other Control Data) **TG-SNF**–Transmission Group Sequence Number Field	
2B	**VRPRQ**–Virtual Route Pacing Request **VRPRS**–Virtual Route Pacing Response **VR-CWRI**–Virtual Route Change Window Reply Indicator **VRRWI**–Virtual Route Reset Window Indicator **VR-SNF-SEND**–Virtual Route Send Sequence Number Field	
4B	**DSAF**–Destination Subarea Address Field	
4B	**OSAF**–Origin Subarea Address Field	
2B	(Other Control Data) **MPF**–Mapping Field	Reserved
2B	**DEF**–Destination Element Field	
2B	**OEF**–Origin Element Field	
2B	**SNF**–Session Sequence Number Field	
2B	**DCF**–Data Count Field	

FID4 TH

Fig. 5. Transmission header format 4.

transport network transmission header. Figure 5 shows the format identifier type 4 (FID4) transmission header required for packets traversing the subarea path control network. In what follows, we shall explain the purpose of all the fields in the header.

Note that in the FID4 transmission header there are origin and destination subarea address fields (OSAF and DSAF) in addition to origin and destination element address fields (OEF and DEF). Boundary function must provide translation from the abbreviated addresses contained in FID2 and FID3 headers to the full network addresses required in FID4 transmission headers and vice versa. To perform this transformation, the subarea node takes advantage of the information contained in the received headers as well as prior knowledge of the configuration of peripheral nodes—that is, knowledge of the physical attachment configuration and the data link control address of a peripheral node will be used in determining the network address of that node. Address translation is the routing component of boundary function path control. In addition to address translation, the boundary function node will determine the logical path on which the message is to travel (virtual route number, explicit route number), as well as the transmission priority (transmission priority field) to be used for that message. Additional information contained in the FID4 header will be discussed in later sections of this paper.

Another path control function is the blocking and segmenting of messages. In some instances, a communications path may be used more efficiently if the messages to be transmitted across that path are of a size different from the lengths of the originally generated messages. If the message (basic information unit) is too long to be efficiently transmitted, the message may be segmented into several smaller messages. Alternatively, if the throughput capability of the communications path between two subarea nodes is sufficiently high to warrant simultaneous transmission of groups of messages, then multiple messages (path information units) may be combined or blocked into a single message (basic transmission unit).

Two specific advantages may be gained through segmenting. First, the transmission of multiple segments may be overlapped where the path of the message traverses multiple nodes or parallel links between two nodes. The transmission time for the example in Fig. 6 is reduced by 33 percent as a result of being able to overlap the transmission of multiple segments. Secondly, the use of a shorter transmission unit results in more favorable error characteristics—that is, the probability of a segment requiring retransmission is lower in proportion to the decrease in the length of the segment.

Segment reassembly capability is provided by using either the mapping field (MPF) or the virtual route sequence number in the transmission header. MPF is used to indicate segment order between peripheral nodes and boundary nodes by the following encoding:

10 = first segment of message
00 = middle segment of message
01 = last segment of message
11 = whole message.

There is an exposure to the undetected loss of middle segments as these segments are not uniquely sequenced. If FID3 transmission headers are used, no session sequence numbers are provided. If FID2 headers are employed, all segments of a message will contain the same sequence number. However, this exposure is limited to the transmission between the peripheral node and the boundary subarea node and is minimized by the

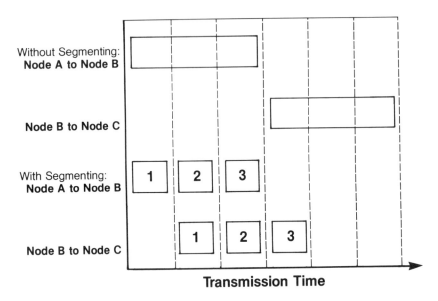

Fig. 6. Segmenting performance enhancement.

use of unique data link control sequence numbers on each segment. At the boundary node, messages may be reassembled, transmitted as segmented by the peripheral node, or further segmented as required for transmission through the transport network.

Sequence numbers are generated by path control at a boundary node prior to transmission over the virtual route. These virtual route send sequence numbers are session independent and distinct from the session sequence numbers (SNF) generated by the transmission control element. The virtual route sequence number is unique for each segment and will allow detection of a missing segment at the message's destination. Current implementations guarantee correct sequencing between adjacent subarea nodes (see Section V). Consequently, a virtual route sequence number error is detected but resequencing at the message's destination is not performed.

Typically, blocking is done between nodes that support FID4 transmission headers to gain throughput by better utilizing a high bandwidth facility such as an I/O channel of a host processor. Each message or path information unit (PIU) included in a blocked basic transmission unit (BTU) retains its own individual transmission header. A single set of data link control headers is used to transmit several PIUs, resulting in some overhead reduction over the I/O channel. At the destination of the BTU, the individual PIUs may be deblocked using the data count field in the transmission header of each PIU and routed to independent sessions as appropriate. Note that the transmission headers generated by element nodes (FID2 and FID3) have no data count field. Consequently, these messages cannot be blocked.

C. Intermediate Node Path Control

As mentioned earlier, path control also exists in the intermediate subarea nodes with or without boundary function. The intermediate node path control function consists of routing messages to the appropriate adjacent subarea node based on information contained in the FID4 transmission header. If path control finds a message for the current subarea node, then it is routed to the local boundary function path control element. Once path control has determined that the message is indeed destined for a subarea node other than its own subarea node, the destination subarea address and the route specification information in the FID4 transmission header are used in conjunction with local routing tables to determine the path to be taken by the message. Intermediate function path control will then schedule the message for transmission on that path.

With this understanding of the function of path control in boundary and intermediate network nodes, it is now appropriate to examine the mechanism that connects the subarea nodes to form SNA's transport network.

V. Transmission Groups

The basic element of connectivity for an SNA transport network is the transmission group (Fig. 7). The transmission group forms a logical connection between any two subarea nodes and may be comprised of one or more physical links between the two nodes. A multilink transmission group provides parallel links between two subarea nodes.

Multiple transmission groups, up to a maximum of 255, may also be defined between any two adjacent subarea nodes. A transmission group (TG) is thus defined at a given node by the specific transmission group number and the adjacent subarea. Multilink transmission groups provide a single queue, multiple server environment as sessions have a routing affinity for a transmission group rather than a specific link. One configuration alternative between two adjacent nodes might be to place all satellite links in one transmission group, all terrestrial links in transmission groups by speed, and all highly secure links in yet another transmission group. Multilink transmission groups provide enhanced reliability for connectivity, while multiple transmission groups between two subarea nodes allow the specification of alternate paths between the nodes.

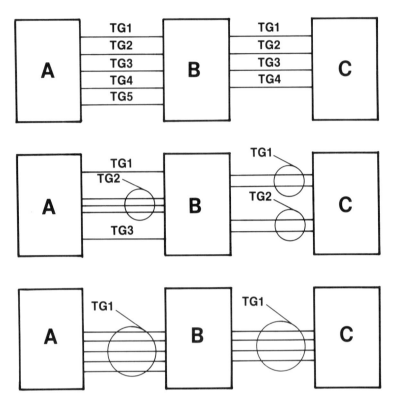

Fig. 7. Transmission group options. (a) Single link transmission groups. (b) Multilink transmission groups. (c) Single multilink transmission group.

Several possible configurations of transmission groups are shown in Fig. 7. Note that there are five physical links connecting node A with node B and four physical links connecting node B with node C. In Fig. 7(a), the five links connecting A and B are treated as five distinct transmission groups. The links adjoining B and C are also treated as independent transmission groups. In Fig. 7(b), the five links are grouped into three transmission groups, and the four links between B and C form two transmission groups. Finally, in Fig. 7(c), there is one transmission group defined between nodes A and B and one transmission group between nodes B and C. Although in all three cases the total physical capacity of the communications channels between nodes A, B, and C could be the same, it will be seen that the management of this capacity is distinctly different.

The transmission group is the basic component in the definition of end-to-end physical paths. Failure of a transmission group, therefore, results in a disruption of service for an end-to-end path through the network. In

Fig. 7(a), the five transmission groups between nodes A and B enable the specification of five distinct physical paths between these nodes, but the restriction of a transmission group to a single physical link means that the physical path through the network will fail if the specific link that defines the transmission group fails. A transmission group is active as long as any link associated with the transmission group is active. Therefore, in the case of multilink transmission groups, the transmission group will continue to provide the logical connection as long as any link associated with that transmission group is operational. In instances of multilink transmission groups as in Figs. 7(b) and 7(c), the logical connection between nodes A and B will continue to exist, although with degraded throughput capacities, even though one or more links (but not all links) associated with the transmission group fail.

The single message throughput rate of a transmission group may be traded off against the reliability characteristic of multilink transmission groups. The instantaneous throughput capability of a single 9600-bit/s link for a single message is certainly greater than that of a transmission group consisting of four 2400-bit/s links, but the latter has significantly better reliability. Typically, multiple transmission groups will be defined to provide different levels of service for traffic between two subarea nodes. As an example, consider again the configurations shown connecting A and B in Fig. 7(b). Suppose that transmission group 1 in this instance is a satellite link, that transmission group 2 is composed of three high-speed terrestrial links, and finally, that transmission group 3 is a low-speed terrestrial link.

Messages will be transmitted over the appropriate physical path according to their individual service requirements. These requirements are reflected in the class of service (COS) selected for a given session (see Section VI).

Although it is possible to have included all five physical links in one transmission group, the result could be inefficient due to resequencing delays. To minimize the resequencing required to maintain original order, the elements of a transmission group should be as homogeneous as possible. Messages transmitted over a multilink transmission group may arrive out of order as the result of:

1. varying length messages;
2. nonhomogeneous link characteristics (e.g., link speed);
3. link errors.

Any of the above conditions may result in loss of FIFO order across the transmission group. Consequently, messages will be held until resequencing can occur. At that time, the messages will be released by the transmission group.

In SNA networks, transmission groups are implemented in such a way as to mask the potential out-of-sequence characteristics of the physical

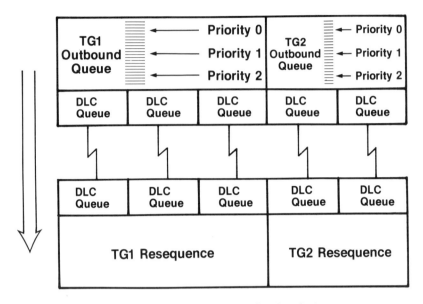

Fig. 8. TG queue structure (one direction view).

connection. As shown in Fig. 8, a transmission group outbound PIU queue may service multiple data links. The transmission group receiver will guarantee that messages of the same transmission priority exit the transmission group in the same order that they entered the transmission group outbound queue. This is accomplished through the use of a transmission group sequence number generated by the transmission group scheduler at the outbound queue and placed in the transmission header of that message.

Messages are placed on the appropriate transmission group outbound queue in a priority sequence determined by the transmission priority field (TPF) and network priority indicator in the FID4 transmission headers. Three values are defined for the transmission priority field:

00 = low priority
01 = medium priority
10 = high priority.

These values are associated with the logical path (virtual route) over which a session flows. Consequently, a priority will be established for a session at its initiation and will be unchanged for the duration of the session. A message will be inserted on the transmission group outbound queue in FIFO order within its priority class, e.g., a message with TPF = 01 will be placed ahead of all messages with TPF = 00 and behind all messages with TPF = 01 or TPF = 10. Note that this will not affect message sequence within a session as all messages for a given session will have the same priority. The use of transmission priorities allows more critical traffic to preempt less important messages. This is especially beneficial when the network is heavily loaded. It also allows traffic from one class of service to get ahead of that for another, as we shall see in the next section.

The network priority indicator is used to allow certain control messages to overtake other messages regardless of transmission priority. These other messages immediately go to the top of the transmission group outbound queue behind any other messages flowing at network priority.

Some products may provide implementation-dependent means for lower priority messages to be guaranteed eventual transmission. As an example, messages on a transmission group outbound queue may be aged by the transmission group sequence number to prevent lockout. When the sequence number reaches a specified (modulo) value, all current messages on the queue could be logically moved to the highest priority partition of the queue. Other techniques may also be used for this purpose.

Each link in a transmission group comprises a full pair of data link control stations, each with its own independent link addressing, error recovery procedures, statistics gathering, etc. In the event that an error occurs on a data link, a copy of the affected message will be retransmitted on that link. No new traffic will be scheduled for the degraded link until that message is successfully transmitted. The original message will simultaneously be sent on an alternate link in the same transmission group. This is done to minimize the resequencing delay resulting from the error in the transmission of the original message and to avoid session damage by link failures. Multiple copies of the same message will be detected by the receiving side of the transmission group. If the transmission group sequence number of a received message is lower than the next expected, the message is discarded as a duplicate. If the TG sequence number is higher than expected, it is held in the TG PIU resequence queue as out-of-order. Integrity of the transmission group sequence numbers is provided by monitoring the wrap of the sequence numbers and performing a "sweep" of the data link outbound queues. Each link outbound queue must be cleared, e.g., by transmission and acknowledgment of a specific control message. This will result in all existing messages being acknowledged before the sequence number wrap occurs. Any outstanding out-of-sequence messages at that point will be determined to be permanent errors, and appropriate notification will occur.

The existence of multiple transmission groups between subareas supports the definition of multiple physical paths between origin and destination subarea nodes. The provision of transmission priorities allows the specification of multiple logical paths on a single physical path. Alternate paths with the class of service concept described in Section VI provide a vehicle for the partitioning of network traffic by service requirements, as well as an enhancement for session recovery in the event of a path failure. The creation of these paths and the control of routing on them is a key responsibility of path control.

VI. Class of Service

The end user's view of route selection is formally defined through the class of service interface. Class of service specification provides the user control of the use of the underlying transmission facility, such as priority, throughput, cost, delay, security, and integrity. Other parameters that may be associated with class of service include private leased lines, public switched lines, terrestrial lines, satellite facilities, etc. The class of service name (COSNAME) may be provided either implicitly or explicitly by the user when a session is initiated. Specification of COSNAME may be logically viewed as selection of a transport network service level for a particular session. Existence of multiple COSNAMEs usually implies multiple physical paths between subarea pairs, but the definition and actual selection of the physical path that provides the desired service level is transparent to the user. In some instances, several COSNAMEs may be used to provide paths giving minimum hop count, maximum throughput, all terrestrial links, maximum security, etc. In other cases, COSNAMEs may reflect multiple transmission priorities on a single physical path.

The request for session initiation includes specification of the originating and destination subareas. Multiple COSNAMEs may be defined for each subarea pair. Each COSNAME defined for an origin/destination subarea pair translates to a list of virtual routes, where a virtual route may be thought of as a logical point-to-point path between the origin and destination subarea. A virtual route is uniquely identified by the subarea address fields of the two end nodes of the virtual route (VR) and the virtual route identifier (VRID). The virtual route identifier is specified by the virtual route number and the transmission priority field discussed in Section V. Current implementations allow up to eight virtual route numbers between any two subarea nodes and three levels of transmission priority. Consequently, it is possible to define as many as 24 virtual routes between any two subarea nodes. The VRID list associated with the COSNAME represents the defined logical connections between the given subareas that can provide the level of service associated with the COSNAME.

The VRID list is assumed to be in order of preference. At session initiation, a mechanism is provided for manipulation of the order of the list. Through this user exit, load balancing may be accomplished by establishing concurrent sessions between two nodes over different routes. Parameters such as the number of sessions active on a given virtual route may be available to assist in this process. Following any necessary reordering of the VRID list, an attempt will be made to establish the session on the first virtual route in the list. If it is determined that this virtual route is not available, then the next virtual route will be tried. If the list is exhausted without successful activation of a virtual route, then the common session control manager will be notified that no route is available in the specified class of service.

Class of service plays an important role in recovery for SNA sessions. If the path associated with a session fails, then it is possible to attempt reestablishment of the session through specification of the same class of service. The first available virtual route in the associated VRID list will be used for reestablishment of the session. If the class of service fails (i.e., if between the subareas all virtual routes on the list for that class of service fail), then the user has the option of selecting an alternate class of service for completion of the session. Although all existing paths between the two end nodes could be included in a single class of service, the use of multiple classes of service provides notification of a service level degradation in the case where all paths of a given service level have failed.

VII. Virtual Routes

A virtual route is a logical duplex connection between two subarea nodes (see Fig. 9). Multiple virtual routes may be defined between a subarea pair, and message traffic for multiple independent sessions may flow concurrently on a single virtual route. The primary objective of the virtual route concept is to enable the management of origin/destination (end-to-end) subarea protocols without concern for the physical nodes and transmission groups over which the virtual route passes. Given that through COSNAME a virtual route has been determined for a session, virtual route control in the subarea node provides the mapping of messages for that session from its virtual route to the appropriate physical path (explicit route). Virtual route control creates a virtual route control block (VRCB) for each virtual route that terminates in the subarea node. The VRCB provides segmenting and virtual route sequence number control for its associated virtual route, as well as managing the flow control for the virtual route. Finally, virtual route control maps messages from the local half-sessions (one end of a session) to the appropriate explicit route. Messages destined for the local subarea node are passed to virtual route control from the explicit route control. The routing component of virtual route control directs the message to its destination half-session using the appropriate VRCB.

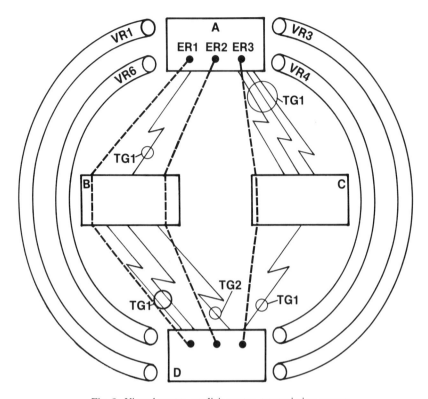

Fig. 9. Virtual routes, explicit routes, transmission groups.

VIII. Explicit Routes

The actual physical components of the logical path are referred to collectively as the explicit route for the associated virtual route. SNA has chosen to use the concept of static physical route definition [12] rather than dynamic adaptive routing alternatives for several reasons. Dynamic routing networks are complex to design and may cause recovery difficulties as the determination of specific link failure and affected messages is complicated by the lack of physical path affinity for the messages. Adaptive algorithms appear no more efficient [13] than static designs, and in fact may be less efficient in commercial usage where message order integrity is critical. Consequently, SNA has selected multilink transmission groups and multiple fixed routes to provide enhanced reliability and recovery rather than adaptive routing techniques. Each explicit route is individually testable and the explicit route concept provides control over the links and nodes traversed by a given path.

The physical path between two subarea nodes may be specified by the ordered set of transmission groups through which traffic is to pass between the two end point subareas. For a given explicit route, only one transmission group may be specified between adjacent subarea nodes. The specification of transmission groups must include the adjacent subarea nodes to remove ambiguity. As an example, in Fig. 9, ER2 consists of Subarea A, TG1, Subarea B, TG2, Subarea D. This represents a bidirectional physical path, but each direction of transmission may be assigned a unique explicit route number (ERN). The reversibility of explicit routes is required to simplify failure notification by allowing simultaneous flow of failure detection to both ends of the associated virtual routes along those routes themselves rather than by some other routes. For completeness, then, the specification of an explicit route must include the ERN for each direction (ERN and reverse ERN) and an ordered indication of the subareas connected by the ERN. Current implementations provide for the possibility of eight ERNs per subarea pair and allow multiple virtual routes to be mapped to a single explicit route.

IX. Routing

A virtual route is a logical end-to-end connection. Virtual routes are therefore known only in the origin and destination subarea nodes, where the virtual routes terminate. Here the messages are mapped by virtual route control onto the correct explicit route. Intermediate node routing is based solely on the explicit route number and destination subarea fields of a message's FID4 transmission header and represents the primary function of explicit route control [12]. Figure 10 shows the relationship of explicit route functions with other path control components. While at the boundary nodes explicit route control maps messages to and from virtual route control, the explicit route control component of intermediate nodes routes traffic to the appropriate transmission group using routing tables assembled during system generation. Although SNA does not specify the format of routing tables, Fig. 11 illustrates the explicit routing concept used in SNA. Explicit route control inspects the FID4 transmission header and determines the message's destination subarea (B in the example) and the explicit route number (2) for the message. These two values are used to access an element in the routing table that specifies the next subarea to which the message is to be transmitted (M) and the transmission group number to be used (N) (recall that multiple transmission groups may exist between two subarea nodes).

Current SNA implementations do not use origin subarea as a routing parameter. Consequently, if two explicit routes having common explicit

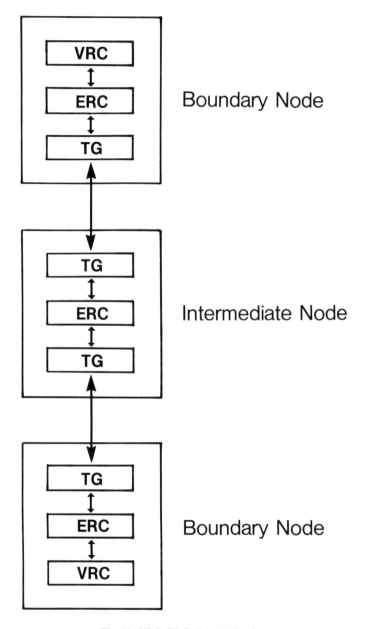

Fig. 10. VRC, ERC, TG relationships.

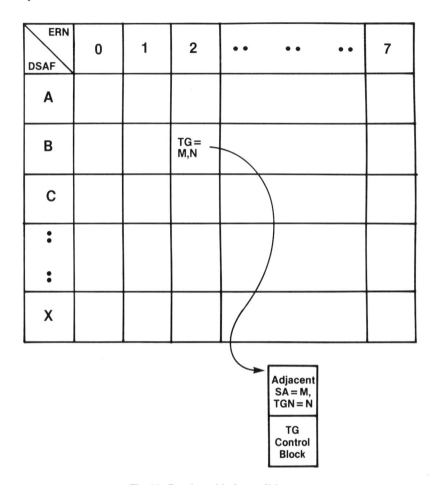

Fig. 11. Routing table for explicit routes.

route numbers and destination subareas intersect at an intermediate node, they will be merged regardless of origins. Care must be taken to recognize this situation in defining route configurations.

X. Explicit Route Activation

Explicit routes are generally in one of three states: Inoperative, Operative, or Active. An explicit route is said to be Inoperative if at least one transmission group in the explicit route definition is inoperative (no links operative). If all transmission groups that form the explicit route are operative, then the explicit route is said to be operative. Both end node explicit route managers will have received a network control (explicit route operative) request (NC_ER_OP). An NC_ER_OP message is generated by the explicit route manager in each subarea node when a transmission group attached to that node becomes operative (at least one operative link), providing a connection to an adjacent subarea node. NC_ER_OP flows across the newly operative transmission group from both subareas and specifies the subareas connected by the transmission group, the transmission group number (TGN) of the transmission group, and a list of operative explicit routes.

This list represents the additional connectivity achieved by the transmission group becoming operative. It is, in fact, a statement by the adjacent subarea node of its current routing capability and is generated from the operative entries in its explicit route status table. The operative explicit route fields in the NC_ER_OP list all destination subareas that may now be accessed over the new transmission group. A mask is provided for each subarea indicating which explicit route numbers may be used to access that subarea.

The node receiving the NC_ER_OP message will update its routing status tables and modify the operative explicit route fields by eliminating bits in the mask representing explicit route numbers that are not valid beyond the current node (route terminates in the current node). The NC_ER_OP is then propagated to all adjacent subarea nodes, except the subarea node from which it was received. The process is repeated until all masks in the operative explicit route fields contain only zeros (no valid explicit route numbers) or all subareas have been notified. The flow pattern of NC_ER_OP results in automatic notification of the Operative state of an explicit route to the end nodes of the route when all associated transmission groups have been activated.

A similar flow results in the event of a transmission group failure (last link inoperative). In this case, the request is network control (explicit route inoperative), NC_ER_INOP, and the information content is similar to NC_ER_OP. NC_ER_INOP eventually reaches the end nodes of each affected explicit route, causing the explicit routes to be set Inoperative and notification to be sent to the virtual route manager for appropriate action relative to the virtual routes mapped to the affected explicit routes.

An explicit route remains in the Operative state until a network control (explicit route activate) request (NC_ER_ACT) has been sent by the explicit route manager and a network control (explicit route activate reply) message (NC_ER_ACT_REPLY) has been received. As a result of the successful exchange of these two messages, an explicit route number will be defined for each direction of the explicit route and the length of the explicit route will be determined in units of transmission groups (used in global flow control). The explicit route can now be set to the Active state. The route will remain active until connectivity is lost as a result of a transmission group failure. Such an occurrence results in all explicit route managers that receive the associated NC_ER_INOP request resetting the affected explicit routes in the Inoperative state. The explicit route managers then notify the appropriate virtual route managers that the affected virtual routes are inoperative.

XI. Session Path Activation

A session cannot be established until an appropriate path has been activated. Selection of a class of service provides a list of potential paths in the form of the VRID list. The virtual routes in this list are usually in one of two states, Reset or Active. Reset state implies that no buffer resources are allocated to a virtual route and a VRCB does not exist for that virtual route, although the underlying explicit route may have been activated earlier. The virtual route will leave the Reset state as the result of a network control (activate virtual route) request (NC_ACTVR) flowing successfully on the explicit route, entering the Active state. This means that the virtual route managers at both end nodes have created VRCBs to support the virtual route to explicit route mapping.

Common session control, the element of SNA responsible for session activation/deactivation, passes the selected VRID list from the SSCP to the virtual route manager [1]. After any desired reordering of the list, the virtual route manager determines if the first virtual route in the VRID list is Active by searching for the corresponding VRCB. If the virtual route is Active, the address of the VRCB is returned to common session control and the session initiation continues. Otherwise, the virtual route manager determines through the explicit route manager if the underlying explicit route is Active. If this is the case, the virtual route manager creates a VRCB for the virtual route and sends an NC_ACTVR request to the virtual route manager at the destination subarea. The NC_ACTVR request includes specification of both send and receive ERNs, an initial virtual route sequence number, and minimum and maximum virtual route pacing window sizes (see Section XII).

The destination virtual route manager will attempt to allocate required buffer resources and create a VRCB for the specified virtual route. If successful, the virtual route will be set to the Active state and a positive response will be sent to the origin virtual route manager, causing the virtual route to be set Active there and the address of the VRCB to be returned to common session control. Otherwise, a negative response is sent to the origin virtual route manager and the next virtual route in the VRID list is processed.

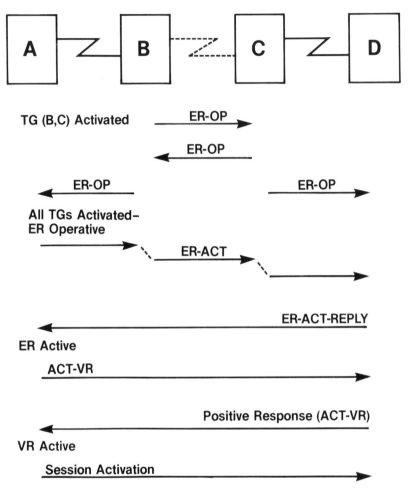

Fig. 12. Route activation sequence.

If the explicit route is in the Operative state, then the explicit route manager issues NC_ER_ACT. If the explicit route is successfully activated, then virtual route activation proceeds as described above. An Inoperative explicit route will result in consideration of the next virtual route in the VRID list. When the VRID list is exhausted, common session control is notified that the class of service has failed.

The relationship of SNA routing commands in creating a session path is illustrated in Fig. 12. The protocols defined for the activation of a route are structured to prevent the occurrence of a deadlock condition in this operation [14]. The next section will describe the protocols defined to prevent deadlock conditions in the allocation of resources for network traffic.

XII. Flow Control

Economic considerations in the physical implementation of a network generally lead to constraints on the throughput capability of the network. The design points selected with respect to processing and storage capacity of nodes and bandwidth of communication links are usually such that peak loads will exceed the throughput capability of the network. Such a network should respond to increased loads with a monotonic increase in throughput, with stabilization near the maximum throughput of the system in overload conditions. Mechanisms (see Chapter 13) must be in place to prevent degradation of throughput under these circumstances and, above all, to avoid network deadlock (see Chapter 13). SNA provides flow control mechanisms that attempt to avoid deadlock conditions without penalizing network throughput in lightly loaded situations.

SNAs primary flow control mechanisms are based on a window pacing concept [13]–[18]. Network traffic is measured in units of windows (see Fig. 13). A transmitter is allowed to send a window, k messages, upon receipt of transmit authorization from the receiver. In Fig. 13, $k = 4$. The first message in a window will contain a request for authorization to transmit another window of messages. The receiver may respond to this request before the entire window has arrived depending on resource status in the node. Consequently, the pacing response may overlap the transmission of the current window of messages and may result in a second window being transmitted before the first window has been completely received. The window pacing mechanism therefore limits the number of messages introduced into the network by the given transmitter to $2k - 1$, where k is the current window size. The various slopes in Fig. 13 reflect different levels of congestion and thus different transmission delays. Note that larger window sizes may result in shorter waiting times at the sender or receiver but run the risk of creating congestion delays in the network. Pacing attempts to balance flow between origin and destination.

Window pacing is employed on both a session basis and a virtual route basis. Session pacing protects the end user, and VR pacing protects the network resource along the VR. Session-level pacing, a local flow control mechanism designed to control the admission of data into the path control network, may be provided in two stages. The first stage is from the peripheral node to its supporting boundary node. The second stage is from that boundary node to the other end user, typically an application resident in a host. The window sizes are specified independently for the two stages at

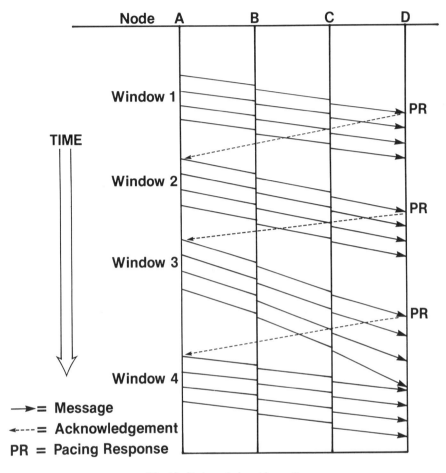

Fig. 13. Pacing window (size = 4).

the time the session is created and remain fixed for the duration of the session. The primary objective of session-level pacing is to match the input data rate of the source end user to the capability of the destination end user to receive and handle the data. The decision to respond to a pacing request is based solely on the resource status of the receiving application; session-level pacing does not reflect resource utilization status within the path control network. Session-level pacing is a transmission control layer responsibility; the flow control mechanism for the path control layer is provided by virtual route pacing.

Virtual route pacing is the global flow control mechanism of SNA. It is intended to regulate the flow of traffic through the transport network by monitoring the utilization of path control network resources and modifying input rates for virtual routes accordingly. (Recall that multiple independent sessions may flow on a single virtual route and that, as shown in Fig. 9, multiple virtual routes may share the physical resources of the transport network.) Input traffic for a virtual route is again measured in units of windows and control is accomplished through the same pacing request/response mechanism used in session pacing, but the traffic on a virtual route or on a given link in the path control network is much more variable than the traffic on a single session. Consequently, studies [17] have shown that significantly improved network throughput may be attained by dynamically adjusting the virtual route window as the network load fluctuates. Although the virtual route is bidirectional, the following discussion of virtual route window management will be based on a single direction view for clarity.

Minimum and maximum virtual route window sizes (WS_MIN) and (WS_MAX) are established when a virtual route is activated (NC_ACTVR). The minimum window size corresponds to the "hop count," the length of the explicit route measured by the number of transmission groups in the underlying explicit route. The maximum window size is typically set to some multiple of the explicit route length, e.g., three times WS_MIN. The virtual route window size is dynamically adjusted between these limits to reflect the current throughput capability of the network.

Five bits are defined in the FID4 transmission header (see Fig. 5) to support virtual route pacing. The virtual route pacing request (VRPRQ) bit is set on in the first message of each window by the transmitter of the window. Upon receipt of a message with VRPRQ on, the receiver may send a control message with the virtual route pacing response (VRPRS) bit on to indicate that the receiver can accept another window of messages. If the receiver cannot allocate resources for another window, then the VRPRS will be withheld until resources are determined to be available. Isolated VRPRS messages, sent independently of any particular request and without correlation of sequence numbers, have the network priority indicator set in the FID4 transmission header, allowing them to overtake all other messages. When the sender receives VRPRS it may then transmit another window of messages. The sender maintains a virtual route pacing count that represents the number of messages the sender has been authorized to transmit on the virtual route. Each time the sender receives a VRPRS it increments the virtual route pacing count by the current window size. A value of one is subtracted from the virtual route pacing count whenever a message is transmitted on the virtual route. As long as the virtual route pacing count is positive, the sender may continue to transmit messages on the virtual route. When the virtual route pacing count is equal to the current window size, the VRPRQ bit is set on in the next message, representing the first message of a new window.

The action taken if congestion is detected by an intermediate network node is dependent on the level of congestion as measured by implementation-dependent parameters. For example, a subarea node may define congestion on a path by the transmission group outbound queue lengths on that path. Minor congestion results in the intermediate network node setting the change window indicator (CWI) bit in messages that encounter the congestion. The receiver of CWI notes the existence of congestion on the associated virtual route and will set the change window reply indicator (CWRI) bit in the next VRPRS sent to the transmitter for that virtual route. The CWRI may also be set by an end node if congestion exists in that node itself. If severe congestion is detected, then the reset window indicator (RWI) bit is set on in any message flowing on that explicit route in a direction opposite to the message that encountered the severe congestion.

Although the global flow control mechanism is coupled with virtual routes, the detection of congestion in the intermediate network nodes is based on the status of explicit route components. The intermediate routing function is based on explicit routes as intermediate network nodes have no knowledge of virtual routes. If a transmission group or intermediate node

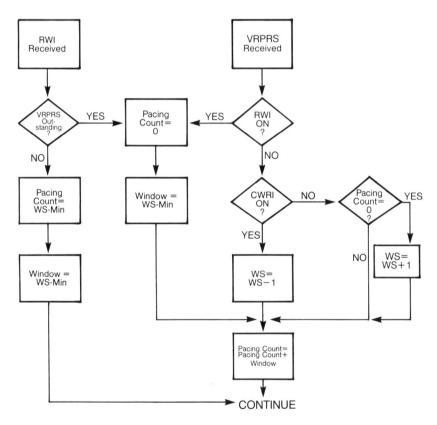

Fig. 14. VR window control.

experiences a lack of resource availability, all virtual routes flowing through that element may be affected. Consequently, all sources of messages flowing on that explicit route will be notified and the windows of all notified virtual routes utilizing that explicit route will be adjusted accordingly.

When an end node receives a message with RWI on, the window size for the corresponding virtual route is immediately set to WS_MIN ("slammed"). If the RWI was received in a VRPRS, the virtual route pacing count is set equal to the new window size and the next window of messages is transmitted. Otherwise, the current virtual route pacing count is examined. If it is less than or equal to WS_MIN, no action is taken. If the current pacing count exceeds WS_MIN, it is set equal to WS_MIN and processing continues.

When an end node receives a VRPRS without RWI set on, then CWRI is examined. If CWRI is set on, then the current window size is decremented by one to a minimum of WS_MIN. If CRWI is not set on, then the window size is incremented by one if the virtual route pacing count equals zero. Otherwise, the window size is unchanged as the implication is that the virtual route is operating satisfactorily with current window size value. The window size will not be incremented beyond WS_MAX. Management of the virtual route pacing count and window size is summarized in Fig. 14.

Although the virtual route is bidirectional and WS_MIN and WS_MAX are the same in both directions, there is no correlation between the two window sizes after the virtual route has been activated. The window sizes are independently modified according to network congestion detected in either direction along the virtual route.

XIII. Summary

This chapter has presented a tutorial on the transport network of SNA, especially the path control layer. The path control network consists primarily of subarea nodes connected by transmission groups, although path control functions are also seen in peripheral nodes. The routing structure of SNA is built on the transport network through the concepts of explicit routes and virtual routes. These concepts provide the definition of multiple static routes between end nodes in the transport network. The end user's interface to routing is the class of service, a facility for path selection and recovery that masks the physical attributes of routes from the end user. The protocols for path activation are designed to layer the management of route control and prevent deadlock occurrence in route activation. Flow control mechanisms are defined to manage the utilization of path control resources, allowing maximum throughput in overload conditions while not artificially restraining the network when traffic is light.

Definition of the path control layer is critical to the success of SNA. The functions of path control are typically transparent to the end user, but must create a network that is both flexible in configuration and throughput capabilities and reliable in the provision of paths through the network. These network attributes are apparent to the end user only in their absence. The goal of path control is continued unawareness.

References

[1] *Systems Network Architecture Format and Protocol Reference Manual: Architecture Logic*, Order Number SC30-3112, IBM Corp., Data Processing Div., White Plains, NY 10504.

[2] E. H. Sussenguth, "Systems network architecture: A perspective," in *ICCC 1978 Conf. Proc.*, Kyoto, Japan, 1978.

[3] R. J. Cypser, *Communications Architecture for Distributed Systems*. Reading, MA: Addison-Wesley, 1978.

[4] P. E. Green, Jr., "The structure of computer networks," and this book, Chapter 1, also in *IBM Syst. J.*, vol. 18, pp. 202–222, 1979.

[5] *Reference Model of Open Systems Architecture*, Int. Standards Org. Document ISO/TC97/XC16/N117, Nov. 1978.

[6] L. Pouzin and H. Zimmerman, "A tutorial on protocols," *Proc. IEEE*, vol. 66, Nov. 1978.

[7] V. G. Cerf and P. T. Kirstein, "Issues in packet-network interconnection," *Proc. IEEE*, vol. 66, Nov. 1978.

[8] S. Wecker, "Computer network architecture," *Computer*, vol. 12, Sept. 1979.

[9] R. A. Donnan and J. R. Kersey, "Synchronous data link control: A perspective," *IBM Syst. J.*, pp. 140–162, 1974.

[10] J. H. McFadyen, "Systems network architecture: An overview," *IBM Syst. J.*, vol. 15, pp. 2–23, 1976.

[11] J. P. Gray and T. B. McNeill, "SNA multi-systems networking," *IBM Syst. J.*, vol. 18, pp. 263–297, 1979.

[12] R. R. Jueneman and G. S. Kerr, "Explicit path routing in communication networks," in *ICCC 1976 Conf. Proc.*, Toronto, Ont. Canada, 1976.

[13] H. Rudin and H. Muller, "Dynamic routing and flow control," *IEEE Trans. Commun.*, vol. 28, pp. 1030–1040, July 1980.

[14] V. Ahuja, "Routing and flow control in systems network architecture," *IBM Syst. J.*, vol. 18, pp. 298–314, 1979.

[15] L. Kleinrock, *Queuing Systems, Volume 2: Computer Applications*. New York: Wiley, 1976.

[16] G. A. Deaton and D. J. Franse, "A computer network flow control study," in *ICCC 1978 Conf. Proc.*, Kyoto, Japan, 1978.

[17] G. A. Deaton, "Flow control in packet switched networks with explicit path routing," in *Proc. Int. Symp. Flow Control in Comput. Networks*, Versailles, France, 1979.

[18] M. Reiser, "A queueing network analysis of computer communication networks with window flow control," *IEEE Trans. Commun.*, vol. COM-27, Aug. 1979.

12

Routing Protocols

Mischa Schwartz and Thomas E. Stern

I. Introduction

In this chapter, we provide an overview of routing techniques used in a variety of computer communication networks in current operation. These include the public data networks TYMNET and TRANSPAC (the former is a specialized common carrier network based in the United States, but with connections to Europe as well; the latter is the French government PTT data network), ARPAnet, the U.S. Department of Defense Computer Network, and the commercial network architectures SNA (Systems Network Architecture) and DNA (Digital Network Architecture), developed by IBM and Digital Equipment Corporation, respectively. The networks are all examples of store-and-forward networks with data packets* moving from a source to a destination, buffered at intermediate nodes along a path. The path is defined simply as the collection of sequential communication links ultimately connecting source to destination.

The routing algorithms used in these networks all turn out to be variants, in one form or another, of shortest path algorithms that route packets from source to destination over a path of least cost. The specific cost criterion used differs among the networks. As will become apparent in the discussion following, some networks use a fixed cost for each link in the network, the cost being roughly inversely proportional to the link transmis-

---

*We use the word packet here to represent a self-contained block of user data, of possibly varying size, that will traverse the network as one cohesive unit. In some networks, this is synonymous with a message. In others, a message may be broken at the source node, into several smaller packets. For this reason, we make no real distinction between the two, and we shall, in fact, sometimes use the words interchangeably.

sion capacity in bits per second. For a network with equal capacity links, minimization of the path cost generates a minimum hop path. Links with measured congestion and/or high error rates may be assigned higher costs, steering traffic away from them. Costs may also vary with the type of traffic transmitted—whether interactive, asynchronous terminal type, synchronous traffic, or file transfers between computers. Other networks attempt to estimate average packet time delay on each link and use this to assign a link cost. The resultant source-destination path chosen tends to provide the path of minimum average time delay.

Since a least cost routing algorithm is used in all cases, we provide in the next section a unifying discussion of least cost routing to further demonstrate the similarities in the network algorithms.

Although the basic routing procedures are similar, differing primarily in the choice of a link cost function used to establish the minimum cost path, the routing techniques used tend to differ in implementation and the place at which the algorithms are run. The routing algorithm may be run in centralized fashion by a central supervisory program or Network Control Center, or may be carried out in a decentralized or distributed way with individual nodes in the network running the routing algorithm separately. In the former (centralized) case, global information about the network required to run the algorithm (current topology, line capacity, estimated link delays if required, condition of links and nodes, etc.) need only be kept by the central supervisor. Path setup is then accomplished through routing messages sent to each node along the path selected. In the latter (distributed) case, the required information must be exchanged among nodes in the network. This implies some means of disseminating changes in topology (nodes and links coming up or going down), congestion, and estimated time delay information if used in the algorithms. In the next section, we discuss two least cost routing algorithms, which are the basis for routing procedures in many networks.

The routing procedures adopted also differ in how dynamic they are—how rapidly and in what manner they adapt, if at all, to changes in network topology and/or traffic information. In some cases, routes are fixed during the time of a user session. (This is the length of a call from sign-on or connect time to sign-off or disconnect time.) A node or link failure during a session will then abort the call or may, in some cases, cause a new route to be selected, transparent to the user. In other cases, paths may be changed during a session (although unknown to the user and relatively slowly to avoid stability problems).

Once the path has been determined, routing tables, set at each node, are used to steer individual packets to the appropriate outgoing link. An example appears in Fig. 1. A typical node N in a network is shown, with three neighboring nodes X, Y, Z to which it is connected. In part (b) of the

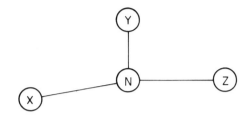

PACKET IDENTIFICATION	NEXT NODE ASSIGNMENT
(1,4)	X
(1,5)	Y
(2,4)	X
(2,5)	Z
(2,6)	Y
⋮	⋮

Fig. 1. Routing at a node in a network. (a) Current node and neighbors. (b) Routing table.

figure, a partial routing table is shown, associating individual user packets with an appropriate outgoing line leading to one of the neighboring nodes. The packet identification requires two numbers. The two numbers could be source and destination address, or they could be a mapping of these two fields into a corresponding pair given by the incoming link number and a number associated with that link. (This is variously called the logical record number, the logical link number, next node indicator etc.) The source-destination addresses could also be combined into one unique network-wide virtual circuit number, although this becomes difficult to monitor and assign with large networks. If all packets routed to a particular destination follow the same path, only a destination address is required to determine the proper outgoing link. (This would be the case, for example, if the paths chosen are independent of message class, type, etc.)

It is obvious that routing procedures play an important role in the design of data networks. Together with the techniques of flow and congestion control, they are implemented as part of the transport level or end-to-end protocols of networks. In layer protocols, this is the level just above the data link level that ensures correct transmission and reception of packets between any neighboring nodes in a network.

Because of their importance to the proper operation of data networks, routing techniques have received a great deal of attention in recent years. They have been variously classified as deterministic, stochastic, fixed, adaptive, centrally controlled, or locally controlled [1].

The fixed versus adaptive classification is particularly vague, since all networks provide some type of adaptivity to accommodate topological changes (links and/or nodes coming up or going down, new topologies being established). In the past, the distinction had been made primarily on the basis of individual packet handling. In the original ARPA routing algorithm, routing tables could be updated at intervals as short as 2/3 s [2]. Routing changes were made by individual nodes in a decentralized manner. As a result, individual packets in a message could follow diverse routing paths. The ARPA adaptive routing algorithm was adopted by a number of other networks as well [3], [4]. The French Cigale network used a related decentralized algorithm [5].

The hope was that by adapting on a packet-by-packet basis, the network could be made more responsive to changes in traffic characteristics and to topology, enabling packets to arrive at their destinations more rapidly, as well as avoiding failed links and/or nodes and regions of congestion. This was the case to some extent, yet the ARPA experience indicated some fundamental problems arising—there were problems with message reassembly at the destination, packet looping, adaptation problems ("too rapid a response to the good news of added links and too sluggish a response to the bad news of deleted links") [2], etc. As a result, the ARPA algorithm has been changed, making it less dynamic.

Although these routing techniques will be called adaptive in the sense of responding to network changes, the time constants are considerably longer. In the case of the new ARPA algorithm, changes may take place about every 10 s. Details appear in Section III.

If the algorithms used in most of these networks are adaptive and of the shortest path type, how then are they to be distinguished? We have already indicated that they may differ in the cost criterion used, and as to whether the computations are done centrally or on a distributed basis. The rate of adaptation is another distinguishing characteristic. This has also been noted already—the ARPA network, as an example, will change routes, if necessary, every 10 s. TYMNET and SNA make changes from session to session only. DNA changes paths only when necessary.

Other differences arise due to the actual implementation: the size of routing tables, the routing overhead required, the time required to set up a path or change one if necessary; all of these will be found to differ in the networks to be described. Other differences will be noted during the discussion.

Interestingly, shortest path single routes turn out not to be optimum if the long-term average *network* time delay is to be minimized. In this case, multiple or "bifurcated" paths arise [1], [6]. Packets at a node are assigned to one of several outgoing links on a probabilistic basis. Bifurcated routing has not as yet been used in routing algorithms implemented in operating networks, although there are plans to incorporate this procedure in future routing mechanisms for the Canadian DATAPAC network [7].

In Section II, we provide a more detailed treatment of routing procedures in networks, focusing, as already noted, on shortest path (least cost) algorithms. In Section III, we then describe the routing implementations currently found in TYMNET, ARPAnet, TRANSPAC, and the two commercial network architectures, IBM's SNA and Digital Equipment's DNA. In these last two cases, the routing procedures adopted are part of the overall protocol design and do not refer to a specific network implementation.

II. Structure of Routing Procedures in Packet-Switched Networks

Efficient utilization and sharing of the communications and nodal processing resources of a packet-switched communication network require various types of control, perhaps the most important of these being packet routing, that is, selecting paths along which packets are to be forwarded through the network. The objective of any routing procedure is to obtain good network performance while maintaining high throughput. "Good performance" usually means low average delay through the network, although many other performance criteria could be considered equally valid. Since poor routing algorithms often lead to congestion problems, and conversely, local congestion often requires at least temporary modification of routing rules, the routing problem cannot be completely divorced from that of congestion control, which is the subject of Chapter 13. Nevertheless, in this paper, we restrict ourselves to routing under the assumption that the better the routing algorithm, the less congestion is likely to occur.

While routing procedures can be set up within a network more or less independently of the protocols seen by the users (i.e., the devices external to the network), the choice of an appropriate routing procedure is influenced to some extent by the transport protocols operating at the network/user interface. It is convenient to classify these as either *virtual circuit-oriented* or *message-oriented*. In the former case, a device or a process within a device (e.g., an application program within a computer), prepares to communicate with another device by exchanging a number of control messages with the network. The purpose of these messages is to determine whether the destination device is connected and ready to receive messages, to agree on certain aspects of the transmission protocol, and to set up a virtual circuit (VC) from source to destination.* Figure 2 illustrates three VCs connecting terminals $T1$, $T2$, $T3$ to a host H. The VC appears to the external devices as

---

*VCs set up in this manner are termed "switched" VCs, in contrast to "permanent" VCs, which require no call setup procedure.

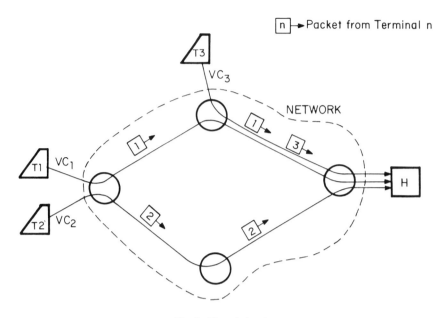

Fig. 2. Virtual circuits.

if it were a dedicated line; under normal operation, individual data packets arrive at the destination essentially without loss or error and in the proper sequence. It is important to note, however, that *within* the network, packets from many different virtual circuits are generally sharing the same communication lines; errors, losses, and changes of packet order may occur. However, it is the function of the internal network protocols to correct for all of these effects. In the message-oriented case, communication is on a message-by-message basis. Each message or packet (often called a *datagram* in this case) must therefore contain its own destination address, but no preliminary control messages are required to set up a communication path.

A. Functions of Routing Procedures

In an idealized situation where all parameters of the network are assumed to be known and not changing, it is possible to determine a routing strategy which optimizes network performance for some class of users, e.g., minimizes average network delay for the interactive user or maximizes throughput for the batch user. The routing problem posed in this form is equivalent to the multicommodity flow problem well known in the operations research literature, and has been treated extensively in the communications network context [6], [8]–[11]. Changing situations in real networks such as a line failure or a change in the traffic distribution, necessitate some degree of adaptivity. Any adaptive routing procedure must perform a number of functions:

1. Measurement of the network parameters pertinent to the routing strategy.
2. Forwarding of the measured information to the points(s) [Network Control Center (NCC) or nodes] at which routing computation takes place.
3. Computation of routing tables.
4. Conversion of routing table information to packet routing decisions. (This may include dissemination of a centrally computed routing table to each switching node as well as the conversion of this information to a form suitable for "dispatching" packets from node to node.)

Typical information that is measured and used in routing computation consists of states of communication lines, estimated traffic, link delays, available resources (line capacity, nodal buffers), etc. The pertinent information is forwarded to the NCC in a centralized system and to the various nodes in a distributed system. In the distributed case, two alternatives are possible: (1) forward only a limited amount of network information to each node (i.e., only that which is required for computing its local routing decisions), or (2) forward "global" network information to all nodes. (See Section III A1 for a comparison of these two strategies in a specific network.) Based on the measured information, "costs" can be assigned to each possible source-destination path through the network. Routing assignments may be based on the principle of assigning a single path to all traffic between a given pair of source/destination nodes, or else traffic for a given source/destination pair might be distributed over several paths, resulting in the *multiple path*, or *bifurcated routing* procedure mentioned in Section I. In the latter case, single paths might still be maintained for each virtual circuit (if a VC-oriented protocol is used). This case is illustrated in Fig. 2, wherein VC_1 and VC_2 involve the same source/destination nodes, but take different paths. (Bifurcated routing on a packet basis is illustrated in Fig. 3.) While maintenance of single paths for each VC is not an optimal procedure, it has a number of practical advantages, an important one being the fact that packets always arrive at their destination in the proper order. It is therefore not surprising that most of the networks currently in operation use VC-oriented protocols with single-path routing per VC. These paths generally remain fixed for the duration of operation of the VC, unless a failure occurs.

Once one thinks in terms of single-path routing, it is natural to choose the "shortest" or, more generally, the *least cost* path whenever alternate paths exist. The path cost can, of course, be assigned using whatever cost functions seem appropriate (see above), the only essential property being

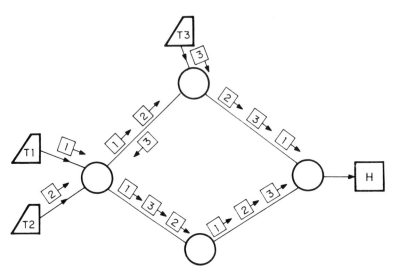

Fig. 3. Bifurcated routing.

that the *path* cost is computed as the sum of the costs of the *links* comprising that path. In such a case, the routing problem is equivalent to that of finding the shortest path through a graph, wherein link "length" is understood to have the more general meaning of link "cost." The set of shortest paths from all source nodes to a common destination node in a network forms a tree with the destination as root node. Thus, it is clear that if single-path routing on a source/destination basis is to be used, the path of a packet is uniquely determined by its destination alone. (Optimal bifurcated routing on a packet basis also only requires destination information.) On the other hand, single-path-per-VC routing requires either explicit or implicit VC identification for each packet; source/destination information alone is insufficient. This is because each time a new VC comes into operation, the costs determining the shortest path may be different since they generally change with time as network operating conditions change. Thus, VCs between the same source/destination pairs, established at different times, may take different paths as illustrated in Fig. 2.

B. Shortest Path Algorithms

The shortest path problem described above has received much attention in the literature. A variant of this problem, that of finding the k shortest paths between source and destination, is also applicable to the routing problem. (One is often interested in two or three alternate routes ranked in order of cost.) This too has been extensively treated. Since most operating networks use some version of shortest path routing, we discuss in this section the two algorithms most commonly used in communication network shortest path calculations. Algorithm A, due to Dijkstra [12], [13], is adapted to centralized computation, while B, a form of Ford and Fulkerson's algorithm [14], is particularly useful in distributed routing procedures. Since they are simple and intuitive, we present them informally, aided by an example.

Consider the network of Fig. 4(a) in which the numbers associated with the links are the link costs. (It is assumed for simplicity that each link is bidirectional with the same cost in each direction. However, both algorithms

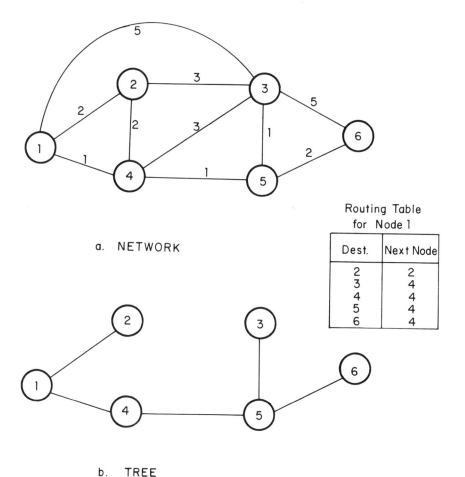

Routing Table
for Node 1

a. NETWORK

Dest.	Next Node
2	2
3	4
4	4
5	4
6	4

b. TREE

Fig. 4. Example of shortest path routing.

are applicable to the case of links with different costs in each direction.) We first use algorithm A to find shortest paths from a single source node to all other nodes. The algorithm is a step-by-step procedure where, by the k th step, the shortest paths to the k nodes closest to the source have been calculated; these nodes are contained in a set N. At the $(k + 1)$th step, a new node is added to N, whose distance to the source is the shortest of the remaining nodes outside of N. More precisely, let $l(i, j)$ be the length of the link from node i to node j, with $l(i, j)$ taken to be $+\infty$ when no link exists. Let $D(n)$ be the distance from the source to node n along the shortest path *restricted to nodes within N*. Let the nodes be indicated by positive integers with 1 representing the source.

(1) Initialization. Set $N = \{1\}$, and for each node v not in N, set $D(v) = l(1, v)$.

(2) At each subsequent step, find a node w not in N for which $D(w)$ is a minimum, and add w to N. Then update the distances $D(v)$ for the remaining nodes not in N by computing

$$D(v) \leftarrow \text{Min}\left[D(v), D(w) + l(w, v) \right]$$

Application of the algorithm to the network of Fig. 4(a) is shown in Table I, and the resultant tree of shortest paths appears in Fig. 4(b), together with a *routing table* for node 1, indicating which outbound link the traffic arriving at that node should take. (It should be clear that the same algorithm can be used to find shortest paths *from* all nodes to a common *destination*.)

Now consider algorithm B. This is an iterative procedure, which we will use in the same network to find shortest paths from all nodes to node 1, considered now as the common *destination*. To keep track of the shortest paths, we label each node v with a pair $(n, D(v))$, where $D(v)$ represents the current iteration for the shortest distance from the node to the destination

Table I. Algorithm A

Step	N	$D(2)$	$D(3)$	$D(4)$	$D(5)$	$D(6)$
Initial	$\{1\}$	2	5	1	∞	∞
1	$\{1,4\}$	2	4	1	2	∞
2	$\{1,2,4\}$	2	4	1	2	∞
3	$\{1,2,4,5\}$	2	3	1	2	4
4	$\{1,2,3,4,5\}$	2	3	1	2	4
5	$\{1,2,3,4,5,6\}$	2	3	1	2	4

and n is the number of the next node along the currently computed shortest path.

(1) Initialization. Set $D(1) = 0$ and label all other nodes $(\cdot, +\infty)$.

(2) Update $D(v)$ for each nondestination node v by examining the current value $D(w)$ for each adjacent node w and performing the operation

$$D(v) \leftarrow \underset{w}{\text{Min}} \left[D(w) + l(v, w) \right]$$

Update of node v's label is completed by replacing the first argument n by the number of the adjacent node which minimizes the above expression. Step (2) is repeated at each node until no further changes occur, at which time the algorithm terminates.

Table II illustrates the procedure for the network of Fig. 4(a). Two complete cycles of updates are required, after which no further changes occur and the iteration is complete. The tree of shortest paths generated is, of course, the same as that of Fig. 4(b). In this case, the nodes were updated in numerical order; however, any arbitrary order, cyclic or acyclic, will work. For each nondestination node, the first argument of its final label indicates the next node on the shortest path to the destination, and thus supplies the necessary routing information (for this destination *only*).

A word of comparison is now in order. Construction of routing tables based on algorithm A requires a shortest path tree calculation for each node in the manner described above. The tree is constructed with the particular node chosen as source (root) node, and the routing information that is generated is used to construct the table for that node as illustrated in Fig. 4(b). The tree can then be discarded. It should be noted that tree construction for each node requires *global* information about the network. Construction of a routing table using algorithm B requires repeated application of the algorithm for each *destination* node, resulting in a *set* of labels for each node, each label giving the routing information (next node) and distance to a particular destination. Note that in this case, the algorithm can be conveniently implemented in a *distributed* fashion, in which case each node requires only information from its neighbors.

Evaluation of the comparative merits of the two algorithms depends on a number of factors: amount of overhead required in passing measured

Table II. Algorithm B

Cycle	Node →	2	3	4	5	6
Initial		$(\cdot, \infty)$	$(\cdot, \infty)$	$(\cdot, \infty)$	$(\cdot, \infty)$	$(\cdot, \infty)$
1		$(1, 2)$	$(2, 5)$	$(1, 1)$	$(4, 2)$	$(5, 4)$
2		$(1, 2)$	$(5, 3)$	$(1, 1)$	$(4, 2)$	$(5, 4)$

information to the point(s) at which computation is performed, amount of data to be stored, complexity of the computation, speed with which the algorithm can respond to changes in link costs, etc. These comparisons can only be made meaningful in the context of a specific network. See Section III A 1, for an example, namely ARPAnet.

Finally, it should be noted that the algorithms described here have been assumed to be operating under *static* conditions of topology and link costs. (Their convergence has been proved in the literature for this case only.) In some applications, the link costs are defined to depend in some fashion on link traffic, which in turn depends, through the routing algorithm, on link cost; the result is a feedback effect. By studying the dynamics of such situations, it has been shown [15] that poor choices of link cost functions can, in fact, produce instabilities in the resultant traffic patterns. Stability can, however, be ensured by making the link costs sufficiently insensitive to link flow.

C. Packet Routing Implementation

As indicated in Section II A, computation of the routing tables does not complete the routing procedure. These tables must be converted to a form appropriate for dispatching packets from node to node. In this section, we describe a method which underlies a number of schemes used for implementing routing on a single-path-per-VC basis in some existing or proposed systems [16], [17]. The essence of the procedure is that each VC has a *path number* (PN) associated with each link it traverses; if two VCs share a link, they obtain different path numbers on that link. Each packet carries the appropriate PN, which is updated or "swapped" as the packet traverses the network. The updating procedure is determined by, and replaces the routing table, at each node. The PN contains all information necessary for routing; thus, the packet need not carry a VC number. To illustrate, consider a set of four active virtual circuits traversing the network of Fig. 5. The second column of Table III indicates the node sequence for the paths chosen for these VCs. (Note that VC_1 and VC_2 have the same source/destination node pair, but different paths.) Let $PN(n)$ be a path number associated with a path on a link outbound from node n; each link will have as many path numbers as there are distinct active VCs sharing that link. The remaining columns of Table III show how a sequence of PNs is assigned at each node, serving to identify uniquely the path to be followed by a packet on each VC. When a packet is received on an inbound line at a node, its PN must be updated, and the packet must be placed on the proper outbound line or released to its destination. At each node, a simple table lookup procedure can perform this function. In Table IV we show the necessary table for node 4. Note that it is derived directly from the routing information in Table III.

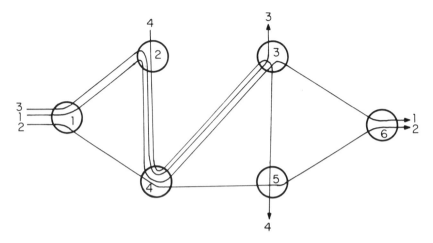

Fig. 5. Example of routing implementation.

Table III. Path Numbers

VC#	Path	PN(1)	PN(2)	PN(3)	PN(4)	PN(5)
1	1-2-4-3-6	1	1	1	1	—
2	1-4-5-6	1	—	—	1	1
3	1-2-4-3	2	2	—	3	—
4	2-4-3-5	—	3	1	2	—

Table IV. Routing at Node 4

Arriving from node	Old PN	New PN	Next node
1	1	1	5
2	1	1	3
2	2	3	3
2	3	2	3

The PN used in this section is roughly equivalent to the *logical record number* used by TYMNET [16] (see Section III A 2) and the *next node indicator* (NNI) once proposed for explicit routing [17]. It might be thought that it would be simpler to tag each packet with a unique VC number rather than using the procedure outlined here. However, there will generally be far more active VCs in the network (perhaps thousands) than there are distinct VCs sharing a link (up to 256 in the case of TYMNET, for example). Thus, the PN approach is generally more efficient in memory requirement and table lookup time than any method using VC numbers.

III. Examples of Routing Procedures Used in Practice

A. Computer and Data Networks

1. ARPAnet, A Computer Network *

ARPAnet [18] was created in 1969 as an experiment in computer resource sharing. Beginning with four nodes in 1969, it now runs as an operational system with over 100 computers connected to 56 nodes throughout the continental United States, Hawaii, and Europe. It is a distributed network with at least two paths between any pair of nodes. Most of its lines are 50-kbit/s synchronous links. It is a store-and-forward packet-switched network in which the transport protocol is message-oriented. Messages longer than the maximum packet length are segmented into up to 8 packets at the source node and are reassembled at the destination node. This requires special provision for buffer allocation at the nodes to prevent various types of lockups (a significant problem in the early stages of network development).

The network was originally operated with a distributed adaptive routing algorithm of the minimum cost, i.e., shortest path, type wherein link cost was evaluated in terms of measured link delay. Since the measured delays were determined by queue lengths encountered along a packet's transmission path, these quantities varied rapidly with time. Routing was on an individual packet basis where each packet was forwarded along the path that was perceived by the forwarding node to be the shortest in time to the packet's destination at the time of transmission. Since adaptivity was quite rapid, and different nodes could have different views of network conditions, perceptions of shortest paths could change during the period the packet traversed the network, typically ten to several hundred milliseconds. The shortest path algorithm used was essentially our algorithm B (Section II B), with information necessary for node updates passed among neighbors at $2/3$-s intervals. Details of the algorithm can be found in [19]. A number of difficulties appeared in the algorithm, and it underwent several modifications [2] from the time it was implanted until May 1979 when it was replaced by a basically different procedure [20].

The new routing algorithm is distributed in the sense that each node independently computes its own routing tables using what is called a *shortest path first* algorithm (essentially our algorithm A with some modifications). That is, each node computes a shortest path tree with itself as the

---

*The authors are indebted to Dr. John McQuillan of Bolt Beranek and Newman for providing information on ARPAnet.

root node. Since algorithm A requires availability of global network information at the node doing the routing computation, this procedure can also be viewed as a "partially" centralized method.

Link costs are evaluated in terms of time delays on the links. Each node calculates an estimate of the delay on each of its outbound links by averaging the total packet delay (processing, queueing, transmission, retransmission, propagation time) over 10-s intervals. (One of the problems with the first algorithm was that delay estimates were obtained too frequently to be accurate.) Since all nodes must be informed of any changes in link time delays, a "flooding" technique is used in the new method for forwarding the measured delays throughout the network. Each node transmits to all its neighbors delay information for all of its outgoing links. It also acts as a repeater, broadcasting to all of its neighbors the link delay information it has received from other nodes. (Transmitting delay information back to the adjacent node from which it was received provides an automatic positive acknowledgment mechanism.) Duplicate delay information packets are dropped, so that while the information propagates to all nodes in the network, it does not circulate indefinitely. To reduce the amount of communication overhead involved in this information exchange, the 10-s average link delay measurements are not always transmitted. Only when the *change* in link delay since the last transmission exceeds a certain threshold does a new transmission take place. The threshold is reduced as time increases since the previous transmission. (However, a change in the status of a line is reported immediately.) The total communication overhead involved in delay update exchanges is less than 1 percent.

Since a complete execution of algorithm A at each update requires considerable computation, the algorithm has been modified so that "incremental" computation can be performed. When a single link delay changes (or if a link or node is added or deleted from the network), each node does a *partial* computation to restructure its shortest path tree. (This, of course, implies that each node must store the most recently updated tree as a basis for future updates, imposing an additional memory requirement.) Also, to take care of the case where link or node failures cause a complete partition of the network, an indication of "age" is inserted in each delay update packet. In this way, "out of date" delay information can be recognized and discarded when lines are reconnected and routing tables are recomputed. Operational results indicate that complete processing of a routing update at a node requires several milliseconds on the average.

A series of tests were performed with the algorithm under actual operating conditions, revealing a number of its features: it responds fairly rapidly (100 ms) to topological changes (one of the problems with the earlier algorithm was that it responded too slowly to line failures); it usually does minimum hop routing, but under heavy load conditions it spreads traffic over lines with excess capacity; it can respond to congestion by choosing paths to avoid congested nodes; and it seems to be stable and free of sustained looping.

Based on the information available at this time, the new algorithm seems to show some advantages over the old in terms of speed of response to changing topology, stability, and suppression of looping. These advantages are apparently attained without undue overhead. It must be kept in mind that in going from algorithm B to A, many other aspects of the routing scheme were also changed, most importantly, the procedure for estimating and forwarding link delay information. Many of the problems encountered using algorithm B were due to the extremely rapid updating that was used based on information whose accuracy did not warrant such rapid adaptivity.

2. TYMNET *Routing Algorithm*

TYMNET is a computer-communication network developed in 1970 by Tymshare, Inc. of Cupertino, CA. It has been in commercial operation since 1971 [1], [21], [22]. Originally developed for time-shared purposes, it has more recently taken on a network function as well, and is classified by the Federal Communications Commission as a value-added specialized carrier. As of 1978, the network had 300 nodes in operation and was growing at the rate of 2 nodes/week [16]. Almost all nodes are connected to at least two other nodes in the network, giving rise to a distributed topology with alternate path capability. The network is designed primarily to handle interactive terminal users, although it does handle higher-speed synchronous traffic as well. The lines connecting the nodes range in speed from 2400 to 9600 bit/s. The network covers the United States and Europe, with connections also made to the Canadian Datapac Network. Trans-Atlantic lines are cable with satellite backup. Satellites are avoided, where possible, for interactive users because of the substantial delay involved.

Individual user data packets or logical records, each preceded by a 16-bit header incorporating an 8-bit logical record number to be discussed below and an 8-bit packet character count, are concatenated to form a physical record of at most 66 8-bit characters, including 16 bits of header and 32 bits of checksum for error detection [1]. These data packets can range in length from a few characters to a maximum of 58 characters. (Physical records are transmitted as soon as available, without waiting for a specified size logical record to be assembled.)

TYMNET routing is set up centrally on a virtual circuit, fixed path, basis by a supervisory program running on one of four possible supervisory computers in the network.

A least cost algorithm [1], [16] is used to determine the appropriate path from source to destination node over which to route a given user's packets. The path is newly selected each time a user comes on the network, and is maintained unchanged during the period of the user connection or session. (In the event of an outage, the session is interrupted and a new routing path has to be computed. In TYMNET I, the version of TYMNET that has operated to the present, this could take up to 2.5 min as the supervisor learned of the incident and established the new topology. In the newer TYMNET II, which is gradually replacing the earlier version, rerouting in the event of an outage is carried out by the supervisor in a manner transparent to the user.) The algorithm used by the supervisor is a modification of Floyd's algorithm, a variation of our algorithm *B*.

Integer-valued costs are assigned to each link, and costs are then summed to find the path of least cost. The cost assignments depend on line speed and line utilization. Thus, the number 16 is assigned to a 2400-bit/s link, 12 to a 4800-bit/s link, and 10 to a 9600-bit/s link. A penalty of 16 is added to a satellite link for low-speed interactive users. This shifts such users to cable links, as noted above.

A penalty of 16 is added to a link if a node at one end complains of "overloading." The penalty is 32 if the nodes at both ends complain. Overload is experienced if the data for a specific virtual circuit have to wait more than 0.5 s before being serviced. This condition is then reported by the node to the supervisor. An overload condition may occur because of too many circuits requesting service over the same link, or it may be due to a noisy link with a high error rate, in which case the successive retransmissions which are necessary slow the effective service rate down as well. The penalty used in this case serves to steer additional circuits away from the link until the condition clears up.

Details of the specific algorithm used appear in [16]. In the absence of overloading, the algorithm tends to select the shortest path (least number of links) with highest transmission speed. As more users come on the network, the lower-speed links begin to be used as well. In lightly loaded situations, users tend to have relatively shorter time delays through the network. The minimum hop paths, favored in the lightly loaded case, also tend to be more reliable than ones with more links. Users coming on in a busy period may experience higher time delays due both to congestion and to the use of lower speed lines. The use of the overload penalties tends to spread traffic around the network, deviating from the shortest path case, but attempting to reduce the time delay. In practice, the average response time for interactive users is 0.75 s [16].

It takes 12 ms for the supervisor to find the least cost path using this algorithm [23]. Once the path has been selected, the supervisor notifies each of the nodes along the path, assigning an 8-bit *logical record number* to each link on that path. (This allows up to 256 users or channels to share any one link. In practice, the maximum number ranges from 48 for a 2400-bit/s line to 192 for a 9600-bit/s line. In addition, one number or channel is reserved for a node to communicate with the supervisor and one channel is reserved for communications with the neighboring node.) The supervisor also associates a logical record number on an incoming link to a node with a number on the appropriate outgoing link setting entries in routing tables, called permuter tables in TYMNET terminology. This process, described in more detail later, is basically the same as the method of *path number swapping* described in Section II C. In the TYMNET II version of the network, the nodal computers themselves establish the routing table sizes and entries, as well as the buffers associated with them, relieving the supervisor of this burden.

Routing information is sent to a particular node in a 48-bit supervisory record with the usual 16 bits of logical record overhead as part of a normal physical record. The data transmission overhead due to the dissemination of this routing information is calculated, on a worst case basis, to be 1.6 percent [23]. This assumes that the circuit to be set up is 4 links long, with 5 nodes to be notified (the average path in TYMNET is 3.1 links) during a busy period in which an average of 1 user/s requests entry to the network. The supervisory overhead is taken as distributed equally over a minimum of 8 outgoing 2400 bit/s links from the supervisor. This calculation does not assign any physical record overhead to the supervisory logical record. The assumption is made that there are always data waiting to be transmitted and that the supervisory record is piggybacked onto a normal data record, as noted earlier.

Each node acknowledges receipt of the routing information, again doing this as part of a physical record. (Nodes, in addition, report any link outages to the supervisor as part of a 48-bit record transmitted every 16 s.)

The procedure at a node for forwarding an incoming data packet (logical record) to the appropriate outgoing link, or to either a host computer or terminal if at the destination node, proceeds as follows. As noted earlier, there is a routing or permuter table associated with each link at a node. Each logical record number in either direction on the link is associated with an entry in the table. That entry, in turn, corresponds to the address of a pair of buffers at the node, one for each direction of data flow (inbound and outbound). For L links at a node, L permuter tables are needed, each receiving up to 256 buffer addresses. An error-free physical record arriving at a node is disassembled into its component data packets (logical records). Each data packet is steered by the permuter table entry to its appropriate buffer. Data in buffers destined for terminals and/or computers associated with this node are then transferred to the appropriate device. This node thus represents the destination node for these logical records. Logical records waiting in transit buffers are handled differently. A physical record for a given outgoing link is created, under program control, by scanning sequentially the entries in the permuter table for that link. As each buffer address is read, a determination is made as to whether its *pair* has had data entered. If so, the data are then formed into a logical record with their corresponding new logical record number. This logical record is incorporated in the physical record and is transmitted out over the link.

A specific example appears in Fig. 6 [23]. Figure 6(a) shows a typical two-link virtual circuit connecting nodes numbered 5, 7, and 10. In this example, terminal data enter the network via a terminal port at node 5, destined for a Host computer connected to node 10. The link connecting nodes 5 and 7 is labeled 1, as seen at the node 5 side, and 2 as seen at the node 7 side. Similarly, the link connecting nodes 7 and 10 is labeled 3 at the node 7 side and 1 at the node 10 side.

Figure 6(b) portrays the logical record number assignments and permuter table entries in detail, node by node. (Eight possible logical record numbers only have been assumed for simplicity.) The logical record numbers 4 and 6 have been assigned to this virtual circuit over the two links shown, respectively. At node 5, the entry node, the number 3 in entry 4 in the permuter table for link 1 indicates that data with logical record number 4 are to be found in buffer 2, the mate of buffer 3.

At node 7, data coming from link 2 are stored in buffers designated by the contents of the permuter table for link 2 at that node. Continuing with this example, data arriving at that link with logical record 4 are to be further transmitted over outgoing link 3 to node 10. Their outgoing logical record number is to be changed to 6. To accomplish this, note that the contents of entry 4 of permuter table 2 and entry 6 of the permuter table 3 are paired together. Data arriving over incoming link 2 are stored in buffer 8. They are read out over link 3 when the entries for the permuter table for that link are scanned, entry 6 pointing to buffer 9, the mate of buffer 8. At node 10, the destination node for this virtual circuit, data arriving with logical record 6 are stored in buffer 100 of that node and are then transferred to the appropriate Host.

3. Routing in TRANSPAC*

TRANSPAC, the French public packet-switching service [24], began operation in December 1978 with ten nodes (soon to be expanded to twelve) in a

---

*The authors are indebted to J. M. Simon of TRANSPAC for providing information used in preparing this section.

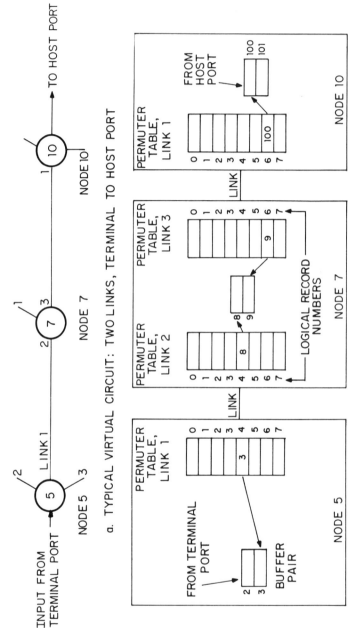

a. TYPICAL VIRTUAL CIRCUIT: TWO LINKS, TERMINAL TO HOST PORT

b. PERMUTER TABLES AND LOGICAL RECORD NUMBERS

Fig. 6. Routing example, TYMNET.

distributed network configuration. As is the case with most public packet-switching services, the transport procedures for TRANSPAC follow the X.25 international standard protocol. Thus, this is a virtual-circuit-oriented system, and the routing procedures discussed below reflect this orientation. For purposes of reliability, there are at least two 72-kbit/s lines, following different physical paths, connecting each node to the remainder of the network. Each node consists of a control unit (CU) (a CII Mitra 125 minicomputer) to which are attached a number of switching units (SU). Each incident link is controlled by an SU, which executes all data link procedures. The SUs also execute the access protocols for customers connected to the node. Routing is handled by the CU, using information from the Network Management Center (see below).

Network control is partially decentralized through six local control points which handle a certain amount of statistics gathering and perform test and reinitialization procedures in case of node or line failures. However, general network supervision, including the bulk of routing computation, is exercised through a single Network Management Center (NMC).

Routes in TRANSPAC are assigned on a single-path-per VC basis. The algorithm of interest to us here is that which governs the assignment of a route to a switched virtual circuit, i.e., a VC which is established temporarily in response to a "call request." The call request takes the form of a *Call Packet*, emitted by equipment connected to the originating network node, and requesting connection to a specified destination. The path that eventually will be retained by the switched VC is identical to that taken by the Call Packet as it is forwarded through the network. Routing of the Call Packet is effected through routing tables stored at each node; as indicated in Section II, the tables associate a unique outbound link with each destination node. The network as currently configured has two classes of nodes. One class is connected in a distributed fashion, with alternate route capability. The second class consists of nodes homing in via a single link to a node of the first class. Node 5 in Fig. 7 is an example of a node of the first type; node 6 is a node of the second type. Messages destined to nodes of the second type are routed to the "target" node to which they are connected. In Fig. 7, messages destined for node 6 have node 5 as a target node.

The routing tables for the network are constructed in an essentially centralized fashion, using a minimum cost, i.e., shortest path criterion. Link costs are defined in terms of link resource utilization. Thus, the cost assigned to a link varies dynamically with network load. We shall first describe the method of evaluation of link cost and then the routing algorithm [25], [26]. Consider a full duplex link k connected between nodes m and n. Let $C_m(k)$, $C_n(k)$ be the cost assigned to link k as perceived by nodes m and n, respectively, and let $C(k) = \text{Max}[C_m(k), C_n(k)]$ be the "combined" estimate of link cost. The quantities $C_i(k)$ are the basic data on

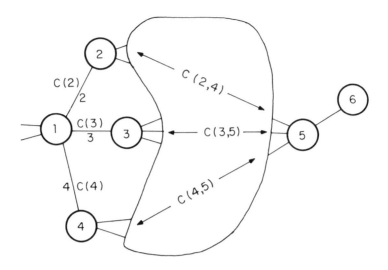

Fig. 7. Routing example, TRANSPAC.

which routing computation is based; they are determined locally by each node's CU which gathers estimated and measured data from its associated SU's. Link cost is defined as a function of the level of utilization of two types of resources: line capacity and link buffers. The utilization of these quantities is evaluated both by estimation (based on the parameters of the active VCs using the link) and by measurement. The cost $C_i(k)$ is set to infinity if either the link is carrying its maximum permissible number of VCs or it has exceeded a preset threshold of buffer occupancy. Otherwise, $C_i(k)$ is defined as a piecewise constant increasing function of average link flow, quantized to a small number of levels and including a "hysteresis" effect. A typical function is shown in Fig. 8, with the arrows indicating the

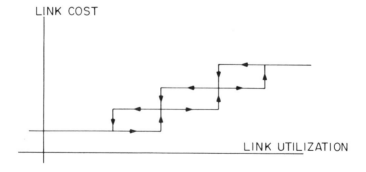

Fig. 8. A typical link cost relation, TRANSPAC.

way link cost changes as a function of changing utilization. The nodes send updated values of their $C_i(k)$'s to the NMC whenever a change occurs; these events are infrequent owing to the combined effect of coarse quantization and hysteresis. At the NMC, the costs perceived by the nodes at both ends of each link are compared to form $C(k)$ as defined above.

The major part of the routing computation takes place at the NMC, but some local information is used at each node. The procedure is illustrated by an example in Fig. 7 in which a Call Packet arriving at node 1 (which may be either the originating node or an intermediate one) is to be forwarded through one of the adjacent nodes 2, 3, 4 to the target node 5, and finally to the destination node 6. Let $C(k, n)$ (computed by the NMC) be the total cost associated with the minimum cost path between nodes k and n. Node 1 determines the "shortest" route to node 5 by choosing the value of k which minimizes $C(k, 5) + \text{Max}[C(k), C_1(k)]$, $k = 2, 3, 4$. In this way, node 1 chooses the intermediate node that would have been chosen by the NMC, unless the value of $C_1(k)$ has changed recently. Ties are resolved by giving priority to the shortest hop path. Because of the way in which link costs are defined, the routing procedure becomes a minimum hop method upon which is superimposed a bias derived from the level of link resource utilization.

Although the TRANSPAC routing algorithm has many of the features of a typical centralized routing procedure, its operation departs from being purely centralized by allowing the final routing decision to be made locally, based on a combination of centrally and locally determined information. This is similar to the concept of "delta routing" suggested by Rudin [27].

By examining the current topology of the network [24], one can deduce the order of magnitude of the computational load at the NMC. The $C(k, n)$'s must be determined for all k and n belonging to the subset of all possible target nodes. Only six out of the twelve currently planned network nodes are in this category. Furthermore, rather than doing a complete shortest path computation to determine these quantities, the designers chose to limit the shortest path computation to a minimization over a prescribed subset of four or five paths joining each pair of nodes. Thus, the computation of all pertinent $C(k, n)$'s involves at most 75 path length evaluations.

At this writing, the network has recently entered its operational phase, with 300–400 subscribers as compared to an expected full load population of 1500. It is reported that the routing algorithms are operating satisfactorily, without undue overhead.

B. Commercial Network Architectures

The examples discussed thus far have all been operational networks. Specific physical implementations exist, although the networks have been steadily growing and changing their topologies. In the two examples discussed in this section, we focus on another type of distributed network architecture for which routing procedures become important. These are the network protocols introduced by most large computer system manufacturers during the past decade or so to enable private users to configure their own computer networks. Such networks are being increasingly developed to handle such diverse tasks as distributed processing, distributed database handling, and computer resource sharing. A computer manufacturer's protocol is designed to enable a user to interconnect a variety of computer systems and terminals in any desired configuration. All of these network protocols tend to follow a layered architecture, starting at the lowest level, that of setting up physical connections, continuing to the next, data link level, which controls the flow of data packets between neighboring nodes, then proceeding to the transmission or transport level, involved with end-to-end (source to destination) control of packet flow, routing, and congestion control, and finally concluding, at the highest levels, with several levels of "handshaking" between users or programs at the two ends. Other chapters in this book discuss these network protocols in detail.

In this section, we describe the routing procedures defined for distributed versions of the IBM Systems Network Architecture (SNA) and the Digital Equipment Corporation's Digital Network Architecture (DNA), which are described in Chapters 11 and 10, respectively. These are both relatively recent developments since earlier versions of both SNA and DNA were tailored primarily to star- or tree-type network configurations with no real need for routing. It will be noted that, unlike the network examples discussed previously, where networking is essentially transparent to the user, it is left to the user of either SNA or DNA to configure his own network. There is a certain flexibility in the routing procedures as well, with the user free to define his own link costs and paths to be taken. This is, of course, not the case in the earlier networks described.

1. IBM's Systems Network Architecture (SNA)*

The early versions of SNA, appearing in 1974, were designed for single-computer system tree-type networks [28], [29]. In these networks, it is apparent that routing was not really a significant problem. Later versions of SNA allow two or more such single-system networks to be interconnected, leading to the concept of cross-domain networking [28]. Here, too, routing requirements were quite simple. IBM's latest SNA architecture, termed SNA 4.2 [30], envisions multiple computer systems interconnected to form a distributed network. Routing thus plays an important role in the architecture.

---

*The authors are indebted to Dr. James P. Gray of IBM for help with this section.

The routing procedure chosen for SNA incorporates predetermined fixed paths from source to destination. A multiplicity of possible routes is provided to increase the probability that a route will be available when needed to achieve load leveling, to provide alternate route capability in the event of node/link failures or congestion, and to provide different types of services for different classes of users [30], [31]. For example, batch traffic would normally be routed differently from interactive traffic. (Not only are the response time requirements different, calling usually for different capacity links, as noted earlier in discussing the TYMNET routing procedure, but one would not normally want to have batch traffic interfering with, and hence slowing down, interactive traffic. In SNA 4.2, this can be done by assigning a lower transmission priority to batch traffic.) Some traffic may require high security handling and will therefore be routed differently.

Multiple routing is provided at two levels: when first initiating a session, the user specifies a name corresponding to a particular class of service. Examples of classes of service include low response time, high capacity lines, more secure paths, etc. Associated with each class of service name is a list of possible virtual routes for use by sessions specifying that name. This list provides load balancing and backup capability. A particular session uses only one of these virtual routes at a time. This corresponds to the first level of multiple routing. Each virtual route provides a full-duplex connection between source and destination nodes, and can support multiple users or sessions. Each virtual route in turn maps into a so-called explicit route, the actual physical path from source to destination. It is this path that has been precalculated to provide the desired performance. Multiple explicit routes will exist, on a unidirectional basis, between any source–destination nodal pair. The multiple explicit routes provide the second level of multiple route control noted earlier. In the current SNA 4.2 release, up to eight explicit routes can be made available between any source–destination nodal pairs. Several virtual routes may use the same explicit route.

Although explicit routes are established by the source node on a unidirectional basis, explicit routes are used in pairs that are physically reversible. This simplifies user notification of route failure.

Up to 24 virtual routes are currently available between any pair of nodes. These are grouped into three levels of transmission priority, with eight possible virtual route numbers associated with each level. The entire set of virtual routes, each identified by a virtual route number and transmission priority, is stored in a virtual route identifier list. Class of service names are then associated with subsets of this list, in some preassigned order. A user setting up a session specifies his class of service name. He is then assigned to the first virtual route in the virtual route list that is available or can be activated. Multiple sessions may be assigned to the same virtual route. The same virtual route is defined by four fields—the source and destination addresses, a virtual route number, and the transmission priority.

The explicit route corresponding to a specific virtual route is, in turn, defined by the source and destination addresses and an explicit route number. Each explicit route number represents one of the eight distinct routes possible between any source-destination nodal pair. A given explicit route is made up of a sequence of logical links connecting adjacent nodes along the path.

The term transmission group is used for logical link in the SNA terminology. Transmission groups may consist of multiple physical links. Thus, a set of parallel physical links between any two nodes can be divided into one or more transmission groups. This adds flexibility to the transmission function: physical links may be combined in parallel to provide higher capacity, links may be dynamically added or deleted without disruption, and scheduling of links is employed to optimize the composite bandwidth or capacity available. But the use of multiple-link transmission groups means that data packets or blocks may arrive out of sequence. Out-of-order blocks must thus be reordered at the receiving end of each transmission group along the composite path.

Routing of data packets is carried out by examining the destination address and explicit route number as a packet arrives at an intermediate node along the path. An explicit routing table at each node associates an appropriate outgoing transmission group with the destination address and explicit route number. An example of such a table at a particular node appears in Fig. 9. The letters represent the transmission groups to which packets with the corresponding address, route number pair are directed. By changing the explicit route number for a given destination, a new path will be followed. This introduces alternate route capability. If a link or node along the path becomes inoperative, any sessions using that path can be reestablished on an explicit route that bypasses the failed element. Explicit routes can also be assigned on the basis of type of traffic, types of physical media along the path (satellite or terrestrial, for example), or other criteria,

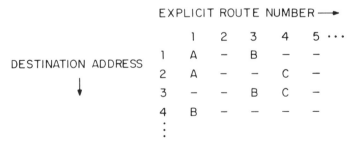

Fig. 9. Explicit routing table, SNA.

as already noted. Routes could also be listed on the basis of cost, the smallest cost route being assigned first, then next smallest cost route, etc.

Note that the explicit routing concept is similar to that adopted by TYMNET in its virtual circuit approach. Here the path selected may be changed by the source node, however, by choosing a new explicit route number. In essence, a variety of alternate routes is laid out in advance. This introduces the alternate route capability noted above. In the current TYMNET approach, the central supervisor must set up a new path if one is desired.

The concept of explicit routing, as first enunciated and as noted in Section II earlier, is somewhat broader than the one described here [17]. There, rather than using a fixed explicit route number, a variable "next node index" (NNI) field was proposed for the packet header. The combination of the destination address and the NNI field then directs the packet to the appropriate outgoing transmission group. The NNI is changed at the same time as well. This allows more explicit routes to be defined than through the use of a fixed explicit route number. The idea is similar to the (variable) logical record number concept used by TYMNET. In addition, some form of intermediate or local node routing capability could be introduced through the use of the NNI. For by changing the NNI locally, a new path from that point on will be followed. This makes it possible to introduce alternate route capability along the initial path chosen in the event of localized congestion or some other delaying phenomenon. The British NPL, in a series of network simulation experiments., has shown the benefits of alternate route capability [32]. Rudin has proposed as well a routing strategy that combines centralized routing with a measure of local adaptability [27]. The general idea of explicit routing thus enables centralized, distributed, and local routing strategies (or some combination of them) to be introduced into the network. In the current IBM implementation, however, only precalculated routes are used.

Three steps are required to activate a route. The individual links of the transmission groups forming the explicit route must be brought up. The explicit route is then activated. Finally, the virtual route to be used that maps into this explicit route must be activated. Special command packets are used for this purpose [31]. For example, an explicit route is activated by transmitting a specific activate command from node to node along the path. This packet verifies the routing tables of the nodes along the path. It ensures loop-free routes by checking the routing tables of nodes along the route. It verifies that there are no packets along the path with the same source–destination address pairs. It also measures the length of the explicit route in hops. Activation of the explicit route is considered completed when verified by a reply command from the destination. If the activation of the first-choice virtual route and its associated explicit route fails, the second-choice virtual route is tried, repeating with the third choice, and so on, if necessary.

The user is involved in setting the routing tables, and hence in route definition in the SNA architecture. Thus, the user can define the routes he desires, given his physical topology, by providing table entries at system definition time. The user can also ensure that a session is established on a desired route. For unique or specialized requirements, the user can write a user-exit routine that is invoked during session establishment. This exit can assign a session to a specific route.

2. Routing in Digital's DNA*

Digital Equipment Corporation's network architecture is called Digital Network Architecture, or DNA for short. It provides the interfaces and protocols that enable users to create their own networks using Digital Equipment Corporation Systems. The family of network products supporting DNA is generally called DECnet. DNA and DECnet were first introduced in 1973.

As does the IBM SNA, DNA employs a layered architecture. Six levels have been defined, as shown in Fig. 10 [33]. The Transport Layer shown in the figure was sufficiently simple in the Phase II DECnet implementations introduced in 1978 so as to be encompassed within the Network Services Layer. Phase II provides for point-to-point connections with no routing capability required. The next phase, Phase III DECnet, will have provision for store-and-forward distributed topologies requiring routing, flow and congestion control, and a network management capability. For this phase of DECnet, the Transport Layer has been defined and provides the necessary routing and congestion control features. In this section of the paper, we focus on routing in Phase III of DECnet.

The routing procedure adopted by Digital Equipment Corporation is based on a variation of the distributed shortest path algorithm (our algorithm B), with each node carrying out its own calculations. It is similar to the protocol analyzed by Tajibnapis [34] which has been implemented on the Michigan MERIT Computer Network. The routing algorithm adapts to changes in network topology (it does not use traffic flow information), and so needs to be invoked only when a link or node in the network comes up or fails. Unlike the IBM SNA approach, routing is done on a packet-by-packet or datagram basis, as contrasted to a virtual circuit service.

To carry out the least cost routing procedure, each link in the network is assigned a fixed cost. The specific cost is set by the user, but is approximately inversely proportional to link capacity. (Note that these assignments are then roughly similar to those used by TYMNET.) Paths with

*The authors are indebted to Anthony Lauck of the Digital Equipment Corporation for providing information used in preparing this portion of the paper.

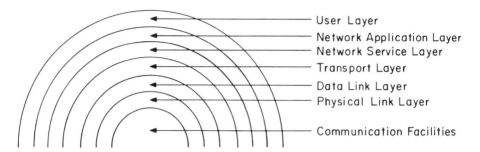

User Layer
Network Application Layer
Network Service Layer
Transport Layer
Data Link Layer
Physical Link Layer

Communication Facilities

Fig. 10. DNA layered architecture.

high capacity links are favored. These costs are used by each node to derive
a routing database (or routing table) which lists the cost to each destination
using each of the node's outgoing lines. An example appears in Fig. 11(a).
(Each node in the network is assigned a unique address. Naming and
addressing are carried out at a level higher than the Transport level.)

Packets going to a particular destination are routed to the output link
with the smallest cost. In the example of Fig. 11(a), packets going to
destination C would take output line 2 with a cost of 2 units. Those going to
destination B would take output line 1. The listing of minimum cost
outgoing lines, one for each destination, that is used in routing the packets
is kept in a second database, called the forwarding database. An example
appears in Fig. 11(b) for the routing table of Fig. 11(a). (A third, Boolean,
database indicates whether each destination is reachable or not. This is
discussed briefly later.)

As noted earlier, these tables are changed only on receipt of routing
messages, triggered by a line (or node) coming up or going down. Specifically, a node, on learning that one of its links or a neighboring node has
either been brought up or has failed, will update its tables. If the minimum
cost to any destination has changed, the cost information is broadcast using
a routing message to all the neighbors. These nodes, in turn, add to the cost
forwarded for each destination the link cost for the link over which the
message has arrived. The sum is then entered in the routing database.
Minimization is then carried out row by row (i.e., for each destination), and
the forwarding database is changed. If the resultant cost changes, this is, in
turn, broadcast, using routing messages, to all neighbors. In this way,
changes percolate throughout the network.

Routing messages contain 16 bits per destination, with a maximum of
128 nodes allowed at present. The routing message thus consists of a
maximum of 256 bytes. Of the 16 bits, 11 are used to transmit total cost
information and 5 bits represent a hop count that is transmitted as well.

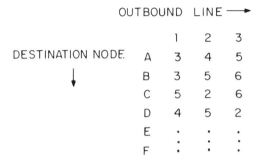

a. ROUTING DATA BASE

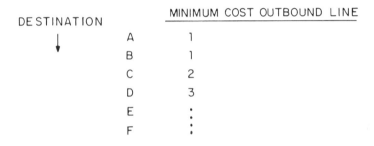

b. FORWARDING DATA BASE

Fig. 11. Typical nodal routing tables, DNA routing protocol. (Similar tables are kept at each node.)

This hop count is incremented by 1 at each node, and is used for reachability analysis. To avoid indefinite ping-ponging, one node adding 1, its neighbor adding 1, back and forth, a destination is declared unreachable if the hop count reaches a specified maximum. This maximum could be one more than the maximum path length, it could be the diameter of the network, etc.

Packets going to an unreachable destination are discarded. However, there is an option of notifying the source that a particular destination is unreachable through the use of a "return to sender" packet. This would be used on setting up a connection or initializing the operation of the network.

If a link fails, packets queued on that link are discarded as well. To maintain end-to-end (source to destination) integrity, an acknowledgment and time-out procedure is carried out by the higher-level Network Service

Layer of DNA. (The lower-level digital data communications message protocol—DDCMP—provides link, or node-to-node, error control as well. This is, of course, similar to link error control carried out by HDLC, SDLC, and other data link control protocols [1].)

How does a node know if a link is down? This is based on the number of retransmissions of packets needed. If the number 7 is reached the link is declared down. In addition, provision is made for transmitting a low-priority "Hello" message to a neighboring node that has not been heard from for a while. If there is no acknowledgement, the node is declared down.

The actual software implementation of the routing procedure involves three processes: a *decision process*, which receives routing messages; an *update process*, which updates the routing tables; and a packet *forwarding process*, which uses the forwarding database to route the packets. Normally, the third process only is used. The first two are run only when changes in the network topology dictate changes in the routing table. Provision is made to check the routing algorithm periodically, if desired, with the use of a timer. Such a check might be made once a minute, for example. Although the forwarding database (minimum cost paths) is normally used for routing, the entire routing database is retained as well at each node. This is required to run the distributed routing algorithm when needed. The routing database can also be used to provide alternate path capability as well, if desired, or if necessary.

Some additional factors provided by the DNA phase III Transport Layer in addition to routing include a packet lifetime control and a congestion control mechanism. The packet lifetime control is used to bound the time a packet spends in the network. A nodal visit count is kept in each data packet. If the number is too large, the packet is purged. The congestion control involved is the one analyzed by Irland [35]. The queues at each outbound link at a node are limited in size. Packets are discarded if the number queued will exceed this maximum value. Priority is, however, given to transit messages (those already in the network, as contrasted to packets originating at the node in question).

IV. Conclusions

After a brief discussion of routing in general, we have presented the basic features of routing procedures currently used in five representative packet-switched communication networks and network architectures. While the networks were chosen to represent a broad spectrum of operational characteristics, it is interesting to note that there are many similarities in their routing algorithms. At the same time, there is a great deal of diversity in the manner in which these algorithms are implemented. Most of the networks use some variation or approximation of a shortest path routing strategy. However, each network defines the "length" or "cost" of a communication link differently. Some use centralized computation, some decentralized, and some use a hybrid of the two. Adaptivity ranges from the bare minimum necessary to react to line failures to more sophisticated procedures sensing and responding to queueing delays, error rates, and line loading. Undoubtedly, a larger set of representative networks would have yielded a still richer set of alternative schemes for information gathering, routing computation, and packet forwarding. One can conclude from this survey that while the routing function is central to the smooth and efficient operation of packet-switched networks, no one scheme can be identified as "best." Many viable alternatives exist at all levels of the routing function.

References

[1]   M. Schwartz, *Computer Communication Network Design and Analysis.* Englewood Cliffs, NJ: Prentice-Hall, 1977.

[2]   J. M. McQuillan, G. Falk, and I. Richer, "A review of the development and performance of the ARPANET routing algorithm," *IEEE Trans. Commun.*, vol. COM-26, pp. 1802–1811. Dec. 1978

[3]   T. Cegrell, "A routing procedure for the TIDAS message-switching network," *IEEE Trans. Commun.*, vol. COM-23, pp. 575–585, June 1975.

[4]   F. Poncet and C. S. Repton, "The EIN communications sub-network: Principles and practice," in *Proc. 3rd ICCC*, Toronto, Ont., Canada, Aug. 1976, pp. 523–531.

[5]   J. L. Grangé and M. I. Irland, "Thirty-nine steps to a computer network," in *Proc. 4th ICCC*, Kyoto, Japan, Sept. 1978, pp. 763–769.

[6]   L. Fratta, M. Gerla, and L. Kleinrock, "The Flow Deviation Method: An Approach to Store-and-Forward Communication Network Design," *Networks*, vol. 3. New York: Wiley, 1973, pp. 97–133.

[7]   W. Older and D. A. Twyver, personal communication.

[8]   J. M. McQuillan, "Interactions between routing and congestion control in computer networks," in *Proc. Int. Symp. Flow Contr. in Comput. Networks*, Versailles, France, Feb. 1979, J. L. Grangé and M. Gien, Eds., Amsterdam: North-Holland, pp. 63–75.

[9]   M. Schwartz and C. Cheung, "The gradient projection algorithm for multiple routing in message-switched networks," *IEEE Trans. Commun.*, vol. COM-24, pp. 449–456, Apr. 1976.

[10]   R. Gallagher, "An optimal routing algorithm using distributed computation," *IEEE Trans. Commun.*, vol. COM-25, pp. 73–85, Jan. 1977.

[11]   T. E. Stern, "A class of decentralized routing algorithms using relaxation," *IEEE Trans. Commun.*, vol. COM-25, pp. 1092–1102, Oct. 1977.

[12]   E. W. Dijkstra, "A note on two problems in connection with graphs," *Numer. Math.*, vol. 1, pp. 269–271, 1959.

[13]   A. V. Aho, J. E. Hopcroft, and J. D. Ullman, *The Design and Analysis of Computer Algorithms.* Reading, MA: Addison-Wesley, 1974.

[14]   L. R. Ford, Jr. and D. R. Fulkerson, *Flows in Networks.* Princeton, NJ: Princeton Univ. Press, 1962.

[15] D. P. Bertsekas, "Dynamic behavior of a shortest path routing algorithm of the ARPANET type," presented at the Int. Symp. Inform. Theory, Grigano, Italy, June 1979.

[16] A. Rajaraman, "Routing in TYMNET," presented at the European Computing Conf., London, England, May 1978.

[17] R. R. Jueneman and G. S. Kerr, "Explicit routing in communications networks," in *Proc. 3rd ICCC*, Toronto, Ont., Canada, Aug. 1976, pp. 340–342.

[18] D. C. Walden, "Experiences in building, operating, and using the ARPA network," presented at the 2nd U.S.A.–Japan Comput. Conf., Tokyo, Japan, Aug. 1975.

[19] J. M. McQuillan, "Adaptive routing algorithms for distributed computer networks," BBN Rep. 2831, May 1974.

[20] J. M. McQuillan *et al.*, "The new routing algorithm for the ARPANET," *IEEE Trans. Commun.*, vol. COM-28, pp. 711–719, May 1980.

[21] L. Tymes, "TYMNET—A terminal oriented communication network," in *1971 Spring Joint Comput. Conf.*, AFIPS Conf. Proc., vol. 38, 1971, pp. 211–216.

[22] J. Rinde, "Routing and control in a centrally-directed network," in *1977 Nat. Comput. Conf., AFIPS Conf. Proc.*, vol. 46, 1977, pp. 603–608.

[23] —, "TYMNET I: An alternative to packet technology," in *Proc. 3rd ICCC*, Toronto, Ont., Canada, Aug. 1976, pp. 268–273.

[24] A. Danet, R. Despres, A LaRest, G. Pichon, and S. Ritzenthaler, "The French public packet switching service: The TRANSPAC network," in *Proc. 3rd ICCC*, Toronto, Ont, Canada, Aug. 1976, pp. 251–260.

[25] J. M. Simon and A. Danet, "Contrôle des ressources et principes du routage dans le réseau TRANSPAC," in *Proc., Int. Symp. Flow Control in Comput. Networks*, Versailles, France, Feb. 1979, J. L. Grangé and M. Gien, Eds. Amsterdam: North-Holland, pp. 33–44.

[26] J. M. Simon, personal communication.

[27] H. Rudin, "On routing and "Delta-routing": A taxonomy and performance comparison of techniques for packet-switched networks," *IEEE Trans. Commun.*, vol. COM-24, pp. 43–59, Jan. 1976.

[28] R. J. Cypser, *Communications Architecture for Distributed Systems*, Reading, MA: Addison-Wesley, 1978.

[29] P. E. Green, "An introduction to network architectures and protocols," *IBM Syst. J.*, vol. 18, no. 2, pp. 202–222, 1979.

[30] J. P. Gray and T. B. McNeill, "SNA multiple-system networking," *IBM Syst. J.*, vol. 18, no. 2, pp. 263–297, 1979.

[31] V. Ahuja, "Routing and flow control in systems network architecture," *IBM Syst. J.*, vol. 18, no. 2, pp. 298–314, 1979.

[32] W. L. Price, "Data network simulation experiments at the National Physical Laboratory, 1968-1976," *Comput. Networks*, vol. 1, no. 4, pp. 199–210, 1977.

[33] Digital Network Architecture, General Description, AA-H202A-TK, Digital Equipment Corp., Maynard, MA, Nov. 1978.

[34] W. D. Tajibnapis, "A correctness proof of a topology information maintenance protocol for distributed computer networks," *Commun. Ass. Comput. Mach.*, vol. 20, pp. 477–485, July 1977.

[35] M. Irland, "Buffer management in a packet switch," *IEEE Trans. Commun.*, vol. COM-26, pp. 328–337, Mar. 1978.

13

Flow Control Protocols

Mario Gerla and Leonard Kleinrock

I. Introduction

A packet-switched network may be thought of as a distributed pool of productive resources (channels, buffers, and switching processors) whose capacity must be shared dynamically by a community of competing users (or, more generally, processes) wishing to communicate with each other. Dynamic resource sharing is what distinguishes packet switching from the more traditional circuit-switching approach, in which network resources are dedicated to each user for an entire session. The key advantages of dynamic sharing are greater speed and flexibility in setting up users connections across the network and more efficient use of network resources after the connection is established.

These advantages of dynamic sharing do not come without a certain danger, however. Indeed, unless careful control is exercised on the user demands, the users may seriously abuse the network. In fact, if the demands are allowed to exceed the system capacity, highly unpleasant congestion effects occur which rapidly neutralize the delay and efficiency advantages of a packet network. The type of congestion that occurs in an overloaded packet network is not unlike that observed in a highway network. During peak hours, the demands often exceed the highway capacity, creating large backlogs. Furthermore, the interference between transit traffic on the highway and on-ramp and off-ramp traffic reduces the effective throughput of the highway, thus causing an even more rapid increase in the backlog. If this positive feedback situation persists, traffic on the highway may come to a standstill. The typical relationship between effective throughput and offered load in a highway system (and, more generally, in many uncontrolled, distributed dynamic sharing systems) is shown in Fig. 1.

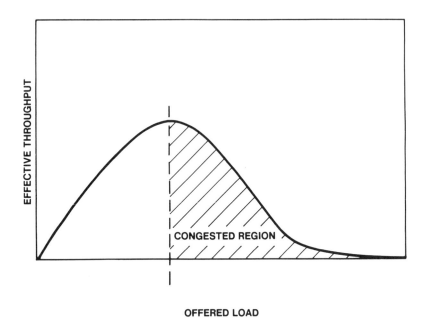

Fig. 1. Effective throughput versus offered load in an uncontrolled distributed dynamic sharing system.

By properly monitoring and controlling the offered load many of these congestion problems may be eliminated. In a highway system, it is common to control the input by using access ramp traffic lights. The objective is to keep the interference between transit traffic and incoming traffic within acceptable limits, and to prevent the incoming traffic rate from exceeding the highway capacity.

Similar types of controls are used in packet-switched networks, and are called *flow control* procedures. As in the highway system, the basic principle is to keep the excess load out of the network. The techniques, however, are much more sophisticated since the elements of the network (i.e., the switching processors) are intelligent, can communicate with each other, and therefore can coordinate their actions in a distributed control strategy.

Internal network congestion may also be relieved by rerouting some of the traffic from heavily loaded paths to underutilized paths. It is important to understand, however, that *routing* can reduce and, perhaps, delay network congestion; it cannot prevent it. We do not discuss the interactions between routing and flow control in this chapter. The interested reader is referred to the routing protocol survey by Schwartz and Stern in Chapter 12.

The main functions of flow control in a packet network are:

1. Prevention of throughput and response time degradation and loss of efficiency due to network and user overload,
2. deadlock avoidance,
3. fair allocation of resources among competing users, and
4. speed matching between the network and its attached users.

Throughput degradation and deadlocks occur because the traffic that has already been accepted into the network (i.e., traffic that has already been allocated network resources) exceeds the nominal capacity of the network. To prevent overallocation of resources, the flow control procedure includes a set of constraints (on buffers that can be allocated, on outstanding packets, on transmission rates, etc.) which can effectively limit the access of traffic into the network or, more precisely, to selected sections of the network. These constraints may be fixed, or may be dynamically adjusted based on traffic conditions.

Apart from the requirement of throughput efficiency, network resources must be fairly distributed among users. Unfortunately, efficiency and fairness objectives do not always coincide. For example, referring back to our highway traffic situation, the effective throughput of the Long Island Expressway could be maximized by opening all the lanes to traffic from the Island to New York City during the morning rush hour, and in the opposite direction during the evening rush hour. This solution, however, would also maximize the discontent of the reverse commuters (and we all know how dangerous it is to anger a New Yorker)! In packet networks, unfairness conditions can also arise (as we will show in the following sections); but they tend to be more subtle and less obvious than in highway networks because of the complexity of the communications protocols. One of the functions of flow control, therefore, is to prevent unfairness by placing *selective* restrictions on the amount of resources that each user (or user group) may acquire, in spite of the negative effect that these restrictions may have on dynamic resource sharing, and, therefore, overall throughput efficiency.

Flow control can be exercised at various levels in a packet network. The following levels, shown in Fig. 2, are identified and discussed in this paper.

(1) Hop Level. This level of flow control attempts to maintain a smooth flow of traffic between two neighboring nodes in a computer network, avoiding local buffer congestion and deadlocks. (We shall devote Section III to the discussion of this form of flow control.)

(2) Entry-to-Exit Level. This level of flow control is generally implemented as a protocol between the source and the destination switch, and has the purpose of preventing buffer congestion at the exit switch (Section IV).

(3) Network Access Level. The objective of this level is to throttle external inputs based on measurements of internal (as opposed to destination) network congestion (Section V).

(4) Session Level. This is the level of flow control associated with user sessions, i.e., the protocols which provide for the reliable delivery of packets on the "virtual" connection between two remote processes. Its main purpose is to prevent congestion of user buffers at the process level (i.e., outside of the network) (Section VI).

Some authors reserve the term *flow control* for the senior level, and refer to the other three levels of control as *congestion control* [34]. This terminology is used to emphasize the physical distinction between the first three levels, which are realized in the communication subnet (and therefore are the responsibility of the network implementer) and the fourth level, which is realized in the user devices (and therefore is the responsibility of the network customer). In this paper, we have chosen to use the term flow control for all four levels.

The design of an efficient flow control strategy for a packet network is a complex task in many ways. The most critical issue is the fact that flow control is a multilayer distributed protocol involving several different levels. At each level, the flow control implementation must be consistent and compatible with other protocol functions existing at that level. Furthermore, the interactions between different levels must be carefully studied in order to avoid duplication of functions on one hand, and lack of coordination on the other.

The purpose of this chapter is to provide a taxonomy of flow control mechanisms based on the above-defined multilevel structure. First, we review problems, functions, and performance measures of flow control. Then, for each level we survey the most representative flow control techniques that have been proposed and/or implemented, providing a performance comparison among techniques at the same level, and discussing the interaction between techniques at different levels. Finally, we briefly mention some new flow control issues raised by novel computer network applications.

II. Flow Control: Problems, Functions, and Measures

Our overall problem is to identify mechanisms which permit efficient dynamic sharing of the pool of resources (channels, buffers, and switching processors) in a packet network. In this section, we first describe and use some toy examples to illustrate the congestion problems caused by *lack* of control. Then we define the functions of flow control and the different levels at which these functions are implemented. Finally, we introduce performance measures for the evaluation and comparison of different flow control schemes.

A. Loss of Efficiency

The main cause of throughput degradation in a packet network is the *wastage* of resources. This may happen either because conflicting demands by two or more users make the resource unstable (e.g., collisions on a random access channel); or because a user acquires more resources than strictly needed, thus starving other users (e.g., a slow sink fed by a fast source may create a backlog of packets within the network which prevents other traffic from getting through). The two resources that are most commonly "wasted" in a packet network are *communications capacity* and *storage capacity*.

Buffer wastage is an indirect consequence of limited nodal storage: a given end-to-end packet stream may be blocked at an intermediate node along the path because all of the buffers at that node have been "hogged" by other streams. This may happen even if channel bandwidth is plentiful along the path of our blocked stream, thus causing an unnecessary loss of throughput. The source of this throughput degradation is that some users unnecessarily monopolize (i.e., waste) the buffers at some congested node.

A simple example of throughput degradation caused by buffer interference is shown in Fig. 3. Two pairs of hosts, (A, A') and (B, B'), are

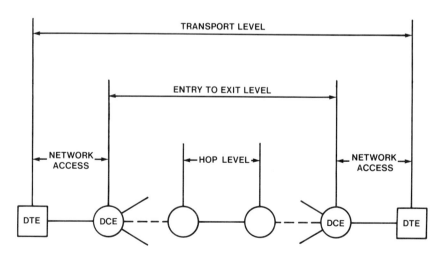

Fig. 2. Flow control levels.

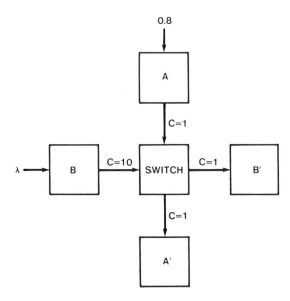

Fig. 3. Buffer interference example.

engaged in data transmission through a single network node. Access line speeds (in arbitrary units) are given in the figure. The traffic requirement from A to A' is constant and is equal to 0.8 (measured in the same units as the line speed). The requirement from B to B' is variable, and is denoted by λ. When λ approaches 1, the output queue from the switch to host B' grows indefinitely large filling up all the buffers in the switch. Packets arriving when all the buffers are full are discarded, and are later retransmitted by the source host (we refer to this model as the *retransmit model*). If we plot the total throughput, i.e., the sum of (A, A') and (B, B') delivered traffic as a function of λ (as in the solid curve of Fig. 4), we note that for $\lambda = 1$, the throughput experiences a sharp drop from 1.8 to 1.1. The drop is due to the fact that the switch can handle the entire user demand $= \lambda + 0.8$ for $\lambda < 1$; while for $\lambda \geq 1$, the switch buffers become full, causing overflow. Consequently, large queues build up in both the A and B hosts. With a heavy load, the rate of packet transmissions (and retransmissions) from B is 10 times the rate from A because of the difference in line access speeds. Thus, packets from B have a 10 times better chance of being accepted when a buffer becomes free than packets from A, leading to a 10 to 1 imbalance in effective throughput. Since the (B, B') throughput is limited to 1, the (A, A') throughput is reduced to 0.1 (i.e., one tenth of the AA' throughput), yielding a total throughput $= 1.1$ for $\lambda \geq 1$.

In this example, we have observed a *decrease in useful throughput* caused by an *increase of offered load* beyond the critical system capacity.

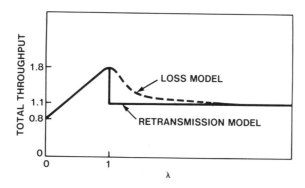

Fig. 4. Throughput degradation of system of Fig. 3 due to buffer interference.

This throughput degradation is typical of congested systems, and is often taken as a definition of congestion as was mentioned in connection with Fig. 1. (i.e., a system is "congestion-prone" if an increment in offered load causes a reduction in throughput) [27].

In the previous example, we assumed that dropped packets would be retransmitted from the host. A similar analysis can be carried out assuming that dropped packets are lost (*loss model*). The throughput versus offered load performance is similar to that of the retransmit model, although the drop is somewhat smoother in this case (the dashed curve of Fig. 4).

Throughput degradation effects, caused by inefficient allocation (and therefore wastage) of buffers are found also in multinode networks as reported by several studies [27], [13], [18]. To prevent this type of degradation, proper buffer allocation rules are generally established at each node, as soon described.

Another cause of throughput degradation is channel wastage. This problem manifests itself very clearly in multiaccess channels (e.g., packet satellite, or packet radio channels), when users transmit packets at random times without prior coordination (random access). A well-known example is offered by the ALOHA channel [23]. Packets that collide are lost, thus causing channel wastage and consequently, throughput degradation. Congestion prevention in multiaccess channels is discussed in Chapter 6. Also, it is clear that unnecessary retransmissions of a packet represent another form of channel wastage. Yet another manifestation is the use of unnecessarily long paths in a network (e.g., looping in routing algorithms).

B. Unfairness

Unfairness is a natural byproduct of uncontrolled competition. Some users, because of their relative position in the network or the particular

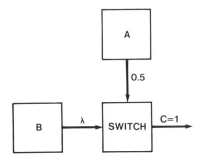

Fig. 5. Example of unfairness.

selection of network and traffic parameters, may succeed in capturing a larger share of resources than others, and thus enjoy preferential treatment.

One example of unfairness has already been given in Figs. 3 and 4 where the $(B-B')$ flow is allowed to exceed the $(A-A')$ flow by a factor of 10. Another obvious example of unfairness is offered by the single switch loss model in Fig. 5. The speed of the output trunk is 1. Hosts A and B are injecting data into the switch with rates 0.5 and λ, respectively. For fairness, the output trunk should be equally shared by the two hosts. However, the *loss model* performance results shown in Fig. 6 indicate that for large values of λ, host B captures the entire output trunk bandwidth, reducing the A throughput to zero. As previously observed, for $\lambda \gg 0.5$ host B has a far better chance to seize free buffers in the switch than host A. Specifically, the ratio of A packets to B packets in the switch at heavy load is roughly equal to $0.5/\lambda$. Thus, the ratio of A throughput to B throughput is also $0.5/\lambda$, explaining the behavior in Fig. 6.

Cases of unfairness have been reported in many multinode network studies, and several "fairness" techniques have been proposed. Unfortunately, the problem of fairness is considerably more difficult to deal with

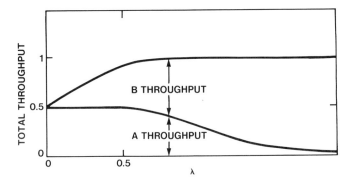

Fig. 6. Performance of system shown in Fig. 5.

than the problem of total throughput degradation because a general, unambiguous definition of fairness is not always possible in a distributed resource sharing environment.

C. Deadlocks

A deadlock condition manifests itself by a (total or partial) network crash. Deadlocks often occur because of a cyclic wait of resources to become available. That is, one user is holding a portion of the resources that he currently needs and is waiting for another user to release the remaining resources necessary to complete his task and this user is waiting for yet a third user, etc., such that the sequence of "waiting" users closes into a cycle, and it is immediately seen that no user in the cycle can make any progress [3]. Thus, the throughput for this subset of users is reduced to zero.

Deadlocks are likely to occur in a network when the offered load exceeds network capacity. For a simple example of a deadlock, consider two switches, A and B, connected by a trunk carrying heavy traffic in both directions (see Fig. 7). Under the heavy traffic assumption, node A rapidly fills up with packets directed to B; and vice versa, B fills up with packets directed to A. If we assume that dropped packets are retransmitted, then each node must hold a copy of each packet (and therefore a buffer) until the packet is accepted by the other node. This may result in an endless wait in which a node holds all of its buffers to store packets being transmitted to the other node, and keeps retransmitting packets to the other node waiting for buffers to be freed there. Consequently, no useful data are transferred on the trunk. It turns out that this type of deadlock (known as direct store-and-forward deadlock [19]) is relatively easy to prevent by setting simple restrictions on buffer usage at each node. A more extensive discussion of deadlocks will be given in Section III.

It is important to point out that buffer deadlocks are possible only in networks which retransmit dropped packets, i.e., which save a copy of a packet at each node while transmitting the packet to the next node on the path, and retransmit a copy of the packet in case of overflow (retransmit model). If dropped packets are not retransmitted (i.e., a loss model), the

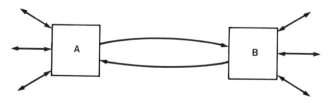

Fig. 7. Deadlock example.

sending node is not required to save a copy of the packet until acceptance at the next node, thus removing a necessary condition for deadlocks. Thus, lossy networks are deadlock free; however, an additional recovery mechanism for lost packets must then be provided at the end-to-end level, as is done for example in DNA (Chapter 10).

D. Flow Control Functions

Flow control may be defined as a protocol (or more generally, a set of protocols), designed to protect the network from problems related to overload and speed mismatches. Solutions to the three problems just discussed (maintaining efficiency, fairness and freedom from deadlock) are accomplished by setting rules for the allocation of buffers at each node and by properly regulating and (if necessary) blocking the flow of packets internally in the network as well as at the network entry points. Actually, multiple levels of flow control are generally implemented in a real network, as we shall see.

Efficiency and congestion prevention benefits of flow control do not come for free. In fact, flow control (like any other form of control in a distributed network) may require some exchange of information between nodes to select the control strategy and possibly some exchange of commands and parameter information to implement that strategy. This exchange translates into channel, processor, and storage overhead. Furthermore, flow control may require the dedication of resources (e.g., buffers, bandwidth) to individual users, or classes of users, thus reducing the statistical benefits of complete resource sharing. Clearly, the tradeoff between gain in efficiency (due to controls) and loss in efficiency (due to limited sharing and overhead) must be carefully considered in designing flow control strategies. This tradeoff is illustrated by the curves in Fig. 8, showing the effective throughput as a function of offered load. The ideal throughput curve corresponds to perfect control as it could be implemented by an ideal observer, with complete and instantaneous network status information. Ideal throughput follows the input and increases linearly until it reaches a horizontal asymptote corresponding to the maximum theoretical network throughput. The controlled throughput curve is a typical curve that can be obtained with an actual control procedure. Throughput values are lower than with the ideal curve because of imperfect control and protocol overhead. The uncontrolled curve follows the ideal curve for low offered load; for higher load, it collapses to a very low value of throughput and, possibly, to a deadlock.

Clearly, controls buy safety at high offered loads at the expense of somewhat reduced efficiency. The reduction in efficiency is measured in terms of higher delays (for light load) and lower throughput (at saturation).

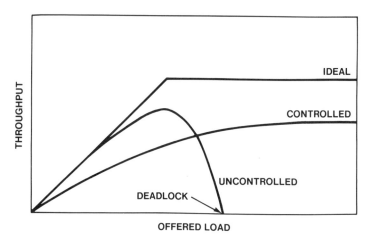

Fig. 8. Flow control performance tradeoffs.

Furthermore, experience shows that flow control procedures are quite difficult to design and, ironically, can themselves be the source of deadlocks and degradations. In particular, when one controls flow, one places *constraints* on the flow. If one cannot meet a constraint, then the result is a deadlock. Or, if one is slow in meeting the constraint, the result is a throughput degradation.

E. Levels of Flow Control

Flow control in a packet network can be best described as a multi-layered structure consisting of several mechanisms operating independently at different levels. Since flow control levels are closely related to (and sometimes imbedded in) protocol levels, it is helpful for us to begin by briefly reviewing the network protocol structure, pointing to the flow control provisions existing at each level [17]. The flow control level structure will then be defined following the protocol structure model.

Figure 9 depicts the typical protocol layer architecture implemented in a packet network, using as a reference a network path connecting user devices called DTEs (data terminal equipment) through a number of intervening communications switches called DCEs (data circuit terminating equipment). For the user-to-network (i.e., DTE-to-DCE) interface, a standard set of protocol levels is now being defined by ISO and ANSI [9]. For the internode protocols within the communications subnetwork, there is less emphasis on standardization since different network manufacturers tend to select different solutions to best exploit their equipment capabilities. In spite of these differences, it is still possible to define a set of reference levels for

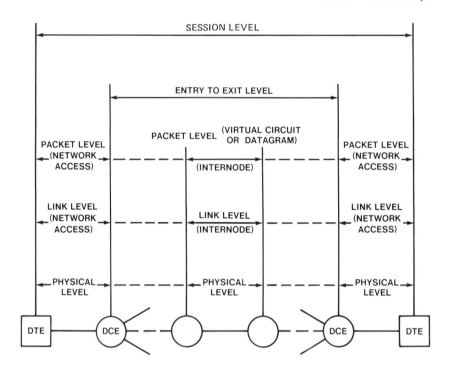

Fig. 9. Network protocol levels. (DTE: Data terminal equipment, e.g., host, terminal. DCE: Data circuit terminating equipment, e.g., switching processor.)

internal network protocols which closely parallel the DTE–DCE interface protocol levels.

Starting from the bottom of the protocol hierarchy, we have the *physical level* which has the function of activating and deactivating the electrical connection between the nodes. No flow control functions are assigned to this level.

Above the physical level, we have the *link level* which serves the purpose of transporting packets reliably across individual physical links. One of the functions of this protocol is related to flow control, and consists of retransmitting packets that are dropped because of congestion at the receiving node. In some protocols, a congested receiver may stop the sender by using appropriate commands (e.g., RNR: receiver not ready, in HDLC and SDLC; or, XOFF in asynchronous terminal connections). As mentioned before, we find two different types of links in the network: the internal (or node-to-node) link and the network access link. Correspondingly, we have (at the same level in the protocol hierarchy) two types of link protocol: the *network access protocol* and the *node-to-node protocol*. Typical examples of link protocol implementation are HDLC, SDLC, and X.25 level 2 (which is a subset of HDLC).

Above the link level, we have the *packet level protocol*, which defines the procedures for establishing end-to-end user connections through the network and specifies the format of the control information used to route packets to their destinations. Two different versions of packet protocol exist: the *virtual circuit* protocol and the *datagram* protocol.

When the virtual circuit (VC) implementation is used, a "virtual" circuit connection must be set up between a pair of users (or processes) wishing to communicate with each other *before* the data transfer can be started. The establishment of this circuit implies dedication of resources of one form or another along the network path. A typical virtual circuit implementation, used in Transpac [7], assigns a fixed path to each connection at setup time. A virtual circuit ID number, stamped in the packet header, uniquely identifies the packets belonging to a connection, and is used to route packets to the destination using routing maps stored at each intermediate node at setup time. From the flow control point of view, the VC protocol has the distinguishing feature of permitting *selective* flow control on each individual user connection. This selective flow control can be applied at the internode level as well as at the network access level. Since a fixed path is maintained for the entire user session, the selective flow control can also be extended from entry to exit switch and if so desired, even from entry to exit DTE.

In contrast to the virtual circuit implementation, the datagram implementation does not require any circuit setup before transmission. Each packet is independently submitted to the network, and explicitly carries in its header all the information required for its delivery to destination [34]. Selective flow control, on a connection by connection basis, is not available in the datagram implementation since the packet header does not contain specific connection information (it merely posts source and destination DTE addresses).

Above the packet protocol, we find (within the subnet only) the *entry-to-exit* (ETE) protocol. The objective of this protocol is the reliable transport of single and multipacket messages from network entry to network exit node. Important functions of this protocol which are related to flow control are the reassembly of multipacket messages at the exit node and the regulation of input traffic using buffer allocation and windowing techniques. Some network implementations, e.g., DNA, do not have the ETE level of protocol. In this case, the ETE functions are relegated to higher-level protocols.

The highest level of network protocol which has impact on flow control is the *session protocol*. This protocol provides for the reliable delivery of packets on the "virtual" connection between two remote processes. One of the flow control related functions of this protocol is the protection of destination buffers. The goal is to regulate the flow so as to make the most efficient use of network resources, while avoiding buffer overflow at the destination. "Window" and "credit" schemes are generally used for this purpose.

The above network protocol review has identified various flow control functions and capabilities built into different levels of protocols, and has brought to our attention the fact that each protocol level has its own distinct flow control responsibilities. It is now clear that the classification into the four types of flow control procedures mentioned earlier parallels the classification of network protocols. Recall that there is

1. hop (or node-to-node) level (Section III),
2. network access level (Section V),
3. entry-to-exit level (Section IV), and
4. session level (Section VI).

The diagram in Fig. 2 illustrates these levels of flow control for a typical network path. A comparison with Fig. 9 reveals the close relationship between flow control and protocol level structures.

Unfortunately, the true system behavior is far more complex than our models and classifications attempt (or can afford) to portray. Therefore, actual networks may not always mechanize all of the above four levels of flow control with distinct procedures. It is quite possible, for example, for a single flow control mechanism to combine two or more levels of flow control. On the other hand, it is possible that one or more levels of flow control may be missing in the network implementation. The matrix in Fig. 10 provides a synopsis of the main network implementations and flow control schemes that will be surveyed in this paper. It is seen that some of the schemes cover more than one level.

	ARPA			TRANSPAC	SNA			GMDNET	
	CQL	RFNM	NCP	X.25	SDLC	VR PACING	SESSION PACING	I-C	SBP
HOP LEVEL	●			●	●	●		●	●
NETW. ACC.				●			●	●	
ENTRY-EXIT		●		●		●	●		●
SESSION			●	NOT DEFINED			●	NOT DEFINED	

Fig. 10. Classification of a sample of actual flow implementations.

F. Performance Measures

We wish to define a quantitative measure of flow control performance for various reasons. First, we wish to be able to "tune" the parameters of a given flow control scheme so as to optimize a well-defined performance criterion. Second, we wish to carefully weigh performance benefits against overhead introduced by flow control. Third, we are interested in comparing the performance of alternative flow control schemes in quantitative terms.

Throughput efficiency (where throughput is expressed in packets/s) is probably the most common measure of flow control performance. Total effective throughput (sum of all the individual contributions) is evaluated as a function of offered load. This representation is particularly useful to determine the critical load in an uncontrolled system and to assess the throughput efficiency of a controlled network at heavy load.

Another common measure is the *combined delay and throughput performance*. The delay-vs.-throughput profile allows us to determine the delay overhead introduced by the controls (which the throughput versus offered load curve did not display). In general, it gives us a more complete picture of system performance than does throughput behavior alone. In fact, a system may be designed to deliver high throughput at heavy load, and yet it may experience intolerable delays at light load.

A more compact measure of combined throughput and delay performance is offered by the concept of *power* [13], [24]. The simplest definition of power is the ratio of throughput over delay; it is, therefore, a function of the offered load. In fact, it defines the "knee" of the throughput–delay profile as that point where power is maximized, and as shown in Fig. 11 this knee occurs where a ray out of the origin is tangent to the performance profile [24]. A very nice characterization of this maximum power point is

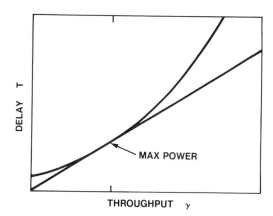

Fig. 11. Delay, throughput, and power.

such that it occurs when the average buffer occupancy at each intermediate node on the path is unity. In [25], it was shown that blocking due to loss systems could easily be included in a more general definition of power (by multiplying the simple definition by one minus the blocking probability); this leads to system designs whose optimum operating point is easily found and which corresponds to the operating point one would intuitively choose.

In some important cases, power is maximized for a value of offered load which is approximately half of the saturation load [24]. The maximum power value reflects both delay performance (at light load) and throughput performance (at heavy load) and therefore, represents a good figure of merit of the flow control implementation. Much more general definitions of power are also studied in [25].

III. Hop Level Flow Control

A. Objective

The objective of hop level flow control (HL) is to prevent store-and-forward buffer congestion and its consequences, namely, throughput degradation and deadlocks. Hop level flow control operates in a local, "myopic" way in that it monitors local queues and buffer occupancies at each node and rejects store-and-forward (S/F) traffic arriving at the node when some predefined thresholds (e.g., maximum queue limits) are exceeded. The function of checking buffer thresholds and discarding (and later retransmitting) packets on a network link is often carried out by the data link control protocol.

This locality of the control does not preclude, however, possible end-to-end repercussions of hop level flow control due to the "backpressure" effect [i.e., the propagation of buffer threshold conditions from the congested node upstream to the traffic source(s)]. In fact, the backpressure property is efficiently exploited in several network implementations (as soon described).

Store-and-forward congestion has two unpleasant consequences: throughput degradation and deadlocks. These conditions were described in Sections II A and II C, respectively. In the remainder of this section, we survey and compare a number of hop level flow control procedures, specifically designed to eliminate these problems.

B. Classification of Hop Level Control Schemes

The hop level flow control scheme can play the role of arbitrator between various *classes of traffic* competing for a common buffer pool in each node. A fundamental distinction between different flow control schemes is based on the way the traffic entering a node is subdivided into classes.

One family of hop flow control schemes distinguishes incoming packets based on the output queue they must be placed into. Thus, the number of classes is equal to the number of output queues; the flow control scheme supervises the allocation of store-and-forward buffers to the output queues. Some limit (fixed or dynamically adjustable) is defined for each queue; packets beyond this limit are discarded. Hence, the name *channel queue limit* schemes is generally given to such mechanisms (see Section III C).

Another important family of hop flow control schemes distinguishes incoming packets based on the "hop count" (i.e., the number of network links that they have so far traversed). This implies that each node keeps track of $N - 1$ classes of traffic, where $N - 1$ is the number of different hop counts, and N is the number of nodes in the network (note that if loopless routing is assumed, no network path can exceed $N - 1$ hops in length), and allocates a (fixed or adjustable) number of buffers to each class. We will refer to this family of schemes as *buffer class* schemes (see Section III D).

A third family distinguishes packets based on the virtual circuit (i.e., end-to-end session) they belong to. This type of scheme requires, of course, a virtual circuit network architecture; it assumes that each node can distinguish incoming packets based on the virtual circuit they belong to and keep track of a number of classes equal to the number of virtual circuits that currently traverse it. Note that the number of classes varies here with time (since virtual circuits are dynamically created and released), as opposed to the previously mentioned schemes where the number of classes is merely a function of the topology. Upon creation, a virtual circuit is allocated a set of buffers (fixed or variable) at each node. When this set is used up, no further traffic is accepted from that virtual circuit. We will refer to this family of schemes as *virtual circuit hop level* schemes (see Section III E).

Many other traffic subdivisions are possible: for example, a traffic class may be associated with each traffic source; with each traffic destination; or with each source–destination node pair. Indeed, these are all legitimate and, in many respects, well justified choices for a link level flow control scheme. However, we will restrict our study to the three schemes just mentioned, since these are the only schemes which have been extensively analyzed in the published literature and implemented in real networks.

Apart from traffic class distinctions, another parameter that is often used to characterize and classify hop flow control schemes is the degree of dynamic sharing of the store-and-forward buffers. Here, several possibilities exist, namely:

1. fixed, uniform partitioning of buffers among buffer classes (no sharing);

2. buffer partitioning proportional to traffic in each class (no sharing);
3. overselling (i.e., the sum of the buffer limits, one for each class, is larger than the total buffer pool); and
4. dynamic adjustment of buffer limits based on relative traffic fluctuations.

The following sections discuss each hop flow control class in more detail.

C. Channel Queue Limit Flow Control

In the channel queue limit (CQL) scheme, the traffic classes correspond to the channel output queues, and there are restrictions on the number of buffers each class can seize. We may define the following versions of the CQL scheme [20].

(1) Complete Partitioning (CP). Letting N be the number of output queues, and n_i be the number of packets on the ith queue and B the buffer size, we have the following constraint:

$$0 \leq n_i \leq B/N, \qquad \forall i$$

(2) Sharing with Maximum Queues (SMXQ). Let b_{max} be the maximum queue size allowed (where, $b_{max} > B/N$); we have the following constraints:

$$0 \leq n_i \leq b_{max}, \qquad \forall i$$

$$\sum_i n_i \leq B.$$

(3) Sharing with Minimum Allocation (SMA). Let b_{min} be the minimum buffer allocation which is guaranteed to each queue (typically, $b_{min} \leq B/N$). The constraint then becomes

$$\sum_i \max(0, n_i - b_{min}) \leq B - Nb_{min}$$

(4) Sharing with Minimum Allocation and Maximum Queue. This scheme combines (2) and (3) in that it provides for a minimum buffer guarantee and a maximum buffer allocation for each queue at the same time.

The above options assume that the buffer limit parameters are fixed in time and are the same for all queues. Additional flexibility may be introduced in these schemes by allowing the buffer parameters to change dynamically in time and from queue to queue based on traffic fluctuations.

Having defined a number of CQL flow control options, we now proceed to show that this form of flow control can eliminate the performance degradation and deadlock effects mentioned in Section II. Referring first to Fig. 2, we note that in the presence of CQL flow control, the traffic component (B, B') will no longer be permitted to seize all the buffers in the switch. Therefore, traffic can now flow freely from A to A', and the throughput degradation effect is removed. Similarly, the deadlock condition depicted in Figs. 6 and 7 cannot occur since the buffers in node A cannot be taken over completely by the channel (A, B) queue. Therefore, some buffers in A will always be available to receive packets from node B.

Some form or another of CQL flow control is found in every network implementation.The ARPAnet IMP (Interface Message Processor) has a shared buffer pool with minimum allocation and maximum limit for each queue, as shown in Fig. 12 [30]. Of the total buffer pool (typically, 40 buffers of one packet), two buffers for input and one buffer for output are

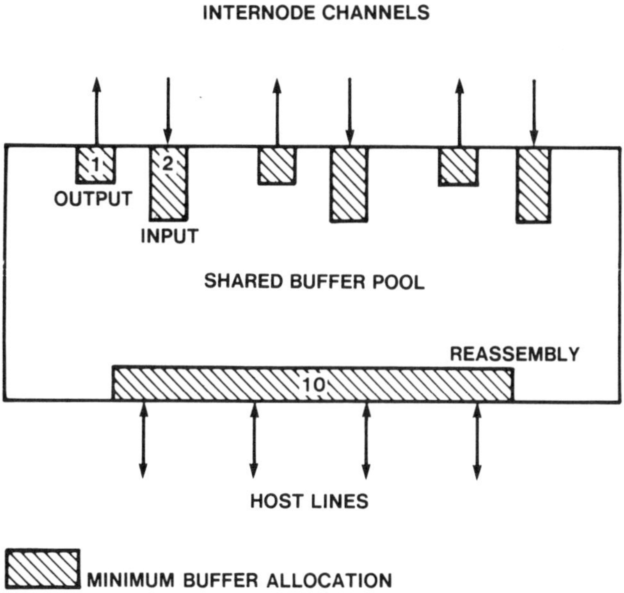

Fig. 12. Buffer allocation in ARPAnet IMP (1972 version).

Total buffer pool = 40 packet buffers

	minimum allocation	maximum allocation
Reassembly	10	20
Internode input queue	2	
Internode output queue	1	8
Total internode queues (i.e., total S/F buffers)		20

permanently allocated to each internode channel. Similarly, ten buffers are permanently dedicated to the reassembly of messages directed to the hosts. The remaining buffers are shared among output queues and the reassembly function, with the following restrictions: reassembly buffers ≤ 20, output queue ≤ 8, the total store-and-forward buffers ≤ 20.

Next we proceed to the evaluation and comparison of CQL implementations, and briefly review the main results available in the published literature [18],[20]. We first report on some throughput degradation conditions observed in absence of flow control. Figure 13 from [18] shows throughput performance as a function of link load for a variety of buffer control policies. The curve labeled "unrestricted sharing" corresponds to a system without flow control. We notice that, for increasing input load, the throughput of the uncontrolled system reaches a peak and then degrades asymptotically to unity. This behavior confirms the throughput degradation predictions made in Section II.

Throughput degradation is easily corrected with the introduction of CQL flow control, as shown by the remaining curves in Fig. 13. The "no sharing" system (i.e., complete partitioning of the buffer pool among the outgoing queues) is, as expected, the most conservative scheme and least efficient with respect to throughput. The best scheme is the "optimal sharing" scheme, which corresponds to optimally reselecting a new buffer limit for each level of traffic (i.e., dynamic SMXQ). A heuristic approximation of the optimal scheme is offered by the "square root scheme," a load

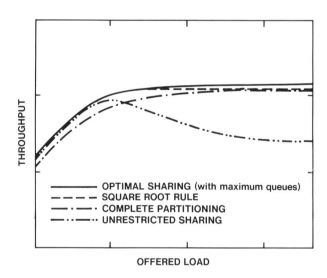

Fig. 13. Single switch buffer and allocation model. Throughput versus load behavior for various buffer management schemes (unbalanced load pattern).

invariant scheme with fixed buffer limit $= \sqrt{B/N}$, where B is the total number of buffers and N is the number of output channels. The square root scheme is simpler to implement than the optimal scheme since it does not depend on traffic load and, therefore, does not require the reoptimization of the buffer limit values as a function of traffic pattern changes, and yet, it was shown to be practically as efficient as the optimal sharing for a number of cases [18].

Kamoun [20] used a similar switch model to investigate the sharing with minimum allocation (SMA) scheme. The results, obtained in a balanced load environment, show no substantial difference between SMXQ and SMA; in fact, neither scheme is consistently better over the entire range of offered loads. We conjecture, however, that with strongly unbalanced traffic SMA would exhibit better "fairness" since SMA guarantees minimum throughput (with low delay) for each output channel even when the shared portion of the buffer pool is captured by a few heavily loaded queues.

Summarizing various published results, we may state that CQL flow control is necessary to avoid throughput degradation, unfairness, and direct store-and-forward deadlocks. Furthermore, it seems that almost any form of CQL implementation will provide the minimum required protection. The safest scheme (for fairness reasons) seems to be the combination of SMXQ and SMA, which imposes a maximum and minimum limit on each queue (incidentally, this was the scheme used in ARPAnet).

D. Structured Buffer Pool (SBP) Flow Control

We have shown in the previous section that CQL flow control eliminates direct store-and-forward deadlocks. However, there is another, more general form of deadlock which can arise in packet networks, namely, *indirect store-and-forward deadlocks* [19]. Figure 14 illustrates a typical indirect store-and-forward deadlock situation. Suppose that unfavorable traffic conditions in the ring topology shown in Fig. 14 cause each queue to be filled with Q_{max} packets, where Q_{max} is the limit imposed by the CQL strategy. Furthermore, assume that the packets at each node are directed to a node two or more hops away [e.g., all packets queued on link (A, B) are directed to C]. In these conditions, no traffic can move in the network since all the queues are full. Thus, we have a deadlock even if the network is equipped with CQL flow control (which is known to prevent direct store-and-forward deadlocks)!

Prevention of indirect store-and-forward deadlocks is obtained with the "structured buffer pool" strategy proposed by Raubold *et al.* [37]. In this strategy, packets arriving at each node are divided into classes according to the number of hops they have covered. For example, packets entering a

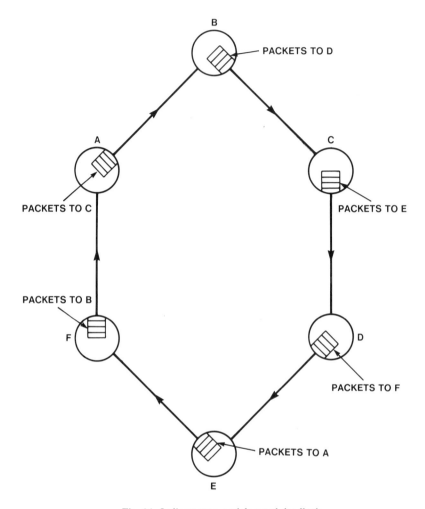

Fig. 14. Indirect store-and-forward deadlock.

node from the host belong to class 0 of that node, since they have not yet covered any hops. The highest class H_{max} corresponds to packets that have traversed H_{max} hops, where H_{max} is the maximum path length in the network (a function of the topology and the routing algorithm). The highest class H_{max} also includes all the packets that have reached their destinations and are therefore being reassembled into messages before delivery to the hosts. The nodal buffer organization reflects this class structure as shown in Fig. 15.

Each packet class has the right to use a well-defined set of buffers. Class 0 can access only the buffers available in set 0. Buffer set 0 is large

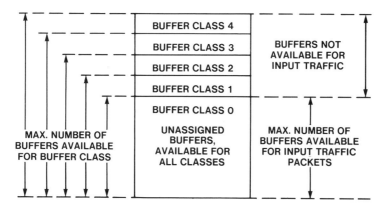

Fig. 15. Structured buffer pool.

enough to store the largest size message entering the network. Class $i + 1$ can use all the buffers available to class i, plus one additional buffer. Finally, class H_{max} can access all the buffers available to class $H_{max} - 1$, plus a number of buffers sufficient to reassemble the largest message to be delivered to any destination (this provision is necessary, although not sufficient, to avoid "reassembly deadlocks," as will be shown in Section IV).

Under normal traffic conditions, only set 0 buffers are used. When the load increases beyond nominal levels, buffers fill up progressively from level 0 to level H_{max}. When at a given node the buffers at levels $\leq i$ are full, arriving packets which have covered $\leq i$ hops are discarded. Thus, in case of congestion, "junior" packets are dropped in the attempt to carry "senior" packets to their destination. This is a desirable property, since senior packets correspond to a higher network resource investment.

It can easily be shown that this strategy eliminates deadlocks of both the direct and indirect type [37]. To prove this, we consider the "resource graph" [3] associated with the packet-switched network. In this graph, there is an arc associated with each packet in the network. The arc originates from the buffer currently occupied by the packet and terminates in the (currently unavailable, but awaited) buffer in the next node on the path. A deadlock occurs if and only if there is a cycle in the graph, i.e., there is a chain of arcs which starts from one buffer, and terminates at the same buffer. The existence of cycles can easily be recognized in the deadlock situations depicted in Figs. 6 and 14.

With the structured buffer pool, however, no cycle can occur in the resource graph since each arc starts from a buffer of class i and points to a buffer of class $i + 1$ (recall that a packet gains seniority at each hop; an illustration of this property is shown in Fig. 16. Thus, both direct and indirect store-and-forward deadlocks are prevented.

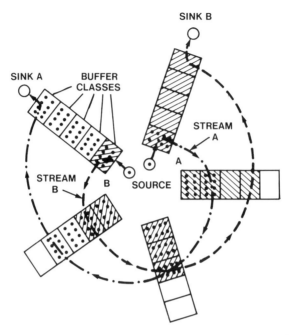

Fig. 16. Access to buffer classes. Example for two data streams. Dotted areas: buffers available for stream A. Hatched areas: buffers available for stream B.

The SBP method was developed by the GMD group in Darmstadt, Germany, for implementation in GMDNET, an experimental packet switch network [37]. Before implementation, an extensive simulation effort was carried out to verify and evaluate the performance of all the network protocols, and of the SBP procedure in particular [13]. Early simulation results showed that the proposed flow control scheme was effective in eliminating deadlocks, but was not successful in preventing throughput degradation when the offered load exceeded the critical threshold (some SBP simulation experiments with typical packet switch network topologies showed that the throughput in heavy load conditions was four to five times lower than the maximum throughput).

To correct the loss of throughput efficiency under heavy loads, additional constraints were imposed on the number of buffers that each traffic class could seize. The most dramatic improvement was obtained by limiting the number of class 0 buffers that could be seized by input packets (i.e., packets entering the network from external sources). In the absence of this constraint, input packets had the tendency to monopolize all class 0 buffers, leaving only a "thin" buffer layer for the transit traffic to circulate. The control of input traffic, known as "input flow control" in GMDNET is a form of network access flow control and will be discussed more extensively in Section V.

Additional improvements in the SBP scheme were obtained in the case of datagram networks, by setting a specific buffer size constraint $L(i)$ on each class i[13]. (In other words, instead of having a nested buffer pool in which class i can access all buffers available to class $i - 1$, plus one buffer, a different constraint is set on each class). The constraint $L(i)$ was dynamically adjusted to adapt to the relative demands of the various classes. It is interesting to note that the deadlock prevention property is *not* affected by dynamic changes in buffer class size (as long as at least one buffer is dedicated to each class at all times).

E. Virtual Circuit (Hop Level) Flow Control

We recall that packet switch networks can be subdivided into two broad classes: datagram (DG) networks and virtual circuit (VC) networks. In DG networks, each packet in a user session is carried through the network independently of the other packets in the same session; that is, packets in the same session may follow different routes, and may be delivered out of sequence to the destination. In VC networks, a physical network path is set up for each user session and is released when the session is terminated. Packets follow the preestablished path in sequence. Sequencing and error control are provided at each step along the path.

The previously mentioned flow control schemes, namely, CQL and SBP, are applicable to both DG and VC nets. In addition, VC nets permit the application of *selective flow control* to each individual VC stream (VC flow control). There are two forms of VC flow control.

(1) Hop level (or stepwise) VC flow control, which controls VC flow at each hop along the path, and is designed to avoid S/F buffer congestion; and

(2) Source–sink (or end-to-end) VC flow control, whose function it is to adjust source rate to sink rate so as to maximize VC throughput, yet avoiding sink buffer congestion.

In this section we will mainly deal with VC hop level (VC-HL) flow control; we discuss end-to-end VC flow control in more detail in Section IV.

The basic principle of operation of the VC-HL scheme consists of setting a limit M on the maximum number of packets for each VC stream that can be in transit at each intermediate node. The limit M may be fixed at VC setup time, or may be dynamically adjusted, based on load fluctuations. The buffer limit M is enforced at each hop by the VC-HL protocol, which regulates the issue of transmission "permits" and discards packets based on buffer occupancy.

The advantage of VC-HL (over CQL and SBP) is to provide a more efficient and prompt recovery from congestion by selectively slowing down the VCs directly feeding into the congested area. By virtue of backpressure, the control then propagates to all the sources that are contributing to the congestion, and reduces (or stops) their inputs, leaving the other traffic sources undisturbed. Without VC-HL flow control, the congestion would spread gradually to a larger portion of the network, blocking traffic sources that were not directly responsible for the original congestion, and causing unnecessary throughput degradation and unfairness.

As in the case of CQL and SBP schemes, various buffer sharing policies can be proposed. At one extreme, M buffers can be dedicated to each VC at setup time; at the other extreme, buffers may be allocated, on demand, from a common pool (complete sharing). It is easily seen that buffer dedication can lead to extraordinary storage overhead, since there is, generally, no practical upper bound on the number of VCs that can simultaneously exist in a network; furthermore, the traffic on each VC is generally bursty, leading to low utilization of the reserved buffers. For these reasons, most of the implementations employ dynamic buffer sharing.

The shared versus dedicated buffer policy also has an impact on the deadlock prevention properties of the VC-HL scheme. With buffer dedication, the VC-HL scheme becomes deadlock free. This can easily be deduced by considering the resource graph and recognizing that the graph cannot contain loops, since virtual circuits are loopless by construction. (For deadlock freedom, it actually suffices that at least one buffer be reserved for each virtual circuit.) If, on the other hand, no buffer reservations are made and buffers are allocated strictly on demand, deadlocks may occur unless additional protection (e.g., the SBP scheme) is implemented.

In the following, we briefly describe three different versions of VC-HL flow control implemented in existing networks and report on some performance results.

TYMNET is probably the earliest VC network developed [39]. As distinct from most VC networks, TYMNET uses a "composite" packet internode protocol. This means that data from different VCs traveling on the same trunk can be packed in the same envelope, for the purpose of link overhead reduction. TYMNET is a character-oriented network in the sense that data flows on a virtual circuit in the form of characters, rather than packets (i.e., characters are assembled into packets at the entry node, and are then disassembled at the exit node). The character-oriented nature of TYMNET implies that VC-HL buffer allocation is based on character (rather than packet) counts.

In TYMNET [39], a throughput limit is computed for each VC at setup time according to terminal speed, and is enforced all along the network path. Throughput control is obtained by assigning a maximum buffer limit (per VC) at each intermediate node and by controlling the issue of transmission permits from node to node based on the current buffer allocation. Periodically (every half second), each node sends a backpressure vector to its neighbors, containing one bit for each virtual circuit that traverses it. If the number of current buffered characters for a given VC exceeds the maximum allocation (e.g., for low speed terminals—10 to 30 characters/s— the allocation is 32 characters), the backpressure bit is set to zero; otherwise the bit is set to one. On the transmitting side, each VC is associated with a counter which is initialized to the maximum buffer limit and is decremented by one for each character transmitted. Transmission stops on a particular VC when the corresponding counter is reduced to zero. Upon reception of a backpressure bit $= 1$, the counter is reset to its initial value and transmission can resume.

The effect of backpressure from an individual hop back along the VC in TYMNET constitutes a good example of the "hybrid" character of many practical flow control implementations, since we see here a mixture of hop level and transport level flow control. This was pointed out earlier in connection with Fig. 10, and we shall encounter other examples as we proceed.

TRANSPAC, the French public data network, is a VC network which uses X.25 as an internode protocol [42]. One of the distinguishing features of Transpac is the use of the throughput class concept in X.25 for internal flow and congestion control. Each VC call request carries a throughput class declaration which corresponds to the maximum (instantaneous) data rate that the user will ever attempt to present to that VC. Each node keeps track of the aggregate declared throughput (which represents the worst case situation), and at the same time, monitors actual throughput (typically, much lower than the declared throughput) and average buffer utilization. Based on the ratio of actual to declared throughput, the node may decide to *oversell* capacity, i.e., it will attempt to carry a declared throughput volume higher than trunk capacity. Clearly, overselling implies that input rates may temporarily exceed trunk capacities, so that the network must be prepared to exercise flow control. Packet buffers are dynamically allocated to VCs based on demand (complete sharing), but thresholds are set on individual VC allocations as well as on overall buffer pool utilization. Of particular interest is the impact of overall buffer pool thresholds on VC-HL. Three threshold levels [S_0, S_1, and S_2 (where $S_0 < S_1 < S_2$)] are defined and are used in the following way:

1. S_0: do not accept new VC call requests;
2. S_1: slow down the flow on current VCs (by delaying the return of ACKs at the VC level); and
3. S_2: selectively disconnect existing VCs.

The threshold levels S_0, S_1, and S_2 are dynamically evaluated as a function of declared throughput, measured throughput, and current buffer utilization.

Another example of a VC network is offered by GMDNET [13]. As we mentioned before, GMDNET applies SBP flow control. In addition, it applies I-control (individual control) on each virtual circuit. I-control consists of two components: end-to-end flow control and hop level flow control. End-to-end and hop level flow control are implemented using variable size windows PUL_E and PUL_L, respectively (PUL = packet underway limit). The window is defined as the maximum number of packets that a sender is allowed to transmit before receiving an ACK, or permit [5]. The windows PUL_E and PUL_L are dynamically adjusted based on sink congestion and intermediate node congestion, respectively; their values may vary within predefined ranges ($1 \leq PUL_E \leq W_E$; $1 \leq PUL_L \leq W_L$) [37], [13]. The buffer pool is completely shareable, without specific reservations for individual VCs.

Simulation results on the performance of the I-control scheme lead to the following important conclusions.

(1) I-control alone cannot prevent throughput degradation, unfairness, and deadlocks. Experimental results clearly show that an I-controlled network without SBP becomes deadlocked immediately after the applied load exceeds the critical value (this confirms our prediction that VC flow control without specific buffer reservations for individual VCs cannot prevent deadlocks).

(2) The end-to-end component of I-control is very effective in preventing network congestion in the case of source rates exceeding sink rates. Without I-control (i.e., the SBP control alone), a fivefold throughput degradation was observed in a typical network overload experiment.

IV. Entry-to-Exit Flow Control

The main objective of the entry-to-exit (ETE) flow control is to prevent buffer congestion at the exit node due to the fact that remote sources are sending traffic at a higher rate than can be accepted by the hosts (or terminals) attached to the exit node. The cause of the bottleneck could be either the overload of the local lines connecting the exit node to the hosts, or the slow acceptance rate of the hosts. The problem of congestion prevention at the exit node becomes more complex when this node must also reassemble packets into messages, and/or resequence messages before delivery to the host. If fact, reassembly and resequence deadlocks may occur, which require special prevention measures.

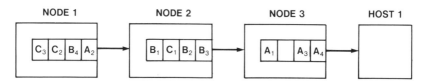

Fig. 17. Reassembly buffer deadlock.

In order to understand how reassembly deadlocks can be generated, let us consider the network path shown in Fig. 17, where three store-and-forward nodes (node 1, node 2, and node 3, respectively) relay traffic directed to host 1. In the situation depicted in Fig. 17, three multipacket messages A, B, and C are in transit towards host 1. Without loss of generality we assume that the maximum message size is 4 packets and that 4 packet buffers are dedicated to messages being assembled at a node; furthermore, a channel queue limit $Q_{max} = 4$ is set on each trunk queue, for hop level flow control. We note from Fig. 17 that message A (which has seized all four reassembly buffers at node 3) cannot be delivered to the host since packet A_2 is missing. Packet A_2, on the other hand, cannot be forwarded to node 2 since the queue at node 2 is full. The node 2 queue, in turn, cannot advance until reassembly space becomes available in node 3 for B or C messages. Deadlock!

A very similar order of events leads to resequence deadlocks as shown in Fig. 18. Assume that a sequence of single packet messages $A, B, \ldots, K$ originating from host 2 and directed to host 1 is traveling through a three-node network. If messages must be delivered in sequence, messages B, C, D, E in node 3 cannot be transmitted to host 1 until message A is received at node 3. However, due to store-and-forward buffer unavailability in node 2, message A cannot reach node 3. Deadlock!

Various schemes can be used to prevent these types of deadlocks. In the ARPAnet, for example, reassembly deadlocks are avoided by requiring a reassembly buffer reservation for each multipacket message entering the network; resequence deadlocks are avoided by discarding out-of-sequence messages at the destination. Other networks (e.g., TELENET) have sufficient

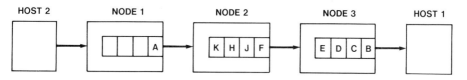

Fig. 18. Resequence deadlock.

nodal storage to permit out-of-sequence messages to be accepted at a destination node with the understanding that these may be discarded later if storage congestion occurs; again, the existence of a source copy saves the day. These and other schemes are discussed in more detail in the following sections.

While the main objective of ETE controls is to protect the exit node from congestion, an important byproduct is the prevention of global (i.e., internal) congestion. Virtually all ETE controls are based on a window scheme that allows only up to W sequential messages to be outstanding in the network before an end-to-end ACK is received. If the network becomes congested (this may occur independently of destination node congestion), messages and ACKs incur high end-to-end delays. These delays, combined with the restriction on the total number of outstanding messages, effectively contribute to reduce the input rate of new packets into the network.

Several varieties of ETE flow control schemes have been proposed and implemented. We first describe four representative examples, and then briefly review some analytical and simulation models for the performance evaluation and comparison of such schemes.

A. ARPAnet RFNM and Reassembly Scheme

ETE flow control in ARPAnet is exercised on a host-pair basis [30], [23]. Specifically, all messages traveling from the same source host to the same destination host are carried on the same logical "pipe." Each pipe is individually flow controlled by a window mechanism. An independent message number sequence is maintained for each pipe. Numbers are sequentially assigned to messages flowing on the pipe, and are checked at the destination for sequencing and duplicate detection purposes. Both the source and the destination keep a small window w (presently, $w = 8$) of currently valid message numbers. Messages arriving at the destination with out-of-range numbers are discarded. Messages arriving out of order are discarded since storing them (while waiting for the missing message) may lead to potential resequence deadlocks. Correctly received messages are acknowledged with short ETE control messages called RFNMs (ready for next message). Upon receipt of an RFNM, the sending end of the pipe advances its transmission window, accordingly.

RFNMs are also used for error control. If an RFNM is not received after a specified time out (presently about 30 s), the source IMP sends a control message to the destination inquiring about the possibility of an incomplete transmission. This technique is necessary to keep source and destination message numbers synchronized and also to request a retransmission from the host in the case of message loss.

The window and message numbering mechanisms described so far support ETE flow control, sequencing, and error control functions in the ARPAnet. A separate mechanism, known as reassembly buffer allocation [30], is used to prevent reassembly deadlocks. Each multipacket message must secure a reassembly buffer allocation at the destination node before transmission. This is accomplished by sending a reservation message called a REQALL (request for allocation) to the destination and waiting for an ALL (allocation) message from the destination before attempting transmission. To reduce delay (and, therefore, increase throughput) of steady multipacket message flow between the same source–destination pair, ALL messages are automatically piggybacked on RFNMs, thus eliminating the reservation delay for all messages after the first one. If a pending allocation at the source node is not claimed within a given time out (250 ms), it is returned to the destination with a "giveback" message. Single-packet messages are transmitted to their destinations without buffer reservation. However, if upon arrival at the destination, all the reassembly buffers are full, the single-packet message is discarded and a copy is retransmitted from the source IMP after an explicit buffer reservation has been obtained. Some pitfalls inherent in such schemes are described in [23].

B. SNA Virtual Route Pacing Scheme

The IBM systems network architecture (SNA) is an architecture aimed at providing distributed communications and distributed processing capabilities between IBM systems [15], [16]. SNA was first announced in 1974. Since then, the original set of functions which supported single rooted networks (i.e., single host) have been enhanced to support multiple-domain (i.e., multiple host) networking. In this paper, we refer to SNA release 4.2 [16].

SNA devices can be subdivided into four main categories: host computers (e.g., system/370), communications controllers (e.g., 3704 and 3705), terminal cluster controllers, and terminal devices (e.g., TTYs, CRTs, readers, and printers). Distributed communications with full routing, flow control, and global addressing capabilities are provided only on store-and-forward networks interconnecting host computers and communication controllers. These nodes are called *subarea* nodes in SNA. Terminals and terminal cluster controllers are considered *peripheral* nodes and are connected into the high level net at subarea nodes, which provide the necessary boundary functions (e.g., global/local address conversion, etc.). Thus, for purposes of this section, SNA can be viewed as the usual two-level network architecture, with terminals and terminal cluster controllers at the lower level, and hosts and communications controllers at the higher level.

SNA is essentially a virtual circuit network, in the sense that each user session is associated with a physical route at session setup time. The routing policy is a static, multipath policy which maintains up to eight distinct routes between each source–destination pair in the high-level network (i.e., between subarea nodes). These routes are called ERs (explicit routes), to distinguish them from VRs (virtual routes) defined below. ERs are defined as an ordered sequence of network trunks, and are uniquely identified by ER numbers. When a failure is detected on an ER currently being used, the next ER on the list is "switched in." One difficulty here is that the list of ERs must be updated by the network designer each time the network topology is changed.

Next, virtual routes (VRs) are defined between each source–destination node pair of the high-level network. A VR is essentially a virtual pipe which is constructed on top of an ER and is subject to flow control. Three sets of VRs, each with a different level of priority are maintained between each subarea node pair. Each set may consist of up to eight VRs, thus allowing for up to 24 VRs between each high-level network node pair. Active VRs are identified by VR numbers and are stored in lists at each node.

At session setup time, the entry node scans the VR list and assigns the user session to the first available virtual route of desired priority. Several user sessions may be multiplexed on the same VR. In turn, several VRs may be multiplexed on the same ER. Finally, several ERs can be multiplexed on the same trunk.

The rationale for the distinction between virtual routes and explicit routes (a unique SNA feature among all VC networks, which typically associate a virtual route with a fixed path) is to " ...insulate the virtual route layer from the physical configuration" [16]. As a consequence, user packets are driven through the network using the ER ID number, while the VR ID number needs to be checked only at the end points of the path. This feature considerably reduces storage and processing overhead with respect to conventional VC schemes, which typically require large maps at each intermediate node to store the information relative to all virtual circuits traversing that node.

In the high-level network, flow control is applied independently to each VR from entry to exit node. This scheme, known as *VR pacing* is actually a combination of ETE and hop level flow control. It is based on a window mechanism, in which the entry node must request (and obtain) permission from the exit node before sending a new group of k packets, where k is the window size. The destination may grant (or delay) such permission depending on local buffer availability. The window size k varies from h to $3h$, where h is the path hop length. The value of k is dynamically adjusted not only by the exit node, but also by any intermediate node along the path on the basis of its buffer availability [1]. The fact that both the end node and the intermediate nodes can "modulate" the window size k makes VR pacing a hybrid ETE and hop flow control scheme. Details are given in Section XII of Chapter 11.

In addition to VR-pacing control, which operates between subarea nodes, the SNA architecture provides also for *session level pacing* which, for terminals and clusters, extends beyond subarea nodes and indivudally flow controls each user session between terminal and host computer. Session pacing is discussed in Section VI.

C. GMD Individual Flow Control

In GMDNET, entry-to-exit flow control is exercised individually on each virtual circuit, hence the name of individual flow control assigned to the scheme [37]. We recall that GMDNET is a VC network in which a fixed route is assigned to each user session at session setup time.

The main purpose of entry-to-exit flow control in GMDNET is to protect the exit node from overflow caused by low sink rates. When the source host rate exceeds the sink host rate, the flow control mechanism intervenes to slow down inputs from the source host into the entry node. This is achieved by maintaining a window of outstanding packets between entry and exit node for each virtual circuit. The window must be large enough to permit each virtual circuit to efficiently utilize the bandwidth available on the path. GMD simulation experiments have shown that $w = h + 1$ (where h is the hop length of the path) is a satisfactory choice under nominal load conditions. Window size can be reduced if the sink is slow in accepting packets. More precisely, when for a given VC the queue waiting to be transferred from exit node to sink reaches the value w, further arrivals to the exit node within that VC are discarded and a negative ACK is returned to the source node. Each negative ACK causes a window size reduction of 1 at the source node, until the minimum window size $w = 1$ is reached. Each positive ACK, on the other hand, increases window size by 1, until the maximum window size $w = h + 1$ is reached. In this way, window size is dynamically controlled in the range 1 to $h + 1$ by positive and negative acknowledgments [37].

In addition to the entry-to-exit flow control, each hop of the virtual circuit is also independently flow controlled (see Section III). The two layers of flow control, entry-to-exit and hop, are logically separated one from the other, in that the ETE window is controlled by exit buffer occupancy, while hop window is controlled by intermediate node congestion.

Packets within the same virtual circuit must be delivered to the host in sequence, and in case of multipacket messages, must be reassembled before delivery to the host. Fixed path routing and link level sequencing imply that packets arrive at their destination in sequence. This sequencing property, and the fact that a number of buffers sufficient to reassemble the largest size packet is permanently dedicated to traffic leaving the network, preclude the possibility of reassembly deadlocks and eliminate the need for reassembly buffer allocation schemes of the type implemented in ARPAnet.

D. DATAPAC Virtual Circuit Flow Control

The Canadian public data network, DATAPAC, implemented with the Northern Telecom SL-10 Packet Switching System provides virtual circuit services using an internal transport protocol built on top of a datagram subnetwork [28]. Flow control is exercised from entry to exit node on a virtual circuit basis, although no physical path is actually assigned to each virtual circuit, as was the case with SNA and GMDNET. The absence of a fixed path leads to some complications in the resequencing and loss recovery procedures, which will soon be discussed.

In DATAPAC, a virtual circuit is provided between the two end points of each user session. The virtual circuit is implemented at the concatenation of three protocol segments: a packet level X.25 protocol from the source device (i.e., data terminating equipment or DTE) to entry node (i.e., data communications equipment or DCE), an internal protocol from entry DCE to exit DCE, and a packet level X.25 protocol from exit node (DCE) to destination node (DTE). Each one of these protocol segments is flow controlled by a window mechanism. Of particular interest to us is the fact that window controls on these three segments are synchronized so as to provide a means of matching source DTE transmission rate with destination DTE acceptance rate. Window control synchronization is achieved by withholding the return of ACKs on a window if the downstream window is full.

As an example, let us assume that all windows are of size $w = 3$, and that the window between entry and exit DCE is full (i.e., there are three outstanding packets). The next packet arriving from the source DTE to the entry DCE will be accepted (assuming buffer space is available), but will not be immediately acknowledged; rather, the ACK will be withheld until an ACK from the exit DCE is received, thus opening up the downstream window [28].

Within the concatenated window mechanism the entry-to-exit flow control serves the function of promptly reflecting back to the source an exit segment congestion situation by withholding ACKs. Recall that in GMDNET the entry-to-exit flow control provided a similar service by dynamically adjusting the window with positive or negative ACKs. In DATAPAC, things are complicated, however, by the fact that the window mechanism is used not only for flow control, but also for sequencing, packet loss recovery, and duplicate detection. These latter functions are not required in the GMDNET, since sequencing is enforced there by the fixed path routing policy, and packet loss could occur only if a node along the path failed, in which case the virtual circuit would be automatically reinitialized.

The use of window ACKs for loss recovery in DATAPAC leads to the following problem. If the exit DCE does not return to the entry DCE an ACK for a correctly received packet (because the exit segment is congested), the entry DCE will retransmit the packet after a time out, under the assumption that the packet was lost (or was dropped by the exit DCE for lack of resequence space). If no ACK is received after a specified number of retransmissions, the entry DCE will clear the virtual circuit. In order to minimize the generation of duplicate packet, and avoid the unnecessary interruption of user sessions, the value of time out must be carefully adjusted as a function of window size and other network parameters.

E. Performance Models

The great majority of entry-to-exit flow control mechanisms are based on the window scheme. Critical parameters in the window implementation are the size of the window, and if error and loss recovery are to be provided, the retransmission time-out interval. Several analytic and simulation models have been developed recently to investigate the impact of these parameters on throughput and delay performance. This section briefly surveys some of the most significant contributions in this area.

We start with the Kleinrock and Kermani model of a single source-to-destination stream flow controlled by a window mechanism [26]. The network entry-to-exit delay is simplified as an $M/M/1$ queue delay, and the round trip delay therefore follows an Erlang-2 distribution. (This approximation is supported by simulation experiments showing that more accurate delay assumptions do not significantly change the nature of the results.) The exit node has finite storage and delivers packets to the destination host on a finite capacity channel. Consequently, the exit node may occasionally overflow and drop packets. To provide for transmission integrity, the entry node will retransmit an unacknowledged packet after a time-out interval. This simplified window model is solved analytically, yielding the optimal (i.e., minimum delay) window size and time-out interval for a given throughput requirement and destination buffer storage size.

In a subsequent paper [22], the same authors propose an adaptive policy (the "look-ahead" policy) for the dynamic adjustment of window size to time-varying traffic rate. In the proposed policy, the window size is dynamically controlled by the queue size at the exit node. Numerical results show that the delay versus throughput performance of the adaptively controlled scheme is somewhat superior to the performance of a scheme operated under static control, in which the window is adjusted in accordance with the traffic volume. These results are very encouraging, and are consistent with simulation experiments on dynamic window control carried out in multinode networks [1], [13].

The models in [26], [22] approximate the network as a single queue and therefore do not offer insight into the dependence of window size w on the window of intermediate hops. This issue is addressed by a simple multihop model developed by Kleinrock in [24]. In this model a packet stream from a single destination is transmitted across the network on a k-hop network path. Infinite buffer storage and negligible error rates are assumed on each hop. The stream is flow controlled by a window mechanism. In this model, as the window size w increases, the end-to-end delay grows without limit while the throughput asymptotically reaches the path capacity. In order to find a meaningful criterion for the optimization of w, the concept of "power" as defined in Section II F is used. We find that power is optimized by $w = k$. This implies that, at optimum, there should be on the average one packet in each intermediate queue. This result agrees with our intuition that the "entry-to-exit pipe should be kept full (in fact, *just* full)" for satisfactory performance. The general validity of this result is confirmed by actual window implementations. In fact, the SNA pacing scheme allows the window to dynamically vary from h to $3h$, where h is the number of intermediate hops. Similarly, the GMD individual flow control scheme uses a maximum window of $h + 1$.

The main limitation of the two previous models is the single-source, single-destination traffic assumption which excludes interference at a given node by other traffic traversing it. The model by Pennotti and Schwartz [32] includes the effect of interference in an approximate fashion in that it represents a virtual link situation in which end-to-end link traffic flowing on a multihop path must compete at each hop with external traffic. This is essentially a "one-hop" interference model in which some external traffic λ is injected into one node along the path and is transmitted to the next node on the path, where it then is removed from the network. The purpose of this study is to evaluate the possible path congestion caused by an increase in the virtual link rate λ_0, both with and without flow control. Congestion is defined as the relative average increase in time delay experienced by external users due to an increase in λ_0, taking $\lambda_0 = 0$ as a reference. Without flow control, congestion rapidly grows to infinity even for moderate values of λ_0. By introducing end-to-end window control which limits to w the number of packets outstanding on the virtual link at any one time, congestion can be bounded for any value of λ_0. The value of the upper bound varies with w, and decreases for decreasing w, as expected.

As an alternative to window flow control, hop flow control was also implemented in the Pennotti and Schwartz model by setting a limit on the number of link packets that would be stored at each intermediate node [32]. This scheme exhibited essentially the same performance as the window scheme. The above experiments show that flow control (either window or hop) can be used effectively to maintain fairness in a multiuser environment with conflicting requirements; that is, by adjusting the window parameter w, one can balance the relative user throughputs as desired.

The previously mentioned model offers some insight into multiuser flow control, but suffers from the limitation that only one virtual circuit can be flow controlled at a time, the remaining traffic components being kept constant. To remove this limitation, a number of multiple source, multiple destination models with selectively controlled user pairs have been developed. These models combine ETE flow control with network access flow control, and therefore may be regarded as hybrid models. Wong and Unsoy analyze a simple 5-node network to which individual entry-to-exit window control as well as isarithmic control are applied [41]. The isarithmic scheme is a network access flow control scheme which controls the total number of packets allowed in the entire network (see Section V for additional details). The major finding of this study is the fact that isarithmic control alone is not enough to guarantee efficient network operation. In fact, under some unfavorable traffic situations, one node pair may capture most of the permits, starving other pairs and leading to unfairness and to overall performance degradation. Similar results were found by Price in a series of simulation experiments [36]. The problem is corrected by introducing individual entry-to-exit flow controls in addition to isarithmic control.

The exact analysis of multinode networks with individually controlled node pairs becomes impractical for topologies with more than five to six nodes because of the rapidly increasing computational complexity of exact solution techniques [41]. To circumvent this problem, Reiser recently proposed an approximate solution technique based on a mean value analysis which is computationally affordable even for large networks, and which reaches a typical accuracy of 5 percent in throughput and 10 percent in delay [38]. With this technique it is now possible to analyze the interaction of various flow control schemes in a much more realistic environment (i.e., large networks; varied traffic patterns) than was possible with previous methods. Important design problems such as the optimization of window parameters for all source–destination pairs in order to maximize network throughput (within given fairness constraints), now become approachable. In particular, mean value analysis was used to study the interplay between routing and window flow control in [12b].

In spite of the previously mentioned advances in computational solution techniques, some window flow control issues are still too complex to be attacked analytically. For example, the dynamic control of window size in a multinode network is not amenable to a network-of-queues model even with the approximate solution methods. In these cases, simulation is still the leading performance evaluation tool [13], [1], [36].

V. Network Access Flow Control

A. Objective

The objective of network access (NA) flow controls is to throttle external inputs based on measurements of internal network congestion. Congestion measures may be local (e.g., buffer occupancy in the entry node), global (e.g., total number of buffers available in the entire network), or selective [e.g., congestion of the path(s) leading to a given destination]. The congestion condition is determined at (or is reported to) the network access points and is used to regulate the access of external traffic into the network.

NA flow control differs from HL and ETE flow control in that it throttles external traffic to prevent *overall internal buffer congestion*, while HL flow control limits access to a specific store-and-forward node to prevent *local congestion and store-and-forward deadlocks*, and ETE flow control limits the flow between a specific source–destination pair to prevent *congestion and reassembly buffer deadlocks at the destination.* The distinction, however, is not quite so clearcut, since as we mentioned earlier, both HL and ETE schemes indirectly provide some form of NA flow control by reporting an internal network congestion condition back to the access point either via backpressure (HL scheme), or via credit slowdown (ETE scheme).

Three NA flow control implementations will be discussed: the isarithmic scheme, a global congestion prevention scheme based on the circulation of a fixed number of permits [8]; the input buffer limit scheme, a local congestion scheme which sets a limit on the number of input packets stored at each node [27], [13]; and the choke packet scheme, a selective congestion scheme based on the delivery of special control packets of that name from the congested node back to the traffic sources [29].

B. The Isarithmic Scheme

Since the primary cause of network congestion is the excessive number of packets stored in the network, an intuitively sound congestion prevention principle consists of setting a limit on the total number of packets that can circulate in the network at any one time. An implementation of this principle is offered by the Isarithmic scheme proposed for the National Physical Laboratories network [8], [35].

The isarithmic scheme is based on the concept of a "permit," i.e., a ticket that permits a packet to travel from the entry point to the desired destination. Under this concept, the network is initially provided with a number of permits, several held in store at each node. As traffic is offered by a host to the network, each packet must secure a permit before admission to the high-level node is allowed. Each accepted packet causes a reduction of one in the store of permits available at the accepting node. The accepted data packet is able to traverse the network, under the control of node and link protocols, until its destination node is reached. When the packet is handed over to the destination subscriber, the permit which has accompanied it during its journey becomes free and an attempt is made to add it to the permit pool of the node in which it now finds itself.

In order to achieve a viable system in which permits do not accumulate in certain parts of the network at the expense of the other parts, it is necessary to place a limit on the number of permits that can be held in store by each node. If then, because of this limit, a newly freed permit cannot be accomodated at a node (overflow permit), it must be sent elsewhere. The normal method of carrying the permit in these circumstances is to "piggy-back" it on other traffic, be this data or control. Only in the absence of other traffic need a special permit-carrying packet be generated.

A simulation program was developed by NPL to evaluate the performance of the isarithmic scheme in various network configurations and in the presence of different network protocols [35]. The main conclusion of these simulation studies was that the isarithmic scheme is a simple congestion prevention mechanism which performs well in uniform traffic pattern situations, but may lead to unnecessary throughput restrictions, and therefore, to poor performance in the case of nonuniform, time-varying traffic patterns. In particular, in the presence of high bandwidth data transfers, there is the possibility that permits are not returned to the traffic sources rapidly enough to fully utilize network capacity (the "permit starvation" problem). This would be the case when the destination node redistributes the overflow permits randomly in the network. If, on the other hand, the destination systematically returns all the permits to the source, the source–destination pair may end up capturing most of the network permits, thus causing unfairness. Tradeoffs between different permit distribution schemes are investigated with an analytical model in [41]. Finally, a delicate problem in isarithmic control is the bookkeeping of permits, to avoid unauthorized generation or disappearance of permits.

In spite of the above limitations, the isarithmic scheme proved to be very effective in *weakly controlled* networks (namely, networks without hop level flow control), eliminating congestion and deadlocks that had occurred without flow control. Some simulation experiments were also carried out on networks with hop level control (specifically CQL), and with a simple form of local access control (one buffer on each output queue was reserved for store-and-forward traffic). For this class of networks (called *strongly controlled* networks), it was found that the network performance did not show congestion tendencies even without isarithmic control in the case of a fixed routing discipline. When the fixed discipline was replaced with an adaptive routing discipline, it was found that the network would become easily congested since the simple form of network access control implemented would not prevent external traffic from flooding all the queues in the entry node. Again, the introduction of the isarithmic scheme was successful in eliminating the congestion problem for the adaptive routing case [36].

Critical parameters in the isarithmic scheme design are the total number of permits P in the network and the maximum number of permits L that can be accumulated at each node (permit queue). Experimental results show that optimal performance is achieved for $P = 3N$, where N is the total number of nodes, and $L = 3$. An excessive number of permits in the network would lead to congestion. An excessive value of L would lead to unfairness, accumulation of permits at a few nodes, and throughput starvation at the others.

C. Input Buffer Limit Scheme

The input buffer limit (IBL) scheme differentiates between input traffic (i.e., traffic from external sources) and transit traffic, and throttles the input traffic based on buffer occupancy at the entry node. IBL is a *local* network access method since it monitors local congestion at the entry node, rather than global congestion as the isarithmic scheme does. Entry node congestion, on the other hand, is often a good indicator of global congestion because of the well-known backpressure effect which propagates internal congestion conditions back to the traffic sources.

The function of IBL controls is to block input traffic when certain buffer utilization thresholds are reached in the entry node. This flow control approach clearly favors transit traffic over input traffic. Intuitively, this is a desirable property since a number of network resources have already been invested in transit traffic. This intuitive argument is supported by a number of analytical and simulation experiments proving the effectiveness of the IBL scheme.

Many versions of IBL control can be proposed. Here, we describe and compare four different implementations that have been experimentally evaluated.

The term input buffer limit scheme refers to a scheme restricting the number of buffers made available to input traffic and was first introduced by the GMD research group [37], [13]. The scheme proposed for GMDNET is a by-product of the nested buffer class structure used to allocate buffers to different classes of traffic. We recall from Section III D that the ith traffic class consists of all the packets that have already covered i hops. Input traffic is assigned to class zero (zero hops covered). Traffic class zero is entitled to use buffer class zero, which is a subset of the nodal buffer pool (in general, class i is entitled to use all buffer classes $\leq i$). Thus, input packets are discarded when class zero buffers are full. The size of buffer class zero (referred to as input buffer limit) was found to have a significant impact on throughput performance under heavy loads. Simulation experiments indicate that for a given topology and traffic pattern there is an optimal input buffer limit which maximizes throughput for heavy offered load. The use of lower or higher limits leads to a substantial drop in throughput [13].

A version of IBL control that is simpler than the GMD version was proposed by Lam [27] and analytically evaluated in an elegant model. Only two classes of traffic—input and transit—are considered in this proposal. Letting N_T be the total number of buffers in the node and N_I the input buffer limit (where $N_I \leq N_T$), the following constraints are imposed at each node:

1. number of input packets $\leq N_I$, and
2. number of transit packets $\leq N_T$.

The analytical results confirm simulation results independently obtained by the GMD group. There is an optimal ratio N_I/N_T, which maximizes throughput for heavy offered load, as shown in Fig. 19. A good heuristic choice for N_I/N_T is the ratio between input message throughput and total message throughput at a node. As shown in the figure, throughput

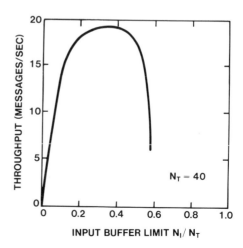

Figure 19. Input buffer limit scheme: throughput versus buffer limitation for heavy offered load.

performance does not change significantly even for relatively large variations of the ratio N_I/N_T around the optimal value, thus implying that the
IBL scheme is robust to external perturbations such as traffic fluctuations
and topology changes. One shortcoming of this model is that all nodes in
the net are assumed to have the same blocking probability, a somewhat
unrealistic assumption.

A scheme similar to Lam's IBL scheme has been earlier proposed by
Price [35]. In order to prevent input traffic from monopolizing the entire
buffer pool, one buffer in each output queue was reserved for transit traffic.
This is essentially equivalent to setting an input buffer limit $N_I = N_T - C$,
where C is the number of output channels. Simulation studies showed that
this simple network access control based on source buffer utilization was
quite successful in single level networks.

Kamoun [21] proposes yet another version of IBL control, in which an
input packet is discarded if the *total* number of packets in the entry node
exceeds a given threshold (whereas in Lam's scheme an input packet is
discarded when the number of *input* packets exceeds a given threshold).
Transit packets, instead, can freely claim all the buffers. The scheme is
called drop-and-throttle flow control (DTFC) policy since a transit packet
arriving at a full node is dropped and lost (loss model); while all previous
schemes assumed link level retransmission of overflow packets (retransmit
model). The DTFC scheme was analyzed using a network of queues model
[21]. The results, shown in Fig. 20, clearly indicate that there is an optimal
threshold value L which maximizes throughput for each value of offered
load. Below the threshold, the network is "starved"; above the threshold, the

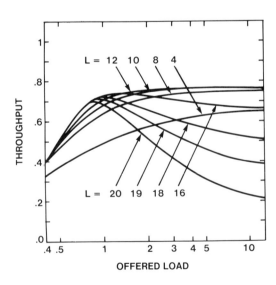

Figure 20. Throughput versus
load for a 121-node network for
drop-and-throttle flow control.

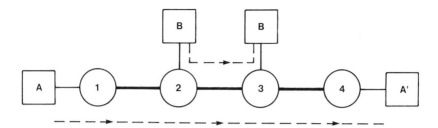

Fig. 21. Unfairness condition produced by input buffer limit and drop-and-throttle flow control schemes.

network is congested. A similar scheme, referred to as the *free flow* scheme, is described and analyzed by Schwartz and Saad in [41]. Preliminary results indicate that, while free flow and IBL throughput performances are compatible, the free flow scheme offers substantial delay improvements.

We have pointed out that IBL control prevents congestion by favoring transit traffic over input traffic. In most cases (indeed, in all cases analyzed in the previously referenced studies), this favoritism leads to throughput improvements. In some cases, however, *unfairness* may result. Consider, for example, the 4-node network shown in Fig. 21. In this network, two file transfers, A to A' and B to B', respectively, are simultaneously competing for trunk $(2, 3)$. Node 2 sees traffic A as transit traffic, so it gives it preferential treatment over traffic from B. Consequently, the A–A' packet stream can acquire more buffers in node 2, and thus achieve better throughput performance than the B–B' stream. The unfairness is particularly dramatic when DTFC is used. With the DTFC policy, if the A-packet queue in node 2 exceeds the buffer threshold (this could easily occur if $C_{23} < C_{12}$), B packets cannot be accepted by node 2. Consequently B traffic is completely shut off until the A–A' file transfer is completed.

D. Choke Packet Scheme

The choke packet (CP) scheme, proposed for the Cyclades network [29], is based on the notion of trunk and path congestion. A trunk (link) is defined to be congested if its utilization (measured over an appropriate history window with exponential averaging) exceeds a given threshold (e.g., 80 percent). A path is congested if any of its trunks are congested. Path congestion information is propagated in the network together with routing information, and thus each node knows hop distance and congestion status of the shortest path to each destination.

When a node receives a packet directed to a destination whose path is congested it takes the following actions:

(1) If the packet is an *input* packet (i.e., it comes directly from a host), then the packet is dropped.

(2) If the packet is a *transit* packet, it is forwarded on the path; but a "choke" packet (namely, a small control packet) is sent back to the source node informing it that the path to that destination is congested and instructing it to block any subsequent input packets to this destination. The path to the destination is gradually unblocked if no choke packets are received during a specified time interval.

This is a greatly simplified description of the CP scheme. Several other features (which are essential to make the scheme workable) are discussed in [29].

It is clear that the CP scheme attempts to favor transit traffic over input traffic, much in the same way as the IBL scheme did. The basic difference between the two schemes is the fact that IBL uses a local congestion measure, namely, the entry node buffer occupancy, to indiscriminately control all input traffic; whereas, CP uses a path congestion

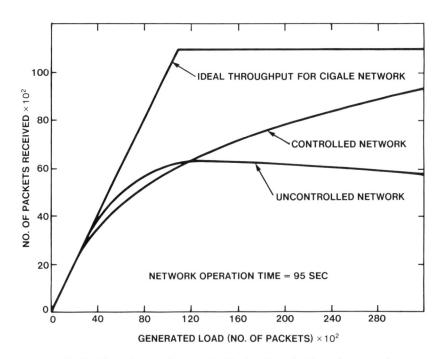

Fig. 22. Throughput performance in Cigale with and without flow control.

measure to exercise *selective* flow control on input traffic directed to different destinations.

Simulation experiments based on the Cigale network topology are given in Fig. 22 and show that the CP scheme can introduce substantial throughput improvements (with respect to the uncontrolled case) in sustained load conditions, asymptotically achieving the ideal performance for infinite load [29].

VI. Session Level Flow Control

A. Objectives

A transport protocol is a set of rules that govern the transfer of control and data between user processes across the network. The main functions of this protocol are the efficient and reliable transmission of messages within each user session (including packetization, reassembly, resequencing, recovery from loss, elimination of duplicates) and the efficient sharing of common network resources by several user sessions (obtained by multiplexing many user connections on the same physical path and by maintaining priorities between different sessions to reflect the relative urgency).

For efficient and reliable reassembly of messages at the destination host (or more generally, the DTE), the transport protocol must ensure that messages arriving at the destination DTE are provided adequate buffering. The transport protocol function which prevents destination buffer congestion and overflow is known as *session level flow control*. Generally, this level of flow control is based on a "credit" (or window) mechanism as discussed earlier. Specifically, the receiver grants transmission credits to the sender as soon as reassembly buffers become free. Upon receiving a credit, the sender is authorized to transmit a message of an agreed-upon length. When reassembly buffers become full, no credits are returned to the sender, thus temporarily stopping message transmissions [5].

The credit scheme described above is somewhat vulnerable to losses, since a lost credit may hang up a connection. In fact, a sender may wait indefinitely for a lost credit, while the receiver is waiting for a message. A more robust flow control scheme is obtained by numbering credits relative to the messages flowing in the opposite direction. In this case, each credit carries a message sequence number, say N, and a "window size" w. Upon receiving this credit, the sender is authorized to send all backlogged messages up to the $(N + w)$th message. With the numbered credit scheme, if a credit is lost then the subsequent credit will restore proper information to the sender [45].

Besides preventing destination buffer congestion, the credit scheme also indirectly provides global network congestion protection. In fact, store-and-forward buffer congestion at the intermediate nodes along the path may cause a large end-to-end credit delay, thus slowing down the return of credits to the sender, and consequently, reducing the rate of fresh message input into the network.

B. Implementations

Several versions of the transport protocol are in existence, each incorporating its own form of transport level flow control. Here, we briefly describe four representative implementations.

The earliest example of transport protocol implementation is the original version of the ARPAnet network control program (NCP) [4]. NCP flow control is provided by unnumbered credits called "allocate" control messages (see Section IV D). Only one allocate could be outstanding at a time (i.e., window size $W = 1$).

The French research network Cyclades provided the environment for the development of the transport station (TS) protocol [50]. In the TS protocol, the flow control mechanism is based on numbered credits, each credit authorizing the transmission of a variable size message called a letter. Flow control is actually combined with error control in that credits are carried by acknowledgment messages.

The transmission control program (TCP) was a second generation transport protocol developed by the ARPAnet research community in order to overcome the deficiencies of the original NCP protocol [5]. As in the TS protocol, flow and error control are combined in TCP. As a difference, however, error and flow control are on a byte (rather than letter) basis. This allows a more efficient utilization of reassembly buffers at the destination.

In SNA, the transport level flow control is provided by session pacing. The purpose of session-level pacing is to prevent one session end from sending data more quickly than the receiving session end can process the data [16]. As in TCP and TS, session-level pacing is based on a window concept, in which the receiving end grants "credits" to the sending end based on its buffer availability and processing capability. As a difference, however, subarea nodes in SNA can control the inbound flow from a cluster controller into the network by intercepting and withholding the credits (called pacing responses in SNA) for a given session, if the subarea node buffers are congested or if the virtual route (VR) transmission queue for that session is congested. Specifically, session-level pacing responses are intercepted at the entry node to exercise *network access* flow control from the terminal into the high-level network [16]. Thus, session pacing may be viewed as a hybrid form of transport level flow control, which is obtained by concatenating a network access level segment (from the terminal to the high-level network node) and an entry-to-exit level segment (controlled by virtual route pacing).

VII. Conclusions and Directions for Further Research

In this chapter we have proposed a taxonomy of flow control mechanisms based on a multilevel structure. We have defined *four levels of flow control* and have shown how these levels are actually embedded into corresponding levels of protocols. To the extent that these levels can be independently defined, the analysis, design evaluation, and comparison of flow control schemes is greatly simplified, since any complex control structure can be decomposed into smaller modules, and each module individually analyzed. The overall performance is then obtained by studying the interaction of the various modules.

Recent advances in queueing theory have led to reasonable success in the *modeling and analysis of individual levels* of flow control. We have reported on several performance results, and have used such results to compare different schemes.

In real life, however, some control structures defy the simple, hierarchical representation here proposed, and seem to combine two or more levels into *hybrid flow control solutions* (see Fig. 10). This is particularly common in homogeneous networks (e.g., SNA) in which a single manufacturer is responsible for the implementation of both DCE and DTE equipment and, therefore, has more freedom in the design of the various flow control levels.

The existence of multiple levels of flow control and the possible integration of some of these into hybrid arrangements immediately brings up a very critical issue in flow control which requires further study, namely, the *interaction between levels*. Given that we understand the throughput and delay implications of each specific level of flow control, we still have to study the combined effect when these levels are operating simultaneously in the network. For instance, network experience seems to indicate that a network equipped with a very conservative hop level flow control, such as the SBP scheme in GMDNET or the VC-HL scheme in TYMNET, does not require strong network access or ETE flow control schemes since network congestion situations are immediately reported back to the entry node by back pressure through the hop level [36]. This type of issue can be fully investigated only by developing models which include multiple levels of flow control. An interesting example in this direction was the combined isarithmic and entry to exit flow control model presented in [47]. More research is required in this area.

Hybrid packet and circuit networks are now emerging as a solution to multimode (voice and data; batch and interactive) user requirements [11]. These networks must be equipped with novel flow control mechanisms. In fact, if the network were to apply conventional flow control schemes to the packet-switched (P/S) component only, leaving the circuit-switched (C/S) component uncontrolled, then the C/S component would very likely capture the entire network bandwidth during peak hours. If this does not cause congestion, since the C/S protocol is not as congestion prone as the P/S protocol, it certainly creates unfairness. Some form of flow control on C/S traffic which is sensitive to the relative P/S load is therefore required.

The *integration of voice and data* requirements in packet-switched networks has been vigorously advocated in recent years on grounds of improved efficiency and reduced cost [14]. Unfortunately, little attention has been given to the fact that integrated networks require a complete redesign of the conventional flow control schemes since voice traffic cannot be buffered and delayed in case of congestion. Priorities are of help only if the voice traffic is a small fraction of the total traffic. For the general case, new flow control techniques must be developed for voice. These techniques should be *preventive* in nature, i.e., they should block calls before congestion occurs, rather than *detecting* congestion and then attempting to *recover* from it, as is the case for most of the conventional flow control schemes for data [10], [31].

Routing and flow control procedures have traditionally been developed independently in packet networks, under the assumption that flow control must keep excess traffic out of the network, and routing must struggle to efficiently transport to destination whatever traffic was permitted into the network by the flow control scheme. It seems, however, that routing and flow control can be brought together into useful cooperation in virtual circuit networks, where a path must be selected before data transfer on a user connection begins [12], [12c]. In this case, the routing algorithm can be invoked first to determine whether a path of sufficient residual bandwidth is available. If no path is available, the virtual circuit connection is blocked immediately at the entry node by the network access flow control level, thus *preventing* congestion rather than allowing it to occur and then attempting to *recover* from it. A combined routing and flow control strategy is implemented in TYMNET [39], and is described in more detail in Section IV of Chapter 12.

Challenging flow control problems exist in *multiaccess broadcast networks*. In single hop multiaccess systems, congestion prevention and stability mechanisms are well understood, and are usually directly embedded in the channel access protocol [46]. In distributed multihop multiaccess systems (e.g., multihop ground radio networks), congestion prevention becomes a very hard problem because of the interaction between buffer and channel congestion. Conventional flow control schemes used in hardwired nets cannot be directly applied. In particular, the hop level flow control should be revised to combine the buffer allocation strategy with the retransmission control strategy. Some pioneering work in this direction is reported in [2], [48], [43].

Finally, growing user demands require the *interconnection* of networks which may implement different flow control policies and which may even be built on different media (e.g., satellite, radio, cable, or optical fiber). These networks are interconnected by gateways which provide for internet routing and flow control, as well as for protocol conversion between two adjacent networks [44], [6]. It appears that a new level of flow control must therefore be defined in our hierarchy, namely, the gateway-to-gateway level. This level should be designed to prevent the congestion of gateways along the path, and should be supported by explicit gateway-to-gateway protocols for the exchange of status information. The status information should include buffer occupancy at the gateway, and load conditions in the adjacent networks, and could probably be exploited also for gateway routing. Functionally, the gateway-to-gateway protocol is positioned between the entry-to-exit protocol and the session protocol hierarchy in Fig. 2. All the other levels remain unchanged. The actual implementation of the gateway-to-gateway flow control will be dependent on the internet protocol used. If the CCITT X.75 Recommendation, which is an extension of the X.25 virtual circuit concept to internet connections [45], is adopted, the gateway-to-gateway flow control will be virtual-circuit oriented, and will be exercised on a connection-by-connection basis. Alternatively, datagram-oriented gateway level flow control schemes can also be implemented.

The design of efficient gateway flow control schemes is very challenging. It requires *vertical* consistency between the gateway level and all the other levels implemented in each individual network as well as *horizontal* consistency across the various networks on the internet path. Specifically, the gateway level flow control must be able to balance loads between extremely diverse network environments such as point-to-point, satellite, cable, and ground radio. These design requirements further emphasize the need for continuing research in *multilevel* flow control models in order to understand the vertical interactions between the various levels in the hierarchy, as well as the horizontal interactions between the various segments of a flow control chain along an internet path.

In summary, we have presented a framework for the study of flow control, showing that flow control mechanisms have advanced somewhat beyond simply being "a bag of tricks" [34], and indeed can be conceptually organized into a useful and well-structured system of controls. This structure is extremely helpful in the survey and comparison of existing flow control implementations, as well as in the development of flow control models. In particular, complex control systems can be (and should be) decomposed into smaller modules, thus simplifying the analysis of each module as well as the analysis of interactions between different modules. Furthermore, the proposed flow control structure is sufficiently flexible to permit extensions in response to new networking technologies and applications.

Although our focus has been on flow control models and performance criteria, we expect that the proposed structure will prove to be useful also for the actual implementation of flow control techniques. One must be aware, of course, of the fact that in actual networks, it is not always possible to develop and update flow controls in a well structured fashion. The designer, in fact, is usually confronted with a number of constraints imposed by the preexisting protocol structure (in which flow control mechanisms must be embedded) and by limited storage and processing resources. The designer must therefore avoid overburdening the switch with overly sophisticated flow control mechanisms, and creating inconsistencies and possibly deadlocks. These constraints, together with the fact that flow control is a distributed multilevel control function that cannot be confined to a well-defined modular "black box," make flow control design a very hard task. It is our strong opinion, however, that the only way to prevent flow control implementations from degrading to the state of an uncontrollable "bag of tricks" is to identify an underlying structure in the early stage of flow control design, and to continuously verify this structure during the various updates of protocols and flow control procedures.

Indeed, it is important that one be able to subject a proposed flow control algorithm to various tests of correctness, consistency, and proper termination [33], [49]. This is, in general, a very difficult task whose solution requires advances in the frontier of computer science. Unfortunately, since it is relatively difficult to create efficient, deadlock-free, flow control algorithms, we cannot totally ignore this need for verification. Moreover, many difficulties with flow control procedures often arise due to errors in the detailed implementation of otherwise correct algorithms. Consequently, it is important that a modular approach to flow control design be taken, that the code itself be confined to isolated portions of the network operating system (rather than sprinkled through thousands of lines of code), and that the mechanisms be simple enough to be understood and tested via simple procedures.

References

[1] V. Ahuja, "Routing and flow control in systems network architecture," *IBM Syst. J.*, vol. 18, no. 2, pp. 298–314, 1979.
[2] G. Akavia and L. Kleinrock, "Performance tradeoffs in distributed packet-switching communication networks," Dep. Comput. Sci., School of Eng. Appl. Sci., Univ. of California, Los Angeles, Tech. Rep. UCLA-ENG-7942, Sept. 1979.

[3]   P. Brinch-Hansen, *Operating System Principles.* Englewood Cliffs, New Jersey, Prentice-Hall, 1973.

[4]   S. Carr *et al.*, "Host/host protocol in the ARPA network," in *Proc. Spring Joint Comput. Conf.*, 1970, pp. 589–597.

[5]   V. G. Cerf and R. Kahn, "A protocol for packet network intercommunication," *IEEE Trans. Commun.*, vol. COM-22, May 1974.

[6]   V. G. Cerf, "DARPA activities in packet network interconnection," in *Interlinking of Computer Networks* (NATO Advanced Study Inst. Series). Reidel.

[7]   A. Danet *et al.*, "The French public packet switching service: The Transpac network," in *Proc. Int. Conf. Comput. Commun.*, Toronto, Ont., Canada, Aug. 1976.

[8]   D. W. Davies, "The control of congestion in packet-switching networks," *IEEE Trans. Commun.*, vol. COM-20, June 1972.

[9]   H. C. Folts, "International standards in computer communications," in *Proc. Nat. Telecommun. Conf.*, Nov. 1979, pp. 59.5.1–59.5.5.

[10] J. Forgie and A. Nemeth, "An efficient packetized voice/data network using statistical flow control," in *Proc. Int. Conf. Commun.* Chicago, IL, June 1977.

[11] M. Gerla and D. DeStasio, "Integration of packet and circuit transport protocols in the TRAN data network," in *Proc. Comput. Network Symp.*, Liege, Belgium, Feb. 1978.

[12] M. Gerla, "Routing and flow control in virtual circuit computer networks," in *Proc. INFO II Int. Conf.*, July 1979.

[12b] M. Gerla and P. O. Nielson, "Routing and flow control interplay in computer networks," *ICCC Proc.*, Atlanta, November, 1980.

[12c] M. Gerla, "Bandwidth control in X.25 networks, *PTC Proc.*, Hawaii, January 1981.

[13] A. Giessler *et al.*, "Free buffer allocation—An investigation by simulation," *Comput. Networks,* vol. 2, pp. 191–208, 1978.

[14] I. Gitman and H. Frank, "Economic analysis of integrated voice and data networks," *Proc. IEEE*, pp. 1549–1570, Nov. 1978.

[15] J. P. Gray, "Network services in systems network architecture," *IEEE Trans. Commun.*, vol. COM-25, pp. 104–116, Jan. 1977.

[16] J. P. Gray and T. B. McNeill, "SNA multiple-system networking," *IBM Syst. J.*, vol. 18, no. 2, 1979.

[17] P. E. Green, "The structure of computer networks," this book, Chap. 1; also in *IBM Syst. J.* no. 2, 1979.

[18] M. Irland, "Buffer management in a packet switch," *IEEE Trans. Commun.*, vol. COM-26, pp. 328–337, Mar. 1978.

[19] R. E. Kahn and W. R. Crowther, "A study of the ARPA computer network design and performance," Bolt Beranek and Newman, Inc., Tech. Rep. 2161, Aug. 1971.

[20] F. Kamoun, "Design considerations for large computer communications networks," Ph.D. dissertation, Univ. of California, Los Angeles, Eng. Rep. 7642, Apr. 1976.

[21] F. Kamoun, "A drop and throttle flow control (DTFC) policy for computer networks," Proceedings of the 9th Int. Teletraffic Congr., Spain, Oct. 1979.

[22] P. Kermani and L. Kleinrock, "Dynamic flow control in store and forward computer networks," *IEEE Trans. Commun.*, vol. COM-27, Feb. 1979.

[23] L. Kleinrock, *Queueing Systems: Volume II. Computer Applications.* New York: Wiley-Interscience, 1976.

[24] L. Kleinrock, "On flow control in computer networks," in *Proc. Int. Conf. Commun.*, June 1978.

[25] L. Kleinrock, "Power and deterministic rules of thumb for probabilistic problems in computer communications," in *Proc. Int. Conf. Commun.*, June 1979.

[26] L. Kleinrock and P. Kermani, "Static flow control in store and forward computer networks," *IEEE Trans. Commun.*, vol. COM-27, Feb. 1979.

[27] S. Lam and M. Reiser, "Congestion control of store and forward networks by buffer input limits," in *Proc. Nat. Telecommun. Conf.*, Los Angeles, CA, Dec. 1977.

[28] R. Magoon and D. Twyver, "Flow and congestion control in SL-10 networks," in *Proc. Int. Symp. Flow Control Comput. Networks*. Versailles, France, Feb. 1979.

[29] J. C. Majithia *et al.*, "Experiments in congestion control techniques," in *Proc. Int. Symp. Flow Control Comput. Networks*, Versailles, France, Feb. 1979.

[30] J. M. McQuillan *et al.*, "Improvements in the design and performance of the ARPA network," in *Proc. Fall Joint Comput. Conf.*, 1972.

[31] W. E. Naylor, "Stream traffic communication in packet-switched networks," Ph.D. dissertation, Dep. Comput. Sci., School Eng. Appl. Sci., Univ. of California, Los Angeles, Sept. 1977.

[32] M. Pennotti and M. Schwartz, "Congestion control in store and forward tandem links," *IEEE Trans. Commun.*, Dec. 1975.

[33] J. Postel, "A graph model analysis of computer communications protocols," Ph.D. disseration, Univ. of California, Los Angeles, Jan. 1974.

[34] L. Pouzin, "Flow control in data networks—Methods and tools," in *Proc. Int. Conf. Comput. Commun.*, Toronto, Ont. Canada, Aug. 1976.

[35] W. L. Price, "Data network simulation experiments at the National Physical Laboratory," *Comput. Networks*, vol. I, 1977.

[36] W. L. Price, "A review of the flow control aspects of the network simulation studies at the National Physical Laboratory," in *Proc. Int. Symp. Flow Control in Comput. Networks*, Versailles, France, Feb. 1979.

[37] E. Raubold and J. Haenle, "A method of deadlock-free resource allocation and flow control in packet networks," in *Proc. Int. Conf. Comput. Commun.*, Toronto Ont., Canada, Aug. 1976.

[38] M. Reiser, "A queueing network analysis of computer communication networks with window flow control," *IEEE Trans. Commun.*, pp. 1199–1209, Aug. 1979.

[39] J. Rinde, "Routing and control in a centrally directed network," in *Proc. Nat. Comput. Conf.*, Dallas, TX, June 1977.

[40] J. Rinde and A. Caisse, "Passive flow control techniques for distributed networks," in *Proc. Int. Symp. Comput. Networks*, Versailles, France, Feb. 1979.

[41] M. Schwartz, and S. Saad, "Analysis of congestion control techniques in computer communication networks," in *Proc. Int. Symp. Comput. Networks*. Versailles, France, Feb. 1979.

[42] J. M. Simon and A. Danet, "Controle des ressources et principes de routage dans le reseau TRANSPAC," in *Proc. Int. Symp. Comput. Networks*. Versailles, France, Feb. 1979.

[43] J. Silvester "On spatial capacity of packet radio networks," Ph.D. dissertation, Dep. Comput. Sci., School Eng. Appl. Sci., Univ. of California, Los Angeles, Mar. 1980.

[44] A. C. Sunshine, "Interconnection of computer networks," *Comput. Networks*, vol. 1, 1977.

[45] A. C. Sunshine, "Transport protocols for computer networks," in *Protocols and Techniques for Data Communications Networks*, F. Kuo, Ed. Englewood Cliffs, NJ: Prentice-Hall, 1980.

[46] F. Tobagi, "Multiaccess link control," this book, Chap. 6.

[47] J. W. Wong and M. S. Unsoy, "Analysis of flow control in switched data networks," in *Proc. Int. Fed. Inf. Processing Soc. Conf.*, Aug. 1977.

[48] Y. Yemini and L. Kleinrock, "On a general rule for access control or, silence is golden...," in *Proc. Int. Symp. Flow Control Comput. Networks*, Versailles, France, Feb. 1979.

[49] P. Zafiropulo, "A new approach to protocol validation," in *Proc. Int. Conf. Commun.* June, 1977.

[50] H. Zimmermann, "The Cyclades end-to-end protocol," in *Proc. 4th Data Commun. Symp.*, Quebec, P. Q., Canada, Oct. 1975, pp. 7:21–26.

[51] Schwartz and Stern, "Routing protocols," this book, Chap. 12.

PART V

Higher-Layer Protocols

The protocol layers discussed so far serve the purpose of providing a connectivity path between the two end users that hides those peculiarities of the network involved in sending messages back and forth between them. These include the fact that the message may have to be steered across a succession of intervening nodes and lines, that errors in transmission may have to be recovered from, that congestion of *network* resources (lines, buffers) may have to be prevented, that alternate paths may sometimes have to be substituted, and so forth. We now turn to the remaining functions needed to allow the end users to communicate. Those functions that we now discuss reflect the needs of the end users themselves, not those of the network. They are essentially those functions that would remain to be done even if the end users could be plugged together with a hypothetical ideal communication channel having no errors, adequate bandwidth, and a guaranteed sequential message delivery, albeit with a statistically varying time of propagation.

One of the functions we must consider is the need of the end users not to send messages to each other when they are not supposed to. This involves not only such actions (partially covered already in Chapter 13) as controlling flow *rates* (for example, to make sure that a high execution rate CPU does not overdrive a low acceptance rate line printer) but other user limitations on message exchange. For example, it is usually considered part of the function of the communication software to respect the end users' idiosyncrasies on exchange of requests and responses. A terminal may expect to receive a related chain of messages each representing a line of text, with the terminal not being expected to request another chain until the first one is completed. If a recovery operation is required during this process, the unit of information to be recovered is the entire chain. Such protocols are embodied in Layer 5, the Session layer of the OSI model presented earlier in Chapter 2, and have been most extensively developed in SNA, where they are called "data flow control" as will be described in Chapter 16. (We have already met a simpler form of this in the message-versus-packet option of the NSP layer of DNA, Chapter 10).

The other function of the higher-level protocols has to do with *presentation*, the form in which the messages generated by one end user are to be presented to the other. This is handled in the highest protocol layer (Layer 6 of the OSI model or Presentation Services of SNA). The simplest example of this question is that of code conversion; an application program may generate alphanumeric characters from one alphabet whereas a terminal may be expecting to receive another. But in practice the problems solved by the presentation layer are more extensive than this. As a more complex example, it should be possible ideally for an application program to have a two-dimensional view of a screen full of characters in some standard format, while the other end user (the terminal) has a serial-by-character view of the same screen; it is up to the two presentation layer protocol partners to make the transformation—perhaps all at one end, all at the other, or partially by each end. An example of the last of these three options is the *virtual terminal* convention in which each end makes a conversion to and from the code and format convention of a hypothetical but physically nonexistent standard terminal type. In this way, if there are M application presentation conventions to be accommodated and N terminal conventions, only $M + N$ pieces of software have to be developed rather than $M \times N$ of them.

In the first chapter of this part, Chapter 14, Nippon Telegraph and Telephone's DCNA architecture is described, with emphasis on the higher layers. Then in Chapter 15, an extensive discussion is given of the presentation issues for terminal support, both the virtual terminal approach and an alternative strategy. Chapter 16, after a brief treatment of SNA data flow control, gives an extensive discussion of presentation layer issues, including the subject of Logical Unit Types, which are roughly analogous to Virtual Terminal conventions. An interesting point made at the end of this chapter is that as cheap microcomputers become more prevalent, a certain simplification becomes possible: one needs only those presentation conventions having to do with program–program communication (avoiding the present variety of terminal–terminal or program–terminal conventions) since each terminal can be regarded from the other end as consisting of a program in execution.

To conclude this part, Chapter 17 discusses the Videotex class of protocols, now being widely exploited by telephone administrations and cable TV companies to bring flexible alphanumeric and graphics displays inexpensively to home and business users.

14

DCNA Higher-Layer Protocols

Iwao Toda

I. Introduction

The problem of designing protocols for heterogeneous computer networks may be considered as one consisting of two subproblems.

The first subproblem is how to design *lower-level communication protocols* for transferring data between computers and other equipment of different types which participate in the computer network. The solution to this problem has been considerably simplified by the CCITT Recommendation X.25 for interfacing with public data networks. It has been shown elsewhere [1] that somewhat expanded versions of X.25 can be defined as lower-level protocols to be applied to the network using leased lines as well.

The second subproblem is how to design *higher-level communication protocols* concerned with the mechanism for using and managing *network resources*, i.e., processing power, files, data bases, and I/O devices existing in the computer network. The characteristics of these resources and the interfaces between the resources and local users vary greatly among different computer types within a heterogeneous computer network.

Therefore, a network model should be built that is abstract enough to relieve the protocol designers of concerns about the heterogeneity of various resources.

In order to decide upon an abstract model of network resources, the following problems should be resolved:

1. What network resources should be defined as common to all computer types?
2. How should the network resources be managed for efficient joint usage among different computer types?

3. How should the network resources be seen and used by the networkwide users?

A similar approach has been taken in the design of SNA [2], DNA [3], DCA [4], and other computer network architectures. However, another level of abstraction will be required for wider applicability to more heterogeneous environments, such as open systems interconnection [5].

This chapter discusses a viewpoint about all protocol levels, but focuses particular attention on the design of higher-level communication protocols adopted in *Data Communication Network Architecture* (DCNA). DCNA is an architecture for heterogeneous computer networks which has been developed jointly by Nippon Telegraph and Telephone Public Corporation (NTT) and four Japanese computer/communications manufacturers (Nippon Electric, Hitachi, Fujitsu, and Oki Electric Industry).

II. The DCNA Model

The DCNA model for defining higher-level communication protocols has been designed based on the following premises:

(1) The network consists of different types of computers, communication control processors, terminals, communication circuits, etc.

(2) The method of communication involves various telecommunication means, e.g., public packet-switched networks, leased lines, telephone networks, circuit-switched networks, and host I/O channels.

(3) The *lower-level communication functions*, i.e., data transfer functions between equipment, are realized by means of the lower-level protocols. These consist of the X.25 protocols and their expanded versions [1], including routing, flow control, acknowledgment, and other functions.

(4) To realize the *higher-level communication functions*, i.e., functions for sharing network resources by computers, standard higher-level protocols should be defined among different computer types taking into account performance, ease of extension, and ease of implementation.

The DCNA model consists of three submodels [6]. The first submodel is the *basic model*, which describes the network resources and associated mechanisms. The second submodel is the *logical network model*, which describes the mechanisms for managing network resources. The third submodel is the *virtual network model*, which describes the mechanisms for using network resources.

III. The Basic Model

The basic model clarifies the network resources which are used in common by different computer types, as well as the mechanisms for

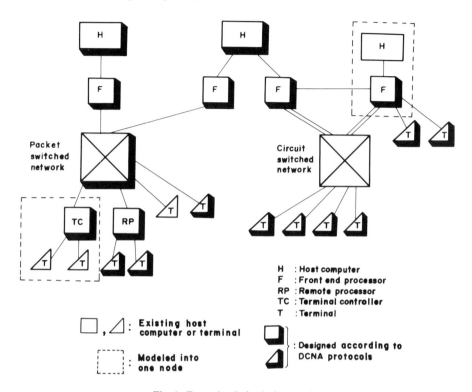

Fig. 1. Example of physical network.

accessing such resources [7], [8]. It represents a logical view of the physical computer network by mapping various physical components into the logical elements defined in the following.

A. Constituent Elements

The constituent logical elements of the basic model are *nodes* and *links*. A node is a type of logical equipment which models a physical network component, e.g., a host computer, a terminal, a public packet-switched network, or certain other equipment.

An example of a physical network and a basic model associated with it are shown in Fig. 1 and Fig. 2.

A node comprises a set of (logical) network resources and a set of (logical) mechanisms for accessing them. Each node is given a unique network address. Five types of nodes (N_5–N_1) are defined; they model such physical network components as host computers (N_5), front end processors (N_4), public packet-switched networks (N_3), and terminals (N_2 or N_1).

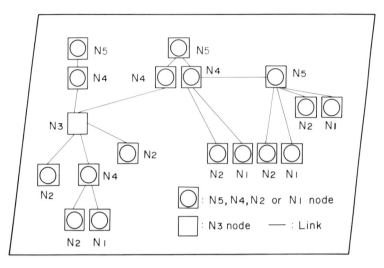

Fig. 2. Example of basic model.

Network resources of a node are defined as processing power, files, data bases, and I/O devices. These particular resources were chosen as the network resources associated with a node because (1) these resources are basic in computer usage, and (2) they are generally used in conventional on-line systems.

A link models a physical medium, e.g., a leased line, a telephone circuit, a circuit-switched network connection, or a host I/O channel, which exists between the physical components modeled into nodes. A link is defined as a logical medium for transferring information between adjacent nodes.

B. Layered Structure of Node Mechanisms

A node of the basic model comprises a set of resources and associated mechanisms. These mechanisms are, in general, partitioned into two subsets: the C-machine, which executes lower-level and higher-level communication protocols, and the P-machine, which consists of sources or sinks of information transferred by use of such protocols.

As a degenerate case, certain nodes, e.g., a public packet-switched network or relay computer, consist solely of C-machines.

One requirement of each P-machine is the initial establishment of the node and the links which are incident to the node.

A C-machine performs communication functions in cooperation with one or more other C-machines. The protocols are the rules defined between several C-machines in order to perform the communication functions.

To make it easier to modify and extend the protocols, the C-machine is divided into an ordered set of four *levels*. Each of these is defined as a collection of communication mechanisms which are more or less dependent upon each other. These levels are, from the bottom, the *physical level*, the *data link level*, the *transport level*, and the *function control level*.

The transparent, i.e., unchanging format, data transfer functions between two arbitrary nodes are performed by the mechanisms of the physical, data link, and transport levels. They are called lower-level communication functions. The other communication functions, such as network management (for overall management of resources and their uses), message transfer (for the use of processing power), virtual terminal access (for the use of processing power and I/O devices), or virtual file system access (for the use of processing power and files), are performed by the mechanisms of the function control level. They are called higher-level communication functions.

To simplify interfaces between adjacent levels and to make the levels more independent of one another, the data transfer functions (which each level, except the physical level which provides a link to the data link level, provides to the next higher level) are expressed by logical paths, i.e., *D-link*, *T-path*, and *F-path*, as shown in Fig. 3. For information passed between adjacent levels, three types of data transfer units, i.e., *data link unit*, *transport unit*, and *data unit*, corresponding to the logical paths are defined, as well as the *information unit*, which is exchanged between a P-machine and its associated C-machine. The transport level and the function control level are capable of multiplexed use of the D-links and T-paths, respectively, provided by the levels below them.

The transport level and the function control level are each further divided into *sublevels*.

In principle, there is the following difference between levels and sublevels:

(1) The set of functions of each level is self-contained; the control informations for a level are meaningful only within that level and transferred along a logical path independently of those for other levels. Thus, control information is not shared across the boundary between adjacent levels.

(2) The set of functions of each sublevel is not completely self-contained; the control informations for the sublevels of a level may be handled collectively in order to reduce the frequency of control information transfers. Thus, control information is shared across the boundary between adjacent sublevels within a level.

The concept of sublevels is introduced to avoid the overhead associated with creating more levels. (To make it easier to modify or extend protocols, it would be desirable to distinguish between as many levels as possible.

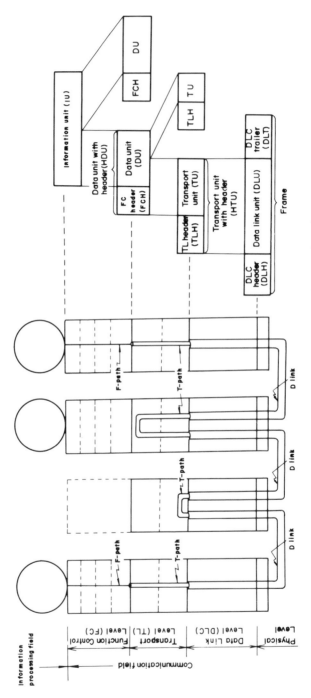

Fig. 3. Protocol levels, logical paths, and data transfer units.

Table I. Summary of Protocols at Each Level

Level	Sublevel	Typical Protocols					
		Message Transfer	Virtual Terminal	Virtual File System	Job Transfer	Data Base	(other)
Function Control Level (FC)	Application Function Sublevel	--					
	System Function Sublevel	--					
	Fundamental Attribute Processing Sublevel	--					
	Data Unit Control Sublevel	--					
Transport Level (TL)	Transport Unit Control Sublevel	Setting up and clearing T-path. Segmenting a data unit into transport units (TUs) and assembling TUs to form a data unit. TU sequence control, flow control to prevent congestion, transfer acknowledgment to prevent loss, and error recovery (based upon CCITT X.25 Packet Level protocol and its extension).					
	Routing Control Sublevel	Addressing and routing. Blocking TUs to form a data link unit and deblocking data link units into TUs.					
Data Link Level (DLC)		Transparent transfer control between adjacent nodes. (High-Level Data Link Control Procedures)					
Physical Level (PL)		Electrical and physical control of communication media.					

However, creating additional levels would increase the overhead due to such factors as the need for independence in the manipulation of control information at each level.)

An outline of the protocols for each level and sublevel of a C-machine is given in Table I.

C. Function Control Level

Various mechanisms are defined at the function control level for accessing the network resources of other nodes by using transparent data transfer functions provided by the transport level and other lower levels [9]–[13].

These mechanisms of the function control level are divided into four sublevels.

(1) *The data unit control* (DUC) sublevel consists of mechanisms for setting up and clearing of F-paths between P-machines and for data transfer over the F-paths. These mechanisms are provided in common with various kinds of higher level communication functions, such as network management, message transfer, virtual terminal access, and virtual file system access.

(2) *The fundamental attribute processing* (FAP) sublevel consists of mechanisms for code conversion, etc. These mechanisms are provided in common with various kinds of higher-level communication functions similar to those at the DUC sublevel.

(3) *The system function* (SYF) sublevels consists of basic mechanisms which are specific to each kind of higher-level communication function, but not specific to each application.

(4) *The application function* (APF) sublevel consists of additional mechanisms specific to each kind of higher-level communication function and also specific to each application.

A summary of the protocols of the various sublevels of the function control level is given in Table II. An example of the construction of a function control level header is shown in Fig. 4.

Table II. Summary of Protocols at Each Sublevel of the Function Control Level

Sublevel	Typical protocols
Application Function (APF) Sublevel	System function extension and other application-specific protocols.
System Function (SYF) Sublevel	Basic protocols for message transfer, Virtual Terminals, Virtual File System, and network management.
Fundamental Attribute Processing (FAP) Sublevel	Code conversion. Data compression and restoration. Data encryption and decryption.
Data Unit Control (DUC) Sublevel	Setting up and clearing F-paths (Activation of SCPs and UCPs). T-path multiplexing control. Superposition of Function Control Level positive response on a Transport Level acknowledgment. Priority control. Sequencing control for data units. Data unit chain control and response control. Transmission control. Bracket control.

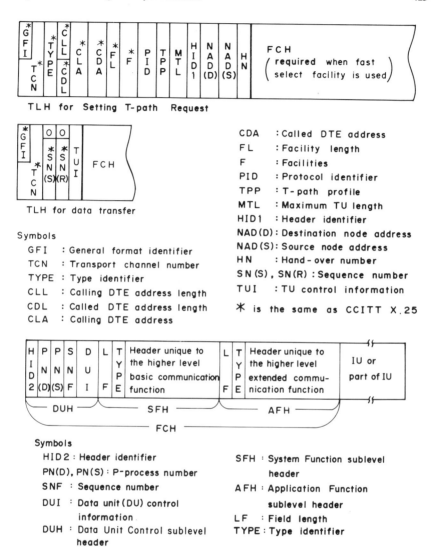

Fig. 4. Example of function control level header configuration. (a) Relation between TLH and FCH. (b) Contents of function control level header.

IV. Logical Network and its Protocols

The logical network (LN) model is a model clarifying the mechanisms for managing network resources; it models the logical relationships of management programs and/or system operators in charge of the management of the computer network equipment.

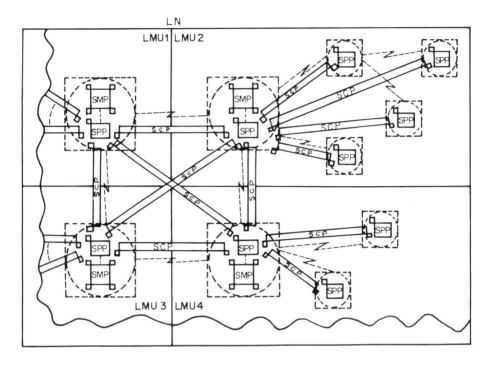

LN : Logical Network   LMU : LN Management Unit
SMP : System Management Process   SPP : System Processing Process
SCP : System Communicating Process   ___ : Node or link

Fig. 5. Example of logical network management structure.

The logical network is defined as a combination of one or more *logical network management units* (LMU). Each LMU consists of one or more *system processing processes* (SPPs), *a system management process* (SMP), and *system communicating processes* (SCPs). (See Fig. 5.)

An SPP models the management program and/or system operator of a host computer, a terminal, etc. An SMP models the network management program and/or network management operator residing on a host computer or communication control processor. An SCP models the execution of communication functions between two management programs, etc. In other words, an SCP offers higher-level communication functions between SPPs on the basis of data transfer functions realized by an F-path.

A. SPP Characterization

SPPs are characterized by the following statements:

(1) One SPP is defined on the P-machine of each basic model node.

(2) Each SPP has a unique process address which is the concatenation of a node address and a process number.

(3) An SPP uses the mechanisms of the P-machine and manages the network resources of its own node as well as the links incident to it.

(4) Through communication functions offered by the SCP, the SPP can communicate in order to exchange management information with another SPP.

B. SMP Characterization

SMPs are characterized by the following statements:

(1) One SMP is defined in each LMU on the P-machine of one node of type N_5 or N_4 in the LMU.

(2) An SMP has no process address, i.e., there is only one SMP in an LMU.

(3) An SMP uses the mechanisms of the P-machine and manages SPPs and SCPs of an LMU and coordinates with other LMUs.

(4) An SMP cannot directly use a communication function offered by an SCP, i.e., communication is done for the SMP through the SPP on the same node. This is a restriction to simplify SMP characteristics.

C. SCP Characterization

SCPs are characterized by the following statements:

(1) One SCP is defined between the SPP of each node in the LMU and the SPP of the node which has the SMP of the LMU.

(2) An SCP is identified by a pair of SPP addresses.

(3) An SCP uses the mechanisms and protocols of the function control level of the C-machine and offers higher-level communication functions, including the establishment and maintenance of F-paths between SPPs.

D. LN Management Protocols

An outline of the protocols for the management of the logical network is shown in Table III.

Table III. Summary of Protocols for Management of the Logical Network.

Function Category	Physical Level Management	Connection Management for Circuit Switched Link	Information Management for Data Link Control	Activation/deactivation Management for Data Link	Failure Management	Maintenance/operation Management
Function	DTE-DCE interface control. e.g., control of ON/OFF condition for circuits in X.21	Connection control for circuit switched network	Management control information such as DLC system constants, routing tables, etc.	Activation/deactivation control for data link	Failure/recovery notification	Activation/deactivation control for maintenance/operation function
Associated Commands	Activate Link, Deactivate Link, etc.	Activate Connect In, Connect Out, etc.	Set Control Vector, etc.	Contact, Contacted, etc.	Inoperative, Recovered, etc.	Execute Test, Start Dump, etc.

V. The Virtual Network and its Protocols

The virtual network (VN) model is a model for clarifying the mechanisms of network resource usage. As several sets of interrelated applications, e.g., time-sharing applications and information retrieval applications, may be run in a single computer network sharing the common network resources, the virtual network models a set of interrelated applications from the viewpoint of the network resource users. (See Fig. 6.)

A. Composition of the Virtual Network

The virtual network is defined as the combination of one or more virtual network management units (VMU). A VMU is conceptually defined as being independent of LMUs. For example, a VMU can be defined over two or more LMUs, while two or more VMUs can be defined within an LMU.

Each VMU consists of *user processing processes* (UPPs), a *user management process* (UMP), *user communicating processes* (UCPs), and *virtual network resources* managed by the UMP and the UPPs. (See Fig. 7.)

A UPP models the application programs and/or terminal operators, etc., of a host computer. A UMP models the application service management programs, etc., of the host computer. A UCP models the execution of the communication functions between two application programs, etc. In other words, a UCP offers higher-level communication functions between UPPs on the basis of data transfer functions realized by an F-path.

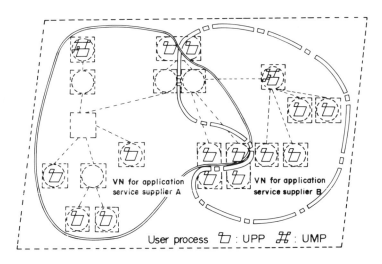

Fig. 6. Virtual networks and user processes.

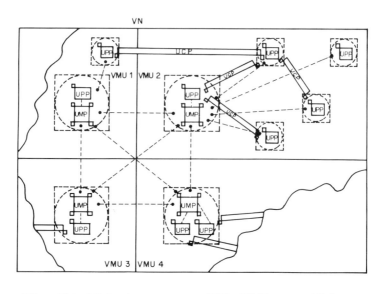

Fig. 7. Example of virtual network management structure.

A UPP can be assigned virtual network resources. The virtual network resources correspond to the network resources defined in the basic model, as modeled from the viewpoint of the virtual network.

The reasons for defining UPPs so as to have virtual network resources are (1) access rights to the use of network resources from a UPP of another node, passwords and other security checks, and the use status of resources can be defined for each virtual network; and (2) the form of communication for use of various network resources can be standardized as UPP–UPP communication.

B. UPP Characterization

UPPs are characterized by the following statements:

(1) For each P-machine of the basic model, an arbitrary number of UPPs can be defined.

(2) Each UPP has a process name as well as a unique process address which is the concatenation of a node address and a process number.

(3) A UPP can use the mechanisms of the P-machine and execute arbitrary information processing functions.

(4) A UPP can, by means of the communication functions offered by the UCP, use the virtual network resources of another UPP.

C. UMP Characterization

UMPs are characterized by the following statements:

(1) One UMP is defined for each VMU on the P-machine of one node of type N_5 or N_4 in the VMU. (A UMP and an SMP may or may not be defined on the same P-machine.)

(2) A UMP has no process address, i.e., there is only one UMP in the VMU.

(3) A UMP cannot directly use a communication function provided by an SCP, i.e., communication is done for the UMP through the SPP on the same node.

(4) A UMP uses the P-machine mechanisms and manages the UPPs and UCPs of a VMU and coordinates with other VMUs.

[*Note*: The following are defined as the VMU management functions of a UMP:

(1) Address conversion of the UPP name.

(2) Registration and look-up of the sets of C-machine option mechanisms.

(3) Checking of communication qualifications, registration, and checking of passwords, etc.

(4) Storage of other control information needed for UPPs to communicate.]

D. UCP Characterization

UCPs are characterized by the following statements:

(1) An arbitrary number of UCPs can be set up between UPPs which request to communicate.

(2) Permission by the UMP is needed for setting up a UCP.

(3) A UCP is identified by a pair of UPP addresses.

(4) A UCP uses the mechanisms and protocols of the function control level of a C-machine and offers higher-level communication functions, including the establishment and maintenance of F-paths between UPPs.

E. VN Management Protocols

An outline of the protocols for virtual network management is shown in Table IV.

Table IV. Summary of Protocols for Management of the Virtual Network

Function Category	UMP Management	VMU Management	UPP Management	UCP Management	Failure Management
Function	Activation/ deactivation control of UMP	Synchronize control of VMU	Activation/ deactivation control of UPP	Activation/ deactivation control of UCP	Failure/ recovery notification
Associated Commands	Activate UMP, Deactivate UMP, etc.	UMP Start, Terminate VMU, etc.	Activate UPP, Deactivate UPP, etc.	Initiate, Control Initiate, etc.	Request Partial VMU Initiation, etc.

VI. Message Transfer Protocols

The *message transfer protocols* are protocols to be obeyed by a UCP between UPPs in order to send and receive a message. For a UPP to communicate with another UPP, a UCP must be set up between both UPPs. Setting up a UCP is done with the permission of the UMP or UMPs which manage these UPPs of a virtual network.

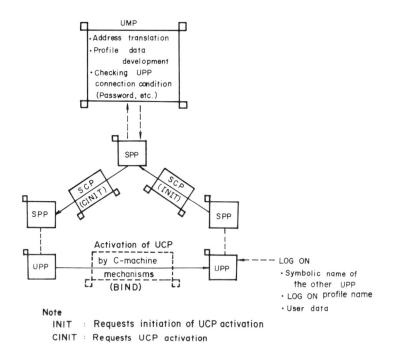

Fig. 8. User communicating process activation.

A UPP wishing to communicate must send to the UMP the name of the partner UPP and information for specifying the type of higher-level communication function desired, e.g., message transfer, virtual terminal access. This information is transferred by communication between SPPs within the logical network.

The UMP, after checking communication qualifications, etc., sends the information needed for activation of a UCP to the requested UPP or the requesting UPP. An example of the procedure protocol for activating a UCP is shown in Fig. 8.

VII. Virtual Terminal Protocols

As stated earlier, a terminal, like a computer or other equipment, may be modeled as a node consisting of a P-machine and a C-machine.

On the other hand, there exists another category of various terminals which has been in existence without conforming to architecture specifications. The concept of a *virtual terminal* (see the next chapter) is introduced in order to unify the handling of both terminal categories existing in the physical network.

A virtual terminal models terminal functions from the viewpoint of the application programs in a host computer. As shown in Fig. 9, a virtual

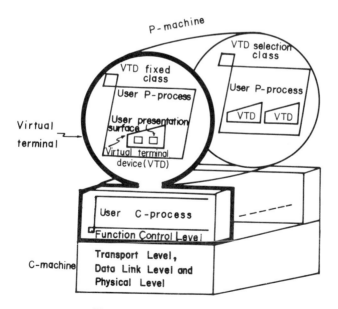

Fig. 9. Virtual terminal on a node.

terminal consists of a UPP with virtual terminal devices (VTD) and a UCP which executes the virtual terminal protocol.

The virtual terminal devices model terminal devices, as virtual network resources assigned by the SPP at the time of virtual network initiation to the UPPs which comprise the virtual terminal.

The UCP, in accordance with the virtual terminal protocol, outputs the message sent by the sending UPP to the virtual terminal device.

The reasons for modeling the terminal functions by a virtual terminal in this way are as follows:

(1) Application programs may treat various kinds of physical terminals uniformly.

(2) Several virtual terminals may be defined corresponding to a single physical terminal, making it easier for several applications to use the same terminal.

(3) An existing terminal may be converted to a virtual terminal UPP, i.e., the case in which one node is formed by combining a remote processor having mechanisms for executing virtual terminal protocols with an existing terminal.

There are two classes of virtual terminals: the *VTD-fixed class* and the *VTD-selection class*.

A virtual terminal of the VTD-fixed class has only one virtual terminal device, while a virtual terminal of the VTD-selection class may have several

Table V. Example of Virtual Terminal Device Control Functions

Class	Area definition	Formatting control	Editing control
Character Class	Enable Presentation Inhibit Presentation	Space Backspace Bell	
Line Class	Maximum Presentation Column Set Left Margin Set Right Margin Set Column Tab. Reset Column Tab.	Carriage Return Line Feed New Line Horizontal Tab.	Erase in Line Delete Character Insert Character Erase in Field
Page Class	Maximum Presentation Line Set Top Margin Set Bottom Margin Set Line Tab. Reset Line Tab. Field Definition	Form Feed Vertical Tab. Set Activate Position Select Vertical Channel	
Area Class	Area Definition		Delete Line Insert Line Erase Column Delete Column Insert Column

virtual terminal devices. With the VTD-fixed class, it is not necessary for a sending UPP to distinguish between different devices, and control is simple. With the VTD-selection class, control is needed for device selection and device contention.

In a single virtual terminal device, several *user presentation surfaces*, of which there are three types (character control, picture control, and binary control), may be defined, and each may be controlled independently.

Information for the selection of virtual terminal class, virtual terminal device activation/deactivation, and control of virtual terminal devices and of user presentation services is stipulated as the virtual terminal protocols.

As an example of virtual terminal protocols, formatting and editing control protocols are shown in Table V.

VIII. Virtual File System Protocols

A *virtual file system*, from the viewpoint of application programs on a computer, models the file system functions of other computers. This is done in the same way as with virtual terminals; a virtual file system consists of a UPP having *virtual files* (VF), and a UCP which executes virtual file system protocols.

A virtual file models the files of a file system.

The UCP complies with the virtual file system protocols in executing requests from a sending UPP for access to a virtual file, transfer of a virtual file, etc.

The reasons for modeling file systems as virtual file systems are the same as the reasons for modeling terminals as virtual terminals.

A virtual file consists of two or more units called blocks. The first block consists of such file attribute information as file name, file size, and block length; the second and remaining blocks are for data.

Four types of virtual files are defined as *nonorganized files*, *sequential files*, *indexed files*, and *direct files*.

In nonorganized files, only the file transfer functions are defined. Partial transfer is also possible by specifying the number of blocks.

In the other three types of files, or *organized files*, both file transfer functions and file access functions are defined. In these organized files, records are defined as data access units independently of blocks. There are both fixed-length and variable-length records.

In sequential files, the records can be retrieved in the order in which they were stored. In indexed files, several keys may be defined within records, and records can be retrieved either by specifying these keys or in the order of the keys. In direct files, a record can be accessed by specifying the position in which it is arranged.

Table VI. Virtual File System Protocols

Type of protocol	Command	Function
File Transfer Protocol	SFT	Requests initiation of transfer of virtual file
	R.SFT	Gives yes/no reply to SFT
	GO	Requests virtual file attribute information and initiation of data transfer
	EFT	Requests completion of transfer of virtual file
	R.EFT	Gives reply to EFT
File Access Protocol	OPEN	Requests initiation of access to virtual file
	R.OPEN	Gives yes/no reply to OPEN
	CLOSE	Requests conclusion of access to virtual file
	R. CLOSE	Gives reply to CLOSE
	READ	Requests input of one or more record from virtual file
	WRITE	Requests output of one or more record from virtual file
	REWRITE	Requests update of one record in virtual file
	START	Indicates initiation point for access in virtual file
	DELETE	Requests deletion of one record in virtual file
	DISAT	Requests retrieval of virtual file attribute information
	R. DISAT	Returns a yes/no and attribute information to DISAT
	UPDAT	Requests renewal of virtual file attribute information
	R. UPDAT	Gives yes/no reply to UPDAT

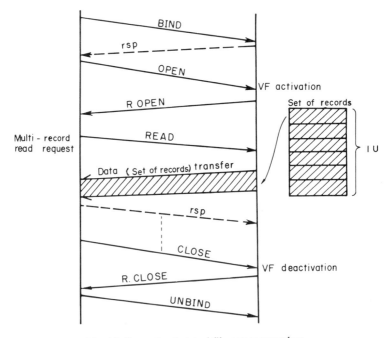

Fig. 10. Example of virtual file access procedure.

A summary of virtual file system protocols is given in Table VI. An example of a procedure for file access by means of these protocols is shown in Fig. 10.

IX. Conclusions

The DCNA is a network architecture for heterogeneous computer networks; it defines higher-level protocols to make possible the common use of various network resources among different computer types. These protocols involve functions which are thought to be basic to computer usage, such as network management, message transfer, virtual terminal access, and virtual file system access functions.

The DCNA higher-level protocols have the following characteristics.

(1) They are defined on two network models—a logical network model, with respect to the management of network resources, and a virtual network model, with respect to the usage of network resources. These models describe the various network resources uniformly and independently of their mode of use. The virtual network model is a basis for defining virtual terminals and virtual file systems and for facilitating the common use of terminals and files by several sets of application.

(2) After partitioning a C-machine into four basically independent levels, some levels are further decomposed into sublevels in order to allow for flexibility without deteriorating performance. Specifically, the protocol modifications and extensions are made easier by placing the basic parts of the higher-level communication functions in the system function sublevel and the extension parts into the application function sublevel.

The logical structure and higher level protocols of the DCNA have been discussed, as well as the philosophy for modeling the higher level communication functions. With the further development of heterogeneous computer networks expected in the future, it is anticipated that various higher level protocols, which take into account the subjects discussed in this paper more broadly, will be standardized.

References

[1] H. Ohba, S. Yoshitake, S. Mutoh, and T. Nishimura, "End-to-end protocol based on CCITT X.25 and its implementation," in *Proc. 4th ICCC*, Sept. 1978, pp. 281–287.

[2] IBM Corp., "Systems network architecture format and protocol reference manual: Architectural logic," IBM Form SC30-3112, Mar. 1976, June 1978.

[3] G. E. Conant and S. Wecker, "DNA: Architecture for heterogeneous computer networks," in *Proc. 3rd ICCC*, Aug. 1976, pp. 618–625.

[4] J. P. McGovern, "DCA—A distributed communications architecture," in *Proc. 4th ICC*, Sept. 1978, pp. 359–367.

[5] "Reference model of open systems interconnection," ISO/TC97/SC16 N227, July 1979.

[6] T. Kawaoka, T. Abe, and A. Shiraishi, "A logical structure for a heterogeneous computer communication network architecture," in *Proc. 4th ICCC*, Sept. 1978, pp. 510–524.

[7] I. Toda and H. Nakata, "Basic concepts of data communication network architecture," *Information Processing* (in Japanese), vol. 20, pp. 153–160, Feb. 1979.

[8] K. Naemura, T. Kawaoka, M. Miyazawa, and K. Morino, "Data communication network architecture—Objectives and fundamental concepts," *Rev. Elec. Commun. Lab.*, vol. 27, pp. 297–311, June 1979.

[9] K. Naemura and T. Abe, "Descriptions of data communication network architecture (1)," *Information Processing* (in Japanese), vol. 20, pp. 237–246, Mar. 1979.

[10] K. Naemura and M. Mashio, "Descriptions of data communication network architecture (2)," *Information Processing* (in Japanese), vol. 20. pp. 438–447, May 1979.

[11] T. Abe, M. Mashio, H. Nakata, and T. Tajima, "Protocol design for data communication network architecture," *Rev. Elec. Commun. Lab.*, vol. 27. pp. 312–337, June 1979.

[12] M. Sobami and T. Abe, "Data communication network architecture development," *Japan. Telecommun. Rev.*, vol. 20. pp. 308–312. Oct. 1978.

[13] *DCNA Protocol Manuals*. DCNA-P1010, P1020, P1030, P1040, P1050 (in Japanese), Nippon Telegraph and Telephone Eng. Bureau, Oct. 1978.

15

Terminal Support Protocols

John D. Day

I. Introduction

Terminal protocols provide basic services for the users of computer networks. Terminal protocols establish mechanisms that allow efficient and flexible terminal access to networks. Terminal protocols not only allow a user to access a timesharing service through the network, but can also be used as a character-oriented network interprocess communication facility. Many of the problems encountered in terminal protocols recur in more complex forms in the more sophisticated protocols (e.g., network mail protocols, distributed data base protocols).

In this chapter, we will be concerned primarily with protocols for heterogeneous networks. Protocols for homogeneous networks generally are a subset of the heterogeneous network protocols in terms of the scope and of the mechanisms they use. In order to expose the reader to as wide a variety of the problems found in these protocols as possible and to do it in a reasonable amount of space, we will restrict our discussion to heterogeneous network protocols.

A computer communications protocol is typically designed as one of several successive layers of protocols. Protocols are layered for many of the same reasons that large software systems are organized into layers. The layers provide a means to aggregate related functions. In addition, a protocol layer provides a transparent service for the next higher level, so that modifications to a lower level do not affect a higher level. In much of the protocol literature, the terms "lower level" and "higher level" are used to denote the absolute (rather than relative) position of the protocol. In this usage, the term "lower level" is applied to protocols concerned primarily with the reliable transfer of data across the network. The term "higher level" is applied to protocols concerned primarily with performing remote operations. More descriptive labels might be "communications protocols" (for lower-level protocols) and "resource sharing protocols" (for higher-level protocols).

II. Terminal Access to Networks

Probably the most common application of computer communications today is for terminal access. Terminal access is commonly provided by terminal-concentrator networks. These networks are organized into a star or a tree topology. Terminals and terminal concentrators are connected by point-to-point lines to the central data processing center. The point-to-point lines and in some cases the terminal concentrators of a terminal-concentrator network can be replaced with a packet switched network. Replacing a terminal-concentrator network by a packet-switched network can significantly reduce costs and also increase reliability.

Terminal access to a network may be provided in one of three basic ways: through a large computer, through a network access machine or "minihost," or through a direct interface.

When a large computer (or "host") is connected to a network, terminals attached to the large computer may access the network using special network access software in the host. The terminal user executes a program on the host that allows connections with other hosts to be opened and closed. Since the host can support complex software, this technique can provide a sophisticated network terminal user environment.

In the second approach, a minicomputer is dedicated to providing many of the network terminal user services available to the terminal user accessing a network through a large computer, but at considerably less cost. Several of these "minihost" systems [1, 2, 7, 10, 25, 27, 28] have been developed. Some are oriented to providing a convenient human interface [1, 2]. Some support specialized peripherals such as graphics displays or plotters [7] and digital voice equipment [28]. Others use artificial-intelligence-based systems to provide very sophisticated user facilities [2].

In a third approach, the network itself provides a facility through which terminals can be directly connected to the network via dialup or permanent connections. Once connected, the terminal user then issues commands to the network. The command language allows the user to open and close connections to host computers and to set certain terminal-specific parameters. In the ARPAnet, this facility was called the Terminal Interface Processor [25] or TIP. In the nomenclature of the CCITT it is called the Packet Assembler Dissembler [9] or PAD. The command languages provided by the TIP and the PAD are cryptic and primitive. The TIP and PAD are functionally

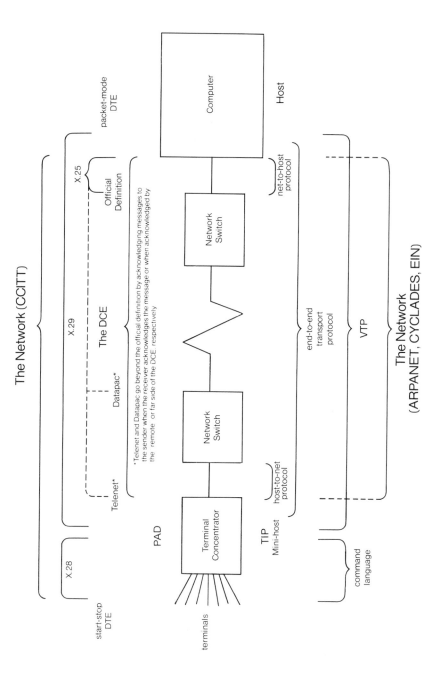

Fig. 1. Depending on your view of the network, a terminal concentrator may be a host or an interface.

almost identical, but are architecturally distinct. In the ARPAnet, the TIP is considered architectually to be a host (with very limited capabilities). Although the TIP software resides in the packet switch, it appears to all other hosts and to the switching software as a host connected to the network. The CCITT on the other hand considers the PAD to be part of the network, an interface between two kinds of Data Terminating Equipment (DTE): the Packet Mode DTE (or the computer) and the Start–Stop Mode DTE (or the terminal). There is considerable controversy surrounding these two viewpoints. (See Fig. 1.) Although the first appears to be conceptually clean and efficient, the second supposedly provides certain economic and growth advantages for some networks.

III. The Need for Terminal Protocols

Terminal handling has always been problematic, but with networks the problem is further complicated. If a network were no more than a different technology providing the equivalent of point-to-point lines, networking would not compound the terminal handling problem. Data generated by a terminal could simply be "packaged" and transferred over the network to the computer, and vice versa. However, one of the major advantages of networking is that a terminal user can potentially establish communication with any computer attached to the network. Conversely then, each computer on the network must be prepared to handle every kind of terminal that may access the network at large.

Although terminals exhibit broadly similar characteristics, they differ in very significant ways (e.g., line length, the meaning of attentions or "breaks," character sets, cursor addressing conventions, etc.). Most operating systems require a separate piece of software (i.e., a device driver) to handle each kind and make of terminal attached to it. Since most computer installations support only a few kinds of terminals, this variety does not represent an undue burden. However, if this approach were carried over to the network, each host would have to support all n kinds of terminals, supported by each of the m hosts on the network. Thus each host must potentially be able to support $m \times n$ terminals in order to allow any user to connect to it. Clearly, this is impractical.

Terminal-oriented protocols are designed to reduce this "$m \times n$" problem to a manageable size by establishing conventions for handling the terminals connected to the network.

Two basic approaches to terminal protocols have emerged. One approach [9] attempts to parametrize the differences between terminals. The protocol is used by the host to set the various terminal parameters to the requested values. The other approach [6, 12, 16, 24, 29, 31, 32, 33, 34] defines a network Virtual Terminal (VT). The terminal side of a connection maps the output of its terminal into the VT format for transmission to the host. The host then maps the VT format into its local form. This reduces the "$m \times n$" problem to an "$m \times 1$" problem. Each host on the network must support one new terminal type (the VT) when it joins the network. The next two sections will discuss the parametric and virtual terminal approaches in more detail.

IV. Parametric Terminal Protocols

The parametric approach has been pursued primarily by the national PTTs (Postal, Telegraphy, and Telephony Ministries) within the CCITT and in the U.S. by Telenet. The CCITT has approved protocols to define a Packet Assembler/Disassembler (PAD). These have been designated X.28 and X.29. Recommendation X.28 defines the protocol for use between the start/stop mode DTE (the terminal) and the PAD. Recommendation X.29 defines the protocol for use between the PAD and the packet-mode DTE (PDTE) (the host). (There is also a Recommendation X.3, which defines the PAD.)

CCITT Recommendation X.25 defines the protocol for data transfer between the packet-mode DTE (the host) and the Data Communicating Equipment or DCE (the network). X.29 uses the user data fields defined by X.25 to exchange control information and user data between the PAD and the host. It may seem that X.29 is being used in an end-to-end fashion on top of the X.25 protocol. From the point of view of the CCITT, this is not the case. The PAD is part of the network or DCE. Thus, X.29 is not being used end-to-end even though the PAD may be some distance from the computer. X.29 is an interface.

X.29 provides several PAD Messages which are used to control the PAD and to indicate certain conditions. The PAD parameters can be inspected and modified by the use of the READ, SET, and SET AND READ Messages. For example, a PDTE may send a SET PAD Message to a PAD to set the line length parameter (called line folding in X.29). The SET Message has as an argument a list of pairs of parameter codes and parameter values. The parameter code indicates which parameter is to be modified and the parameter value contains the new value of the parameter. This ⟨CODE, VALUE⟩ pair is repeated for each parameter that is to be modified. The PAD replies to one of these messages with a PARAMETER INDICATION Message which gives the current or new values of parameters in the same format as the SET or READ. A list of the PAD parameters defined as of January 1979 can be found in Table I.

Table I. PAD Parameters According to CCITT Recommendation X.3

PAD Recall	Provides the means to leave data transfer state and return to PAD command state.
Echo	Determines whether or not the PAD echos characters received from the terminal.
Data Forwarding Signals	Allows the terminal or host to specify when buffered characters are to be transmitted to the host.
Idle Timer Selection	Allows the terminal or host to specify a time interval for buffered characters to be transmitted if no forwarding signal has been received.
Ancillary Device Control	Provides flow control between the PAD and the terminal (with PAD as receiver of data).
Suppress PAD Signals	Allows PAD service signals to be suppressed.
Break Signal Semantics	Allows the terminal or host to select the action of a break signal.
Discard Output	Allows the PAD to discard all data received from the host.
Carriage Return Padding	Allows the terminal or host to specify the number of padding characters after a carriage return.
Line Folding	Allows the PAD to automatically fold lines greater than a specified length.
Flow Control	Provides flow control between the PAD and the terminal (with the terminal as receiver).

Most terminals provide a "break" facility. Its primary purpose is to allow the terminal to abort an operation or discard output. When the terminal user generates a "break" character at his terminal, the PAD will send an X.25 Interrupt followed by an INDICATION OF BREAK Message. The Interrupt packet travels outside the normal data flow. The exact semantics of the "break" condition are determined by the PAD parameters. Other PAD Messages are provided for indicating errors, resetting the PAD connection, and clearing the PAD.

The PAD protocols do not provide generic functions as found in the Virtual Terminal Protocols discussed below. The data stream consists of IA5 (International Alphabet No. 5) characters. (ASCII is essentially IA5 with national options.) It is assumed that the application in the host knows what the terminal will do with the characters. It is also assumed that the terminal will do what is intended. At present, the PAD has only been defined for scroll-mode terminals (e.g., a simple TTY). It is unclear how it will be used to support more sophisticated devices. Experience with X.25 has shown that to ensure reliable communications an end-to-end transport protocol is required on top of X.25 or that equivalent end-to-end facilities be added to X.25 [17, 21]. It is very unclear how the use of an end-to-end protocol on top of X.25 can be extended to use with X.29 in a consistent manner.

Another aspect of X.29 which exacerbates this problem is that X.29 uses a facility (the Q-bit) of the lower-level X.25 protocol to distinguish PAD control messages from data. It may be difficult for some systems to support this mixing of levels.

The Interactive Terminal Interface (ITI) [35] used by Telenet is very similar to X.29. There are two major differences between the two. First, Telenet supports a much more extensive set of parameters (including such things as Tab Padding, Transmit on Timer, six parameters for 2741 operation, Manual/Automatic Connection, etc.). To some degree ITI indicates the kinds of additions to X.29 we can expect in the future. Second, Telenet's ITI supports what is called a virtual terminal mode. The Telenet VT described is not as fully developed as the ones we will discuss below. This VT supports only a very primitive scroll terminal. The only generic functions provided by ITI are the go-ahead (for half-duplex operation), the interrupt process, the abort output, and the break functions.

The parametric approach is most successful when the primary purpose is to handle existing terminal types [3]. The PAD provides a basic, transparent mode of operation, which places most of the burden of terminal handling on the PDTE or the host. The PAD parameters allow the PDTE to shift some of this burden to the PAD. As the PAD is used to support more and more complex terminals, the number of parameters required increases rapidly. X.29 has 12 parameters; an early version of Telenet's ITI had 20-some parameters which have since grown to more than 50. The PAD protocols do not allow PAD-to-PAD communication and it is unlikely that it will allow the PDTEs to use the PAD protocols for communication between themselves. However, symmetrical operation has been mentioned as a point for further study. Many of these problems can be avoided by using the virtual terminal approach.

V. Virtual Terminal Protocols

The VTP approach has been used by the ARPAnet in the U.S. [12, 34], by the CYCLADES network in France [24], by the GMD network in West Germany [33], by the European Informatics Network (EIN) built for the European Economic Community (EEC) [32], and has been proposed for the Belgian University Network [6]. (Some vendors of networks advertise that they provide a virtual terminal protocol. However, on closer inspection one finds that their "virtual" terminal is identical to the terminals sold by these vendors. Also these protocols often do not provide any means for extensions or negotiations. These protocols are intended for homogeneous systems and will not be considered here.) In the VTP approach, the user composes input at the terminal. Before this input is transferred across the network it is translated into the VT format. When the host receives the data from the network, it then translates this VT form into the form expected by its terminal handling software. The application then receives the data as if it had come from a local terminal. The major advantage of this approach is that it avoids the "$m \times n$" problem while allowing relatively sophisticated terminal usage. Many conventional operating systems such as the Burroughs MCP or Honeywell MULTICS have used this canonical form approach for many years with great success. Depending on the detail with which the VT is defined, applications may use network terminals without any loss of sophistication.

A. Background

The ARPAnet Telnet protocol [12, 34] was the first Virtual Terminal Protocol. Telnet (acronym for Telecommunications Network) is a very simple protocol intended for use by scroll-mode terminals. It is based on three principles: the concept of the network virtual terminal, the concept of negotiations (or negotiated options), and a symmetrical view of terminals and processes. The Telnet protocol has been remarkably successful within the ARPAnet. The two major design successes of Telnet are the symmetrical view of terminals and the negotiated options. The scroll-mode VT was adequate for most ARPAnet applications. Further development of the Virtual Terminal was left for later. Protocol research in the ARPAnet terminated in 1973, so that many of the improvements that were intended were never made. Since that time almost all protocol research has been done in Europe.

While Telnet focused primarily on the symmetry and negotiation issues, the Europeans have focused their attention on the definition of a virtual terminal model that could be used in a wider range of applications. There are several centers in Europe that have been investigating the design of VTPs: Schicker and Duenki in Zurich [30]; Bauwens and Magnee at Liege [6]; Schulze at Darmstadt [33], Higginson at University College London [18]; and Barber at the National Physical Laboratory in England [3, 4]. Two basic VTP organizations have emerged in this research. In the earlier work [24, 31, 32], symmetric operation was ignored. This led to a model in which the combination of the real terminal and the software to convert to the protocol appeared as a virtual terminal to the application program. Later, Schulze [33] proposed the use of a shared communications variable as the basis of a common data structure. Although this approach allows symmetric operation, it does so with considerable loss of asynchrony and efficiency. Recently, a more flexible approach [19] has been used to provide symmetrical operation without the use of a common data structure. This protocol uses an organization much like the two-NVT organization found in Telnet.

The European investigations into VTPs have made two major contributions: (1) a well-defined virtual terminal and (2) the development of a model for attentions or interrupts. Both are crucial in a general VTP.

The following sections will discuss in detail these and other major aspects of virtual terminal protocols. But before doing that let us consider the environment in which VTPs will be developed and used.

B. VTPs in a Layered Architecture

The virtual terminal protocols described in this paper were defined to be used directly on top of an end-to-end transport service, such as the Host-Host Protocol in the ARPAnet or the Transport Station protocol in CYCLADES. Since the design of these VTPs, there has been much activity by the International Organization for Standardization (ISO) in the development of a standard networking architecture for interconnecting heterogeneous ("open" in the terminology of ISO) systems [20]. This work which is being done by ISO/TC97/SC16 (Open Systems Interconnection) has defined a seven-layer architecture (see Chapter 2). The first four layers (physical, link, network, and transport) of this architecture are concerned with the reliable transfer of data. The upper three layers (session, presentation, and application) are the domain of higher-level protocols and are of concern here. Layer 4 (the transport layer) corresponds to the transport service in the ARPAnet or CYCLADES. However, the VTPs described in this paper incorporate functions found in both the session and presentation layers. Most of the functions of a VTP are concerned with creating and maintaining the virtual terminal. These transformation functions are considered to be functions of the presentation layer. The functions of dialogue control and data delimiting (if used in a VTP) are considered to be session layer functions. The VTP designs described here are basically sound although they must be partitioned to correspond to the SC16 architecture. As yet, no one has proposed a VTP consistent with the SC16 architecture. However, one should expect that one or more proposals may be made by the time this article appears in print, or soon after.

C. VTP Architecture

The purpose of a VTP is to facilitate the use of terminals in a heterogeneous environment. Several different models have been proposed for organizing a VTP. In this section we compare the overall organization of various VTPs and consider global aspects of VTP operation such as terminal classes, phases of operations, and extensions.

VTP Models and Symmetry

In the large majority of cases a VTP will be used by a user at a terminal accessing an application program. However, in a network it is often very useful to be able to support terminal-to-terminal and application-to-application configurations. The terminal-to-terminal configuration is very useful for record communications and certain kinds of teleconferencing applications and other applications. At first, one might think that connecting two application programs together would not require a VT. Indeed programs designed to interact with other programs probably would not require a VTP to mediate communications. However, if one wishes to connect two programs together which were originally intended for use by a user at a terminal, a VTP can be very useful in facilitating such an arrangement. This arrangement occurred many times in the ARPAnet. The Telnet protocol was used in just this manner. For example, the interactive graphics system, OLS, at UCSB was connected to the algebraic manipulation system, MACSYMA, at MIT. Thus, users of OLS could use MACSYMA to algebraically simplify equations before graphing them [26].

Designers of Virtual Terminal Protocols have proposed several models as the basis for a VTP. The earliest of these was the Telnet model. In Telnet, a VTP connection is seen as two virtual terminals with the keyboard of one connected to the presentation unit (or display) of the other and vice versa. (See Fig. 2). This model takes a symmetric view of terminals and processes. The representation used by a local terminal or process is mapped onto its virtual terminal "keyboard." The virtual representation is sent to the presentation unit of the remote virtual terminal where it is mapped to the representation of the remote host. Each virtual terminal represents the state as seen from the point of view of its associated host. In the Telnet protocol, echoing is controlled by means of a negotiation sequence which allows echoing to be done by none, one, or both VTs. (The default case is for each VT to echo for its local partner.) This model allows for considerable asynchrony between the two systems. In some applications, the information

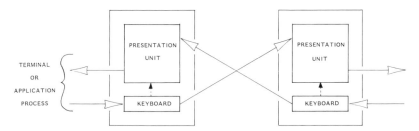

Fig. 2. The Telnet virtual terminal model. (The dotted line indicates the ability to echo characters locally or remotely.)

"displayed" by the two VTs may differ for a time. In other cases, the information may differ radically for long periods of time.

In some of the European VT models [6, 29, 30, 31, 32] that have been proposed, the Virtual terminal is considered from the point of view of the host. The virtual terminal is defined as a combination of the real terminal and whatever adaptation functions are required to make the real terminal appear as a virtual terminal as seen from the host. (See Fig. 3.) At the host, there is an adaptation function which converts the virtual terminal format into the local representation expected by the host. This model is asymmetrical. It cannot support terminal-to-terminal or process-to-process interactions. If the host needs to determine the current disposition of the VT, a command must be sent to it and a reply must be generated. In order to prevent the reply from being invalidated before it is delivered by subsequent input from the user, this model relies heavily on an alternating dialogue mode to control contention for the VT. Much less asynchrony is allowed by this model. The alternating dialogue (or half-duplex) mode is seen by the designers as the primary mode of usage. (This is probably related to the greater abundance of half-duplex terminal systems in use among European researchers than among U.S. researchers.) All input from the terminal is displayed locally. No echo control is provided as in Telnet.

Another VTP model suggested by Schulze [33] is based on the "shared communication variable." The essence of this approach is to transplant the "single-site" model into the network environment. In this VTP, each side takes turns accessing a single virtual data structure. This virtual data structure is provided by a lower-level protocol. This protocol is able to give the illusion of a single data structure by having a copy of the data structure at each host and restricting access to only one user at a time. This approach cannot support the asynchronous, full-duplex dialogues found in many systems. By taking a centralized approach rather than a distributed approach and not allowing asynchrony, this approach can incur considerable overhead in resolving contention for the data structure. (Other flaws in the "shared communication variable" approach appear when it is applied to broadcast protocol applications or distributed data bases, e.g., maintaining multiple copies of the "shared variables" reliably and consistently.) This model does not consider the problem of echo control.

Fig. 3. Asymmetrical VTP architecture (after Bauwens and Magnee [6]).

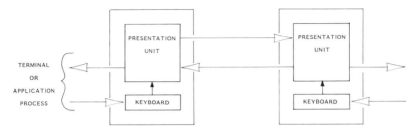

Fig. 4. INWG virtual terminal model.

In the INWG VTP [19] each side has a VT which represents that side's view of the state of the VT session (see Fig. 4) much like the Telnet model. This model explicitly recognizes the asynchronies present in the network. Input from the local user is written on the local data structure and transmitted over the network to be entered in the remote data structure. In asynchronous full-duplex or "free-running" dialogue mode, the contents of the two data structures may be different owing to the concurrency of the applications and variable network delays. (The same data are written on both, but the order may differ. Control of echo is not provided.) This "free-running" dialogue mode can provide greater efficiency by allowing messages to be sent at any time. In fact, for some applications it may even be desirable that the two data structures be different. This model is symmetrical and thus can support terminal-to-terminal and process-to-process configurations.

The VT Data Structure

Regardless of the network architecture of a virtual terminal protocol, a central component of all of the virtual terminals is the data structure. This data structure is an abstract representation of the data being "displayed" on the VT. This data structure is defined to have certain properties and parameters. For example, a scroll-mode VT has a one-dimensional data structure; a paged terminal, a two-dimensional data structure; and a data entry terminal, a two-dimensional data structure within which data elements can have special attributes such as protection, highlighting, etc. (Other properties such as overprinting or character replacement may also be defined.) A pointer to the current character position in the current line is associated with the data structure. Various VT primitives (such as "move cursor" or "erase protected") are defined by the protocol to modify and to manipulate this data structure (see below for more detail). There are also several VT parameters (such as line and page length) that may be associated with the data structure. These are set by means of the negotiation mechanism described below.

Phases of Operation

It is useful to consider a VTP session as consisting of several phases. Depending on the level of sophistication of the VT, the following phases of operation are well defined in proposed VTPs:

(1) Establishment Phase. This phase is entered whenever the VT service is requested until a VTP connection is completely established.

(2) Negotiation Phase. This phase is entered whenever one side or the other wishes to negotiate the use of new terminal primitives, parameters, or classes; or new parameter settings.

(3) Form Definition Phase. This phase is peculiar to data entry terminals. It is entered whenever a form is being defined on the terminal's presentation unit.

(4) Data Phase. This phase is entered during the normal exchange of data between the two partners.

(5) Synchronous Attention Phase. This phase is entered whenever an attention or out-of-band signal is sent that must be coordinated with a particular point in the normal data stream. (See section below on attentions.)

(6) Termination Phase. This phase is entered whenever the VT service is requested to terminate VT service on this connection.

Special phases may be envisioned for other major classes of terminals. These phases of operation are not always strictly enforced in all VTPs, but are very useful in organizing and describing a VTP.

Extensions

The ultimate terminal has not yet been defined, and probably never will be. Therefore, a VTP must provide a general framework within which future terminal functions can be accommodated. VTP extensions can be categorized into three major categories: terminal primitives, terminal parameters, and terminal classes. A VTP should provide a mechanism by which new terminal primitives can be defined to allow new operations to be performed on the data structure. New terminal parameters are required to allow new properties of the data structure to be defined. Although not independent of the last two, it is useful in a VTP to allow new terminal classes to be defined. Terminal classes define the minimal set of primitives and parameters and the nature of the data structure that must be supported. A VTP may support several classes and combinations of primitives and parameters. These are selected during a negotiation phase. In many cases a terminal class can be seen as a macro defining a specific set of primitives and parameters. A VTP user will negotiate a terminal class and then perhaps negotiate the use of additional primitives and parameters (or parameter settings) to fit his requirements. An excellent example of a VTP designed to take advantage of this kind of extensibility is the VTP defined by INWG [19]. This VTP specification defines the basic elements of the protocol and the rules for specifying terminal classes, primitives, and parameters, and then defines the basic set of classes, primitives, and parameters according to these rules.

D. Elements of a VTP

Negotiation

All VTPs define a negotiation mechanism that is used to negotiate and to select the terminal class to be used, the primitives and parameters to be used, and the parameter settings to be used. Two basic negotiation mechanisms have been used in the VTPs discussed here: the one used by Telnet [34], and the one found in most of the European VTPs [6, 16, 19, 30].

The Telnet protocol negotiation mechanism can be initiated by either side. Besides negotiating whether or not a particular option is to be in effect, the mechanism also allows one to specify, when appropriate, which side is to perform the function. For example, a user may negotiate the Echo option and specify whether echoing is to be done locally or remotely with respect to the initiator of the negotiation.

Four commands support option negotiation (DO, DONT, WILL, and WONT). WILL ⟨option name⟩ is sent by either party to indicate that party's willingness to begin performing the option. DO ⟨option name⟩ and DONT ⟨option name⟩ are the positive and negative acknowledgments. Similarly, DO ⟨option name⟩ is sent to request that the other party begin performing the option. WILL ⟨option name⟩ and WONT ⟨option name⟩ are the positive and negative acknowledgments (see [12, 34] for a more complete description). Each option specification defines the conditions for terminating the negotiation of that option.

Telnet only provides for extensions to the protocol along one dimension. Although they are not explicitly constrained by Telnet as such, the negotiable options are primarily terminal-related parameters. The ability to negotiate the use of new terminal commands or to negotiate new terminal classes to modify the basic NVT model is not provided by the protocol.

The scroll-mode terminal is the only terminal model that Telnet can efficiently support. Experiments with extending Telnet to handle more complex terminals have shown that major inefficiencies develop (see for example [13]). The only reasonable way for new terminal commands or primitives (e.g., position the cursor) to be introduced without modifying the protocol is to use the subnegotiation mechanism.

In the European VTPs, the negotiation mechanism is somewhat different. Since the two VTs (in those models where there are two) are more tightly coupled, a negotiated function is not seen as occurring at one site or the other. The function is either performed by the VT or it is not. Each VT supports the function for its local user whether terminal or process. This negotiation mechanism defines five primitives. The Request Parameters Range and Indicate Parameters Range primitives are used to determine what facilities are supported by the remote implementation. (In Telnet, a Status option fulfills this function.) The Set Parameter Value, Agree, and Disagree primitives are used to select specific values and to agree or disagree to their use. In the asymmetric VTPs, negotiation is mediated by the application side only. It determines what parameter values it will select within the range supported by the terminal side. In the symmetrical VTPs, negotiation can be initiated by either side. This requires that a mechanism be defined to prevent infinite cycling of proposal and counterproposal. The European VTPs attempt to define a single mechanism applicable to all negotiations for terminating negotiation. (As opposed to the Telnet scheme of letting each negotiable function define an algorithm for termination.) In the INWG VTP, an octet containing a random number is sent with each set primitive. If a disagreement occurs, when both try to set the value of the parameter the suggested value with the largest random number prevails. More experience with negotiations is required before it will be clear which scheme is the better.

Terminal Primitives and Parameters

There are two kinds of VTP primitives: primitives used to control the virtual terminal and to establish its parameters, and primitives used to modify the data structure. The control-related primitives are used in the negotiation sequence and to control auxiliary devices. The data-structure related primitives are used to format and enter text in the data structure (see Table II).

Terminal Parameters are used to characterize the VT and the data structure. They include properties such as line length, page size, overprint/erase (whether a character is overprinted or replaced when two different characters are stored in the same position), and the selection of auxiliary devices. These parameters characterize the nature of the data structure and the VT. To some extent they also determine how data in the data structure will be transformed into what is shown to the user at his real terminal.

Table II. Minimum Parameters and Primitives Required by the INWG VTP

Primitives	Parameters
Scroll Mode	
Agree	Terminal Class
Disagree	Line Length
Request	Erase/Overprint
Indicate	Dialogue Mode
New Line	Auxiliary Data Structure
Start of Line	
Text Segment	
Purge	
Asynchronous Attention	
Synchronous Attention	
Paged Mode	
Scroll Mode Primitives	Scroll Mode Parameters
Delete All	Page Size
Position	
Data Entry Terminal Mode	
Paged Mode Primitives	Paged Mode Parameters
Attribute[a]	
Delete Attribute	
Erase Unprotected	
Next Protected Field	

[a]Attributes are protected/unprotected fields, and three levels of display: Nondisplay, Normal, and Intensified.

Attentions

The use of attentions, or out-of-band signals, has also been a question of much concern to designers of VTPs. Attentions are used to provide the "break" function found in many terminals and other out-of-band control functions. There are essentially two kinds of attentions that are required in a VTP: the asynchronous attention, which is independent of the data stream, and the synchronous attention, whose action must be coordinated with a point in the data stream. The first poses no problems, but there are certain race conditions that make providing the second more difficult. An excellent solution to this problem was first proposed in [14] and later developed in detail by Bauwens and Magnee in [5].

The basic issues that the attention mechanism must address are as follows:

1. Whether or not data are to be purged.
2. The dialogue mode after the attention (full and half duplex).
3. If half duplex, which side has the turn.

In the Duenki and Schicker scheme the attention carries these pieces of information which provide the remote user with a means to flush data, to

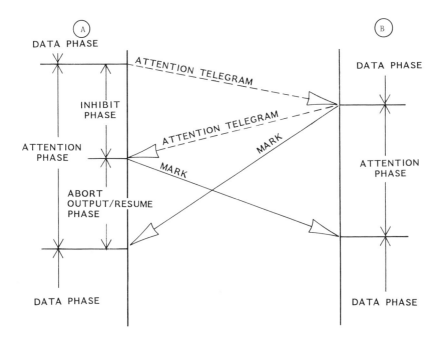

Fig. 5. Handling an attention condition. *A* denotes the process which initiated the attention. *B* denotes the process which receives the attention. (After Bauwens and Magnee [6].)

request that the "turn" be given to it, and to send other out-of-band signals. (In addition, most of the VTPs provide 8 or 16 bits for the terminal classes or user applications to define.)

The mechanism described by Duenki and Schicker assumes that the transport service provides reliable delivery of out-of-band signals, often called telegrams. In addition, only one attention from either side may be outstanding. The attention mechanism consists of the telegram sent out-of-band and a data mark that is sent in the normal data stream. The mark acknowledges that an attention has been received and also indicates the point in the data stream at which the attention phase ends and a new data phase begins. As seen by the initiator of an attention, the procedure goes as follows (see Fig. 5):

The initiator

- Stops accepting keyboard and network messages.
- Transmits an attention telegram specifying dialogue possibilities, purge information, etc.
- Awaits a responding attention telegram with the remote partner's request specifying the same information.
- Reevaluates the dialogue mode and location of the turn according to a distributed algorithm.

- Transmits a "mark" which carries the confirmation of this "negotiation" and signals the beginning of the next data phase.
- Accepts incoming messages, discarding or displaying them according to the attention information received until a mark is received.
- Reinitializes the dialogue mode, and continues processing.

The sequence for the receiver of an attention is very similar:

- Respond with an attention telegram.
- Issue a mark in the data stream.
- Wait for the incoming mark discarding or displaying data according to the parameters of the attention telegram.
- Continue normal processing when the mark arrives.

The above was freely adapted from the Duenki and Schicker paper [14]. For a detailed discussion showing how various deadlocks and races are avoided by this scheme, the interested reader should consult the paper by Bauwens and Magnee.

Dialogue Control

There are two major modes of dialogue found in terminal systems: full duplex or free-running and half-duplex or alternating. In free-running mode either side can send whenever it pleases. The protocol and its users are assumed to be able to sort out what is happening. In alternating mode the situation is more structured. One side is given the turn. That side sends everything it has and then gives the turn to the other side, who can then send. In the European VTPs alternating mode is enforced across the network. Only one implementation may send data at a time. In Telnet, the situation is more loose. Message traffic between the two VTs is always in free-running mode. However, when alternating mode is used, control information is also sent with the data that allows the interface between the VT and the real terminal or process to be controlled in an alternating mode. The superiority of one method over the other is a trade-off between response time and buffer requirements. The Telnet scheme may give the user better response time since data queued by the VTP may be written to the terminal or process as soon as the turn is relinquished. In the European VTPs the user would have to wait for the turn to be sent to the remote partner and for a reply to come back. However, if a user held the turn for some time, the Telnet scheme might cause the user with the turn to incur considerable difficulties because of the amount of data queued.

Data Delimiters

The problem of data delimiting in VTPs has not been explored in any detail as yet. The most common delimiter is the end-of-line. Many VTPs will buffer an entire line before sending it to the remote partner. However, in some applications more sophistication is desired. In these cases, it is desirable for the VTP to buffer data until a particular character or class of characters is encountered, and then forward the data. This aspect of VTPs has not been adequately explored. The best example of such a facility is the Remote Controlled Transmission and Echo option in Telnet [12, 34]. This facility was defined to increase the efficiency of several major application systems such as NLS [15] a sophisticated text editing, text manipulation, and retrieval system in the ARPAnet that do sophisticated echoing for the user.

VI. Summary

Virtual Terminal Protocols make the interworking of terminals and hosts in a heterogeneous environment possible with very little overhead. At the same time, a single VTP provides a framework which can accommodate a variety of terminal classes including those prevalently in use today (scroll, data entry, etc.) and those we can expect to be prevalent in the future (graphics, intelligent terminals, etc.)

As one can readily see from the above discussion, there is a fair amount of variety within the domain of VTPs. A recent survey by Magnee, Endrizzi, and Day [23] investigates, in much more detail than is possible here, the differences in the various European models. Work in this field is proceeding at a fairly fast pace. A proposal for a standard VTP can be expected by the end of 1983, if not before. VTP work in the U.S. very nicely complements the work that has been done in Europe. Hopefully, a standard VTP will combine the best of both Telnet and the European proposals.

VII. Conclusions

This chapter has discussed in some detail two basic approaches to terminal protocols, the parametric and virtual approaches. The PAD protocols which characterize the parametric approach are more concerned with the support of current telecommunication requirements, while the VTPs are aimed at the more general communications environment likely to evolve in the future. Currently, most users of computer networks use one host. In essence, the network is replacing point-to-point lines. The PAD protocols are designed for this environment. The PAD protocols parametrize basic terminal handling characteristics; but assume that the host knows how to manipulate the presentation unit. In a very real sense the parametric approach tends to keep users tied to one major host or vendor. Since the host must have a fair amount of knowledge about the terminal, it is difficult for users to easily take advantage of the opportunities provided by the network. In fact, the users can be expected not to rely heavily on the network and remain strongly tied to the mainframe vendor.

In the future, we can expect users to use several hosts of different manufacturers. The VTP will then become a necessity as users break out of these essentially closed groups. However, this does not mean that the PAD and VTP approaches are diametrically opposed. The VTP is primarily concerned with manipulating the presentation unit, which the PAD is not. Compatibility between the PAD and VTP can be achieved by making the Virtual terminal one of the kinds of "terminals" a PAD can support. Or, if the "real terminal" is sufficiently sophisticated it can implement the VTP directly and use the PAD protocols as a more sophisticated transport service.

References*

[1] P. A. Alsberg, J. F. Bailey, D. S. Brown, and J. R. Mullen, *Intelligent Terminals as User Agents.* Trends and Applications 1976: Micro and Mini Systems, IEEE 76CH1101-5C, Gaithersburg, MD 1976.

[2] R. H. Anderson "Advanced intelligent terminals as a user's network interface," Proc. Comput. Conf., Fall 1975, 11th IEEE Computer Society Conference, 1975.

[3] D. L. A. Barber, "The role and nature of a virtual terminal," *Comput. Commun. Rev.,* vol. 7, no. 3, p. 5; also in Proc. NCC'76, 1976.

[4] D. L. A. Barber, "The real virtual terminal," *INWG Protocol Note* # 64, 1977.

[5] E. Bauwens and F. Magnee, "Remarks on negotiation mechanism and attention handling," S.A.R.T. 77/12/13. *INWG Protocol Note* # 72, 1977.

[6] E. Bauwens and F. Magnee, "The Virtual Terminal Protocol for a Belgian University Network," Proc. Comput. Network Protocols Symp., Liege, Belgium, 1978.

[7] W. J. Bouknight, G. R. Grossman, and D. M. Grothe, "The ARPA network terminal service—A new approach to network access," Proc. 3rd Data Commun. Symp., 1973.

[8] R. T. Braden, "NETCRT—A character display protocol," *ARPANET RFC* # 205, 1971.

[9] CCITT, "Proposals for draft provisional recommendations for interworking between non-packet mode and pocket mode DTE," *CCITT Study Group VII Temporary Document* no. 62-E, Geneva, 1977.

[10] G. L. Chesson, "The network UNIX system," Proc. 5th Symp. on Operating System Principles, Austin, TX, 1975.

---

*Items in the Reference list marked with a NIC number have been archived by the ARPA Network Information Center, Stanford Research Institute, Menlo Park, CA 94025. Items marked with an RFC number are a series of Requests for Comments maintained at the NIC by the ARPA Network Working Group. The ARPAnet Protocol Handbook is edited by Elizabeth Feinler and Jon Postel and is produced for the Defense Communication Agency. Copies are available from the U.S. National Technical Information Service, 5285 Port Royal, Springfield, VA 22161, order number ADA 052 594/9WC. Items marked with INWG numbers are the working papers of IFIP Working Group 6.1 (International Network Working Group) and can be obtained from Alex McKenzie, Bolt Beranek and Newman, 50 Moulton St., Cambridge, MA 02138.

[11] G. Cosell, and D. Walden, "Telnet issues," *ARPANET RFC* # 435, 1973.

[12] J. Davidson, W. Hathaway, J. Postel, N. Mimno, R. Thomas, and D. Walden, "The ARPANET Telnet protocol: Its purpose, principles, implementation, and impact on host operating system design," Proc. 5th Data Commun. Symp., 1977.

[13] John Day, "Telnet data entry terminal option," *ARPANET RFC* # 731, 1977.

[14] A. Duenki, and P. Schicker, "Symmetry and attention handling: Comments on a virtual terminal," EIN/ZHR/77/03, *INWG Protocol Note*, 1977.

[15] D. C. Englebart, R. W. Watson, and J. C. Norton, "The augmented knowledge workshop," AFIPS Proc. NCC, June, 1973.

[16] EPSS Liason Group, "An interactive terminal protocol," HLP(CP)(75)2 INWG General Note 94, 1975.

[17] F. R. Hertweck, E. Raubold, and F. Vogt, "X.25 based process-process communication," Proc. Symp. Comput. Network Protocols, Liege, Belgium, 1978.

[18] Peter L. Higginson, "Restructured version of ESP 25—Part C; Chapter 2—Packet assembler for the adaptation of asynchronous character terminals to the virtual terminal," *INDRA Note* No. 640, Dept. of Statistics and Computer Science, University College, London, 1977.

[19] IFIP WG 6.1. "Proposal for a standard virtual terminal protocol," *INWG Protocol Note* 91, 1978, also in Proc. Symp. Comput. Network Protocols, Liege, Belgium, 1978.

[20] International Standards Organization, "Reference model for open system architecture," ISO/TC97/SC16/N46 revised, 1978. Available from National Standards Bodies.

[21] Y. Jacquemart, "Network interprocess communication in an X.25 environment," Proc. Symp. Comput. Network Protocols, Liege, 1978.

[22] Richard Luca, "Zones—A solution to the problem of dynamic screen formatting in CRT-based networks," Proc. 4th Data Commun. Symp., Quebec, 7–9 October, p. 1-1, 1975.

[23] F. Magnee, A. Endrizzi, and J. Day, "Virtual terminal protocols—A survey," *Computer Networks* 3, pp. 299–314, 1979.

[24] N. Naffah, "Protocole appareil virtuel-type ecran," TER 536, *Reseau CYCLADES*, *IRIA*, Rocquencourt, France, 1976.

[25] S. M. Ornstein, *et al.*, "The terminal IMP for the ARPA computer network," *Proc. SJJCC* 1972 pp. 243–254.

[26] W. Parrish, and J. R. Pickens, "MIT-Mathlab meets UCSB-OLS," *ARPANET RFC* # 525, 1973.

[27] T. N. Pyke, Jr., "Network access techniques: Some recent developments," *Proc. 3rd Texas Conf. Comput. Syst.*, Austin, TX, 1974.

[28] D. L. Retz, "ELF—A system for network access," *IEEE Intercon Conf. Rec.*, New York, 1975.

[29] Peter Schicker, "Virtual terminal protocol (Proposal 2)," EIN/ZHR/75/5 *INWG Protocol Note* # 30, 1975.

[30] P. Schicker, and A. Duenki, "Virtual terminal definition and protocol," EIN/ZHR/76/019a, *INWG Protocol Note* # 51, 1976.

[31] P. Schicker, and A. Duenki, "The virtual terminal definition," EIN/ZHR/77/1086, *Computer Networks* 2, pp. 429–441, 1978.

[32] P. Schicker, and H. Zimmerman, "Proposal for a scroll mode virtual terminal," EIN/CCG/77 02, *INWG Protocol Note* # 62.

[33] G. Schulze, and Joachim Borger, "A virtual terminal protocol based upon the 'shared communication variable' concept," Proc. Symp. Comput. Network Protocols, Liege, 1977.

[34] Telnet Protocol Specification, NIC#18639. 1973. Also in the *ARPANET Protocol Handbook*, 1973.

[35] Telenet Corp. Interactive Terminal Interface Specification, Telnet Corp., Washington, D.C., 1977.

16

SNA Higher-Layer Protocols

Verlin L. Hoberecht

I. Introduction

A. Systems Network Architecture (SNA) LU-to-LU Sessions

A comprehensive network architecture which addresses the meaningful exchange of information between end users must address a number of basic requirements. This first requirement involves transporting messages from one network node to another over common carrier or privately owned communication facilities. It also involves message routing when the source and destination nodes of a message are separated by one or more intermediate nodes, all connected by communication links. These SNA functions are dealt with in Chapter 11. The second requirement is the definition of the content of the messages such that they can be understood and used by both end users. How this requirement is met is the subject of this chapter.

This chapter assumes the architectural framework of SNA as depicted in Fig. 1. The sources and destination of messages flowing through the path control network are network addressable units.

End users, for example, application programs or terminal operators, are associated with network addressable units called logical units, usually referred to as LUs. Each LU has a unique network address indicated by na_i (see Fig. 1). The ability for two end users to exchange information is obtained by establishing a logical connection, called a session, between the two LUs associated with the two end users. Once established, the two end users are able to send and receive information to and from each other. A pair of network addresses is associated with each message flowing through the path control network. In Fig. 1, na_j identifies a typical destination LU and na_i identifies an origin LU.

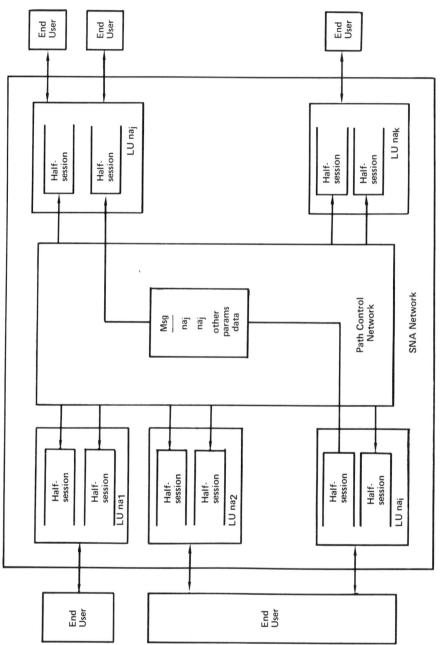

Fig. 1. SNA network overview.

B. Session Level Message Format

The subject of this chapter is the syntax and semantics of the messages which flow between two LUs on LU-to-LU sessions and the protocols used by one LU to manage functions performed by a remote LU. The general format of these messages when viewed at the point at which they are passed from the sending LU to the path control network (or where they are passed from the path control network to the receiver LU) is a binary bit string divided into two parts

where (1) RU denotes request unit or response unit, and (2) RH denotes RU header.

The functions encoded in the RH and RU will be discussed in more detail in the following sections. The exact syntax of these headers is given in [2]. At this point, it should be understood that in addition to carrying the information being exchanged between end users, the same general message format is used to carry control information between the associated LUs.

II. General Purpose Function and Protocols

SNA has defined a number of functions and protocols which are fundamental to end user to end user communication but are independent of the end user to end user application. These functions are performed by the LUs and are referred to as session level protocols. This section briefly describes a number of these functions and protocols, most of which are concerned with data flow control.

A. Request–Response Protocols

Suppose that a session has been established between two LUs and that one of the LUs sends a request unit (RU) to the other LU. There are many instances in which the sender requires a positive confirmation that the request unit was received by the other LU independent of the syntax or semantics of the content of the RU. Thus, there are circumstances in which the sender of a request unit requires the receiver to return a response unit. There are also many circumstances in which there is no requirement for a response unit to be returned, and it would be inappropriate to burden the network with unnecessary response units.

This request–response protocol is managed through the use of certain bits in the RH (RU header). One bit is used to indicate whether the RU is a request or a response unit. If a request is being sent, the sender uses other bits to indicate whether or not a response is to be returned and if so, whether it is to be a definite response or an exception response. Exception responses are only returned when exception conditions are detected. If a definite response is indicated, a response will always be returned.

The sender of response units uses the same bit positions in the RH to indicate that the RU is a response and the type of response being returned, i.e., a positive response or an exception response. A positive response is sent when a definite response was requested and there were no errors or exceptions. A response is sent when either a definite response was requested or an exception response was requested and an error or exception condition was detected. An RH with a response type indicator is always followed by a 4-byte response unit containing data which define the nature of the error.

The basic request–response protocol just described allows several different modes of operation. For example, by requesting a definite response and not sending additional requests until the definite response is received, the sending end user limits the extent to which it gets ahead of the receiving end user. This mode simplifies greatly the protocols for recovery and resynchronization following a session failure.

Another operating mode is for an LU to send multiple request units before it has received a response to the first. This is done to overcome the delay encountered in transporting messages from the sender to the receivers and to keep the receiver "fully utilized." In this mode, a sender gets ahead of the receiver. This causes no problem until an exception response is received by the request sender. This response must be correlated with the appropriate request, and then appropriate error recovery steps must be taken including disposition of the requests which were sent subsequent to the request having the exception condition.

B. Request Unit Chains

In many applications, the unit of information to be sent from one end user to another can be most easily handled as a string of request units. Examples are the data to print a report, the data for a display screen update, or the content of a file which is being transferred.

Such a unit of information is handled as a chain of request units. (See Fig. 6 of Chapter 11 for an illustration of the case where each RU is not further segmented, but is handled by path control as one segment.) The sender delimits the chain by setting appropriate bits in the RH's to indicate:

1. first RU of a chain,
2. middle RU (there may be more than one),
3. last RU of a chain, and
4. only RU of a chain.

C. Half-Duplex, Flip/Flop Protocol

Many applications involve a conversational mode of operation in which one LU sends requests for a period of time and then enters a state in which it is prepared to receive and process requests. This general mode of operation requires a protocol for the sending LU to notify the receiving LU that it is changing its state from send to receive and that the other LU should change its state accordingly. This is accomplished by the sending LU setting the change direction indicator bit in the RH of the last request unit it sends.

D. Half-Duplex Contention Protocol

In some conversational applications, the session may go into an "idle state" in which neither party has any information to send. A modification to the HDX flip/flop protocol is made to allow the two parties to go into an idle state at the end of an RU chain. The conversation can be resumed by either party. If both should try to resume the conversation at the same time as depicted in Fig. 2, the contention is resolved according to a rule selected at the time the session was established.

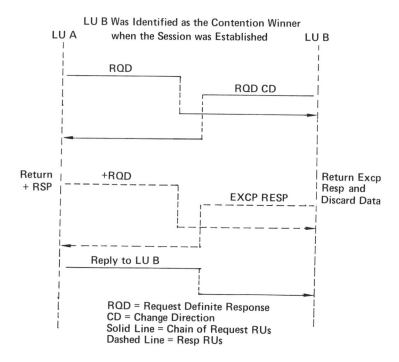

Fig. 2. Example of half-duplex contention request/response protocol.

E. Full Duplex Protocol

The path control network of SNA has the capability to support sessions in which data can be flowing concurrently in both directions between the two LUs. However, there has not been a general requirement to develop and implement LUs which use this protocol.

F. Brackets

Within the scope of this section, the word transaction means a series of conversational exchanges between two LUs. One of the LUs initiates the transaction by sending a request unit chain to the second LU. The second LU sends a request unit chain to the first LU in reply. The cycle may be repeated until the transaction is complete.

Now assume that either of the LUs of a session can initiate a transaction; however, once a transaction is initiated, it is most desirable that it not be interrupted by the initiation of a second transaction by the other LU. This then leads to the definition of a brackets protocol which defines how the boundary of a noninterruptable unit of work involving conversational exchanges is identified and how the two LUs are synchronized to work on a single transaction at a time.

The sender sets begin bracket and end bracket indicators in the request unit headers. There is also a protocol established at the time the session is started which gives one of the LUs the privilege of unilaterally initiating a bracket while the other LU must bid for and receive permission from the first LU to begin a bracket.

The example illustrated in Fig. 3 assumes that LU-B has received permission to begin a bracket.

G. Session Pacing*

In general, an LU is allowed to send request units when they are available to be sent. In some instances, the sending of a request unit may be held up while the LU waits for a definite response. In other cases, the sending of request units is held up due to the restrictions of HDX protocol.

However, there are still circumstances in which it is possible for a sending LU to overrun the receiving LU. This situation is prevented through *session pacing*.

Whether or not pacing is used in a session is determined at the time the session is established along with a number N, called the pacing window.

---

*See Chapter 13.

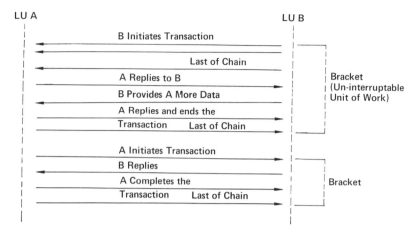

Fig. 3. Pictorial representation of a bracket.

The sending LU sends N request units, with the pacing indicator on in the header of the first request unit. The sending LU then waits for a response with the pacing indicator on before it sends another group of N request units.

The receiving LU sends a response with the pacing indicator on when it has received a request header with the pacing indicator on and it is able to handle N more request units.

H. RU Categories and SNA Layers

The preceding sections discussed a number of general purpose functions that are encoded in the RH. There are also a number of general purpose functions which are encoded as RUs. RUs on LU-to-LU sessions fall into three categories:

1. session control,
2. data flow control, and
3. function management (FM) data.

The category of the RU following an RH is indicated by the encoding of RU category bits in the RH.

The three RU categories are associated with three different layers of an LU half-session. This association is depicted in Fig. 4. The RUs of a particular category are used to carry control information and data from its associated layer in one half-session to the corresponding layer in the other half-session.

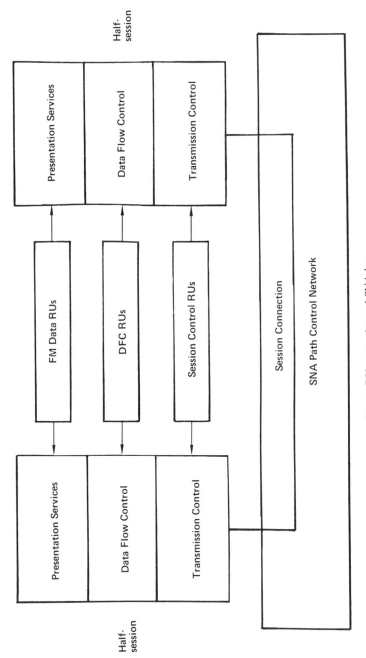

Fig. 4. RU categories and SNA layers.

FM data RUs are the RUs which carry end user data and are the RUs used to manage end user defined application-dependent functions.

Session and data flow control RUs are used by the LUs to control and manage the session. Session control and data flow control are independent of the nature of the FM data carried on the session. A complete detailed definition of these RUs can be found in [2]. However, a brief summary of each category follows.

I. Session Control RUs

Session control RUs are concerned with establishing a session, reestablishing a session following a session failure, and ending the session. The fundamental RU is the bind RU. It carries the parameters which establish the protocols which will be used during the session from the sending LU to the receiving LU. For example, the bind RU specifies session protocols such as

1. operating mode, e.g., HDX flip/flop;
2. maximum RU size;
3. pacing count;
4. whether or not multiple request exception response chains will be sent; and
5. bracket termination rules.

The bind RU also specifies the nature of the FM data that will be used on the session. There is also an unbind RU to end the session. Other session control RUs are used to reestablish a session following a session failure.

J. Data Flow Control RUs

The title of this section gives a general idea of the functions of the RUs in this category. Data flow control RUs have been defined to

1. allow the sender to cancel an RU chain which has been started:
2. quiesce and resume the flow of FM data on the session;
3. provide an LU the means by which it will be allowed to begin a bracket;
4. send a change in LU status, for example, to notify the other LU that a resource which has been reported temporarily unavailable is now available;
5. provide the means for an LU in receive state to signal the other LU that the sending LU should stop sending and pass control to the receiving LU so that it can send.

As an example, the format of the signal RU is shown in Fig. 5. Others are defined in [2].

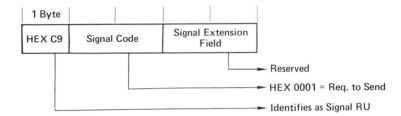

Fig. 5. Format of *signal* RU.

III. LU Types

The preceding discussion has briefly described or outlined a number of functions which are essential to end user to end user communications. These functions are independent of the nature or character of the end user and the information being exchanged between them.

Given a pair of specific end users and using these functions, it is possible to define a set of protocols for exchanging messages between the two end users. However, is it possible to define two classes of end users and a set of message exchange protocols which are applicable to any pair of end users formed by taking one from each class? The answer to this important question is yes. It has been done for the following:

1. program-to-keyboard/printer terminal,
2. program-to-keyboard/display terminal,
3. keyboard/printer terminal-to-keyboard/printer terminal, and
4. program-to-program.

These four sets of message exchange protocols are part of the definitions of LU session types 1, 2, 4, and 6, respectively. An introduction to and a more detailed description of these LU session types can be found in [3].

An examination of the message exchange protocols of LU session types 1 and 2 will reveal that they are very similar. The significant difference between LU 1 and LU 2 is due to differences in the FM data handled by these two LU session types.

However, there are two factors which cause significant differences in message exchange protocols. The first factor is the relationship between the two parties of the session. Is it a peer relationship or a master/subordinate relationship. LU session types 1 and 2 support a master/subordinate relationship. LU session types 4 and 6 support a peer relationship. The second factor is related to the role or extent of an end user operator in recovery.

Message exchange protocols between peers are symmetric. Message exchange protocols between master and subordinate are not. This is reflected in such protocol rules as the following:

(1) The master is responsible for recovery.

(2) The master establishes the context in which the data are to be understood. For example, the program establishes the format of the screen which determines what information the operator can enter.

The second factor is related to the role or extent of an end user operator in recovery. The operators of the terminals involved in LU type 4 sessions play a key role in recovery if there has been a session failure. In some circumstances recovery may involve telephone conversations between the two operators as they resynchronize their work.

In contrast, the logic for recovery in program-to-program communication must be handled without operator intervention. This leads to the definition of recovery protocols for LU 6 sessions which are not required in LU 4 sessions.

Table I is a summary [4] of products which have implemented support for LU session types 1, 2, 4, and 6.

Table I. Implementations of LU Types

Product	LU Session type 1	LU Session type 2	LU Session type 4	LU Session type 6
IMS/VS	√	√	√	√
CICS/VS	√	√	√	√
RES	√		√	
NOSP	√	√		
JES 2	√			
JES 3	√			
POWER/VS	√			
TSO	√	√		
NCCF	√	√		
VSPC	√	√		
TCAM	√	√		
3630	√			
DPPX	√	√		
DPCX	√	√		
3270	√	√		
3767	√			
3770	√			
3790	√	√		
S/32	√			
S/34	√		√	
S/38	√		√	
5250			√	
6670			√	

IV. Function Management (FM) Data

The raw form of all RUs is a binary bit string. In order for an RU to carry information it is necessary to impose a structure on the bit string, define syntactical relationships between the elements of the structure, and define the meaning or semantics of the structural elements. We shall now discuss how this is handled for the end user data expressed in the FM data RUs.

Different structures, syntax, and semantics are defined for carrying different kinds of information. More than one structure and syntax can be defined to carry a particular kind of information. That is, there is not necessarily a one-to-one relationship between a particular kind of information and a unique structure, syntax, and semantics for carrying that kind of information. However, for two parties to communicate, that is, exchange information, they must agree on the structure, syntax, and semantics of the bit strings carried in the RUs they exchange with each other.

A. Coded Character Data

One structure that can be imposed on a bit string is to divide it into n-bit bytes and assign a standard meaning to each unique value or code point that can be represented with n-bits. ASCII is an example of such a standard which defines a set of meanings for 7-bit bytes. EBDCIC is another example which defines a set of meanings for 8-bit bytes. (See Chapter 5 for detailed coding.)

Both EBCDIC and ASCII divide the definitions into two groups. The first group of definitions assign graphic characters to specific code points; the second group assigns control functions to the remaining code points.

Information which can be expressed as a string of alphanumeric characters and special symbols can be carried in an RU by assigning each character and special symbol an n-bit code and creating a coded character data stream. However, to communicate this information from a program to a terminal operator requires a transformation of the binary coded form of the information to a visual form (usually in two dimensions), which can be read by the operator. This function of transforming the information and presenting it to the end user in a form which is understandable by the end user is called presentation services. Presentation services require control codes to manage the presentation of the information in the desired format. We shall now describe several ways in which presentation services carries out these functions.

B. SNA Character String

The SNA Character String [3] is a set of EBCDIC control codes that has been defined for use on SNA sessions to enable one end of the session to manage functions available at the other end. It should be understood that the functions represented by this set of codes are not new or original with SNA. They have evolved from the functions which were used to control the earliest keyboard printer terminals. It should also be noted that some of the EBCDIC control codes have an ASCII equivalent. However, EBCDIC has 64 code points for control while current 7-bit ASCII standard has only 32.

The full set of SNA Character String functions will not be defined here. This information is available in [3]. However, the following functions are listed to give the reader a general idea of the nature of SNA Character String functions:

NEW LINE
FORM FEED
BACK SPACE
HORIZONTAL TAB
VERTICAL TAB
CARRIAGE RETURN

The syntactical nature of a string of graphic characters and SNA Character String controls requires that the receiver process the string sequentially by character. In printing (or displaying) the information carried in the string, the graphic characters are printed (or displayed) left-to-right, top-to-bottom. Control functions are executed when encountered.

The SNA Character String controls are designed to give the sending end user full control over how the graphic character data being sent to the other end user are to be presented. The position at which a particular graphic character is printed is determined by the data and controls which have preceded it. Since the information to be conveyed to the receiving end user may be dependent on where certain graphic character data are printed, either absolutely or relative to other printed data, the sending end user must be responsible for managing the presentation of the data to the receiving end user. The SNA Character String controls are not designed to share or delegate presentation control to the receiver. That is, the SNA Character String controls are based on a certain distribution of function between sender and receiver. A change in the distribution of function changes the functions which must be encoded and carried in the RU. A prerequisite for two end users to be able to communicate is a complementary distribution of function.

C. 3270 Display Data Stream

The 3270 display data stream is a character coded data stream with a number of interesting exceptions.

The 3270 data stream is composed of EBCDIC coded graphic characters, EBCDIC coded controls, and positionally defined commands, control, and status information. The syntax for graphic characters is the same as when used with SNA Character String controls, i.e., consecutive graphic characters are displayed left-to-right, top-to-bottom.

The syntax of the 3270 data stream is not a pure character coded data stream because of the positionally defined commands, control, and status information.

1. Commands and Write Control Character

The first two bytes of the first RU in an RU chain being sent to a display are a command byte and a write control character. Semantics for different values of the command byte include

ERASE/WRITE,
WRITE,
READ (modified fields),
READ FULL BUFFER, and
ERASE ALL UNPROTECTED FIELDS.

The write control character is bit encoded and controls such functions as

UNLOCK KEYBOARD,
SOUND AUDIBLE ALARM,
RESET MODIFIED DATA TAGS, and
PRINT.

These semantics are only associated with the first two bytes of an RU chain being sent to the display. The same bit values for a byte appearing elsewhere in the data stream will have a different semantic. Similarly on input, the first three bytes of the chain are positionally defined. The first byte identifies the event which caused the input to be sent, such as depression of the enter key or the depression of a program function key by the operator. The second and third bytes report the position of the cursor.

2. Orders

The character coded controls of the 3270 data stream have a different general syntax and a significantly different set of semantics from SCS. This is due to the different orientation of the two data streams. SCS is oriented to describing how to format and print a page of graphic characters. The 3270 data stream is oriented towards efficiently writing data into a buffer where each character position on the display screen has a one-to-one correspondence to a byte position in the buffer. The relative position and format of the information on the display screen is determined by where the data are written into the buffer. An update to the buffer of information which is being displayed is reflected as a change or update to the information showing on the display screen.

A number of character coded controls, called orders, have been defined for the 3270 data stream to support this mode of operation. The dominant architectural characteristics of the 3270 data stream are determined by two of these orders, SET BUFFER ADDRESS and START FIELD.

(*a*) *Set Buffer Address Order.* The set buffer address order, like all other 3270 data stream orders, has a unique code which allows it to be included in the data stream with coded graphic characters and other orders. The special syntax of the set buffer address order uses the two bytes which follow the order to define a buffer address.

When writing data into a buffer, each coded character in the data stream is examined to determine whether it is a graphic character or an order. If it is a graphic character it is written into the buffer and the pointer which was used to address that location is incremented to the next buffer location. If the coded character is an order, the specific order is identified and executed.

The set buffer address order causes the pointer to the buffer to be updated with the address contained in the two bytes immediately following the order. The next byte of data to be written into the buffer will be written into this location.

There are a number of observations to be made. First, the sequence of data in the 3270 data stream does not necessarily correspond to the reading sequence of the data (i.e., left-to-right, top-to-bottom) as it appears on the display screen. For example, data which are displayed at the bottom of the display screen may be written into the buffer before data which are shown at the top of the screen.

Secondly, the set buffer address order and the two bytes following are not written into the buffer.

Thirdly, the semantics of the two bytes following the set buffer address order are not defined by EBCDIC but are defined by the syntactical context of the set buffer address order.

Fourth, it should be noted that the two bytes following the set buffer address order specify a buffer address value not a row or column position on the display screen. That is, the data stream semantics are not oriented to or coupled with the display screen space. The buffer space is mapped to the screen space by display hardware. This mapping may be fixed and simple, or it is possible to provide a buffer which is larger than the screen space and a mapping which makes the screen space a window through which one views the buffer. By "moving" the window (or the buffer behind the window), one is able to look into different parts of the buffer.

(b) *Start Field Order*. The special syntax of the start field order defines the byte immediately following the order as an attribute byte. Execution of the start field order when writing to the buffer causes the attribute byte to be written into the buffer and encoded or tagged in such a way that it can be distinguished from the graphic characters which have been written into the buffer. The pointer used to address the buffer is incremented to point to the next location of the buffer. The start field order is not written into the buffer. Since there is a one-for-one relationship between buffer positions and screen positions, the attributes written into the buffer take up character spaces on the screen.

Attributes written into the buffer delimit fields of graphic characters. The particular value of an attribute byte determines the display attributes of the field following the attribute bytes. These display attributes are

1. protected/unprotected,
2. intensity,
3. alphanumeric/numeric only,
4. light pen selectable, and
5. an indication of whether or not the field has been modified, e.g., changed from the keyboard.

An unprotected field is one into which the operator can key graphic characters. A protected field is one into which the operator is prevented from keying in graphic characters.

Similarly, the operator is prevented from keying nonnumeric data into fields which are unprotected, numeric only.

These examples show how a data stream can be created by a program to control the format of the information shown on the display screen and also control the operations that can be performed on the displayed data by the operator.

A discussion of the full set of 3270 data stream orders will not be presented in this chapter. If the reader is interested, more details on the 3270 data stream can be found in [3]. However, it is of some interest to discuss how the 3270 data stream has been extended to accommodate new functions.

3. Extended Attribute Functions

How does one extend the 3270 data stream to support

1. multiple graphic character sets,
2. color, and

3. highlighting
   reverse video,
   blinking, and
   underscore?

The use of multiple graphic character sets means that different symbols are to be associated with different instances of a particular graphic character code. Similarly, the color and highlighting attributes are to be applied to individual graphic characters. This simply requires that this additional information must be written into the buffer with each character. The question is, how should this additional information be expressed in the data stream by the program which is controlling the display?

(*a*) *Start Field Extended Order*. One solution is to make it possible to set the extended attributes for all the graphic characters in a field to the same value. That is, all characters will have the same color or all symbols come from the same character set. This has been accomplished by defining a new order with its own unique code and with a new syntax for the bytes following the order. This order is called START FIELD EXTENDED. The general syntax of the order is to allow a variable number of attributes to be defined for the field.

The first byte following the order is a 1-byte binary integer specifying the number of attributes being defined. Each attribute is defined by two bytes. The first byte specifies the type of attribute, and the second byte specifies the value. For example, type = color, value = red, or type = highlight, value = underscore. Type = 3270 field attribute indicates that the following byte contains the attribute values defined with the START FIELD order.

(*b*) *Set Attribute Order*. Another order, the SET ATTRIBUTE order, has been defined to allow the program to specify different attributes for different characters in the same field. The syntax for the SET ATTRIBUTE order is the same as the syntax of the START FIELD EXTENDED order. The set attribute order does not cause any data to be written into the buffer; it establishes the attribute values that will be associated with graphic characters when they are subsequently written into the buffer. This order can be used to change the color of the characters within the same field.

4. Summary—3270 Data Stream

As was stated at the beginning of the discussion of the 3270 data stream, it is a character coded data stream with a number of interesting exceptions. First, there were the command and write control character bytes whose semantics were determined by their position in the data stream. Second, there were the bytes whose semantics were determined by their syntactical relationship to character coded controls called orders. Finally, we note the concept of an order which introduces a variable length context and has a type-value syntax which easily accommodates new semantics.

This discussion has shown how a program is able to control or manage the functions of a display using what is fundamentally a character coded data stream. There is no single best way to represent functions and controls in the data stream. What is absolutely essential is that both sender and receiver use the same data stream architecture.

D. Function Management Headers

1. New Function Management Requirements

Suppose one uses LU Session type 1 message exchange protocols and SCS coded character controls for program-to-keyboard/printer communication. How does one extend this architecture to treat the keyboard/printer as an operator's console and support additional I/O devices such as

1. One or more additional printers,
2. Card printers,
3. Card punches,
4. Diskettes, and
5. Disk storage.

The new functions to be managed from the program involve selecting the I/O component to be used for receiving or sending data to the program. It also involves sending commands and setup information to the selected component.

Commands must be provided to enable the program to

1. SELECT a particular device or data set,
2. SUSPEND I/O with a selected device or data set,
3. BEGIN I/O with another device or data set,
4. END the I/O operation,
5. RESUME the last suspended I/O operation, and
6. END-ABORT the active I/O operation.

The setup information that must be specified includes

1. electronic forms control information,
2. identification of the form to be mounted,
3. the number of copies to be created,
4. compaction table, and
5. the prime compression character.

Commands for managing I/O with disk storage include

1. Create data set,
2. Add record,
3. Erase record,
4. Scratch data set,
5. Password, and
6. Execute program.

Execute program causes the named program to be scheduled for execution after the LU-to-LU session has been ended.

Much of the information carried by the parameters associated with the above commands is not easily or conveniently represented with character coded byte strings. The general requirement is to establish a framework or structure in which the semantics of the data are determined by position, not by code value.

2. The Solution—Function Management Headers

The solution to this requirement is an architected structure called a function management header (FMH). If FM headers are used they must appear beginning with the initial bytes of the request unit (RU) of a chain. Whether or not FM headers are present is indicated by an FMH Indicator bit in the request header (RH).

The first two bytes of all FM headers have the same semantics. The first byte of an FM header defines its length. The first bit of the second byte indicates whether or not another FM header follows. The remaining seven bits of the second byte identify the FM header type. The semantics of the remaining bytes in the FM header are a function of the FM header type field. Syntactical relationships may be defined between certain fields. For example, a specific value in one field may require that a certain field must also be present, whereas the field will be absent for other values.

For example, if certain field values indicate that the selected device is disk storage, then the field which specifies data set name must also be present.

3. General Applicability of Function Management Headers

Although FM headers were invented to give programs control over terminals and work stations having an operator's console and multiple I/O devices of different types, the generality of the architecture of FM headers has led to the definition of FM headers which are applicable to program-to-program communication. Specifically, FM headers have been defined for CICS-to-CICS, CICS-to-IMS, and IMS-to-IMS communications.

E. Structured Fields

1. New Function Management Requirements

A number of functional enhancements to the IBM 3270 Information Display System required the definition of new data stream constructs to give programs the means to manage these new functions. One of these enhancements gives the program the ability to define and manage multiple buffers called partitions. Another enhancement gives the program the ability to load the display character generator with the bit images of application defined graphic symbols.

(*a*) *Multiple Partitions.* The multiple partition feature capitalizes on the fact that the basic semantics of the 3270 character coded data stream [3] is oriented towards writing to a buffer not to the display screen. This feature gives the program the ability to define and write into multiple buffers. It also gives the program the ability to define a mapping of each buffer (partition) to a portion of the display screen called a viewport, because it gives the operator a view into a portion of the buffer. By defining multiple viewports it is possible to have portions of multiple partitions showing on the display screen at the same time.

The capacity of a partition may exceed the display capacity of its viewport. By appropriately changing the mapping parameters it is possible to display different portions of the partition. That is, one may scroll the partition buffer past the viewport on the display screen.

(*b*) *Programmed Symbols.* The image of a graphic character or symbol can be defined by setting on the appropriate bits of a binary matrix of known resolution to create a representation of the symbol. If the dimension of the matrix is 9×16, the image of a symbol can be defined with 144 bits. Other resolutions and aspect ratios will require fewer or more bits.

The programmed symbol feature provides the program with the ability to load the display character generator with the binary images of the symbols which are to be associated with different EBCDIC graphic character code points.

Since character coded data structure, syntax, and semantics are not applicable for giving representation to the binary bit image of graphic symbols, a new kind of structure was required for carrying image information.

Similarly, the character coded structure syntax and semantics of the basic 3270 data stream was not readily adaptable to carrying the information and control requirements of the multiple partition feature.

2. The Solution—Extend the 3270 Data Stream

The key to extending the functional capability of the basic 3270 data stream was to define a new, additional command called "write structured field." The semantics of this command are that the data following the command are to be interpreted according to the architecture of structured field data streams, not according to the architecture of 3270 character coded data.

(a) *Structured Field Format.* A structured field data stream is simply a string of structured fields where each structured field is of the following general format:

Length	ID	Information Field

where (1) *length* is a 16-bit field which defines the length of the structured field; (2) *ID* uniquely identifies the structured field and implies the format and semantics of the information field. The ID is used to determine the procedure or logic that must be used to extract the information carried in the information field bit string; and (3) the *information field* is a bit string.

(b) 3270 *Extended Data Stream.* Approximately 28 structured fields have been defined for the 3270 Extended Data Stream to give programs the ability to manage the enhanced functions of the 3270 display systems.

For example, one of these structured fields is used to load the programmed character set. The first 13 bytes of the structured field contain the length, the ID value which identifies it as the load programmed character set structured field, and a number of control parameters. These parameters specify such controls as the local ID of the character set, the size of the matrix used to define the image of the graphic symbols, the manner in which the matrix was converted to a linear bit string, and the manner in which the bit string may have been compressed. The semantics of the bits in the first 13 bytes of the structured field are determined by their position.

The remaining bits of the structured field are the binary images of graphic symbols.

A 30-byte structured field is used to create a new partition. Again the semantics of the bits are determined by their position in the structured field, not by their value.

An 8-byte structured field is used to change the mapping parameters such that a different portion of the partition buffer is displayed on the screen.

3. Generality of Structured Fields.

Although the general format for structured fields was defined to provide an architectural base for encoding the functions required by a program to manage and utilize the capabilities of an enhanced 3270 display system, the generality of this architecture makes structured fields applicable to all new function management requirements.

F. Summary—Function Management Data

SNA defines three categories of RUs. One of these, function management (FM) data RUs, is used to carry the information exchanged between end users. The raw form of all RUs is a binary bit string. In order to carry information, a structure, syntax, and semantics must be imposed on the bit string. In order for two end users to communicate they must use a common data stream architecture, i.e., structure, syntax, and semantics.

This section on FM data has focused on the architecture of data streams used for program-to-terminal communication. The basic architecture for these data streams is pre-SNA and reflects a distribution of function which gives the program responsibility for managing the terminal. The program is in full control of how the information will be formatted and presented to the terminal operator. The program is also responsible for establishing the context in which the operator enters data to be read by the program.

The data streams used for program-to-terminal communication are based on the use of coded character data, a structure in which the semantics of a particular byte of data is defined by its value, not by its position. As the functional capabilities of terminals increased, it has been necessary to increase the number of functions to be encoded in the data stream so that the program can have control over and make use of these new functions.

The number of functions to be controlled by the program has quickly exceeded the number of code points available for encoding control functions. This has led to two fundamental extensions to a pure coded character data stream architecture and the introduction of structured fields.

The first extension defined special semantics for the initial bytes of a data stream. This architectural technique is used by the 3270 data stream to identify the first byte of an output data stream as a command and the second byte as a write control character.

This architectural technique is also used with SCS data streams when FM headers are used. In the case of the 3270 data stream, the command and write control character must always be present. In the case of SCS data streams, FM headers are optional; the presence or absence of FM headers is indicated by a bit in the RH.

The second architectural extension uses coded character controls to establish a context in which new semantics can be defined. The 3270 data stream orders make use of this technique.

Specific structured fields were introduced to handle new functions to be provided with 3270 display systems. However, the general format for structured fields defines a data object with four important properties:

(1) The data construct is self-delimiting.

(2) There are no constraints on the structure, syntax, or semantics which can be imposed on the bits in the information field.

(3) The data construct is self-identifying. The ID field identifies the structure, syntax, and semantics which have been imposed on the information field.

(4) Structured fields can be strung together to form a data stream. This data stream is capable of carrying all information which can be represented in a binary bit string structure.

V. Impact of Advancing Electronic Technology

The general effect of advancing electronic and communications technology is to lower the costs of logic, storage, and communications. This is most dramatically reflected in the storage and computing power being placed in terminals. The functional enhancements in terminals which lead to extensions of data stream architecture are also a reflection of these trends.

Host program management of a terminal via communications is not a simple process. Communication delays also introduce human factors problems. The process becomes more complex as more functions to be managed by the program are added to the terminal.

A point will be reached where program management of the terminal will be most easily accomplished by placing the program in a cluster controller or the terminal. Instead of program-to-terminal communication, we will have program-to-program communication.

The shift to program-to-program communication from program-to-terminal communication will be accompanied by a change in data stream structure and semantics. Terminal control semantics will be replaced by program oriented data structures and semantics.

The emphasis will shift from controlling the receiver to sending information to the receiver which the receiver has been programmed to process. The critical requirement will be to identify easily the many different pieces of information the receiver has been programmed to handle. A second important requirement will be for the sending program to select the receiving program which is to process the data stream.

Function management headers have been defined to perform this function. Structured fields seem to be ideally suited for carrying the different pieces of information a receiver has been programmed to process. The structured field ID is used to invoke the program code which can extract the information carried in the information field. What it does with this information depends entirely on the design and intent of the receiving program.

In summary, advances in electronic and communication technology will cause a shift to program-to-program communication from program-to-terminal communication. This shift will be accompanied by a change in data stream semantics which deemphasizes the concept that the sender is controlling or managing the receiver. The orientation will be a peer relationship between sender and receiver and the emphasis will be on the exchange of information. SNA function management headers and structured fields provide a solid architectural base for defining data streams to support program-to-program communications.

References

[1] J. D. Atkins, "Path control: The network level of SNA," this book, Chapter 11.
[2] SNA *Format and Protocol Reference Manual*, Data Processing Div., IBM Corp., White Plains, NY 10504, Order SC-30-3112.
[3] *SNA Logical Unit Types*, Data Processing Div., IBM Corp., White Plains, NY 10504, Order GC-20-1868-1.
[4] *SNA: Introduction to Sessions Between Logical Units*, Data Processing Div., IBM Corp., White Plains, NY 10504, Order GC-20-1869-1, pp. 3–7.

17

Videotex Terminal Protocols

Paul E. Green, Jr.

I. Introduction

In this chapter we shall describe certain higher-level terminal protocols that began with experimentation by the telecommunication administrations in Europe and which have recently become important computer communication components. They are rapidly being standardized by standards bodies, notably the CCITT. The services based on these protocols have proved to have such high function, such low terminal cost, and such good ease of use that they appear to be on their way to an explosive growth in Europe, Japan, and North America, especially if the protocols can be widely standardized.

A major problem in explaining these protocols is to untangle the confusing jargon used to describe them. Many of their names are almost identical, and additionally it is often ambiguous whether a name applies to a protocol or to the service offering that uses it. As with other chapters in this book we shall discuss the protocols, not the services. We begin by attempting to put the various terms into the common framework of Fig. 1. The terminology adopted is that given in Refs. 1–3.

The term *Videotext* (note the final "t") is often (but not universally) used to describe message services and protocols based on standard home television receivers as the presentation media, supported with suitable hardware adaptors of modest cost. The adaptors contain some form of storage for the screen image and also logic to transform the arriving byte stream into the image. Key sets on the adaptors may range from a simple one with the digits 0–9 to one with these plus a QWERTY keyset plus function keys.

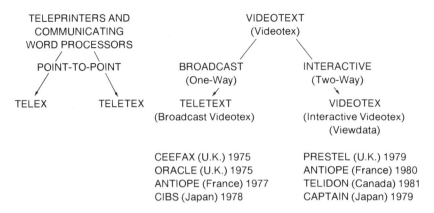

Fig. 1. Basic terminology, showing some important implementations and their field trial dates.

Teletext (again note the final "t") refers to one-way information *broadcast*, during the invisible vertical retrace interval, from a central CPU, over the cable or free space transmission medium, of byte streams defining screens of information (e.g., shopping information, weather reports, and many others). The transmitter cycles through all the frames (or "pages"). A given "page" may be selected for interception, storage in the buffer within the adaptor, and then for display, by keying the page number into buttons on the adaptor. The number of pages one can choose from is limited to 100–200 since it takes several retrace times to transmit one page and the transmitting station must cycle through all the pages in no more than, say, 30 s in the worst case, which is about as long a response time as the viewer is apt to tolerate. In spite of these limitations, Teletext seems destined for wide usage, particularly in homes, because of the low adaptor cost. In cable TV situations where it is economical to dedicate 100% of a channel's duty cycle to Teletext, instead of just the retrace interval, the number of pages available with reasonable response time is in the many thousands.

Teletext is sometimes referred to as *Broadcast Videotex* and the term *Interactive Videotex* is used for what will be called *Videotex* in this chapter. When the former convention is used, *Videotex* refers to what we are calling *Videotext*. Our *Videotex* is sometimes referred to as *Viewdata*.

Teletext is not to be confused with *Teletex*, the latter being an up-graded form of *Telex*, the service providing message exchange between keyboard-printer terminals so prevalent in Europe (*Telex* or *Teletype* in North America). The upgrade from Telex to Teletex involves increasing the speed from below 300 to 2400 bit/s and up, sending the message from an electronic buffer memory in the sending machine to a similar buffer in the receiving one, and allowing the latter to receive while unattended or while being used for a different ongoing typewriter or word processor function.

It is necessary to discuss Teletex along with the two forms of Videotext because the protocols must be coordinated. This is because it is expected that some users with Teletex terminals will in certain situations want to receive and print out Teletext pages without having to buy another terminal; similarly the same combination of TV receiver and Teletext adaptor ought to be upgradable to a Videotex terminal. The Videotex protocols described in this chapter are closely related to those being considered for use with Teletext.

Videotex is a two-way *interactive* process. Again the terminal is a TV receiver plus an adaptor, but the adaptor is somewhat more complex than a Teletext adaptor. Videotex can be used over telephone lines or over cable TV systems that provide bidirectional transmission. It is certain to have great potential for business or personal use because it is capable of supporting a full repertoire of interactive data processing services with terminal costs based on the use of consumer TV receivers and the scale economies of combining the home and business terminal market and the common Teletext and Videotext adaptor market. Not only is an interactive system using Videotex likely to be somewhat cheaper than one using commercial CRT-keyboard terminals, but the screens presented to the user can reach high levels of sophistication with low message overhead through the use of terminal microprocessors.

Videotex service, like Teletex has always been aimed at the user with a color receiver. Also, both have had, almost from the beginning, some form of graphics capability, i.e., the presentation of stationary two-dimensional diagrams and figures to go along with the usual alphanumerics. For early offerings, these graphics presentations were fairly crude, approximating (by use of the "alphamosaic" option, to be described shortly) those available in the earliest TV electronic games. The "alphageometric" option, first introduced in the Canadian Telidon system, potentially provides, within the resolution capability of the attached TV display, graphics displays whose flexibility approaches at the high end that of good commercial graphics terminals. At the low end, alphageometric terminal costs may be expected to approach (but never quite reach) those of alphamosaic terminals.

In this chapter, we shall discuss four successively newer protocols, Prestel [4], Antiope [5], Telidon [6], and PLP [7] (the American Telephone and Telegraph Company's Videotex Presentation Level Protocol). The Prestel protocol was developed by the British Post Office, Antiope by the Centre Commun d'Etudes de Télévision et Télécommunications, and Telidon by the Department of Communications, Canada. (Recent statements by DOC indicate that Telidon is being changed to comform to PLP. In this chapter we shall describe the published version of Ref. 6.) Of the four, all but PLP have been implemented to some extent in services or trials bearing the same name. Since we shall discuss here the architecture, not the implementation, the reader should keep in mind that not all the functions attributed to Telidon, for instance, have yet seen field usage. We shall also be referring to the "CCITT Recommendation," Ref. 8, which is the latest draft document attempting to pick from these four the appropriate features for international agreement.

In addition to the four protocols to be described here, we should mention that of the Character And Pattern Telephone Access Information Network (CAPTAIN) [9] developed jointly by Nippon Telegraph and Telephone Corp. and the Ministry of Posts and Telecommunications. Because of the special problems posed by full-screen Kanji character presentation, this system is somewhat different from the other four.

There are five sorts of information to be somehow encoded and sent to the Videotex terminal for conversion into the proper patterns on the TV raster:

(1) *Alphanumeric Option.* This involves sending the identities of letters and numerals to be displayed left–right and top–bottom, and is concerned, roughly speaking, with those byte patterns of standard alphabets not used for the data link control function described in Chapter 4, Fig. 2.

(2) *Alphamosaic Option.* When this option is in effect, a given byte stands for one of 64 patterns of light and dark which are placed on the screen instead of alphanumeric characters. The cell formerly occupied by an alphanumeric character is now occupied by one of the 64 possible two-wide three-high patterns of light and dark. Clearly, so long as the terminal displays rows of cells contiguously in the vertical direction, simple low-resolution graphics may be displayed in this way at a low additional terminal cost.

(3) *DRCS Option* (Dynamically redefinable character sets). We have already met the powerful notion of down-line loading of special custom character shapes in Chapter 16. In the DRCS option of Videotex (at least the more modern versions), the loadable characters are not restricted to shapes that occupy one standard character cell, because the latter can be of arbitrary size. In principle, this not only allows special alphanumeric or mosaic characters, but also other shapes to be created, stored, and then displayed on command. In practice the more elaborate such figures take an impractically long time to transmit. Clearly, with DRCS, more logic and memory are required in the adaptor than with alphanumeric and mosaic byte streams and transmission time is large. Most of the simpler services to date are limited to these two options for this reason.

(4) *Alphageometric Option.* Many limitations of mosaic and DRCS graphics, including inefficiency in transmission channel utilization, are removed by substituting for character or mosaic identities certain serial instructions to a microcomputer in the terminal telling it what picture to draw. For example, a circle is specified by the one of a repertoire of *Picture*

Description Instructions (PDIs) that specifies "circle" and gives also the location of two diametrically opposite points (plus such *attributes* as color, interior shading, and line texture).

(5) *Alphaphotographic Option.* Various proposals exist for transmitting still color images that are to be displayed full-screen or in an inset. Some of these have been tried experimentally, but since no consensus has been reached even on which general approach to take, we shall not be very much concerned with this option.

Before proceeding to a discussion of the protocol by which one option is selected, and more detail for each, we emphasize that these protocols fit into the layered architecture at the presentation or protocol conversion level (Chapters 1 and 2). In what follows, it is assumed that whatever link control, routing, session establishment, and other protocols are required are already functioning.

II. Shifting between Videotex Options

The selection of one of the Videotex options amounts to selecting a character set or code table appropriate to each. Figure 2 shows the layout of a standard 7-bit code, such as ASCII (Chapter 4, Fig. 2). Following computer jargon, let us refer to each possible pattern of seven bits as a *code point*. All code points for which *both* two least significant bits are 0 are reserved for *control codes* and therefore belong to the "*C*" set, the rest to the "*G*" set.

The *C*0 set (Ref. 8) is shown in Fig. 3. Note that in the figure decimal numbers corresponding to the rows and column bit patterns are spelled out so that we can designate a given code point as "(column)/(row)"; for example ESC ("escape") is 1/11.

Among the code points in the *C*0 set, as shown in Fig. 3, there are five (SO, SI, SS2, SS3, and ESC) which allow an arbitrarily rich variety of "extensions" or "shifts," (analogous to upper case on a typewriter) to different interpretations of both the *C* set and the *G* set, and also allow shifting back again. The way this has all been standardized by ISO (Ref. 10) is summarized in Figure 4. The dotted area in the center of the figure indicates the *in-use code table* (repertoire of *C* and *G* points used by both protocol partners.) Columns 0 and 1 of the in-use table practically always contain the *C*0 set of Fig. 3. As shown by the arrowheads, the shift characters (ESC, etc) have the effect of bringing a new load into the receiver's in-use table, or (in the case of *C*1, to be discussed) into an extra piece of storage.

Let us suppose that the *G*0 set is in use, usually corresponding to the alphanumeric option. (the *G*0 code set is shown in Fig. 5.) Suppose the

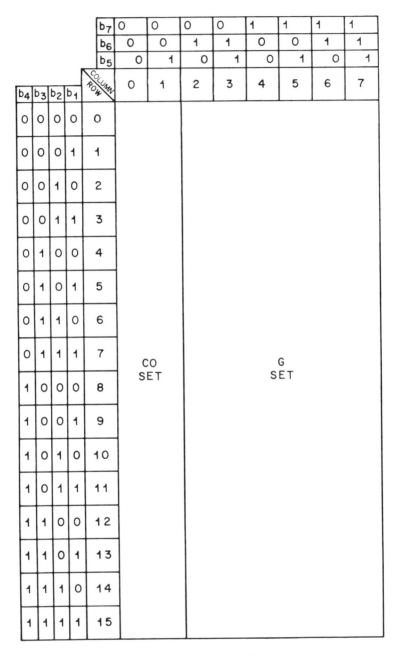

Fig. 2. Seven-bit in-use table.

ROW＼COLUMN	0	1
0	NUL	②
1	②	③
2	②	③
3	②	③
4	②	③
5	ENQ	②
6	②	②
7	①	②
8	APB	CAN
9	APF	SS2
10	APD	①
11	APU	ESC
12	CS	①
13	APR	SS3
14	SO	③
15	SI	③

Fig. 3. The standard CCITT CO control set of code points. 1 = Reserved for future study, 2 = Data link control characters (Chap. 4), 3 = Reserved device control characters. Others include APF = active position forward, APB = active position backward, APD = active position down, APU = active position up, APR = active position return, APH = active position home (upper left corner), CS = clear screen and return to home position, SP = space. (Ref. 8)

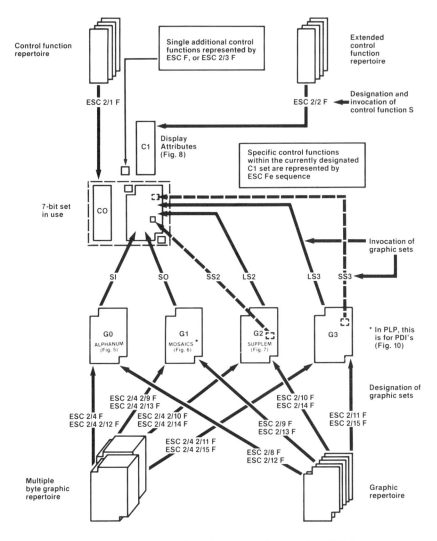

Fig. 4. Extension scheme for 7-bit Videotex codes. (Ref. 9)

sending protocol partner wishes to shift to the alphamosaic option (given in many implementations by $G1$), one of two forms of which is given in Fig. 6, and after a while shift back to alphanumerics. To perform the first shift he sends the SHIFT OUT control code SO (i.e., $0/14$), which has the effect of overlaying $G1$ onto $G0$ in the in-use table and later on SHIFT IN (SI = $0/15$) to shift back again. (SO and SI are "locking" in that their effect persists until there is another shift.) And similarly for sets $G2$ and $G3$ using the SS

COLUMN ROW	2	3	4	5	6	7
0	SPACE	0	@	P	`	p
1	!	1	A	Q	a	q
2	"	2	B	R	b	r
3		3	C	S	c	s
4		4	D	T	d	t
5	%	5	E	U	e	u
6	&	6	F	V	f	v
7	'	7	G	W	g	w
8	(	8	H	X	h	x
9	)	9	I	Y	i	y
10	*	:	J	Z	j	z
11	+	;	K		k	
12	,	<	L		l	|
13	−	=	M		m	
14	.	>	N		n	
15	/	?	O	①	o	▨

Fig. 5. Alphanumerics: the CCITT G0 code set.

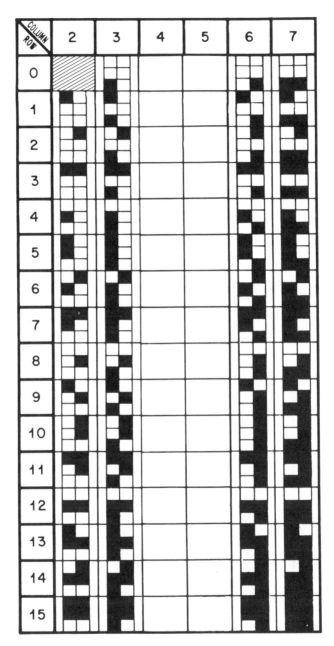

Fig. 6. Alphamosaics: the CCITT G1 code set for serial mode.

(SINGLE SHIFT) control codes, except that the in-use G set reverts to the previous in-use set $G0$ or $G1$ after a single character. For example, $G2$ (Fig. 7) is used for special symbols (e.g., #) and for diacritical marks required in many languages. The shift back after a single character saves a shift back byte. Code points from Column 4 are *non*spacing—so that if it is desired to display "ñ", sending " ̃ " followed by "n" causes first " ̃ " to be displayed in the *active position* on the screen, then "n" to be added in the same place; only then does the active position move to the next cell. Code points in columns 2, 3, 5, 6, and 7 are *spacing* code points, as are all of $G0$, $G1$, and $G2$. (As shown in Fig. 4, ISO has recently added two new locking-shift characters LS2 and LS3 which are available as substitutes for SS2 and SS3 when desired.)

It is to be expected that, CCITT standard G sets notwithstanding, different Videotex services will choose to adopt slightly different $G0$, $G1$, $G2$, and $G3$ sets. In the terminal adaptor, the standard character sets $C0$ and $G1$–$G3$ (if used) are stored in read-only memory (ROM). A terminal that may from time to time need to receive frames from different systems can (at the expense of more memory) have a library of these and (as shown at the bottom of Fig. 4) a member F of this library can be designated for potential use in the in-use table by sending ESC (i.e., $1/11$) followed by the x character shown, followed by the prearranged F character.

Conceivably it may be desired to change even the $C0$ set. As shown in the top part of Fig. 4, some member F of a library of $C0$ sets of 32 code points can be brought in upon receipt of ESC followed by $2/1$, followed by F. A 32 code point *extension* (not replacement) to whatever $C0$ set is in use, the $C1$ set, can be brought into the extra piece of storage from the $C1$ library upon reception of ESC, $2/2$, F, where F is the byte designating the library number. The $C1$ set is used to control the attributes of the presented elements, as will be described in Sections IV and VI.

To date, the CCITT has agreed upon the code points shown in Figs. 5–7, and also agreed on an alternate form of Fig. 6, and a $C1$ set, both for the so-called parallel mode of alphamosaics. Whether "serial" or "parallel" treatment of the arriving byte stream at the receiver is to be preferred has been a somewhat arcane controversy that has existed between the British Prestel and French Antiope proponents and boils down to whether or not to save on storage in the adaptor in exchange for having to leave a space horizontally every time a color change occurs. This is touched on in Section IV. The controversy is in the process of being resolved by the proposal [11] of CEPT (Conference of European Post and Telecommunication Administrations), whose scheme for accommodating both Prestel and Antiope is being considered by CCITT along with PLP. Among several other additional things that the CEPT proposal includes is a set of 32 more characters which, when added to those of Fig. 6, provided somewhat more attractive graphics.

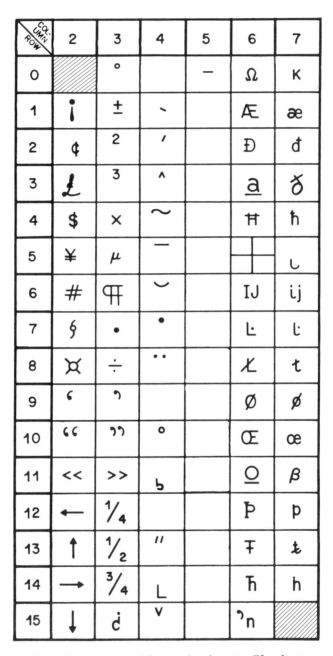

Fig. 7. Supplementary alphanumerics: the CCITT G2 code set.

III. Dynamically Redefinable Character Sets

DRCS is analogous to the alphamosaic option except that instead of 64 standardized characters (Fig. 6), a set of up to 96 (16 rows, 6 columns) customized characters can be down-loaded, each having potentially up to the full screen resolution. These new characters are to be presented as before, namely, occupying standard character cells in left-right top-down raster order on the screen. DRCS is used mainly for the following:

(1) Special characters, for example those found in hotel and restaurant guides (knife-and-fork, Maltese cross), may be defined and loaded downline in preparation for eventual access by the terminal to a database of such material.

(2) Line drawings may be built up from suitably chosen character shapes. In our example of a circle, the character set would be a set of suitably chosen arcs.

Using DRCs, large transmission time is exchanged for the expense of anticipating the building into the terminal ROM a large number of alphabets.

DRCS has been implemented experimentally in several trial Videotex services, at least on a pilot demonstration basis, but the details differ widely. The CCITT has adopted no detailed standard to date [8]. One architectural description is that given as part of AT & T's PLP document [7]. As we shall see, the special C1 control set (Fig. 8) that PLP defines supports a rich repertoire of options. One way to downline loading a character after the C1 set is brought into the in-use table, is to send DEFDRCS, followed by the bit pattern specifying which code point is to have its presented character shape defined, followed by a bit string defining the pattern of dark–light within a character cell (details unspecified), followed by END. Then the character shape of the next code point in increasing order is similarly downline loaded.

PLP has a way of defining dynamically the new DRCS character size, which then applies to the entire screen while it is presented. Earlier protocols do not have this option.

IV. Specifying Color and Other Attributes of Alphanumerics and Alphamosaics

So far in the discussion, we have vaguely referred to alphanumeric, mosaic, or dynamically reloadable characters as "patterns of light and dark." In actual use, however, it is necessary to be more specific, in fact, to consider several *attributes* of the symbol presented in a character cell, for

COLUMN / ROW	4	5
0	DEF MACRO	PROTECT
1	DEFP MACRO	EDC$_1$
2	DEFT MACRO	EDC$_2$
3	DEF DRCS	EDC$_3$
4	DEF TEXTURE	EDC$_4$
5	END	WORD WRAP ON
6	REPEAT	WORD WRAP OFF
7	REPEAT TO EOL	SCROLL ON
8	REVERSE VIDEO	SCROLL OFF
9	NORMAL VIDEO	UNDER LINE START
10	SMALL TEXT	UNDER LINE STOP
11	MED TEXT	FLASH CURSOR
12	NORMAL TEXT	STEADY CURSOR
13	DOUBLE HEIGHT	CURSOR OFF
14	BLINK START	BLINK STOP
15	DOUBLE SIZE	UNPRO-TECT

Fig. 8. Control set C1 for AT & T's PLP. (Ref. 7.)

example:

- Height and width of the character cell, which determines the number of characters per line and lines per screen.
- Color.
- Background color.
- Whether background is a color or is material from some other transmission, e.g., a live TV picture (*transparency*).
- Blinking or steady, and if blinking, what color is on when the character is off.

These attributes are set by one sort of protocol for alphanumerics, alphamosaics, and DRCS characters and by a completely different scheme for alphageometrics in Telidon. In PLP, attribute coding uses a single unified set of commands, as described at the end of Section V. In this section we shall confine the discussion to the CCITT proposals for alphanumerics, alphamosaics, and DRCS, deferring alphageometric attribute control to the next section.

The CCITT defines two alternative *modes* for attribute encoding: *serial* and *parallel*. The serial mode (introduced by Prestel) assumes that changes in character attribute occur only in interword spacings where a BLANK occurs anyhow and that for mosaics one does not object to a blank cell whenever the attribute (e.g., color) changes. (Prestel graphics can often be spotted by looking for such dark spaces horizontally at color boundaries.) This inconvenience buys the implementation simplicity of having all the character cells of a frame appear sequentially in the frame buffer; that is, the frame buffer is a map of the frame presented. Any byte defining an attribute of all characters to follow (until changed by the arrival of the next attribute byte) is stored in the buffer but is displayed as a blank (i.e., the background color), by the following protocol.

Prestel, Antiope, and CCITT specify $C1$ sets in which, unlike PLP's $C1$ set (Fig. 8), the foreground and background colors are designated by specific code points. To set a new attribute, say *yellow*, one sends ESC followed by the $C1$ code point for yellow followed by the character string to be displayed. Before the "yellow" byte can reach the frame buffer it is intercepted and interpreted by the color control circuitry, then the most significant bit is complemented from 1 to 0, and only then is the character stored in the frame buffer. Since the $C1$ set is drawn from columns 4 and 5 of the code table and needs to be distinguished from the corresponding character codes upon reception on the line, the preceding ESC tells the receiver to treat any following column 4 or 5 character as a $C1$ code point, and to flip the bit before storing in the frame buffer. Since all $C0$ characters (i.e., 0 high-order bit) are treated by the display circuitry as BLANK anyhow, the desired nondisplay is achieved. It should be pointed out that by convention, normally arriving $C0$ bytes (including ESC) never reach the frame store, only those with a 1 least significant bit (unless preceded by ESC).

All of this means that in serial mode the number of bytes of frame store need be no larger than the number of character positions on the screen, and the frame store is a map of the screen appearance byte by byte. The originators of the parallel mode (Antiope) reasoned that such parsimoniousness was unwarranted and suggested an approach which would allow every attribute to change as frequently as with every new character position over the entire screen, if one were willing to pay for several times the storage in this extreme case. The $C1$ set (again lying in columns 4 and 5 and again invoked by preceding each with an ESC) is slightly different from the serial mode $C1$ set. Now, however, the arriving $C1$ bytes are not bit-flipped and used as spacing characters in the frame store but are stored elsewhere, the amount of extra storage required depending on how many of them are permitted to appear per frame, an implementation option. As the "active position" progresses (left–right and top–down) the most recent set of attributes can be considered to "move with it." The active position does not move unless a character ($G0$, $G2$, and most of $G1$) arrives or some *format effector* like backspace (APB in Fig. 3) arrives. (Remember that $G0$, $G2$, and most of $G1$ are spacing characters.)

It is clear that the blank-producing property of the Prestel serial mode could be repaired by a new protocol that uses the backspace character APB to revisit the otherwise blank screen position, and assumes some extra storage for the attribute changes. This is what is done in the British Prestend proposal.

Other attributes defined by code points in the $C1$ set include blinking ("flash") and stop blinking ("steady").

V. Attribute Specification in Telidon and PLP

When the mode of graphics presentation is geometric rather than mosaic, a different way of specifying the attributes is required. Instead of preceding a string of characters with a single $C1$ byte (e.g., *yellow*), one precedes the particular Picture Description Instruction (PDI) for the graphic element to be drawn (e.g., a circle) by one or more PDIs just for attributes. Both Telidon and PLP provide an extendable number of different colors, as follows. Each PDI (of any kind) consists of an *opcode* of one byte, followed by one or more *operands*, each of which consists of one or more bytes of *numeric information* needed in executing the PDI function. In our example of a circle to be drawn in yellow, the PDI that causes the circle to be drawn is preceded by the one that causes the circle to be yellow. The operand field of the former, consisting of one of more bytes, specifies one of a number of different colors available, which depends on the number of bytes of operand. For color control, there are six bits of each operand byte available for color (arranged GRBGRB) so that, even with one byte, 63 resolvable colors are available, plus either transparent or black (compared to the 7 in the C1-based Prestel and Antiope schemes just described). With half a byte, 7 are available in principle with PLP. If more resolvable colors are needed, additional operand bytes can be appended.

An important property of Telidon and PLP is that terminals of varying degrees of complexity can simultaneously receive the same presentation material. Color resolution is one example. The simplest color terminal with only 7 colors would be programmed to ignore operand bits beyond the first half byte of the operand. At the same time, if the lower-order bytes are present, the more expensive terminals could display a larger number of different colors.

Resolution is another example of this coexistence feature. A point on the usable portion of the TV display (the *unit screen*) has its x value expressed by some binary number between 0 and $+1$, and similarly with its y value. Then an operand expressing position may consist of several bytes, the first expressing x and y to 3-bit precision; adding the next gives 6-bit precision, and so forth. Terminals with poorer resolution simply ignore the lower-order bits and display the same material as higher function terminals, but with degraded resolution.

The specification of the colors is left in more or less the form just described in the Telidon architecture [6], but PLP has dealt with it in great generality [7]. In particular, the use of *color maps* allows the increased flexibility of downline loading of colors to high-function terminals just as DRCS does for character shapes. Two color opcodes are available with PLP, SET COLOR and SELECT COLOR. These can be used for one of three *color modes*, 0, 1, or 2 that can be set via the SELECT COLOR PDI:

0—This is the scheme just described. The in-use drawing color is explicitly defined by the arrival of the SET COLOR PDI with the operands giving the color values as just described. (Each operand byte has bits GRBGRB.) The color remains in use and is applied to later arriving byte streams, until changed, for example by a later SET COLOR PDI.

1—The color is *indirectly* specified. SET COLOR is used to downline load a particular color value (given by the operand) into a particular address in a look-up table, the color map. The address is given by the operand of a preceding SELECT COLOR PDI with a particular bit set to 0 in its opcode. By repeating this process, the map can be built up, and then a particular entry later invoked by sending SELECT COLOR with the opcode bit set to 1.

2—This mode is identical to color mode 1 except that both foreground and background color are specified in the operand of SELECT COLOR which is then twice as long. (Mode 1 assumes that the background color already in use is the desired one.)

If this is confusing, it is helpful to keep in mind that the operand of SET COLOR is always a set of bits specifying a color, while that of SELECT COLOR gives a table address. PLP includes a complete definition of the encoding of colors to an arbitrary number of significant bits. It also includes a PDI for blinking whose parameters include such things as the two colors, their time duration, and it even allows different concurrent blinking of different parts of the screen.

Telidon and PLP handle attributes for text characters (alphanumerics and mosaics) somewhat differently. PLP is slightly more general in this respect. Color is handled as just described for geometrics. Others are controlled by the TEXT PDI, which commands that a choice of these attributes be applied to the characters.

- Character size (in terms of fractions of the unit screen vertically and horizontally).
- Character rotation (right-side-up, 90°, upside-down, or 270°).
- Cursor style (three standard styles, plus a code point for invoking one custom cursor.) The cursor is a special mark (e.g., underline) used in alphanumeric, mosaic, and DRCS to indicate the position of the next received character. It also exists in alphageometric mode, where it may or may not be related to the position of the drawing point.
- Direction of cursor advance (right, left, up, down).
- Intercharacter spacing (including proportional).
- Interrow spacing.

The character size encoding is extendable in its fineness of spatial resolution by appending extra bytes as described earlier for colors and screen resolution.

VI. The Alphageometric Option

As we have indicated, this option exploits modern LSI technology by exchanging terminal logical complexity for speed and lowered communication costs when graphics are to be presented. Instead of regarding the screen as consisting of an array of character positions as with alphamosaics, the screen is regarded as a continuous area on which any point may be defined by a set of coordinates to whatever resolution the screen resolution and terminal memory cost will permit. A given complex shape having various colors, textures of solid fill, and bordering line texture can be built up at the receiver from a sequence of received Picture Definition Instructions. Figure 9 shows an example using the Telidon protocol. Notice Note 3, which points

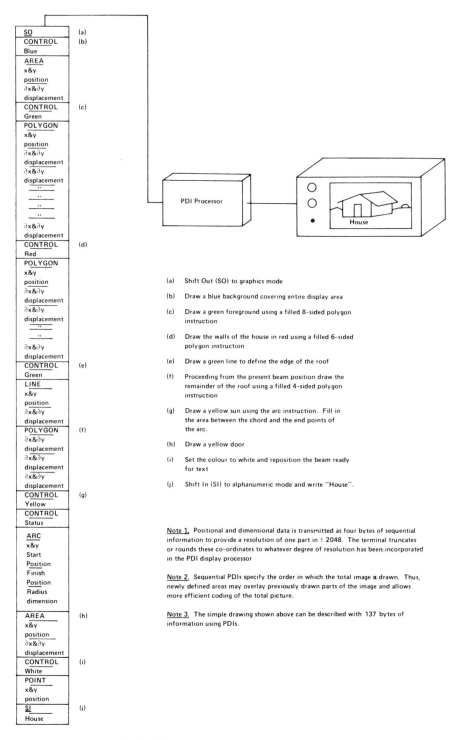

Fig. 9. Example of Telidon's use of a PDI sequence to define an image. (Ref. 6.)

out that only 137 bytes had to be transmitted. Conceivably, this same diagram could be generated by DRCS but at the expense of an enormously long byte stream.

The reader may have wondered how the shifting procedure described in Section II brings into the in-use table the C and G sets required for the alphageometric option. The answer is that the proper $C1$ set (Fig. 8) is brought into the extra storage for columns 4 and 5 by ESC followed by 2/2 as explained in Section II, while the new $G1$ set (Fig. 10) which includes the PDI opcode code points is brought into the $G1$ table from the library by ESC, 2/9, F and thence into the in-use table (columns 2–7) by SO. The code points shown in Figs. 8 and 10 are for PLP. The CCITT alphageometric code points for $G1$, adopted from Telidon, are slightly different, as indicated by the shading in Fig. 10. Unless otherwise specified, PLP uses $G0$ for alphanumerics and $G2$ for supplementary characters like everyone else, but relegates the alphamosaics to $G3$ (not $G1$) and uses $G1$ for PDI code points.

We shall now discuss in more detail the PLP alphageometric protocol. The PDIs required to construct geometric shapes include POINT, LINE, ARC, RECTANGLE, and POLYGON. The INCREMENTAL LINE PDI is used to construct images that consist of sequences of points. DOMAIN controls the picture element (pel) size used in executing these six commands, FIELD makes inset areas, and TEXTURE controls texture of lines and interior fill.

DOMAIN includes in its operand one or more bytes to define the dimensions dX and dY of the *logical pel*, the width and height of the spot used to draw the geometric figure. (It does not operate on alphanumeric or mosaic characters.) This ability to control the "stroke width" of a diagram is an important advantage of PLP over its predecessors. Incidentally, one could think of Prestel or Antiope alphamosaics on a 40×20 character screen of vertically contiguous characters as having a fixed stroke width of $1/60$ of the screen vertically and $1/80$ horizontally—not very fine resolution, when compared to some 200×240 pels intrinsically available through the RF input or up to 500×600 by going directly into the "RGB" color video amplifiers. DOMAIN also has operand bits that specify how many bytes are to be used in the operands of POINT, LINE, etc. to define an x, y coordinate.

TEXTURE sets up line textures (solid, dotted, dashed, or dot-dashed) and fill textures (solid, vertical hatched, horizontal hatched, cross hatched, plus four programmable textures). TEXTURE also allows highlighting of filled rectangles, arcs, and polygons, e.g., drawing their perimeters in black.

The PDIs DOMAIN, TEXTURE, BLINK, SET COLOR, and SELECT COLOR (and one or two others) that we have already discussed are *control* PDIs since they control attributes of the presentation. The second class of PDIs, the six *geometric primitives* (POINT, LINE, ARC, RECTANGLE, POLYGON, and INCREMENTAL LINE) are used to create within the unit screen graphic images

COLUMN ROW	2	3	4	5	6	7
0	C O N T R O L	R E C T				
1						
2						
3						
4	P O I N T	P O L Y				
5						
6						
7			NUMERIC DATA			
8	L I N E	I N C R				
9						
10						
11						
12	A R C	C O N T R O L				
13						
14						
15						

Fig. 10a. Picture Definition Instruction (PDI) code points for PLP. Basic layout. Adapted from Ref. 7.

COLUMN / ROW	2	3	4	5	6	7
0	RESET	RECT (OUT-LINED)				
1	DOMAIN	RECT (FILLED)				
2	TEXT	SET & RECT (OUT-LINED)				
3	TEXTURE	SET & RECT (FILLED)				
4	POINT SET (ABS)	POLY (OUT-LINED)				
5	POINT SET (REL)	POLY (FILLED)				
6	POINT (ABS)	SET & POLY (OUT-LINED)				
7	POINT (REL)	SET & POLY (FILLED)	NUMERIC DATA			
8	LINE (ABS)	FIELD				
9	LINE (REL)	INCR POINT				
10	SET & LINE (ABS)	INCR LINE				
11	SET & LINE (REL)	INCR POLY (FILLED)				
12	ARC (OUT-LINED)	SET COLOR				
13	ARC (FILLED)	CONTROL STATUS (WAIT)				
14	SET & ARC (OUT-LINED)	SELECT COLOR				
15	SET & ARC (FILLED)	BLINK				

Fig. 10b. Picture Definition Instruction (PDI) code points for PLP. Specific code points. Shading indicates additions made to Telidon. Adapted from Ref. 7.

that have the attributes given in the operands of the currently effective control PDIs. Each geometric PDI has four possible forms, and thus four possible opcodes (See Fig. 10).

POINT is the most basic primitive and sets in its operand (one or more bytes) the x–y coordinates at which to commence drawing (the current *drawing point*). It may or may not actually draw the dot, and for each of these options x, y may be specified either in absolute value or as a displacement from the preexisting drawing point. This accounts for the four forms of POINT.

LINE is used to draw a straight line, in the currently commanded color and texture, between an initial drawing point and a final one. After execution, the latter becomes the new drawing point. LINE (ABSOLUTE) and LINE (RELATIVE) both start from the current drawing point and go to either an absolute x, y value or by a displacement, respectively. SET AND LINE (ABSOLUTE) specifies both points in absolute coordinates and SET AND LINE (RELATIVE) specifies the initial point absolutely and the final one relatively.

ARC draws arcs from an initial to a final point through an intermediate point, or it draws circles. In the latter case, the initial and final points are coincident and the third point is taken to be diametrically opposite. ARC (OUTLINED) and SET AND ARC (OUTLINED) use two or three operands, respectively, to define the three points. In the former, the current drawing point is implicitly the starting point. ARC (FILLED) and SET AND ARC (FILLED) do the same except that the space between the arc and a chord joining the end points is filled with the in-use color and texture. Four RECTANGLE commands do much the same things, the RECT PDIs specifying in the operands the x and y dimensions, and in the case of SET AND RECT PDIs, the starting point additionally.

POLYGON is used to draw a series of lines connecting up to 256 (or more) points, the initial and final point coinciding. The number of vertices, each of which can be acute or obtuse, is determined solely by the number of operands. This PDI allows figures to be built up in the manner of "connect-the-dots" puzzles, but with the restriction that in the filled versions the figure must be a simple closed one; that is, no two nonadjacent sides may cross. The four opcodes are different from one another in the same way as those for ARC and RECTANGLE.

INCREMENTAL POINT is preceded by a FIELD PDI which establishes a *field* or rectangular drawing area within which INCREMENTAL POINT operates. (FIELD also can be used to make an inset area for text and can define a terminal-operator-usable region for user input and text editing.) The operands of FIELD give the placement, height, and width of the field. With INCREMENTAL POINT, the alphaphotographic option can be implemented, although very tediously. An image can be described as a string of color specifications that replace the in-use color attributes but no other attributes, and which are deposited in a raster sequential manner within the field, pel by pel. Horizontal flyback occurs automatically upon reaching the edge of the field. When the top or bottom of the field is reached, instead of a vertical retrace, as with TV, the image begins to scroll within the field area until the operand is terminated.

Perhaps the most sophisticated alphaphotographic approach is Picture Prestel [12] which uses run-length coding techniques and special data compression algorithms based on human color perception to cut down on transmission and storage requirements.

VII. Other Features of PLP

We have seen how the big step in Videotex protocol transmission economy and generality came when Telidon introduced the alphageometric option. The further refinements added in the PLP protocol of AT & T have not only filled in some of the missing gaps in Telidon—e.g., actual color and texture encodings—but have also made important extensions of function.

Perhaps the most important of these is the *Macro-PDI* function. This capability allows any presentation byte string to be downline loaded to the terminal and represented with a single character name, say X. Subsequently, whenever a suitable macro-PDI with operand X is received, the entire buffered string is processed and the results presented, as though it had just been received. Up to 96 macro-PDIs can be defined simultaneously, corresponding to the 96 code points in a G set. Macro-PDIs can be nested within macro-PDIs.

The string called X can be so designated with the DEF MACRO control character from $C1$ (Fig. 8) followed by X followed by the byte string, followed by END (or another DEF MACRO or a DEFP MACRO, a DEFT MACRO or a DEF DRCS, for which see Section III). DEEP MACRO works just like DEF MACRO except that in addition to storing the string it concurrently executes it.

DEFT MACRO gives the terminal the important new function of *sending* Videotex byte strings from the terminal to the CPU or another terminal. In our example, the key X on the QWERTY keyset could then become a function key triggering the execution in the CPU of user-written code.

To summarize the other features that PLP adds to its predecessors, we list (1) the provision of a user (*unprotected*) inset on the screen for use in text editing, for example, and implemented using FIELD; (2) downline loadable textures using DEF TEXTURE; (3) a choice of cursor shapes; (4) alphaphotographic capability using INCR POINT; (5) reverse video (swapping the in-use drawing and background colors); (6) scrolling; (7) underlining;

(8) proportional spacing; (9) "word wrap," i.e., causing a string of characters that might be many lines long to have a "line feed-carriage return" function occur when each line is full; and (10) code points for 8-bit alphabets. (Since Teletex uses such alphabets, there are important Videotex–Teletex compatibility issues here.) Functions (1), (6), (7), (8), (9), and (10) offer obvious word processing possibilities.

VIII.   Conclusions

In this chapter we have traced the evolution of Videotex architecture and protocols from alphanumerics to alphageometrics, from the original Prestel to PLP. Although the protocol proposals are evolving rapidly, the services based on them are not always that easy to change when there is a large base of installed terminals. Therefore, the reader may expect to find even the oldest material in this chapter to be of current interest.

It is tempting to speculate on whether the next few improvements will be major or minor. It is the author's opinion that they will be minor. The architects have done their work at the basic level to the extent that protocol details are in place for as rich a variety of character and graphics function as will be needed over the next few years. The problem now is not only to reach wide agreement between contending parties, but to make these services widely available; and this requires good head-end software systems and lower terminal costs. Three key factors will influence terminal costs: the availability of standard Videotex LSI chips, lower memory cost, and a move by TV manufacturers to provide new receivers with access to the direct color "RGB" inputs, bypassing the resolution-degrading RF and IF amplifiers.

References

[1] E. Sigel, Editor, *Videotext, the Coming Revolution in Home/Office Information Retrieval*, New York: Harmony Div. of Crown Publishers, 1980.

[2] Butler Cox and Partners Ltd., *International Standardization*, vol. 2 of Videotex Report Series, 26-30 Holborn Viaduct, London EC1A2BP, Oct. 1980.

[3] Conference Proceedings, *Viewdata 1981*, Oct. 1981, Argyle House, Northwood Hills HA6IT5, Middlesex, U.K.

[4] K. E. Clarke, The Post Office Viewdata Service, *J. Royal Television Soc.*, vol. 17, no. 5.

[5] B. Marti *et al.*, The Antiope Videotex System, *IEEE Trans Consumer Electron.*, July 1979.

[6] H. G. Bown, C. D. O'Brien, W. Sawchuk, and J. R. Storey, *Picture Description Instructions for the Telidon Videotex System*, Commun. Res. Ctr. Technical Note 699-E, Dept. of Commun., Ottawa, November 1979.

[7] *Videotex Standard Presentation Level Protocol*, Am. Tel. and Telegraph Co., 5 Wood Hollow Rd., Parsippany, New Jersey 07054, May 1981.

[8]   *International Information Exchange for Interactive Videotex*, CCITT Draft Recommendation S.100, Document AP-VII-No. 88E, Geneva, 1980.

[9]   T. Kumamoto and S. Ohkoshi, CAPTAIN System Features, Proc. of *Viewdata '80* pp. 95–105, March, 1980, Argyle House, Northwood Hills, HA6 IT5, Middlesex, U.K.

[10] *Code Extension Technique for use with the 7- and 8-bit Coded Character Sets*, ISO-2022.2, International Standards Organization, Torino, May 1981.

[11] *Current Status of Harmonization for Videotex Display Aspects and Transmission Coding for 26 Countries of Europe*, Contribution D41 to CCITT Study Group VIII, Geneva, Oct., 1981.

[12] K. E. Clarke, The Application of Picture Coding Techniques to Viewdata, Proc. IEEE Consumer Electronics Conference, Chicago, June 1980.

PART VI

Network Interconnection

Having completed our journey through the various computer network protocol layers, we now turn our attention to the first of two large areas of current research and development interest that lie outside the subject of providing better design for protocol layers.

The topic of the present section is the interconnection of otherwise autonomous networks. There are several motivations for wanting to make such interconnections. Having a single large network may be impractical because of address space limitations, limitation on how much one network management operator can handle, the need to localize the effect of configuration changes, and the existence of nonoverlapping patterns of ownership and organizational jurisdiction. As to the last of these, the increasingly relaxed attitude of regulatory bodies (particularly in the U.S.) toward unregulated interenterprise communication acts to encourage the interconnection of networks belonging to different corporations with some commonality of interests, for example, a large manufacturer and one of its suppliers.

The connection may be between homogeneous networks (e.g., ones using the same release level of the same computer manufacturer's networking products) or it may be a heterogeneous interconnection. Clearly the least difficult inhomogeneity to handle is one between different release levels of a common product line (e.g., SNA or DNA) or different variants of a common design (e.g., different X.25-based packet-switched networks or different ARPAnet structures). However, the big challenge to be met in the next few years concerns inhomogeneous network interconnections that will require significant protocol conversions across many protocol layers. The surface has barely been scratched on this problem, and yet it will surely have to be solved, because all the evidence indicates that at the same time that pressures to interconnect are growing, implementations based on different network architectures are prospering independently.

The mechanism by which the interconnection is effected at the point of contact is the *gateway*, a special node that belongs simultaneously to the two networks. The gateway may be implemented as a machine dedicated to the purpose or it may be a special piece of software running in a CPU that is also running user applications.

Depending partly on the amount of inhomogeneity, the gateway may involve all of the protocol layers or only the lower ones. For example, if only the addressing, routing, and network flow control functions need to be managed separately, a gateway functioning only up through the network level (Part IV) would suffice. The gateway would splice together two access path portions involving only these lower layers; there would be only two end users. The higher layers would be absent in the gateway. The other extreme would be to have a special application program ("pass through") within the same gateway serving simultaneously at the end of two separately established and managed access paths within the two networks. It might be the case that conversion at all protocol layers, including those described in Part V would be required in these very inhomogeneous interconnections.

In the present volume, all we can hope to present on this evolving topic is a sampling of the research and experimentation in progress. Chapters 18 and 19 both describe approaches that involve only the lower protocol layers of the interconnected networks. Chapter 18 provides an overview of the subject and treats two homogeneous interconnection examples which are being handled in different ways: the CCITT X.75 recommendation for interconnecting X.25-based packet networks, and the ARPAnet Interconnect structure. Chapter 19 describes a completely worked out and proto-typed system built at Xerox Palo Alto Research Center to interconnect such varied networks as the contention-based Ethernet in-plant networks and a packet radio network.

18

Internetwork Protocol Approaches

Jonathan B. Postel

I. Introduction

The motivations for constructing computer networks—data and program exchange and sharing, remote access to resources, etc.—are also motivations for interconnecting networks. This follows from the observation that the power of a communication system is related to the number of potential participants.

This chapter first discusses a few key concepts involved in computer communication networks. The view that computer networks provide an interprocess communication facility is presented. The datagram and virtual circuit services are compared. The interconnection device or gateway is discussed. The relation of the interconnection issues to the Open Systems Architecture is described.

In this chapter, two approaches to internetworking are characterized: the public data network system as implied by the CCITT X.75 recommendation and the ARPA experimental internetwork. These two systems illustrate the virtual circuit and the datagram approaches to network interconnection respectively. The vast majority of the work on interconnecting networks falls into one of these two approaches.

II. Interprocess Communication

While discussing computer communication, it is useful to recall that the communication takes place at the request and agreement of processes, i.e., computer programs in execution. Processes are the actors in the computer communication environment; processes are the senders and receivers of data. Processes operate in computers or hosts. It should be noted that

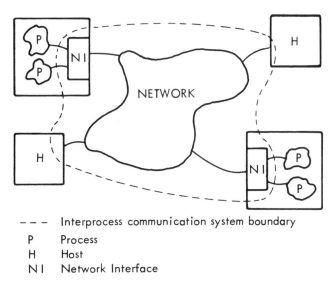

---   Interprocess communication system boundary
P   Process
H   Host
N I   Network Interface

Fig. 1. Communications network.

terminal–host communication can likewise be implemented as interprocess communication (see Chapters 15 and 16).

The protocols used in constructing the communications capability provide an interprocess communication system. Figure 1 shows how the combination of the network and the host network interface (hardware and software) can be viewed as providing an interprocess communication system.

When a new host computer is to be connected to an existing network, it must implement the protocol layers necessary to match the existing protocol used in the network. The new host must join the networkwide interprocess communication system so the processes in that host can communicate with processes in other hosts in the network.

The interconnection of networks require that the processes in the hosts of the interconnected networks have a common interprocess communication system. This may be achieved by converting the networks to a new interprocess communication system, by converting one or more levels of protocol to new protocols, or by translating between pairs of interprocess communication systems at their points of contact.

III. Datagrams and Circuits

Two types of service are commonly discussed as appropriate for the network-provided interprocess communication service: datagrams and virtual circuits.

Datagrams are one-shot simple messages. They are inherently unreliable since they travel one-way and are not acknowledged. Datagrams may also arrive in a different order than sent (at least in some networks). Datagrams are simple to implement since they do not require the networks or gateways to record and update state information (e.g., sequence numbers). Datagrams must carry complete address information in each message. The transmission of datagrams by a process is via send and receive actions.

Virtual circuits (or connections) are designed to be reliable and to deliver data in the order sent. Implementation of virtual circuits is complicated by the need for networks or gateways to record and update state information. Virtual circuits are created through an exchange of messages to set up the circuit; when use terminates, an exchange of messages tears down the circuit. During the data transmission phase, a short form address or circuit identifier may be used in place of the actual address. To use a virtual circuit a process must perform actions to cause the virtual circuit to be created (call setup) and terminated, as well as the actions to send and receive data.

Datagrams provide a transaction-type service while virtual circuits provide a connection-type service. Each of these services is needed in a general purpose communication environment. Datagrams are most efficient for transaction-type information requests such as directory assistance or weather reports. Virtual circuits are useful for terminal access to interactive computer systems or file transfer between computers.

IV. Gateways

Two or more networks are connected via a device (or pair of devices) called a gateway. Such a device may appear to each network as simply a host on that network (Fig. 2).

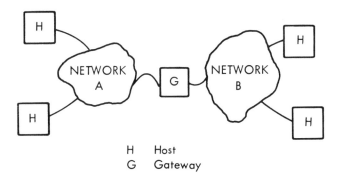

H   Host
G   Gateway

Fig. 2. Interconnected networks.

Some gateways simply read messages from one network (unwrapping them from that network's packaging), compute a routing function, and send messages into another network (wrapping them in that network's packaging). Since the networks involved may be implemented using different media, such as leased lines or radio transmission, this type of gateway is called a media-conversion gateway.

Other gateways may translate the protocol used in one network to that used in another network by replacing messages received from the first network with different messages having the same protocol semantics but with the syntax of the second network. This type of gateway is called a protocol-translation gateway.

It should be clear that the distinction between media conversion and protocol translation is one of degree: the media-conversion gateways bridge the gap between differing link and physical level protocols, while protocol-translation gateways bridge the gap between differing network and higher-level protocols.

The translation approach to network interconnection raises several issues. Success in protocol translation seems inversely correlated with the protocol level. At the lower levels, protocol translation causes no problems because the physical level and link levels are hop-by-hop in nature. It should be noted, though, that different protocols even at these low levels may have impact on the reliability, throughput, and delay characteristics of the total communication system.

At the network and transport levels, the issues of message size, addressing, and flow control become critical. Unless one requires that only messages that can be transmitted on the network with the smallest maximum message size be sent, one must provide for the fragmentation and reassembly of messages. Fragmentation and reassembly is the division of a long message into parts for transmission through a small message size network, and the reconstruction of those parts into the original message at the destination. The translation of addresses is a difficult problem when one network or transport level protocol provides a larger address space than the corresponding protocol to be translated to. When end-to-end flow control mechanisms are used, as they commonly are in transport level protocols, difficulties arise when the units controlled are different, for example, when one protocol controls octets and the corresponding protocol controls letters. More difficulties arise with potential difference in the model of flow control. For example, there may exist a difference between pre and post allocation, or between the allocation of buffer space and the allocation of transmission rate.

At higher levels, the problems are more difficult because of the increased state information kept and the lower likelihood of one-to-one translation of individual protocol messages. A further difficulty is that each level further multiplexes the communication so that each connection or

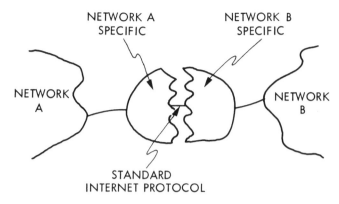

NETWORK A
SPECIFIC

NETWORK B
SPECIFIC

NETWORK
A

NETWORK
B

STANDARD
INTERNET PROTOCOL

Fig. 3. Gateway halfs.

stream or channel or virtual circuit must be separately translated. In spite of the difficulties some advocate the translation approach, and there are some successful demonstrations of high-level translation gateways for terminal access and file transfer. While the number of different protocols remains small the translation approach is workable, but as the number of protocols grows to N, the number of translations needed grows to N squared.

It should be pointed out that neither of the specific interconnection approaches discussed in this chapter attempts higher-level protocol translation.

Gateways may be thought of as having a "half" for each network they interconnect. One could model the operation of a gateway as having each gateway-half contain procedures to convert from a network-specific protocol into a standard protocol and vice versa (Fig. 3).

V. Relation to Open Systems Interconnect

In relation to the open systems architecture discussed in Chapter 2, the interconnection of networks focuses on levels 3 and 4.

To review, the Open Systems Interconnect defines the following levels of protocol:

Level	Function
7	Application
6	Presentation
5	Session
4	Transport
3	Network
2	Link
1	Physical

The lower levels, the physical and the link levels are hop-by-hop in nature and present no interconnection issues in terms of compatibility, though there may be some performance concerns.

The higher levels, the session level, the presentation level, and the application level, have so many compatibility requirements that it seems quite unlikely that interconnection of different protocols at those levels will be workable.

Thus, it is at the network level and the transport level that the interconnection of networks exposes issues of concern. The network level corresponds roughly to the interface to datagram service, and the transport level corresponds to the interface to virtual circuit service.

In some networks, the network level and datagram service have been hidden from the user, forcing consideration of network interconnection at the transport level.

VI. Interconnection of X.25 Networks

Introduction. The public data networks (PDNs) that follow the CCITT X.25 recommendation are to be interconnected via an interface specified in CCITT recommendation X.75. Recommendation X.25 specifies the interface between the customer's equipment, called the Data Terminal Equipment (DTE); and the network equipment, called the Data Circuit-terminating Equipment (DCE). Recommendation X.25 implies a virtual circuit operation. Thus, the PDNs offer an interface to a virtual circuit transport level protocol. Figure 4 shows the model of a PDN virtual circuit [1]. Chapter 8 discusses recommendation X.25.

The interface between two PDNs specified in recommendation X.75 is quite similar to that in recommendation X.25. The equipment on either side of this interface is called a Signalling TErminal (STE). The STE–STE interface is much like the DTE–DCE interface. The STE–STE interconnection is a split gateway with each gateway-half in a physical device controlled

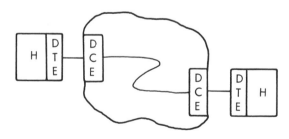

Fig. 4. PDN virtual circuit.

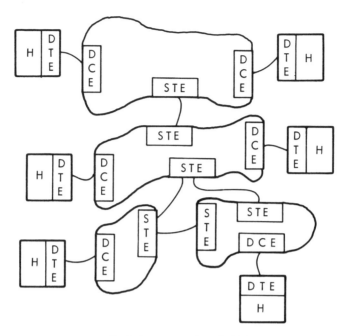

Fig. 5. Interconnection of PDNs.

by the PDN connected to that gateway-half [2]. Figure 5 shows the interconnection of PDNs.

The interconnection of PDNs via X.75 interfaces results in a series of virtual circuits. Each section is a distinct entity with separate flow control, error recovery, etc. Figure 6 shows a PDN transmission path with two virtual circuits (VCs) and five separate flow control (FC) steps.

Addressing. The address field is variable in length up to 15 digits, with each digit coded in a 4-bit field. The maximum address is then 60 bits (about 8 octets).

Routing. The user has no influence over routing used. To create the series of virtual circuits, a series of call setups establishes a fixed route (between pairs of STEs at least). State information must be kept for each call in the source and destination DTEs and DCEs and in each STE in the route.

Buffering and Flow Control. Each portion of the total path is a distinct virtual circuit. Each virtual circuit has an independent flow control (and particular to that PDN). In addition, there is flow control across each STE–STE interface. All this flow control is on a per call basis. This stepwise flow control may introduce delay in the total path that could be avoided with an end-to-end scheme.

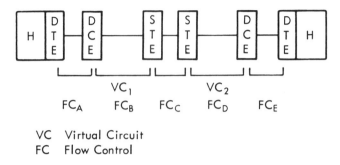

VC   Virtual Circuit
FC   Flow Control

Fig. 6. PDN transmission path.

There are some concerns about the interaction of two types of flow control implemented in PDNs. One type allows one message in transit from source DCE to destination DCE at any one time. The other allows multiple messages to be in transit, the number being determined by the flow control window.

Acknowledgment. Each portion of the total path has an acknowledgment. The user to network interface also has an acknowledgment. This local acknowledgment means only that the first PDN has accepted the message for transmission, not that it has arrived at the destination.

Recovery. The X.25 and X.75 recommendations do not specify how the PDNs deal with errors internally. If unrecoverable errors occur, the network will signal a Reset, which apparently means that the virtual circuit still exists, but the flow control is reset and messages may have been lost. More serious errors result in the call being cleared.

Because of the fixed route nature of the multinet path, a STE failure disrupts the communication.

Security. The X.25/X.75 recommendations do not provide any security features.

Header Structure. Once the call is established, a header is only 3 octets. The call setup headers are substantially longer, typically 20 octets, but possibly as large as 166 octets. There is a trade-off between header size and state information kept; in the PDNs, the trade-off has been made toward small headers and large state. The details of the headers are shown in Appendix 1.

Summary. The most important aspect of the interconnection of PDNs is that service provided to the using process is a virtual circuit with essentially the same properties a single PDN would have provided. This is done by concatenating a series of virtual circuits to provide the total path, resulting in a fixed route through a set of network interconnection points.

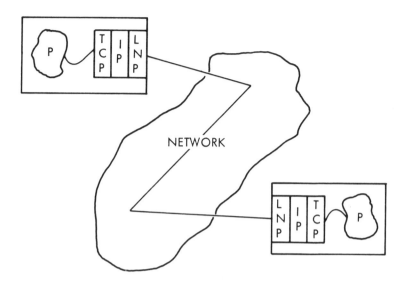

Fig. 7. End-to-end connection.

VII. Interconnection of ARPA Research Networks

Introduction. The ARPA sponsored research on interconnections of networks has led to a two-level protocol to support the equivalent function of the PDN's X.25/X.75 service. The ARPA sponsored work on networks has developed an Internet Protocol (IP) [3], and a Transmission Control Protocol (TCP) [4].

TCP is a logical connection transport protocol and is a level-4 protocol in the OSI model of protocol structure. The IP is a datagram protocol. The collection of interconnected networks is called an internet. IP is the network protocol of the internet and this is a level-3 protocol in the OSI model. The actual networks used are of various kinds (e.g., the ARPAnet, radio networks, satellite networks, and ring or cable networks) and are referred to as local networks even though they may span continents or oceans. The interface to a local network is a local network protocol or LNP. Figure 7 shows the model of an end-to-end connection.

In the ARPA mode, the networks interconnect via a single device called a gateway. A gateway is a host on two or more networks. Figure 8 shows the ARPA model of the interconnection of networks.

Each network addresses a gateway on it in the same way it addresses any other host on it. The information required to deliver a message to a destination in the internet is carried in the IP header. The IP is implemented in the gateways and in hosts. A sending host prepares a datagram (which is

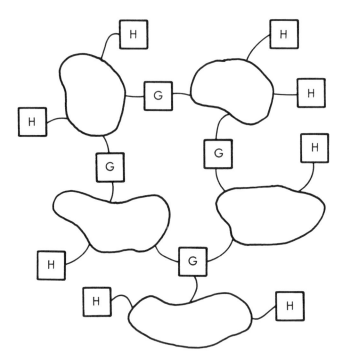

Fig. 8. ARPA model of interconnection of networks.

an IP header and the original message) and then selects a gateway in its own net to forward the datagram. The sending host then sends the datagram wrapped in a local network packet to that gateway.

A gateway receives a packet from one of the local networks to which it is attached and unwraps the IP datagram. The gateway then examines the IP header and determines the next gateway (or destination host) address in one of the local networks it is directly connected to. The gateway then sends the datagram with its IP header in a new local net packet to that gateway (or host).

The IP has no provision for flow control or error control on the data portion of the message (the IP headers are checksummed). There are no acknowledgments of IP messages. The IP is simple and the gateway may be implemented in small machines. A key point is that a gateway has no state information to record about a message. At the IP level, there are no connections or virtual circuits.

The IP does not provide a service equivalent to the PDN's X.25/X.75. To provide that type of end-to-end reliable ordered delivery of data the ARPA internet uses TCP.

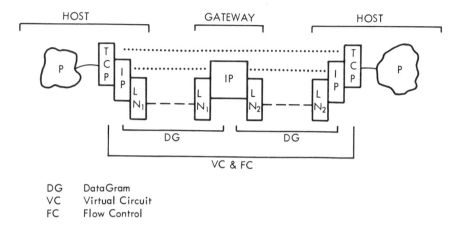

DG   DataGram
VC   Virtual Circuit
FC   Flow Control

Fig. 9. ARPA model of transmission path.

TCP uses end-to-end mechanisms to ensure reliable ordered delivery of data over a logical connection. It uses flow control, positive acknowledgments with time out and retransmission, sequence numbers, etc., to achieve these goals. Figure 9 shows the conceptual transmission path in this interprocess communication system, pointing out the datagram (DG) path between the IP modules and the virtual circuit path between the TCP modules at the source and destination and the flow control (FC) at that level.

ARPA has used these techniques to interconnect several very different networks including the ARPAnet, packet radio nets, a satellite net, and several local networks.

Addressing. The size of the address in this experimental system is fixed. The IP provides a one octet network field and a three octet host field. Also a one octet protocol identifier in the IP header may be considered address information. This protocol identifier allows the IP module to demultiplex datagrams to higher-level modules on the basis of protocol, e.g., TCP vs. some other protocol. The TCP provides a two octet port field. The total of the address length is then seven octets. Provision has been made for a host to have several addresses, so the host field is sometimes called the logical host field. The total address is the concatenation of the network, host, protocol, and port fields.

Routing. Normally, the user has no influence over the route used between the gateways. There is no call setup and the route may vary from one message to the next. No state information is kept in the gateways.

A user might insert a source routing option in the IP header to cause that particular message to be routed through specific gateways.

Buffering and Flow Control. There is no flow control mechanism in the IP. The gateways do not control the flow on connections for they are unaware of connections or any relation between one message and the next message. The gateways may protect themselves against congestion by dropping messages. When a gateway drops a message because of congestion, it may report this fact to the source of the message.

The TCP uses end-to-end flow control using windows on a per logical connection basis.

Acknowledgment. The IP has no provision for acknowledgments. The TCP uses acknowledgments for both error control and flow control. The TCP acknowledgments are not directly available to the user.

Recovery. Errors in a network or gateway result in a message being dropped, and the sender may or may not be notified. This inherent unreliability in the IP level allows it to be simple and requires the end-to-end use of a reliable protocol.

TCP provides the reliable end-to-end functions to recover from any lost messages. The TCP uses a positive acknowledgment, time out, and retransmission scheme to ensure delivery of all data. Each message is covered by an end-to-end checksum.

Because of the potential for alternate routing, the end-to-end communication may be able to continue despite the failure of a gateway.

Security. The IP provides an option to carry the security, precedence, and user group information compatible with AUTODIN II. The enforcement of these parameters is up to each network, and only AUTODIN II is prepared to do so.

The TCP end-to-end checksum covers all the address information (source and destination network, host, protocol, and port), so that if the checksum test is successful the address fields have not been corrupted.

Header Structure. The IP header is 20 octets (plus options, if used), but there is no call setup and no gateway state information. Thus, at the IP level, the header size vs. state information trade-off has been made toward large header and little (no) state information.

The TCP header is 20 octets (plus option, if used). There is a connection establishment procedure called the "three-way handshake," and significant state information is kept. In this case, there are both large headers and large state tables. The details of the headers are shown in Appendix 2.

Summary. The ARPA networks are interconnected by using a common datagram protocol to provide addressing (and thus routing) information and an end-to-end transport protocol to provide reliable sequenced data connections.

This model has evolved from the ARPAnet experience, in particular from the internetwork protocol model suggested in a paper by Cerf and Kahn [5].

VIII. Conclusion

Both the PDNs and the ARPA networks are interconnected by establishing standard protocols. The PDNs provide a virtual circuit service by concatenating the virtual circuit services of the individual networks. The ARPA networks use two levels of protocol to provide both datagram and virtual circuit services.

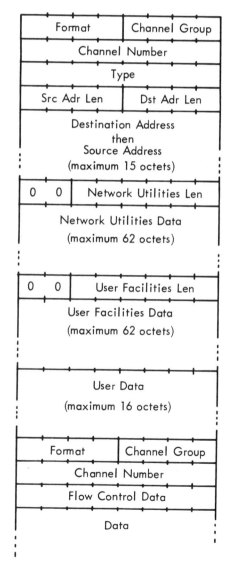

Fig. 10. X.75 Packet.

Additional discussion of the interconnection of PDNs is provided in
[6, 7]. In Chapter 19 Boggs *et al.* present in detail another example of
network interconnection using the datagram approach.

The issues of network interconnection have been discussed for at least 5
years (for example, McKenzie [8]). The recent expositions by Sunshine [9],
by Cerf and Kirstein [10], and by Gien and Zimmermann [11] are particularly recommended.

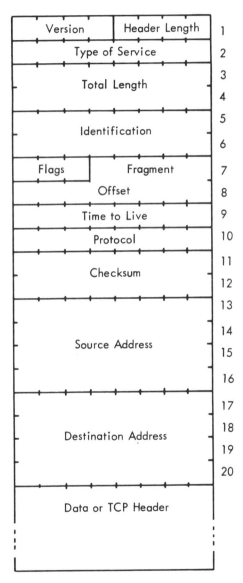

Fig. 11. IP format.

Appendix 1

X.75 Header Formats. The Call Request and Data packet formats are illustrated in Fig. 10. These typify the X.75 packet formats. All the X.75 packets are the same in the first two octets. The Format field indicated the type of packet.

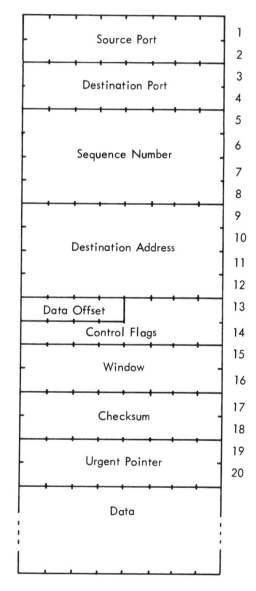

Fig. 12. TCP format.

Call Request. The call request packet is variable in length from a practical minimum of 11 octets to an unlikely maximum of 160 octets. *Data.* The Data packet has a three octet header.

Appendix 2

ARPA Protocol Header Formats. Every datagram carries the basic IP header. Every TCP segment transmitted carries the basic TCP header. *Internet Protocol (Fig. 11).* The ARPA IP has a basic header of 20 octets, and may carry a variable number of options up to a total length of 60 octets. *Transmission Control Protocol (Fig. 12).* The basic TCP header is 20 octets, and the header may be up to 60 octets long if options are used.

References

[1] "Recommendation X.25/interface between data terminal equipment (DTE) and data circuit-terminating equipment (DCE) for terminals operating in the packet mode on public data networks," CCITT Orange Book, vol. 7, International Telephone and Telegraph Consultative Committee, Geneva.

[2] "Proposal for provisional recommendation X.75 on international interworking between packet switched data networks," in CCITT Study Group VII Contribution No. 207, International Telephone and Telegraph Consultative Committee, Geneva, May 1978.

[3] DARPA, "DOD standard internet protocol," IEN-128, Defense Advanced Research Projects Agency, National Technical Information Service ADA079730, January 1980.

[4] DARPA, "DOD standard transmission control protocol," IEN-129, Defense Advanced Research Projects Agency, National Technical Information Service ADA082609, January 1980.

[5] V. Cerf, and R. Kahn, 'A protocol for packet network intercommunication, "*IEEE Trans. Commun.*, COM-22, 5, 637–2648, May 1974.

[6] G. Grossman, A. Hinchley, and C. Sunshine, "Issues in international public data networking," *Comput. Networks*, 3, 4, 259–266, September 1979.

[7] V. DiCiccio, C. Sunshine, J. Field, and E. Manning, "Alternative for interconnection of public packet switching data networks," *Proc. Sixth Data Commun. Symp.*, ACM/IEEE, 120–125, November 1979.

[8] A. McKenzie, "Some computer network interconnection issues," *Proc. Nat. Comput. Conf.*, AFIPS, 857–859, 1974.

[9] C. Sunshine, "Interconnection of computer networks," *Comput. Networks*, 1, 3, 175–195, January 1977.

[10] V. Cerf, and P. Kirstein, "Issues in packet-network interconnection." *Proc. IEEE*, 66, 11, 1386–1408, November 1978.

[11] M. Gien, and H. Zimmermann. "Design principles for network interconnection," *Proc. Sixth Data Commun. Symp.*, ACM/IEEE, 109–119, November 1979.

19

A Specific Internetwork Architecture (Pup)

David R. Boggs, John F. Shoch, Edward A. Taft, and Robert M. Metcalfe

I. Introduction

Research in network interconnection techniques has been motivated by the desire to permit communication among diverse, geographically distributed computing resources and users interconnected by a wide variety of network technologies.

It is the purpose of an internetwork architecture to provide a uniform framework for communication within a heterogeneous computing, communication, and applications environment. The work described in this chapter represents one internetwork architecture, known as *Pup*, in widespread regular use within Xerox. The name referred originally to the abstract design of a standard internetwork datagram (the PARC Universal Packet), but has expanded in usage to include the whole hierarchy of internetwork protocols as well as a general style for internetwork communication.

To assist in understanding the design of the Pup protocols, it is useful to characterize briefly the environment in which this architecture has evolved.

The computational environment includes a large number of "Alto" minicomputers [11], [31], and other personal computers capable of high-quality interaction with human users. Supporting these are various specialized server systems that are shared among many users and provide access to expensive peripherals such as large disks, magnetic tapes, and high-quality

527

printers. Additionally, there are several general-purpose time sharing systems providing customary services for terminal users.

The communications environment includes several different individual network designs. The dominant one is the "Ethernet" communications network, a local-area broadcast channel with a bandwidth of 3 Mbit/s [15]. Long-haul communication facilities include the ARPAnet, the ARPA packet radio network, and a collection of leased lines implementing an ARPAnet-style store-and-forward network. These facilities have distinct native protocols and exhibit as much as three orders of magnitude difference in bandwidth.

The applications to be supported include a wide range of activities: terminal access to the time sharing services, electronic mail, file transfer, access to specialized data bases, document transmission, software distribution, and packet voice, to name just a few. We would also like to facilitate more ambitious explorations into the area generally referred to as "distributed computing."

This chapter is organized as follows. In Section II we discuss some of the design issues which have emerged in the formulation of the Pup architecture, while Section III provides more detail on the protocols themselves. Section IV describes briefly some of our operational experience with the present implementation. The final section presents a retrospective critique of the work, highlighting some areas which merit further attention.

II. Design Principles and Issues

Constructing an architecture for internetwork protocols is, first and foremost, an exercise in design: identifying individual issues, exploring alternative solutions, and then knitting these pieces together to form the final result. Along the way, many compromises are made as one trades off among different criteria: functionality, efficiency, generality, ease of implementation, extensibility, and others.

In this section we enumerate some of the major design issues confronted in the development of a network architecture and describe, in general terms, the choices made in the development of Pup. (Several of these and other issues are enumerated in [2] and [17].) From this discussion the broad outlines of Pup will emerge; the section that follows provides more specific detail about the actual design.

A. The Basic Model: Individual Networks Connected with Gateways

As with most internetwork models, one envisions a collection of heterogeneous networks, connected with a set of *internetwork gateways* to form a loosely coupled system known generally as an *internet* [1], [2], [26]. An internet should provide the ability for any two hosts to communicate, so long as their own local networks are interconnected.

An important feature of the Pup internet model is that the hosts *are* the internet. Most hosts connect directly to a local network, rather than connecting to a network switch such as an IMP, so subtracting all the hosts would leave little more than wire. Gateways are simply hosts in the internet that are willing to forward packets among constituent networks. Thus, most of the properties of the internet are primarily artifacts of host software. The architecture must scale gracefully, and in particular must allow for the existence of a degenerate internet consisting of a single local network and no gateways.

B. Simplicity

One of the guiding principles in designing Pup has been the desire for simplicity. Pup is a framework for computer communications research, and simplicity is one of the best ways to minimize restrictions and maximize flexibility for experimentation. Attempting deliberately to eliminate un-needed complexity helps to keep the design open-ended. This in turn makes it easier to incorporate the existing diverse collection of networks and hosts and to accommodate new alternatives as the technology matures. Keeping the design simple helps to avoid building in technological anachronisms.

A second motivation for this principle is the desire to foster efficient implementations of the protocols in the host machines, which are typically quite small. Software overhead must be kept low in order to sustain high-bandwidth local communication, which constitutes the bulk of the traffic; yet the same software must support the full generality of internet-work communication.

C. Datagrams versus Virtual Circuits

There are two major approaches to providing an interface to packet-switched communications: accepting individual *datagrams* or providing a higher level of service in the form of a *virtual circuit*. The two interfaces are not unrelated, since a virtual circuit interface is usually implemented within a network by the use of datagrams. In some sense, datagrams provide access to a network at a lower level, closer to its underlying capabilities. Data-grams are particularly useful in many kinds of transaction-oriented proto-cols. Furthermore, the task of the internet is significantly simplified if it need only transport independent, individually addressed datagrams, without having to maintain the state required to support virtual circuits. If the internet provides a datagram interface, virtual circuit interfaces can be provided by adding appropriate mechanisms at the end points.

Therefore, the basic function provided by the Pup internet is the transport of datagrams; this simple abstraction is the foundation of Pup. The internet does not guarantee reliable delivery of datagrams (called "Pups"); it simply gives its "best efforts" to deliver each one, and allows the end processes to build protocols which provide reliable communications of the quality they themselves desire [14]. The internet has no notion of a connection. It transports each Pup independently, and leaves construction of a connection—if that is the appropriate interprocess communication model—to the end processes. Keeping fragile end-to-end state out of the packet transport system contributes to reliability and simplicity.

D. Individual Networks as Packet Transport Mechanisms

Individual networks within the internet can be viewed simply as *packet transport mechanisms*. As links in the internet they give their best efforts to deliver internet packets, but they do not guarantee reliable delivery. Packets may be lost, duplicated, delivered out of order, after a great delay, and with hidden damage. A network can have any combination of bandwidth, delay, error characteristics, topology, and economics; the routing algorithm should attempt to take these characteristics into consideration.

Encapsulation is an invertible, network-dependent transformation performed on a Pup to permit it to be carried transparently through a network: an abstract Pup is presented at one end, encapsulated for transmission through the net, and decapsulated at the other end, yielding the original Pup. For some networks, encapsulation consists merely of adding headers and trailers. More elaborate transformations may be necessary to pass a Pup through other networks (for example, using low-level acknowledgments or error correction because the network has a high loss rate). Encapsulation and decapsulation take place in a *network-specific driver* in which is vested all knowledge of the encapsulation technique. The internet specification has nothing to say about encapsulation except that it be invisible.

E. Internetwork Gateways

We distinguish two kinds of gateways: *media translators* and *protocol translators*. Media gateways are hosts with interfaces to two or more packet transport mechanisms among which they forward internet datagrams, using the appropriate encapsulation for each. These are the heart of any datagram-based internet. Protocol gateways are hosts which speak two or more functionally similar but incompatible higher-level protocols used to transport information within networks, mapping one higher-level abstraction into the other. (It is clear that a media gateway is just doing protocol translation at the link level, but the distinction is useful given the importance of internet datagrams in this architecture.)

In the Pup internet, media gateways are by definition simple, since all that is required of the translation process is that it preserve the semantics of internetwork datagrams. Protocol gateways are usually more difficult, even when the protocols are similar, since such higher-level protocols provide richer and more specialized semantics and it is not always clear how one should map the functionality of one protocol into another. Development of higher-level protocol translators between different network and internet architectures, e.g., between the ARPAnet file transfer protocol (FTP) and the Pup-based FTP, is a thorny task, but one that must be confronted when interconnecting systems that do not share the necessary lower-level primitives.

F. A Layered Hierarchy of Protocols

Layering of protocols is one of the most effective means for structuring a network design: each level uses the functions of the lower level, and adds some functionality of its own for possible use by the next level. Provided that suitable interfaces are maintained, an implementation at one level can be modified without impacting the overall structure; this helps to simplify both the design and the implementation.

Pup protocols are organized in a hierarchy, as shown in Fig. 1; the details of this figure will be presented in Section III. A level represents an abstraction, to be realized in different ways in different hosts. There are four levels of interest, but there may be more than one protocol at any level except level 1, representing a different use of the underlying layers. (The numbering of layers—and, indeed, the choice of points at which to divide the layers—is arbitrary; there is no relationship between Pup's numbering and that of other designs such as the Open Systems Interconnect, as discussed in Chapter 2.)

The level 0 abstraction is a packet transport mechanism. There are many realizations: an Ethernet channel, the ARPAnet, the ARPA packet radio network, our store-and-forward leased line network, and others. Level 0 protocols include specifications such as hardware interfaces, electrical and timing characteristics, bit encodings, line control procedures, and network-dependent packet formatting conventions. Associated with each packet transport mechanism is a convention for encapsulating Pups.

The level 1 abstraction is an internet datagram. The realization of this abstraction consists of the format of a Pup, a hierarchical addressing scheme, and an internetwork routing algorithm. There is only one box at

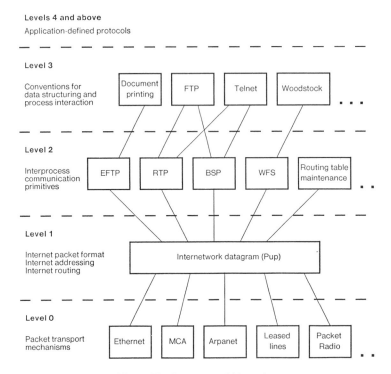

Fig. 1. The Pup protocol hierarchy.

level 1: the internet datagram protocol; it is this layer of commonality which unifies all of the different networks that might be used at level 0, and which makes available a uniform interface to all of the layers above. It is the purpose of this level to provide media independence while maintaining the common properties of the underlying packet networks.

The level 2 abstraction is an interprocess communication mechanism: a way to move bits without saying much about their form or content. Various level 2 protocols provide many combinations of reliability, throughput, delay, and complexity. These protocols can be divided into two classes according to the amount and lifetime of state information kept by the communicating end processes. Connectionless protocols support short-lived interactions; the end processes maintain little state, and usually only during the exchange of a few Pups—no more than a few seconds. Connection-based protocols support sustained interactions, generally requiring substantial state to be maintained at both ends, and for longer periods—minutes to hours.

Level 3 adds structure to the data moved at level 2, as well as conventions for how processes interact. For example, the file transfer protocol (FTP) consists of a set of conventions for talking about files and a format for sending them through a level 2 byte stream protocol connection. These are sometimes referred to as function-oriented protocols [4].

Above level 3 the dividing lines become blurred, and individual applications evolve with their own natural decomposition into additional layers. With respect to layering of protocols, Pup is similar in many ways to the ARPA internet and TCP design [1] and the Open Systems Architecture [32]. Unlike the Open Systems Architecture (and others), Pup often has several alternative boxes which all rest on a lower level and offer different functionality and interfaces to the next higher level.

G. Naming, Addressing, and Routing

Names, addresses, and routes are three important and distinct entities in an internet [19]:

The *name* of a resource is *what* one seeks,
an *address* indicates *where* it is, and
a *route* is *how to get there*.

A name is a symbol, such as a human-readable text string, identifying some resource (process, device, service, etc.). An address is a data structure whose format is understood by level 1 of the internet, and which is used to specify the destination of a Pup. A route is the information needed to forward a Pup to its specified address. Each of these represents a tighter binding of information: names are mapped into addresses, and addresses are mapped into routes. Error recovery should successively fall back to find an alternate route, then an alternate address, and then an alternate name.

The mapping from names to addresses is necessarily application-specific, since the syntax and semantics of names depend entirely on what types of entities are being named and what use is being made of them. This is dealt with at the appropriate higher levels of protocol.

An address field, as contained in a Pup, is one of the important elements of commonality in the internet design. An end process sends and receives Pups through a *port* identified by a hierarchical address consisting of three parts: a *network number*, a *host number*, and a *socket number*. This structure reflects the attitude that the communicating parties are the end processes, not the hosts' protocol handlers; among other things, this permits alternate implementations of a higher-level protocol to coexist in a single machine. (In contrast, the ARPA Internet Project [17] takes the position that the socket abstraction does not belong at the internet level; therefore, ARPA internet addresses contain only network and host numbers. When a packet arrives, it is first demultiplexed by the *protocol type* field in the internet header; higher-level protocols such as the TCP, datagram protocol, and packet voice protocol then impose their own concept of socket if they find it useful, which, as a practical matter, they all do.)

The actual process of routing a packet through the Pup internet uses a distributed adaptive routing procedure. The source process specifies only the *destination address* and not the *path* from source to destination. The internetwork gateways route Pups to the proper network, a network then routes Pups to the proper host, and a host routes Pups to the proper socket.

This routing process is associated with level 1 in the protocol hierarchy, the level at which packet formats and internet addresses are standardized. The software implementing level 1 is sometimes referred to as a *router*. Thus, the routing table itself is kept at level 1; a very simple host (or gateway) would need only levels 0 and 1 in order to route Pups. But the routing table also requires periodic updating, as gateways exchange and distribute their current routing information; this *routing table maintenance* protocol is found logically at level 2 of the hierarchy.

Gateways provide internet routing tables to individual hosts as well as to each other. Hosts use this routing information to decide where to send outgoing packets destined other than to a directly connected network.

H. Flow Control and Congestion Control

Although the terms are often confused, *flow control* and *congestion control* attack two very different problems in packet-switched communication, as discussed in Chapter 13. Flow control is a mechanism used to regulate the behavior of a specific source and destination pair, so that the source does not send data at a rate greater than the receiver can process it. In an internet architecture, flow control remains the responsibility of the end-to-end protocols, particularly those at level 2 supporting regular stream traffic.

Congestion control, as used in this chapter, is a network-wide mechanism, used to control the number and distribution of packets in the network so as to prevent system overload. Internet congestion control is necessary to help protect the gateways from being burdened with excessive traffic.

The Pup datagram-based internet model does not require that the internet successfully deliver every packet that has been accepted. Therefore, an intermediate gateway which suddenly encounters a period of severe congestion is free to discard packets, although the system should be engineered to make this an uncommon event.

If a gateway is forced to discard an incoming packet because of congestion, it should attempt to return some information to the source: an *error Pup* (negative acknowledgment) indicating that a packet had to be discarded in midroute. This error Pup is simply returned to the source port, as identified in the discarded Pup; this is a good illustration of the value of including the socket number as part of the standard internet address. The source process can use this information to modify its transmission strategies, for example, to reduce its offered load (the rate at which it attempts to send Pups along the congested path) and thereby help to relieve the congestion.

Long-term congestion should eventually be reflected in the routing information exchanged among gateways, discouraging subsequent traffic from attempting to pass through a badly congested area.

I. Reliable Transport

Defining datagrams to be less than perfectly reliable is realistic since it reflects the characteristics of many existing packet transport mechanisms. Probabilistic transmission is basic to the theory of operation of network designs such as Ethernet. Even in networks nominally designed to deliver correctly sequenced, error-free packets, occasional anomalies may result from certain hardware or software failures: an ARPAnet IMP may crash while loading the only copy of a packet, or an X.25 virtual circuit may be reset.

As mentioned previously, the Pup internet *always* has the option of discarding packets to relieve congestion, although this is certainly not an optimal strategy. This point is of considerable practical importance when one considers the complicated measures required to avoid deadlock conditions in the ARPAnet, conditions which are a direct consequence of attempting to provide reliable delivery of every packet in a store-and-forward network [13], [14]. Packet management strategies that attempt to guarantee perfect reliability must be designed to operate correctly under *worst case* conditions, whereas strategies that have the option of discarding packets when necessary need operate correctly only under *most* conditions. The idea is to sacrifice the guarantee of reliable delivery of individual packets and to capitalize on the resulting simplicity to produce higher reliability and performance overall.

For some applications, perfectly reliable transport is unneccessary and possibly even undesirable, especially if it is obtained at the cost of increased delay. For example, in real-time speech applications, loss of an occasional packet is of little consequence, but even short delays (or worse, highly variable ones) can cause significant degradation [3], [24].

Reliable delivery requires maintaining state information at the source and destination. The actions of a large class of simple servers, such as giving out routing tables or converting names into addresses, are idempotent (i.e., may be repeated without incremental effects), and a client of that service can simply retransmit a request if no response arrives. These protocols reduce to a simple exchange of Pups, with an occasional retransmission by the client, but with no state retained by the server. (The server may choose to retain answers to the last few requests to improve response time, but this optimization is invisible to the protocol.)

On the other hand, many applications such as file transfer and terminal connection do depend upon fully reliable transmission. In these cases, it is perfectly reasonable to build a reliable end-to-end protocol on top of the internet datagrams. Ultimately, reliability (by some definition) is always required; the issue is where it should be provided. The Pup attitude is that it is the responsibility of the end processes to define and implement whatever form of reliable transport is appropriate to the situation.

J. Packet Fragmentation

It is inevitable that some process will want to send an internet packet which is too large to be directly encapsulated for transmission through an intermediate network that has a smaller maximum packet size. This problem is usually approached with one of two forms of *packet fragmentation* [20].

With *internetwork fragmentation*, an internet-wide design specifies the operations to be performed on a packet that is too large for a network it is about to enter. The internet datagram is fragmented into a number of smaller internet datagrams, thereafter to be transported independently and reassembled at the ultimate destination. This is the approach taken, for example, in the ARPA internet design. It requires every destination to have procedures for reassembly.

Alternatively, one may use *intranetwork fragmentation* (or *network-specific fragmentation*): when presented with an oversize packet, the network-specific driver undertakes to fragment the packet in a manner specific to that network, to be reassembled by the corresponding driver as the packet exits the network (e.g., at the next gateway). This approach confines the fragmentation and reassembly procedures to the level 0 modules of hosts directly connected to the network in which fragmentation is required.

The Pup design does not attempt to provide any form of general internetwork fragmentation. This complex issue has been simply legislated out of existence by requiring that every agent in the internet handle Pups up to a standard maximum size, using network-specific fragmentation where necessary.

K. Broadcast Packets

Broadcast packets are a particularly useful means for locating available resources or distributing information to many hosts at once. Some local networks, such as the Ethernet, directly support transmission of broadcast packets. In store-and-forward systems, however, specialized algorithms are required to propagate a packet efficiently to all hosts [5], [6]; no existing store-and-forward networks support any technique besides brute-force transmission of a packet to every node, although such a capability is now being implemented in the ARPAnet.

Broadcasts may also be expensive since every host that receives one must expend some resources, if only to discard it. In networks where a broadcast involves generating more than one packet, there is the additional cost of creating and transporting the extra copies. Because of their potentially high cost, internet-wide broadcasts are not presently supported in the Pup design. Nor is it clear that such a capability would be desirable, since it would not extend well to a very large internet. The problem of locating distant resources in the internet at reasonable cost is a topic of current research.

But Pups can be broadcast on a single network; they are frequently used to locate nearby resources, or to permit gateways to announce their presence on a network. Implementation of the broadcast procedure is left to the network-specific driver, using the best technique available on that net.

L. Privacy and Security

It must be recognized that in practical internet environments, packets may be delivered to the wrong host, intercepted by another host, or generated by a host masquerading as some other host. To prevent this would require one to interpose some agent between hosts and the internet and to specify a secure access control procedure. This would significantly increase the complexity of the internet, and truly suspicious users would probably not trust it anyway.

Processes are encouraged, however, to ensure the privacy and authenticity of their communication by whatever end-to-end encryption techniques seem appropriate [16]. Particularly vulnerable components, such as gateways and servers, should take precautions to protect their own integrity, but ultimate responsibility rests with the end processes. The Pup internet does not attempt to protect users from traffic analysis or from malicious replay of previous traffic.

III. Implementation

The preceding section has outlined some of the important properties of the Pup architecture and the internetworking issues it addresses. What follows is a more detailed description of the present design of the four major layers in the system.

A. Level 0: Packet Transport

An individual network moves network-specific packets among hosts; the addressing schemes, error characteristics, maximum packet sizes, and other attributes of networks vary greatly. An internetwork packet transport mechanism, however, moves Pups between hosts. The level 0 code which transforms a network into an internet packet transport mechanism is called a *network driver*.

A machine connected to a single network, therefore, has one level 0 network driver; a gateway has one driver for each directly connected network. Only the driver knows about the peculiarities of a network's hardware interface and low-level protocol.

The interface between levels 0 and 1 is very simple. Level 1 passes down a Pup and a network-specific host address, and the driver encapsulates the Pup and does its best to deliver it to the specified host. When a Pup arrives at a host, the driver decapsulates it and passes it up to level 1; if for any reason the Pup looks suspicious (as determined by network-specific error checking), the driver discards it.

Every packet transport mechanism must be able to accept a maximum-size Pup; if the actual network cannot directly encapsulate a packet of that size for transmission, the driver must include some form of intranetwork fragmentation.

A network driver may also be asked to broadcast a packet to all other hosts on that net. On some networks this is straightforward; on others it may require use of a reverse-path forwarding algorithm [6] or brute-force replication of the packet to each destination.

The transport mechanisms do not have to be perfectly reliable, but they should be successful most of the time—a packet loss rate of less than 1 percent is usually acceptable. A network operating for a short time in a degraded mode with a higher loss rate is harmless, so long as the probability is low that Pups will transit more than one net that is in this condition. However, if a network's inherent error characteristics are unfavorable, the driver should take steps to improve its performance, perhaps by incorporating a network-specific low-level acknowledgment and retransmission protocol.

To date, there have been five major types of networks integrated into the Pup architecture, each with a different level 0 driver.

Ethernet. Local Ethernet facilities can very easily serve as transport mechanisms for Pups: a Pup fits in an Ethernet packet with only a few additional words of encapsulation (see Fig. 2), and requires no fragmentation. These systems have good reliability, high speed, and can send broadcast packets [15], [21], [22].

MCA. The Multiprocessor Communications Adapter (MCA), a parallel TDM bus, serves as a local network tying together a limited number of

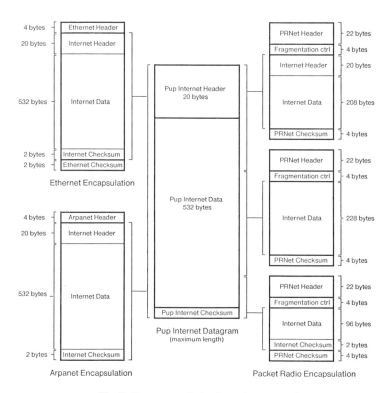

Fig. 2. Pup encapsulation in various networks.

Nova computers [7]. It has good reliability and requires no fragmentation, but does not support broadcast packets. Broadcasts are accomplished by the brute-force method, sending a copy of a broadcast packet to each of the possible hosts.

ARPAnet. To cover longer distances, Pups can be routed through the ARPAnet; the format for encapsulating a Pup in an ARPAnet message is shown in Fig. 2. (Note that ARPAnet Pup transport is based on host–IMP protocol messages, not on host–host protocol streams.) Because the standard maximum Pup length is less than that of an ARPAnet message, the driver itself need not fragment Pups; however, the ARPAnet does perform network-specific fragmentation internally: one "message" containing a Pup may become multiple "packets" within the ARPAnet. Furthermore, the ARPAnet provides increased reliability through the use of its own internal acknowledgment and retransmission protocols. The ARPAnet does not presently support broadcast packets; rather than sending packets to all possible ARPAnet hosts, the network driver does not implement broadcasts at all.

Leased Line Store-and-Forward Network. More frequently, different local networks are interconnected over long distances through the use of a

private store-and-forward network constructed using leased telephone circuits. Similar in spirit to the ARPAnet, this system is used to connect
internetwork gateways. Unlike the ARPAnet, the system does not use
separate packet switches (IMP's), but instead switches packets through the
hosts themselves; that is, the connected hosts include network-specific
drivers that implement a store-and-forward network. This network has its
own adaptive routing procedure, independent of the internetwork routing.
The system is fairly reliable and does not require low-level acknowledgments. At present, the network drivers do not fragment Pups, but they do
promote small packets to the front of transmission queues at intermediate
points to help improve performance for interactive traffic.

Packet Radio Network. On an experimental basis, the ARPA packet
radio network [10] has been used to carry traffic among local networks in
the San Francisco Bay area. The packet radio network was integrated into
the system by building a suitable level 0 network driver [23]. The system
provides good reliability; but due to the relatively small maximum packet
size (232 bytes), the driver must perform fragmentation and reassembly (see
Fig. 2). Though using a broadcast medium, the packet radio protocols do
not support broadcast packets. In this case, the low-level driver includes a
procedure to periodically identify packet radio hosts that might be running
Pup software; when asked to broadcast a packet, the driver sends copies of
it to all such hosts.

To date we have not used any public packet-switched networks, such as
Telenet, as packet transport mechanisms. These systems usually provide
only a virtual circuit interface (X.25) that requires a user to pay for
functionality that may not be needed. Compared to our existing leased line
network, a Telenet-based packet transport mechanism would not be cost-
effective except under conditions of very light traffic volume. We would
prefer to use a service that provided simple, unreliable datagrams; if there
were an appropriate interface, we could dismantle our leased line store-
and-forward network.

B. Level 1: Internetwork Datagrams

This is the level at which packet formats and internetwork addresses
are standardized. It is the lowest level of process-to-process communication.

(1) Pup Format. The standard format for a Pup is shown in Fig. 3. The
following paragraphs highlight the sorts of information required at the
internet datagram level.

The *Pup length* is the number of 8-bit bytes in the Pup, including
internetwork header (20 bytes), contents, and checksum (2 bytes).

The *transport control* field is used for two purposes: as a scratch area
for use by gateways and as a way for source processes to tell the internet

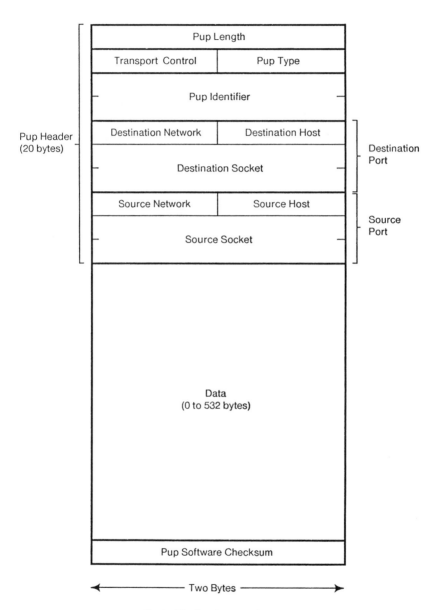

Fig. 3. The Pup internet datagram.

how to handle the packet. (Other networks call this the "facilities" or "options" field.) The *hop count* subfield is incremented each time the packet is forwarded by a gateway. If this ever overflows, the packet is presumed to be traveling in a loop and is discarded. A *trace bit* is specified, for potential use in monitoring the path taken by a packet.

The *Pup type* is assigned by the source process for interpretation by the destination process and defines the format of the Pup contents. The 256 possible types are divided into two groups. Some types are *registered* and have a single meaning across all protocols; Pups generated or interpreted within the internet (e.g., by gateways) have types assigned in this space. Interpretation of the remaining *unregistered* types is strictly a matter of agreement between the source and destination processes.

The *Pup identifier* is used by most protocols to hold a sequence number. Its presence in the internetwork header is to permit a response generated within the internet (e.g., error or trace information) to identify the Pup that triggered it in a manner that does not depend on knowledge of the higher-level protocols used by the end processes.

Pups contain two addresses: a *source port* and a *destination port*. These hierarchical addresses include an 8-bit network number, an 8-bit host number, and a 32-bit socket number. Hosts are expected to know their own host addresses, to discover their network numbers by locating a gateway and asking for this information, and to assign socket numbers in some systematic way not legislated by the internet protocol.

There are some important conventions associated with the use of network addresses. A distinguished value of the network number field refers to "this network" without identifying it. Such a capability is necessary for host initialization (since most hosts have no permanent local storage and consequently no *a priori* knowledge of the connected network number), and to permit communication to take place within a degenerate internet consisting of an unidentified local network with no gateways. A distinguished value of the destination host address is used to request a broadcast. Certain values of the socket number field refer, by convention, to "well-known sockets" associated with standard, widely used services, as is done in the ARPAnet.

The *data* field contains up to 532 data bytes. The selection of a standard maximum packet length must reflect many considerations: error rates, buffer requirements, and needs of specific applications. A reasonable value might range anywhere from 100 to 4000 bytes. In practice, much of the internet traffic consists of packets containing individual "pages" of 512 bytes each, reflecting the quantization of memory in most of our computers. But just carrying the data is not enough, since the packet should accommodate higher-level protocol overhead and some identifying information as well. Allowing 20 additional bytes for such purposes, we arrive at 532 bytes as the maximum size of the data field (a somewhat unconventional value in that it is not a power of 2). Thus, there may be between 0 and 532 content bytes in a Pup, so its total length will range from 22 to 554 bytes. Pups longer than 554 bytes are not prohibited and may be carried by some networks, but no internetwork gateway is required to handle larger ones.

The optional *software checksum* is used for complete end-to-end coverage—it is computed as close to the source of the data and checked as close to the ultimate destination as is possible. This checksum protects a Pup when it is not covered by some network-specific technique, such as when it is sitting in a gateway's memory or passing through a parallel I/O path. Most networks employ some sort of error checking on the serial parts of the channel, but parallel data paths in the interface and the I/O system often are not checked.

The checksum algorithm is intended to be straightforward to implement in software; it also allows incremental updating so that intermediate agents which modify a packet (gateways updating the hop count field, for example) can quickly update the checksum rather than recomputing it. The checksum may (but need not) be checked anywhere along a Pup's route in order to monitor the internet's integrity.

(2) Routing. Accompanying the packet format defined at level 1 are the protocols for internetwork routing. Each host, whether or not it is a gateway, executes a routing procedure on every outgoing Pup, as illustrated in Fig. 4. This procedure decides, as a function of the Pup destination port field, upon which *directly connected network* the Pup is to be transmitted (if there is more than one choice), and it yields an *immediate destination host* which is the address on that network of either the ultimate destination or some gateway believed to be closer to the destination. Each routing step employs the same algorithm based on local routing information, and each Pup is routed independently.

Routing information is maintained in a manner very similar to the ARPAnet-style adaptive procedures [12]. The initial metric used for selecting routes is the "hop count," the number of intermediate networks between source and destination. The protocol for updating the routing tables involves exchanging Pups with neighboring gateways and rests logically at level 2 of the protocol hierarchy. This is an example of a connectionless protocol which does not require perfectly reliable transmission for correct operation. Changes in internetwork topology may cause different gateways' routing tables to become momentarily inconsistent, but the algorithm is stable in that the routing tables rapidly converge to a consistent state and remain that way until another change in topology occurs.

A host which is not a gateway still implements a portion of this level 2 routing update protocol: it initially obtains an internetwork routing table from a gateway on its directly connected network, and it obtains updated

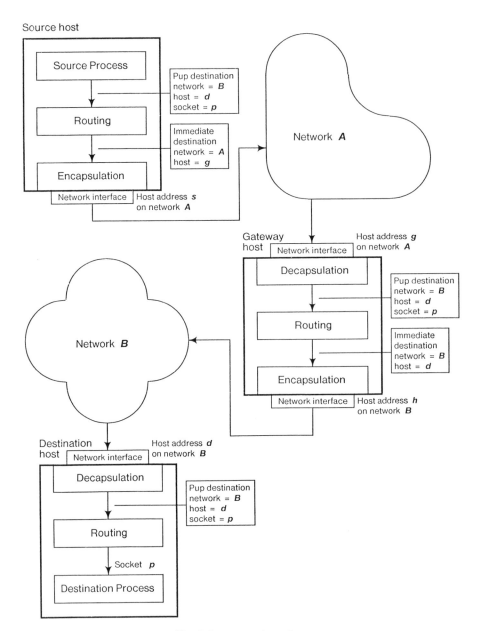

Fig. 4. Internetwork routing.

information periodically. If there is more than one gateway providing connections to other networks, the host can merge their routing tables and thus be able to select the best route for packets directed to any network.

C. Level 2: Interprocess Communication

Given the raw datagram facility provided at level 1, we can begin to build data transport protocols, tailored to provide appropriate levels of reliability or functionality for real applications.

These protocols generally fall into two categories: those in which a connection is established for a sustained exchange of packets, and those in which individual packets are exchanged on a connectionless basis. Connection-style protocols usually transport data very reliably, and transparently.

EFTP—The Easy File Transfer Protocol. This is a very simple protocol for sending files. Each data Pup gives rise to an immediate acknowledgment, and there is at most one Pup outstanding at a time. This protocol is an indirect descendant of the one outlined in [15]. Its simplicity makes this piece of communication mechanism easy to include under conditions of very limited resources. For example, we have implemented a complete EFTP receiver in 256 words of assembly language, for use in a network-based bootstrap and down-line loading process.

Rendezvous and Termination Protocol (RTP). This is a general means to initiate, manage, and terminate connections in a reliable fashion [28]. In normal use, an RTP user initiates a connection by communicating with a well-known socket at some server. That server will spawn a new port to actually provide the service, and the RTP will establish contact with this port. It employs a nonreusable *connection identifier* to distinguish among multiple instantiations of the same connection and to cope with delayed packets without making assumptions about maximum packet lifetimes. RTP also synchronizes Pup identifiers for use in managing the connection.

Byte Stream Protocol (BSP). This is a relatively sophisticated protocol for supporting reliable, sequenced streams of data. It provides for multiple outstanding packets from the source, and uses a moving window flow control procedure. User processes can place *mark bytes* in the stream to identify logical boundaries and can send out-of-band *interrupt* signals. RTP and BSP combined perform a function similar to that of the TCP, with which they share a certain degree of common ancestry [1], [17].

Connectionless protocols do not attempt to maintain any long-term state; they usually do not guarantee reliability, but leave it up to the designer to construct the most suitable system. Their simplicity and ease of implementation make them extremely useful.

Echo. A very simple protocol can be used to send test Pups to an *echo server* process, which will check them and send back a reply. Such servers are usually embedded in gateways and other server hosts, to aid in network monitoring and maintenance. The server is trivial to implement on top of the level 1 facilities.

Name Lookup. Another server provides the mapping from string names of resources to internetwork addresses; this is accomplished by a single exchange of packets. This service is often addressed with a broadcast Pup, since it is used as the first step in locating resources. (The name lookup service itself, of course, must be located at a well-known address. To be useful, it must be widely available; therefore, it is typically replicated at least once per network.)

Routing Table Maintenance. The internetwork routing tables are main-tained by Pups exchanged periodically among internetwork gateways and broadcast for use by other hosts.

Page-Level File Access. The Woodstock file server (WFS), one of the family of file servers available on the internet, provides page-at-a-time access to a large file store [29]. The protocols used for this do not require establishment of a connection, but merely exchange request and response Pups that each carry both commands and file data. This arrangement supports random-access, transaction-oriented interactions of very high per-formance, frequently better than that obtained using local file storage, because the file server's disks are much faster than those typically connected to personal computers.

Gateway Monitoring and Control. There is no single network control center, but individual gateways may be queried from a monitoring program run on any user machine. With suitable authentication, the user may assume remote control of the gateway so as to perform operations such as changing parameters and loading new versions of the software.

Other connectionless protocols are used to access a *date and time server*, an *authentication server*, and a *mail check server* integrated with an on-line message system. These protocols are designed to be as cheap as possible to implement (i.e., without connection overhead) so that such servers may be replicated extensively and accessed routinely without con-suming excessive resources. For example, instances of some of these servers are present in all gateway hosts so as to maximize their availability.

D. Level 3: Application Protocols

Armed with a reasonable collection of data transport protocols at level 2, one can begin to evolve specific applications at level 3. These are supported by various function-oriented protocols [4].

Telnet. Terminal access to remote hosts is provided with an internet-work Telnet protocol, which makes use of the combination of the ren-dezvous and termination protocol (RTP) and the byte stream protocol

(BSP) at level 2. Using the notion of a virtual terminal, Telnet implementations map characteristics of actual terminals into a network-independent representation; a mark byte in the stream and an out-of-band interrupt, for example, are used to signal an "attention." (This approach is a subset of the ARPAnet Telnet protocol, without any of its options such as RCTE [8], [9].)

FTP. The RTP and BSP are again combined as the foundation for an internetwork file transfer protocol (FTP), supporting stream-oriented access to files. The underlying byte streams provide reliable communication, and the major task of FTP is to communicate commands and responses and to sort out different representations of data in different file systems. FTP implementations have been embedded within existing time-sharing systems, and also constitute the core of dedicated, high-capacity file servers.

Printing. Among the important shared resources in the internet are high-quality printing servers. Rather than using the fully developed BSP and FTP, the specialized task of sending unnamed, standard format document files to a printer makes use of the more restricted but much simpler EFTP.

CopyDisk. Given high-performance networks and simple gateways that can forward Pups among them efficiently, it is perfectly reasonable to copy entire disk packs through the internet. The CopyDisk protocol negotiates between the participating machines to ensure that the disks are compatible, and handles error recovery should something break down.

Remote Graphics. Personal display-oriented computers such as the Alto can be used to provide a convivial front end for large programming systems such as Interlisp. The Alto Display protocol is used for exchanging descriptions of graphical structures as well as text; it is similar to the ARPA network graphics protocol, but with extensions to support raster-scanned graphics [24], [25], [30].

Additional applications have included cooperative editing of common documents from multiple machines, audio communication and packet voice, and many others.

As users create new applications, these systems tend to develop their own natural layering of function. Some may require new protocol designs in the existing heirarchy; the Pup architecture permits this degree of flexibility down to the level of the simple internetwork datagram. As we gain experience with new systems, common pieces of design will begin to emerge that might be of more general use; they will eventually find their way into an appropriate place in this hierarchy of communications protocols.

IV. Evolution, Actual Experience, and Performance

The Pup architecture emerged against a background of ARPAnet protocols. Many of its important ideas—and those of its key relative, TCP

—first appeared during the course of a series of meetings of the International Network Working Group (IFIP TC-6 WG6.1) during 1973. Pup and TCP share a number of important principles, most notably that of reliable end-to-end transmission through an internet. Pup subsequently diverged from TCP as the desire for implementation within Xerox required decoupling it from TCP's long and sometimes painful standardization process.

The fundamentals of the Pup design crystallized in 1974 and have remained essentially unchanged since then. During this interval many higher-level protocols have been developed, the implementations have evolved considerably, and the internetwork system has grown to include approximately 1000 hosts, attached to 25 networks of 5 different types, using 20 internetwork gateways. The system is in regular use, is quite stable, and requires little regular maintenance or attention.

From a functional point of view, this internetwork architecture has been able to fulfill the needs of a very diverse community. While the bulk of all traffic is carried by means of a few standard protocols, it has proven extremely valuable to be able to define new protocols—aiming at different points in the space of performance, cost, and functionality—and to fit them into the internet protocol hierarchy at any of several levels.

In terms of performance, the internetwork gateways impose very little overhead because they are so simple. In regions of the internet where multiple high-bandwidth local networks are interconnected directly by a single minicomputer-based gateway, there is almost no noticeable difference between intranet and internet performance. Total throughput in an individual gateway is high, ranging from 400 to 1000 kbit/s (depending on the particular implementation), and the typical delay experienced by maximum-length Pups in the case just mentioned is 2 to 5 ms.

These figures do not represent limits to what is achievable, even with the relatively low-powered machines now being used as gateways, because the gateway software has not been highly tuned for this application but rather is based on general-purpose software packages that are also used in many other hosts. But the current performance is adequate because the internetwork traffic load is typically only a tiny fraction of the capacity of the underlying local network channels. There exists one Alto-based gateway that interconnects three 3-Mbit/s Ethernet channels as well as several 9.6-kbit/s leased lines and a packet radio interface. In general the bottlenecks are not the gateways but rather the slower communication channels; discard of Pups due to congestion in gateways is almost exclusively due to overload of the 9.6-kbit/s lines.

As might be expected, most of the traffic in our local networks is intranetwork, that is, consisting of Pups whose source and destination are on the same network. For example, measurement of one such network has shown a typical volume of 2.2 million packets per day, 72 percent of which are intranetwork packets [22]. Furthermore, of the remaining 28 percent, more than half consist of traffic to or from another nearby local network connected via a single gateway. (This site is served by multiple local networks because it is too large to cover with a single one using existing Ethernet technology, and also because it would exhaust a single network's address space.) The rest of the traffic—some 250 000 packets per day—is transported to or from other campuses in the internet, mostly via the leased line network.

The higher-level protocols, such as the byte stream and FTP, are generally limited in performance by the processor capacity or the secondary storage bandwidth at the source and destination. For example, our BCPL implementation of BSP can maintain a data stream at the rate of about 500 kbit/s between end processes running on Alto minicomputers, at which point both machines are CPU-bound. While it is certainly adequate for most applications, we find this performance somewhat disappointing, and we view it as an indication that BSP—although substantially simpler than say, TCP—is still too complicated a protocol for high-performance communication.

The Pup architecture allows individual networks to be added to the internet system on an ad hoc basis, with no need for central control or coordination except to assign new network numbers. Users sharing a local network can assemble gateways and lease lines to other nearby gateways; they are encouraged to make multiple intergateway connections to provide alternate routes and thereby reduce the probability of being isolated. The gateway software has evolved to the point where if one starts a copy of it on a host having at least one connection to the existing internet, it will automatically obtain the files and other information it needs, announce its availability to the rest of the internet, and begin forwarding Pups.

V. A Retrospective Critique, Possible Improvements, and Future Research

While the architecture works extremely well, there are some lessons to be learned from this experience.

A. Addressing and Routing

The size of address fields is a question of continuing controversy. An 8-bit network number supports up to 256 nets; that is fine for now, but eventually it should be made larger. To date, 256 hosts per net has not been a problem, though it is likely to become one (for example, when the

ARPAnet's new 24-bit addressing convention starts to receive wide use). We have avoided variable-length address fields in the Pup design because they increase per-packet processing costs.

If an internetwork system becomes extremely large, the number of networks becomes so great that it is no longer practical for all hosts to keep routing table entries for all possible destination networks. Area routing strategies may be employed to attack this problem [12]. Alternatively, one may adopt a scheme in which the local routing table becomes a cache of recently used routing information, with routes to specific networks computed and maintained as needed. The problem of locating routes to distant parts of the internet is an area of current research.

One could consider revising the entire notion of a hierarchical address space. Under the current design, it is sometimes necessary to change the host number of a machine which is moved from one net to anther—an operational annoyance. It is conceivable that every host could be given a unique address within a flat address space; a more sophisticated mechanism would then be needed to map addresses into routes, since there would no longer be a network number as part of the address (except perhaps as a hint, to improve performance).

We view with some disfavor nonhierarchical organizations in which internet addresses consist of a concatenation of network-specific addresses [27]. Such arrangements have the effect of fixing the *path* to a given destination and blur the distinction between addressing and routing.

Socket numbers, which are now 32 bits wide, could easily shrink to 16. Originally, 32 bits were assigned to allow inclusion of a unique subfield to distinguish among multiple instantiations of a connection; we now recognize that a better approach is to use a distinct connection identifier at the time a connection is established, as mentioned earlier in the presentation of the rendezvous and termination protocol.

Using hop counts as the metric for routing decisions has worked remarkably well. An obvious drawback, however, is that it considers a hop through a 9.6-kbit/s phone line equally as good as a hop through a 3-Mbit/s Ethernet link. As the topology becomes more richly connected, this will increasingly become a problem. We intend eventually to change the routing algorithms to reflect some consideration of bandwidth and delay, using known techniques based on research into adaptive distributed routing algorithms in the ARPAnet and elsewhere.

We have given little consideration to source routing or other forms of advice (e.g., class of service) provided to the internet routing procedures by source processes. In providing such facilities, one must take great care not to compromise the simplicity of the basic internet datagrams or violate the layering of protocols.

B. Congestion Control and Utilization of Low-Bandwidth Channels

The current congestion control techniques must be regarded as primitive. Discarding Pups and (where possible) notifying the source process when congenstion occurs has the virtue of simplicity, and we believe it is a good general approach; but the present design has several defects. Insufficient information is returned to the source process to enable it to make an informed decision about how to proceed; further, the discard of Pups is haphazard, and no provision is made for fairness. Congestion occurs most often at the entry to slow channels, and under overload conditions the perceived performance of paths through those channels is highly variable.

This is a situation in which it would be appropriate to perform a relatively large amount of computation per packet in order to optimize the utilization of the communication bandwidth. For example, the network-specific driver for a leased telephone circuit could examine the source and destination addresses of Pups to deduce the existence of "conversations," and use this information to share the slow channel more effectively. (The ARPAnet IMPs deduce conversations in precisely this way, though for purposes having to do primarily with flow control rather than congestion control.)

In the same vein, techniques such as code compression, elimination and regeneration of identical internet headers in successive packets, etc., may be implemented in the network-specific drivers for the slow channels, with minimal impact on the end-to-end protocols. Such techniques are used widely in virtual circuit designs, and their applicability is sometimes cited as an advantage of virtual circuits over datagrams [18]. But there is no reason they cannot be employed in a datagram-based internet, so long as the necessary additional computation is done in the right place.

The important point is that optimizing the utilization of the communicatin channel is appropriate only when the channel bandwidth is scarce compared to the computation required to perform such optimization. Where the processing capacity of the end machines is itself the scarce resource, as we have observed in the local network environment, such techniques are highly inappropriate.

C. Pup Types in the Internet Header

The distinction between registered and unregistered Pup types at the level of itnernet datagrams has not turned out to be particularly useful, except in a few cases: Pups of type "error" and "trace" may be generated from within the internet without knowledge of the higher-level protocols being employed by the end processes.

D. Performance of Reliable End-to-End Protocols

Present implementations of the byte stream protocol include fairly sophisticated adaptive flow control heuristics that also try to take note of any packets lost due to internet congestion. This approach has worked reasonably well in enabling a source to adapt to the conditions encountered along the path to a particular destination. However, use of networks with highly variable behavior, such as the wide-ranging delays experienced when using the packet radio network, can confound these heuristics. Under unusual circumstances, the flow control procedures have been observed to move suddenly into very unfavorable operating regions. The difficulty involving the radionet has since been solved, but the general design of simple, effective flow control and congestion control procedures is just a very hard problem, particularly procedures intended to adapt dynamically to and make good use of different networks whose performance may vary by nearly three orders of magnitude.

The step from raw Pups to a byte stream may be too large. The byte stream protocol does too much for many applications; it is complex enough that few systems have ever implemented the entire specification. As discussed previously, performance of the BSP, when compared to some other systems, is reasonable; but it does not give a user the full capacity of the underlying networks. In a high-bandwidth local network environment, paying attention to per-packet processing overhead is of extreme importance.

We have considered, but have not yet implemented, a proposal for an intermediate level of functionality: a reliable packet protocol (RPP) that takes care of connection establishment and processes flow control information, but tries not to dictate how a client program should do buffer management. It ensures reliable delivery (i.e., each packet once and only once), but may deliver packets to the client out of order, and does not deliberately attempt to hide packet boundaries. A BSP connection, where that is what is desired, may then be reimplemented as a veneer on top of an RPP connection.

E. Access to the Internet

The present Pup architecture can be characterized as "open": users and applications are permitted, and indeed encouraged, to take advantage of the internet for routine communication. Access to the internet is uncontrolled; as in many network designs, responsibility for access control rests with the host systems, and whatever accounting is performed is for the services rendered by individual servers. In our research and development environment this is ideal, but obviously in some other environments it might not be.

F. Conclusions

The success of Pup as an internetwork architecture depends on a number of important principles. Key among these is the layering of function in such a way that applications may make use of the internet at any of several levels, with the ability to choose among alternative protocols at each level or to develop new ones where necessary. Simple internetwork datagrams constitute the level at which media independence (through encapsulation) is achieved; they are also the unit of direct process-to-process communication. This is crucial both to flexibility and to performance, particularly in an internetwork environment dominated by relatively lightweight hosts and high bandwidth local networks.

During 1976, the Pup internet reached a level of functionality roughly equivalent to that provided by the standard ARPAnet protocols—byte streams, Telnet, and FTP. From that time to the present we have concentrated on building servers and constructing applications to access them through the internet. We are just beginning to explore that area of interprocess communication traditionally considered the domain of multiprocessors. Some interesting opportunities arise from the availability of 100 or so minicomputers interconnected by a 3-Mbit/s broadcast channel, and by ten or so similar clusters, all interconnected by a store-and-forward network. We believe that the Pup architecture serves as a good foundation for such investigations.

References

[1] V. G. Cerf and R. E. Kahn, "A protocol for packet network intercommunication," *IEEE Trans. Commun.*, vol. COM-22, pp. 637–648, May 1974.

[2] V. G. Cerf and P. T. Kirstein, "Issues in packet-network interconnection," *Proc. IEEE*, vol. 66, pp. 1386–1408, Nov. 1978.

[3] D. Cohen, "Issues in transnet packetized voice communication," presented at the 5th Data Commun. Symp., Snowbird, UT, Sept. 1977.

[4] S. D. Crocker, J. F. Heafner, R. M. Metcalfe, and J. B. Postel, "Function-oriented protocols for the ARPA computer network," in *AFIPS Conf. Proc. Spring Joint Comput. Conf.*, vol. 40, 1972.

[5] Y. K. Dalal, "Broadcast protocols in packet switched computer networks," Stanford Univ. Digital Syst. Lab., Tech. Rep. 128, Stanford, CA, Apr. 1977.

[6]   Y. K. Dalal and R. M. Metcalfe, "Reverse path forwarding of broadcast packets," *Commun. Ass. Comput. Mach.*, vol. 21, Dec. 1978.

[7]   Data General Corp., "Type 4038 multiprocessor communications adapter," Tech. Ref. 014-000002-01, Sept. 1971.

[8]   J. Davidson, W. Hathaway, J. Postel, N. Mimno, R. Thomas, and D. Walden, "The ARPANET Telnet protocol: Its purpose, principles, implementation, and impact on host operating system design," in *Proc. 5th Data Commune. Symp.*, Snowbird, UT, Sept. 1977.

[9]   E. Feinler and J. Postel, Eds., "Telnet protocol specification," in *Arpanet Protocol Handbook*, Jan. 1978.

[10] R. E. Kahn, S. A. Gronemeyer, J. Burchfiel, and R. C. Kunzelman, "Advances in packet radio technology," *Proc. IEEE*, vol. 66, pp. 1468–1496, Nov. 1978.

[11] A. C. Kay, "Microelectronics and the personal computer," *Sci. Amer.*, vol. 237, Sept. 1977.

[12] J. M. McQuillan "Adaptive routing algorithms for distributed computer networks," Ph.D. dissertation, Harvard Univ., Cambridge, MA, 2831, Bolt Beranek and Newman, Rep. 2831, May 1974.

[13] J. M. McQuillan and D. C. Walden, "The ARPANET design decisions," *Comput. Networks*, vol. 1, Aug. 1977.

[14] R. M. Metcalfe, "Packet communication." Ph.D. dissertation, Harvard Univ., Cambridge, MA. M.I.T. Project Mac TR-114, Dec. 1973.

[15] R. Metcalfe and D. Boggs, "Ethernet: Distributed packet switching for local computer networks," *Comm. Ass. Comput. Mach.*, vol. 19, July 1976.

[16] R. Needham and M. Schroeder, "Using encryption for authentication in large networks of computers," *Comm. Ass. Comput. Mach.*, vol. 21, Dec. 1978.

[17] J. Postel, "Internetwork protocol approaches," this book, Chapter 17.

[18] L. G. Roberts, "The evolution of packet switching," *Proc. IEEE*, vol. 66, pp. 1307–1313, Nov. 1978.

[19] J. F. Shoch, "Internetwork naming, addressing, and routing," in *Proc. 17th IEEE Comput. Soc. Int. Conf. (CompCon)*, Sept. 1978.

[20] J. F. Shoch, "Packet fragmentation in internetwork protocols," *Comput. Networks*, vol. 3, Feb. 1979.

[21] J. F. Shoch, "Design and performance of local computer networks," Ph.D. dissertation, Stanford Univ., Stanford, CA, University Microfilms, Aug. 1979.

[22] J. F. Shoch and J. A. Hupp, "Performance of an Ethernet local network—A preliminary report," in *Proc. Local Area Network Symp.*, Boston, MA, May 1979.

[23] J. F. Shoch and L. Stewart, "Interconnecting local networks via the packet radio network," in *Proc. 6th Data Comm. Symp.*, Pacific Grove, CA, Nov. 1979.

[24] R. F. Sproull and D. Cohen, "High-level protocols," *Proc. IEEE*, vol. 66, pp. 1371–1386, Nov. 1978.

[25] R. Sproull and E. Thomas, "A network graphics protocol," *Comput. Graphics*, vol. 8, Fall 1974.

[26] C. Sunshine, "Interconnection of computer networks," *Comput. Networks*, vol. 1, Jan. 1977.

[27] C. Sunshine, "Source routing in computer networks," *ACM Comput. Commin. Rev.*, vol. 7, Jan. 1977.

[28] C. Sunshine and Y. Dalal, "Connection management in transport protocols," *Comput. Networks*, vol. 2, Dec. 1978.

[29] D. Swinehart, G. McDaniel, and D. Boggs, "WFS: A simple shared file system for a distributed environment," *Oper. Syst. Rev.*, vol. 13, Nov. 1979.

[30] W. Teitelman, "A display-oriented programmer's assistant," in *Proc. 5th Int. Joint Conf. on Artificial Intelligence*, Cambridge, MA, Aug. 1977; also available as Xerox PARC Tech. Rep. CSL-77-3.

[31] C. P. Thacker, E. M. McCreight, B. W. Lampson, R. F. Sproull, and D. R. Boggs, "Alto: A personal computer," *Computer Structures: Readings and Examples*, Siewiorek, Bell, and Newell, Eds., 1980.

[32] H. Zimmermann, "A standard layer model," this book, Chapter 2.

PART VII

Formal Specifications and Their Manipulation

Up to now, our mode of defining each protocol we have encountered has been to describe in words what happens. An event occurs in one protocol partner in a given layer. This triggers either another event in the same partner (as with the expiration of a timeout, for example), or the emission of some sort of message unit specified by the protocol's semantics. The arrival of this message unit triggers an event in another protocol partner, being either in an adjacent layer or remotely in the same layer.

Such "informal" descriptions suffice very well for gaining a general idea of what is going on, but when it comes time to actually produce running hardware or software implementations, the imprecision and ambiguity of such descriptions leads to difficulties. This section focuses on how protocols may be *represented* (*specified*) in a totally unambiguous way and on some of the practical consequences of doing this.

One consequence of formal protocol specification is of course to provide a compact and unambiguous way of documenting the protocols and architectures for the use of a product's implementors and others whose products must interact with it. But the benefits go quite a bit beyond this. As we shall see in the ensuing chapters, one may carry out operations on the formal specifications that will *verify* in advance of any implementation whether or not the implementation will work in some sense. And it is also becoming possible to generate real executable programs directly by automatic means from the specification (rather than by *ad hoc* hand programming methods) and have the resulting code be fairly efficient.

There are three basic approaches to formal protocol specifications and the possible manipulations that can be carried out upon them. Each has its particular merits in ease of creating the representation and in how much can be verified using it. Chapter 20 presents an overview of the current state of the art of all three. In the *transition model* approach (discussed in detail in

Chapter 21), each protocol partner, or *entity*, is represented as a *finite state machine* (FSM), or an equivalent Petri net. We have met examples of FSMs in Chapters 3, 7, and 8. An event in the action of one of the entities is portrayed as a transition from one state to another. In the *abstract program* approach (which Chapter 22 discusses at length), an event is portrayed as the execution of a line of code or an entire procedure in the abstract program. The *hybrid* approach uses a combination of the two techniques. Hybrid techniques are described in Chapters 23 and 25.

If one wants to carry out verification of real protocols in a real system development environment, the transition model approach to representation (Chapter 21) has proved to be quite practical. This is because of the relative lack of specialized knowledge required to use it and the fact that one can automate the search through the space of all possible combinations of states of the FSMs looking for such pathologies as deadlocks and spurious responses to unanticipated message arrivals. The price paid for this convenience is that verification is only a test that the representation is free of a limited set of defects, not that it provides a required set of services to the next higher protocol layer. Also, clever tricks or restrictions are required to avoid an explosion in state space size (for example, instead of allowing message sequence number to be a variable, it may be necessary to allow it to take on integer values only up to 2 or 3). The size of the space of all possible states of all protocol entities acting jointly is the product of those of the individual entities.

Other things that contribute to the state explosion are the need to have more than two protocol partners (as with multiple access, routing, or distributed directory protocols) and to allow a complex message transmission medium between the partners (the protocol layers below the one being examined), for example, one that can lose an occasional message.

In principle, these two problems, limited range of guarantee and state explosion, can be avoided in the abstract program class of representation discussed in Chapter 22. It is possible to construct a service level specification (for example, that a stream of messages inserted at one end will arrive eventually and in sequential order at the other) and prove, for example using the Floyd–Hoare program verification approach, that the protocol representation will satisfy it. The protocol representation is in terms of program statements whose execution (if proven correct) converts a stated precondition into a stated postcondition. State space explosions are avoided because the pre- and postconditions can express clusters of states (e.g., sequence numbers as a variable). Also an abstract program is inherently executable, if compiled down to a suitable machine interface. In spite of these advantages, abstract program approaches have not proved very practical in a development environment, because they require a great deal of special knowledge and skill to apply and because complete automation of the process of proving individual programs seems to be some years away.

Hybrid approaches are the ones that seem to be receiving the most attention. The state transition part of the model captures the control aspects of the protocols while variables and data are easily handled by the program part of the model. A hybrid representation approach motivated along these lines is described in Chapter 23.

The idea of being able to execute directly the protocol representation is a particularly valuable consequence of protocol formalization. One reason is that it circumvents much of the expense and error susceptibility of hand coding. Such a motivation has led to the hybrid model described in Chapter 25, in which both FSM and program parts of the model are expressed in a variant of one of the standard programmming languages.

20

A Survey of Formal Methods

Gregor V. Bochmann and Carl A. Sunshine

I. Introduction

As evidenced by the earlier chapters in this book, increasingly numerous and complex communication protocols are being employed in distributed systems and computer networks of various types. The informal techniques used to design these protocols have been largely successful, but have also yielded a disturbing number of errors or unexpected and undesirable behavior in most protocols. This chapter describes some of the more formal techniques which are being developed to facilitate design of correct protocols.

As they develop, protocols must be described for many purposes. Early descriptions provide a reference for cooperation among designers of different parts of a protocol system. The design must be checked for logical correctness. Then the protocol must be implemented, and if the protocol is in wide use, many different implementations may have to be checked for compliance with a standard. Although narrative descriptions and informal walk-throughs are invaluable elements of this process, painful experience has shown that by themselves they are inadequate.

In the following sections, we shall discuss the use of formal techniques in each of the major design steps of specification, verification, and implementation. Section II clarifies the meaning of specification in the context of a layered protocol architecture, identifies what a protocol specification should include, and describes the major approaches to protocol specification. Section III defines the meaning of verification, discusses what can be verified, and describes the main verification methods. Section IV provides pointers to some important case histories of the use of these techniques. For detailed examples, we refer to the subsequent chapters of this book, which generally provide additional support for the points which we have had to treat briefly in this survey. A complete bibliography may be found in [18], and complementary surveys in [44], [8], [33], [43].

II. Protocol Specification

As noted above, protocol descriptions play a key role in all stages of protocol design. This section clarifies the meaning of specification in the domain of communication protocols, identifies the major elements that comprise a specification, and presents the major methods for protocol specification.

A. The Meaning of Specification

We assume that the communication architecture of a distributed system is structured as a hierarchy of different protocol layers, as described in earlier chapters. Each layer provides a particular set of *Services* to its users above. From their viewpoint, the layer may be seen as a "black box" or machine which allows a certain set of interactions with other users (see Fig. 1). A user is concerned with the nature of the service provided, but not with how the protocol manages to provide it.

This description of the input/output behavior of the protocol layer constitutes a *Service Specification* of the protocol. It should be "abstract" in the sense that it describes the types of commands and their effects, but leaves open the exact format and mechanisms for conveying them (e.g., procedure calls, system calls, interrupts, etc.). These formats and mechanisms may be different for users in different parts of the system, and are defined by an *Interface Specification*.

Service Specifications

Specifying the service to be provided by a layer of a distributed communication system presents problems similar to specifying any software module of a complex computer system. Therefore methods developed for software engineering [36], [31] are useful for the definition of communica-

Fig. 1. Services provided by a protocol layer.

tion services. Usually, a service specification is based on a set of *Service Primitives* which, in an abstract manner, describe the operations at the interface through which the service is provided. In the case of a transport service, for example, some basic service primitives are *Connect, Disconnect, Send,* and *Receive.* The execution of a service primitive is associated with the exchange of parameter values between the entities involved, i.e., the service providing and using entities of two adjacent layers. The possible parameter values and the direction of transfer must be defined for each parameter.

Clearly, the service primitives should not be executed in an arbitrary order and with arbitrary parameter values (within the range of possible values). At any given moment, the allowed primitives and parameter values depend on the preceding history of operations. The service specification must reflect these constraints by defining the allowed sequences of operations directly, or by making use of a "state" of the service which may be changed as a result of some operations.

In general, the constraints depend on previous operations by the same user ("local" constraints), and by other users ("global" constraints). Considering again the example of a transport service, a local constraint is the fact that *Send* and *Receive* may only be executed after a successful *Connect.* An example of a global constraint is the fact that the "message" parameter value of the first *Receive* on one side is equal to the message parameter value of the first *Send* on the other side.

Protocol Specifications

Although it is irrelevant to the user, the protocol designer must be concerned with the internal structure of a protocol layer. In a network environment with physically separated users, a protocol layer must be implemented in a distributed fashion, with *Entities* (processes or modules) local to each user communicating among one another via the services of the lower layer (see Fig. 2). The interaction among entities in providing the

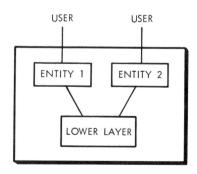

Fig. 2. Internal structure of a protocol layer.

layer's service constitutes the actual *Protocol*. Hence a protocol specification must describe the operation of each entity within a layer in response to commands from its users, messages from the other entities (via the lower layer service), and internally initiated actions (e.g., timeouts).

Abstraction and Stepwise Refinement

The specifications described above must embody the key concept of *Abstraction* if they are to be successful. To be abstract, a specification must include the essential requirements that an object must satisfy and omit the unessential. A service specification is abstract primarily in the sense that it does not describe how the service is achieved (i.e., the interactions among its constituent entities), and secondarily in the sense that it defines only the general form of the interaction with its users (not the specific interface).

A protocol specification is a refinement or distributed "implementation" of its service specification in the sense that it partly defines how the service is provided (i.e., by a set of cooperating entities). This "implementation" of the service is what is usually meant by the design of a protocol layer. The protocol specification should define each entity to the degree necessary to ensure compatibility with the other entities of the layer, but no further. Each entity remains to be implemented in the more conventional sense of that term, typically by coding in a particular programming language. There may be several steps in this process until the lowest-level implementation of a given protocol layer is achieved [20], [11].

B. What a Protocol Definition Should Include

A protocol cannot be defined without describing its context. This context is given by the architectural layer of the distributed system in which the protocol is used. A description of a layer should include the following items [28].

1. A general description of the purpose of the layer and the services it provides.
2. An exact specification of the service to be provided by the layer.
3. An exact specification of the service provided by the layer below, and required for the correct and efficient operation of the protocol. (This of course is redundant with the lower layer's definition, but makes the protocol definition self-contained.)
4. The internal structure of the layer in terms of entities and their relations.

5. A description of the protocol(s) used between the entities including:
   a. An overall, informal description of the operation of the entities.
   b. A protocol specification which includes
      i. a list of the types and formats of messages exchanged between the entities;
      ii. rules governing the reaction of each entity to user commands, messages from other entities, and internal events.
   c. Any additional details (not included in point b), such as considerations for improving the efficiency, suggestions for implementation choices, or a detailed description which may come close to an implementation.

Reference [8] presents an example of these items for a simple data transfer protocol.

C. Specification Methods

Descriptions of communication services and protocols must be both easy to understand and precise—goals which often conflict. The use of natural language gives the illusion of being easily understood, but leads to lengthy and informal specifications which often contain ambiguities and are difficult to check for completeness and correctness. The arguments for the use of formal specification methods in the general context of software engineering [36] apply also in our context.

Protocol Specifications

Most of the work on formal specification of protocols has focused on the protocol itself and not on the service it provides. A variety of general formalisms such as state diagrams, Petri nets, grammars, and programming languages have been applied to this problem and in many cases adaptations or extensions to facilitate protocol modeling have been made [14]. These techniques may be classified into three main categories: transition models, programming languages, and combinations of the first two.

Transition models are motivated by the observation that protocols consist largely of relatively simple processing in response to numerous "events" such as commands (from the user), message arrival (from the lower layer), and internal timeouts. Hence state machine models of one sort or another with such events forming their inputs are a natural model. However, for protocols of any complexity, the number of events and states required in a straightforward transition formalism becomes unworkably large. For example, to model a protocol using sequence numbers, there must be different states and events to handle each possible sequence number [37]. Models falling into this category include state transition diagrams [4], [50], grammars [25], [47], Petri nets and their derivatives [35], [46], L-systems [19], UCLA graphs [37], and colloquies [30].

Programming language models [24], [41], [6], [21] are motivated by the observation that protocols are simply one type of algorithm, and that high-level programming languages provide a clear and relatively concise means of describing algorithms. These models are described in Chapter 22. Depending on how high level and abstract a language is used, this approach to specification may be quite near to an implementation of the protocol. As noted above, this proximity is a mixed blessing, since unessential features in the program are often combined with the essential properties of the algorithm. A major advantage of this approach is the ease in handling variables and parameters which may take on a large number of values (e.g., sequence numbers, timers), as opposed to pure state machine models.

Hybrid models [45], [16], [10], [40], [3] attempt to combine the advantages of state models and programs. These typically employ a small-state model to capture only the main features of the protocol (e.g., connection establishments, resets, interrupts). This state model is then augmented with additional "context" variables and processing routines for each state. In such hybrid models, the actions to be taken are determined by using parameters from the inputs and values of the context variables according to the processing routine for each major state. For example, the sequence number of an arriving message may be compared with a variable giving the expected next sequence number to determine whether to accept the message, what the next state should be, and how to update the expected sequence number. Bochmann and Gecsei [10] have demonstrated the potential for trading off the complexity of the state model with the amount of context information for a given protocol. (Other techniques for managing the complexity of protocols are discussed in Section III C.)

As noted above, one major goal of protocol specification is to provide a basis for implementation. Some specification methods facilitate this goal more than others. Programming language specifications may be quite close to implementations (but often lack the desired degree of abstraction). Direct implementation of transition or hybrid model specifications by some form of interpreter or "compiler" is also relatively straightforward [11]. In many cases, these implementation methods have been at least partially automated [40], [47], [22], [2].

Service Specifications

It is only recently that the need for comprehensive protocol service specifications has been realized [3], [39], [43]. Initial efforts at formal service specifications have been directed towards applying general software engineering methodology. As noted in Section II A, definition of the primitive operations supported by the layer (e.g., *Send, Connect*) is a basic feature of any specification. In abstract machine type specifications, internal "states" of the layer are also defined. These states are used in defining the effects of each operation, and may be changed as a result of the operation [38].

Other specification methods that do not require definition of explicit states may also be used. I/O history type methods define the allowed input and output sequences of the layer and their relation to each other (e.g., that the sequence of messages delivered is identical to the sequence of messages sent) [20], [3]. Algebraic specifications [23] provide another way of defining the allowed sequence of operations. Sunshine [42] provides a comparison of several of these methods, but work in this area is just beginning.

III. Protocol Verification

In its broadest interpretation, system validation aims to assure that a system satisfies its design specifications and (hopefully) operates to the satisfaction of its users. Validation activity is important during all design phases, and may include testing of the final system implementation, simulation studies, analytical performance predictions, and verification. Verification is based on the system specification, and involves logical reasoning. Therefore it may be used during the design phase before any system implementation exists, in order to avoid possible design errors. While testing and simulation only validate the system for certain test situations, verification allows, in principle, the consideration of all possible situations the system may encounter during actual operation.

A. The Meaning of Verification

Verification is essentially a demonstration that an object meets its specifications. Recalling from Section II that *Services* and *Protocol Entities* are the two major classes of objects requiring specification for a protocol layer, we see there are two basic verification problems that must be addressed: (1) the protocol's *Design* must be verified by analyzing the possible interactions of the entities of the layer, each functioning according to its (abstract) protocol specification and communicating through the underlying layer's service, to see whether this combined operation satisfies the layer's service specification; and (2) the *Implementation* of each protocol entity must be verified against its abstract protocol specification.

The somewhat ambiguous term "protocol verification" is usually intended to mean this first design verification problem. Because protocols are inherently systems of concurrent independent entities interacting via (possibly unreliable) exchange of messages, verification of protocol designs takes on a characteristic communication oriented flavor. Implementation of each entity, on the other hand, is usually done by "ordinary" programming techniques, and hence represents a more common (but by no means trivial) program verification problem that has received less attention from protocol verifiers.

The service specification itself cannot be verified, but rather forms the standard against which the protocol is verified. However, the service specification can be checked for consistency [20]. It must also properly reflect the users' desires, and provide an adequate basis for the higher levels which use it. Unfortunately, techniques to achieve these latter goals are still poorly understood.

It is important to note that protocol verification also depends on the properties of the lower-layer protocol. In verifying that a protocol meets its service specification, it will be necessary to assume the properties of the lower layer's service. If a protocol fails to meet its service specification, the problem may rest either in the protocol itself, or in the service provided by the lower layer.

Most of the verification work to date has been on design rather than implementation, and we shall focus on design verification in the remainder of this section. While a protocol design need only be verified once, each different implementation must be verified against the design.

B. What Can Be Verified

The overall verification problem may be divided along two axes, each with two categories. On one axis, we distinguish between general and specific properties. On the other we distinguish between safety and liveness.

General properties are those properties common to all protocols that may be considered to form an implicit part of all service specifications. Foremost among these is the absence of deadlock (the arrival in some system state or set of states from which there is no exit). Completeness, or the provision for all possible inputs, is another general property. Progress or termination may also be considered in this category since they require minimal specification of what constitutes "useful" activity or the desired final state.

Specific properties of the protocol, on the other hand, require specification of the particular service to be provided. Examples include reliable data transfer in a transport protocol, copying a file in a file transfer protocol, or clearing a terminal display in a virtual terminal protocol. Definitions of these features make up the bulk of service specifications.

On the other axis, safety has the usual meaning that if the protocol performs any action at all, it will be in accord with its service specification. For example, if a transport protocol delivers any messages, they will be to the correct destination, in the correct order, and without errors. Liveness means that the specified services will actually be completed in finite time. In the case of logical verification, which is the subject of this report, it is sufficient to ascertain a finite time delay. In the case that the efficiency and responsiveness of the protocol is to be verified, it is clearly necessary to determine numerically the expected time delay, throughput, etc.

C. Verification Methods

Approaches to protocol verification have followed two main paths: reachability analysis and program proofs. Within the scope of this paper, we can only outline these two approaches. The references cited in Section IV provide more details on particular techniques.

Reachability analysis is based on exhaustively exploring all the possible interactions of two (or more) entities within a layer. A composite or global state of the system is defined as a combination of the states of the cooperating protocol entities and the lower layer connecting them. From a given initial state, all possible transitions (user commands, time-outs, message arrivals) are generated, leading to a number of new global states. This process is repeated for each of the newly generated states until no new states are generated (some transitions lead back to already generated states). For a given initial state and set of assumptions about the underlying layer (the type of service it offers), this type of analysis determines all of the possible outcomes that the protocol may achieve. Chapter 24 provides a clear exposition of this technique.

Reachability analysis is particularly straightforward to apply to transition models of protocols which have explicit states and/or state variables defined. It is also possible to perform a reachability analysis on program models by establishing a number of "break points" in the program that effectively define control states [24]. Symbolic execution (see the following) may also be viewed as a form of reachability analysis.

Reachability analysis is well suited to checking the general correctness properties described above because these properties are a direct consequence of the structure of the reachability graph. Global states with no exits are either deadlocks or desired termination states. Similarly, situations where the processing for a receivable message is not defined, or where the transmission medium capacity is exceeded are easily detected. The generation of the global state space for transition models is easily automated, and several computer aided systems for this purpose have been developed [16],

[50], [37]. The major difficulty of this technique is "state space explosion" because the size of the global state space may grow rapidly with the number and complexity of protocol entities involved and the underlying layer's services. Techniques for dealing with this problem are discussed below.

The program proving approach involves the usual formulation of assertions which reflect the desired correctness properties. Ideally, these would be supplied by the service specification, but as noted above, services have not been rigorously defined in most protocol work, so the verifier must formulate appropriate assertions of his own. The basic task is then to show (prove) that the protocol programs for each entity satisfy the high-level assertions (which usually involve both entities). This often requires formulation of additional assertions at appropriate places in the programs [41], [6].

A major strength of this approach is its ability to deal with the full range of protocol properties to be verified, rather than only general properties. Ideally, any property for which an appropriate assertion can be formulated can be verified, but formulation and proof often require a great deal of ingenuity. Only modest progress has been made to date in the automation of this process.

As with specification, a hybrid approach promises to combine the advantages of both techniques. By using a state model for the major states of the protocol, the state space is kept small, and the general properties can be checked by an automated analysis. Other properties, for which a state model would be awkward (e.g., sequenced delivery), can be handled by assertion proofs on the variables and procedures which accompany the state model. Such combined techniques are described in [16] and [10].

While a large body of work on general program verification exists, several characteristics of protocols pose special difficulties in proofs. These include concurrency of multiple protocol modules and physical separation of modules so that no shared variables may be used. A further complication is that message exchange between modules may be unreliable requiring methods that can deal with nondeterminism. A few early applications of general program verification methods to protocols are cited in Section IV and in Reference 42. Chapter 22 provides a detailed example of this technique.

A particular form of proof that has been useful for protocols with large numbers of interacting entities (e.g., routing protocols) may be called "induction on topology" [33]. The desired properties are first shown to be true for a minimum subset of the entities, and then an induction rule is proved showing that if the properties hold for a system of N entities, they also hold for $N + 1$ entities.

When an error is found by some verification technique, the cause must still be determined. Many transitions or program statements may separate the cause from the place where the error occurs, as for example when the acceptance of a duplicate packet at the receiver is caused by the too rapid reuse of a sequence number at the sender. In some cases the protocol may be modeled incorrectly, or the correctness conditions may be formulated incorrectly. In other cases, undesired behavior may be due to transmission medium properties that were not expected when the protocol was designed (e.g., reordering of messages in transit). Even when an automated verification system is available, considerable human ingenuity is required to understand and repair any errors that are discovered.

Another approach to achieving correct protocols that has been proposed recently is based on constructive design rules that automatically result in correct protocols. In one approach [50], described in Chapter 24, design rules are formulated which guarantee that the specifications obtained for a set of interacting entities will be complete. For each send transition specified by the designer, the rules determine the corresponding receive transition to be added to the partner entity. In another case [34], the specification of a second entity is determined by a design rule such that it will operate with a specified first entity to provide a given overall service.

A major difficulty for protocol verification by any method is the complexity of the global system of interacting protocol entities, also termed "state space explosion." The following methods may be used to keep this complexity within manageable limits.

(1) Partial Specification and Verification. Depending on the specification method used, only certain aspects of the protocol are described. This is often the case for transition diagram specifications which usually capture only the rules concerning transitions between major states, ignoring details of parameter values and other state variables.

(2) Choosing Large Units of Actions. State space explosion is due to the interleaving of the actions executed by the different entities. For example, the preparation and sending of a protocol data unit by an entity may usually be considered an indivisible action which proceeds without interaction with the other entities of the system. The execution of such an action may be considered a single "transition" in the global protocol description.

A particular application of this idea is to consider only states where the transmission medium is empty. Such an "empty medium abstraction" [4] is justified when the number of messages in transit is small. In this case, previously separate sending and receiving or sending and loss transitions of different entities can be combined into single joint transitions of both entities.

(3) Decomposition into Sublayers and/or Phases. The decomposition of the protocol of a layer into several sublayers and/or phases of operation simplifies the description and verification, because the protocol of each part may be verified separately [52]. An example of this idea is the decomposition of HDLC into the sublayers of bit stuffing, checksumming, and

elements of procedure, and the division of the latter into several components as described in [9].

(4) Classifying States by Assertions. Assertions which are predicates on the set of all possible system states may be formed. Each predicate defines a set (or class) of states which consists of those states for which the predicate is true. One may then consider classes of states collectively in reachability analysis instead of considering individual states. By making an appropriate choice of predicates (and therefore classes of states) the number of cases to be considered may be reduced considerably. This method is usually applied for proving safety of protocol specifications given in some programming language [41], [6], and forms the basis for symbolic execution [13]. Typically, the assertions depend on some variables of the entities and the set of messages in transit (through the layer below).

To illustrate the possible savings in the number of cases to be analyzed, consider the state of an entity receiving numbered information frames. Instead of treating all possible values of a sequence counter variable explicitly as different states, it may be possible to consider only the three cases where the variable is "less than," "equal to," or "greater than" the number in the information frame received.

(5) Focusing Search. Instead of generating all possible states, it is possible to predetermine potential global states with certain properties (e.g., deadlocks), and then check whether they are actually reachable [16].

(6) Automation. Some steps in the analysis process may be performed by automated systems [13], [16], [20], [24], [50], [37], [13]. However, the use of these systems is not trivial, and much work goes into representing the protocol and service in a form suitable for analysis. Human intervention is needed in many cases for distinguishing between useful and undesired loops, or for guiding the proof process.

IV. Uses of Formal Techniques

We give in the following a (certainly incomplete) list of cases where formal methods were successfully used for designing data communication and computer network protocols. In some cases, the formal specification was made after the system design was essentially finished, and served for an additional analysis of correctness and efficiency, or as an implementation guide. In other cases, the formal specification was used as a reference document during the system design.

Standards

Call establishment in the CCITT X.21 protocol has been modeled with a state transition-type model and analyzed with a form of reachability analysis [49]. The analysis checked for general correctness properties of completeness and deadlock, and uncovered a number of completeness errors (i.e., a protocol module could receive a message for which no processing was defined).

Virtual circuit establishment in the CCITT X.25 protocol has been modeled with a state transition model and analyzed by a manual reachability analysis [3], [1], [7]. It was found that several cycles with no useful progress could persist after the protocol once entered certain unsynchronized states.

A formal specification method was used during the design of several interface standards for the interconnection of minicomputers with measurement and instrumentation components [26], [48]. The relatively concise description of the protocols was used as means for communication between the members of the standard committees and for the verification of the design. It is also part of the final standard documents.

The HDLC link protocol has been specified with a regular grammar model [25] that incorporated an indexing technique to accommodate sequence numbering. The same protocol has also been specified with a hybrid model combining state transitions with context variables and high-level language statements [9]. The latter specification also heavily employed decomposition to partition the protocol into seven separate components, and was used in obtaining an implementation of the HDLC link level procedures of X.25 [11].

ARPAnet

Connection establishment in a transport protocol (TCP) for the ARPAnet has been partially modeled with a hybrid state transition model and validated with a manual reachability analysis [45]. An automated reachability analysis [24] was also used on a simplified model and revealed an error in sequence number handling, and incorrect modeling of the transmission medium.

A simplified version of the ARPAnet IMP–IMP link protocol has been analyzed with a transition model augmented with time constraints to show that proper data transfer requires certain time constraints to be maintained between retransmission, propagation, and processing times [35].

A simplified version of the ARPAnet communications subsystem has been modeled with a high-level programming language, and verified using partially automated program proving techniques [20], [21]. A software engineering system (called *Gypsy*) was used which provides a unified language for expressing both specifications and programs so that high-level specifications in the design can be progressively refined into detailed programs. Program modules can be both comprehensively verified in advance, or checked against their specifications at run time for the particular inputs which occur.

Connection establishment between a requester and a shared server process (the ARPAnet Initial Connection Protocol) has been modeled with a state transition model and analyzed by an automated reachability analysis [37]. The analysis showed that one of a pair of simultaneous requests for service might be rejected. A revised version of the protocol was shown to eliminate this error. The same analysis technique was also used to validate a simple data transfer protocol.

Other Examples

The end-to-end transport protocol of the French computer network Cyclades was first specified in a semiformal manner using a high-level programming language. This specification was the basis for the different protocol implementations in different host computers. Some of these implementations were obtained through a description in a macrolanguage, derived from the original protocol specification [51]. The same specification was also the basis for simulation studies which provided valuable results for the protocol validation and performance evaluation [29], [17]. A formalized specification of the protocol has also been given using a hybrid model with state machines augmented by context information and processing routines [15].

The procedures for the internal operation of the Canadian public data network Datapac were described by a semiformal method using state diagrams and a high-level programming language for the specification of the communicating entities [32]. This description was very useful for doing semiformal verifications of the protocols during the design phase, and served as a reference document during the implementation and testing phases of the system development.

IBM's SNA has been specified with a hybrid model using state machines augmented by context information and processing routines, as detailed in Chapter 25. Hierarchical decomposition is heavily used to create a large number of more manageable modules. The model provides a basis both for automated verification of general properties, and for compilation of executable code.

The Message Link Protocol [12] for process-to-process communication has been formally specified in a hybrid model. A formal service specification was also given, and the design has been partially verified by a manual reachability analysis using symbolic execution [5]. The verification uncovered a synchronization problem that has been corrected in a more recent version of the protocol.

V. Conclusions

The specification of a protocol layer must include definitions of both the services to be provided by the layer, and the protocol executed by the entities within the layer to provide this service. "Design verification" then consists of showing that the interaction of entities is indeed adequate to provide the specified services, while "implementation verification" consists of showing that the implementations of the entities satisfy the more abstract protocol specification. A useful subset of design verification may be described as verification of "general properties" such as deadlock, looping, and completeness. These properties may be checked in many cases without requiring any particular service specification.

Although protocol specifications must serve many purposes, verification and implementation are two critical tasks which require rigorous or formal specification techniques in order to be fully successful. Formal protocol specifications are more precise than descriptions in natural language, and should contain the necessary details for obtaining compatible protocol implementations on different system components. The cases mentioned in Section IV demonstrate that formal methods may be used profitably for the specification, verification, and implementation of communication protocols. However, a great deal of work remains to be done in improving verification techniques and high-level system implementation languages, in integrating performance (efficiency) analysis with analysis for logical correctness, and in automating these analysis techniques.

Most published papers on protocol verification present some particular verification technique, and demonstrate this technique by discussing its application to a simple protocol of more or less academic nature. This is not surprising, considering the short history of this specialized discipline. Some *a posteriori* verifications of protocol standards of general concern have been presented pointing out certain difficulties with the adopted procedures [1], [7], [49]. These verification efforts were based on a state reachability analysis, and in one case [49] an automated system was used. The results will influence the implementation of these protocols, and may have an impact on future revisions of the standards.

We believe that more effort should be spent on the logical verification of protocols during the design phase. Based on a formalized description method, this effort may in the future be simplified by the use of interactive automated systems for protocol verification. The same protocol specification used for the verification should also serve as an official definition of the protocol, and could be transformed, possibly through a semiautomated process into a usable protocol implementation [40], [22], [11]. It is clear that such an approach would increase the reliability of the protocols, decrease compatibility problems, and lower the cost of the protocol implementations.

References

[1] D. Belsnes and E. Lynning, "Some problems with the X.25 packet level protocol," *ACM SIGCOMM Comput. Commun. Rev.*, vol. 7, pp. 41–51, Oct. 1977.

[2] D. Bjorner, Finite state automation—definition of data communication line control procedures," in *Fall Joint Comput. Conf., AFIPS Conf. Proc.*, 1970.

[3] G. V. Bochmann, Chapter 23 of this book.

[4] G. V. Bochmann, "Finite state description of communication protocols," *Comput. Networks*, vol. 2, pp. 361–372, Oct. 1978.

[5] G. V. Bochmann, "Formalized specification of the MLP," "Specification of the services provided by the MLP," and "An analysis of the MLP," Univ. Montreal, Dep. d'I.R.O., June 1979.

[6] G. V. Bochmann, "Logical verification and implementation of protocols," in *Proc. 4th Data Commun. Symp.*, Quebec, Canada, 1975, pp. 8-5–8-20.

[7] G. V. Bochmann, "Notes on the X.25 procedures for virtual call establishment and clearing," *ACM SIGCOMM Comput. Commun. Rev.*, vol. 7, pp. 53–59, Oct. 1977; see also [4].

[8] G. V. Bochmann, "Specification and verification of computer communication protocols," chapter 5 in *Advances in Distributed Processing Management*, T. A. Rullo, ed., Philadelphia, PA: Heyden & Son, 1980.

[9] G. V. Bochmann and R. J. Chung, in "A formalized specification of HDLC classes of procedures," in *Proc. Nat. Telecommun. Conf.*, Los Angeles, CA, Dec. 1977, Paper 3A.2.

[10] G. V. Bochmann and J. Gecsei, "A unified model for the specification and verification of protocols," in *Proc. IFIP Congress*, 1977, pp. 229–234.

[11] G. V. Bochmann and T. Joachim, "Development and structure of an X.25 implementation," *IEEE Trans. Software Eng.*, vol. SE-5, pp. 429–439, Sept. 1979.

[12] G. V. Bochmann and F. H. Vogt, "Message link protocol—Functional specifications," *ACM SIGCOMM Comput. Commun. Rev.*, vol. 9, pp. 7–39, Apr. 1979.

[13] D. Brand and W. H. Joyner, Jr., "Verification of protocols using symbolic execution," *Comput. Networks*, vol. 2, pp. 351–360, Oct. 1978.

[14] A. Danthine, Chapter 21 of this book.

[15] A. S. Danthine and J. Bremer, "An axiomatic description of the transport protocol of Cyclades," presented at Prof. Conf. Comput. Networks and Teleprocessing, Aachen, Germany, Mar. 1976.

[16] A. S. Danthine and J. Bremer, "Modeling and verification of end-to-end transport protocols," *Comput. Networks*, vol. 2, pp. 381–395, Oct. 1978.

[17] A. Danthine and E. Eschenhauer, "Influence on the node behavior of a node-to-node protocol," in *Proc. 4th Data Commun. Symp.*, Oct. 1975, pp. 7-1–7-8.

[18] J. Day and C. Sunshine, Eds. "A bibliography on the formal specification and verification of computer network protocols," *ACM SIGCOMM Comput. Commun. Rev.*, vol. 9, Oct. 1979.

[19] C. A. Ellis, "Consistency and correctness of duplicate database systems," in *Proc. 6th Symp. Op. Syst. Principles*, Purdue Univ., West Lafayette, IN, Nov. 1977; *ACM Op. Syst. Rev.*, vol. 11, pp. 67–84, 1977.

[20] D. I. Good, "Constructing verified and reliable communications processing systems," *ACM Software Eng. Notes*, vol. 2, pp. 8–13, Oct. 1977; also Rep. ICSCA-CPM-6, Univ. Texas at Austin.

[21] D. I. Good and R. Cohen, "Verifiable communications processing in GYPSY," Univ. Texas at Austin, Rep. ICSCA-CPM-11, June 1978.

[22] M. G. Gouda and E. G. Manning, "Protocol machines: A concise formal model and its automatic implementation," in *Proc. 3rd Int. Conf. Comput. Commun.*, Toronto, Canada, 1976, pp. 346–350.

[23] J. V. Guttag, E. Horowitz, and D. R. Musser, "Abstract data types and software validation," *Commun. Ass. Comput. Mach.*, vol. 21, Dec. 1978.

[24] J. Hajek, "Automatically verified data transfer protocols," in *Proc. 4th Int. Comput. Commun. Conf.*, Kyoto, Japan, Sept. 1978, pp. 749–756; also see progress Rep. in *ACM SIGCOMM Comput. Commun. Rev.*, vol. 8, Jan. 1979.

[25] J. Harangozo, "An approach to describing a link level protocol with a formal language," in *Proc. 5th Data Commun. Symp.*, Utah, 1977, pp. 4-37–4-49.

[26] IEEE Standard 488-1975; see also D. E. Knoblock, D. C. Loughry, and C. A. Vissers, "Insight into interfacing," *IEEE Spectrum*, May 1975.

[27] IFIP WG 6.1, "Proposal for an internetwork end-to-end transport protocol," INWG Gen. Note 96.1; also in *Proc. Comput. Network Protocols Symp.*, Univ. Liege, Belgium, Feb. 1978, p. H-5.

[28] International Organization for Standardization, TC97/SC 16/N380 and N381, "Guide lines for the specification of services and protocols," 1981.

[29] G. LeLann and H. LeGoff, "Verification and evaluation of communication protocols," *Comput. Networks*, vol. 2, pp. 50–69, Feb. 1978.

[30] G. LeMoli, "A theory of colloquies," *Atla Frequenza*, vol. 42, pp. 493-223E–500-230E, 1973; also in *Proc. First European Workshop on Comput. Networks*, Arles, France, Apr. 1973, pp. 153–173.

[31] B. Liskov and S. Zilles, "Specification techniques for data abstractions," *IEEE Trans. Software Eng.*, vol. SE-1, pp. 7–18, Mar. 1975.

[32] F. Mellor, W. J. Olden, and C. J. Bedard, "A message-switched operating system for a multiprocessor," in *Proc. COMPSAC'77*, IEEE, Chicago, IL, 1977, pp. 772–777.

[33] P. M. Merlin, "Specification and validation of protocols," *IEEE Trans. Commun.*, vol. COM-27, pp. 1671–1680, Nov. 1979.

[34] P. Merlin and G. V. Bochmann, "On the construction of communication protocols," *Proc. International Conf. on Computer Communication*, Atlanta, October 1980.

[35] P. M. Merlin and D. J. Farber, "Recoverability of communication protocols—Implications of a theoretical study," *IEEE Trans. Commun.*, vol. COM-24, pp. 1036–1043, Sept. 1976.

[36] D. L. Parnas, "The use of precise specifications in the development of software," in *Proc. IFIP Congress 1977*, pp. 861–867.

[37] J. B. Postel, "A graph model analysis of computer communications protocols," Ph.D. thesis, Comput. Sci. Dep., Univ. California, Los Angeles, UCLA ENG-7410, 1974.

[38] L. Robinson, K. N. Levitt, and B. A. Silverberg, *The HDM Handbook*, vol. I-III, SRI Int., 1979.

[39] A. M. Rybczynski and D. F. Weir, "Datapac X.25 service characteristics," in *Proc. Fifth Data Commun. Symp.*, 1977, pp. 4-50–4-57.

[40] G. D. Schultz *et al.*, Chapter 25 of this book.

[41] N. V. Stenning, "A data transfer protocol," *Comput. Networks*, vol. 1, pp. 99–110, Sept. 1976.

[42] C. A. Sunshine, "Formal methods for communication protocol specification and verification," The Rand Corp., N-1429, Nov. 1979.

[43] C. A. Sunshine, "Formal techniques for protocol specification and verification," *Comput. Mag.*, vol. 12, pp. 20–27, Sept. 1979.

[44] C. A. Sunshine, "Survey of protocol definition and verification techniques," *Comput. Networks*, vol. 2, pp. 346–350, Oct. 1978.

[45] C. A. Sunshine and Y. K. Dalal, "Connection management in transport protocols," *Comput. Networks*, vol. 2, pp. 454–473, Dec. 1978.

[46] F. J. W. Symons, "Modeling and analysis of communications protocols using numerical Petri nets," Dep. Elec. Eng., Univ. Essex, England, Tech. Rep. 152, May 1978.

[47] A. Y. Teng and M. T. Liu, "A formal model for automatic implementation and logical validation of network communication protocols," in *Proc. Comput. Networking Symp.*,

Nat. Bureau Standards, Dec. 1978, pp. 114–123.

[48] C. A. Vissers and B. V. D. Dolder, "Generative description of DIN 66 202(E)" German, English, Twente Univ., Rep. 1261, 1881, Mar. 1977.

[49] C. H. West and P. Zafiropulo, "Automated validation of a communications protocol: The ccitt X.21 recommendations," *IBM J. Res. Develop.*, vol. 22, pp. 60–71, Jan. 1978.

[50] P. Zafiropulo *et al.*, Chapter 24 of this book.

[51] H. Zimmermann, "The Cyclades end-to-end protocol," in *Proc. Fourth Data Commun. Symp.*, 1975, pp. 7-21–7-26.

[52] S. S. Lam and A. U. Shankar, "Protocol projections: a method of analysing communication protocols," *Proc. Nat. Telecom. Conf.* 1981, pp. E3.2.

21

Protocol Representation with Finite State Models

André A. S. Danthine

I. Introduction

Although the problem of process cooperation has been under thorough study since 1965, the development of distributed systems and computer networks has increased its importance. Now the problems associated with communication between entities located in the same machine have been supplemented by those due to the characteristics of the communication medium and the disparities of environment in terms of space, time, and function.

The cooperation between two communicating entities is governed by a set of rules called a protocol. When the two communicating entities are connected to the same bus, the protocol is based on electrical signals. When the two communicating entities are located in different environments, the protocol is based on message exchanges. Any line protocol is an example of such a situation.

A computer network is generally represented as a set of distributed processes organized in a hierarchical structure.

In Fig. 1, we show a three-layer model with the application layer at the top, the transmission layer at the bottom, and the transport layer in between. The transmission layer may consist, e.g., of a set of private lines, a circuit-switching network or a packet-switching network. The transport layer provides a transport service to the processes located in the top layer. This requires an interface protocol between the upper layer and the transport layer. Another interface protocol is needed between the transport layer and the transmission layer.

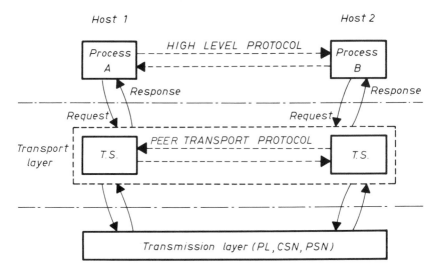

Fig. 1. A computer network as a three-layer structure.

From Fig. 1, it is clear that the communication between process A and process B involves a set of chained interface protocols. However, most modern networks have introduced the concept of end-to-end or peer protocols which govern the interaction of processes located at the same level of the hierarchy.

In Fig. 1, a peer protocol symbolized by dashed lines exists between processes located in the upper layer and also in the transport layer. We assumed that the transport service is provided by two distributed processes called transport stations (TSs). The cooperation between these two processes is governed by a peer transport protocol.

We would like to survey, using finite-state models, the problem of protocol modeling, starting with a simple protocol and moving with increasing complexity to the network protocols. But it is not without interest to consider first the design methodology.

The designer first builds a basic scenario. This involves the simultaneous definition of the basic messages and of the basic sequence of these messages. He then looks into alternative situations and during this process may introduce new messages and new sequences. In general, he also has to introduce scenarios for error recoveries. This gives rise to additional messages and increases the list of acceptable sequences.

Except for very simple cases, the protocol has reached a level of complexity which requires a systematic approach to be able to validate the design. A description based on a natural language is not adequate. There is, therefore, a strong need for a formal model at the design level. This formal model must also be usable for formal verification.

It is not certain that a model suitable for design and verification will also fit the needs of the implementers. If another formal model is more appropriate to their needs, the mapping from one model to the other must preserve the verification results.

II. Interface Protocol

As already indicated, interface protocols occur between adjacent layers of a network hierarchy. In an interface protocol, first there exists a direct exchange capability and second, interest is limited to the exchanges taking place in the dashed rectangle of Fig. 2.

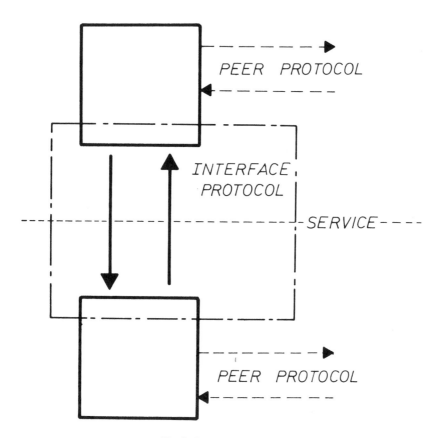

Fig. 2. Interface protocol.

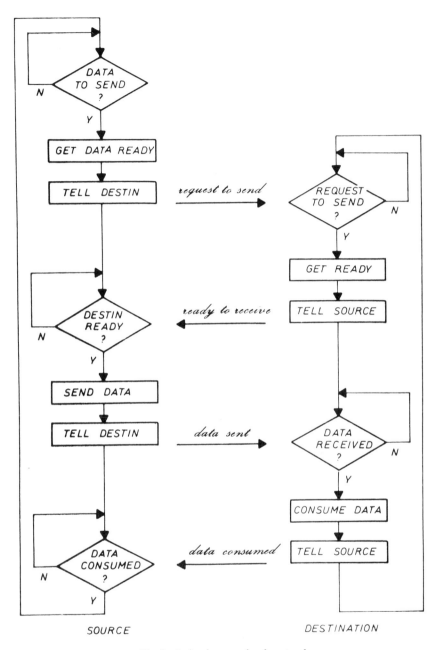

Fig. 3. A simple example of protocol.

A. A Simple Example

For an example of such an interface protocol, let us consider the flowcharts of Fig. 3. This protocol is based on a master–slave relationship between source and destination and the exchange of messages takes place in a half-duplex mode.

In any protocol, we have to consider two parts. The first one is concerned with the synchronization between the two entities at the "process level." This covers the exchange of messages which has to take place before they are able to send data. This exchange is often called the "control phase." The second part is concerned with the synchronization between the two entities at "data level." This covers the message exchange which takes place when data are transferred and which is sometimes called the "data phase."

For the protocol of Fig. 3, the pair *request to send* and *ready to receive* is concerned with the synchronization at the process level. The pair *data sent* and *data consumed* is related to the synchronization at the data level.

From the flowchart of the source, it is clear that the two events directly related to the protocol are the arrival of the two messages *ready to receive* and *data consumed*. The arrival of data to send will be considered as internal to the source process but outside the dashed rectangle of Fig. 2.

The flowchart of Fig. 3 is already a model of the protocol. Let us now look at other possible modeling techniques.

B. Finite State Machine

A *finite state machine* or automaton is a 5-tuple (X, I, O, N, M) where X is a finite set of states; I is a finite set of inputs; O is a finite set of outputs; N is a state transition function $(N: I \times X \to X)$; M is an (action and) output function $(M: X \times I \to O)$. N and M express the behavior of the automaton. If, in any given state, an input is received, the (action and) output function will indicate (the action and) the output to generate and the state transition function will indicate the new state of the automaton. Incoming messages belong to the set of inputs and outgoing messages to the set of outputs, but we may have to introduce, in the set of inputs, "internal events" or "null events" which are necessary to model events occurring outside of the specifications of the protocol but in direct connection with its behavior.

There exist several representation methods for a finite state machine but the most widely used is the state transition diagram [1]–[5]. From Fig. 3, two finite state machines may be defined, one for the source and one for the destination. They are represented as state transition diagrams in Fig. 4.

For the source finite state machine (FSM), we have as inputs the two messages and two "internal events." The first one (i.e., 1) is related to the

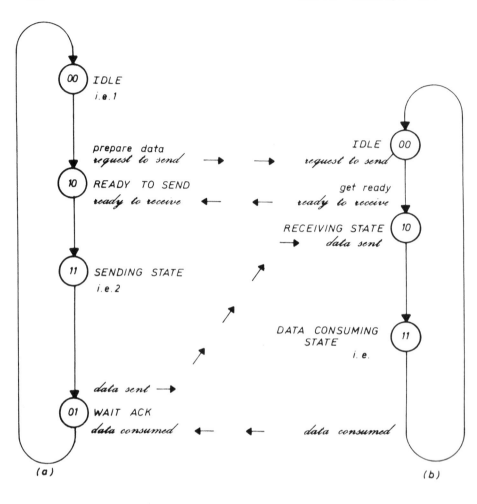

SOURCE   DESTINATION

Fig. 4. State transition diagrams for the source and the destination of Fig. 3 (names of states are in capital letters, italic is used for messages, and lower case is used for local action or internal event, abbreviated i.e.).

arrival of data to send. The second one (i.e., 2) is a true internal event and is related to the end of data transmission. These two internal events model the relationship between the protocol process and its environment. The same thing is true for the internal event introduced in the destination FSM.

From Fig. 4, it is clear that our model gives rise to four states for the source FSM and three states for the destination FSM. It is always possible to introduce additional states. For example, we may introduce between IDLE and RECEIVING STATE, a state such as PREPARING TO RECEIVE DATA. This would, however, imply that we are not only modeling the protocol but also some details of the process which implement it.

Up to now we have considered the source and the destination separately, but we may take a more global view and try to model the global FSM, i.e., the dashed rectangle of Fig. 2. The state space of the global FSM belongs to the Cartesian product of the two state spaces but is in fact a subset of it. With the four and three states of Fig. 4, we end up with only seven states instead of twelve: $\{00/00; 10/00; 10/10; 11/10; 01/10; 01/11; 01/00\}$.

The state transition diagram is not the only representation which may be used in connection with finite state automata. Another representation uses state transition matrices [3], [6]–[8]. The Appendix gives an example of such a representation for the protocol of Fig. 3.

Another possible representation is based on *decision tables*. The decision table of Fig. 5 corresponds to the source FSM of Fig. 3. In a given state and for any possible input, we find in the table the next state and the output function, if any. From Fig. 5 it is clear that in any given state, most of the

Input / State	i.e. 1.	Ready to receive	i.e. 2.	Data consumed
x_1 (00)	x_2 / OI	x_1 / –	x_1 / –	x_1 / –
x_2 (10)	x_2 / –	x_3 / –	x_2 / –	x_2 / –
x_3 (11)	x_3 / –	x_3 / –	x_4 / OII	x_3 / –
x_4 (01)	x_4 / –	x_4 / –	x_4 / –	x_1 / –

Fig. 5. Decision table of the source. The outputs are *OI: request to send, OII: data sent,* —: no output.

inputs will give rise neither to a state transition nor to an output generation. This indicates that we do not expect to receive such inputs in this given state. These "unexpected" inputs are not represented in Fig. 4.

C. Petri Nets

Petri nets [9], [10] were used initially to study the interconnection properties of concurrent and parallel activities. It is not surprising that they have been of interest in the modeling of protocols [11]–[13].

A Petri net (Fig. 6) consists of places (nodes, conditions) and transitions (events) which are connected by directed arcs. A directed arc connects either a place to a transition or a transition to a place. The places from which there are arcs incident to a transition are called the input places of that transition. The output places of a transition are similarly defined to be those which are connected to the transition by arcs which originate at the transition and terminate at the place.

A place may have one or several tokens or it may be empty. The transition obeys the following rules of operation:

(1) A transition is said to be *enabled* or *firable* if each of its input places contains at least one token.

(2) The firing of an enabled transition consists of removing one token from each of its input places and adding one token to each of its output places.

(3) The firing of an enabled transition takes zero time but may not occur immediately. The firing of an enabled transition may be considered to depend on an outside authority. Notice that if all conditions are met to run a job (enabled transition), it does not mean that the job will be go immediately into the "running" state.

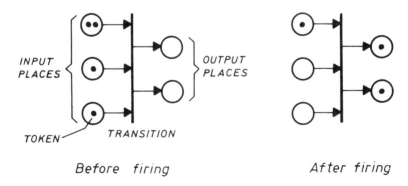

Fig. 6. Petri net principle.

Figure 6 is a representation of the formal definition of a Petri net which is 4-tuple

$$C = (P, T, I, O)$$

where

P is a set of places (conditions)	$P = \{p_1, \cdots, p_k\}$
T is a set of transitions (events)	$T = \{t_1, \cdots, t_n\}$
I is the input function	$I(t_k) = \{p_i, p_j, \cdots\}$
O is the output function	$O(t_1) = \{p_m, p_n, \cdots\}$

For the simple protocol of Fig. 3, it is possible to construct the Petri nets of Fig. 7 with the Petri net of the source on the left and that of the destination on the right. Our comments about the source FSM and its internal events are illustrated here. The internal event 1 is here the arrival of a token in B; and internal event 2 is the firing of t_3. Notice also that the CONSUME DATA of Fig. 3 appears here as an interaction with the environment.

A token distribution amongst the available places in a Petri net is called a marking. From an initial marking of a Petri net, it is possible to construct the set of markings reachable from it. Each marking represents a state of a process and defines a state machine called a token machine [11]–[12]. The token machine of the source is represented in Fig. 8.

Each arc of the token machine is labeled with the name of the transition that affects it. However, we very often have peripheral places, i.e., places receiving their token from outside the limits of the process we intend to model. In the source process of Fig. 7, B, D, and G are peripheral places. The introduction of a token in such a peripheral place results from a transition located outside the process and in the token machine the arc is labeled by the name of the place where the token is introduced. The same situation exists with places located inside the model but where the removal of a token depends upon a transition located outside.

Let us compare Figs. 4(a) and 8, which are both derived from the same source process of Fig. 3. The markings A, C, E, and F are, respectively, equivalent to the states 00, 10, 11, and 01. Inputs of the SSM such as *ready to receive* and *data consumed* appear as additional markings in the Petri net (CD and FG in Fig. 8). Finite state machine and Petri net are not strictly equivalent constructs [9], [14]; however, in most problems they will give the same results.

A Petri net provides a detailed model of the conditions related to the information flow in a process and corresponds, in a more abstract form, to a flowchart or a natural language description. As a token machine and a FSM

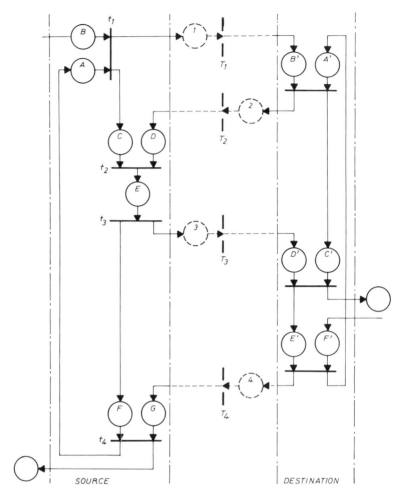

Fig. 7. Petri net for the source and the destination. Initial marking: Token in A and A'. $B = data\ to\ send$, $D = ready\ to\ receive$, $G = data\ consumed$, $B' = request\ to\ send$, $D' = data\ sent$.

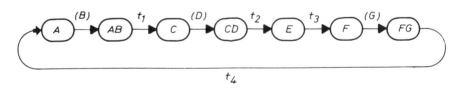

Fig. 8. Token machine of the source process.

are equivalent, it means that a FSM is, as a token machine, the result of a transformation. States are derived from conditions. Therefore, a FSM is not the best tool to use at the very beginning of the design of a protocol. At this stage a Petri net model may be very useful, while the final design may be presented as a classical and more compact FSM.

D. Interface Machine

From Fig. 7, it is possible to obtain the token machine of the destination process. It is also possible to derive the token machine for the global process located inside the dashed rectangle of Fig. 2. A transmission medium with no delay between A and B may even be replaced by a model involving four places (1 to 4) and four transitions (T_1 to T_4) as in Fig. 7.

However, if we take into account the master–slave relationship and the half-duplex characteristic of our protocol, it is possible to introduce the ideal of an *interface machine*. Such a machine does not exist but it may be a useful conceptual tool. Such an interface machine is located between the two processes A and B of Fig. 2 and receives as inputs the messages generated by A and B [Fig. 9 (a)]. Figure 9(b) is the Petri net graph of the interface machine. Figure 9(c) is the state transition diagram associated with the interface machine and Fig. 9(d) is the token machine.

This virtual interface machine places in evidence the fact that, in the example analyzed, *"the knowledge of the state of the source is enough to know the state of the destination and vice versa."* Even if the two processes have only local information, our protocol is such that this local information is equivalent to global information.

The FSM of the interface machine involves four states [Fig. 9(c)]. We mentioned in Section II B that the global FSM involves seven states. Besides the initial states, the only pair of truly equivalent states is the state 11/10 of the global FSM and the state 11 of the interface machine [Fig. 9(c)]. The greater number of states of the global FSM comes from the asynchronous character of the transitions of the source and destination processes and also from the internal events introduced in Fig. 4. This again raises the problem of the boundary between the specifications of the protocol and the specifications of the processes which implement it.

E. Transmission Medium

In the simple example of Section II A, we assumed a perfect transmission medium. We did not consider that a message might be lost. In the general case, we will need to model this transmission medium more realistically because its properties may be essential at the design level (Fig. 10).

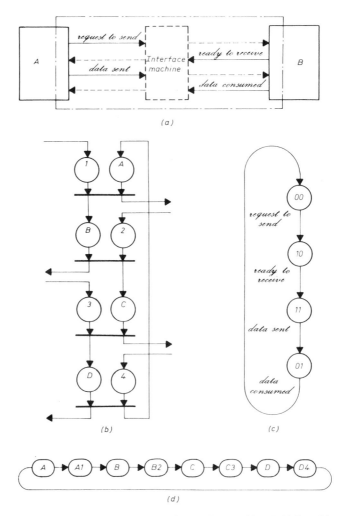

Fig. 9. (a) Interface machine. (b) Petri net of the interface machine. Initial marking: token in *A*. 1 = *request to send*, 2 = *ready to receive*, 3 = *data send*, 4 = *data consumed*. (c) State diagram of the interface machine. (d) Token machine.

The transmission medium must be defined in terms of actions on the messages which may take various forms such as variable delay of transmission, loss of a message, duplication of a message, etc. In such an environment, it is no longer possible to introduce the idea of a unique interface machine because the information about one process no longer allows one to deduce the global state. Even with a perfect transmission medium but with a full-duplex protocol, the interface machine concept has to be discarded.

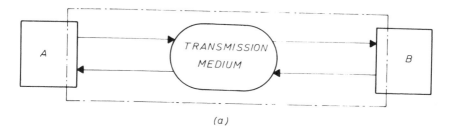

(a)

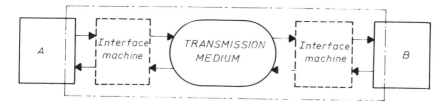

Fig. 10. Interface machine with nonideal transmission medium.

It has been suggested that two interface machines be introduced [Fig. 10(b)] each reflecting the view that each side has about the global state. However, there may be difference between the state of any interface machine and the real global state due to the behavior of the transmission medium. Therefore, the value of interface machines is questionable and we prefer to rely on a global model which involves two local models and a model of the transmission medium.

F. Other Transition Techniques

Besides FSMs and Petri nets, other representation methods have been proposed such as the UCLA graph [15]. Variable structure sequential machines have also been proposed for modeling [16].

In [17], Zafiropulo used a directed graph where only the basic events, message transmission, and reception are represented. The processes are assumed to begin and terminate in state 0. From the directed graph of a local model, it is possible to find one or several paths beginning and ending in state 0, which is a "unilogue." A unilogue is, at the local model level, a possible sequence of events–messages received or transmitted. After identification of all possible unilogues, it is possible to build a "duologue matrix" used for validation. The duologue matrix is related to the search for compatible unilogues. If the transmission medium is not assumed to be perfect, its characteristics are mapped into extensions of the direct graph.

This work, which has been used to validate the X.21 protocol [18], has been extended and automated [19]–[21], as described in Chapter 23.

G. Programming Languages

Our starting point for introducing our simple protocol was flowcharts and it is not surprising that high-level programming languages have been used for modeling the source and the destination processes [22]–[25]. We will return to this later.

III. Peer Protocol

In the Introduction we mentioned the concept of an end-to-end or peer protocol which governs the interaction of processes located at the same level of the hierarchy of a computer network (Fig. 1). The purpose of such a protocol is very often to provide a service to entities located in the next higher level of the hierarchy. For instance, the transport protocol between the two TSs in Fig. 1 is designed to provide a transport service to the processes located in the upper level. It is therefore essential not to limit the model to the "interface between the two TSs" but to include the interface protocol between the user process and a TS (Fig. 11).

The link between the two TSs is a virtual one. The characteristics of such a virtual link may depend upon series of chained interface protocols, and the properties of the transmission medium over the virtual link have to be carefully evaluated.

These considerations eventually lead us to the global model of a peer protocol represented by the dashed rectangle in Fig. 11. It involves the models of two TS and the transmission medium model. A TS is a local entity and the model of it will be called a local model.

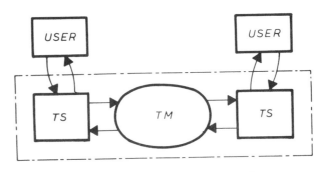

Fig. 11. Global model of a peer protocol.

Any local entity (e.g., the TS in Fig. 11), exchanges messages with its peer entity but interacts also with the user process. The user process requests services from the TS, which has to respond to these requests. This leads us to introduce for the local model two sets of inputs and two sets of outputs.

The rationale for separation is based on the following considerations. Between peer entities there is no reason to introduce a master–slave relationship, and furthermore, the set of output messages of one local model must be the same as the set of input messages of the other. Between a user process and the TS, which are in two different levels of the hierarchy, it may be essential to introduce a master–slave relationship, and furthermore, the interface protocol is a local one. In two locations, it may be different in the extent of the services provided. The set of requests from a user to its local TS and the set of responses from the TS to the user may therefore be different from one location to another.

The differences between the two types of interactions call for a clear separation between the two input sets and between the two output sets involved in the modeling of the local process.

If we compare Figs. 2 and 11, it is clear that in the latter, the two interacting entities are entirely enclosed in the dashed rectangle. All interactions with the environment of a TS are part of the input and output definitions. Here, internal events will now really be internal to the model.

As our global model involves two local models and a transmission medium model, we are back to our initial point, i.e., to model a local process. However, the additional inputs and outputs raise the problem of the usefulness of the methods presented when the complexity increases. As will be seen, it is necessary to extend the methods in order not to be limited to academic examples.

IV. General Local Model

A. State Variables and Context Variables

When the number of states becomes very large, any type of state machine is difficult to apply and all transition diagram becomes unusable. This dimensionality problem may be overcome by decomposition techniques.

In an instance of a program, the status word is only part of the complete state of the process. The information associated with the status word is supplemented by a set of context variables. Following the same approach to overcome the dimensionality problem in protocol modeling, it has been proposed to associate with a set of states, a set of context variables

[7], [30]. Transitions involving context variables are described by a set of procedures. Using such an extended model, it has been possible to completely model the transport protocol for Cyclades [4] and to verify certain aspects of it [8], [31].

During this study, two basic questions were raised. (1) How do we separate state and context variables? (2) What are the relationships between the procedure, execution and the state transition?

The second question will be considered later. Let us try to address the first one.

The protocols we are interested in are based on message exchanges and the interface with the upper level is based on requests and responses (Fig. 1). The general structure of any input to the local process may be assumed to be the following:

$$\langle \text{op. code}\rangle\langle\text{parameter vector}\rangle$$

The operation code indicates the kind of request or message, e.g., $\langle\text{send letter}\rangle$, $\langle\text{ack}\rangle$, etc.

The parameter vector is used to transmit additional information in connection with this $\langle\text{op. code}\rangle$ and we have, therefore, a dependency relationship which may be used to separate state and context.

Let us define

$I = \{\langle\text{op. code}\rangle\langle\text{parameter vector}\rangle\}$

$I_1 = \{\langle\text{op. code}\rangle\}$

$I_2 = \{\langle\text{parameter vector}\rangle\}$

$I \subset I_1 \times I_2$.

The cardinal number of the finite set I_1 of the operation codes is in general much smaller than the cardinal number of the finite domain of the discrete parameter vector space. A small cardinal number for the input set is a necessary condition for limiting the number of states of the FSM. Therefore, adopting a FSM model with the input set I_1 is a possible way to overcome the dimensionality problem.

To any input from the set, I_1 (basic input) will correspond a state or a set of states in the FSM. As the parameter vector has a dependency relationship with its $\langle\text{op. code}\rangle$, we may associate with a state (or a group of states) a set of context variables selected in connection with the elements of the parameter vector. The dependence of the $\langle\text{parameter vector}\rangle$ on the $\langle\text{op. code}\rangle$ will be mapped into a dependency of the context variables on the state variables. Roughly speaking, $\langle\text{op. code}\rangle$ will change state variables and $\langle\text{parameter vector}\rangle$ will modify context variables. We will return to this point in Section IV E.

B. Petri Nets

If the problem of dimensionality of the FSM has to be considered, the same is true for the Petri net. In order to get a usable tool to describe complex and real situations, Nutt [32] introduced the concept of an *evaluation net* which, like a Petri net, is also made up of transitions interconnected by directed arcs to locations (places), but here the transitions obey the following rule: a transition fires if the set of input and output locations *satisfied the definition of that particular transition* causing one token to be removed from each location of a *prespecified subset* of input locations and one token to be placed on each location of a *prespecified subset* of the output locations. Furthermore, the time required for each execution of a transition is part of the specification of the net. This extension allows one to introduce time as a measure of the net performance.

Nutt introduced several evaluation net primitives:

(1) The *T*-transition is a transition involving one input location and one output location. The *T*-transition is enabled if the input location is full (contains one token) *and* the output location is empty (contains no token). Here, the state of the output locations has to be verified before enabling the transition. The *F*-transition with one input and two output locations and the *I*-transition with two input locations and one output location also require empty output locations to enable the transition.

(2) The *X*-transition is reproduced in Fig. 12. In the *X*-transition, a hexagon has been introduced. It represents a *resolution location* which is a special type of input location whose status may be 0 (i.e., empty), 1 (i.e., full) or $\varnothing$ (i.e., undefined). The two output arcs have also been marked with a 0 or a 1 and the *X*-transition definition is the following: the *X*-transition is enabled if the input location is full (contains one token) *and* the resolution location status is defined (0 or 1) *and* the output location corresponding to the value of the resolution location status is empty. The firing of an enabled transition consists of removing the token from the input location, putting one token in the output location corresponding to the value of the resolution location status and changing the resolution location status to be "undefined." As previously mentioned, the transition time is specified for each transition.

As the resolution location status returns to the undefined state, the complete specification of the *X*-transition implies a *resolution procedure* which is activated when a token is placed in the input location. One purpose of this resolution procedure is to define the status of the resolution location.

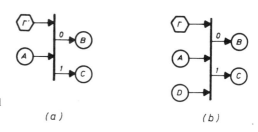

Figure 12. *X*-transition. (a) As defined by Nutt [32]. (b) As used in [13].   *(a)*   *(b)*

The resolution procedure includes an expression of the form

$$M:[\,p_1 \rightarrow S(r):= i; p_2 \rightarrow S(r):= 1 - i\,]$$

where $S(r)$ is the status of r, i is either 0 or 1, and p_1 and p_2 are two predicates.

If p_1 is true, the status is set to i and further evaluation of the procedure is discontinued. Otherwise, p_2 is evaluated and if it true, the status of r is set to $1 - i$. When both predicates are false, the status of r remains undefined and the procedure need not be evaluated again until one of the arguments of the predicates changes its value.

The purpose of the *resolution procedure* is to prepare the firing of the transition by setting the value of r to 0 or 1. One may also introduce a *transition procedure* which is executed at the firing time.

Another important extension of the classical Petri net introduced by Nutt is the concept of *attribute token*. A token may be a simple token only denoting occupancy or it may be an *attribute token*, i.e., a vector representing a set of attributes, some or all of which may change as the token flows through the net. A *transition procedure* may reference *and* alter value attributes of tokens as they flow through the associated transition. They may also reference and alter *environment variables*, i.e., global variables that may be accessed by any procedure in the net. A *resolution procedure* may reference but not alter token attributes and environment variables.

Since in general the execution of a *resolution procedure* is immediately followed by the execution of an associated *transition procedure*, we will not here distinguish any further between the two and will only refer to a *resolution procedure* which in the first step may reference (but not alter) token attributes and environment variables in order to set the value of r, and in second step depending upon the value of r, may proceed further and alter token attributes and environment variables.

C. Time Petri Net

The time Petri net is another extension of the classical Petri net. Introduced by Merlin [11]–[12], it consists in adding two time values to each transition of a Petri net. The first time value associated with the transition i will be noted $t * i$ and denotes the minimal time that must elapse from the time that all the input conditions of a transition are enabled until this transition can fire. The second time value associated with the transition i will be noted $t * * i$ and denotes the maximum time that the input conditions can be enabled and the transition does not fire. We always have $t * i < t * * i$ and a Petri net is a special case of a time Petri net with $t * i = 0$ and $t * * i = \infty$.

The time concept introduced here is completely different from the transition time of Nutt. Time Petri nets are useful in protocol modeling, for instance to model the discarding of a token received under some conditions (token absorber) or to model a retransmission mechanism based on a timeout.

D. Combined Petri Net

A combination of the time Petri net and the X-transition of Nutt has been used to model the Cyclades transport protocol in the following way [13]. We already know the general structure of an input (request or message):

$$\langle \text{operation code} \rangle \langle \text{parameter vector} \rangle$$

Therefore, the occurrence of an input with a given operation code is not represented by a simple token but by an attribute token. The occurrence of a request or of a message must first be checked with an input condition and therefore the transition will have two input locations [Fig. 12(b)]. When an awaited request or an awaited message occurs, the protocol has to check the parameter vector associated with it and make a basic evaluation. Such an evaluation may be expressed with the help of predicates and the X-transition is just what is needed to model it. Eventually, we end up with the basic module of Fig. 13.

The occurrence of an input with a given $\langle \text{op. code} \rangle$ will be indicated by a token in location A. Location B will be used for marking the condition under which the request or message will not be discarded.

(1) If the token is missing in B when a token appears in A, we must provide a mechanism which removes the token in A without firing f_1. Such a mechanism, not represented in Fig. 13, involves an arc from location A to a

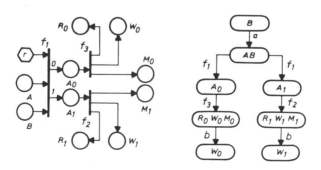

Fig. 13. Basic module (left) with its token machine (right).

transition f_0 used to absorb the unwanted token. To avoid any interference between transitions f_0 and f_1, we will set ($t * 0 > t ** 1$).

(2) If the condition B is not missing when A occurs, the resolution procedure r may be activated and will decide to put a token in A_0 or A_1 or not to fire f_1 immediately. From a conceptual point of view, we may say that the case 1 where a token is placed in A_1 means that the request is accepted and that the case 0 where a token is placed in A_0 means that the request is not accepted. In both situations, the token resulting from the firing of transition f_1 will eventually fire the transition f_2 or f_3. The most that such a firing may do is

(a) to pass a message to the next unit (token in M_i);
(b) to send a reply to the origin of the request or message received (token in R_i) and
(c) to set a waiting condition for another incoming message or request (token in W_i).

On the right-hand side of Fig. 13, the token machine associated with the basic module has been reproduced. Transitions between states (markings) are due to transitions firing (f_1, f_2, and f_3), to token arrival (a) or to token removal (b). For simplicity, we assume that if the output location involves a message M_1 and a response R_1, both proceed further at the same time.

In our model we will need the concept of environment variables that may be accessed by any procedure in the net and we will allow a resolution procedure to alter these variables. Returning to Fig. 13 and assuming a token in the B location when a token in A arrives, the general structure of a resolution procedure involves

(1) checking up on available resources;
(2) setting or updating of environment variables; and
(3) selection of an output location by evaluation of predicates.

The predicate evaluation may involve the availability of resources, the matching of the parameter vector associated with the input A with the global variables, and so on.

Without environment variables and resolution procedures, the number of places and consequently of markings would be too numerous and the model would not be usable. By keeping the parameter vector information at the environment variable level, it is possible to gain a partial control of the dimensionality problem. To every ⟨op. code⟩ we associate a place like A in Fig. 13 and introduce environment variables and resolution procedures to deal with the parameter vectors. As an example, it has been possible to develop a model with 28 places for the basic control phase of Cyclades protocol [13].

In our two state transition models (extended FSM of Section IV A and extended Petri net of this section), we have now introduced very equivalent ideas. With the FSM, we had state variables and context variables. With the Petri net we have the markings and the environment variables. With the FSM, we had a procedure execution and a state transition. With the Petri net we have a resolution procedure and a firing.

To complete this comparison we would like to point out that one of the main attractions of Petri net oriented models lies in the insight they give into the mechanisms of the protocol. With the basic module of Fig. 13, a lot of questions are raised when a protocol is analyzed. But such a tool will even be more useful at the design stage. For instance, if we want to define the way to interpret a request to open a link issued by the user process to its TS (Fig. 11), we may use the basic model of Fig. 13.

The occurrence of the request ⟨open link⟩ will put a token in place A. A syntactically correct request may be rejected if the source process does not have the access rights to the service or if the TS does not have the resources and does not want to queue the request. If the request is rejected the firing of f_1 will put a token in A_0. The firing of f_3 will put a token in R_0, i.e., will send a negative response to the source of the request. Places like M_0 (message sent to the other TS) and W_0 (waiting condition) are not necessary in this example. If the request is accepted, the firing of f_1 will put a token in A_1. A message will be sent to the remote TS (token in M_1) and a waiting condition will be set (token in W_1). The introduction of a place like R_1 would mean that the source will receive a reply with the following semantic: your request has been accepted by your local TS. However, the designer may prefer to avoid all partial replies and wait until the end of the processing of the request by all distributed entities before reporting back to the source. If so, places like R_1 very often have to be dropped.

In summary, for every received request or message, the designer will tailor the basic module (Fig. 13), define environment variables, and define resolution procedures to determine the processing of the information included in parameter vectors.

E. Finite State Machine Decomposition

In our Petri net, we have attribute tokens and states represented by markings and environment variables. Furthermore, transitions are completed by resolution procedures.

In Section IV A complex inputs were introduced, basic state variables were supplemented by context variables, and state transitions by procedure executions. We would like here to formalize this approach and propose the replacement of a unique FSM model by a two-step process involving two

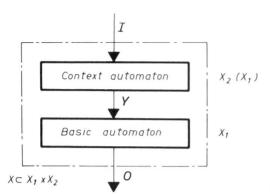

$X_2 (X_1)$

X_1

$X \subset X_1 \times X_2$

Figure 14. Decomposition of a finite state automaton into context and a basic automata.

successive FSMs (Fig. 14) [31]. The second FSM is, of course, equivalent to the set of procedures.

Let us expand our previous definitions and define

X_1 as the finite set of states of a basic automaton

X_2 as the finite set of states of a context automaton

with $X \subset X_1 \times X_2$.

The first step involves the FSM defined as the 5-tuple $X_1 \times X_2 \times 1_1 \times 1_2, Y, P, Q$, where Y is a set of output symbols

$$P: 1_1 \times 1_2 \times X_1 \times X_2 \to X_2$$

$$Q: 1_1 \times 1_2 \times X_1 \times X_2 \to Y$$

As only X_2 is modified by the state transition this FSM will be called the context automaton. To define more precisely the transition and the output functions we may use the following notation:

$$P[X_1 \times 1_1]: X_2 \times 1_2 \to X_2$$

$$Q[X_1 \times 1_1]: X_2 \times 1_2 \to Y$$

which means that the mappings from $X_2 \times 1_2$ into X_2 or Y depend upon the values of the basic automaton state and the input symbol (op. code). The second step involves the FSM defined as the 5-tuple

$$X_1 \times X_2, Y, 0, F, G$$

where

$$F: Y \times X_1 \to X_1$$

$$G: Y \times X_1 \times X_2 \to 0 \times 0$$

The introduction of the Cartesian product 0×0 in the output mapping function G is necessary, as an element of Y may generate two outputs. The input symbol of this FSM is the output symbol of the first one. As only X_1 is modified by the state transition this FSM will be called the basic automation. The decomposition process is summarized in Fig. 15.

To understand why the mapping G depends upon X_2, we must remember that any response or output message has the following structure:

⟨op. code⟩ ⟨parameter vector⟩

and if we define

0_1: finite set of output symbols (op. code),

0_2: finite domain of a discrete parameter vector space,

the output set 0 is a subset of the Cartesian product $0_1 \times 0_2$. To construct the parameter vector of an output we need the values of some of the context variables.

The behavior of the two automata may be summarized as follows: when a request or input message is received, the op. code is first examined and, depending on the basic state, the input is accepted or rejected (neglected). If accepted, the processing of this input will involve the parameter vector of the input and the value of the context state, the net result of the processing being the generation of an output symbol y and the possible

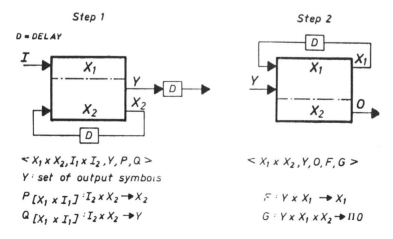

Fig. 15. Finite state automaton as a two-step process.

modification of the context state. For a pair of op. code and basic state we may have several possible elements of Y which are to be selected depending on the values of the parameters associated with the op. code and of the context state. For instance, an input message for opening a liaison, received in a given basic state, may be mapped into one output symbol if there is parameter agreement or into another output symbol if there is parameter disagreement.

Therefore, the cardinal number of Y is in general greater than the cardinal number of I_1 but much smaller than the cardinal number of I and thus, one of the goals, which was to overcome the dimensionality problem, has been achieved, at least for the basic automaton.

When the output symbol y is passed to the basic automaton the context state is already updated. The basic automaton is a classical FSM with a state transition and output generation depending upon the input symbol and the basic state. The complete output generation implies the concatenation of the op. code and of a parameter vector depending on context state X_2. If the parameter vector is neglected the output mapping of the minimal basic automaton becomes $G': Y \times X_1 \to 0_1 \times 0_1$.

One may prove that this decomposition is always possible and with this two-step process we have now answered the second question of Section IV A.

F. Hybrid Models

In Section IV B, extended Petri nets were associated with resolution procedures. In Section IV E the second FSM was normally described by a set of procedures. This combination of a transition model and an abstract program is called a hybrid model.

In [33], Bochmann also proposed a hybrid model involving a FSM part plus additional state variables, and concluded that "since reachability analysis of state machines seems to be more amenable to algorithmic methods than verifying (and finding) program assertions, the above tradeoff may have important implications for future automated methods of protocol verification." The hybrid model of [33] is based on Keller's model [34], itself very close in concept to the evaluation net of Nutt [32].

The model of [33] has been used in [35] for the HDLC protocol. In this example, it is interesting to notice the heavy use of functional partitioning which is another way to reduce the dimensionality problem of the finite state machine. This decomposition method has been used in [36] for modeling SNA.

In [37], Sunshine raises an interesting objection against the use of a programming language as a specification tool: "a program, even in a 'high level language,' is usually not a satisfactory specification because it is

impossible to separate the essential features of what the program is supposed to do from the particular way chosen to accomplish those functions."
As almost all hybrid models are using programming languages at least
partially, Sunshine's objection concerns the whole protocol community. Our
personal opinion is that, even with formal models like FSM, it is extremely
difficult to model only the protocol and to avoid completely the process
which will implement it. This was pointed out in Section II F.

Owing to the limitations of transition models, the interest in hybrid
models is increasing. They have also been used in [38] and are mentioned as
a natural extension by several authors.

As FSM and abstract program are equivalent constructs, it is possible
to represent protocols as abstract programs. This will be developed in
Chapter 22. The dimensionality problem is no longer an issue at the
representation level but verification remains a very difficult problem.

V. Global Model

If we have the model of the two peer entities of Fig. 11, we still need a
model of the transmission medium to be able to consider the complete
end-to-end protocol. The nondeterministic aspect of the transmission
medium model does not allow the use of the same modeling techniques and
this raises additional difficulties. As this is related to the verification
aspects, it will not be treated in this paper. Let us just say that reachability
analysis is the basic method for transition-oriented models and that assertion proving is the cornerstone of models based on programming languages.
Of course, hybrid models require both methods. Additional information
about verification aspects may be found in [35], [37], [39] and in other
chapters of this book.

VI. Conclusion

The problem of modeling protocols in order to validate or verify or
implement them has now reached a level of development which allows
practical problems to be solved.

The generalization of the hybrid approach is certainly not an accident.
In the long run, the superiority of reachability analysis versus program
assertions or the converse will probably depend upon their relative capability in terms of automated methods.

At the modeling level, there are quasiequivalent tools starting from
Petri nets and evolving to programming languages through automata theory,

grammars, and formal languages. The past experience of people will probably decide their choice. It is, therefore, more important to stress the similarities of these methods than to focus on their differences, and we hope to have contributed to this goal.

Appendix: State Transition Matrices for Fig. 3

If we represent inputs and outputs by unit vectors, it is possible to express the state transition and the output functions by matrices whose elements are logical functions of the state

$$x = N(x) \cdot i \quad \text{and} \quad o = M(x) \cdot i$$

For instance, for the source FSM, if we used the following input vectors i:

$$\text{internal event, } 1 = \begin{bmatrix} 1 \\ 0 \\ 0 \\ 0 \end{bmatrix}, \qquad \text{ready to receive} = \begin{bmatrix} 0 \\ 1 \\ 0 \\ 0 \end{bmatrix}$$

$$\text{internal event, } 2 = \begin{bmatrix} 0 \\ 0 \\ 1 \\ 0 \end{bmatrix}, \qquad \text{data consumed} = \begin{bmatrix} 0 \\ 0 \\ 0 \\ 1 \end{bmatrix}$$

and the following output vectors

$$\text{request to send} = \begin{bmatrix} 1 \\ 0 \end{bmatrix}, \qquad \text{data sent} = \begin{bmatrix} 0 \\ 1 \end{bmatrix}$$

with the following states:

$$x_1 = [0,0]^T = (\text{idle}) \qquad\qquad x_2 = [1,0]^T = (\text{ready to send})$$

$$x_3 = [1,1]^T = (\text{sending state}) \qquad x_4 = [0,1]^T = (\text{data consumed})$$

we have

$$N(x) = \begin{bmatrix} p(x_1 + x_2 + x_3) & p(x_2 + x_3) & p(x_2) & p(x_2 + x_3) \\ p(x_3 + x_4) & p(x_2 + x_3 + x_4) & p(x_3 + x_4) & p(x_3) \end{bmatrix}$$

where

$$p(x_i + x_j) = 1 \qquad \text{if state is } x_i \text{ or } x_j$$

$$= 0 \qquad \text{otherwise}$$

and

$$M(x) = \begin{bmatrix} p(x_1) & 0 & 0 & 0 \\ 0 & 0 & p(x_3) & 0 \end{bmatrix}$$

References

[1] D. Bjorner, "Finite state Automaton—Definition of data communication line control procedures," *AFIPS Proc.*, Vol. 37, FJCC, Houston, November 1970, pp. 477–491.

[2] H. Kawashima, K. Futami, and S. Kand, "Functional specification of call processing by state transition diagrams," *IEEE Trans. Comm. Tech.*, Vol. COM-19, October 1971, pp. 581–587.

[3] R. E. Rusbridge and A. Langsford, "Formal representation of protocols for computer networks," Report AFRE-R-7826, UKAEA, Harwell, England, December 1974, 20 p.

[4] A. A. S. Danthine and J. J. Bremer, "An axiomatic description of the transport protocol of cyclades," *Rechnernetze und Datenfernverarbeitung*, Aachen 1976, Springer-Verlag, pp. 259–273.

[5] G. V. Bochmann, "Finite state description of communication protocols," *Proc. Comput. Network Protocols Symp.*, Univ. of Liege, February 1978, pp. F3-1 to F3-11, and *Comput. Networks, 2*, 4/5, October 1978, pp. 361–372.

[6] R. W. Stutzman, "Data communication control procedures," *Comput. Surv.*, Vol. 4, No. 4, December 1972, pp. 197–220.

[7] A. A. S. Danthine and J. J. Bremer, "Communication Protocols in a Network Context," *Proc. ACM Interprocess Comm. Workshop*, Santa Monica, March 1975, pp. 87–92.

[8] A. A. S. Danthine and J. J. Bremer, "Modeling and verification of end-to-end protocols," SART 77/11/13, *Third European Network User's Workshop*, IIASA, Laxenburg, Austria, April 19–20 1977, 17 p.

[9] J. L. Peterson, "Petri nets," *ACM Comput. Surveys*, Vol. 9, No. 3, September 1977, pp. 223–251.

[10] R. C. Chen, "Representation of Process Synchronization," *Proc. ACM SIGCOMM/SIGOPS Interprocess Commun. Workshop* 1975.

[11] P. M. Merlin, "A methodology for the design and implementation of communication protocols," *IEEE Trans. Commun.*, Vol. COM-24, No. 5, June 1976, pp. 614–621.

[12] P. M. Merlin and D. J. Farber, "Recoverability of Communication Protocols. Implications of a theorical study," *IEEE Trans. Commun.*, Vol. COM-24, No. 9, September 1976, pp. 1036–1043.

[13] A. Danthine, "Petri nets for protocol modeling and verification," *Proc. Comput. Networks and Teleprocessing Symp.*, Budapest, Hungary, October 1977, Vol. II, pp. 663–685.

[14] P. M. Merlin, "Specification and validation of protocols," *IEEE Trans. Commun.*, Vol. COM-27, No. 11, November 1979, pp. 1671–1680.

[15] J. Postel, "A graph model analysis of computer communications protocols," Ph.D. dissertation, UCLA-ENG 7410, January 1974, 184 p.

[16] L. Mezzalira and F. A. Schreiber, "Designing colloquies," *1st Europ. Workshop on Comput. Networks*, Arles, April 1973, pp. 351–363.

[17] P. Zafiropulo, "Protocol validation by duologue-matrix analysis," *Proc. Intern. Commun. Conf.*, Chicago, June 1977, pp. 259–263, and *IEEE Trans. Commun.*, Vol. COM-26, August 1978.

[18] C. H. West and P. Zafiropulo, "Automated validation of a communication protocol: The CCITT X.21 recommendation," *IBM J. Res. Dev.*, Vol. 22, No. 1, January 1978, pp. 60–71.

[19] H. Rudin, C. H. West, and P. Zafiropulo, "Automated protocol validation: One chain of development," *Proc. Comput. Network Protocols Symp.*, Univ. of Liege, February 1978, pp. F4-1 to F4-6 and *Comput. Networks*, 2, 4/5, October 1978, pp. 373–380.

[20] C. H. West, "An automated technique of communications protocols validation," *IEEE Trans. Commun.*, Vol. COM-26, No. 8, August 1978.

[21] C. H. West, "General technique for communication protocol validation," *IBM J. Res. Dev.*, Vol. 22, No. 4, July 1978.

[22] G. V. Bochmann, "Logical verification and implementation of protocols," *Proc. 4th Data Commun. Symp.*, Quebec, October 1975, pp. 7-15 to 7-20.

[23] N. V. Stenning, "A data transfer protocol," *Comput. Networks*, Vol. 1, No. 2, September 1976, pp. 99–110.

[24] D. Brand and W. H. Joyner, "Verification of Protocols using symbolic execution," *Proc. Comput. Network Protocols Symp.*, Univ. of Liege, February 1978, pp. F2-1 to F2-7 and *Comput. Networks*, 2, 4/5, October, 1978, pp. 351–360.

[25] J. Hajek, "Automatically verified data transfer protocols," *Proc. Int. Comput. Commun. Conf.*, Kyoto, September 1978, pp. 749–756.

[26] J. Harangozo, "Protocol definition with formal grammars," *Proc. Comput. Network Protocols Symp.*, Univ. of Liege, February 1978, pp. F6-1 to F6-10.

[27] A. Y. Teng and M. T. Liu, "A formal approach to the design and implementation of network communication protocol," *Proc. COMPSAC* 78, Chicago, pp. 722–727.

[28] A. Y. Teng and M. T. Liu, "A formal model for automatic implementation and logical validation of network communication protocol," *Proc. Comput. Networking Symp.*, N. B. S., Gaithersburg, Maryland, December 13, 1978, pp. 114–123.

[29] J. C. Day, "A bibliography on the formal specification and verification of computer network protocols," *Proc. Comput. Network Protocols Symp.*, Univ. of Liege, February 1978.

[30] A. A. S. Danthine and J. J. Bremer, "Definition, representation et simulation de protocoles dans un contexte reseau," *J. AIM Mini-Ordinateurs et Transmission de Donnees*, Liege, janvier 1975, pp. 115–126.

[31] A. Danthine and J. Bremer, "Modeling and verification of end-to-end transport protocols," *Proc. Comput. Network Protocols Symp.*, Univ. of Liege, February 1978, pp. F5-1 to F5-12 and *Comput. Networks*, 2, 4/5, October 1978, pp. 381–395.

[32] G. J. Nutt, "Evaluation nets for computer system performance analysis," *AFIPS Conf. Proc.*, Vol. 41 Part 1, 1972, pp. 279–286.

[33] G. V. Bochmann and J. Gecsei, "A unified method for the specification and verification of protocols," *Proc. IFIP Congress*, Toronto 1977, pp. 229–234.

[34] R. M. Keller, "Formal verification of parallel programs," *CACM*, 7, 1976, pp. 371–384.

[35] G. V. Bochmann and R. J. Chung, "A formalized specification of HDLC classes of procedures," *Proc. Nat. Telecommun. Conf.*, Los Angeles, December 1977, pp. 03A..2-1 to 2-11.

[36] R. J. Sundstrom, "Formal definition of IBM's system network architecture," *Proc. Nat. Telecommun. Conf.*, Los Angeles, December 1977, 3A1.

[37] C. Sunshine, "Formal techniques for protocol specification and verification," *IEEE Comput. Mag.*, August 1979, 21 p.

[38] C. A. Sunshine and Y. K. Dalal, "Connection management in transport protocols," *Comput. Networks*, 2, 6, December 1978, pp. 454–473.

[39] C. A. Sunshine, "Survey of protocol definition and verification techniques," *Proc. Comput. Network Protocols Symp.*, Univ. of Liege, February, 1978, and *Comput. Networks*, 2, 4/5, October 1978, pp. 346–350.

Specifying and Verifying Protocols Represented as Abstract Programs

Brent T. Hailpern

I. Introduction

Network protocols form the cornerstone upon which distributed systems are built. Because of their fundamental importance, protocols must be designed with care so that they work correctly. In this chapter we discuss the techniques that have evolved for specifying and verifying protocols. In particular, we concentrate on those techniques that model protocols as abstract parallel programs.

In order to specify a protocol, one must describe what the protocol should do, what the protocol should not do, and how the protocol should react to external stimuli. The implementation of a protocol is an implicit specification; the protocol is specified to behave exactly as does the implementation. We prefer, however, to specify the protocol abstractly and to leave until later those details of the implementation that do not affect our idea of how the protocol should behave.

To verify a protocol, one describes some desirable property (or properties) of the protocol. One then proves that the specification of the protocol satisfies that property.

We are interested in two kinds of properties of network protocols: *safety* and *liveness*. Safety properties are of the form "bad things will not happen." Partial correctness—if an operation terminates, then the correct result will occur—is a safety property. (In other words, it will not happen that the operation terminates with an incorrect result.) Note that a program can be partially correct by never terminating. Another example of a safety property is "the number of acknowledgments sent does not exceed the number of messages received." Note again that a program that never sends any acknowledgments would satisfy this safety property. In order to state that a program makes progress—that it does something—we use liveness properties. Liveness properties have the form "good things will happen" (for example, "the program will terminate" and "acknowledgments will be sent"). In general, we use safety properties to state that if something is done, then it is done correctly; we use liveness properties to state that the something is done.

How should we evaluate a technique for specifying a protocol? There are many criteria: how easy is it to implement the specification, how easy is it to use the specified protocol (if the only information provided is the specification), how easy is it to prove properties of a specification, and how easy is it to prove that a given implementation meets its specification? We will not attempt to rate the techniques described in this report, but rather to discuss some of their strengths and weaknesses.

First we briefly discuss four techniques for specifying and verifying protocols. In Section III we describe the hierarchical view of network protocols and the importance of this view in abstract-program techniques. Section IV presents a brief overview to the Floyd/Hoare approach to verifying programs. Section V describes those abstract-program techniques that deal only with safety properties of protocols. Section VI discusses those techniques that use *temporal logic* in order to specify and verify both safety and liveness properties of protocols. Finally, we give an overview of automatic verification of network protocols expressed as abstract programs.

II. Overview

We will describe four approaches to specifying network protocols: informal, transition model, abstract program, and mixed model. (The majority of this paper will be concerned with the abstract-program approach.) In the informal approach, the protocol is specified in a natural language (for example, English). The input/output characteristics are described along with the expected responses to external stimuli. Verification consists of describing how the protocol responds in every conceivable situation. The informal approach is not reliable enough for most applications; English is imprecise and can lead to ambiguities. In addition, without some formal model it is difficult to guarantee that all circumstances are being considered.

The most commonly used formal techniques are based upon transition models in which the protocol is described as a set of finite state machines (or similar systems such as Petri nets). Each machine represents a component of the network (for example, reader, writer, and communication medium). Transitions correspond to external stimuli (for example, receipt of a message). To verify the correctness of a protocol, one forms the system state space as the cross product of the state spaces of the protocol's component machines. One then performs a reachability analysis on the set of system states. Deadlock is detected when a reachable system state with no exit transitions is discovered. Bochmann, Sunshine, and Danthine have written excellent surveys on the transition-model approach. (See Chapters 20, 21, and 23. Also see Sunshine's survey [35].)

The transition-model approach is superior to the informal approach because the former permits less ambiguity. Another advantage of the transition model is that generating the system state space and performing the reachability analysis can be automated [15, 36]. Such automatic verification reduces the possibility that some situation (combination of states) may be forgotten. The main disadvantage of the transition-model approach is that as the complexity (number of states) of the protocol increases, the number of systems states and hence the length of the proof grows exponentially. (This phenomenon is known as "state-space explosion.")

In the abstract-program approach, the protocol is described as a parallel program (in a language such as Concurrent Pascal). The program may serve as the specification or as an abstract implementation. If it serves as the specification, then various properties of the program can be proved (such as freedom from deadlock and correct data transfer). If, instead, the program represents an implementation, then the task is to show that this implementation meets the properties stated in the specification. Verification follows the standard Floyd–Hoare technique [9, 16] described below. This approach will be discussed in more detail in the remainder of this paper.

The mixed-model approach [2] is an attempt to combine the best features of the transition-model and abstract-program techniques. Variables are associated with the states to record sequence numbers and other information that is not easily represented in a reasonable number of states. The resulting representations are smaller than the corresponding pure finite state machine representation. The proof technique, however, is no longer simple because the system state space involves more than the simple cross product of the individual machine state spaces; it also involves the variables, the values of which are potentially unbounded.

III. The Hierarchical View of Network Protocols

In all of the techniques described below, protocols are specified and verified in the context of the hierarchical framework used throughout this volume. In this view, the various functions of the network are separated into layers. Each layer uses the services provided by the next lower layer as primitive instructions. In turn, each layer provides services to be used by the next higher layer. For example, one protocol layer can define a bit data type in terms of high and low voltages. The next layer can define characters in terms of bits, and so on. A layer need not define a new data type; it can provide some other service. For example, if one layer provides a message data type and an unreliable transmission medium (that is, messages can be lost), then the next layer can provide the same message data type with a reliable medium.

Each level of a protocol is specified and verified in terms of the services provided by the next lower level and by the services it provides to the next higher level. There are three advantages to using this hierarchical structure when specifying protocols: the layers to be designed are all of a reasonable size and complexity, the layers can be designed independently as long as the interfaces (service specifications) have been precisely defined, and alternative implementations for a layer can be interchanged without affecting the correctness of the rest of the protocol. In addition, each part of the protocol can be verified independently—proving its specification in terms of the specifications of the operations it uses. This independence simplifies the task of verifying large protocol systems.

IV. The Floyd–Hoare Technique for Verifying Programs

The Floyd–Hoare technique consists of attaching logical statements, called *assertions*, to the program to describe the program state (that is, the value of the program variables) at each control point. One can think of the control points of a program as being the different values of the program-counter. For parallel programs, there is a control point between each atomic (indivisible) operation. For example, in a program that adds up a series of positive integers, we can assert that after the addition of each integer in the series, the new partial sum equals the old partial sum plus the added integer.

In addition to these "local" assertions, one develops *invariant assertions* (or *invariants*). Invariants are also logical statements about the program variables and control points, but they describe properties of the program that are always true (that is, true at each and every control point). Using the example above, we can state that the value of the partial sum is always nonnegative. These assertions and invariants allow one to abstract information from the representation of the program state. One can then reason about classes of states (avoiding the state-space explosion of the transition-model reachability analysis).

To describe the behavior of a program statement, we associate two assertions, called the *precondition* and *postcondition*, with that statement. If S is a statement and P and Q are the pre- and postconditions, respectively, then we write

$$\{P\}\ S\ \{Q\}$$

to mean that if P is true before S executes, and if S terminates, then Q will be true after S terminates. For each programming language, rules are developed to derive the pre- and postconditions for each type of statement in that language.

In addition to describing the properties of individual statements, pre- and postconditions can be used to specify the properties of procedures and functions. No additional notation is needed, just rules for proving that the precondition of a procedure and the code of that procedure suffice to prove the postcondition of the procedure. Pre- and postconditions are used to specify the actions of the low-level operations that a given protocol uses (such as "send" and "receive"), as well as the actions of the protocol procedures themselves. (Note that there is no restriction that the pre- and postconditions must specify deterministic procedures. Hence, unreliable transmission media may be described easily using this technique [5], [13], [14], [33].)

The Floyd–Hoare technique deals only with sequential programs. Owicki and Gries [22] describe the additional concepts needed to verify safety properties of parallel programs.

V. Specifying and Verifying Safety Properties

In this section we discuss five abstract-program approaches to specifying and verifying safety properties of network protocols. We first discuss the early work of Bochmann that introduced the idea of treating protocols as abstract programs. Next we describe Stenning's approach, which is similar to Bochmann's, but with more formal proofs. Thirdly, we discuss Krogdahl's protocol skeletons for specifying and verifying classes of protocols. Then we describe Schindler's specification technique. Finally, we present an overview of the work of Bremer and Drobnik; their technique is especially suited to specifying and verifying safety properties of distributed systems.

Bochmann

Bochmann [1] made one of the earliest attempts at specifying and verifying a protocol using an abstract program. He cited three properties that a protocol specification method should have:

1. A protocol can be specified in a comprehensive form; in particular, the complete definition of a protocol can be partitioned into different levels of abstraction;

2. the specification of a protocol allows proving certain properties of the protocol and its operation, proving in particular that the error recovery is effective, and that all possible situations of erroneous behavior have actually been considered;
3. given the specification of a protocol, its implementation is simple, and part of the implementation may be obtained automatically.

He went on to say that no method then existed that satisfied all three requirements, but that useful tools for specifying and proving properties of parallel processes did exist. Note the emphasis on the hierarchical view of protocols and the necessity for both precise specification and formal verification; these concepts permeate the other techniques that we will discuss.

Bochmann presented, as an example, a simple data transfer protocol based upon HDLC [7]. The protocol was specified in a "free-style Pascal." The program structure was event driven, with statements of the form "when event X occurs perform actions Y and Z." In many ways, the structure was similar to a transition model: the states were specified by the values of the variables at each "station," and the state transitions were represented by events.

Bochmann partially verified the protocol by stating three safety invariants that described the number of messages sent and received by each station. He presented the outline of a proof for these invariants in terms of other simpler invariants. The proof was not formal, but at that time there was no good theory for verifying the correctness of parallel programs.

It should be noted that Bochmann intended (in this paper) that the program code be the specification of the protocol. Invariants were meant to describe certain properties of the protocol.

Stenning

Independently of Bochmann, Stenning was attacking the problem of specifying and verifying data-transfer protocols using abstract programs [34]. He also described his protocol in a procedural manner (that is, by program code). Stenning, however, specified the safety properties of his primitive operations and the safety criteria that the procedures of the protocol were supposed to fulfill (using the Floyd–Hoare notation described above). As in Bochmann, the program can be considered as the specification and the safety assertions as properties that have been proved of this specification. Alternatively, the safety properties can be considered to specify the protocol and the program to be a sample implementation.

Stenning's proof technique was more formal than that of Bochmann. His code was very close to standard Pascal, which enabled him to rely on the standard Pascal rules for deriving pre- and postconditions. He provided specifications for the behavior of those statements that were not strictly Pascal. He outlined the proofs of eleven invariants and presented a rigorous proof of the final system invariant.

Krogdahl

Krogdahl [18] developed the technique of *protocol skeletons* for describing and verifying safety properties of classes of protocols. A protocol skeleton includes the "essence" of what is necessary for a protocol to be safe (there is no notion of timers or time-out conditions). The skeleton consists of a set of operations for the stations (processes) of the protocol system. The operations use only variables local to the associated station and any incident communication medium (FIFO queues). There are two restrictions on the execution of these operations: within one station operations must be executed sequentially, and associated with each operation there is a condition that has to be met before the operation can be initiated. The specification of the operations themselves uses an Algol-like language.

After the operations have been developed one proves a system invariant that describes the safe operation of the protocol. The variables referred to by the invariant may be accessed only by the specified operations. The proof of the invariant follows the standard Floyd–Hoare technique (that is, assuming that the invariant assertion is true before an operation is executed, show that the operation preserves the invariant's validity). Because only the specified operations can access the invariant's variables and because the specified operations always preserve the invariant, any order of execution of the specified operations is safe. (Note that seemingly unsafe sequences are prevented by the condition clauses of the operations that state when it is safe to execute the operation in question.) Different protocols can be developed that use the operations in different orders—with respect to the invariant all of these protocols will be safe.

Schindler, Didier, and Steinacker

Schindler, Didier, and Steinacker [29], [30], [31], [32] have been working to precisely specify the X.25 packet level protocol with the goal of developing a system in which the implementation can be automatically generated from the specification. Though one of their objectives is that their specification system be easily verifiable, they have not detailed any verification techniques.

They divide the problem into the specification of a number of *protocol machines*. (A protocol machine is a special purpose abstract machine with only a few meaningful execution sequences—namely, those consistent with its protocol [31].) Each protocol machine consists of a number of modules (data abstractions). Each module consists of specifications of a state vector (the variables of the module), functions accessing the state vector, admissible execution sequences of these functions, and interface specifications.

The functions in a module enforce restrictions and conventions, provide data transfer, and implement internal routines (such as buffering and multiplexing). Unlike most other specification techniques, these functions are allowed to have side effects; they may affect the state vectors of other modules. The authors claim that if properly controlled, such side effects allow for a more natural specification and implementation than would be possible without side effects.

In order to specify a function, one provides the following information: a precondition, an if-condition, and a postcondition. The pre- and postconditions have the usual meanings; the if-condition has the form

IF sem-cond THEN T.postcond ELSE F.postcond.

The meaning of this if-condition is "if the function begins with 'sem-cond' true and if it terminates, then when it terminates 'T.postcond' will be true; if the function begins with 'sem-cond' false and if it terminates, then when it terminates 'F.postcond' will be true." On the surface, the if-condition could be merged with the pre- and postconditions. However, all conditions must be based on predicates (functions that return true or false) also specified in the protocol. Pre- and postconditions must consist of predicates that do not alter the system state—they may be safely checked to see if the function may be executed in a particular circumstance. The evaluation of the sem-cond, however, may call predicates from a lower-level module that do affect the system state—these predicates may have side effects. Therefore, if-conditions should only be checked if the function is actually being executed. The if-conditions are used to model the side effects of the functions that they specify.

Bremer and Drobnik

Bremer and Drobnik [5] use additional hierarchical structure in their technique in order to further simplify the task of specification and verification. They explicitly specify the lower-level services that the protocol is provided (which they call the *transmission subsystem service*) and the higher-level services that the protocol is to provide (which they term the *protocol service*). These two services specify what the protocol must do. The verification problem, then, is to show that a given implementation satisfies the constraints specified by these two services.

They expand the pre- and postcondition notation in order to describe more completely the intricacies of a distributed environment. This additional information is stated in terms of three conditions that must be true during different phases of an operation's execution. The environment of the call to an operation must guarantee that the *execution condition* of the operation remains true as long as execution of the operation has not terminated. Similarly, the operation guarantees that the *invariant condition* remains true as long as execution has not completed. Finally, the *completion condition* must become true in order for the operation to terminate. Bremer and Drobnik do not give a formal theory for deriving these conditions, but they do present many examples of the conditions.

In order to simplify the programming and verification of the parallel processes, Bremer and Drobnik further decompose each protocol layer into two levels: the *concurrency level* and the *distribution level*. The concurrency level provides a high-level description of the protocol without specifying the distribution of the parts of the protocol among the component processes. The distribution level allocates the functions defined in the concurrency level among the different processes. The verification task involves showing that the distribution level program, using the transmission subsystem services, correctly implements a set of operations that the concurrency level (correctly) uses to implement the protocol service.

Bremer and Drobnik have outlined proofs of the alternating bit protocol, the HDLC link protocol (in a multipoint environment), and a decentralized directory management protocol. They note that the split between the concurrency and distribution levels reduces the complexity of designing, implementing, and verifying protocols.

VI. Temporal Logic Techniques

The techniques described above involve only safety properties of protocols; that is, assertions that the protocol cannot reach an undesirable state. Liveness properties—assertions that the protocol will progress—refer to the future occurrence of a certain event. For example, we can say that an operation *will* terminate, that a message *will* be sent, or that an acknowledgment *will* be received. Conventional logic formulas are inadequate for expressing and reasoning about liveness, because they cannot refer to any state other than the present one. In an attempt to reason about liveness properties of protocols, Hailpern, Lamport, Owicki, Melliar-Smith, and Schwartz have adopted the notation of temporal logic [10], [20], [26], [27], which provides operators for making assertions about future program states. (Hailpern, Owicki, and Lamport [14], [25] discuss rules for deriving and proving temporal assertions about programs.)

The simplest form of temporal logic includes two temporal operators: □ (henceforth) and ◇ (eventually). The formal definitions of these operators are stated in terms of sequences of states in a program computation. Informally, we may interpret the formula $\Box P$ as meaning that P is true now and will remain true forever. The eventually operator is the dual of the henceforth operator; the informal interpretation of $\Diamond P$ is that either P is true now or P will be true at some time in the future. As an example, the statement "the operation P will terminate" can be written as

$$\text{at } P \supset \Diamond(\text{after } P)$$

where "at P" is an assertion that is true if the program is just about to execute operation P. Similarly, "after P" is true immediately after executing operation P. (The statement would be read as "if 'at P' is true, then eventually 'after P' will be true.") Other, more complex, temporal operators are also used in the papers discussed below, but these two operators, henceforth and eventually, give much of the flavor of the logic.

Hailpern and Owicki

Hailpern and Owicki [13], [14] model a protocol system as a set of interacting modules that represent the logical units of the system (for example, transmitter, receiver, and communication medium). (Each module is either a *process* or a *monitor*. A process is an active program component —a procedure with its own program-counter. A monitor is a synchronized data abstraction, that is, a collection of data and procedures that access that data where only one process can access a given monitor at a time.) Hailpern and Owicki exploit this modularity in their specifications and proofs. All low-level operations are specified by safety and liveness inference rules. Each module, in turn, is specified by safety invariants and liveness commitments (the temporal statements that correspond to invariants) that must be verified directly from the code of that module. In constructing the system proof, only the verified properties of the modules are used; the internal implementation is ignored. This method is hierarchical in that any level of abstraction may be assumed as long as the inference rules of the constituent operations are specified.

In addition to temporal logic, Hailpern and Owicki use *auxiliary history variables* [12], [17], [23], [24] to record the interactions between the modules of the protocol system. (Auxiliary variables are used only in the proof of a program. They record information as do normal variables, but they may affect neither the value of any normal variable nor the control flow of the program. History variables have the ability to record an unbounded sequence of values—all the messages sent through a communication medium, for example.) One frequently stated safety property of a link protocol is that the output is an initial subsequence of the input (that is, the output history may be no longer than the input history and corresponding elements of the two histories are equal). This safety invariant would be stated as

$$\text{out} \le \text{in}$$

where $\le$ indicates "initial subsequence," *in* represents the input history, and *out* represents the output history. Histories also facilitate liveness statements. For example, to state "if message X has been received, then acknowledgment Y will eventually be sent" we would write

$$X \in \text{in} \supset \Diamond(Y \in \text{out})$$

Hailpern and Owicki have verified the safety and liveness of the alternating bit protocol, two versions of Stenning's data transfer protocol, and Brinch Hansen's multiprocessor network [6].

Lamport, Schwartz, and Melliar-Smith

Lamport, Schwartz, and Melliar-Smith have divided the task of defining and verifying protocols into two parts: *service-level specification* and *network-level specification*. This separation is similar to that of Bremer and Drobnik; the service level defines the operations available to the users of the protocol, and the network level represents an abstract specification of the essential details of the protocol implementation. The goal is to verify the service level from the network level and to verify the network level from the protocol code.

A major difference between this technique and that of Hailpern and Owicki is that the latter relies on large-scale synchronized units, such as monitors where this technique is defined in terms of fine grain atomic operations (possibly as small as changing the parity of a bit). A second difference is that this technique does not use history variables or any kind of auxiliary variable. (The Hailpern–Owicki technique relies heavily on the use of auxiliary variables.) By not using auxiliary variables, the programmer avoids describing properties of the protocols in terms of variables that are not actually implemented in the program. However, input/output relationships, such as out $\le$ in, are more difficult to describe without the use of auxiliary histories.

In describing the service-level specification, Lamport and Schwartz [21] rely on Lamport's notation for stating the safety properties of concurrent processes [19]. In Lamport's notation, the formula $\{P\}\ S\ \{Q\}$ is interpreted to mean "if execution is started anywhere inside S (including at its beginning) with predicate P true, then P will remain true so long as control remains in S—and Q will become true if and when S terminates." This

notation allows for multiple (visible) control points during the execution of
S, allowing for interference with S by other processes. Liveness statements
take the same form as in Hailpern and Owicki: $P \supset \Diamond Q$ (if the program
ever reaches a state in which P is true, then it will eventually reach a state in
which Q is true).

The service-level specification of the alternating bit protocol is extremely simple, it consists of four assertions for each of the two operations
give and *take*. The assertions do not mention the existence of the alternating
bit, because it is transparent to the user. Lamport and Schwartz have
attempted to specify only those properties that would be relevant to a user
of the protocol.

Schwartz and Melliar-Smith [33] describe the network-level specification. While the service level did not include implementation details, the
network level is specified in terms of sequence numbers, timers, and internal
control points. The resulting assertions (about safety and liveness properties) are correspondingly more complex. These invariants involve additional
temporal operators to describe the duration of one event in relation to
another event. As with the service-level specification, the network-level
specification has been stated in a way that avoids overspecification. For
example, messages and acknowledgments can occasionally be ignored, and
decisions as to when sequence numbers are updated are left to the implementer (as long as the network-level specifications are met).

Lamport, Schwartz, and Melliar-Smith have not, as of yet, verified the
service level in terms of the network level. Neither have they verified the
network level in terms of a sample implementation. The main direction of
their current research is the development of higher-level temporal operators
to "bring the level of expression closer to the level of conceptualization of
the requirements."

VII. Automated Verification

One drawback of the techniques described above is that they are paper
and pencil exercises. As such, they are limited in size to the amount of
specification and verification that one person (or a few people) can do.
There are some attempts, however, to automate the verification of network
protocols using an abstract program model. In this section, we will discuss
the protocol work of Brand and Joyner, and the Gypsy, SARA, and AFFIRM
projects. All four systems are general program provers that have been
adapted to the task of proving the correctness of protocols.

Brand and Joyner

Brand and Joyner's verifier [3], [4] was designed and implemented as a
part of a general purpose verifier oriented towards microcode verification.

The protocols are stated in an Algol-like language and are verified using *symbolic execution*.

The goal of symbolic execution is to create a proof tree, a node of which represents a class of states of the system at one point in time. The root of the tree represents all initial states in which the protocol can begin; the leaves represent all possible final states. Associated with each node is a predicate list that describes the class of states represented by that node. For example, an IF statement generates two cases, one with the test true, the other with the test false; correspondingly, one branch leads to those states in which the test is true and the other branch leads to those states in which the test is false. To prove that a program has a given end result, one must show that all final states (leaves) have that result true. Parallelism is modelled (in the standard way) as nondeterminism, that is, the execution of two processes do not overlap, but may be arbitrarily interleaved.

In some sense this technique is another form of reachability analysis with the predicates acting to reduce the state-space explosion by combining states into classes. Alternatively, the proof technique can be thought of as a predicate transformation technique; the possible consequences of each program statement contribute a branch to the tree, the nodes of which describe the new situation after the statement's execution.

In proving the correctness of the HDLC protocol [4], Brand and Joyner's verifier produced a tree with 131 leaves. To verify all of these cases, 1347 theorems had to be proved, of which the verifier was able to prove 80% automatically. The remaining 20% required knowledge of modular arithmetic that the verifier did not have.

The Gypsy Project

Gypsy [12] is intended to provide an effective, practical language for developing large (concurrent) software systems that are formally verified. Gypsy systems are built out of well-defined subsystems so that proofs of the system and of each subsystem are mutually independent. Process coordination is accomplished strictly through message buffers; formal specifications are stated in terms of buffer transaction histories. The language syntax is similar to that of Pascal.

DiVito [8] has taken the first steps to specifying and verifying the alternating bit protocol with Gypsy. The major difficulty is modeling the unreliable nature of the communication medium; the transmitter and receiver processes easily fit the Gypsy paradigm. The problem with the medium is that Gypsy restricts all communication between processes to message buffers—buffers that do not lose or corrupt messages. Therefore, the current line of research is to modify Gypsy to accept unreliable media.

The SARA System

The SARA system [28] has grown out of the UCLA-graph transition model. SARA, however, has been augmented to be equivalent to the abstract-program systems discussed elsewhere in this survey. The SARA paradigm allows a program to be modeled in three domains: *control flow, data flow,* and *interpretation.* The control graphs are similar to Petri nets. Each node has input logic, which describes the conditions that must exist for a node to be initiated. Similarly, each node has output logic, which dictates the arcs along which the node passes control upon termination. Control is represented by tokens on the control arcs; the tokens move as a result of actions by the nodes. The data graphs describe static collections of data. The interpretation links events in the control graph to transformations of the data, using a PL/I-like syntax.

Razouk and Estrin have used SARA to model the X.21 interface between Data Terminal Equipment (DTE) and Data Circuit-terminating Equipment (DCE) on a public data network [28] (based upon the work of West and Zafiropulo [36]). Using the resulting model, the automatic verification system discovered 14 deadlocked states. They further extended their analysis to include what they called the "intent" of the interface specification. That is, those states in which the components of the protocol did not agree on the status (empty or not empty) of the communication medium were examined as possible violators of the "intent." They then used formal verification techniques (invariants) to determine if these states were indeed errors. This technique is not a complete verification of a protocol, but it does allow for the verification of vital aspects of a system.

The AFFIRM Project

The last system that we will discuss is AFFIRM [11]. In AFFIRM, data structures are specified in terms of *constructors, extenders,* and *selectors.* Constructors create the objects of a given data type. Extenders are more complicated operators built up from the constructors. Selectors compute the value of functions with arguments of the given data type. (For example, "insert," "remove," and "newlist" might be constructors in a list data type; "joinlists" and "sortlist" might be extenders; "listlength" and "frontvalue" might be selectors.) The actions of these operators are defined by a set of axioms. An automatic theorem prover is used to prove properties of these user-defined data types based upon the set of axioms.

The basic structure of AFFIRM has been generalized in order to prove the correctness of protocols. The "data object" is equated with the "state" of the protocol. The "constructors" become "events." (Sample events include send, receive, and timeout.) Thus a sequence of events are treated as the concatenation of a series of constructors. Gerhart gives the following example. The state

$$RcvS \left(TimeoutS(RcvR(Send(Init, m)))\right)$$

represents one state reached after the sequence of operations

$$Init, Send(m), RcvR, TimeoutS, RcvS$$

Each "state" includes the value of the variables at that time. Therefore, the "selectors" return the values of these variables. (Examples include the contents of the transmission medium and the current sequence number.) Finally, the AFFIRM "axioms" define the "transitions" of the protocol; they specify the legal relationships between states.

The AFFIRM project has verified safety properties of a simple message system, a transport protocol, the alternating bit protocol, and a version of Stenning's data transfer protocol. They are currently attempting to verify FTP (ARPAnet's File Transfer Protocol).

VIII. Conclusion

We have discussed some techniques for specifying and verifying network protocols expressed as abstract programs. The different techniques emphasized different aspects of the problem: specification, safety verification, safety and liveness verification, and automatic verification. It is as yet unclear which of the techniques will turn out to be the best for the specification/verification task, especially since most of them have been tested only against simple link-level protocols.

At a recent workshop held at USC's Information Sciences Institute, a number of researchers in the field met to compare techniques for specifying and verifying network protocols. All were to provide a specification and proof of the alternating bit protocol. Not only were all of the proofs different, but none of the specifications agreed as to what the alternating bit protocol was. If anything, this should indicate the desperate need for tools to precisely specify and rigorously verify network protocols. Extending the hierarchical approaches described in this paper should help simplify this formidable task. Pursuing the various versions of temporal logic should give us a handle on the elusive liveness properties. Finally, automatic verification becomes a necessity as more complex protocols are designed.

References

[1] Gregor V. Bochmann, "Logical verification and implementation of protocols," *Fourth Data Commun. Symp.*, (Quebec City) pp. 7.15–7.20, IEEE, October 1975.

[2] Gregor V. Bochmann and Jan Gecsei, "A unified method for the specification and verification of protocols," *Proc. IFIP Cong. 77*, pp. 229–234. North Holland Publishing Company, 1977.

[3] Daniel Brand and William H. Joyner, Jr., "Verification of protocols using symbolic execution," *Comput. Networks*, vol. 2(4/5), pp. 351–360, September/October 1978.

[4] Daniel Brand and William H. Joyner, Jr., "Verification of HDLC," IBM Research report RC7779, Yorktown Heights, New York, July 1979.

[5] J. Bremer and O. Drobnik, "A new approach to protocol design and validation," IBM Research Report RC8018, Yorktown Heights, New York, December 1979.

[6] Per Brinch Hansen, "Network: A multiprocessor program," *IEEE Trans. Software Eng.* vol. SE-4(3), pp. 194–199, May 1978.

[7] "Data communication—High level data link control procedure—Elements of procedures (independent numbering)." Draft International Standard ISO/DIS 4335, September 1976. See also ISO TC97/SC6, Document 1005.

[8] Benedetto L. DiVito, "A mechanical verification of the alternating bit protocol," ICSCA-CMP-21, University of Texas, Austin, June 1981.

[9] Robert W. Floyd, "Assigning meanings to programs," *Proc. Symp. Appl. Math.* XIX, pp. 19–32, American Mathematical Society, 1967.

[10] Dov Gabbay, Amir Pnueli, Sharon Shelah, and Yonatan Stavi, "On the temporal analysis of fairness," *Seventh Annual ACM Symp. on the Principles of Programming Languages*, (Las Vegas) pp. 163–173, January 1980.

[11] Susan L. Gerhart, "Protocol specification and verification: A progress report" Technical report AFFIRM MEMO-18-SLG, USC Information Sciences Institute, February 1980.

[12] Donald I. Good and Richard M. Cohen, "Principles of proving concurrent programs in Gypsy," *Sixth Annual ACM Symp. on Principles of Programming Languages*, (San Antonio) pp. 42–52, January 1979.

[13] Brent T. Hailpern and Susan S. Owicki, "Verifying network protocols using temporal logic." *Proceedings Trends and Applications 1980: Computer Network Protocols*, (Gaithersburg), pp. 18–28, IEEE Computer Society, May 1980.

[14] Brent T. Hailpern, *Verifying Concurrent Processes Using Temporal Logic.* Ph.D. thesis, Computer Science Department, Stanford University, 1980. Technical report 195, Computer Systems Laboratory, Stanford University, August 1980.

[15] J. Hajek, "Automatically verified data transfer protocols," *Evolutions in Computer Communications: Proceedings of the Fourth International Conference on Computer Communication*, (Kyoto) pp. 749–756, North Holland Publishing Company, 1978.

[16] C. A. R. Hoare, "An axiomatic basis for computer programming." *Commun. ACM*, vol. 12(10), pp. 576 + , May 1969.

[17] John H. Howard, "Proving monitors," *Commun. ACM*, vol. 19(5) pp. 273–279, May 1976.

[18] Stein Krogdahl, "Verification of a class of link-level protocols," *Bit*, vol. 18, pp. 436–448, 1978.

[19] Leslie Lamport, "The Hoare logic of concurrent programs," *Acta Informatica*, vol. 14, pp. 21–37, 1980.

[20] Leslie Lamport, "Sometime" is sometimes "not never": On the temporal logic of programs," *Seventh Ann. ACM Symp. Principles of Programming Languages*, (Las Vegas), pp. 174–185, January 1980.

[21] Leslie Lamport and Richard L. Schwartz, "Notes on a service specification for the alternating bit protocol," In preparation, Computer Science Laboratory, SRI International, June 1980.

[22] Susan S. Owicki and David Gries, "Verifying properties of parallel programs: An axiomatic approach," *Commun. ACM*, vol. 19(5), pp. 279–285, May 1976.

[23] Susan S. Owicki, "Specifications and proofs for abstract data types in concurrent programs," in F. L. Bauer and M. Broy, eds., *Program Construction*, pp. 174–197. Springer Verlag, 1979.

[24] Susan S. Owicki, "Specifications and verification of a network mail system," in F. L. Bauer and M. Broy, eds., *Program Construction*, pp. 198–234. Springer Verlag, 1979.

[25] Susan Owicki and Leslie Lamport, "Proving liveness properties of concurrent programs," to appear in ACM Transactions on Programming Languages and Systems, 1982.

[26] Amir Pnueli, "The temporal logic of programs," *Eighteenth Ann. Symp. Foundations of Comp. Sci.* (Providence) pp. 46–57, IEEE, October 1977.

[27] Amir Pnueli, "The temporal semantics of concurrent programs," *Semantics of Concurrent Computation*, pp. 1–20. Springer-Verlag, 1979.

[28] Rami R. Razouk and Gerald Estrin, "Validation of the X.21 interface specification using SARA," *Proc. Trends and Applications 1980: Comput. Network Protocols*, (Gaithersburg) pp. 155–167, IEEE Computer Society, May 1980.

[29] Sigram Schindler, Jochen Didier, and Michael Steinacker, "Design and formal specification of an X.25 packet level protocol implementation," *Proc. Compsac78*, (Chicago), pp. 686–691, IEEE Computer Society, November 1978.

[30] Sigram Schindler, "Synchronized data types and their suitability for protocol implementations," *Proc. Twelfth Hawaii Int. Conf. System Sci.*, (Honolulu), pp. 18–27, Western Periodicals Company, 1979.

[31] Sigram Schindler and Michael Steinacker, "A formal specification of an X.25 protocol machine," *Proc. Trends and Applications 1979: Adv. Syst. Technol.*, (Gaithersburg), pp. 54–64, IEEE Computer Society, May 1979.

[32] Sigram Schindler and Michael Steinacker, "A uniform protocol machine organization for the transport layers of the ISO/ TC-97/ SC16/ reference model," *Proc. Trends and Applications 1979: Adv. Syst. Technol.*, (Gaithersburg), pp. 65–73, IEEE Computer Society, May 1979.

[33] Richard L. Schwartz and P. M. Melliar-Smith, "Temporal logic specification of distributed systems," Proceedings of the Second International Conference on Distributed Systems, Paris, April 1981.

[34] Norman V. Stenning, "A data transfer protocol," *Comput. Networks*, vol. 1(2), pp. 99–110, September 1976.

[35] Carl A. Sunshine, "Formal techniques for protocol specification and verification," *Computer*, vol. 12(9), pp. 20–27, September 1979.

[36] C. West and P. Zafiropulo, "Automated validation of a communications protocol: The CCITT X.21 recommendation," *IBM J. Res. Dev.* vol. 22(1), pp. 60–71, January 1978.

23

A Hybrid Model and the Representation of Communication Services

Gregor V. Bochmann

I. Introduction

Different approaches have been used for the formal specification and verification of communication protocols. As explained in Chapter 20, most of these approaches use finite state transition diagrams or programs written is some high-level programming language or both. The purpose of this chapter is threefold.

First, in Section II, we review some experience with a general transition model, which we called a "unified" approach [1] because it involves state transitions and programming language elements. We believe that such an approach is appropriate for the formal specification of protocols, the specification of the services provided, and the verification of correct operation. In Section IV, we point out certain similarities between finite state transition and programming language approaches to verification. Knowledge of the indicated references may be useful, but are not necessary for the understanding of these sections.

Second, we discuss these issues by considering, as an example, the HDLC classes of procedures.

Third—and this is the main part of the chapter in Section III—we describe a method for specifying the communication service provided by a protocol. While certain aspects of this method are related to our "unified" approach, we believe that most elements of the method are of general validity and applicability. In fact, the method is related to software engineering methods [2] for specifying software modules. However, certain elements of our method are specific to protocols due to their distributed nature.

II. A General Transition Model

For a given communication layer of a distributed computer system, we assume that the protocol is specified by separate descriptions for both entities executing the protocol, as shown in Fig. 1. We explain in this section the main features of a general transition model [1] which is based on Keller's transition model [3] for parallel programs. We also discuss the relation of this model to other protocol description methods, and the importance of modularization which may lead to the subdivision of a given communication layer into several sublayers or protocol modules. Without giving the complete definitions which may be found in the literature, these concepts are explained using the HDLC classes of procedures as an example. The complete HDLC specifications, based on this method, may be found in [4]. An experience of using these specifications for the implementation of X.25 link level procedures is described in [8].

A. The Description Method

In our general transition model, an entity is described by the set of possible states in which it may be, and the possible state transitions (which are assumed to exclude one another in time). The possible states are generally described by two components:

1. a finite state transition diagram, and
2. a set of program variables which each may assume certain values.

The state of the entity is characterized by (1) a token which indicates the active place in the transition diagram, and (2) the values of the program

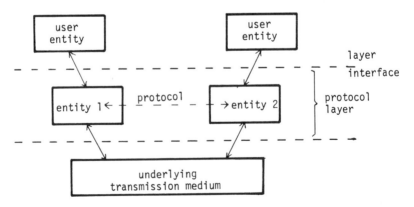

Fig. 1. A protocol layer within a layered system architecture.

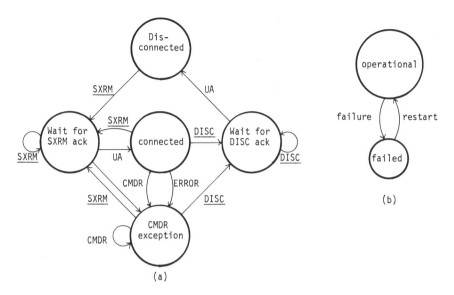

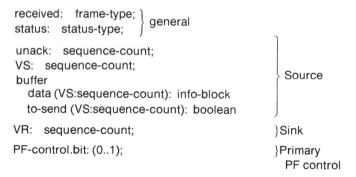

(a)

Fig. 2. State transition diagrams for the primary link setup module of an HDLC station. (a) Operational procedure which may be discontinued due to a failure. [The diagram is hierarchically dependent on the *operational* state of diagram (b).] (b) Diagram showing the possible failure and restart transitions.

variables. As an example, Fig. 2 shows the transition diagram of an HDLC module which operates the link setup and disconnection procedure. The state space of a complete HDLC station is defined by this and similar diagrams (one for each of the modules shown in Fig. 4) and the program variables shown in Fig. 3.

The operation of an entity is defined by the possible state transitions. These transitions are indicated in the transition diagram (see, for example,

```
received:   frame-type; ⎫
status:    status-type;  ⎬ general

unack:   sequence-count;
VS:    sequence-count;
buffer                              } Source
    data (VS:sequence-count): info-block
    to-send (VS:sequence-count): boolean

VR:   sequence-count;               } Sink

PF-control.bit: (0..1);             } Primary
                                      PF control
```

Fig. 3. Program variables of HDLC station.

Table I

Transition	Enabling predicate	Action	Meaning
Primary station:			
SXRM	PF-control.bit = 1	send-unnumbered (SXRM);	SXRM is SNRM or SARM depending on the mode to be set
UA	received.kind = UA	init (source); init (sink); init (transmission);	Initialize the source and sink components
DISC CMDR ERROR	PF-control.bit = 1 received.kind = CMDf Status in [invalid-control-field, invalid-info, invalid-size, invalid-NR]	send-unnumbered (DISC); init (transmission); init (transmission);	Frame received contained an error to be resolved by a higher-level recovery procedure at Primary
OTHER	. . .	init (transmission);	In certain states, the reception of certain kind of frames is simply ignored (not shown in the transition diagrams)
I	buffer.to-send (VS) and VS ≠ (unack + window) mod modulus	send-info (VS, VR, buffer.data (VS)); VS := (VS + 1) mod modulus;	When there is an I frame to be sent, which lies within the send window, send it
I =	received.kind = I and received.NS = VR	unack := received.NR; VR := VR + 1; init (transmission)	If I frame is in sequence, pass data to user

Fig. 2); however, additional information must be provided. For instance, each transition, when executed, may change the values of the program variables and interact with the user entity through the upper layer interface or with the underlying transmission medium through the lower interface (see Fig. 1). A given transition may only be executed when its *enabling predicate*, i.e., a Boolean expression depending on the program variables, is true. This additional information may be given in the form of a table, as shown in Table I. For example, the $\underline{I}$ transition, which sends an information (I) frame to the peer entity, may only be executed when a data block is *to be sent* and not too many I frames are *unack*nowledged. When executed, the action of the transition sends an I frame and updates the value of the send variable VS.

B. Relation to Other Description Methods

It has been pointed out ([5]; see also Chapter 20, Section II C) that most protocols contain certain aspects that are naturally described by finite state (FS) transition diagrams and other aspects that are better described by program variables and executable statements written in some programming language. The HDLC procedures provide a typical example. The link setup and disconnection procedure is described relatively completely by the FS transition diagram of Fig. 2, whereas the data transfer, exemplified by the $\underline{I}$ and $I_=$ transitions given in Table I, essentially involves program variables and statements. Different approaches have been taken to cope with this situation (see, for example, Chapter 20).

The approach of attempting to write complete descriptions in the FS model is limited because most protocols are so complex that the resulting FS descriptions become too large to be useful. However, partial descriptions in the FS model may be very useful. For example, the FS descriptions of X.21 and X.25 are of this kind. We note that even a relatively complete FS description and analysis [7] of the simple "alternating bit" protocol ignores the contents of the exchanged user messages. The partial description approach corresponds to keeping only the FS transition diagram of our general transition model (in the case of the HDLC procedures, for example, keeping Fig. 2 and ignoring Fig. 3 and Table I). But it is clear that such a description, and a protocol analysis based on it, must be complemented with additional information.

On the other hand, the FS aspects may be eliminated from the description of a protocol in the general transition model by replacing each FS transition diagram, which contains one token, by a variable which indicates the place of the token in the diagram, together with appropriate enabling predicates and update actions for the transitions. Such a transformation is straightforward, and is usually performed in order to obtain an implementation of the protocol.

C. Modularization

Most protocols implemented in a given layer of a hierarchical system are so complex that a conceptual subdivision into several sublayers or functions is very useful. In this case, each sublayer or function corresponds to a module within each entity executing the protocol. The different modules of an entity are relatively independent of one another. In the examples which we have considered, i.e., the link level HDLC procedures [4], the X.25 packet level procedures [8], and the ML Protocol [9] providing transport and session layer functions, the following concepts were sufficient to naturally describe the interactions between the modules within one entity, and different entities through a layer interface. We note that all, except the second concept, are also applicable to FS models.

Complete Independence. Each module is described by a separate transition model.

Shared Variables. The modules are independent, except that the transitions of one module may update the program variables of the other module,

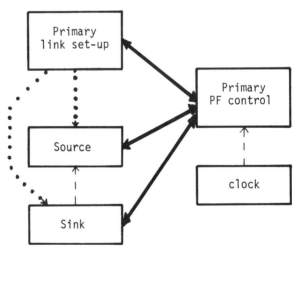

NOTATION:

◆——→ direct coupling

●●●→ hierarchical dependence

— — → update of shared variable

Fig. 4. Modules of an HDLC primary station and their relation.

thus influencing its behavior. Figure 4 shows a possible modular decomposition of an HDLC primary station. In this example, a shared variable is used to indicate a time-out condition to the *P/F-bit control* module, and the variable *unack* of the *source* module is accessed by the *sink* module when a piggybacked acknowledgment arrives.

Hierarchical Dependence [4]. A module *B* is hierarchically dependent on a module *A* if *B* enters its initial state whenever *A* enters a particular state, which we call the *activating state* for *B*, and the transitions of *B* are only possible while *A* remains in the activating state. In the example of Fig. 4, hierarchical dependence is used to describe the fact that the data transfer executed by the *source* and *sink* modules is only active when the *link setup* module is in the *connected* state (see Fig. 2).

Direct Coupling [4], [7]. This concept introduces a strong synchronization between certain transitions of different modules. Two transitions of different modules are directly coupled if they can only be executed jointly (only when both respective enabling predicates are true). This mechanism may be used to describe the local interaction of an entity through the upper layer interface with its user or through the lower interface with the underlying transmission medium (see Section III). In a more general form, where a given transition is directly coupled alternatively to several transitions of the other module, this concept was also used for describing the interaction between the *P/F-bit control* module and the other modules of an HDLC station [4], as indicated in Fig. 4. In fact, each sending and receiving transition of the other modules must be coordinated with a transition of the *P/F-bit control* module which checks the validity of the P/F-bit sent or received.

III. Specification of Communication Service

The specification of the communication service provided by a given protocol layer (see Fig. 1) defines what the user entities have to know about the protocol layer they use, without being concerned with the details of the protocol. We distinguish the local and the global properties of a communication service. The local properties of the service are those which characterize the local interaction of one user entity through a service access point (see Section II of Chapter 2) with an entity providing the service, ignoring what happens at the other access points of the same layer. Given that we consider a *communication* service, the local properties leave an important aspect unspecified, namely, the relation between what happens at the different access points of the layer. In most cases the communication service may be characterized as connections between a pair of access points. The global properties, then, specify the relationship between the two access points of a connection. Therefore they are sometimes called the "end-to-end" properties of the communication service. We note that the distinction between local and global properties is not "exclusive" since the specification of the global properties of a service usually implies (i.e., includes) its local properties. We include in the following only some simple examples. A complete service specification along the lines discussed here may be found in [14].

A. Local Properties

In this subsection, we concentrate on the local properties of a communication service. These properties clearly determine the local interface through which a user entity accesses the service. The properties may be considered to be the *abstract specification* for the local interface, which must be satisfied in each local system. At the end of the section, we comment on how this abstract interface may be refined in order to give rise to a particular interface implementation.

1. A Directly Coupled Interface

We assume that both entities that interact through the interface are described by a general transition model, as explained in Section II. We describe the interaction between the two entities by direct coupling. In particular, certain transitions of the service-providing entity are directly coupled with certain transitions of the user entity. If we do not want to specify the operation of the user entity (which is usually the case), we may simply give a list of *interface transitions* which may be executed by the user entity subject to some (unspecified) enabling predicates, and which are directly coupled with transitions of the service-providing entity. For example, for the entity using the HDLC link layer service, we may define the interface transitions given in Table II. We note that the flow control at the interface is automatically present since a pair of directly coupled transitions may only be executed when the corresponding enabling predicates in both entities are true and no other transition is in progress. Parametrized transitions may be used for passing value parameters between the two entities, such as the *data* parameter in the case of the $\downarrow D$ and $\uparrow D$ transitions.

2. Abstraction

While the conceptual operation of the interface may be described by directly coupled transitions, as explained above, we discuss in the following three further abstractions which lead to simpler interface descriptions. The first two abstractions are based on the fact that the user entity does not

Table II

Interface transition of user entity	Coupled transition of HDLC station (see fig. 2 and Table I)
$\downarrow$Open$_{request}$	*SXRM* starting in *disconnected* or *connected* state
$\uparrow$ Open$_{indication}$	*SXRM* starting in *CMDR exception* state
Open$_{confirmation}$	UA starting in *Wait for SXRM ack* state
$\downarrow$Close$_{request}$	DISC starting in *connected* state
$\uparrow$ Close$_{indication}$	DISC starting in *CMDR exception* state
Close$_{confirmation}$	UA starting in *Wait for DISC ack* state
$\downarrow$ D(data:info-block)	A transition appending the *data* parameter into the *buffer* variable of the source module
$\uparrow$ D(data:info-block)	$I_=$ where the *data* parameter is equal to *received.data*
Fail	failure

need to (and should not) know the operation of the protocol which provides the service. The same considerations apply also in the general context of software engineering for the specification of the service provided by a software module. The last abstraction is particular to the context of communications.

Ignoring the Operation of the Protocol. The order in which the interface transitions may be executed by the user entity is clearly determined by the direct coupling and the order in which the transitions of the service-providing entity may be executed. Let us consider the example of the layer interface for the HDLC protocol. We may deduce from the information in Table II and Fig. 2 that the interface transitions may be executed in the order shown in Fig. 5. (This diagram is obtained from the diagram of Fig. 2 by merging the *Connected* and *CMDR exception* states, and replacing the transition labels according to Table II. We note that this derivation is generally not so simple because the interaction between the two protocol entities may limit the transition possibilities.)

Combining Interface Transitions into "Service Primitives." Continuing with the example above, we see in Fig. 5 that certain interface transitions are always followed by the same next transition. We may therefore combine these transitions into a single one, thus simplifying the overall transition diagram. Adopting the following combinations

$\downarrow$Open$_{request}$	Open$_{confirmation}$	$\equiv \downarrow$Open
$\uparrow$ Open$_{indication}$	Open$_{confirmation}$	$\equiv \uparrow$Open
$\downarrow$Close$_{request}$	Close$_{confirmation}$	$\equiv \downarrow$Close
$\uparrow$ Close$_{indication}$	Close$_{confirmation}$	$\equiv \uparrow$Close

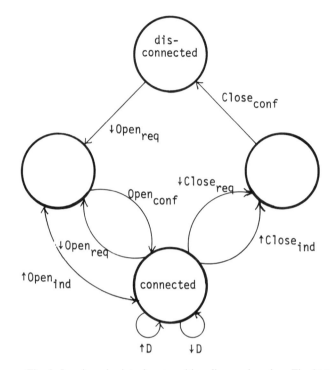

Fig. 5. Local service interface transition diagram based on Fig. 2(a).

leads to the interface transition diagram of Fig. 6. We call the remaining (partially combined) interface transitions *service primitives* [15].

Ignoring the Source of Initiation. The symbols "↑" and "↓" in the names of the service primitives have been introduced to explicitly indicate whether the execution of the primitive is initiated by the service providing entity ("↑") or the user entity ("↓"). In the case of the data transmission primitives ↑ *D* and ↓ *D*, this distinction is clearly important. In the case of the link setup or disconnection primitives, however, this distinction is not always important, in which case one may make abstraction from it. In particular, the diagram of Fig. 6 does not require this distinction; neither does the specification of the global properties of the service discussed in the next section. We therefore drop the symbol "↑" or "↓" whenever this distinction is of no importance.

If we consider the exchange of parameter values between the interacting entities during the execution of a service primitive, the situation may become more complicated. In the case of a primitive for establishing a virtual circuit through a packet-switched data network, for example, a *distant subscriber address* parameter value is provided by the initiating entity, while a *response* parameter value is returned by the other entity.

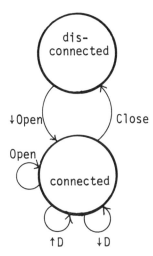

Fig. 6. Simplified local service interface transition diagram.

Independently of which entity initiates the primitive, this fact may be described by the following notation:

VC-Establishment ($\rightarrow x$: distant subscriber address, $\leftarrow y$: response code).

3. Discontinuation of Service Primitives

As shown in Figs. 5 and 6, the concept of hierarchical dependence (see Section II C) may be used to indicate that the normal link layer service is only available as long as the physical circuit is *operational*. Since a *Fail* interface transition may occur any time in the *operational* state, link establishment primitives, for example, will be "interrupted" by a failure which occurs after an Open$_{req}$ transition and before the corresponding Open$_{conf}$ transition (see Fig. 5). We say that the service primitive is *discontinued*. In Fig. 6, this possibility is not shown explicitly, but it must be taken into account. We conclude that whenever the layer interface description involves some hierarchical dependence, the possibility of discontinuation for the dependent service primitives must be considered.

Another example of discontinuation is given by the virtual circuit data transmission service where, according to X.25, the transfer of a complete user sequence (i.e., variable length data block) between the DTE and the network may be "interrupted" by a reset or circuit clear.

4. Interface Implementation

It is clear that many details must be added to the abstract interface specification suggested in this section in order to obtain an interface implementation. However, these details may be chosen differently for each local implementation, whereas the abstract interface properties discussed in this section must be valid for every actual interface. In particular, the mechanisms for implementing flow control and the distinction between which entity initiates a service primitive may be implemented in quite different ways. For instance, the use of message queues between the service-providing entity and its user would be a particular way of implementing the interface.

B. Global Properties

An interface description, as discussed in Section III A, defines the service primitives and the order in which these primitives may be executed at a local interface between a user and a service-providing entity. Here we concentrate on the global properties of a communication service, which are those aspects that make the service useful for *communication*. The local service interface description for the HLDC protocol, for example, states that sending and receiving of user data blocks is possible in the *connected* state (see Fig. 6). Only the global properties state that the first block received at one end is equal to the block first sent at the other hand.

The global properties of a communication service usually have two aspects: (1) restrictions on the order in which the service primitives at the two ends of a connection may be executed, and (2) restrictions on the possible parameter values exchanged. An example of the second aspect is given above; an example for the first aspect is the fact that (usually) the number of possible receive executions at one end is always smaller than or equal to the number of send executions performed at the other end.

Speaking about the execution order of service primitives at different service access points (in usually different locations) brings up the problem of how such an order can actually be observed or enforced. We assume, for the present purposes, that the execution order at different locations can be determined by some hypothetical observer or with sufficiently well synchronized real time clocks.

We use the following notation. Given two service primitives A and B, "$A \Rightarrow B$" means that the beginning of the execution of A is earlier (in real time) than the end of the execution of B (that is, there may be a causal influence of A on B, or equally, B is not earlier than A). The notation "$A \Leftrightarrow B$" means that $A \Rightarrow B$ and $A \Leftarrow B$ holds (that is, there is some instant (in real time) when both service primitives are in progress). We say that A and B are *simultaneous*.

For many purposes, instead of considering the execution order to be defined in respect to the real time, it may be adequate to consider that the execution order defined by the global properties of the service determine

(1) $\langle \text{Link Seq} \rangle ::=$ empty

$$::= \quad \langle \text{Link Seq} \rangle \ \langle \text{Open Seq} \rangle \ \left\{ \begin{array}{c} \text{Close} \\ \Uparrow \\ \text{Close} \end{array} \right\}$$

(2) $\langle \text{Open Seq} \rangle = \left\{ \begin{array}{c} \text{Open} \\ \Updownarrow \\ \text{Open} \end{array} \right\} \langle \text{Data Seq} \rangle$

$$::= \quad \langle \text{Open Seq} \rangle \ \left\{ \begin{array}{c} \text{Open} \\ \Updownarrow \\ \text{Open} \end{array} \right\} \langle \text{Data Seq} \rangle$$

(3) $\langle \text{Data Seq} \rangle ::= \langle \text{Fifo Seq 12} \rangle \| \langle \text{Fifo Seq 21} \rangle$, i.e. arbitrary interleaving of data transfer in both directions

(4) $\langle \text{Fifo Seq 12} \rangle ::= \left\{ \begin{array}{cccc} \downarrow D(x_1) & \downarrow D(x_2) & \ldots \ldots & \downarrow D(x_n) \\ \Downarrow & \Downarrow & & \\ \uparrow D(x'_1) & \uparrow D(x'_2) & \ldots \uparrow D(x'_m) & \end{array} \right\}$

where $0 \leq m \leq n$ and $x_i = x'_i$ for $i = 1, 2, \ldots m$
$\langle \text{Fifo Seq 21} ::= \rangle \ldots$ (similarly)

(5) Discontinuation due to a failure: The execution sequences defined above for entity 1 and entity 2 may be "interrupted" by a local *Fail* transition, such that the last primitive executed by an entity may be discontinued. If A $\Rightarrow$ B holds between executions of two service primitives the following is true: A is completely suppressed due to the failure implies that B is discontinued or completely suppressed.

Fig. 7. Global properties of the link layer communication service.

some partial order of events which represents some "logical time" as discussed by Lamport [10].

A Possible Notation. A possible notation for specifying the global properties of a communication service are production rules of a particular form. We adopt the usual convention of writing the nonterminal symbols in brackets $\langle \cdots \rangle$, and writing the possible productions after the symbol "$::=$". Each production is defined in terms of (possibly other) nonterminals and terminals which are written in the form $\{^X_Y\}$. X and Y are sequences of service primitives which describe a possible pair of corresponding execution sequences at the respective ends of a connection. More details are given in the Appendix.

As an example, Fig. 7 contains a possible specification of the global properties of an HDLC link layer service. Rule 2, for instance, states that an $\langle \text{Open Sequence} \rangle$ consists of *Open* primitives executed simultaneously at both ends of the connection followed by a $\langle \text{Data Sequence} \rangle$ with possibly further repetitions. The $\langle \text{Data sequences} \rangle$ are defined by rules 3 and 4, and rule 1 defines the possible global execution sequences which consist of a repetition of an $\langle \text{Open Sequence} \rangle$ followed by a pair of simultaneous *Close* primitives executed at the two ends of the connection. (We note that the rules of Fig. 7 imply the "local" transition rules given in Fig. 6 which apply separately at each end of the connection.)

Restrictions on the possible parameter values may be stated for each of the production rules. In the case of Fig. 7, the only parameters exchanged are the user data sent and received (see parameters x in rule 4a of Fig. 7). In the case of the establishment of a virtual circuit, using the service primitive given in Section III A 2), the following rule may apply:

$$\langle \text{VC Open} \rangle ::= \left\{ \begin{array}{c} \text{VC-Establishment} (x, y) \\ \updownarrow \\ \text{VC-Establishment} (x', y') \end{array} \right\}$$

where $y = y'$, x is the subscriber address of the entity executing the "lower" part, and x' is the subscriber address of the entity executing the "upper" part.

C. Elements for a Communication Service Specification

We conclude from the foregoing discussion that the specification of a communication service for a given protocol layer should contain the following elements:

(1) An informal explanation of the service provided and the functions included in the layer: this part is given in natural language. It should give an overall understanding of the purpose and operation of the layer.

(2) A list of service primitives available at the layer interface: this part describes precisely each of the service primitives individually.

(3) Local properties determining in which order the service primitives may be executed at one service access point without regard to other access points within the same layer.

(4) Global properties relating the execution order and exchanged parameter values at different access points: this is the essential part of the communication service specification.

(5) Grade of service considerations: they specify quantitative properties such as throughput, delay, etc., and also indicate in which situations and with which probabilities certain malfunctions, such as undetected errors and failures, may occur. [In contrast to this, points (2)–(4) above concentrate on qualitative properties of the service which are always satisfied.]

We believe that any communication service specification that does not contain the equivalent of the elements (2)–(5) must be considered incomplete. Elements (2)–(4) are discussed in the foregoing sections. We believe that formal methods, similar to those described here, may be useful for specifying these elements in a more precise manner.

IV. Protocol Verification

Instead of giving a review of protocol verification (which may be found in Chapter 20) or describing any particular approach to verification, we give in the following some remarks which show the relation of the previous sections with the problems of protocol verification, and which show also, we hope, that many approaches to verification are basically very simple.

A. What Should be Verified?

The term *protocol verification* usually means to ascertain that the entities executing a given protocol together with the underlying transmission medium (see Fig. 1) actually provide the specified communication service to the user entities in the layer above. It is therefore necessary to determine the service actually provided (based on the specification of the underlying transmission service and the definition of the communicating entities) and compare it with the communication service specified. Let us assume that we want to verify that the service actually provided is equal to the service specified. The proof may be divided into two parts.

(1) Partial correctness: to show that every execution sequence of service primitives at different access points (in particular, at the two ends of a connection, and including specific parameter values) that is actually possible satisfies the constraints imposed by the service specification.

(2) Effective progress: to show that every execution sequence of service primitives that satisfies the service specifications is actually possible, and that no situations of deadlock or starvation or infinite loops without progress exist.

B. Various Kinds of Assertions

The use of *assertions* is a well-known technique for the verification of sequential programs and has been extended for use with parallel programs. Similar techniques also apply to the verification of protocols. The basic idea consists of defining an *invariant assertion*, or briefly *invariant*, i.e., a Boolean expression depending on the state of the system which is always true (i.e., as long as no state transition is in progress). Since this technique was developed for verifying programs, it seems natural to use it for verifying protocols that are defined in terms of program variables and executed statements. In this case, the invariants typically involve the program variables of both entities and the state of the underlying transmission medium (i.e., the "messages" in transit) [5], [11].

It is interesting to note that certain approaches to the verification of protocols based on FS description techniques may be shown to be based on a particular form of invariant assertions. For example, the equations given in [7] for the *adjoint states* of a protocol are such that the following assertions are always true when the underlying medium is empty (i.e., no "message" in transit). If a_i ($i = 1, 2, \ldots, n$) are the possible states for entity 1, and s_1 and s_2 are the actual states of entity 1 and entity 2, respectively, then the assertion

$$s_1 = a_i \text{ implies } s_2 \text{ is an element of } Adj(a_i)$$

holds for every possible state a_i. This is not surprising since the definition of *adjoint state*, roughly speaking, is as follows. The adjoint states $Adj(a_i)$ of a given state a_i are those states of entity 2 in which entity 2 may possibly be when entity 1 is in state a_i.

Another example is the detection of incompleteness or overspecifications as described by Zafiropulo et al. (see, for example, [12]). Their main idea is as follows. Given an FS protocol definition, an invariant assertion of the following form is derived for each possible state a_i ($i = 1, 2, \ldots, n$) of entity 1:

$$s_1 = a_i \text{ implies the messages} \ldots \text{may now be received}$$
$$\text{by the entity 1, but no other messages}$$

Given such assertions, it is easy to check whether the definition of entity 1 includes all necessary receiving transitions and no unnecessary ones. It is sufficient to verify, for any given state a_i, that the definition foresees the handling of exactly those received messages which are mentioned in the corresponding assertion.

In the case of a protocol definition in terms of the general transition model described in Section II where the state of an entity is defined by an FS transition diagram and certain program variables, invariant assertions are in general of the following form:

$$s_1 = a_i \text{ and } s_2 = b_j \text{ implies } Assertion_{ij}$$

where a_i and b_j are possible states of the entities 1 and 2, respectively, and $Assertion_{ij}$ is a Boolean expression depending on the program variables of both entities and possibly also on the state of the underlying transmission medium [13].

As an example, we give the following invariant assertion which may be derived from the definitions of the HDLC procedures given in Figs. 2 and 3 and Table I and the assumption that each frame received without error notification is an exact copy of a frame sent by the other entity:

$s_1 =$ connected and $s_2 =$ connected implies

$$\left[\begin{array}{l} \text{entity 2. received. kind} = I \text{ and} \\ \text{entity 2. received. NS} = \text{entity 2. VR} \\ \text{implies entity 2. received. data} = \\ \qquad \text{entity 1. buffer. data (entity 2. VR)} \end{array} \right]$$

This assertion is important for the verification of correct data transfer of the HDLC procedures. It specifies conditions under which a data block received by entity 2 is equal to the corresponding data block in the buffer of entity 1. Given the definitions of the service primitives $\downarrow D$ and $\uparrow D$ (see Table II) and the transition $I_=$ (see Table I), this invariant assures that the data blocks received by the user from entity 2 are the same as those submitted by the user to entity 1. This is what rule 4 of the service specification in Fig. 7 postulates.

We conclude that the above invariant assertion proves the partial correctness of the HDLC protocol, as far as rule 4 of the service specification is concerned. However, it does not imply effective progress, which would mean that each data block submitted to entity 1 will eventually be delivered to the user by entity 2. For proving this, we must rely on the underlying transmission service not to make "too many" transmission errors. A more detailed discussion of a simple protocol verification example in the context of the general transition model is given in [1].

V. Conclusions

In the framework of distributed system architecture involving a hierarchy of different protocol layers, the clear delimitation between the different layers becomes an important issue. The delimitation between a given layer and its user is given by the layer interface which is characterized by the communication service provided through that interface. For the description of the layered architecture of a distributed system, the service specifications for the individual layers seem to be the main tool. For instance, one objective for a layered system architecture is the possibility to change the protocol adopted in a given layer without affecting the other layers of the system. During such a change, the protocol of that layer clearly changes, while the service provided must remain unchanged.

Because the communication service definitions play such an important role in the design of distributed systems, great care should be taken for their exact specification. This paper presents a possible formal approach to the specification of communication services. While a finite state approach seems to be useful for many aspects of communication protocol specification and verification (although not all), we feel that, for the specification of communication *services*, the finite state approach alone is insufficient. It seems that important service characteristics are naturally described by constraints on parameter values which are exchanged over the interface during the execution of the service primitives. The two aspects of *order of execution* and *exchanged parameter values* seem to correspond to the two aspects of our general transition model described in Section II, namely, *state transitions* and *program variables*.

Appendix: Notation for Specifying Global Properties of Communication Services (as Used in Fig. 7)

Our notation is an extension of BNF, which is used for specifying formal grammars and the syntax of programming languages.

A *terminal* symbol stands for the execution of a service primitive and is represented by the name of that primitive. The *nonterminal* symbols, written in brackets, $\langle \cdots \rangle$, stand for the set of execution sequences that may be generated from them (see below). Sequential execution of service primitives is expressed by writing terminals or nonterminals in the usual order from left to right. A production rule is written in the form

$$\langle \text{some terminal} \rangle ::= X_1 X_2 \cdots X_n$$

where each X_i ($i = 1, \ldots, n$) is a terminal or nonterminal symbol. Such a rule specifies that the set of execution sequences that are generated from $\langle$some nonterminal$\rangle$ includes all the sequences that are obtained by the successive execution of sequences generated by the X_i. (A terminal symbol X only "generates" the execution of the service primitive it stands for.)

For example, the rules

$$\langle LS \rangle ::= \text{empty}$$

$$\langle LS \rangle ::= \langle LS \rangle \langle OS \rangle \text{Close}$$

specify that the empty sequence (no execution) may be generated from $\langle LS \rangle$ (first rule) and any sequence that is a repetition of sequences generated by $\langle OS \rangle$, each followed by the execution of the Close primitive (repeated application of the second rule, with final application of the first rule).

We have adopted the following extensions to BNF:

1. Grouping of service primitives executed at different service access points:
   a. The symbol

$$\left\{ \begin{array}{c} X \\ Y \end{array} \right\}$$

   stands for the execution of the service primitives X and Y at the two respective access points of a connection. No specific order of execution is assumed between these two primitives.
   b. The symbol

$$\left\{ \begin{array}{c} X \\ \Downarrow \\ Y \end{array} \right\}$$

   means the same as $\{{}^X_Y\}$, but X is executed not later than Y (see Section III B).
   c. The symbol

$$\left\{ \begin{array}{c} X \\ \Updownarrow \\ Y \end{array} \right\}$$

   means the same as $\{{}^X_Y\}$, but X and Y are executed simultaneously (see Section III B).
2. Parallel execution: Parallel and independent execution of two processes results in an overall execution order which is an arbitrary interleaving of the execution sequences of the two processes. We write $\parallel$ to indicate this parallel execution.
3. Constraints on parameter values: Parameters of service primitives are written in parentheses, $(\cdots)$. They represent the actual values of the parameters during the execution of the primitives. Conditions that must be satisfied by these values are associated with the production rules (see, for example, rule 4).

References

[1] G. V. Bochmann and J. Gecsei, "A unified model for the specification and verification of protocols," in *Proc. IFIP Congr.* 1977, pp. 229–234.
[2] D. L. Parnas, "The use of precise specifications in the development of software," in *Proc. IFIP Congr.* 1977, pp. 861–867.

[3] R. M. Keller, "Formal verification of parallel programs," *Commun. Ass. Comput. Mach.*, vol. 19, pp. 371–384, July 1976.

[4] G. V. Bochmann and R. J. Chung, "A formalized specification of HDLC classes of procedures," in *Proc. Nat. Telecommun. Conf.*, Los Angeles, CA, Dec. 1977, pp. 03A. 2-1–2-11; reprinted in *Advances in Computer Communications and Networking*, W. W. Chu., Ed. Dedham, MA: Artech House, 1979.

[5] N. V. Stenning. "A data transfer protocol," *Comput. Network* vol. 1 pp. 99–110, Sept. 1976.

[6] G. V. Bochmann and C. Sunshine, "A survey of formal methods," Chapter 20 of this book.

[7] G. V. Bochmann, "Finite state description of communication protocols," in *Proc. Comput. Network Protocols Symp.*, Univ. Liège, Liège, Belgium, Feb. 1978, pp. F3-1–F3-11; and *Comput. Networks*, vol. 2, pp. 361–372, Oct. 1978.

[8] G. V. Bochmann and T. Joachim, "Development and structure of an X.25 implementation," *IEEE Trans. Software Eng.*, vol. SE-5, pp. 429–439, Sept. 1979.

[9] G. V. Bochmann and F. H. Vogt, "Message link protocol—Functional specifications," *ACM Comput. Commun. Rev.*, vol. 9, pp. 7–39, Apr. 1979.

[10] L. Lamport, "Time, clocks and the ordering of events in a distributed system," *Commun. Ass. Comput. Mach.*, vol. 21, pp. 558–565, July 1978.

[11] G. V. Bochmann, "Logical verification and implementation of protocols," in *Proc. 4th Data Commun. Symp.*, ACM/IEEE, 1975, pp. 8-15–8-20.

[12] P. Zafiropulo *et al.*, "Protocol analysis and synthesis using a state transition model," Chapter 24 of this book.

[13] G. V. Bochmann, "Combining assertions and states for the validation of process communication," in *Constructing Quality Software*, P. G. Hibbard and S. A. Shuman, Ed. North-Holland, 1978, pp. 229–232.

[14] G. V. Bochmann, "Specification of the services provided by the MLP," Univ. Montreal, Montreal, P.Q., Canada, Tech. Rep., 1979.

[15] In the formal description techniques developed for OSI (ISO TC 97/SC16 N380 and 381) the term "service primitive" is used for individual, non-combined abstract interface transitions.

24

Protocol Analysis and Synthesis using a State Transition Model

Pitro Zafiropulo, Colin H. West, Harry Rudin, D. D. Cowan, and Daniel Brand

I. Introduction

The growing trends both to increase the sophistication of functions implemented in information-handling systems and to distribute these functions in different processes has resulted in an enormous growth in complexity. This complexity is particularly acute in the interactions or protocols which specify how these processes are synchronized and communicate with one another. However, formal methods are gradually being introduced to describe these interactions; see chapters 20, 21, 23, and 25 as well as [1]–[5].

The benefits of using such formal methods have already proven to be substantial: the imprecise interpretation which is characteristic of prose description has been eliminated, formal proofs are now possible, and the door is opened to techniques for computer-aided validation and computer-supported synthesis or design of such interactions or protocols. It is these last two areas, computer-aided validation of protocols and computer-supported synthesis of protocols, that this paper examines. These have been the main lines of research in protocols at the IBM Zurich Research Laboratory. This work has been guided by two main objectives:

1. automation of these techniques using computers, and
2. primary concern with the logical structure of a protocol as opposed to a protocol's intended function.

The first objective is to provide automated tools to lighten the task of the designer while at the same time achieving a thorough analysis in the face of great complexity. A concern primarily with the logical structure of interaction also guarantees widespread applicability.

In recent years, there has been a sharp increase in activity in the area of formally expressed protocols, and the work of many individuals should be referenced here. Instead, the reader is referred to Chapter 19 and the papers of Sunshine [6] and Merlin [7]. Furthermore, protocols were the subject of a conference held in Liège early in 1978; the Proceedings provide an excellent overview of the field [8].

Both our work in validation and in synthesis is based on logical structural properties derived from notions of physical causality and completeness [9]. In the case of validation, a protocol is examined for these properties by means of a reachability analysis similar to that suggested by Sunshine [3] and Bochmann [10] and implemented in an automated validation system [11]. Hajek has also developed a validation system using state-transition techniques [12].

In validating protocols such as the CCITT X.21 and X.25 and Data Flow Control from IBM's SNA, we have found that the designer(s) of a protocol usually does not foresee all the structural properties of the design, in that the protocol may be incomplete or logically inconsistent [13], [14]; see also Chapter 25. From this experience, we feel well justified in examining only the limited aspect of logical structure in protocols. In theory, compared with assertion-proving techniques we test for little; in practice these few tests have turned out to be very effective.

An automated validation process is usually intended for a protocol in an advanced stage of development, while for a protocol in the early stages of design, a synthesis technique is preferable. This paper describes two methods of analyzing protocol behavior, and both techniques can be used for either validation or synthesis. The first method, the perturbation technique, has already been implemented as an automated validation system which has had extensive use in examining existing protocols. The second method based on a set of production rules has been incorporated into an automated synthesis system. A protocol developed through the use of these production rules will be free of the same errors guaranteed by the perturbation approach. Our initial attempt at protocol synthesis [15] is one of the earliest in the field.

The techniques of validation and synthesis and the tools described in this paper have widespread applicability to the entire field of cooperating processes since a protocol is a very general concept. We quote the definition given by Merlin [7] to indicate this generality: "Given a system of cooperating processes such that the cooperation is done through the exchange of messages, a protocol is the set of rules which governs this exchange." This statement implies that protocols are not just concerned with the correct transfer of data, but pervade all areas where interaction between processes is inherent.

II. Modeling of Protocols

A model with which to represent protocols and interaction examples is required; we employ a representation similar to the one proposed by Bartlett *et al.* [16] and used by Bochmann [10]. Figure 1 shows a simple access authorization protocol in which each interacting process is modeled by a finite-state graph, and the two initial states are identified by states labeled 0. The messages exchanged between the processes are represented by integers. Message transmission is represented by the negative value of the corresponding integer, and message reception by its positive value. For example, the message ACCESS-REQUEST is represented by the integer 1, its generation is represented by traversal of the arc labeled -1 in process A, and its reception by traversal of the arc labeled $+1$ in process B. The integer representation is a notational detail, but one that is compact and which lends itself to numerical manipulation. This model using finite-state graphs can be used to represent both nonideal communication channels (i.e., ones which lose and distort messages) and interactions between more than two processes (see Appendix A).

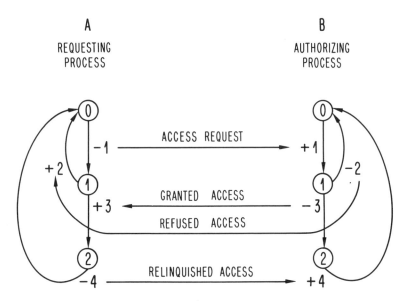

Fig. 1. Simple access authorization protocol.

III. Types of Design Errors

We make two basic assumptions about protocols and interactions. First, we are not concerned with explicit time constraints such as transmission and response delays, and second, we assume the processes to be correctly initialized (all in their zero or reset states) prior to the start of an interaction. Within this framework we can handle four potential design errors, namely, state deadlocks, unspecified receptions, nonexecutable interactions, and state ambiguities. Figure 2 shows a two-process interaction example that exhibits all these errors, each of which is explained separately in the following sections. Although the form of these design errors is syntactic, their successful resolution must consider their semantic intent. Since we are not concerned with the semantics or meaning of the interaction, messages in Fig. 2 are given no descriptive identifiers. Other potential design errors can be formulated; for example, channel overflow has been incorporated into the automated validation system [1].

A. State Deadlocks

Different types of deadlocks are definable within the context of process interactions but we shall only be concerned with state deadlocks. We define: a state deadlock occurs when each and every process has no alternative but to remain indefinitely in the same state. Stated differently, a state deadlock is present when no transmissions are possible from the current state of each

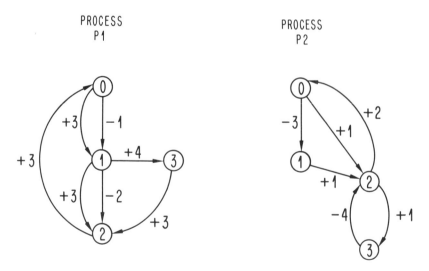

Fig. 2. Two-process interaction example containing various design and potential design errors.

process and when no messages are in transit, i.e., all channels are empty. This type of deadlock occurs in the interaction of Fig. 2 when $P1$ transmits message 1 at the same time that $P2$ transmits message 3. As a result both $P1$ and $P2$ enter states 1 and then 2 where they must wait to receive messages (no transmissions possible). As no further messages are in transit, the processes have no alternative but to wait indefinitely in these states.

State deadlocks usually represent errors but there are exceptions. Protocols may be designed to terminate in states with no exit when their function is complete. We therefore consider state deadlocks as potential errors that must be detected. Their evaluation is then a matter of semantics.

B. Unspecified Receptions

An unspecified reception occurs when a positive arc that can be traversed is missing, in other words when a reception that can take place is not specified in the design. For example, if in Fig. 2 $P2$ transmits message 3, and $P1$ on receiving message 3 transmits message 2, then state 1 of $P2$ will receive message 2, yet this reception is not specified in the design.

Unspecified receptions are harmful since in the absence of adequate recovery procedures, occurrence of an unspecified reception causes the respective process to enter an unknown state via a transition not specified in the design. As a consequence, the occurrence of an unspecified reception causes the subsequent behavior of the interaction to be unpredictable.

Protocols can be protected by state-check mechanisms [2], [4]. These mechanisms initiate recovery procedures when states receive messages which they are not designed to accept. Unfortunately, in the case of unspecified receptions, recovery procedures can adversely modify the interaction semantics as the occurrence of an unspecified reception is not caused by an operational malfunction yet is handled in the same manner. For example, if a connection setup protocol contains an unspecified reception and such a reception occurs in every connection setup attempt, then the ensuing recovery procedures will not fulfill the intended purpose, namely, to set up a connection. In other words, error recovery procedures should not be invoked unless the error for which they have been designed has occurred.

Thus, unspecified receptions are design errors. They are more common than expected: a number of unspecified receptions were identified in the CCITT X.21 interface version of 1976 [13]. These were brought to the attention of CCITT and are reflected in the current X.21 working papers.

C. Nonexecutable Interactions

A nonexecutable interaction is present when a design includes message transmissions and receptions that cannot occur under normal operating conditions. A nonexecutable interaction is equivalent to dead code in a computer program and is illustrated in Fig. 2. No normal interaction sequences can cause state 2 of $P2$ to receive message 1, hence state 3 is not entered and message 4 cannot be generated. Consequently, state 3 of $P1$ cannot be reached.

The creation of nonexecutable interactions must be treated with great caution. If the designer erroneously believes that state 2 of $P2$ can receive message 1 during normal operation, then the nonexecutable interaction represents a design error. On the other hand, if the designer's intention is to create recovery actions to handle abnormal conditions, and he purposely wants $P2$ to enter state 3 if abnormal (error) conditions cause state 2 to receive message 1, then it does not represent a design error. In order to distinguish between normal and abnormal conditions, it is probably good design practice to design and validate a protocol for normal operation before adding recovery actions.

D. Stable-State Pairs and State Ambiguities

A stable-state pair (x, y) is said to exist when a state x in one process and a state y in the other can be reached with both channels empty. In such a case, states x and y coexist until the next transmission occurs. Monitoring stable-state pairs is useful for detecting loss of synchronization, i.e., the presence of unintended stable-state pairs or the absence of intended ones. A case of special interest is when ambiguity occurs among stable states. A state ambiguity exists when a state in one process can coexist stably with several different states in the other process. Figure 2 contains state ambiguities. For example, if both processes are in their initial states (state 0), and $P1$ transmits messages 1 followed by 2 while $P2$ only receives messages, then $P1$ reaches state 2 while $P2$ returns to state 0. Thus, state 0 of $P2$ can coexist stably with both state 0 and state 2 of $P1$. State ambiguity is closely related to the adjoint-state concept [10]: state ambiguity implies that the cardinal number of the corresponding adjoint-state set is greater than 1.

State ambiguities do not necessarily represent errors but they must be treated with caution. If, for example, the designer's intention was that state 0 of $P1$ coexist stably solely with state 0 of $P2$, then the identified state ambiguity does represent an error. We therefore consider state ambiguities as potential design errors that need monitoring. State ambiguities are detectable via an examination of syntax; their evaluation is a matter of semantics.

IV. Analyzing Interactions

In this section we describe techniques to detect the presence of design and potential design errors in an interaction or protocol. Our first approach was based on an analysis of dialogues of interaction between communicating processes [9], [17], [18]. It was significantly improved and generalized in a method based on a technique of perturbation [11]. This technique is a reachability analysis conceptually similar to one proposed by Sunshine [3]. This perturbation method has been programmed and has successfully detected errors in protocols.

A. The Perturbation Analysis

We describe the perturbation method by analyzing in Fig. 3 the example of Fig. 2. A system state consisting of a two-dimensional array is defined where the elements on the main diagonal represent the individual process states (element 1, 1 is state of $P1$ and so on) and each off-diagonal element i, k represents the message content of the communication medium from process Pi to process Pk. Figure 2 represents a two-process interaction; hence the system states SS in Fig. 3 are 2×2 arrays.

One begins by defining $SS0$ which is the initial system state. It consists of both processes in $S0$ (state 0) and both channels empty (represented by E). $SS0$ is then "perturbed" into all possible successor states reachable by executing a single transition in one of the individual processes $P1$, $P2$ (in

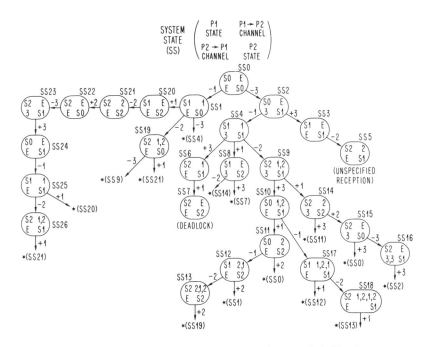

Fig. 3. Corresponding reachability tree for the example in Fig. 2.

Fig. 2). Thus, either $SS1$ is entered by $P1$ transmitting message 1 ($P1$ enters $S1$ and places 1 in channel $P1 \to P2$) or $SS2$ is entered by $P2$ transmitting message 3 ($P2$ enters $S1$ and places 3 in channel $P2 \to P1$).

The procedure continues by perturbing each of these new system states in turn. Thus considering $SS2$, either $SS3$ is entered by $P1$ receiving message 3 ($P1$ takes 3 from channel $P1 \to P2$ and enters $S1$) or $SS4$ is entered by $P1$ transmitting message 1 ($P1$ enters $S1$ and places 1 in channel $P1 \to P2$). The procedure continues until no new system states are created, thus indicating that all reachable system states have been determined. Asterisks in the ensuing reachability tree indicate system states that have been previously generated by perturbation of earlier states.

The method has the attractive property that it creates the reachability tree for any n-process interaction by simply defining the system states as $n \times n$ arrays. For example, the system states for a three-process interaction are 3×3 arrays, each consisting of three process states and six channels, some of which may remain empty. Certain types of interactions can cause unbounded growth in the number of messages in transit (see Section VI). In order to contain such unlimited growth, bounds are set on the channel-storage capacity. These bounds make it possible to detect when a prescribed channel-storage capacity is exceeded.

B. Error Detection via Analysis

Deadlocks are identified in a reachability tree by system states with all channels empty (E in Fig. 3) and no departing transitions. For example, the deadlock described in Section III A ($P1$ and $P2$ in $S2$) is identified by $SS7$. Such system states represent deadlocks because there are no further receptions (all channels empty) and no possible further transmissions (no departing transitions).

Unspecified receptions are identified by system states with no departing transition to absorb the next output from one of the channels. For example, the unspecified reception discussed in Section III B (message 2 cannot be received in $S1$ of $P2$) is identified by $SS5$, where the next $S1 \to S2$ channel output is message 2, yet there is no transition out of $SS5$ to absorb that message.

Stable-state pairs (tuples for many-process interactions) are identified in the reachability tree by system states having all channels empty. State ambiguities are identified by a particular process state appearing in a plurality of such system states. For example, the state ambiguity discussed in Section III D is identified by state $S0$ of process $P2$ appearing in both system states $SS0$ and $SS22$. Figure 3 identifies other ambiguities, for example, $SS3$, $SS24$ represent an ambiguity with respect to $S1$ of $P2$.

Nonexecutable interactions are identified as state transitions present in the design that are absent in the reachability tree. For example, $P2$ in Fig. 2 contains a -4 arc which never appears in the tree of Fig. 3.

V. Synthesizing Interactions

An alternative to testing an existing design for errors is to create from the outset a design devoid of the errors considered here. In this section we shall describe a mechanism (or tool) which is used interactively by a designer to create a protocol or interaction. The tool prevents the occurrence of unspecified receptions and immediately notifies the designer of the presence of state deadlocks and ambiguities. This immediate response has the advantage that at this point in time, the designer has the most insight into the resolution of the design problem. The tool is based on three production rules which create only those arcs needed to prevent unspecified receptions. A tracking algorithm then specifies where and when to apply the rules. Both tracking algorithm and production rules have been automated using a novel programming method called data-directed design [19], [20]. The rules are based on a study of the cause-and-effect relationships that occur when two entities exchange messages. They are currently limited to two-process interactions.

A. Production Rules

Three rules governing the derivation of two-process interactions are described in this section and proofs for their necessity and sufficiency are given in Appendix B. These rules are a modification of an earlier version which was developed [15] but was found to be incomplete. The relative simplicity of the rules rests on the fact that they are designed to produce tree-structured graphs. Section V B shows how interactions can be constructed from such graphs. We now explain the rules.

The first rule specifies all receptions of a message whose transmission directly succeeds the reception of a previous message. Consider Fig. 4(a) where $P2$ upon receiving message x transmits message e. If $P1$ transmits no further messages before receiving e, then it receives e in the state entered upon transmitting x. Hence a $+e$ arc is appended to $-x$ in $P1$. On the other hand, if $P1$ transmits y before e is received, then e is received after y is transmitted. Hence a $+e$ must be appended to $-y$. We append $+e_y$ instead to note the fact that in this case messages e, y occur concurrently, or collide. Two messages are said to collide when neither is received before the other is transmitted. As we shall see, identifying collisions via subscripts is necessary for Rule 3. The subscript refers to all collisions. Thus, as shown in Fig. 4(a)

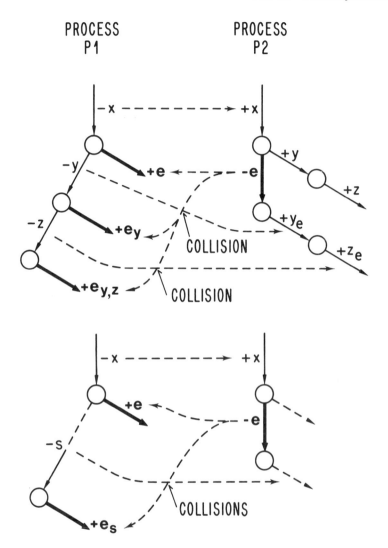

Fig. 4. Derivation of production Rule 1.

if z is also transmitted before e is received, then we append $+e_{y,z}$ to $-z$. We now formulate the first rule using the generalized example in Fig. 4(b) where $-s$ represents a transmission sequence.

Rule 1. If $-e$ is appended to $+x$ then
    (a) append $+e$ to $-x$;
    (b) append $+e_s$ to every negative arc sequence $-s$ attached to
       $-x$.

Part (a) specifies collisionless receptions whereas part (b) specifies all receptions associated with collisions.

The second rule specifies all receptions of a message whose transmission directly succeeds the transmission of a previous message. Consider Fig. 5(a) where P2 transmits e directly after transmitting x. Therefore, P1 can receive e directly after x. Hence, $+e$ is appended to $+x$ in P1. If P1 transmits y before receiving x, then not only do y and x collide but y and e also collide. Then e is received after $+x_y$ and we append $+e_y$ to $+x_y$. Finally, if P1 transmits z after traversing $+x_y$ but before receiving e, then e is received after z is transmitted. In this case e collides with both y and z, hence $+e_{y,z}$ must be appended to $-z$. Similar circumstances hold true if P1 transmits z'. We now formulate the second rule using the generalized example shown in Fig. 5(b) where $-s$ and $-s'$ represent transmission sequences.

Rule 2. If $-e$ is appended to $-x$ then
  (a) to every $+x$ and $+x_s$ append $+e$ and $+e_s$, respectively;
  (b) to every negative arc sequence $-s'$ attached to $+x$ or $+x_s$ append $+e_s$, and $+e_{s,s'}$, respectively.

A third production rule is necessary because new cause-and-effect mechanisms come into play when a negative arc is appended to a subscripted reception. Consider Fig. 6(a) where P2 transmits e directly after receiving $+w_x$, i.e., after receiving a w that collides with an x. Message e is the next P2 transmission after x. Therefore, P1 receives e directly after x. But w is received before e is transmitted, hence P1 can only receive e after transmitting w. Therefore, P1 can only receive e after it both transmits w and receives x. Hence, $+e$ must be appended to $+x_w$. The arc $+e$ is not indexed because, as shown in Fig. 6(a), no collisions are associated with its transmission. If, on the other hand, P1 transmits y before receiving x, then x collides with both w and y, whereas e collides only with y. Hence, $+e_y$ is appended to $+x_{w,y}$.

Finally, the mechanism of the third reception case $+e_{y,z}$ is identical to that of $+e_{y,x}$ in Fig. 5(a). We now formulate the third rule using the generalized example in Fig. 6(b) where $-s$ and $-s'$ represent transmission sequences and " ... " stands for an arbitrary message sequence.

Rule 3. If $-e$ is appended to $+v_{...,u}$, then within the tree with root $-v$
  (a) append $+e$ to $+u_{...,v}$ and $+e_s$ to every $+u_{v,s}$;
  (b) to every negative arc sequence $-s'$ attached to $+u_{...,v}$ or $+u_{...,v,s}$ append $+e'_s$ or $+e_{s,s'}$, respectively.

Part (b) of Rule 3 describes the same specification mechanism as part (b) of Rule 2.

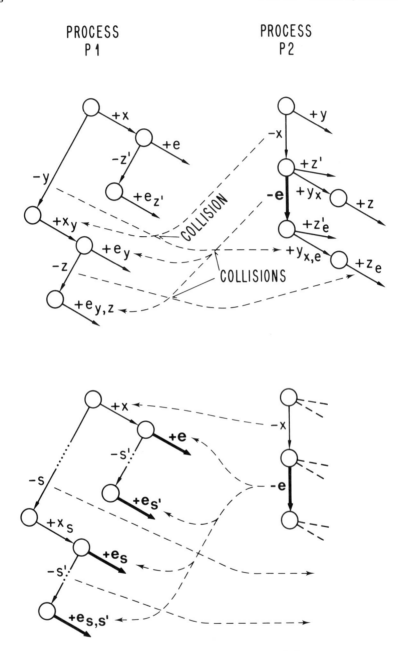

Fig. 5. Derivation of production Rule 2.

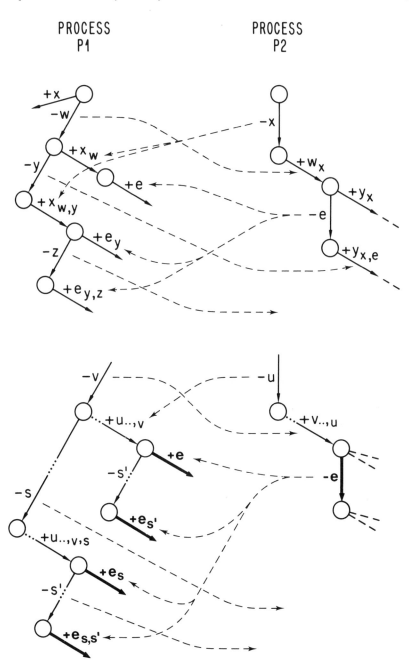

Fig. 6. Derivation of production Rule 3.

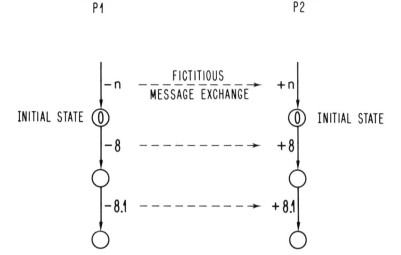

Fig. 7. Example showing minor notational extensions.

A few notational conventions simplify application of the production rules. For example, entering the initial states via a fictitious message exchange as shown in Fig. 7 enables Rules 1 or 2 to specify reception arcs appended to initial states. Furthermore, to generate only exercisable sequences, the rules require that every negative arc within one process be uniquely specified. The ensuing problem of representing different transmission instances of a same message is solved as follows. The first transmission of a message 8 is represented by -8, the second transmission is represented by -8.1, and so on (see Fig. 7). The eleventh occurrence would be specified as 8.10 and would be considered different from 8.1.

B. On Using the Rules

We require an algorithm that specifies where and when to apply the rules. The algorithm is based on an incremental design approach requesting designer intervention whenever semantic-dictated decisions are needed. The designer creates state diagrams, but in order to describe the algorithm, we will consider tree structures. Consider the design portrayed in Fig. 8(a). The algorithm begins by automatically creating the fictitious message exchange $(-n, +n)$, which initializes both processes. It then requests a first design action. The designer complies and creates the transmission of message 1 in $P1$ by specifying $P1,(0) - (-1) \rightarrow (1)$, where $P1$ is the process considered, 0

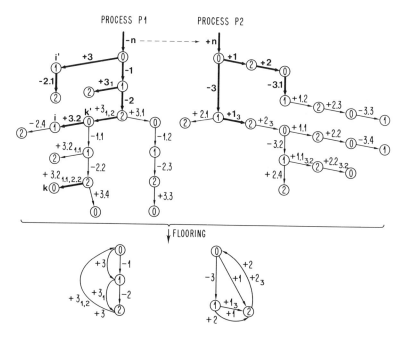

Fig. 8. Synthesis design example. Thickly lined arcs in (a) are explicitly discussed in the text.

is the departure state, 1 the entry state, and -1 is the message transmitted. The algorithm then invokes Rule 2 (-1 is appended to $-n$) which creates $P2,(0) - (+1) \rightarrow (?)$ and requests the designer to specify the entry state identified by $(?)$. He specifies this as state 2. The algorithm again requests the next designer action which is $P2,(0) - (-3) \rightarrow (1)$. This new arc is appended to a reception, hence Rule 1 is invoked and creates the arcs $P1,(0) - (+3) \rightarrow (?)$ and $P1,(1) - (+3_1) \rightarrow (?)$. The designer then specifies the entry states as 1 and 2, respectively. This specification causes the node representing state 1 to appear twice. We are building trees, and tree nodes have at most one entry arc, hence state names may appear more than once.

Creating arc -3 in $P2$ causes arcs -3 and $+1$ to have a common origin, namely, state 0. Hence, it is possible for $P2$ to receive message 1 after transmitting message 3. This reception can be specified by reapplying Rule 1 to arc -1. But a much simpler method is to duplicate arc $+1$, append it to arc -3 and index it accordingly. Indexing is necessary, for this arc can only be traversed if messages 1, 3 collide. We call this reception-replication. The algorithm automatically executes reception-replication, thereby creating the arc $P2,(1) - (+1_3) \rightarrow (?)$ with the designer then specifying "?" to be state 2.

The next designer action is to create the transmission $P1,(1) - (-2) \rightarrow$ (2). At this point the tree structure $P1$ contains two copies of state 1. Hence, the algorithm appends a second transmission $P1,(1) - (-2.1) \rightarrow (2)$ to the second copy of state 1 (in general, if state i transmits message e, then arc $-e$ is appended to the first created node i, arc $-e.1$ to the second created node i, etc. and the rules are applied in the creation sequence). The algorithm then invokes Rule 2 for arc -2 and Rule 1 for arc -2.1. This creates reception arcs in $P2$. One such arc is $P2,(2) - (+2) \rightarrow (?)$. The designer specifies its entry state as 0 ("?" set to 0). He thereby creates a cycle which enables $P2$ to retransmit message 3. The algorithm takes care of this by automatically appending an arc -3.1 to the arc $+2$ and invoking Rule 2 which in turn creates further receptions, and so on. In this way the algorithm adds arcs to the trees. This tree growth would continue indefinitely if it were not for a termination mechanism that halts the growth when the configuration of Fig. 8(a) is reached. The designer could then enter a further message transmission if he so wished. The above-mentioned termination mechanism is an important part of the algorithm and is described in Section V D.

It is worth noting that when the algorithm creates a duplicate arc such as $+3.2$ (duplicate of $+3$ because $+3$ and $+3.2$ have same departure state) in $P1$, then its entry state must be equal to that of the original arc $+3$ and hence, no designer intervention is needed.

When the designer is finished, the algorithm collapses the tree structures by using a "flooring" operation to obtain the finite-state graphs of the actual interaction, shown in Fig. 8(b). The flooring operation drops all decimal fractions from message numbers and merges identical states and arcs in each tree. It is important to note that the algorithm masks the complexity of the tree structures from the designer by displaying all arc identifiers without decimal fractions and by not displaying duplicate arcs. The designer therefore need not even realize that the algorithm uses trees as internal representation. The reader will note that the interaction we have just designed (Fig. 8) is very similar to that of Fig. 2. In fact, it is the same interaction devoid of unspecified receptions and of nonexecutable interactions. The monitoring of deadlocks and ambiguities during the synthesis process is discussed in the next section.

C. Error Prevention via Synthesis

The algorithm together with the production rules specify those and only those positive arcs that must be created to prevent unspecified receptions. Hence, it is not possible to create nonexecutable interactions (see Section III C).

Every time an arc pair $(-e; +e)$, $(+e_y; +y_e)$ or $(+e\ldots, {}_y; +y\ldots, {}_e)$ is created the corresponding entry states (i, k) represent a stable-state pair. Hence, stable-state pair monitoring is quite easy. A state deadlock (see Section III A) is present if for such a pair neither state has a negative departing arc. The algorithm monitors state deadlocks by testing for the absence of negative departing arcs in every created stable state pair.

State ambiguities (see Section III D) can be monitored in the following way. Every time a new stable-state pair (i, k) is created, it is stored in a list. If the list already contains a pair (i, x) or (x, k), then a state ambiguity is identified.

D. Termination

As mentioned in Section V B, the design rules could be applied continually, defining infinite trees. It is necessary to stop the growth at a point when continuation cannot reveal any new information about the protocol. This section presents a method for termination.

Termination is achieved by deleting negative arc copies. When the algorithm creates a new tree node, it tests whether certain repetition criteria are fulfilled. If they are, the node is marked "dead." Dead nodes are a form of duplicate nodes. They are treated differently in that a transmission arc as well as its corresponding reception arcs are deleted if they all turn out to be appended below dead nodes. Thus, in the example of Fig. 8, the whole process is complete because all further arcs are deleted.

We now describe the criteria that define a node dead. Consider the situation where the algorithm specifies an arc $+e$ with entry node i. This node i is marked "dead" if there already exists an arc $+e'$ with entry node i', where e, e' represent the same message, the nodes i, i' represent the same state, and i' has no dead-node predecessors. For example, in process $P1$ of Fig. 8(a), the entry node i of arc $+3.2$ is dead. This is so as $P1$ already contains an arc $+3$ with entry node i' where i, i' represent the same state 0, 3.2 and 3 the same message and i' has no dead predecessors. Similarly, if the algorithm specifies an arc $+e_s$ with entry node k, then k is marked dead if there already exists an arc $+e'_{s'}$ with entry node k' where in addition to the above requirements being fulfilled, s and s' represent the same message sequence. For example, in process $P1$ of Fig. 8(a), the entry node k of arc $+3.2_{1.1,\,2.2}$ is dead. This is so because $P1$ already has an arc $+3_{1,2}$ with entry node k' where $(1.1, 2.2)$, $(1, 2)$ represent the same message sequence, k and k' the same state, 3.2 and 3 the same message, and k' has no dead-node predecessors.

Appendix C shows that this method is valid, i.e., it will not cause any receptions to be missed in the graph. It also shows that it will terminate the growth of the trees for any protocol where both channels are bounded. The unbounded-channel case is discussed in the next section.

VI. The Unbounded Channel

In this section we consider interactions that can lead to unbounded growth in the number of messages transmitted by one process but not yet received by the other. One example of such an interaction is shown in Fig. 9. $P2$ can transmit message 3 after every message reception. Assume $P2$ does this and that at the same time $P1$ transmits messages 1 and 2 with sufficient speed so that it receives all messages in state 2. Then for every message $P1$ receives, it transmits two messages. Hence the number of messages in transit, i.e., in the $P1$ to $P2$ channel grows without bound. This is a generic example from which more complicated ones can be derived. Another type of interaction that can lead to unbounded-channel growth are transmission cycles. Such a cycle would be present if in $P1$ of Fig. 9, arc -2 were modified so as to enter state 0. $P1$ would then contain a transmission cycle -1, -2.

The perturbation method (Section IV A) sets bounds on the maximum channel capacity. Hence, a perturbation analysis will always terminate when interactions exhibiting unbounded-channel growth are considered. The same holds true for the synthesis case when one sets upper bounds on the index sequences and on the number of consecutive transmissions. The consequence of these termination mechanisms is that interactions exhibiting unbounded channel growth may not be fully analyzable or synthesizable. This limitation is by no means unique to our termination mechanisms. It is

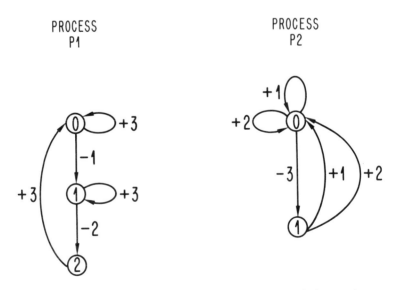

Fig. 9. Interaction exhibiting unbounded-channel growth. Indexing not shown.

a necessary property of all termination mechanisms, as will be proven in a forthcoming paper. Consequently, we can improve termination mechanisms to cover more and more practical protocols, but we must always be prepared for protocols that can never be completely analyzed or synthesized.

It is interesting to consider design criteria that guarantee unbounded-channel capacity and hence, guarantee complete analysis and synthesis. One such criterion is that every cycle in an interacting process that contains one or more transmission arcs must also contain at least one collisionless reception. This limits the channel capacity because when a collisionless reception occurs, the transmitting channel of the receiving process is empty. Hence, the transmitting channel is emptied every time a message generation cycle is traversed, thereby causing the channel capacity to be bounded.

VII. Conclusions

Two approaches to improving protocol correctness have been described. The first, perturbation, is implemented as a method for validating an existing protocol, while the second is a set of production rules applied in a stepwise interactive manner to synthesize a "correct" design. The underlying principles of both approaches are equivalent in that the production rules could be used for validation purposes and the perturbation method could be used for synthesis purposes. Both approaches require limits on the channel content when handling protocols or interactions that exhibit unbounded-channel growth. This limitation can be transformed, for example, into design criteria which when fulfilled prevent unbounded-channel growth. But some form of limitation is a necessary condition for there is no solution to the general problem of reception specification.

In the case of validation, a thorough analysis of CCITT X.21 circuit-switched network interface specification has already been published [13]. Some of the results of applying the perturbation technique to the data-flow-control portion of IBM's SNA network architecture are discussed in [8].

The validation procedure has also been applied to the packet-level portion of the CCITT X.25 packet-switched network interface specification. The results, which were independently discovered by Belsnes and Lynning [21], were submitted by IBM to study group VII of the CCITT [14]. The reader interested in X.25 may wish to examine the issue of *Computer Communication Review* devoted to this topic [22]. In the definition of X.25, it was found that a collision of the DCE-CLEAR-INDICATION message coming from the network could collide with the DTE-CALL-REQUEST coming from the terminal. According to the specification, the network was to identify this collision as a "local procedure error" even though such a collision is allowed by the same protocol specification. Thus, the "procedure-error" indication became ambiguous, being used both for the identification of natural collisions and actual protocol violations. The repair to this anomaly was also validated by the same method [14]. The correction has since been accepted by the CCITT study group VII's Rapporteurs' group.

An experiment was also performed using the protocol synthesis package to try to duplicate the same X.25 level-3 specification. During the redesign of this portion of the protocol (for the error-free channel), the synthesis package demanded that the receptions resulting from the previously mentioned collision be resolved as soon as the developing design makes them possible. Terminating these receptions as recommended [14] leads to the successful complete design.

Our work and that of others in protocol specification and validation has only examined one aspect of a large and important area which perhaps should be called "interaction science." Work of others on such topics as concurrent programming is exploring this science from a different viewpoint. Many of the problems inherent in distributed processing will be resolved as this science develops.

Appendix A: Further Considerations about the Model

The representation described in Section II can be used to model both nonideal communication channels and interactions between more than two processes [16]. This is illustrated by the very simple three-process interaction shown in Fig. 10. Process $P1$ transmits message x to process, $P2$, $P2$ models a nonideal channel from $P1$ to $P3$, and $P3$ receives messages from $P2$. Message x' (generated by $P2$) represents a corruption by the channel of message x, and the arc with identifier 0 represents a nonevent, i.e., a state

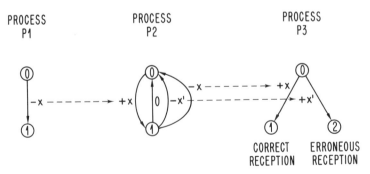

Fig. 10. Interaction example demonstrating how to model many process interactions and how to include communication channels that can lose and distort messages.

transition that generates no messages. $P2$ is initially in state 0. On receiving message x from $P1$ it enters state 1 and can proceed in one of three ways: either it faithfully retransmits x to $P3$ by transmitting x or it corrupts x by transmitting x' to $P3$ or it loses x by traversing arc 0. Thus, $P3$ can either receive message x or a corrupted version x' or no message at all.

Appendix B: Sufficiency and Necessity Proofs for the Production Rules

We present arguments which demonstrate that the production rules, derived in Section V A, are both necessary and sufficient. We say that the rules are sufficient if they create enough arcs to prevent unspecified receptions and that they are necessary if every created arc is needed to prevent unspecified receptions. The proofs assume that arc replication (Section V B) is replaced by repeated application of the rules. We begin with the sufficiency proof and consider Fig. 11.

(1) Assume the rules insufficient and let e be the first message that manifests this, i.e., there exists a state c of $P1$ that can receive e yet this reception is not specified by the rules.

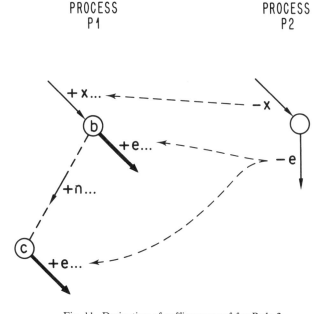

Fig. 11. Derivation of suffiency proof for Rule 2.

(2) Consider first the case that $-e$ is appended to a negative arc $-x$, i.e., that Rule 2 causes this unspecified reception. Later, we will consider $-e$ appended to reception arcs.

(3) By virtue of (2) and the fact that FIFO channels are assumed, message x is always received before message e.

(4) Hence, state c must be below a reception of x; let b be the entry state of that reception.

(5) The path from b to c must contain at least one positive reception arc, say arc $+n$... because otherwise Rule 2 would specify the reception of e in state c.

(6) Since $P1$ would receive message n after x and before e, $P2$ must traverse $-x$ followed by $-n$ followed by $-e$.

(7) But this contradicts our initial assumption that $-x$ then $-e$ be consecutively traversed.

(8) Hence, there is no reception of message e in $P1$ not specified by Rule 2.

We outline the rest of the proof. The above derivation (steps 2–8) is repeated for the case where arc $-e$ is appended to an arc $+x$, i.e., where Rule 1 causes the insufficiency. It is then repeated for the case where arc $-e$ is appended to an arc $+x_s$, i.e., where Rule 3 causes the insufficiency. Since we obtain a contradiction with the assumptions of steps 1 and 2 in all three cases, the rules are sufficient. We now prove with the help of Fig. 12 that the

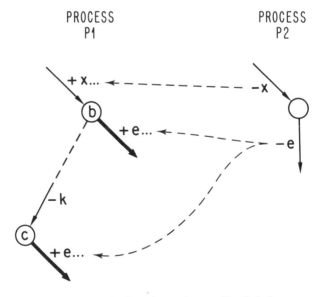

Fig. 12. Derivation of necessity proof for Rule 2.

rules are necessary.

(1) Assume that the rules overspecify and that e is the first message that manifests this, i.e., there exists a state c in $P1$ that cannot receive message e yet the rules specify this reception.

(2) Consider first the case that $-e$ is appended to a negative arc $-x$, i.e., that Rule 2 causes this overspecification. Later, we will consider $-e$ appended to reception arcs.

(3) By virtue of (2) and the fact that FIFO channels are assumed, message x is always received before message e.

(4) Hence, state c must be below a reception of x; let b be the entry state of that reception.

(5) $P1$ enters state b on receiving x, hence state b can receive e, and Rule 2 specifies a reception of e in state b.

(6) $c \neq b$ because otherwise e could be received in state c and the assumptions of (1) would be contradicted.

(7) Since $c \neq b$ and Rule 2 specifies reception of message e by state c, there must be a negative-arc sequence connecting state b to c.

(8) The entry of any negative-arc sequence attached to state b can also receive message e (no time constraints assumed).

(9) By virtue of (7), state c is the entry of such a negative-arc sequence, hence state c can receive message e.

(10) But this contradicts our initial assumption that state c cannot receive e, hence all receptions of e specified by Rule 2 are occurrable.

We outline the rest of the proof. The above derivation (steps 2–10) is repeated for the case where arc $-e$ is appended to an arc $+x$, i.e., where Rule 1 causes the overspecification. It is then repeated for the case where arc $-e$ is appended to an arc $+x_s$, i.e., where Rule 3 causes the overspecification. Consequently, all receptions of e specified by the rules can occur. Hence, the rules are necessary.

Appendix C: Outline of Proof for the Termination Algorithm

We have to prove two facts about ignoring some arcs as described in Section V D:

1. that it will not cause any arcs to be missed in the protocol, and
2. that it will terminate the building of the trees, provided the channels cannot grow without bounds.

The proofs will only be outlined due to space limitations. For the first point consider a situation when a reception $+e_s$ is added to a tree with entry node i, and assume that the node i is declared dead because of a previous reception $+e'_{s'}$ with entry node i'. Let the entry nodes of the transmission arcs $-e$ and $-e'$ be j and j', respectively. Consider two executions: one brings the two processes into nodes i and j, the other into nodes i' and j'. There is no way to distinguish between these two executions because the nodes i and i' represent the same process state, j and j' represent the same process state, and the contents of the two channels are also the same (namely, one channel is empty, the other contains the messages represented by the sequences s and s'). Therefore, no matter how the execution from i, j continues, there must be an equivalent execution where the processes are in states i' and j', respectively. From this, one can prove that for every arc that could possibly be generated (if the design rules were allowed to run forever), there is an equivalent arc attached to an equivalent node generated under the limitations of Section V D.

To show termination, we will show that no infinite branch can be generated in either tree. For the sake of argument assume an infinite branch. First, this infinite branch must contain an infinite number of receptions, for otherwise there would exist a cycle consisting of transmissions only (see Section VI), contradicting our assumption of bounded channels. Secondly, this infinite branch must contain a dead node because there must be a message whose reception is repeated infinitely often along the branch, but there is only a finite number of nonequivalent combinations of channel contents and entry node. Thus, every branch is either finite or contains a dead node. Therefore, there is only a finite number of transmissions that are both transmitted and received above dead nodes. Keeping a finite number of transmission arcs keeps the trees finite.

References

[1] J. Postel, "A graph model analysis of computer communication protocols," UCLA-ENG-741, University of California, Los Angeles, January 1974.

[2] T. Piatkowski, "Finite-state architecture," IBM Technical Report TR-29.0133, Systems Development Division (now Systems Communications Division), Research Triangle Park, North Carolina, August 1975.

[3] C. A. Sunshine, "Interprocess communication protocols for computer networks," Ph.D. thesis, Computer Science Dept., Stanford University, 1975.

[4] IBM Corporation, "Systems network architecture format and protocol reference manual: Architectural logic," Publication SC30-3112-1, File No. S370-30, 1976.

[5] J. Hajek, "Automatically verified data transfer protocols," Proc. Internat. Conf. Comput. Commun., Kyoto, Japan, pp. 749–756, September 1978.

[6] C. A. Sunshine, "Survey of protocol definition and verification techniques," Proc. Comput. Network Protocols Symp., Liège, Belgium, F1-1/F1-4, February 1978.

[7] P. M. Merlin, "Specification and validation of protocols," IEEE Trans. Commun., vol. COM-27, pp. 1671–1680, Nov. 1979.

[8]   A. Danthine (Ed.), *Proc. Comput. Network Protocols Symp.*, Liège, Belgium, February 1978. See also Special Issue on Computer Network Protocols, *Comput. Networks*, vol. 2, no. 4/5, September/October 1978.

[9]   P. Zafiropulo, "Protocol validation by duologue-matrix analysis," *IEEE Trans. Commun.*, vol. COM-26, no. 8, 1187–1194, August 1978.

[10] G. V. Bochmann, "Finite state description of communications protocols," *Proc. Comput. Network Protocols Symp.*, Liège, Belgium, F3-1/F3-11, February 1978.

[11] C. H. West, "General technique for communications protocol validation," *IBM J. Res. Develop.*, vol. 22, no. 1, 393–404, July 1978.

[12] J. Hajek, "Protocols verified by APPROVER," *SIGCOM Comput. Commun. Rev.*, vol. 9, no. 1, January 1979.

[13] C. H. West and P. Zafiropulo, "Automated validation of a communications protocol: The CCITT X.21 recommendation," *IBM J. Res. Develop.*, vol. 22, no. 1, 60–71, January 1978.

[14] IBM Europe, "Technical improvements to CCITT recommendation X.25," Submission to Study Group VII, October 1978.

[15] P. Zafiropulo, "Design rules for producing logically complete two-process interactions and communications protocols," *Proc. Second Internat. Conf. Comput. Software and Applications*, Chicago, pp. 680–685, November 1978.

[16] K. A. Bartlett, R. A. Scantelbury, and P. T. Wilkinson, "A note on reliable full-duplex transmission over half-duplex links," *Commun. ACM*, vol. 12, no. 5, 2260–2261, May 1969.

[17] C. H. West, "An automated technique of communications protocol validation," *IEEE Trans. Commun.*, vol. COM-26, no. 8, 1271–1275, August 1978.

[18] H. Rudin, C. H. West, and P. Zafiropulo, "Automated protocol validation: One chain of development," *Proc. Comput. Network Protocols Symp.*, Liège, Belgium, Paper F4, February 1978.

[19] D. D. Cowan and C. J. P. Lucena, "Some thoughts on the construction of programs—A data-directed approach," *Proc. of Third Jerusalem Conf. Information Technology*, Jerusalem, Israel, August 1978.

[20] D. D. Cowan, J. W. Graham, J. W. Welch, and C. J. P. Lucena, "A data-directed approach to program construction," to appear in *Software Practice and Experience*.

[21] D. Belsnes and E. Lynning, "Some problems with the X.25 packet level protocol," *Comput. Commun. Rev.*, vol. 7, no. 4, 41–51, October 1977.

[22] A. A. McKenzie (Ed.), *Comput. Commun. Rev.*, ACM Special Interest Group on Data Communications, October 1977.

25

Executable Representation and Validation of SNA

Gary D. Schultz, David B. Rose, Colin H. West and James P. Gray

I. Introduction

The 1960s and early 1970s were the design heyday and proving ground for operating systems within single computers and across tightly coupled ones. Today we are experiencing a new design era for coordinating data processing distributed over ensembles of cooperating processors, configured into networks.

Software engineering for operating systems developed layered structuring of systems, top-down design, structured programming, disciplined synchronization (e.g., semaphores) for cooperating processes, and research into proof-of-program-correctness methods. Today's era of *network architectures*, which are specifications of the message formats and interaction protocols for services provided within networks, has had the need for additional design innovations for the changed system context of loosely coupled system components, disparate processor architectures, and widely dispersed groups of people implementing a common network architecture.

This chapter focuses on the evolving specification of IBM's Systems Network Architecture (SNA) and the formal techniques developed to design, describe, and test it. A survey of the flourishing literature on other formal techniques, developed independently of those described here, is outside the scope of this chapter. We refer the reader to Sunshine's extensive survey [1] and other chapters in this book for discussions of parallel advances.

The next section presents a brief overview of SNA. Section III discusses the evolution of the architectural description of SNA into a state-oriented metaimplementation, and the early representations of the metaimplementation in the form of block diagrams, combinational functions, and finite-state machines (FSMs). Section IV describes the development and essential features of the Format and Protocol Language (FAPL). FAPL, based on PL/I, replaces the earlier combinational function flow charts and FSM state-transition graphs by procedures and state-transition matrices, having rigorous semantics and machine-readable syntax. This allows compilation and machine execution of the metaimplementation. In turn, automated validation of the architecture can be performed, as described in Section V. Speculation on the implications and future possibilities of the FAPL description of SNA concludes the chapter.

II. Services and Control Structures of SNA

The purpose of this chapter is twofold: to describe briefly how (and why) SNA is defined by a metaimplementation of a node, and to discuss the formal techniques developed for the specification and validation of the SNA metaimplementation. To do this requires that enough of SNA be defined so that we can explain the rationale for the methodology used to specify the architecture. To the extent that other network architectures are similar, the SNA design approach can be generally applied. See, for example, the discussion in [2] of the application of this approach to ISO's Open Systems Interconnection architecture.

A. Functional Layering and Control of Sessions

The purpose of SNA is to provide means for end users to use data processing services and devices distributed throughout a network. An end user can be a person using a terminal, or an application program executing in a network node. Device media are also regarded as end users when they can be the source or destination of data. With this view of end users and their needs, SNA can be represented as a services network, concentrically layered by function, as shown in Fig. 1.

The top layer provides data formatting and other *presentation services*, as well as connection, or *session*, services allowing an end user to initiate an activation of a session with another end user. *Data flow control* provides functions for sequence numbering and logical chaining of user messages, for correlation of requests and responses between the end users, for control of send–receive concurrency between them, and for bracketing (or serially multiplexing) transactions during the session-active period (e.g., for data-base

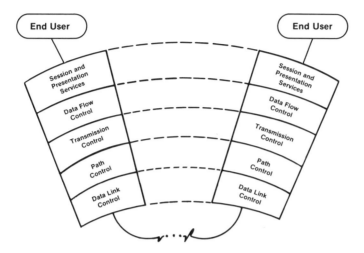

Fig. 1. Functional layers of communication between end users.

applications). *Transmission control* enforces the end-to-end session-level pacing of message traffic between the end users in accordance with the storage and processing available for it, provides other functions related to session control, and enciphers user messages when requested. *Path control* supports the routing and flow control of messages throughout the network, while *data link control* schedules traffic and performs error recovery on the links between adjacent network nodes. For additional details, see Chapter 5 (data link control), Chapter 11 (path control), and Chapter 16 (presentation services and data flow control).

With this model of a network architecture, the task remained to define the protocol boundaries (or interfaces) between adjacent layers, the peer-to-peer (e.g., data flow control to data flow control) protocols, and the message headers and requests and responses exchanged by layer peers. What is lacking in this model is any representation of the partitioning of control for individual end users and their sessions. It is obvious that control and routing need to be exercised on behalf of different end users and different sessions, but the structural components for this control are hidden in a model such as Fig. 1 that deals only with functional layers.

The notion of the *logical unit* (LU) (see Fig. 2) served to fill this particular gap in the simple layered model. An LU serves as a port for an end user to gain access to the network. Each LU contains the functions of the top three layers of Fig. 1, with a control structure imposed. A session now is represented by a *half-session* in each LU and the signaling path

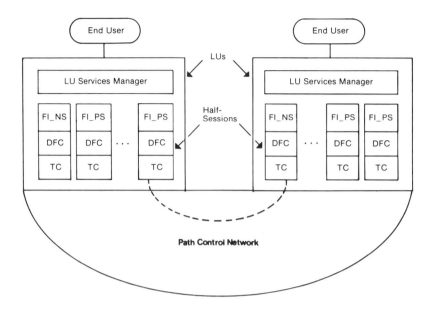

Fig. 2. LUs and the inner path control network.

connecting them through the path control network—the set of all path control and data link control elements in the SNA network.*

The half-sessions contain the same functions as described in the corresponding layer model, but are sensitive to interactions between specific end-user pairs. Based on session parameters exchanged at session activation, the half-sessions provide particular subsets and variations of the layered functions, for example to vary pacing control. The half-sessions also, during the time a session remains active, synchronize and track the sequence of events transpiring at both ends. The top layer of Fig. 1, session and presentation services, is represented by the top layer of the half-sessions and by the LU services manager. The top layer of a half-session, when connected to a half-session in another LU, provides presentation services, as described earlier. The LU services manager intercepts new session initiation (log-on) requests from its end user and represents the end user in a multistep process to activate a new LU–LU session, thereby supporting the session services previously mentioned.

Each LU is represented within the path control network by a *network address* for routing purposes and, external to the SNA network among end

---

*We adopt the convention from [3] of designating an inner network by its outermost layer. Thus, later we refer to the inner network underlying data flow control as the transmission control network.

users, by an *LU name*. End users are thereby freed of routing concerns and can be insensitive to changes in the underlying network configuration.

The directory problem of resolving LU names (used in session-initiation requests) to network addresses supplies the rationale* for an additional type of network addressable unit—the *system services control point* (SSCP). Because of the potential number of LUs a network can contain, a full directory of network addresses may be too large to carry at every node of the network. For this reason, the directory assistance is provided by an SSCP, and an LU–LU session initiation is performed by an LU in conjunction with the SSCP, using an LU–SSCP session.

The top layers of the LU half-sessions are shown in Fig. 2 with differentiated names. SPS, or session presentation services, and SNS, or session network services, distinguish the types of services that are provided for LU–LU and LU–SSCP sessions, respectively. The SSCP (not shown) has a similar services manager and half-session structure, and also attaches to the path control network.

B. The Configuration Model

The model of Fig. 2 is still too simple: it fails to differentiate the underlying node and link configuration, and is therefore not rich enough to deal with the issues of network management and control of real physical networks, in which nodes, links, and their interconnections are of central concern. Also, the model does not deal with the realities of nodes having varying capabilities and roles within the network. The product designer following the architecture has to implement a node; this perspective must be served in an architectural specification.

Figure 3 provides an example of a *configuration model*, which exposes the underlying physical configuration, and illustrates the basic node types, control structures, and interconnections defined in SNA. This model emphasizes the organization of the layer elements into larger control structures —the node itself being one. It allows the relationships of these larger control structures to be exposed and defined. (For simplicity, we suppress the details of path control and data link control elements in this figure.)

The node is the focus of product design, being a partitioning of resources and services that can form a configurable element, interconnected by links to other nodes within a network configuration. A *physical unit* (PU) exists in each node to control the resources associated with the node, perhaps in response to an SSCP request, such as to activate a particular link

---

*Other network services can be selected as rationale, but we choose the directory and routing issues to motivate this overview, and to serve as the integrating theme. For a discussion of other network services, see [3], [4].

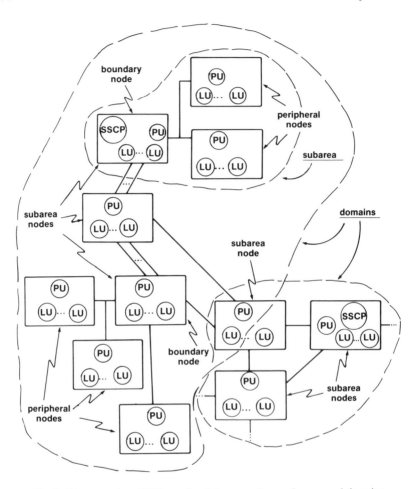

Fig. 3. The network as NAUs, nodes, link connections, subareas, and domains.

to another node. Like the other *network addressable units* (NAUs)—the LU and the SSCP—the PU has a services manager and half-session structure, and uses the path control network.

Each NAU is represented in the path control network by a network address. To facilitate network routing and reduce routing table sizes, the network address has a *subarea address* and an *element address* component; the network as a whole is then partitioned into *subareas*. To reduce the number of nodes responsible for network address routing—and hence sensitive to reconfigurations—only some nodes are involved in network address routing. These are called *subarea nodes*. Other nodes use shorter, local addresses or session identifiers that need be unique only within individual nodes; we refer to these as *peripheral nodes*. (Typically, these are terminals or terminal cluster controllers.) Peripheral nodes attach to SNA networks through subarea nodes, which provide a boundary function for transforming between the local and network addresses. Peripheral nodes, therefore, are not sensitive to changes, additions, or deletions to the network address space. A subarea consists of the PU, the SSCP (if present), and the LUs in a subarea node, along with the PU and LUs in each peripheral node (if any) attaching to it. Each PU or LU in a subarea has a unique element address within the subarea. The PU in the subarea node may dynamically assign a PU or LU in its subarea to a network address. For details of subarea node routing and flow control, see Chapter 11.

To reduce the size of the directory a single SSCP maintains, the responsibility for directory management and assistance is distributed over multiple SSCPs throughout the network, and the network is partitioned into *domains*. A domain consists of an SSCP and the PUs, LUs, links, and link stations that it can activate, deactivate, and control. Serial or concurrent sharing of control of network components is possible, and so domains can overlap. An SSCP knows the network address of every member of its domain, as well as of every other SSCP in the network. It also knows the domain (or SSCP) associated with each LU whose name it is authorized to encounter in a request. The directory assistance (and other functions) related to cross-domain LU–LU session activations involves the cooperation of the SSCPs controlling the separate domains, transparent to the participating LUs. For further discussion of cross-domain session services, see [3], [6]

C. Overview of a Node

With this brief rationale for the network control structures, and the emphasis on the node as the focus of product design, we can now discuss SNA as a node-based architecture. Figure 4 (derived from [3], [7]) provides the architectural overview of a node in its most general representation. It shows a subarea node having a PU (always present), one or more LUs, the boundary function, and an SSCP. The PU controls the physical resources (e.g., links) of the node, while the LUs can be used to partition, allocate, and control the devices associated with end-user communications (Chapter 16).

A peripheral node lacks the SSCP and boundary function (BF) components—consisting of BF.PC, for transforming between network and local addresses, and NAU-like subcomponents (called BF.PUs and BF.LUs) for assisting in session-level control. (The period notation represents decomposition of the larger structure into subcomponents.) The path control element in a peripheral node routes on local addresses or local session

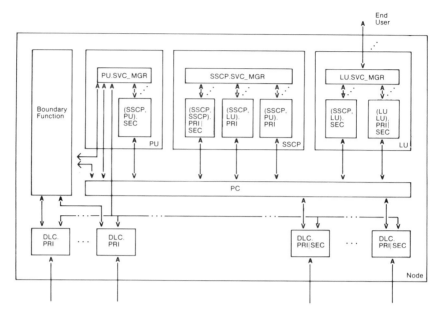

Fig. 4. Overview of an SNA node.

identifiers, rather than on network addresses. Subarea nodes vary from each other only by the presence or absence of an SSCP and boundary function support, and by the number and types of links and LUs they support.

The definition of SNA in the form of a node-based structure, successively refined into substructures, provides an archetypal control structure for implementation groups to follow, without having to reinvent the basic organization from the ground up. Early IBM implementations of SNA have evolved to the metaimplementation structure, while later ones have built upon it from the start.

With this overview of SNA as a layered functional structure on which control structures are imposed, and from which a node definition is derived, we turn in the next section to the design and specification of an SNA node in the form of a state-oriented metaimplementation.

III. State-Oriented Design and Specification

Sundstrom [9] has discussed the futility of relying solely on sequence descriptions and supplementary explanatory prose for the protocol specification of large systems. For a network architecture like SNA, a new approach was needed to remove specification ambiguities and provide greater precision. At the same time that the node structure described in the previous section was evolving, descriptive techniques were being developed to define the SNA protocols and the functional components, or *protocol machines*, within layers, in terms of *states* and *state machines*. This effort was led by T. F. Piatkowski, who set forth the general principles to be followed [10], and developed the basic descriptive tools [11]. Piatkowski proposed that the block diagram of the node be successively refined until the fundamental *finite-state machines* (FSMs) and *combinational functions* (or *logic*) interconnecting them were reached. This approach was rooted in classical FSM theory, such as described in [12]–[14]. Earlier use of FSMs in defining data link controls for an operational data communications system is described in [15]; see also [16], [17] for general discussions of the application of finite-state representations to data link controls.

An FSM is formally defined as a five-tuple:

$$FSM = (S, I, O, FNS, FOUT)$$

where S is a finite *state set*; I is a finite *input set*; O is a finite *output set*; FNS: $S \times I \rightarrow S$ is the *next-state function*, which maps current (state, input) pairs into the next state; and FOUT: $S \times I \rightarrow O$ is the *output function*, which maps current (state, input) pairs into the current output. [The current state itself is a *static* output—like memory, it can be read at any time; *pulsed* output signal(s), such as message units to be forwarded out of the node, can also be issued.]

The FSM provides a representation of a component that has *memory* and tracks the current status of the system. By placing complementary FSMs at the sending and receiving half-sessions, the two ends can retain synchronization with respect to a given protocol. For example, the two ends of an LU–LU session contain complementary FSMs that are sensitive to Bind–Unbind Session request-and-response exchanges, to track session active–reset (and intermediate) states. These FSMs can be checked (via *state checks* on their static outputs) at both ends by other protocol machines to test the validity of other send–receive actions.

The representation of complementary FSMs allows convenient enumeration of all state pairs, (si, sj), where si is the state of FSMi and sj is a state of its complementary (or peer) FSM j. Within a given system context, some of the state pairs may be defined to be invalid, i.e., representing state combinations not allowed (or overlooked) by the architectural specification. A *validation* system can test whether connected complementary FSMs can reach invalid state pairs. A later section describes such a validation system that has been applied to SNA.

The decomposition of the structure into FSMs, and interconnecting routing logic, allowed the specification of protocols in terms of *sequence generators* [3], [9], whose input and output specifications show the relationships and generation of sequenced signals. This removes the necessity to define all possible sequences graphically. (The definition of protocols through comprehensive sequence descriptions was actually performed in IBM in the 1960s for binary synchronous communication (BSC), and later for SDLC; see [18] for application of the technique to the American Standard version of BSC. Even for these relatively contained link controls, the task was formidable.)

In describing the structure and protocols of SNA in this state-oriented fashion, a generic structure of a layer element (e.g., a DFC component within a single half-session) was developed. This is shown in Fig. 5. Each layer element has send and receive subelements, which are coupled with complementary receive and send subelements at the remote peer-layer element. Each send and receive subelement consists of state-independent usage checks (e.g., for message parameter validation), state checks (to reject a state violation on sending or record one on receiving), a message router, and multiple-state FSMs. State checks were (in the original notation) separated out from FSMs into tables, to allow error cases to be separately considered, while the FSMs themselves focused on the basic (normal) function provided. (Now, FAPL allows these easily to be merged.) The

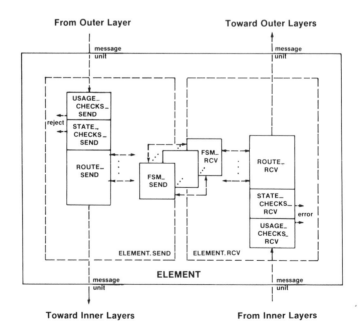

Fig. 5. A generic layer element in SNA.

router sends the message unit to one or more of the FSMs, depending on its content. The FSMs change state according to the input and may produce output messages (to be sent forward), and signals to other FSMs. The FSMs are shown as spanning the send–receive subelements, since local coupling of send–receive FSMs can exist. In the closest coupling, the send–receive FSMs can form a composite FSM, for example in the case of two-way serial (or half-duplex) protocols. More loosely coupled, separate FSMs can exchange signals to synchronize local states.

Piatkowski identified the notion of *friendly* adjacent layers, i.e., those produced by a single implementation group. To avoid a "reject" by a lower layer, and the necessity to "back-out" state transitions already performed in an upper layer, the send checking logic for all friendly layers can be exercised in the uppermost friendly layer.

The checking and routing logic are single-state FSMs, i.e., algorithms without memory. The checking logic was represented in checking tables, or in flowcharts with the routing logic. For general, multiple-state FSMs, a notation of *state-transition graphs* was developed. Figure 6 shows the FSMs defined for the Bind–Unbind protocol machines at both half-sessions. The vertical lines represent the states, while the arrows show the state transitions. Input signals appear above the arrows, and pulsed output signals

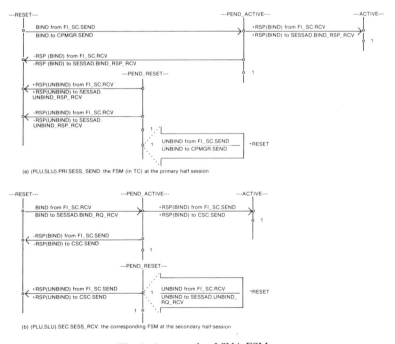

Fig. 6. An example of SNA FSMs.

appear below. The "broad arrow" in the figure is a notational convenience for reducing the number of transition lines in the graph; the predecessor states are identified at the tail ("¬"means logical *not*) and, for added redundancy, numbers identical to the number in the arrow head appear on the state line for each possible predecessor state. Note that the two FSMs are *complementary* rather than *symmetric*, e.g., the primary FSM always sends the Bind, while the secondary always receives it.

In addition to the checking tables, flowcharts, and state-transition graphs, certain special-purpose state machines were defined and represented. These included counters, registers, request–response correlation tables, message-segment accumulators, and queues. Some of these are unbounded in theory and, hence, not FSMs. In practice, SNA protocols can be used to keep these bounded. For example, pacing of message traffic can be used to constrain queue lengths.

This assemblage of descriptive techniques was used in the first edition (1976) of the *SNA Format and Protocol Reference Manual* [3]. The result was a description of an SNA node by a "human-executable" model, or *metaimplementation*. The next step was to establish the framework for a machine-executable version.

IV. Executable Description of SNA

Representation of SNA using state-oriented graphic techniques created great desire among architects, implementers, and testing groups within IBM for a machine-interpretable version. The questions were: How could this translation be done? And what machine-interpretable language should be used? The ensuing debate focused on various requirements. Foremost among these were the needs to keep the official specification understandable to the broad audience of implementers, and to retain the FSM-oriented description.

A leading candidate for the language was PL/I, because of its wide exposure and availability, both inside and outside IBM, and its similarity to the systems programming languages used internally by IBM. Also, PL/I allows structured programming, a required discipline for the executable metaimplementation. The disadvantage of PL/I was that it lacked specialized capabilities for representing FSMs.

One of the authors (Rose) began a pilot project in 1976 to determine if PL/I, suitably augmented, could be used to represent the SNA data flow control layer. This project was successful, and culminated in the definition of the Format and Protocol Language (FAPL) as an augmentation of PL/I. FAPL was then applied generally to the SNA specification. The second edition (1978) of the *SNA Format and Protocol Reference Manual* [3] used a hybrid representation to define the metaimplementation. All flowcharts of the first edition were converted to FAPL procedures, and many (all DFC) state-transition graphs were converted to FAPL state-transition matrices. The conversion is proceeding for future editions.

A. FAPL Language Features

FAPL augments PL/I to provide representations of FSMs and references to them. It also defines general list-handling capabilities, and has features for queued dispatching of procedures. PL/I itself has rich data-variable definition capabilities for representing any special-purpose state machine, such as the required counters, registers, and accumulators mentioned earlier.

Currently, FAPL usage is confined to the following subset of PL/I statements:

assignment statements	DO groups	PROCEDURE
CALL	END	RETURN
DECLARE	IF/THEN/ELSE	SELECT groups

These features are described in the PL/I reference manual [19]. Other features of PL/I, such as data types and built-in functions, are constrained. FAPL extends the PL/I use of the period(.), as a name qualifier for data structures, to procedure and FSM names, as was shown in Fig. 6. This allows showing hierarchical decomposition of *functional*, as well as *data*, components into subcomponents, in a common fashion.

1. Data Entities and List-Handling Facilities

The language extensions to PL/I for list handling are based on concepts used in SIMPL/I [20], a PL/I-based simulation language. Some concepts are used directly, while others are modified slightly.

A basic data-element construct in FAPL is the *entity*. An entity may be sent from one procedure to another, reside on a list, and be created and discarded by FAPL statements. For the SNA metaimplementation, the main use of an entity is to represent a message unit flowing in the network, but other data structures that are to be manipulated in lists are also represented as entities. An entity is defined using an ENTITY statement. Data fields in the entity are defined using the same syntax as for a PL/I DECLARE statement. The difference is that an entity contains header fields preceding the defined data structure; this allows the entity to be manipulated by other

FAPL statements. The CREATE and DISCARD statements allow entities to be generated and destroyed.

FAPL provides high-level list handling statements for managing lists of entities. These extensions allow more succinctness in the metaimplementation representation by subordinating list processing to language features of FAPL. NEWLIST and DESTROY control the existence of lists, and INSERT and REMOVE manipulate list entries. Lists conveniently represent a table of like data structures, such as the request–response correlation tables in SNA data flow control. The SNA definition also uses lists to contain the half-session control blocks for all active sessions. (These control blocks have architected *content* for the metaimplementation; they also have *format* representation in FAPL. They contain all implicit storage for FSM current-state values, and explicit storage for session-activation parameters and session variables.) The SCAN statement provides a convenient method to examine each list entry sequentially. The SCAN group contains statements that can be executed each time a list entry is found with particular attributes.

Data queues are handled as special-case lists. A data queue, like a list, may be defined to contain multiple entities, but a specific data queue or list may contain only one entity type. The INSERT statement provides options that allow first-in, first-out (FIFO) or priority management of a list representing a data queue. REMOVE is used to dequeue.

2. Finite-State Machine Representation

A general, multiple-state finite-state machine (FSM) always has a name using the prefix, FSM_, and is represented in FAPL in the form of a state-transition matrix, illustrated in Fig. 7 (derived from the SNA data flow control definition [3]). This representation allows definition of a complex FSM in a concise form. Inputs and outputs are represented in mnemonic form, and both are defined outside the matrix itself. The primary benefits of the matrix representation are that it allows easy visual verification of the completeness of the inputs considered, and it facilitates consideration of all state and input combinations. It is not as efficient as the state-transition graph in showing predecessor-state relationships; however, it allows easy merging of state error-checking into the basic FSM representation, which the graph form does not. The matrix representation is also easily translated and compiled, as described later.

Each column heading in the matrix contains the state name and state number. Each row heading contains a set of input conditions. The mnemonics used to represent input conditions are defined in an FSM_INPUT_ DEFINITION at the top of the figure. In the input definition section, each input condition mnemonic is associated with a logical test that determines if the input condition is true or false. The mnemonic variables and values,

```
FSM_INPUT_DEFINITION:
                                                              /*
  ┌─────────────────────────────────────────────────────────────┐
  │ THE    SYMBOLS    USED    IN    THE    "INPUTS"   COLUMN   OF   THE │
  │ STATE-TRANSITION MATRIX ARE DEFINED BELOW.                    │
  └─────────────────────────────────────────────────────────────┘
                                                              */
     BC          BCI=BC;
     CANCEL      RQ_CODE=CANCEL;
     EXP         EFI=EXP;
     NORM        EFI=NORM;
     QC          RQ_CODE=QC;
     QEC         RQ_CODE=QEC;
     R           MU_DIRECTION=RECEIVE;
     RELQ        RQ_CODE=RELQ;
     'RESET'     FSMINPUT='RESET';
     RQ          RRI=RQ;
     +RSP        RRI=RSP & RTI=POS;
     S           MU_DIRECTION=SEND;

END FSM_INPUT_DEFINITION;

FSM_QEC_RCV: FSM_DEFINITION CONTEXT(SCB);
```

INPUTS	STATE NAMES---------->	RESET	PEND_ QC	QUIESCED
	STATE NUMBERS---------->	01	02	03
R,RQ,EXP,QEC		-	>(R)	>(R)
S,+RSP,QEC		2	-	-
R,RQ,EXP,RELQ		-	-	-
S,+RSP,RELQ		-	1	1
S,RQ,NORM,QC		>(S1)	3	>(S1)
R,+RSP,QC		-	-	-
S,RQ,NORM, CANCEL		-	-	>(S2)
S,RQ,NORM,¬CANCEL, BC		-	>(S2)	>(S2)
S,RQ,NORM,¬CANCEL,¬BC		-	-	>(S2)
'RESET' /* FROM DFC_RESET */		-	1	1

OUTPUT CODE	FUNCTION
S1	SEND_CHECK_SENSE=X'0809'; /* MODE INCONSISTENCY */
S2	SEND_CHECK_SENSE=X'2006'; /* DATA TRAFFIC QUIESCED */
R	RECEIVE_CHECK_SENSE=X'0809'; /* MODE INCONSISTENCY */

```
END FSM_QEC_RCV;
```

Fig. 7. Example of FAPL FSM.

such as "BCI" and "BC" in the first line, are defined in a PL/I data declaration, not shown. (In Fig. 7, the "R" and "S" indicate whether the DFC layer element is receiving from or sending to its peer element at the remote end of the session. The other values indicate DFC commands or header indications.) The input definition section allows more concise input specification within the matrix itself.

The matrix elements—(row, column) intersections—contain a next-state indicator, optionally followed by an output code in parentheses. The next-state indicator may be the number of the next state, a hyphen (-) to indicate that no state change is called for, a greater-than symbol (>) to indicate that a matrix element selection represents an error condition, or a slash (/) to indicate that a matrix element selection cannot occur because of prior checking in a previously invoked procedure or FSM. The (>) and (/) designations are useful for validation and testing purposes; in essence, they allow representation of specific *assertions* about the expected environment within which the FSM has been designed to operate. (Section V.B.4, "Error Detection," discusses the significance of these symbols for validation in greater detail.) The output code, if present, references an output function description that follows the transition matrix.

When an FSM is referenced, it is assumed that it may have input conditions that test the value of any entity or system variable that exists for which it has addressability. Addressability is provided through a control block that contains pointers to the "current" copy of each entity type. In addition, a specific signal (represented as a character string) may be sent to an FSM as described below.

FAPL provides two modes for referencing FSMs. One is the normal-type FSM reference, in which the next-state and output functions are applied to the current input and state. This type reference is accomplished by

CALL FSM_fsmname[(fsm_input)];

where the brackets indicate that the syntactical element is optional. The other reference mode is a "check" type FSM reference that is invoked by the SEND_OR_RECEIVE_CHECK built-in FAPL function:

IF SEND_OR RECEIVE_CHECK(FSM_fsmname[(fsm_input)]) THEN...

This type of reference does not cause the FSM to change state, or to execute any output function unless the output function is associated with a (>) next-state indicator, representing an error condition. This *checking* FSM reference allows a group of FSMs to be checked for error conditions before any FSMs are allowed to change state, to eliminate "backing-out" of FSM states set before an error is detected. In the SNA metaimplementation, checking-type references of all applicable FSMs always precede normal-type references that may cause state changes.

One byte of storage exists in a control block for each FSM instance (e.g., on a half-session basis) to contain its current-state value. The current state of an FSM may be tested by

IF FSM_fsmname = state_name THEN...

3. Generic FSM References

FAPL allows referring to FSMs by a *generic name* so that one of several FSMs may be selected at execution time, based, for example, on some SNA session-activation parameter. An FSM reference of this form is

$$\text{CALL FSM\_ \# HDX}[(\text{fsm\_input})];$$

This type of reference implies that a variable named #HDX has been assigned the actual name of the FSM to be referenced before the statement is executed. This example (taken from [3]) could result in calling any one of the FSMs: FSM_HDX_FF, FSM_HDX_CONT_WINNER, or FSM_HDX_CONT_LOSER, depending on the name resolution previously performed. Generic names allow greater conciseness of the metaimplementation description where a reference to any of several FSMs can be made, independent of the particular FSM-tailoring resulting from session-activation parameters. In the metaimplementation, the generic name is resolved to a specific name, for the given example, during the session-activation process.

B. Translation from FAPL to PL/I

A FAPL *preprocessor* translates all FAPL language statements to PL/I-compatible statements that can then be compiled by PL/I and executed within the proper environment—a straightforward process. Here we discuss FSM translation, which has some novelty. Each FSM state-transition matrix is translated by the preprocessor to a PL/I procedure. The technique involves generating an array to contain the matrix elements, and addressing the array with the current state value and the input line number that is *true* when the FSM is invoked. During translation, each unique input condition found in an FSM is assigned a number. After scanning the complete FSM, the preprocessor generates two bit-strings for each input line, as shown in Fig. 8 for the FSM of Fig. 7. Each bit-string is equal in length to the number of input conditions used by the FSM, and each bit position corresponds to the input condition of the same number. One string, called the *mask* string, contains a *one*-bit for each input condition that applies to the input line. The other string, called the *match* string, indicates with a *one*- or *zero*-bit whether each applicable input condition should be true or false for this input line. When the FSM is invoked during execution, a bit-string, having the same length as the mask and match bit-strings, is generated, to represent the current value of each input condition to the FSM. This current-input bit-string is then AND-ed with the mask string, and the result compared to the match string for each input line; an equal compare determines the input line-number index into the matrix elements.

C. The Execution Model

In general, SNA does not define, or constrain, processing scheduling or parallelism within an implemented node, because these concerns are so

```
| Input Conditions From Example FSM |
|             (Figure 7)            |
|-----------------------------------|
| Order Encountered | Bit Number    |
|                   | Assigned      |
|-----------------------------------|
|        R          |      1        |
|        RQ         |      2        |
|        EXP        |      3        |
|        QEC        |      4        |
|        S          |      5        |
|        +RSP       |      6        |
|        RELQ       |      7        |
|        NORM       |      8        |
|        QC         |      9        |
|        CANCEL     |     10        |
|        BC         |     11        |
|        'RESET'    |     12        |
```

```
Input Line    Generated Bit Strings
Number
   1          111100000000  <-----  Mask String
              111100000000  <-----  Match String
   2          000111000000
              000111000000
   3          111000100000
              111000100000
   4          000011100000
              000011100000
   5          010010011000
              010010011000
   6          100001001000
              100001001000
   7          010010010100
              010010010100
   8          010010010110  <-----  Input lines 8 and 9 contain
              010010010010          tests for the off condition of
   9          010010010110          an input condition
              010010010000
  10          000000000001
              000000000001
```

Fig. 8. FSM input condition testing (for the FSM in Fig. 7).

implementation dependent. Diverse product contexts, processor architectures, and operating environments cannot easily be served within the framework of a single execution model. Nevertheless, for execution purposes, the FAPL-definition required an execution model for the metaimplementation. A simple one was chosen.

Two procedures, the *node scheduler* and the *node thread-dispatcher*, are defined in FAPL to manage the invocation of the other procedures in the meta-implementation. The node scheduler is the *root* procedure (or the *main* procedure, in PL/I terms) in a single *calling tree* of procedures within the node. It is data-queue driven, responding to the states (occupied, empty) of the data queues defined in the metaimplementation for holding message units as they pass through the node. Upon finding an occupied data queue, the node scheduler initiates the dispatching of a dequeueing *execution thread*, which consists of the successive invocation of all procedures required to process a message unit from its dequeueing to its enqueuing on another data queue, or its exit from the node.

FAPL defines a *dispatching queue*, and a SEND statement, which is used to place a procedure name and pointers to a message unit and other signals on the dispatching queue. The dispatching queue is managed by the node thread-dispatcher, as follows. The node scheduler creates the original entry on the dispatching queue (via SEND), when it finds a data queue from which a message unit can be dequeued; this entry identifies the dequeuing procedure for the data queue. The node scheduler then calls (via CALL) the node thread dispatcher. Upon finding its dispatching queue occupied, the dispatcher removes the first entry from the dispatching queue, creates the necessary execution environment using the pointers contained in the entry, and calls the procedure named in the entry.

The dequeuing procedure dequeues from its data queue and initiates the processing for the message unit. Within a layer, this processing can involve the calling of multiple procedures and FSMs, transparent to the node scheduler and thread dispatcher. To send the message unit to a procedure in another layer for further processing, a procedure (or FSM) executes either INSERT (if a data queue is used) or SEND. This limits a calling subtree to a single layer, and a layer element ultimately returns (via RETURN) to the thread dispatcher, rather than to a procedure in another layer.

Upon regaining control, the thread dispatcher finds as many new entries on its dispatching queue as the number of SENDs executed since it last held control. It then dispatches the next *subthread*, using the new first entry on the dispatching queue, to call a new procedure. This process continues until the thread dispatcher finds its queue empty; it then returns control to the node scheduler, ending the thread.

V. Automated Validation of SNA Data Flow Control

SNA, as a dynamic architecture, is continually being defined, modified, and extended for new products and applications. In an evolving architecture, the automation of error detection is important in order to rapidly evaluate architectural changes.

The development of the FAPL representation has made it possible to consider using automated techniques to validate those parts of the SNA metaimplementation fully defined in FAPL.

In this section we describe how one particular automated technique has been used to validate the data flow control (DFC) layer of SNA. It is not our purpose here to review validation techniques—these are discussed in other chapters in this book.

We have applied the state-perturbation technique, which is discussed in [26] and in more detail in [24]. This is a form of reachability analysis, which exercises a system of finite-state machines that interact via signaling channels modeled as message queues. The technique detects errors representing deadlocks, inconsistent or incomplete design, or loss of synchronization.

The validation procedure has been reformulated as a driver that surrounds two communicating DFC elements; it drives them through their accessible states, searching for error conditions in much the same way as in [24].

The input to the driver consists only of the compiled architecture definition and the parameters defining the session options to be validated. (In particular, it is not driven by test sequences.)

In the following sections, the data flow control layer of SNA is first described. The validation procedure, as modified by one of the authors (West) to match the context of the DFC definition, is then discussed; some sample results of this work are also presented.

A. The Function of Data Flow Control Within SNA

Communication takes place by exchanging message units that have well-defined formats. Each message contains three parts, the transmission header (TH), request/response header (RH), and request/response unit (RU), collectively called a path information unit (PIU). The principal contents of the transmission header are the addresses identifying the source and destination NAUs and the sequence number of the message. The RH identifies whether the message is a command or contains user data, and whether it is a request or a response to a request; the RH also contains a number of other indicators used by DFC. The RU contains control information and/or user data.

The exchange of messages between two half-sessions in both directions is via either the *expedited* flow (EXP) or the *normal* flow (NORM). The two flows have independent sequence numbering schemes and carry different types of messages. The expedited flow has higher priority so that its messages can bypass queues of normal-flow messages at various points within the TC network.

The layers of SNA below DFC, the transmission control elements and the path control network, comprise the TC network, which links two DFC elements. The TC network contains error recovery facilities, which enable it to transport normal- and expedited-flow messages in both directions without loss or mistakes in sequencing. The TC network introduces a delay, which is a function of the overall workload and configuration of the system and is therefore not precisely defined. The session protocols control the synchronization of the states of the communicating half-sessions despite this delay.

The structure of data flow control is shown in more detail in Fig. 9. It is divided into two parts, DFC.SEND and DFC.RCV, which respectively pass requests and responses from FMDS to TC, and vice versa. (FMDS is a generic designation for the higher-level session functions, SPS and SNS, shown in Fig. 2). DFC.SEND and DFC.RCV reference a number of FSMs, some of which are common to both. The FSMs referenced are determined by the optional DFC functions specified when the session is activated. Not all combinations of options are allowed. Permitted combinations are specified by *function management* (*FM*) *profiles*, details of which can be found in [3].

Each FSM is responsible for controlling a particular function of DFC and, in general, communicates with a complementary FSM in the other half-session by means of indicators or command codes in transmitted requests. For example, the chaining protocols permit a large message to be broken up at a higher layer, and sent through the network by DFC as a chain of requests transported as a single logical entity in terms of error recovery. DFC.SEND contains an FSM, CHAIN_SEND, which assures that requests sent conform to the architectural rules for chaining. Its state represents the status of chains underway, enabling it to check the begin-chain and end-chain indicators in the current request, and prevent transmission of

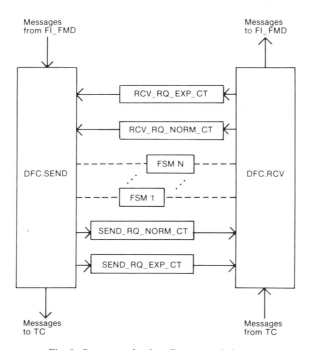

Fig. 9. Structure of a data flow control element.

the request if it would result in an incorrectly structured chain. CHAIN_RCV checks the same indicators on received requests.

Two correlation tables, SEND_RQ_NORM_NORM_CT and RCV_RQ_NORM _CT, are used to correlate responses with previously transmitted normal-flow requests. The first request of a chain creates an entry in SEND_RQ_NORM_CT, which may be updated by subsequent requests in the chain, and removed when a response to the chain is received. RCV_RQ_NORM_CT is used to check that responses sent by FMDS correspond to a previously received chain and that no more than one response to a chain is sent. SEND_RQ_EXP_ CT and RCV_RQ_EXP_CT perform similar functions for the expedited flow.

The definition of all variants of DFC in FAPL comprises some 30 procedures and 26 FSMs, the latter containing over 1200 state transitions. A given example of DFC (selected by means of the "FM profile") within a session is much more compact than this.

B. Adapting the Validation Procedure to Data Flow Control

The protocol validation procedure consists of driving a system through all of its accessible states and examining each for a number of error conditions. In applying it to the validation of DFC, it was necessary to modify the procedure discussed in [24] to take into account the properties of DFC, the environment in which it executes, and the potentially enormous number of system states that a session may reach.

In this section we discuss the modifications that were made, for validation purposes, to the validation procedure and to the version of DFC used as input to the validation system. Some of the properties of DFC that reduce the size of the required computation are also described. Using a simple example, we then show in the following section how the set of protocols constituting a session is validated.

A DFC element in the most general session may reference up to 17 FSMs out of the 26 defined (some of which are complementary, and therefore not present at both ends); these FSMs have up to 9 states each. Thus, in principle, the DFC element may be in any of over a billion possible states. Up to 65,000 requests may be sent before a response is received; each has up to 13 bytes in headers and may generate an entry in a correlation table. The states of the FSMs and the queues in the network, as well as the correlation tables, may all influence the future execution of the session. All must therefore be considered as part of the system state. The potential number of system states to be validated is, at first sight, truly astronomical.

The nature of the DFC layer is such that the number of accessible system states is significantly smaller than the above Cartesian product estimate. The states of individual FSMs, tables, and queues are strongly correlated by the flow of control information within the system, as discussed below.

Furthermore, not all accessible states need be examined. Many of the functions of the DFC layer are loosely coupled, so that subsets of the whole can be validated separately.

1. The Data Flow Control FSM Representation

The individual FSMs that are referenced within a DFC element do not execute asynchronously, but are closely synchronized using a calling tree, as described earlier in the chapter. Thus, they all change state as part of a single execution subthread for the processing of the current message. The individual FSMs, and also the correlation tables, behave as a single, composite FSM, whose total number of states is much less than the Cartesian product of the states of its component machines. A state transition of the composite FSM corresponds to the execution of a subthread, as described in the section on the execution model.

The decomposition of the composite machine into individual FSMs permits a concise representation of the whole without defining directly each individual state of the composite machine. The reachable states of a layer element are not directly stated as part of the architecture definition, but can be derived from it. In validation, they are found by executing the definition and driving it with appropriate inputs.

Although the number of reachable states is much less than the Cartesian product of the states of the component machines, a layer element may still have an extremely large number of states, unless a much lower limit is placed on the number of entries in correlation tables than the architecture allows.

The validation driver does impose a predefined limit and restricts the size of the interaction domain by constraining the number of requests that are sent without a response having been received to two or three. This controls the amount of desynchronization between the communicating half-sessions. The resulting validation is therefore incomplete, but this is not as serious a drawback as might be supposed.

During the development of DFC it was found that, if a loss of synchronization occurs in a complex sequence, it is generally possible to find a related sequence that manifests the error without generating a large number of correlation table entries at any time during the sequence. It appears that most error conditions that can occur in the system will occur within the interaction domain accessible using limited-size correlation tables.

The reason for this lies largely in the design of DFC, which enforces close synchronization of the two half-sessions when significant control information is exchanged.

2. Modeling the Transmission Control Network

The model used for the signaling channels in the earlier validation work [21]–[24] was that of a single FIFO channel queue in each direction between individual pairs of communicating processes. The model of the inner TC network used in DFC validation contains separate *channel queues* for the normal and expedited flows in both directions. [We distinguish these queue representations from the SNA data queues described earlier. The channel queues are *composite* representations of the network of data queues that exist within the inner network underlying the (DFC) elements being validated.]

All messages passing through the network are assigned to the appropriate queue, except normal-flow responses with the queue response indicator (QRI) not set. These pass via the expedited-flow queue, in order to model their ability to pass other normal-flow data in the inner TC network.

The channel queues in the model have a limited size so as to limit the domain of the interaction between the two half-sessions. The validation driver controls the enqueuing and dequeuing of messages in the normal- and expedited-flow channel queues in such a way that all timing combinations of message flow through the network are generated, except for those corresponding to normal-flow messages passing expedited-flow messages, which is not allowed in a real TC network.

3. The Protocol Boundary between DFC and FMDS

DFC controls the flow of information between the FMDS and TC layers, so that in order to exercise the DFC architecture it must be driven by requests and responses from FMDS. When a request or response is sent from FMDS to DFC, the latter always either rejects it with no change of its state, or passes it to TC, having possibly changed the state of one or more FSMs and/or changed a correlation table.

Message rejection is used to prevent the wrong sequencing of messages or the transmission of messages that the session does not allow. The DFC layer does not assume correct ordering or formatting of messages passed from FMDS to DFC. FMDS may attempt to send any message at any time, but those that are incorrect are rejected by DFC.

The usage checks provide a convenient means of reducing the vast number of requests that may be transmitted on a session to the minimal set necessary to exercise all the functions of DFC. Only a few of the many combinations of the bits in a message header need be considered. The function of DFC is independent of address fields and some of the indicators in the RH, such as those controlling pacing and cryptography (which are handled by TC). Only combinations of those message parameters directly referenced by DFC need be considered.

Note that the elimination of unreferenced parameters does not in any way imply a limitation of the validation of the DFC layer, but simply that correct routing, traffic pacing, etc., can only be validated by analyzing the layers of the architecture responsible for such functions.

The subset of requests required to exercise DFC is determined in the following way. A particular type of session is chosen for validation and its session parameters defined in terms of an FM profile and a set of options. Requests containing all combinations of parameters used for the chosen DFC options, and fixed assignments of unused parameters, are generated and passed through the usage checks described above. The set of requests that pass the usage checks generally contains 10 to 100 requests that subsequently drive the session through its accessible states.

When a request passes through DFC, it is assigned a sequence number. Elsewhere, sequence numbers are used to check for correct ordering of messages in the network; within DFC, they are used only for correlation between requests and responses. For the purpose of validation, it is possible to replace the incremental assignment of sequence numbers by fixed assignments, as follows. All requests in the input set for the driver are assigned distinct, fixed sequence numbers. The sequence number assignment in DFC is replaced by one that sets the sequence number on all requests in a chain equal to that of the first request in a chain. In this way, there is no multiplicity of states produced by sequence numbers. The change means that the sequence number generation is not validated, but this can be tested in other ways.

The validation driver correctly formats responses and sends them only if they correspond to an entry in the RCV_RQ_NORM_CT or RCV_RQ_EXP_CT correlation tables, in order to avoid unnecessary rejects.

4. Error Detection

Errors are detected in much the same way as described in [24], but a few differences should be noted.

The earlier work investigated the problem of incomplete design. Design errors were detected by searching for situations where no provision had been made for the reception of an incoming message. While provision for specific inputs can be erroneously omitted in the routing logic or from FSM matrices, the FSM matrix representation of FAPL makes it impossible for the design to be incomplete for any *specified* input, since a transition is specified for all inputs in each state of the FSMs. Two types of next-state indicators, indicating error conditions (>) and cannot-occur conditions (/), can be interpreted as design error indicators. An attempt to execute a (>) while sending a message does not indicate a design error, but merely that an attempt has been made to send a message in violation of the protocol. If one is executed while receiving, a violation of the architectural rules has occurred. In an executing system, it would indicate a failure or the presence of a system component that violates the architecture. During the validation of a session involving metaimplementations of the architecture, it can only indicate an architecture error. An attempt to execute a (/) in such circumstances always indicates a design error.

In validating SNA, it was useful to restrict Bochmann's concept of adjoint states [25] to consider only those system states in which there are no messages underway *and* no entries are in correlation tables. Such states can be characterized as states of the session in which a sender has received all responses to requests that have been sent, and the state of the session will not change until more requests are sent by FMDS. These *stable states* can be examined during a validation run to check for loss of synchronization. Generally, they are few in number and are simply listed by the validation driver.

In principle, assertions concerning the allowed or required combinations of individual FSM states could be formulated, and the detection of erroneous ones automated. However, the number of stable states is small and erroneous ones easily recognized. Errors are therefore simply determined by inspection, there being little point in automating this minor task.

During validation, pointers are maintained, so that it is possible to retrace the message exchanges and state transitions by which it was accessed from the initial system state. This is sufficient information to determine the cause of an error.

C. The Validation Procedure

In this section we show how a session between two DFC elements can be validated, using a model that exercises a simplified version of the DFC chaining protocol. We first describe the behavior of the DFC elements in the session model, then how the driver controls the validation, and finally trace each step in the state generation process.

The model is a session in which only one half-session—the primary—may send requests, the secondary being limited to sending a positive response when it has received a complete chain. The primary DFC element is represented by a single FSM, CHAIN_SEND, and the secondary by CHAIN_RCV; these are shown in Fig. 10(a). The validated session references only the

```
CHAIN_SEND: FSM DEFINITION          CHAIN_RCV: FSM DEFINITION
┌─────────────────────────────┐    ┌─────────────────────────────┐
│  STATE NAMES->│ BETC │ INC  │    │  STATE NAMES-> │ BETC │ INC  │
│ RQ SENT       │ 01   │ 02   │    │ RQ RECEIVED    │ 01   │ 02   │
│───────────────│──────│──────│    │────────────────│──────│──────│
│  BC, EC       │ -    │ >    │    │  BC, EC        │ -    │ >    │
│  BC,¬EC       │ 2    │ >    │    │  BC,¬EC        │ 2    │ >    │
│ ¬BC, EC       │ >    │ 1    │    │ ¬BC, EC        │ >    │ 1    │
│ ¬BC,¬EC       │ >    │ -    │    │ ¬BC,¬EC        │ >    │ -    │
└─────────────────────────────┘    └─────────────────────────────┘
```

(a) Sample FSMs

System State	CHAIN_ SEND State	SEND_RQ_ NORM_CT	PRI-> SEC	CHAIN_ RCV State	RCV_RQ_ NORM_CT	SEC-> PRI	From States	To States
1	BETC	-	-	BETC	-	-	6	2,3
2	BETC	EC	BC EC	BETC	-	-	1	4
3	INC	¬EC	BC¬EC	BETC	-	-	1	5
4	BETC	EC	-	BETC	EC	-	2,8	6
5	INC	¬EC	-	INC	¬EC	-	3,7	7,8
6	BETC	EC	-	BETC	_	+RSP	4	1
7	INC	¬EC	¬BC¬EC	INC	¬EC	-	5	5
8	BETC	EC	¬BC EC	INC	¬EC	-	5	4

(b) Validation of the FSMs in (a)

Fig. 10. A sample validation.

chaining indicator, begin-chain (BC) and end-chain (EC), in normal-flow requests, and there is no expedited flow. As no requests are sent by the secondary, only two correlation tables are referenced: SEND_RQ_NORM_CT in the primary, and RCV_RQ_NORM_CT in the secondary.

A set of four requests is needed to drive this simple session through all of its states. The requests are designated by their chaining indicators. The first is a single-RU chain with both the begin-chain and end-chain indicator set (BC, EC). The other three represent first-of-chain, middle-of-chain, and end-of-chain and are abbreviated as $(BC, \neg EC)$, $(\neg BC, \neg EC)$, and $(\neg BC, EC)$, respectively.

When requests are sent by FMDS, the sequencing for sending correctly formed chains is controlled by CHAIN_SEND. When in the state, Between-Chain (BETC), CHAIN_SEND rejects requests that do not start a chain, and when in the state, In-Chain (INC), it rejects those that start a chain. In the primary, the correlation table SEND_RQ_NORM_CT is used to correlate received responses with previously sent requests. An entry is inserted when a chain is initiated, and deleted when its response is received. The last entry indicates whether a complete chain has been sent (EC) or only a currently incomplete chain $(\neg EC)$.

The secondary is represented by CHAIN_RCV, similar in structure to CHAIN_SEND. The correlation table RCV_RQ_NORM_CT has entries indicating the status of received chains. When an entry corresponding to a complete chain is present (EC), a positive response will be accepted from FMDS, and the entry deleted.

The above summarizes the behavior of the DFC elements in the session. The validation driver is responsible for defining the initial system state of the session in terms of the FSM states and correlation tables, as well as the message queues, PRI → SEC and SEC → PRI, in the TC network. The first line in the table of Fig. 10(b) shows the initial system state, with the FSMs in BETC state and the queues and tables empty. In the validation shown in the table, the driver prevents messages being sent that would result in more than one entry in a queue or table. Starting from the initial system state, the driver tries to generate new system states by sending and receiving all possible messages. Each state so generated is added to the list of reachable system states if it is not identical to one already in the list. Each generated system state is identified by a state number, and the state from which it was entered is shown in the column marked "From States."

When an attempt is made to send the set of requests in the initial system state, $(\neg BC, \neg EC)$ and $(\neg BC, EC)$ are rejected by CHAIN_SEND; (BC, EC) can be sent and leads to state 2, with a complete-chain entry (EC) in SEND_RQ_NORM_CT and (BC, EC) underway from the primary to secondary. Sending $(BC, \neg EC)$ leads to state 3, with a partial-chain entry in the correlation table and CHAIN_SEND in INC, indicating a partial chain has been sent. When an attempt is made to send further requests in states 2 and 3, it is prevented by the driver, as it would result in overflow of the queue in the network.

In both states 2 and 3 the requests underway can be received, leading to states 4 and 5 with the network queues empty, and entries in RCV_RQ_NORM_CT; in state 5, CHAIN_RCV has changed state from BETC to INC.

Further request cannot be sent in state 4 without creating more entries in SEND_RQ_NORM_CT; but the secondary can send a response, thus deleting the entry in RCV_RQ_NORM_CT and resulting in state 6. The requests $(\neg BC, \neg EC)$ and $(\neg BC, EC)$ can be sent in state 5 (leading to states 7 and 8), as they update an entry in SEND_RQ_NORM_CT rather than create a new one. The three last states created lead to already existing states when the message underway is received. The response underway in state 6 deletes the entry in SEND_RQ_NORM_CT when it arrives, and the requests underway in states 7 and 8 produce states 5 and 4 on reception. When all exits from state 8 have been explored, no further states of the system can be reached within the specified limits of the channel queue sizes, and the validation is complete.

The simple example shown contains none of the errors that the technique detects. All reachable system states that do not have full queues or correlation tables have exits to other system states, so that no deadlocks are present. The error conditions (>) shown in the FSM CHAIN_RCV are, in effect, assertions concerning the syntax of chains. As none of these were activated, the validation demonstrates that only correctly formatted chains are received in the interaction domain exercised. The only system state with empty queues and correlation tables is in the initial state; so synchronization is not lost.

D. Sample Validation Results

Figures 11 and 12 show some sample results of applying the validation technique to a recent version of DFC, which had been reformulated in order to correct a few known errors. Prior to validation, a number of test sequences had been run in order to show that the known errors had been corrected. The results were obtained while validating a session for which FM Profile 3 had been specified. This profile has a number of optional

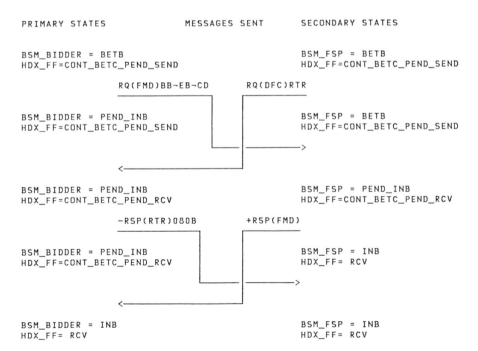

```
PRIMARY STATES                 MESSAGES SENT          SECONDARY STATES


BSM_BIDDER = BETB                                     BSM_FSP = BETB
HDX_FF=CONT_BETC_PEND_SEND                            HDX_FF=CONT_BETC_PEND_SEND

               RQ(FMD)BB-EB-CD          RQ(DFC)RTR


BSM_BIDDER = PEND_INB                                 BSM_FSP = BETB
HDX_FF=CONT_BETC_PEND_SEND                            HDX_FF=CONT_BETC_PEND_SEND

                                                          ------->

            <-------------


BSM_BIDDER = PEND_INB                                 BSM_FSP = PEND_INB
HDX_FF=CONT_BETC_PEND_RCV                             HDX_FF=CONT_BETC_PEND_RCV

              -RSP(RTR)080B            +RSP(FMD)


BSM_BIDDER = PEND_INB                                 BSM_FSP = INB
HDX_FF=CONT_BETC_PEND_RCV                             HDX_FF= RCV

                                                          ------->

            <-------------


BSM_BIDDER = INB                                      BSM_FSP = INB
HDX_FF= RCV                                           HDX_FF= RCV
```

Fig. 11. A sequence leading to a deadlock.

STATE NO.	PRIMARY FSM STATES	SECONDARY FSM STATES
1	BSM_BIDDER=INB HDX_FF=SEND	BSM_FSP=INB HDX_FF=RCV
18	BSM_BIDDER=INB HDX_FF=ERPS	BSM_FSP=INB HDX_FF=ERPR
19	BSM_BIDDER=INB HDX_FF=RCV	BSM_FSP=INB HDX_FF=SEND
20	BSM_BIDDER=BETB HDX_FF=CONT_BETC_PEND_SEND	BSM_FSP=BETB HDX_FF=CONT_BETC_PEND_SEND
164	BSM_BIDDER=BETB HDX_FF=CONT_BETC_PEND_SEND	BSM_FSP=BETB HDX_FF=CONT_BETC_PEND_RCV
170	BSM_BIDDER=BETB HDX_FF=CONT_BETC_PEND_RCV	BSM_FSP=BETB HDX_FF=CONT_BETC_PEND_SEND
186	BSM_BIDDER=PEND_BB HDX_FF=CONT_BETC_PEND_SEND	BSM_FSP=PEND_BB HDX_FF=CONT_BETC_PEND_RCV
187	BSM_BIDDER=PEND_BB HDX_FF=CONT_BETC_PEND_RCV	BSM_FSP=PEND_BB HDX_FF=CONT_BETC_PEND_SEND
469	BSM_BIDDER=BETB HDX_FF=CONT_BETC_PEND_RCV	BSM_FSP=INB HDX_FF=RCV
470	BSM_BIDDER=BETB HDX_FF=CONT_BETC_PEND_RCV	BSM_FSP=BETB HDX_FF=CONT_BETC_PEND_RCV
471	BSM_BIDDER=BETB HDX_FF=CONT_BETC_PEND_SEND	BSM_FSP=INB HDX_FF=RCV
472	BSM_BIDDER=INB HDX_FF=RCV	BSM_FSP=INB HDX_FF=RCV
473	BSM_BIDDER=BETB HDX_FF=CONT_BETC_PEND_RCV	BSM_FSP=INB HDX_FF=SEND
474	BSM_BIDDER=BETB HDX_FF=CONT_BETC_PEND_SEND	BSM_FSP=INB HDX_FF=SEND
475	BSM_BIDDER=PEND_BB HDX_FF=CONT_BETC_PEND_RCV	BSM_FSP=PEND_BB HDX_FF=CONT_BETC_PEND_RCV
711	BSM_BIDDER=INB HDX_FF=SEND	BSM_FSP=INB HDX_FF=SEND

Fig. 12. stable states generated during a validation run.

parameters, of which *half-duplex flip-flop* send-receive mode and *bracket* usage were selected for the validation run described here. The session was further restricted so that only normal-flow single-RU chains were sent, and responses were not allowed to pass requests in the TC network. All channel queues for the TC network and all correlation tables were limited to one entry.

Figure 11 shows a sequence by which a deadlock in the normal flow is reached, as the half-duplex FSMs (HDX_FF) both get into state RCV, where they cannot send requests and there are no outstanding responses. This error was not present in earlier versions of the architecture and proved easy to correct. The ability of the validation system to reconstruct a sequence leading to a system state manifesting an error has always enabled the cause of the error to be easily identified. Error correction may be quite complex, sometimes requiring several iterations before a solution is found that does not introduce further errors.

Figure 12 shows the stable states generated during a validation run. Whereas the validation run generated approximately 900 system states, only 16 were stable states, so that visual inspection could be used to determine if synchronization has been lost. The four system states (469, 471, 473, 474) with bracket-state-managers, BSM_BIDDER and BSM_FSP, in different states, or the two (472, 711) with HDX_FF FSMs both in SEND or RCV, indicate that synchronization has been lost. The other system states are stable without being in error.

The validation run from which these results were obtained also resulted in attempting to execute nine error ($>$) transitions, and required a total of 84 seconds of CPU time on a 370/168, which we believe is negligible compared to the value of the results obtained.

E. Summary Remarks on the Validation

An automated protocol validation technique has been applied to the executable representation of the SNA data flow control layer. So far, a number of subsets of the architecture have been validated. This experience has established the validation technique as a significant tool for the detection of design errors, particularly in newly developed architecture that has not yet been implemented. The technique is completely automated and directly uses a compiled version of the architecture definition. It is able to detect deadlocks, loss of synchronization, and other conditions that should not occur. The detected errors might otherwise only appear under particular timing conditions in a subsequent implementation, and therefore are difficult to detect and reproduce using traditional testing techniques.

The current implementation of the validation system applies only to the data flow control layer of SNA, because it is tailored specifically to the DFC protocol boundaries with adjacent layers. There is no reason why the technique itself could not be applied to other layers of SNA, or to other systems defined in FAPL or in a similar FSM representation.

The technique described should not be considered as performing a complete validation. Not all conceivable types of design errors are detected, and placing explicit limits on channel queue sizes means that the validation is incomplete: there may be session states that are reachable only when the limits are removed. However, a complete validation of such a complex system is probably beyond the capabilities of any currently available validation technique. The main purpose of this work has not been to perform a complete validation, but rather to demonstrate that applying an automated validation technique to an executable, formal representation of a large-scale architecture is an effective way of detecting design errors.

VI. Conclusions and Prospects

The evolution of SNA has seen a steady refinement of formal techniques for its description and validation, resulting from a progressive raising of consciousness within IBM concerning methods to clarify and guide its successful implementation.

Defining SNA in the form of a metaimplementation, as discussed here, has forced meticulous attention to detail and, inevitably, has selected among alternative choices within the architectural specification. Considering that the number of people engaged in designing, implementing, testing, and documenting IBM SNA products worldwide exceeds the number directly participating in its architectural specification by orders of magnitude, the effort on the metaimplementation has not been misplaced. The result has been that architects and implementers think in common terms. They face most of the same concerns regarding function, control, representation, performance, testing, and extendability. The metaimplementation approach has reduced the complexity of coordinating the implementation process, and has been useful in exposing common implementation issues.

The state orientation developed for the metaimplementation is a significant advance that is being transferred more and more to product design. It has also hastened the architectural definition process for extensions to SNA where the analysis of race conditions and error cases is complex by other methods. We expect FSM representation to have a major effect on IBM software technology as the technique disseminates among programmers. (See Landau [27] for a discussion of the application of independently developed FSM-language techniques.)

In the future, we anticipate that the existence of the FAPL description of SNA will shape advances in several areas, just as it has already been useful in the validation process. The compilable version makes it possible to consider ways to shorten the product code-generation process and to devise enhancements for automated testing of products against the architectural specification.

Compiling the FAPL description directly to product code is an exciting concept, but difficult to achieve. A number of problems must be solved before designers can routinely use the compiled FAPL description in this way.

First, the product context itself would need to be taken further into account, especially by the FAPL preprocessor. Product subsetting of the architecture and fixing of free variables, or options, is one such consideration; others concern product control-program and processor environments, as well as product-specific representations of end user and device interfaces. These would seem always to require incorporation of product-specific code.

Second, the FAPL translation and compilation process would require greater emphasis on *efficiency* of object-code generation, for different product-specific subsets of PL/I. Currently, language *descriptive clarity* has been the primary emphasis, although many improvements have been made in the efficiency of the preprocessor since its initial development. FAPL object-code generation will probably never be as efficient as product-specific designs, and manual optimization will likely be required.

Despite these problems, minor success in this area has been achieved. Already, one group has applied manual optimization to a compiled version of data flow control to hasten the design and code-generation process for a new product in development. Other product groups are investigating similar activities.

The testing area provides many opportunities to use the FAPL version more directly. Testing is expensive and time consuming; traditionally, the testing process increases roughly as the square of the number of products for which interconnection pairings (e.g., sessions) are supported and announced. To speed this process, and reduce expense, testing could use the FAPL model as follows. First, the model could be run against itself, and then the two products against it separately; with respect to SNA functions implemented, the products could be seen to work together without ever being specifically tested together. (SNA products cannot be timing dependent on each other.) In this environment, total testing costs would rise linearly with the number of products. Testing costs per product would be proportional to the range of SNA functions implemented by the product.

Testing groups are exploring use of the FAPL model in two contexts. One is in the context of real-time simulation testing; this involves interfacing FAPL code to existing IBM simulation programs, which then connect to products under test. Another use is being considered in the context of tracing. A trace tape captured from the connection of two products could be run against the FAPL code to test the validity of the exchanges between them. In both contexts, work has been started using the compiled FAPL version of data flow control.

The formal techniques described in this chapter should have continuing useful application in the extension and clarification of SNA. They also offer a more formal context for research into questions concerning distributed processing. The consideration of formal descriptive techniques for the specification of network protocols by existing standards bodies is also proceeding. Based on the SNA experience, we believe use of such techniques is worthy of wide support within the technical community.

References

[1]   C. Sunshine, "Formal techniques for protocol specification and verification," *Computer*, vol. 12, No. 9, September 1979, pp. 20–27.

[2]   T. F. Piatkowski, "The ISO-ANSI open systems reference model—A proposal for a systems approach," *Comput. Networks*, vol. 4, No. 3, pp. 111–124, June 1980.

[3]   IBM Corp., *Systems Network Architecture Format and Protocol Reference Manual: Architecture Logic*, IBM Form No. SC30-3112-1 (1978).

[4]   J. P. Gray, "Network services in systems network architecture," *IEEE Trans. Commun.* vol. 25, No. 1, January 1977, pp. 104–116.

[5]   J. D. Atkins, "Path control—The network level of SNA," Chapter 11 in this book.

[6]   J. P. Gray and T. B. McNeill, "SNA multiple-system networking," *IBM Syst. J.*, vol. 18, No. 2, pp. 263–297 (1979).

[7]   IBM Corp., *Systems Network Architecture: Logical Unit Types*, IBM Form No. GC20-1868.

[8]   V. L. Hoberecht, "SNA Higher Layer Protocols" Chapter 16 in this book.

[9]   R. J. Sundstrom, "Formal definition of IBM's systems network architecture," *NTC '77 Conference Record*, vol. 1, pp. 03A: 1-1 to 03A: 1-7, December 1977.

[10] T. F. Piatkowski, "Finite-state architecture," *Proc. 7th Ann. Southeastern Symp. System Theory*, March 1975, Auburn University, Auburn, AL, and Tuskegee Institute, Tuskegee, AL, IEEE Cat. No. 75 CH0968-8C.

[11] T. F. Piatkowski, "Finite-state architecture," IBM Technical Report, TR29.0133, July 1975.

[12] A. Gill, *Introduction to the Theory of Finite-State Machines*, New York: McGraw-Hill (1962).

[13] J. Hartmanis and R. Stearns, *Algebraic Structure Theory of Sequential Machines*, Englewood Cliffs, N.J.: Prentice-Hall, (1967).

[14] E. Moore, *Sequential Machines—Selected Papers*, Reading, MA: Addison-Wesley (1964).

[15] K. A. Bartlett, R. A. Scantlebury, and P. T. Wilkinson, "A note on reliable full-duplex transmission over half-duplex telephone lines," *Commun. Ass. Comput. Mach.* vol. 12, pp. 260–261, May 1969.

[16] D. Bjørner, "Finite-state automaton definition of data communication line control procedures," *Proc. FJCC 1970* vol. 37, pp. 477ff.

[17] J. P. Gray, "Line control procedures," *Proc. IEEE*, vol. 60, No. 11, November 1972, pp. 1301–1312.

[18] "Proposed USA standard, data communication control procedures for the USA standard code for information interchange," *Commun. Ass. Comput. Mach.*, vol. 12, No. 3, March 1969, pp. 166–178.

[19] IBM Corp., *OS PL/I Checkout and Optimizing Compilers: Language Reference Manual*, IBM Form No. GC33-0009-4.

[20] IBM Corp., *SIMPL/I (Simulation Language Based on PL/I) General Information Manual*, IBM Form No. GH19-5035-0 (1972).

[21] P. Zafiropulo, "Protocol validation by duologue matrix analysis," *IEEE Trans. Commun.* vol. COM-26, No. 8, pp. 1187–1194, August 1978.

[22] C. H. West, "An automated technique of communications protocol validation," *IEEE Trans. Commun.*, vol. COM-26, No. 8, pp. 1271–1275, August 1978.

[23] C. H. West and P. Zafiropulo, "Automated validation of a communications protocol: The ccitt X.21 recommendation," *IBM J. Res. Dev.* vol. 22, No. 1, January 1978, pp. 60–71.

[24] C. H. West, "General technique for communications protocol validation," *IBM J. Res. Dev.* vol. 22, No. 1, July 1978, pp. 393–404.

[25] G. V. Bochmann, "Communications protocols and error recovery procedures," *ACM SIGOPS Operating Syst. Rev.*, vol. 9, 1975, p. 45.

[26] P. Zafiropulo, C. H. West, H. Rudin, D. D. Cowan, and D. Brand, "Protocol Analysis and Synthesis Using a State Transition Model" Chapter 24 in this book.

[27] J. V. Landau, "State description techniques applied to industrial machine control," *Computer*, vol. 12, No. 2, pp. 32–40, February 1979.

Index of Acronyms

In most cases an acronym is defined on the page cited. Multiple page references mean that a given acronym has more than one interpretation.

Subject Index